Copyright Exceptions: The Di

Copyright 'exceptions' or 'users' rights' have become a highly controversial aspect of copyright law. Most recently, member states of the European Union have been forced to amend their systems of exceptions so as to comply with the Information Society Directive. Taking the newly amended UK legislation as a case study, this book examines why copyright exceptions are necessary and the forces that have shaped the present legislative regime in the United Kingdom. It seeks to further our understanding of the exceptions by combining detailed doctrinal analysis with insights gained from a range of other sources. The principal argument of the book is that the United Kingdom's current system of 'permitted acts' is much too restrictive and hence is in urgent need of reform, and that paradoxically the Information Society Directive points the way towards a much more satisfactory approach.

ROBERT BURRELL is Reader in Law at the University of Queensland, and Associate Director of the Australian Centre for Intellectual Property in Agriculture. He worked previously at the Australian National University and at King's College, London.

ALLISON COLEMAN is Director of Culturenet Cymru at the National Library of Wales. She was previously Senior Lecturer in Law at the University of Wales, Aberystwyth.

Cambridge Studies in Intellectual Property Rights

As its economic potential has rapidly expanded, intellectual property has become a subject of front-rank legal importance. *Cambridge Studies in Intellectual Property Rights* is a series of monograph studies of major current issues in intellectual property. Each volume will contain a mix of international, European, comparative and national law, making this a highly significant series for practitioners, judges and academic researchers in many countries.

Series editor
Professor William R. Cornish, *University of Cambridge*

Advisory editors
Professor François Dessemontet, University of Lausanne
Professor Paul Goldstein, Stanford University
The Hon. Sir Justice Robin Jacob, The High Court, England and Wales

A list of books in the series can be found at the end of this volume.

Copyright Exceptions: The Digital Impact

Robert Burrell
Allison Coleman

CAMBRIDGE
UNIVERSITY PRESS

CAMBRIDGE UNIVERSITY PRESS
Cambridge, New York, Melbourne, Madrid, Cape Town, Singapore,
São Paulo, Delhi, Dubai, Tokyo

Cambridge University Press
The Edinburgh Building, Cambridge CB2 8RU, UK

Published in the United States of America by Cambridge University Press, New York

www.cambridge.org
Information on this title: www.cambridge.org/9780521123440

© Robert Burrell and Allison Coleman 2005

This publication is in copyright. Subject to statutory exception
and to the provisions of relevant collective licensing agreements,
no reproduction of any part may take place without the written
permission of Cambridge University Press.

First published 2005
Third printing 2006
This digitally printed version 2009

A catalogue record for this publication is available from the British Library

ISBN 978-0-521-84726-1 Hardback
ISBN 978-0-521-12344-0 Paperback

Cambridge University Press has no responsibility for the persistence or
accuracy of URLs for external or third-party internet websites referred to in
this publication, and does not guarantee that any content on such websites is,
or will remain, accurate or appropriate.

For Gita and Amelia
Elizabeth and Sarah

Contents

Preface	*page* xi
List of abbreviations	xiii
Table of cases	xvii
Table of statutes	xxiii

Introduction	1
The exceptions in focus	1
The functions of the exceptions	4
The plan of this work and our argument in outline	6
A note on language	10

Part I Where we are

1 Copyright and freedom of expression — 15
- Recognising the problem — 16
- The idea/expression dichotomy and judicial reaction — 20
- Recognising the conflict — 24
- Resolving the conflict — 35
- Conclusion — 41

2 Fair dealing for the purposes of criticism, review and news reporting and related exceptions — 42
- Fair dealing for the purposes of criticism, review and the reporting of current events: introduction — 43
- Does the exception apply to the work in question? — 44
- Is the use for an approved purpose? — 48
- Is the use fair? — 57
- Attribution of the work — 60
- Summary — 61
- Miscellaneous provisions relating to the communication of information — 62
- Miscellaneous provisions relating to the creation of derivative works — 64
- Other obstacles faced by users — 67
- Conclusion — 78

3	**The public interest defence**	**80**
	The public interest defence in its early form	81
	The recent authorities	91
	Can the same result be achieved by other means?	94
	The objections of principle to a public interest defence	102
	Is a public interest defence legitimate?	103
	Is a public interest defence appropriate?	108
	Is a public interest defence necessary?	109
	Is a public interest defence workable?	111
	Conclusion	111
4	**Exceptions applying to education, research and private study**	**113**
	Fair dealing for the purposes of research or private study	115
	The education exceptions: overview	120
	Things done for the purposes of instruction or examination	120
	Anthologies for educational use	124
	Performing, playing and showing works in educational establishments	124
	Lending of copies by educational establishments	126
	The licensing provisions	126
	Case study: copyright licensing in higher education	130
	Conclusion	135
5	**The library and archive provisions and related exceptions**	**136**
	Overview of the existing exceptions	137
	Defining libraries, archives, museums and galleries and the role of such institutions	138
	Divisions within the 1988 Act	142
	Wider coverage under the directive	143
	The existing library exceptions	145
	Miscellaneous exceptions	160
	Conclusion	162

Part II How we got here

6	**Markets and metaphors**	**167**
	Exceptions, licences and market failure	168
	Copyright as a form of property	180
	Copyright law and notions of balance	187
	Conclusion	191
7	**Copyright in supranational fora**	**193**
	The logic of harmonisation	194
	The Commission's understanding of copyright I: market failure, the copyright balance and property rights	197
	The Commission's understanding of copyright II: harmonisation and the copyright families	201

Contents ix

  Opportunities for participation   208
  The Information Society Directive and the importance of official
  inertia   213
  Summation   215
  The international forum   215
  Conclusion   219

8 Copyright in the domestic arena   220
  Understandings of copyright   221
  The DTI's mandate   226
  Draftsmanship and the inevitable accident   230
  Implementing directives: the method of transposition   235
  European legislation and the erosion of parliamentary control   236
  The role of the judiciary   238
  Conclusion   245

Part III   Where we go from here

9 The fair use panacea   249
  The evolution of the fair use defence and its abolition by the
  judiciary   253
  Protecting parodies   264
  The fair use defence: current practice and future developments   267
  Conclusion   274

10 A model for reform   276
  A flexible system   276
  A workable system   277
  A law of users' rights   279
  The importance of public participation   280
  Working with the Directive: criticism, review and news reporting   282
  Supplementing the Directive: the public interest defence   287
  Working with the Directive: private study and research,
  education, libraries and archives   288
  Summation   297
  The three-step test   298
  Other types of users' rights   299
  Making harmonisation a reality   303
  Changing attitudes   304
  Contractual exclusion and technological measures of protection   306
  Conclusion   310

Appendices

  Copyright, Designs and Patents Act 1988, Part I,
  Chapter III: 'Permitted Acts'   313

  Copyright, Designs and Patents Act 1988, s. 296ZE
  and Schedule 5A   352

Contents

Directive 2001/29/EC of the European Parliament
and of the Council of 22 May 2001 on the
harmonisation of certain aspects of copyright and
related rights in the information society 355

United States Copyright Act 1976, 17 USC, s. 107 375

Bibliography 376
Index 412

Preface

The idea for this book arose out of conversations we had while we were both working at the University of Wales, Aberystwyth. At the time plans for a European Directive to deal with copyright in the 'information society' were at an early stage, but it was already apparent that copyright users were going to struggle to influence the legislative process. We were also concerned that plans for European harmonisation were premature, given that significant doubt remained (and still remains) about some of the directions in which technological developments were taking us. At the same time, however, we did not share the outright opposition expressed by some to any suggestion that copyright exceptions might be harmonised in Europe. In particular, it seemed to us that the United Kingdom's permitted act regime was much too restrictive, and that European harmonisation might provide an opportunity to revisit the entire system of copyright exceptions to an extent that was unlikely to arise in the absence of European intervention in this area.

Our plans for this book have changed considerably since our initial discussions and we have benefited from talking about our ideas with a number of people, including Anne Barron, Lionel Bently, Huw Beverley-Smith, Bill Cornish, Susan Davies, Paul Mitchell and John Phillips. Nevertheless, many of the themes that sparked our interest in this project have remained more or less consistent. We have touched on these themes and on some of the other ideas that inform this work in earlier publications. In particular, it should be noted that Chapter 9 of this book is based on an article written by Robert Burrell and published in the *Intellectual Property Quarterly* in 2001. In writing this book Allison Coleman took principal responsibility for Chapters 4 and 5 and Robert Burrell took sole responsibility for the remainder of this work. We have endeavoured to state the law as at 1 February 2004, but where possible we have tried to take account of later developments.

We are indebted to a number of people for the assistance they provided us during the writing process. In particular we should like to take this opportunity to thank Lionel Bently, Bill Cornish, Peter Drahos, Michael

Handler, Gita Sarda, Brad Sherman, James Stellios and Adrienne Stone for reading and commenting on drafts; Susan Davies, James Hutton and Paul Mitchell for helping with the research; and the Australian National University's Faculties Research Grant Fund and the Monash University Travelling Fellowship Scheme for their financial support for elements of this project. We should also like to thank the Grains Research and Development Corporation and the Rural Industries Research and Development Corporation for their ongoing support for the Australian Centre for Intellectual Property in Agriculture. Finally we should like to thank the staff at Cambridge University Press, in particular Finola O'Sullivan, Brenda Burke, Annie Lovett, Jane O'Regan and Philippa Youngman for their hard work and efficiency.

The publisher has used its best endeavours to ensure that the URLs for external websites referred to in this book are correct and active at the time of going to press. However, the publisher has no responsibility for the websites and can make no guarantee that a site will remain live or that the content is or will remain appropriate.

Abbreviations

AC	*Law Reports, Appeal Cases*
AIPJ	*Australian Intellectual Property Journal*
AIPLA	*American Intellectual Property Law Association*
All ER	*All England Law Reports*
ALR	*Australian Law Reports*
App Cas	*Law Reports, Appeal Cases*
Atk	*Atkyns' Chancery Reports*
Bently and Sherman	L. Bently and B. Sherman, *Intellectual Property Law* (Oxford: Oxford University Press, 2001)
Berne Convention	Berne Convention for the Protection of Literary and Artistic Works
BT	Board of Trade
CAB	Cabinet Office
CDPA	Copyright, Designs and Patents Act 1988
Ch	*Law Reports, Chancery Division*
Cox	*Cox's Equity Cases*
CLR	*Commonwealth Law Reports*
CMLR	*Common Market Law Reports*
Computer Program Directive	Council Directive 91/250/EEC of 14 May 1991 on the legal protection of computer programs
Copinger	K. Garnett, J. Rayner James and G. Davies (eds.), *Copinger and Skone James on Copyright*, 14th edn (London: Sweet & Maxwell, 1999)
Cornish and Llewelyn	W. Cornish and D. Llewelyn, *Intellectual Property: Patents, Copyright, Trade Marks and Allied*

	Rights, 5th edn (London: Sweet & Maxwell, 2003)
CPR	*Canadian Patent Reporter*
CrAppR(S)	Criminal Appeal Reports (Sentencing)
Database Directive	Directive 96/9/EC of the European Parliament and of the Council of 11 March 1996 on the Legal Protection of Databases
DR	*European Commission of Human Rights Decisions and Reports*
Droit de Suite Directive	Directive 2001/84/EC of the European Parliament and of the Council of 27 September 2001 on the resale right for the benefit of the author of an original work of art
East	*East's Term Reports, King's Bench*
ECJ	European Court of Justice
E-Commerce Directive	Directive 2000/31/EC of the European Parliament and of the Council of 8 June 2000 on certain legal aspects of information society services, in particular electronic commerce, in the internal market
ECR	*European Court Reports*
EEA	European Economic Area
EGLR	*Estates Gazette Law Reports*
EHRR	*European Human Rights Reports*
EIPR	*European Intellectual Property Review*
EMLR	*Entertainment and Media Law Reports*
EntLR	*Entertainment Law Review*
EnvLR	*Environmental Law Reports*
Esp	*Espinasse's Nisi Prius Reports*
EU	European Union
EWCA Civ	Court of Appeal Civil Division
F	*Federal Reporter*
F Supp	*Federal Supplement*
FCA	Federal Court of Appeal (Canada)
FCT	Federal Court of Canada, Trial Division
FSR	*Fleet Street Reports*

Guibault	L. Guibault, *Copyright Limitations and Contracts: An Analysis of the Contractual Overridability of Limitations on Copyright* (The Hague: Kluwer Law International, 2002)
HC	House of Commons
HL	House of Lords
HO	Home Office
IFPI	International Federation of the Phonographic Industry
IIC	*International Review of Industrial Property and Copyright Law*
Information Society Directive	Directive 2001/29/EC of the European Parliament and of the Council of 22 May 2001 on the harmonisation of certain aspects of copyright and related rights in the information society
IPJ	*Intellectual Property Journal*
IPQ	*Intellectual Property Quarterly*
IPR	*Intellectual Property Reports*
KB	*Law Reports, King's Bench*
Laddie et al., 2nd edn	H. Laddie, P. Prescott and M. Vitoria, *The Modern Law of Copyright and Designs*, 2nd edn (London: Butterworths, 1998)
Laddie et al., 3rd edn	H. Laddie, P. Prescott, M. Vitoria, A. Speck and L. Lane, *The Modern Law of Copyright and Designs*, 3rd edn (London: Butterworths, 2000)
LCO	Lord Chancellor's Office
LJ Ch	*Law Journal Reports, Chancery*
LO	Law Officers' Department
MacCC	*MacGillivray's Copyright Cases*
NZLR	*New Zealand Law Reports*
QB	*Law Reports, Queen's Bench*
Rental Right Directive	Council Directive 92/100/EEC of 19 November 1992 on rental and lending right and on certain rights related to copyright in the field of intellectual property

Ricketson	S. Ricketson, *The Berne Convention for the Protection of Literary and Artistic Works* (London: Kluwer & QMW, 1987)
RIDA	*Revue Internationale Du Droit D'Auteur*
RPC	*Reports of Patent, Design and Trade Mark Cases*
RSC	Revised Statutes of Canada
Russ	*Russell's Chancery Reports*
SCC	Supreme Court of Canada
SCE	Standing Committee E
Sherman and Bently	B. Sherman and L. Bently, *The Making of Modern Intellectual Property* (Cambridge: Cambridge University Press, 1999)
Shorter OED	*The New Shorter Oxford English Dictionary* (Oxford: Clarendon, 1993)
SI	Statutory Instrument
SR (NSW)	*New South Wales State Reports*
Sterling	A. Sterling, *World Copyright Law*, 2nd edn (London: Sweet & Maxwell, 2003)
Swanst	*Swanston's Chancery Reports*
Tax Cas	*Tax Cases*
Term Directive	Council Directive 93/98/EEC of 29 October 1993 harmonizing the term of protection of copyright and certain related rights
TRIPS	Agreement on Trade-Related Aspects of Intellectual Property Rights 1994
TS	Treasury Solicitor
US	*United States Supreme Court Reports*
USC	United States Code
Ves	*Vesey Junior's Chancery Reports*
WIPO	World Intellectual Property Organization
WIPR	*World Intellectual Property Reports*
WLR	*Weekly Law Reports*
WN	*Weekly Notes of Cases*

Table of cases

A v. B Plc [2003] QB 195   85, 101
A & M Records v. Napster 239 F 3d 1004 (2001)   213, 268
Acohs v. Bashford Consulting (1997) 37 IPR 542   99
AG v. Guardian Newspapers (No 2) [1990] 1 AC 109   92, 104, 106
AGL Sydney v. Shortland County Council (1989) 17 IPR 99   266
Alcolix (1994) 25 IIC 605   207, 284
American Cyanamid v. Ethicon [1975] AC 396   100
American Geophysical Union v. Texaco 60 F 3d 913 (1994)   170, 268
Ashdown v. Telegraph Group [2001] Ch 685; [2002] Ch 149   23, 24,
   31, 53, 54, 55, 92, 93, 94, 100, 101, 103, 180, 189, 239
Associated Newspapers Group v. News Group Newspapers [1986]
   RPC 515   21, 55, 58
Australian Broadcasting Corp. v. Lenah Game Meats (2001) 185
   ALR 1   85
Autodesk v. Dyason [1992] RPC 575   262
Baner v. Sweden (1989) 60 DR 128   105
Banier v. News Group Newspapers [1997] FSR 812   45
Basic Books v. Kinko's Graphics 758 F Supp 1522 (1991)   268
BBC v. BSB [1991] 3 All ER 833   54, 59
Beggars Banquet v. Carlton [1993] EMLR 349   88, 100
Bell v. Whitehead (1839) 8 LJ Ch 141   254
Beloff v. Pressdram [1973] 1 All ER 241   31, 43, 81, 83, 98, 242
Blair v. Osborne & Tomkins [1971] 2 QB 78   185
Bloomsbury Publishing v. News Group Newspapers [2003]
   FSR 842   90
Bonnard v. Perryman [1891] 2 Ch 269   39
British Leyland v. Armstrong Patents [1982] FSR 481; [1986]
   AC 577   96, 184, 185, 242
British Oxygen v. Liquid Air [1925] 1 Ch 383   47, 261
Cala Homes (South) v. Alfred McAlpine Homes East [1995]
   FSR 818   23
Campbell v. Acuff-Rose Music 114 S Ct 1164 (1994)   28, 264, 268

Campbell v. Frisbee [2003] EMLR 76   85
Campbell v. MGN [2003] QB 633; [2004] EMLR 247   84, 85, 86
Canon Kabushiki Kaisha v. Green Cartridge [1997] AC 728   184, 185
Cary v. Kearsley (1802) 4 Esp 168   254
Cary v. Longman and Rees (1801) 1 East 358   254
CBS Songs v. Amstrad [1988] RPC 567   119
CCH Canadian v. Law Society of Upper Canada [2004] SCC 13   48, 58, 117, 118, 119, 173
Cellular Clothing v. Maxton [1899] AC 326   96
Channel Nine v. Network Ten (2002) 55 IPR 112   50, 51, 56, 227
Chiron Corporation v. Organon Teknika (No 10) [1995] FSR 325   98, 99
Cie générale des établissements Michelin – Michelin & Cie v. CAW Canada (1996) 71 CPR (3d) 348   32, 50
Collier Constructions v. Foskett (1990) 19 IPR 44   94, 95
Commonwealth of Australia v. Fairfax (1980) 147 CLR 39   31, 48, 81, 227
Re A Company's Application [1989] Ch 477   86
Copyright Licensing v. University of Auckland (2002) 53 IPR 618   48, 49, 56, 57, 117
Cork v. McVicar (The Times, 31 October 1984)   83, 86
Cornelius v. De Taranto [2001] EMLR 329   98
Corrs Pavey Whiting & Byrne v. Collector of Customs (1987) 10 IPR 53   94, 95
Cream Holdings v. Banerjee [2003] Ch 650   101
De Garis v. Neville Jeffress Pidler (1990) 18 IPR 292   49, 116, 117
Dejonge & Co v. Breuker 235 US 33 (1914)   285
Dennis v. Ministry of Defence [2003] EnvLR 741   99
Dennis v. United States 341 US 494 (1951)   108
Dering v. Earl of Winchelsea (1787) 1 Cox 318   95
Designers Guild v. Russell Williams (Textiles) [2001] FSR 113   22
Deutsche Grammophon v. Metro [1971] ECR 487   194
Distillers v. Times Newspapers [1975] QB 613   31, 55
Doherty v. Allman (1878) 3 App Cas 709   98
Donoghue v. Allied Newspapers [1938] Ch 106   23
Douglas v. Hello! (No 1) [2001] QB 967   90, 101
Douglas v. Hello! (No 5) [2003] EMLR 641   90
Eldred v. Ashcroft 536 US 186 (2003)   23, 24, 219
Eldred v. Reno 239 F 3d 372 (2001)   20
EMI Electrola v. Patricia [1989] ECR 79   194
Ernest Turner v. PRS [1943] Ch 167   86, 239
Express Newspapers v. Liverpool Daily Post [1985] FSR 306   262

Femis-Bank *v.* Lazar [1991] 2 All ER 865   100
Football Association Premier League *v.* Panini [2003] FSR 698; [2004] FSR 1   64, 65, 66, 240
Francome *v.* Mirror Group Newspapers [1984] 1 WLR 892   86, 87
Fraser *v.* Evans [1969] 1 QB 349   81
Fraser *v.* Thames TV [1984] QB 44   90
Glyn *v.* Weston Feature Film Co [1916] 1 Ch 261   92, 95, 106, 264, 266
The Gramophone Co *v.* Leo Feist (1928) 41 CLR 1   257
Gyles *v.* Wilcox (1741) 2 Atk 141   254, 255
Harbottle *v.* National Westminster Bank [1977] 2 All ER 862   100
Harper *v.* Biggs (1907) [1905–1910] MacCC 168   256
Harper & Row Publishers *v.* Nation Enterprises 471 US 539 (1985)   20
Hawkes and Sons *v.* Paramount [1934] 1 Ch 593   65, 239, 261, 262, 263
Heptulla *v.* Orient Longman [1989] FSR 598   23
Holley *v.* Smyth [1998] QB 726   39
Hubbard *v.* Vosper [1972] 2 QB 84   31, 46, 47, 52, 57, 58, 242, 261
Hyde Park *v.* Yelland [1999] RPC 655; [2001] Ch 143   21, 31, 47, 48, 55, 56, 81, 83, 91, 92, 93, 94, 97, 100, 103, 104, 106, 107, 109, 110, 180, 239
Ibcos Computers *v.* Barclays Mercantile Highland Finance [1994] FSR 275   22, 23
Imutran *v.* Uncaged Campaigns [2001] 2 All ER 385   92
Initial Services *v.* Putterill [1968] 1 QB 396   86
IPC Magazines *v.* MGN [1998] FSR 431   64, 65
Jeffrey *v.* Rolls Royce (1962) 40 Tax Cas 443   104
Jersild *v.* Denmark (1995) 19 EHRR 1   37, 59
Jockey Club *v.* Buffham [2003] QB 426   83, 86, 87, 101
Johnstone *v.* Bernard Jones Publications [1938] Ch 599   262
Joy Music *v.* Sunday Pictorial Newspaper [1960] 2 WLR 645   265, 267
Re Keene [1922] 2 Ch 475   104
Keep Thompson Governor Committee *v.* Citizens for Gallen Committee 457 F Supp 957 (1978)   32
Kennaway *v.* Thompson [1981] QB 88   99
Kettles and Gas Appliances *v.* Hordern (1934) 35 SR (NSW) 108   96
Kingdom of the Netherlands *v.* European Parliament and the Council of the European Union [2001] ECR I–7079   274
Lion Laboratories *v.* Evans [1985] QB 526   31, 81, 83, 86, 110, 237, 267

London & Leeds Estates v. Paribas (No 2) [1995] 1 EGLR 102   62
London Regional Transport v. The Mayor of London [2003]
    EMLR 88   84, 87, 102
Ludlow Music v. Robbie Williams [2001] FSR 271   262
Ludlow Music v. Robbie Williams (No 2) [2002] EMLR 585   98
M'Beath v. Ravenscroft (1839) 8 LJ Ch 208   100
Mars v. Teknowledge [2000] FSR 138   81, 89, 185
Mattel v. MCA Records 28 F Supp 2d 1120 (1998)   32
Mattel v. Pitt 229 F Supp 2d 315 (2002)   32
Mattel v. Walking Mountain Productions 353 F 3d 792 (2003)   32
Mawman v. Tegg (1826) 2 Russ 385   254
Maxtone-Graham v. Burtchaell 803 F 2d 1253 (1986)   32
Meeropol v. Nizer 417 F Supp 1201 (1976); 560 F 2d 1061
    (1977)   29, 30
Miller v. Jackson [1977] 1 QB 966   98, 99
Monsanto v. Schmeiser [2001] FCT 256; [2002] FCA 309; [2004]
    SCC 34   186, 187
Moorhouse v. University of New South Wales (1975) 133
    CLR 1   119
Mothercare v. Penguin Books [1988] RPC 113   32
Musical Fidelity v. Vickers [2003] FSR 898   31, 305
Music Vertrieb Membran v. GEMA [1981] ECR 147   39, 194
Network Ten v. Channel Nine [2004] HCA 14   51, 262
New Era Publications v. Henry Holt 695 F Supp 1493 (1988)   32
Newspaper Licensing v. Marks and Spencer [2001] Ch 257   48, 54,
    56, 57, 240
News Verlags v. Austria (2001) 31 EHRR 8   23, 24
Newton v. Diamond 349 F 3d 591 (2003)   262
Nine Network Australia v. Australian Broadcasting Corp (1999) 48 IPR
    333   54, 56
Noah v. Shuba [1991] FSR 14   45
Nottinghamshire Healthcare v. News Group Newspapers [2002] RPC
    962   98
Parfums Christian Dior v. Evora [1998] RPC 166   104
Pasterfield v. Denham [1999] FSR 168   78
PCR v. Dow Jones Telerate [1998] FSR 170   81, 86
Penguin Books v. India Book Distributors [1985] FSR 120   96
Pepper v. Hart [1993] AC 593   245
Plix Products v. Frank M Winstone (Merchants) [1986] FSR 63   22
PPL v. Maitra [1998] 1 WLR 870   98
Princeton University Press v. Michigan Document Services 99 F 3d
    1381 (1996)   170, 268

Pro Sieben v. Carlton [1998] FSR 43; [1999] FSR 610   43, 48, 49, 50, 52, 53, 54, 55, 60, 274
Queen v. James Lorimer & Co (1984) 77 CPR 2d 262   81
R v. Carter [1993] FSR 303   239
R v. Dukett [1998] 2 CrAppR(S) 59   239
Raleigh Cycle v. Miller (1949) 66 RPC 23   98
Ravenscroft v. Herbert [1980] RPC 193   23
Rogers v. Koons 960 F 2d 301 (1992)   26, 28, 50
Ruckelshaus v. Monsanto 467 US 986 (1984)   105
San Francisco Arts and Athletics Club v. US Olympic Committee 483 US 522 (1987)   27
Sayre v. Moore (1785, decision reproduced in Cary v. Longman (1801) 1 East 358)   254
Schnapper v. Foley 471 F Supp 426 (1979)   20
School Books (1972) 3 IIC 394   203, 204
Schweppes v. Wellingtons [1984] FSR 210   265
Series 5 Software v. Clarke [1996] 1 All ER 853   100
Service Corp v. Channel 4 [1999] EMLR 83   81, 83
Shelfer v. City of London Electric Lighting Co [1895] 1 Ch 287   98, 99
Shelley Films v. Rex Features [1994] EMLR 134   90
Sid & Marty Krofft Television v. McDonald's 562 F 2d 1157 (1977)   20
Silhouette v. Hartlauer [1998] 2 CMLR 953   180
Sillitoe v. McGraw Hill Book Co [1983] FSR 545   59, 261
Silver Thistle (1997) 28 IIC 140   207
Skybase Nominees v. Fortuity (1996) 36 IPR 529   21
Slingsby v. Bradford Patent Truck [1906] WN 51   106
SmithKline & French v. Department of Community Services and Health [1990] FSR 617   94, 95
Solar Thompson v. Barton [1977] RPC 537   100, 185
Re a Solicitor (5 November 1996) (Court of Appeal) (*Lexis* Transcript)   88
Sony Corp v. Universal City Studios 464 US 417 (1984)   268
Stovin-Bradford v. Volpoint [1971] Ch 1007   185
Suntrust Bank v. Houghton Mifflin Co 268 F 3d 1257 (2001)   41, 50
Television New Zealand v. Newsmonitor Services [1994] 2 NZLR 91   117, 119
Theakston v. MGN [2002] EMLR 398   85, 101
Theophanous v. Herald & Weekly Times (1994) 182 CLR 104   37
Tidy v. Natural History Museum (1998) 39 IPR 501   78
Time v. Bernard Geis 293 F Supp 130 (1968)   25

Times Newspapers *v.* MGN [1993] EMLR 442   89, 91
Time Warner *v.* Channel 4 [1994] EMLR 1   52, 274
Trebor Bassett *v.* The Football Association [1997] FSR 211   66
Tucker *v.* News Media Ownership [1986] 2 NZLR 716   85
United Wire *v.* Screen Repair Services [2000] 4 All ER 353   185
Universities UK *v.* Copyright Licensing Agency [2002] EMLR 693
    133, 134, 135, 239
University of London Press *v.* University Tutorial Press [1916]
    2 Ch 601   242, 260
W *v.* Egdell [1990] 1 Ch 359   97
Walt Disney *v.* Air Pirates 581 F 2d 751 (1978)   25, 41
Warner Bros *v.* Christiansen [1988] ECR 2605   194
Whittingham *v.* Wooler (1817) 2 Swanst 428   254
Wigginton *v.* Brisbane TV (1992) 25 IPR 58   227
Wilkins *v.* Aikin (1810) 17 Ves 422   254
Williams *v.* Settle [1960] 1 WLR 1072   98
Williamson Music *v.* The Pearson Partnership [1987] FSR 97   50, 266
Woodward *v.* Hutchins [1977] 1 WLR 760   85
Woolgar *v.* Chief Constable of the Sussex Police [2000] 1 WLR 25   86,
    87, 88
World Wildlife Fund *v.* World Wrestling Federation Entertainment
    [2003] EWCA Civ 401   99
Wrotham Park *v.* Parkside Homes [1974] 1 WLR 798   98
Zamacois *v.* Douville [1943] 2 DLR 257   58
ZYX Music *v.* King [1995] FSR 566   106

Table of statutes

United Kingdom

Broadcasting Act 1996
  s. 137   54, 69, 307

Copyright Act 1842
  s. 15   256

Copyright Act 1911
  s. 2(1)   234
  s. 2(1)(i)   258, 259
  s. 2(1)(iii)   234
  s. 2(1)(iv)   124

Copyright Act 1956
  s. 6(1)   232
  s. 6(2)   110
  s. 7   153
  s. 7(5)   156
  s. 9   232
  s. 9(3)   234
  s. 9(4)   234
  s. 15   157
  s. 19   231
  s. 25(1)   257

Copyright and Related Rights Regulations 1996 (SI 1996 No 2967)
  reg. 35   159

Copyright and Related Rights Regulations 2003 (SI 2003 No 2498) 128, 136

Copyright (Application of Provisions relating to Educational Establishments to Teachers) (No 2) Order 1989 (SI 1989 No 1067) 120

Copyright (Certification of Licensing Scheme for Educational Recording of Broadcasts and Cable Programmes) (Educational Recording Agency Limited) Order 1990 (SI 1990 No 879)   128

Copyright (Certification of Licensing Scheme for Educational Recording of Broadcasts) (Open University) Order 2003 (SI 2003 No 187)   128

Table of statutes

Copyright, Designs and Patents Act 1988
- s. 3(3)   63
- s. 4(2)   44
- s. 9(2)(ab)   60
- s. 9(3)   44
- s. 11(2)   44
- s. 18   133, 198
- s. 18(2)   47
- s. 18A(2)   126, 158
- s. 28(1)   69
- s. 28A   76, 150, 301
- s. 29   42, 115, 116, 119, 152, 153, 198
- s. 29(1)   115, 237
- s. 29(1B)   115
- s. 29(1C)   116
- s. 29(2)   116
- s. 29(3)   152
- s. 29(3)(b)   116, 117, 118
- s. 30   43
- s. 30(1)   43, 46, 60
- s. 30(1A)   43, 46, 47, 121
- s. 30(2)   60, 207
- s. 30(3)   60
- s. 31   299
- s. 31(1)   64
- s. 31(3)   65
- ss. 31A–C   237
- ss. 31A–F   299
- ss. 31B–C   222
- ss. 31B–D   170
- s. 31D   222
- ss. 32–36A   120
- s. 32   120, 121, 122, 123, 230, 240
- s. 32(1)   121
- s. 32(2)   122
- s. 32(2A)   121
- s. 32(2B)   121
- s. 32(3)   124, 300
- s. 32(3A)   123
- s. 32(4)   123
- s. 32(5)   231
- s. 33   120, 124
- s. 33(1)   124
- s. 33(2)   124
- s. 33(3)   123
- s. 34   120, 123, 125, 182, 295, 302
- s. 34(1)   125
- s. 34(2)   125, 127
- s. 34(3)   125
- s. 35   120, 125, 127, 129, 170
- s. 35(1)   127
- s. 35(1A)   127
- s. 35(2)   222
- s. 36   120, 127, 128, 129, 170
- s. 36(1A)   128
- s. 36(1B)   128
- s. 36(3)   128, 129, 222
- s. 36A   120, 126, 158, 159, 295, 302
- ss. 37–44A   136
- s. 37   142
- s. 37(2)(a)   146
- s. 38   142, 145, 147, 148, 149, 150, 151, 153, 159
- s. 38(1)   148
- s. 38(2)(b)   148
- s. 38(2)(c)   148
- s. 39   142, 145, 147, 148, 149, 150, 151, 153, 159
- s. 39(2)(b)   148
- s. 40   152
- s. 40(2)(a)   146
- s. 40(2)(b)   147
- s. 40A   142, 145, 158, 295, 302
- s. 40A(1)   158
- s. 40A(2)   158, 159
- s. 41   142, 145, 154, 155

s. 42   142, 145, 155, 156
s. 42(1)   156
s. 42(2)   155
s. 43   142, 145, 146, 150, 151, 152, 153
s. 43(2)(b)   151
s. 43(3)(a)   151
s. 43(3)(b)   151
s. 43(3)(c)   151
s. 44   136, 142, 145, 159, 302
s. 44A   142, 145, 157, 237
s. 44A(1)   157
s. 44A(2)   157
ss. 45–46   62
s. 45(2)   63
s. 46(2)   63
s. 46(4)   62
s. 47   160
s. 47(1)   160
s. 47(2)   160
s. 47(3)   160
s. 48   88
s. 49   136, 160, 161
s. 50(1)   87
ss. 50A–C   5, 235, 237
ss. 50A–D   300
s. 50B   5, 116
s. 50BA   116
ss. 51–53   5, 302
ss. 54–55   5, 182, 302
s. 56   5
s. 57   182
s. 58   63, 87, 237, 285
s. 58(1)   163
s. 59   123, 302
s. 60   170, 222, 237
s. 60(2)   222
s. 61   141, 160, 161
s. 61(2)(c)   161
s. 61(3)   152
s. 61(4)   161
s. 62   233, 234, 299, 300
s. 62(2)   233
s. 62(3)   233
s. 63   160, 162, 299
s. 63(1)   162
s. 63(2)   162
s. 64   66
s. 65   70, 185, 233, 299
s. 66   159, 302
s. 66A   182
s. 68   5, 299
s. 69   5
s. 70   198, 233
s. 71   198
ss. 73–73A   5, 302
s. 74   170, 222, 299
s. 74(4)   222
s. 75   141, 160, 161
s. 75(1)   161
s. 80   77
s. 80(2)(a)   77
s. 80(2)(b)   78
s. 80(3)–(6)   78
s. 80(5)   186
s. 118   133
s. 119   133
ss. 135A–G   6
s. 137   129
ss. 138–140   129
s. 143   127
s. 143(2)   128
s. 163(1)   44
s. 171(3)   81, 237, 241
s. 172(3)   243
s. 174   120
s. 178   60, 62, 118, 122, 148, 149, 158, 231
s. 253   301
s. 296A   69, 307
s. 296B   69, 307
s. 296ZE   306
s. 296ZE(2)   74
s. 296ZE(3)   74

Sched. 1, para. 1(3)   153
Sched. 1, para. 3   150
Sched. 1, para. 16   150, 153
Sched. 5A   74, 306

Copyright (Educational Establishments) (No 2) Order 1989 (SI 1989 No 1068)   120

The Copyright (Librarians and Archivists) (Copying of Copyright Material) Regulations 1989 (SI 1989 No 1212)
   reg. 3(1)   148
   reg. 3(2)   151, 154, 155
   reg. 3(3)   154, 155
   reg. 3(4)   151, 155
   reg. 3(5)   148
   reg. 4(2)(b)(i)   146
   reg. 4(2)(b)(ii)   147
   reg. 4(2)(c)(i)   148
   reg. 4(2)(c)(ii)   148
   reg. 4(2)(d)   148
   reg. 4(3)   146
   reg. 5(2)(a)   154, 155
   reg. 5(2)(b)   154
   reg. 5(2)(c)   154, 155
   reg. 6(2)(a)   155
   reg. 6(2)(b)   155
   reg. 6(2)(c)   155
   reg. 6(2)(d)   155
   reg. 7(2)(a)(i)   151
   reg. 7(2)(b)   151
   reg. 7(2)(c)   151
   Sched. 1, Part A   148, 155
   Sched. 2   145

Copyright (Recording for Archives of Designated Class of Broadcasts and Cable Programmes) (Designated Bodies) Order 1993 (SI 1993 No 74)   161

Copyright (Recording of Folksongs for Archives) (Designated Bodies) Order 1989 (SI 1989 No 1012)
   reg. 3(2)   161

Electronic Commerce (EC Directive) Regulations 2002 (SI 2002 No 2013)
   reg. 2   76
   reg. 17   76
   reg. 18   76
   reg. 19   76
   reg. 19(a)(i)   77
   reg. 19(a)(ii)   77

Government of Wales Act 1998   161

Human Rights Act 1998
   s. 12   100, 101
   s. 12(3)   101
   s. 12(4)   101

Legal Deposit Libraries Act 2003
   s. 6   157
   s. 7   157
   s. 9   160

Table of statutes   xxvii

Limitation Act 1980
  s. 2   147

Patents Act 1977
  s. 70   301

Public Lending Right Act 1979   158

Public Records Act 1958   161

Public Records Act (Northern Ireland) 1923   161

Public Records (Scotland) Act 1937   161

Registered Designs Act 1949
  s. 26   301

Trade Marks Act 1994
  s. 21   301

Unfair Terms in Consumer Contracts Regulations 1999 (SI 1999 No 2083)
  reg. 5(1)   69

European Union legislation

Computer Program Directive
  Art. 5   235
  Art. 6   235
  Art. 9(1)   69, 307

Database Directive
  Art. 6(1)   307
  Art. 8(1)   307

Droit de Suite Directive
  recital 5   196
  Art. 3   303
  Art. 4   303
  Art. 8   195
  Art. 10   195

E-Commerce Directive
  recital 17   76
  Art. 2   76
  Art. 12   76
  Art. 13   76
  Art. 14   76
  Art. 14(1)(a)   77
  Art. 14(1)(b)   77

Information Society Directive
  recital 9   200
  recital 12   196
  recital 16   300
  recital 20   300
  recital 35   292
  recital 37   292
  recital 40   144
  recital 42   293
  recital 60   302
  Art. 1(2)   300
  Art. 5(1)   214, 301
  Art. 5(2)(a)   288, 290, 291, 292, 295, 308
  Art. 5(2)(b)   288, 290, 291, 292, 309
  Art. 5(2)(c)   144, 288, 295, 308

Art. 5(2)(d) 299, 308
Art. 5(2)(e) 308
Art. 5(3)(a) 289, 293, 294, 295, 308
Art. 5(3)(b) 299, 308
Art. 5(3)(c) 214, 282, 284, 285, 287
Art. 5(3)(d) 282, 283, 286
Art. 5(3)(e) 107, 283, 285, 308
Art. 5(3)(f) 283, 285
Art. 5(3)(g) 303
Art. 5(3)(h) 299
Art. 5(3)(i) 299, 300
Art. 5(3)(j) 162, 299, 300
Art. 5(3)(k) 283, 284
Art. 5(3)(m) 299
Art. 5(3)(n) 144, 289, 296
Art. 5(3)(o) 277, 302
Art. 5(4) 282, 288, 289
Art. 5(5) 298
Art. 6 3, 308
Art. 6(4) 307, 308, 309
Art. 9 108, 158, 287, 306

Rental Right Directive
Art. 5 303
Art. 5(1) 158
Art. 5(3) 126, 158

Term Directive 196
recital 9 200

Foreign legislation

Australia

Copyright Act 1905
s. 28 257, 258

Copyright Act 1912 257

Copyright Act 1968
s. 10 228
ss. 40–73 249
s. 40 227
s. 40(2) 228
s. 40(3) 228
s. 42 227
ss. 103A–112E 249
s. 103B 227
s. 103C 227
s. 103C(2) 228
s. 202 301

Austria

Copyright Act 1936 23

Canada

Copyright Act, RSC 1985
ss. 29–30.9 249
ss. 31–32.2 249

France

Intellectual Property Code 1992
Art. 122(5) 49, 284

Germany

Basic Law
Art. 14 203, 204

Copyright Act 1965
Art. 24(1) 49, 207, 284
Art. 45 206
Art. 45a 206
Art. 46 206
Art. 47 206
Art. 48 206
Art. 49(1) 206

Art. 49(2) 206
Art. 50 206
Art. 51 206
Art. 52a 206
Art. 53(1) 205
Art. 53(2) 205
Art. 53(2)(1) 205
Art. 53(2)(2) 205
Art. 53(2)(3) 205

India

Copyright Act 1957
ss. 52(1)(a)–(za) 249

New Zealand

Copyright Act 1994
ss. 40–92 249

Singapore

Copyright Act 1987
ss. 35–74 249

South Africa

Copyright Act 1978
ss. 12–19B 249

Spain

Copyright Act 1996
Art. 39 284

United States

Constitution of the United States
  Art. 1, cl. 8 (the 'copyright clause')
  First Amendment 2, 8, 18, 19, 20, 26, 33
  Fifth Amendment 105

Copyright Act 1976 (17 USC)
  s. 107 4, 249
  s. 108(a)–(i) 249
  s. 1201(a)(1) 270

International instruments

Berne Convention 1886
  Art. 8 2
Berne Convention 1971
  Art. 9(2) 2, 106, 216
  Art. 10(1) 286
  Art. 10bis(2) 65, 285
  Art. 17 106
European Convention on the Protection of Human Rights and Fundamental Freedoms 1950
  Art. 8 85, 109
  Art. 10 23, 109
  Art. 10(2) 34

  Prot. 1, Art. 1 105
TRIPS 1994
  Art. 7 187, 218, 271
  Art. 8 218, 271
  Art. 10 106
  Art. 13 2, 217, 271
WIPO Copyright Treaty 1996
  Preamble 188
  Art. 11 3, 74
WIPO Performances and Phonograms Treaty 1996
  Preamble 188
  Art. 18 3, 74

Introduction

The exceptions in focus

Copyright law seems to have lurched from one crisis to another over recent years.[1] Debates have raged over how new types of subject matter can be accommodated within copyright law,[2] whether the term of protection for copyright ought to be extended, how to respond to the unauthorised distribution of works over the Internet and whether developing countries ought to be forced to adopt Western copyright standards. More recently, controversy has also come to surround the copyright 'exceptions' or 'defences' or 'permitted acts' or 'users' rights' that all modern copyright systems provide so as to privilege certain acts that would otherwise amount to an infringement of copyright. This controversy looks set to continue, with copyright exceptions receiving an unprecedented level of attention from officials, academics and legal practitioners.

In the United Kingdom and elsewhere in Europe the most immediate reason why so much attention has been given to the exceptions is because the European Union (EU) has taken steps towards harmonising this aspect of copyright law as part of the Information Society Directive.[3] This has forced the United Kingdom and other European countries to amend their copyright legislation.[4] However, most countries have sought to minimise the impact of the Information Society Directive, with the

---

[1] Similarly, see Sherman and Bently, p. 1.
[2] Including, for example, multimedia products and electronic databases – questions considered by earlier books in this series. See, respectively, I. Stamatoudi, *Copyright and Multimedia Works: A Comparative Analysis* (Cambridge: Cambridge University Press, 2002); M. Davison, *The Legal Protection of Databases* (Cambridge: Cambridge University Press, 2003).
[3] Directive 2001/29/EC of the European Parliament and of the Council of 22 May 2001 on the harmonisation of certain aspects of copyright and related rights in the information society. Hereafter, the Information Society Directive.
[4] In the United Kingdom the relevant changes were brought into effect by the Copyright and Related Rights Regulations 2003 (SI 2003 No 2498), which came into force on 31 October 2003. The Information Society Directive should have been implemented by 22 December 2003, but the United Kingdom, like most other member states, found it impossible to meet this deadline.

result that significant differences remain between the laws of member states as regards the exceptions. Consequently, questions are likely to arise as to whether countries are complying with their obligations under European law, and the European Commission may seek to revisit this aspect of its harmonisation agenda.

Developments at the European level should also be seen alongside international developments that are turning the exceptions into a source of potential controversy. Although the various international instruments relating to copyright have long contained provisions dealing with this aspect of copyright law,[5] for the most part national governments and legislatures were left with a free hand in this area. Unsurprisingly, this led to 'bewildering differences in national copyright Acts in the area of exemptions and limitations'.[6] More recently, however, the TRIPS Agreement has limited the freedom of member states to provide copyright exceptions. While the relevant provision of TRIPS has its origins in the Berne Convention, the enforcement mechanism of TRIPS means that member states are being forced to treat the TRIPS provision as more than a mere general statement of principle, as was the case under Berne.[7]

A third reason why attention is being focused on the exceptions is that, in the United Kingdom at least, interest in such provisions has coincided with developments in other areas of the law. Most notably, increased interest in the exceptions has coincided with the coming into force of the Human Rights Act.[8] Not only has this created interest generally in the intersection between copyright and the fundamental rights and freedoms guaranteed under that Act (in particular, freedom of expression), it has also furthered interest in the question of the extent to which limitations and exceptions can be found outside copyright law, that is, the circumstances in which human rights law, competition law or the general principles of the common law might operate to limit the rights granted to copyright owners.

A fourth factor that explains why the exceptions are becoming increasingly controversial is that many people are concerned that an interrelated

---

[5] See Berne Convention (1886 text), Art. 8: 'As regards the liberty of extracting portions from literary or artistic works for use in publications destined for educational or scientific purposes, or for chrestomathies ['a collection of selected passages from an author or authors, especially one compiled to assist in learning a language' – *Shorter OED*], the matter is to be decided by the legislation of the different countries of the Union, or by special arrangements existing or to be concluded between them'.
[6] T. Hoeren, *Copyright in Electronic Delivery Services and Multimedia Products* (Luxembourg: European Commission, 1995), p. 12.
[7] The relevant provisions are Art. 9(2) of the Berne Convention and Art. 13 of the TRIPS Agreement. See Chapters 7 and 9 for detailed discussion.
[8] Human Rights Act 1998. The Act came into force on 2 October 2000.

set of technological and legal developments will result in copyright owners being able to exclude the operation of the exceptions. There is a strong international trend towards providing legal protection for 'technological measures of protection', that is, for devices or technologies that are designed to prevent or restrict the reproduction of copyright works.[9] Copyright owners insist that legal protection for technological measures of protection is essential if they are to have the confidence to make their works available in digital form. Critics have argued, however, that protection for technological measures, together with the possibility that owners may seek to exclude the operation of the exceptions through contract, may alter dramatically the relationship between copyright owners and users.

More generally, interest in copyright exceptions has increased as awareness of copyright law and other forms of intellectual property has risen. In particular, those who work with copyright on a day-to-day basis are coming to appreciate the importance of the exceptions to their ordinary working practices. For example, artists are coming to appreciate that whether they need permission to use parts of the cultural environment will largely depend upon the range and scope of the exceptions that any given copyright system provides. Similarly, those working in the education sector have had to confront the fact that because the exceptions relating to education are limited, widespread copying practices in universities and schools constitute an infringement of copyright. Even librarians and archivists, who have long been concerned with copyright, have had to confront new issues as they consider the extent to which they are able to place materials online and provide other digital services for their readers.

If it is possible to point to a number of factors that are coming together to push debates about the exceptions centre stage, it is also important to appreciate that arguments about the exceptions often form part of a wider dispute between those who are in favour of the expansion of copyright and those who would like to see copyright protection curtailed. For example, now that the argument that the digital environment should be entirely unregulated by copyright law has been lost[10] (at least at the political level[11]), those opposed to the operation of copyright in cyberspace have turned their attention to ensuring that copyright is applied in as

---

[9] For evidence of the international trend, see WIPO Copyright Treaty 1996, Art. 11; WIPO Performances and Phonograms Treaty 1996, Art. 18; Information Society Directive, Art. 6.

[10] Compare, most famously, J. Barlow, 'Selling Wine without Bottles: The Economy of Mind on the Global Net', in P. Ludlow (ed.), *High Noon on the Electronic Frontier* (Cambridge, Mass.: MIT Press, 1996).

[11] But see Chapter 10 for a discussion of the possibility that at the social level copyright may increasingly come to be seen as illegitimate.

narrow a form as possible. One way of achieving this is to insist that copyright protection should be subject to a range of broad exceptions. In some respects, therefore, disputes over the exceptions are merely a veneer that disguises more fundamental disagreements about the functions of, and justifications for, a copyright system, and it is unsurprising that the existing literature is deeply divided on the question of whether the exceptions ought to expand or contract. As will become apparent, we are in favour of a liberalisation of the exceptions and hence, broadly speaking, fall into the pro-user camp. Taking the United Kingdom's system of 'permitted acts' as our principal focus, we argue that the current legislative regime is much too restrictive and that user interests have never been accorded the weight they deserve. In order to defend this position it is first necessary to pause and consider the approach to the provision of copyright exceptions in the United Kingdom that has been adopted and the roles such provisions play.

The functions of the exceptions

Although all modern copyright systems provide for circumstances in which copyright will not be infringed by the unauthorised reproduction or presentation of a copyright work, there are two general approaches to the provision of copyright exceptions that can be taken. The first approach is to provide a small number of generally worded exceptions. The second approach is to provide a larger number of much more specific exceptions, encompassing carefully defined activities. Although no country can be said to adhere rigidly to either approach, some countries lean towards one approach rather than the other. The United States, for example, leans towards the first approach. This is because US copyright law contains a broad 'fair use' defence.[12] The effect of this defence is such that any use which a court deems to be 'fair' will be treated as non-infringing. Admittedly, the US Act does seek to provide guidance as to how the question of whether the use was 'fair' is to be determined, but ultimately fair use remains a highly flexible instrument.

In contrast to the United States, the United Kingdom leans heavily towards the second approach. Thus Chapter III, Part I of the Copyright, Designs and Patents Act 1988 consists of more than 60 sections that set out, often in great detail, a wide range of acts that will not infringe copyright. Given the number of exceptions that have been incorporated into the Act, the claim that the current system fails to provide adequate protection for users may well seem extraordinary at first. However, once

---

[12] Copyright Act 1976 (17 USC), s. 107.

Introduction 5

it is appreciated that under UK law the exceptions perform a range of different functions this claim may well seem much more plausible.

Copyright exceptions are most commonly thought of as representing situations in which the legislature has decided to prioritise some other interest over the interests of the copyright owner, and many of the United Kingdom's permitted acts do take this form. It is important, however, to distinguish the provisions that reflect some overriding goal of public policy from permitted acts that have a rather different function and effect. In particular, some permitted acts are provided to deal with the special nature of certain types of work. For example, the Copyright, Designs and Patents Act 1988 contains special provisions relating to computer programs.[13] These provisions are designed to ensure that the copyright owner does not abuse its monopoly in circumstances where the general principles of copyright might seem to offer such an opportunity.[14] Similarly, there are a number of exceptions that only apply to artistic works consisting of the design of a typeface.[15] These exceptions go even further and establish a distinctive and much more limited form of copyright than that which exists in other types of artistic work. (In effect, these exceptions reduce the copyright monopoly to a 25-year term and limit the owner's monopoly to the right to control the production and sale of articles designed to produce the typeface). Still other exceptions are provided to mark out the boundary between copyright and designs law, so that owners are forced to rely on the most appropriate form of protection.[16] The exceptions therefore play an important part in modifying copyright law so as to ensure that it fits different types of subject matter whilst preserving the illusion that copyright law consists of one set of standards and one set of principles that apply equally to all types of work.

Another group of permitted acts should be viewed in the context of industry or media regulation more generally. Here we have in mind the provisions relating to broadcasts which allow copies of broadcasts to be made for the purposes of oversight by a regulatory body,[17] which allow for retransmission of a broadcast by cable[18] and which allow for temporary copies to be made of a work for the purpose of broadcasting.[19] These provisions are best understood as part of a much wider regime of broadcasting regulation which includes regulation of content, 'must

---

[13] CDPA 1988, ss. 50A–50C, and see also s. 56 (transfers of copies of works in electronic form).
[14] For example, s. 50B of the Act provides a decompilation exception, without which a copyright owner's monopoly would extend beyond the boundaries of 'the work' to include the sole right to produce compatible products.
[15] CDPA 1988, ss. 54–55.   [16] *Ibid.*, ss. 51–53.
[17] *Ibid.*, s. 69.   [18] *Ibid.*, ss. 73–73A.   [19] *Ibid.*, s. 68.

carry' obligations for cable service providers, the 'needletime' compulsory licence[20] and oversight and control of licences and licensing schemes by the Copyright Tribunal.

It is important to emphasise that we are not claiming that the above threefold division of the permitted acts is comprehensive or that there are not a number of other, equally plausible, ways of dividing up and thinking about the permitted acts. However, for the reasons given above, it is important to recognise that the permitted acts perform a range of different functions and that they should not all be treated as if they represent circumstances in which Parliament has decided to privilege some other interest over the interests of the copyright owner. Nevertheless, it must equally be recognised that it is the exceptions that reflect some overriding goal of public policy that are the most controversial provisions and those on which litigation and demands for reform most often centre.

The plan of this work and our argument in outline

In order to make the case for reform of the exceptions we have divided this work into three parts. The first part consists of a detailed examination of some of the United Kingdom's existing exceptions. It is important to emphasise that no attempt is made to provide a comprehensive treatment of all of the permitted acts. Rather, we concentrate on those exceptions that relate to the protection of important rights and interests. Our aims in this first part of the book are twofold. First, we set out to demonstrate why exceptions of this type are required. More specifically, we demonstrate in Chapter 1 that copyright has the potential to impose serious restrictions on freedom of expression and that the exceptions have a key role to play in ensuring that copyright does not unduly burden political communication and artistic freedom. Similarly, in Chapters 4 and 5 we emphasise the importance of the exceptions for scholarly research and other forms of study and for the activities of 'institutional users' of copyright, such as educational establishments, libraries, archives, museums and galleries.

Our second aim in the first part of the book is to provide a detailed analysis of current law in those areas on which we have chosen to concentrate. To this end, in Chapter 2 we consider at length the fair dealing exceptions that allow reuse of part of a work for the purposes of criticism, review and news reporting. We also consider a number of related exceptions in this chapter, for example, the provision that allows for the use of records of spoken words. In Chapter 3 we turn to consider whether, in addition to the exceptions considered in Chapter 2, UK law contains

---

[20] *Ibid.*, ss. 135A–G. For background see *Copinger*, para. 29.28.

a public interest defence and, if so, the circumstances in which such a defence might now be available. The final chapters in the first section of the book, Chapters 4 and 5, consider the provisions that apply to research and private study and to establishments such as schools, universities, libraries and archives. In each case, our argument is that the current provisions suffer from a number of serious defects and cause real practical difficulties for those who have to deal with copyright as part of their ordinary working lives. More specifically, we set out to demonstrate that the current provisions are much too inflexible. Not only can this create injustice for particular defendants, at a more general level it prevents courts from responding creatively to technological developments or new artistic practices. Many of the exceptions are also outdated, unnecessarily complicated and bureaucratic. In addition, however, our analysis reveals that considerable uncertainty surrounds the scope and operation of some of the exceptions. This is particularly important, because the strongest argument for the United Kingdom's existing approach to the exceptions (that is, for providing a long list of detailed exceptions) is that it provides certainty, for owners and users alike. If it can be shown that the current system does not in fact provide certainty, the case for reform becomes overwhelming.

By providing a detailed doctrinal analysis of the current provisions together with a consideration of why such provisions are justified and illustrations of some of the practical problems caused by the United Kingdom's current approach, we hope to be able to convince opponents of reform that at least some liberalisation of the permitted acts is desirable. In particular, we hope that advocates of strong copyright protection will recognise that there are some circumstances in which it would be highly undesirable to allow copyright owners to enforce their rights and others in which there is no realistic prospect of owners being able to exercise their rights effectively. We do not accept that it is necessarily naïve to suppose that copyright owners might be persuaded of the case for reform if the problems with the current system are laid out sufficiently clearly, and more generally we are uncomfortable with the tendency amongst some pro-user commentators to portray the copyright industries and their representatives as irredeemably wicked and self-centred.

We also believe that an approach that takes current law and practice as its starting point is preferable to starting with a normative theory of copyright law and attempting to build an ideal system from the ground up. That is, we believe that our approach is preferable to attempts to use a particular justification or set of justifications for copyright to construct an ideal system of rights and exceptions. All too often copyright theorists of various persuasions have applied their preferred visions of copyright much too mechanistically, ignoring the increasingly accepted insight that there needs to be an interaction between our ethical principles and our observations of the world and its complexities.[21] A closely related failing is that many copyright theorists write as if they were designing a copyright law in a state of nature, rather than against the backdrop of an existing body of law that has created a series of expectations around which a variety of actors have structured agreements, understandings and practices. This is not to suggest that our current arrangements are sacrosanct or that particular fundamental reforms are not desirable, but it does mean that all reforms, including reform of the exceptions, must be judged against the disruption they would create as well as against more concrete standards.

In the second part of the book we move away from doctrinal analysis and turn to consider why users have received a poor deal in the United Kingdom. In outline, we argue that a complex set of factors is responsible. Political factors (such as the disparity in lobbying power between owner representative and user groups and the way in which the United Kingdom chooses to implement European legislation), institutional factors (such as the division of departmental responsibilities within government), constitutional factors (such as the mandate of the European Commission), accidental factors (in particular, the effect of poor drafting) and the attitude of the judiciary towards users, all have to be accounted for. In addition, however, we believe that certain widely held beliefs about copyright law and the nature and role of the exceptions have played both a direct and an indirect role in influencing the shape of the current regime. Consequently Chapter 6 is concerned with a number of ideas and assumptions about copyright and the role of the exceptions that have informed and continue to reinforce the current approach. In particular, we criticise the argument that exceptions should only be available in cases of market failure (an argument that is becoming increasingly important in the light of recent technological developments), the idea that the exceptions must be interpreted narrowly because copyright is a property right, and the idea that copyright represents a balance between the interests of owners and users. Thus, for example, we argue that the idea that copyright represents a balance is, at best, an empty rhetorical flourish and, at worst, is a device used to close off debates about the proper boundaries of copyright law.

---

[21] Cf. J. Glover, *Humanity: A Moral History of the Twentieth Century* (London: Pimlico 2001), in particular p. 6, developing Rawls' idea of the 'Reflective Equilibrium', as to which see J. Rawls, *A Theory of Justice* (Oxford: Oxford University Press, 1973), in particular pp. 48–50. See also J. Waldron, *Law and Disagreement* (Oxford: Clarendon, 1999), in particular pp. 5–6, discussing the requirement of 'fit'.

Introduction 9

The remaining two chapters in the second section, Chapters 7 and 8, are concerned respectively with the supranational and domestic legislative and political processes that have produced the current regime. We argue that the interests of users have not been adequately accounted for at either the supranational or domestic level, but that users have struggled to make their voices heard at the supranational level in particular. This provides cause for concern about the effect of a shift in the law-making process in the copyright field from the domestic to the European level. It does not, however, lead us to conclude that the exceptions should be solely a matter for domestic law, since we are also concerned about the practical consequences of differences between national standards for the international marketing of derivative works.

The third section of the book is concerned with options for reform. In Chapter 9 we consider the argument that has frequently been put that the United Kingdom (and other Commonwealth jurisdictions) should move to adopt a general, US-style, fair use defence. We argue against this solution for a number of reasons. Most fundamentally, we believe that a search for a legislative solution is, by itself, potentially fruitless, because it is also important to appreciate the role that the judiciary has played in the emergence of the current system of exceptions. Starting with the history of the copyright exceptions in the United Kingdom, we demonstrate that if judges are unable to protect users at present, this is at least in part because they have divested themselves of a series of tools that could have been used to keep copyright protection within more appropriate bounds. We therefore conclude that any proposal that focuses solely on the need for legislative reform should be treated with caution, and that without a change in judicial attitudes the introduction of a fair use defence might achieve little. Of course, this still leaves open the possibility of arguing for the introduction of a fair use defence coupled with a change in judicial mindset. However, we also argue that the political obstacles to the introduction of a fair use defence are such that it makes more sense to look for alternative ways of reforming the exceptions.

In the final chapter, therefore, we turn to outline our preferred model of reform. Somewhat counterintuitively, we argue that the Information Society Directive provides an opportunity for fundamental reform. Thus far, pro-user commentators have invariably been implacably opposed to the Information Society Directive, probably in large part because the initial proposals for a directive would have dramatically curtailed the range and scope of copyright exceptions across Europe. In contrast, we argue that it is important to look at the final version of the Directive and that if the wording of the Directive were to be followed closely this would result in the introduction of a range of flexible, but not entirely open-ended, exceptions. Provided such provisions were supplemented by a public interest defence (which we argue can be justified within the terms of the Directive) and minimum standards around which institutional users could safely structure their copyright policies, this approach would represent the beginnings of a much better deal for users.

We therefore believe that we are confronted with a rare opportunity for fundamental reform of the exceptions. That this is a result of the Information Society Directive is paradoxical, given the problems users have had in influencing the European legislative process. But it is an opportunity that should nevertheless be seized.

A note on language

As a final introductory point it is perhaps worth saying something briefly about the language we have employed in this study. One of the problems that confronts anyone who wishes to write about copyright 'exceptions' is that there is no neutral language with which to describe the subject matter under consideration. This is because disagreements about how the 'exceptions' ought to be described have formed part of the broader dispute between pro-owner and pro-user commentators. On the one hand, proponents of increased copyright protection tend to prefer the language of copyright 'exceptions'. This indicates that these provisions run counter to the ordinary rule and hence that they ought to be interpreted narrowly – that these provisions are to be treated as 'exceptional'. On the other hand, pro-user commentators tend to prefer to style the 'exceptions' as 'users' rights' or as 'rights of the public'. This suggests that such provisions are to be treated on an equal footing with the rights given to copyright owners. In contrast, we believe that although copyright law *ought* to recognise 'users' rights', it is a mistake to describe the current provisions in these terms. First, as an historical matter, we believe that it is important to recognise that the current system of permitted acts has its origins in those spaces that were left unregulated after copyright was expanded (initially by the judiciary) beyond its role as a system for the regulation of the book trade. To represent the current provisions as if they were purposely designed at their inception to protect the interests of the public may be to underestimate the difficulties of reform. Second, we believe that to refer to the current provisions as users' rights may be to lose a useful means of describing the reforms that are required. Politically, it may be more effective to insist that the current system of 'exceptions' needs to be replaced by a system of 'users' rights'.

We should also say something about our employment of the term 'users' to describe all those who might seek to rely on an exception. It is important to emphasise that this is merely intended to be a shorthand – our analysis does not rest on the importance of recognising 'users' as a class of persons in need of protection.[22]

[22] This is a point to which we return in the final chapter.

Part I

Where we are

1 Copyright and freedom of expression

We begin our analysis of the exceptions in the United Kingdom by considering those provisions that relate to activities such as criticism, review and news reporting. In the next chapter we provide a detailed analysis of the current provisions that relate to such activities, focusing, in particular, on the section 30 fair dealing exceptions. We argue that the current provisions suffer from a number of serious shortcomings. Before turning to consider the current provisions, however, it is necessary to consider why exceptions covering activities such as criticism, review and news reporting are justified – the limits of the current provisions are only a matter of concern if broader exceptions are warranted. A number of justifications have been offered for such provisions. For example, it has been argued that an exception for 'reviews' (in the narrow sense of book reviews, film reviews and the like) can be justified on the economic ground that reviews increase the supply of information to consumers and hence help them to make more informed purchasing decisions.[1] In contrast, although we do not discount other justifications, we seek to demonstrate that rights of criticism, review and so on are necessary to reconcile the potential conflict between copyright and freedom of expression or freedom of information.[2]

In outline, we argue that although the capacity of copyright to interfere with freedom of expression is being increasingly recognised, there has been a tendency amongst judges and commentators alike to downplay the extent of the intersection between the two interests. The explanation for this tendency probably lies in the fact that attempting to reconcile copyright with a broad notion of freedom of expression is a daunting

---

[1] W. Landes, 'Copyright, Borrowed Images and Appropriation Art: An Economic Approach' (2000) 9 *George Mason Law Review* 1, 10.
[2] Freedom of expression and a right of access to information are treated together in the remainder of this chapter because of our particular concern with the importance of freedom of expression for the effective functioning of democratic processes. According to this view freedom of expression is conceived not merely as a right that vests in the speaker for that person's benefit, but also as a right that benefits society by ensuring that the general public has uncensored access to a wide range of views and information. See n. 82 below and accompanying text.

task. Moreover, a broad understanding of copyright's ability to interfere with freedom of expression raises awkward questions about whether a copyright system is ethically justified or constitutionally legitimate at all. Given that even the most strident critics of the current copyright system have stepped back from calling for the outright abolition of copyright,[3] it is hardly surprising that the judiciary and commentators with more moderate reform agendas have sought to present the intersection between copyright and freedom of expression in limited and hence manageable terms. Rather than attempting to downplay the extent of the potential conflict between copyright and freedom of expression, we argue that the intersection between copyright and freedom of expression is much more significant than is normally assumed to be the case. This does not, however, lead us to conclude that copyright should be curtailed drastically, because we subscribe to a model of freedom of expression that can account for the importance of intellectual property protection.

Recognising the problem

There has been scholarly interest in the relationship between copyright and freedom of expression for more than thirty years, but it is only over recent years that this subject has received sustained attention.[4] The increased attention that is being paid to this topic is due in large part to the controversy that has come to surround the intellectual property system. Commentators who are concerned about the expansion of intellectual property rights often seek to cast their objections in human rights terms. In so doing they ensure that their concerns are expressed in a language that has general resonance. In the patent context, for example, this turn to human rights-based arguments has been reflected in debates about whether patent protection for pharmaceuticals can interfere with rights to life, healthcare and development.[5] In the copyright context the main focus has been on the capacity of copyright to interfere with freedom of expression. If the increasingly controversial nature of intellectual property

---

[3] See, e.g., John Perry Barlow, 'Politics and Ownership', paper delivered at the Institute of Contemporary Arts in London, 6 November 2002, unconcerned about the operation of copyright in the analogue environment; J. Boyle, *Shamans, Software and Spleens* (Cambridge, Mass.: Harvard University Press, 1996), p. 172, calling for copyright to be restricted to a twenty-year term and for a more generous fair use defence.

[4] Patterson notes, however, that one of the justifications put forward for the First Amendment during debates on the adoption of a Bill of Rights in the United States was that it would prevent Congress from misusing its powers under the copyright clause of the Constitution: L. Patterson, 'Free Speech, Copyright and Fair Use' (1987) 40 *Vanderbilt Law Review* 1.

[5] See, e.g., P. Drahos, 'Intellectual Property and Human Rights' [1999] IPQ 349, 362.

rights has created interest generally in the relationship between copyright and freedom of expression, in the United Kingdom the coming into force of the Human Rights Act 1998 has increased this interest still further.

The most positive effect of the attention that has been given to the relationship between copyright and freedom of expression over recent years is that the potential conflict between the two interests is now widely, although by no means universally, accepted to be the most controversial potential consequence of providing strong copyright protection. Furthermore, the work that has been done in this field has done a good job of discrediting the argument that there is no tension between copyright and communicative freedom because copyright only extends to protect expression and not underlying ideas or facts (an argument to which we return in the next section). Taken collectively, this work has also developed a range of scenarios that illustrate the scope of the potential conflict between the two interests. However, with one or two notable exceptions, individual commentators have tended to shy away from confronting the full range of circumstances in which copyright can be said convincingly to interfere with freedom of expression. Instead they have chosen to focus on particular issues and problems.

It is instructive to consider why there might be a temptation to downplay the potential conflict between copyright and freedom of expression. In particular, we believe that it is important to recognise that reconciling copyright and freedom of expression is a daunting task. Difficulties arise on a number of levels. Any accommodation requires the articulation of a convincing theory of freedom of expression. Yet any attempt to elaborate such a theory requires consideration of an immense literature. Within this literature we find a host of competing rationales for traditional rights of free speech. Although, in general terms, each of these rationales points towards the importance of freedom of expression, at a level of detail (including the extent to which copyright protection is compatible with freedom of expression) these rationales can point to very different outcomes. Over and above disagreements as to why rights to freedom of expression are justified, we also find commentators who believe that the language of freedom of expression is unable to account for (post)modern conditions,[6] who believe that rights of free speech need to be fundamentally restructured[7] or who subscribe to some variant of

---

[6] See, e.g., R. Coombe, *The Cultural Life of Intellectual Properties: Authorship, Appropriation and the Law* (Durham, N.C.: Duke University Press, 1998), ch. 6.
[7] See T. Streeter, 'Some Thoughts on Free Speech, Language and the Rule of Law', in D. Allen and R. Jensen (eds.), *Freeing the First Amendment* (New York: New York

the critique that in capitalist societies 'the only freedom of the press . . . is for those who own one'.[8]

Having articulated a theory of speech it is then necessary to determine the extent to which freedom of expression can be set off legitimately against other rights and interests, including the interests of copyright owners. This issue will be determined in part by the rationale for freedom of expression that is adopted, but other factors will also come into play. Most obviously, there are a number of different justifications for copyright protection, some of which might justify protection even in circumstances in which copyright protection interferes with freedom of expression. In particular, if copyright protection is justified as a 'natural right' of an author, then the fact that copyright interferes with freedom of expression may not mean that the former has to give way, since the conflict can then be seen in terms of a clash of two, possibly incommensurable, natural rights.

If copyright is justified on some basis other than natural rights or if freedom of expression is seen as a more fundamental natural right than copyright (and few commentators have been willing to go down the path of accepting that copyright imposes a substantial burden on freedom of expression and yet insist that copyright remains justifiable as a natural right of authors), the question then becomes how best to reconcile the conflict between the two. The most obvious solution is to provide a defence covering all situations in which copyright and freedom of expression collide. A number of commentators have adopted this approach. However, the majority of them have also started with the premise that copyright protection, in some form at least, is both justifiable and desirable. The natural temptation, therefore, is to develop a closed list of examples of when copyright can come into conflict with freedom of expression and then to propose the introduction or extension of an exception so as to deal with this narrowly defined set of problem cases.[9] The alternative – that is, to recognise that copyright imposes limitations on freedom of expression in a wide range of circumstances – is unattractive because,

---

University Press, 1995), p. 31, arguing that a variety of traditions dealing, *inter alia*, with pornography and racial issues are premised not on the belief that there should be exceptions to freedom of expression, but rather that freedom of expression itself needs to be reinterpreted.

[8] A. J. Liebling, cited in Streeter, 'Some Thoughts', p. 47.

[9] See also E. Baker, 'First Amendment Limits on Copyright' (2002) 55 *Vanderbilt Law Review* 891, 897: 'Those commentators who see [conflict between copyright and freedom of expression] as only an occasional state of affairs often hope to resolve the conflict by placing discrete limits on copyright – either in the form of constitutionally inspired "fair use" defenses or through a more explicit First Amendment privilege – that would allow the public to receive all ideas.'

having accepted that copyright should give way to freedom of expression, this raises serious questions about whether a copyright system is legitimate at all.

Even if a broad view of the conflict between copyright and freedom of expression does not lead us to conclude that copyright protection is entirely illegitimate, the assumption that copyright should give way to freedom of expression in all circumstances where the two collide would still lead to the introduction of an incredibly broad free speech exception. If we accept that copyright acts as an incentive for the creation of certain types of work in at least some circumstances, such a broad exception might result in the under-production of some types of copyright subject matter. Moreover, other possibilities, such as the provision of a free speech compulsory licence,[10] create awkward problems in the absence of a detailed discussion of what happens to those who cannot afford the licence fee.[11]

It can therefore be seen that recognising a broad overlap between copyright and freedom of expression engenders a number of difficulties. Nevertheless, we believe that it is disingenuous to claim that there is a bright line between circumstances in which copyright protection interferes with freedom of expression and those in which it does not, and think that it is important to recognise that there is a broad spectrum of cases in which copyright can interfere with expressive freedom. In our view, however, this does not necessarily lead to the conclusion that copyright protection should give way to freedom of expression in all circumstances. Rather, we argue that although there are cases in which the threat to freedom of expression is so severe that copyright must give way, there are a range of other circumstances in which there is plenty of room for good faith disagreement about where to draw the boundary between copyright protection and expressive freedom. This is particularly true as regards circumstances in which copyright has the potential to interfere with later creative activities. The important thing to appreciate about the current UK regime, however, is that it manifestly fails to take proper account of the importance of freedom of expression. It will be seen in the next chapter that the current regime fails to protect the right to communicate

---

[10] Cf. M. Nimmer, 'Does Copyright Abridge the First Amendment Guarantees of Free Speech and the Press?' (1970) 17 UCLA Law Review 1180, 1199, proposing a compulsory licence for 'news photographs'; D. Quentel, 'Bad Artists Copy. Good Artists Steal.: The Ugly Conflict Between Copyright Law and Appropriationism' (1996) 4 UCLA Entertainment Law Review 39, proposing a compulsory licence for certain types of appropriation art.
[11] While we may recognise that the effective exercise of political rights is often constrained by a lack of resources, building an ability to pay limitation into freedom of expression in advance is still likely to strike many people as objectionable.

information and to express opinions on important matters. Moreover, although the question of how best to reconcile the interests of copyright owners with the expressive interests of subsequent authors is inherently complex, it is clear that UK law does not begin to accord sufficient importance to the interests of later authors.

We develop our argument by reviewing the earlier literature that has recognised the potential conflict between copyright and freedom of expression. This is a valuable exercise because, to reiterate, within this literature we find a host of convincing examples of when copyright can interfere with freedom of expression. We then turn to explore what can be drawn from these examples and consider how to deal with the conflict between copyright and freedom of expression. But before we go further, it is important to deal with an argument that is still sometimes used to dismiss concerns about the impact of copyright on freedom of expression, namely, that the idea/expression dichotomy prevents any conflict between the two interests.

The idea/expression dichotomy and judicial reaction

The suggestion that copyright can encumber freedom of expression may at first seem implausible, given that one of the founding principles of copyright law is usually said to be that copyright does not give a monopoly over ideas or facts, but only over the author's expression. It can therefore be argued that there is no relationship between copyright and freedom of expression since copyright cannot prevent someone from talking about, writing about or receiving information on any subject whatsoever. The view that the idea/expression dichotomy prevents copyright from impinging on free speech interests has received judicial support in a number of jurisdictions, including the United States,[12]

---

[12] See, e.g., *Sid & Marty Krofft Television* v. *McDonald's* 562 F 2d 1157 (1977), 1170: 'the idea–expression dichotomy already serves to accommodate the competing interests of copyright and the first amendment' (per Carter, Circuit Judge); *Schnapper* v. *Foley* 471 F Supp 426 (1979), 428, referring, *inter alia*, to *Sid & Marty Krofft* and concluding: 'it is well established that there is no conflict between the First Amendment and the copyright laws' (per Smith Jr, District Judge); *Harper & Row Publishers* v. *Nation Enterprises* 471 US 539 (1985), 556: 'The Second Circuit noted, correctly, that copyright's idea/expression dichotomy "strike[s] a definitional balance between the First Amendment and the Copyright Act by permitting free communication of facts while still protecting an author's expression"' (per Justice O'Connor); *Eldred* v. *Reno* 239 F 3d 372, 376 (2001): '[the contested legislation] puts the works on the latter half of the "idea/expression dichotomy" and makes them subject to fair use. This obviates further inquiry under the First Amendment' (per Ginsburg, Circuit Judge). See also W. Gordon, 'A Property Right in Self-Expression: Equality and Individualism in the Natural Law of Intellectual Property' (1993) 102 *Yale Law Journal* 1533, and the other cases discussed therein.

Australia[13] and the United Kingdom. In the United Kingdom in *Associated Newspapers* v. *News Group Newspapers*[14] Walton J dismissed the argument that copyright can conflict with freedom of expression as follows:

> [The defendant] has tried to make a great deal of play on the lines that to grant the injunction would be to interfere with the press's freedom of speech or publication. It seems to me that that is total nonsense. A person is not in any way prohibited from saying exactly what he likes, or publishing exactly what he likes, if he cannot publish it in the precise words which someone else has used, which is the essence of copyright. Freedom of speech is interfered with when someone is not allowed to say what is the truth.[15]

Much the same sentiment seems to have underpinned Mance LJ's statement in *Hyde Park* v. *Yelland*[16] that 'copyright does not lie on the same continuum as, nor is it the antithesis of, freedom of expression'.[17] However, despite there being some judicial support for the view that the idea/expression dichotomy ensures that there is no overlap between copyright and freedom of expression and despite the fact that versions of this argument are still encountered from time to time in the literature,[18] this view is now largely discredited.

The most fundamental problem with the argument that the idea/expression dichotomy prevents copyright from burdening freedom of expression is that this claim rests on a narrow understanding of freedom of expression. First, the assumption that it is always possible to find an alternative means of conveying exactly the same thoughts and ideas is problematic. Freedom of expression extends not merely to the ability to convey a general message, but also to the ability to convey particular subtleties and nuances. Thus, even as regards literary and dramatic works, it is far from obvious that it will be possible in every case to convey exactly the same message using an alternate form of words.[19] As regards visual works, such as paintings, photographs and films, the claim is entirely unpersuasive. Second, even on the assumption that a means of conveying exactly the same message exists, to suggest that the *potential defendant* will,

---

[13] See *Skybase Nominees* v. *Fortuity* (1996) 36 IPR 529, 531: 'the fact that another work deals with the same ideas or discusses matters of fact also raised in the work in respect of which copyright is said to subsist will not, of itself, constitute an infringement. Were it otherwise the copyright laws would be an impediment to free speech, rather than an encouragement of original expression.'
[14] [1986] RPC 515.   [15] *Ibid.*, 517.   [16] [2001] Ch 143.   [17] *Ibid.*, 170.
[18] See, e.g., D. Thomas, 'A Public Interest Defence to Copyright Infringement?' (2003) 14 AIPJ 225, 231.
[19] The same point is made by R. Tushnet, 'Copyright as a Model for Free Speech Law: What Copyright has in Common with Anti-Pornography Laws, Campaign Finance Reform, and Telecommunications Regulation' (2000) 42 *Boston College Law Review* 1, 9–11.

in every case, be able to discover this means of communication is clearly erroneous. As Tushnet has pointed out, freedom of expression 'is not guaranteed only to the well-educated, with thesauruses at their fingertips'.[20] Third, the argument that the idea/expression dichotomy prevents copyright from interfering with freedom of expression ignores the fact that speech will often only be persuasive if it is supported by evidence. Providing this evidence may well involve the reproduction of copyright material.

The argument that the idea/expression dichotomy prevents copyright from burdening freedom of expression is also open to the objection that it rests on a view of the idea/expression dichotomy that bears little resemblance to actual practice. Although it is true to say that copyright does not subsist in very general ideas, it has long been recognised in a range of jurisdictions that copyright protection is not confined to the surface of a work. Consequently, a defendant who tells a similar story in her own words or in a foreign language can infringe copyright in a literary or dramatic work.[21] Similarly, copyright in an artistic work extends to protect the pattern of ideas represented therein – it is only the more general or abstract elements of a work that are excluded from protection.[22] In the light of the fact that copyright extends beyond that which is immediately recognisable as expression, commentators in a number of jurisdictions have doubted whether the idea/expression dichotomy has any explanatory force at all.[23] These doubts have received some judicial support,[24] and more generally judges in the United Kingdom have often shown a

---

[20] *Ibid.*, 16.
[21] See *Designers Guild* v. *Russell Williams (Textiles)* [2001] FSR 113, 121: 'Copyright may be infringed by a work which does not reproduce a single sentence of the original. If one asks what is being protected in such a case, it is difficult to give any answer except that it is an idea expressed in the copyright work' (per Lord Hoffman). Also see Laddie et al., 3rd edn, pp. 97–8 and the cases discussed therein.
[22] See *Designers Guild* v. *Russell Williams (Textiles)* and Laddie et al., 3rd edn, pp. 212–18 and the cases discussed therein.
[23] See Laddie et al., 3rd edn, pp. 97–102; R. Jones, 'The Myth of the Idea/Expression Dichotomy in Copyright Law' (1990) 10 *Pace Law Review* 551; P. Loughlan, 'The Marketplace of Ideas and the Idea/Expression Distinction of Copyright Law' (2002) 23 *Adelaide Law Review* 29.
[24] *Designers Guild* v. *Russell Williams (Textiles)*, 121; *Ibcos Computers* v. *Barclays Mercantile Highland Finance* [1994] FSR 275, 291: 'It should be noted that the aphorism "there is no copyright in an idea" is likely to lead to confusion of thought', and 'The problem may be bedevilled by the "no copyright in an idea" argument' – along the lines of United States Code s.102(b). As I have indicated that has no relevance in United Kingdom law once one goes beyond a mere general idea (at 301–2) (per Jacob J). Also see *Plix Products* v. *Frank M. Winstone (Merchants)* [1986] FSR 63, 92: 'It is no longer universally accepted that there is "no copyright in ideas"' (High Court of New Zealand, per Pritchard J).

reluctance to employ the idea/expression dichotomy when deciding substantive questions such as authorship[25] and infringement.[26]

The argument that the idea/expression dichotomy prevents copyright from imposing a restriction on freedom of expression is therefore incorrect, and even the basic claim that it is possible to convey the same information using a different form of words is potentially misleading. It is also significant that more recent judicial pronouncements have placed less reliance on the idea/expression dichotomy when considering the relationship between copyright and freedom of expression. Thus in the United Kingdom it has been accepted that freedom of expression does at times require that the defendant be able to copy the precise form of a work, albeit only in 'rare' or 'very rare' circumstances.[27] The European Court of Human Rights has also shown a willingness to intervene in the copyright field. In *News Verlags v. Austria*[28] the Court held that the prohibition on the publication of photographs of a person suspected of terrorist offences under the right to privacy in images of persons guaranteed under the Austrian Copyright Act 1936 violated Article 10 of the European Convention on Human Rights. In its most recent decision to touch on the relationship between copyright and the First Amendment, the US Supreme Court placed rather less reliance on the idea/expression dichotomy than in previous cases (although it was still mentioned), preferring to emphasise that the proximity in time between the creation of the copyright clause and the adoption of the First Amendment indicates that copyright is compatible with free speech so long as the legislature does not alter 'the traditional contours of copyright protection'.[29]

---

[25] See *Cala Homes (South) v. Alfred McAlpine Homes East* [1995] FSR 818, 835–6. See also *Heptulla v. Orient Longman* [1989] FSR 598, 609 (High Court of India). But cf. *Donoghue v. Allied Newspapers* [1938] Ch 106, 109.

[26] *Ravenscroft v. Herbert* [1980] RPC 193; *Ibcos Computers v. Barclays Mercantile Highland Finance* [1994] FSR 275.

[27] *Ashdown v. Telegraph Group* [2002] Ch 149. This case is discussed in detail in Chapters 2 and 3.

[28] (2001) 31 EHRR 8. For commentary see I. Simon, 'Picture Perfect' [2002] EIPR 368; R. Burrell and J. Stellios, 'Fair Dealing and Freedom of Expression in the United Kingdom' (2003) 14 AIPJ 45, 50–1. This case can be contrasted with two earlier decisions of the European Commission of Human Rights, *De Geillustreerde Pers v. The Netherlands* (6 July 1976); *France 2 v. France* (15 Jan. 1997). These decisions are discussed in detail by Hugenholtz: B. Hugenholtz, 'Copyright and Freedom of Expression in Europe', in N. Elkin-Koren and N. Netanel (eds.), *The Commodification of Information* (The Hague: Kluwer Law International, 2002), pp. 258–61, who argues that the Commission in these cases 'sidestepped the essence of the conflict between copyright and Article 10'.

[29] *Eldred v. Ashcroft* 537 US 186 (2003), 220–1. For an informative discussion of this aspect of *Eldred* see S. McJohn, '*Eldred*'s Aftermath: Tradition, the Copyright Clause, and the Constitutionalization of Fair Use' (2003) 10 *Michigan Telecommunications and*

Despite the fact that judicial reliance on the idea/expression dichotomy appears be waning, this has not led courts to throw open the question of how copyright protection impacts upon freedom of expression. Rather courts have found other ways of avoiding this line of enquiry, for example by simply asserting that the overlap between copyright and freedom of expression is limited,[30] by focusing on fact-specific tests,[31] or by relying on constitutional and legislative history.[32] This seems to suggest that judges are wary of meeting the challenge of reconciling copyright and freedom of expression. In this context it is worth noting that the UK Court of Appeal referred expressly to the 'floodgates' argument when concluding that the overlap between copyright and freedom of expression is limited,[33] and in the United States it has been suggested that the Supreme Court has recently been motivated by similar concerns.[34] In contrast, we are of the view that attempting to downplay the extent of the intersection between copyright and freedom of expression is unsatisfactory and that the academic work that has been done in this field points to a range of important issues that need to be borne in mind.

Recognising the conflict

Illustrating the problem I

Some proponents of the view that there are circumstances in which freedom of expression requires that defendants be allowed to copy a work have focused on cases in which there is no substitute for the work in question. For example, Melville Nimmer has pointed out that there are works that can make a unique contribution to public understanding and public debate. He gives the example of evidence of atrocities committed by US service personnel during the Vietnam War:

> Consider the photographs of the My Lai massacre. Here is an instance where the visual impact of a graphic work made a unique contribution to an enlightened democratic dialogue. No amount of words describing the 'idea' of the massacre could substitute for the public insight gained through the photographs. The photographic expression, not merely the idea, became essential if the public was to fully understand what occurred in that tragic episode. It would be intolerable if

---

Technology Law Review 95. More generally, see M. Rimmer, 'The Dead Poets Society: The Copyright Term and the Public Domain' (2003) 8(6) *First Monday* (online).

[30] *Ashdown* v. *Telegraph Group* [2002] Ch 149.

[31] *News Verlags* v. *Austria* (2001) 31 EHRR 8, and see Burrell and Stellios, 'Fair Dealing', 51, pointing out that because of the way in which the decision in this case was framed it is open to a range of very different interpretations.

[32] *Eldred* v. *Ashcroft*.   [33] *Ashdown* v. *Telegraph Group*, 167.

[34] See McJohn, 'Eldred's Aftermath', 110.

the public's comprehension of the full meaning of My Lai could be censored by the copyright owner of the photographs.[35]

For Nimmer, the only non-substitutable works are 'news photographs'. Within this category Nimmer also included films, but not other types of graphic work.[36] Spence, however, takes the non-substitutability argument further, arguing that there are some works that have a particular association or carry a special meaning. He gives the example of the 'Internationale', which, he argues, 'with its rich history of political association clearly conveys meanings for which it would not be possible to find an adequate alternative vehicle'.[37]

Spence's expanded view of when a work will not be substitutable shades into a second theme developed by proponents of the view that copyright can restrict freedom of expression, namely, that there are times when free speech demands that others be allowed to turn works to their own political advantage. This argument is developed by Gordon, who argues that people must be given the power to retell, rethink, deconstruct and joke about the narratives that shape their lives.[38] In particular, Gordon has in mind situations where a well-known work is used to convey a message very different from that with which it is normally associated. One example she gives comes from *Walt Disney* v. *Air Pirates*,[39] where the Walt Disney Corporation sued the creators of a comic book aimed at adults that ridiculed the values cherished by Disney.[40] For Gordon

---

[35] Nimmer, 'Copyright', 1197. For a recent analysis of the events at My Lai see J. Glover, *Humanity: A Moral History of the Twentieth Century* (London: Pimlico, 2001), ch. 9.

[36] Nimmer, 'Copyright', 1199. Nimmer concluded that the Zapruder film of the assassination of President Kennedy would also fall into this category and explains *Time* v. *Bernard Geis* 293 F Supp 130 (1968) on this basis. (The *Bernard Geis* case involved a book in which sketches of frames from the Zapruder film were reproduced without the copyright owner's permission. It was held that there was no infringement because the defendant's activities fell within the fair use defence, but for Nimmer this conclusion was based on a misapplication of the fair use factors. An example of a sketch from the *Bernard Geis* case and the frame on which it was based is provided in Edward Samuels' invaluable book, *The Illustrated Story of Copyright* (New York: Thomas Dunne, 2000), p. 203.

[37] M. Spence, 'Intellectual Property and the Problem of Parody' (1998) 114 *Law Quarterly Review* 594, 611.

[38] Gordon, 'A Property Right', 1536, drawing in part on a talk delivered by Salman Rushdie at Columbia University; W. Gordon, 'Reality as Artifact: From Feist to Fair Use' (1992) 55(2) *Law and Contemporary Problems* 93, 101–2.

[39] 581 F 2d 751 (1978), affirming summary judgment of the copyright claim.

[40] See also J. Lawrence, 'Donald Duck v. Chilean Socialism', in J. Lawrence and B. Timberg (eds.), *Fair Use and Free Inquiry: Copyright Law and the New Media*, 2nd edn (Norwood: Ablex Publishing, 1989), in which Lawrence discusses the attempts of the Disney Corporation to persuade the US Treasury Department (which is responsible for customs) to prohibit the importation of *How to Read Donald Duck*. See A. Dorfman and A. Mattelart, *How to Read Donald Duck: Imperialist Ideology in the Disney Comic*, trans. D. Kunzle (New York: International General, 1984) (in this edition a version of Lawrence's essay is reprinted as an appendix).

this provides a clear example of when free speech interests ought to take priority. Other commentators have developed their own examples of when free speech interests ought to prevail. Krieg, for instance, considers the example of the reuse of segments of television commercials in a film that criticises the portrayal of women in advertising.[41] She also argues that it might be appropriate for an artist to reuse a well-known photograph of a middle-aged white policeman that 'symbolise[s] state power and authority' where this image is juxtaposed 'with a news photo depicting black protesters injured by the police during a race riot'.[42]

Krieg focuses on the political dimension of art, but her views are closely allied with a third line of argument, namely, that copyright should not interfere with later artistic expression. Although not always couched in these terms, at least some defences of appropriation art practices,[43] digital sound sampling[44] and parody[45] have been couched in terms of the importance of protecting freedom of artistic expression as an end in itself. An outsider surveying debates in the copyright field might well conclude that appropriation art, sound sampling, parody and similar issues have attracted an undue amount of attention over recent years. Once it is appreciated, however, that these issues provide lenses through which to examine the extent to which copyright might interfere with artistic expression, it is clear that these issues deserve considerable attention.

A variant on the second and third themes outlined above is provided by commentators who have drawn on attacks on romantic notions of authorship to critique copyright law and other forms of intellectual

---

[41] P. Krieg, 'Copyright, Free Speech and the Visual Arts' (1984) 93 *Yale Law Journal* 1565, 1571, considering the example of Jean Kilbourne's *Killing Us Softly* series of films.
[42] *Ibid.*, 1566.
[43] See, e.g., L. Greenberg, 'The Art of Appropriation: Puppies, Piracy and Post-Modernism' (1992) 11 *Cardozo Arts and Entertainment Law Journal* 1, 30, arguing that the decision in *Rogers v. Koons* (discussed below) 'censored the content of permissible artistic speech'; Quentel, 'Bad Artists Copy', 77: 'favouring a First Amendment right over the first author's rights'; P. Drahos, 'Decentering Communication: The Dark Side of Intellectual Property', in T. Campbell and W. Sadurski (eds.), *Freedom of Communication* (Sydney: Dartmouth, 1994), pp. 271–2.
[44] See, e.g., L. Bently, 'Sampling and Copyright Law: Is the Law on the Right Track? Part 2' [1989] *Journal of Business Law* 405, in particular at 412–13; R. Kravis, 'Does a Song by Any Other Name Still Sound as Sweet?: Digital Sampling and Its Copyright Implications' (1993) 43 *American University Law Review* 231, in particular at 273–6, arguing that '[d]igital sampling is a form of art that the law must not forbid'.
[45] See e.g., N. Jacobson, 'Faith, Hope and Parody: *Campbell v. Acuff-Rose*, "Oh, Pretty Woman", and Parodists Rights' (1994) 31 *Houston Law Review* 955, e.g. at 959, arguing that 'The free speech rights of parodists are particularly vulnerable to violation by culturally hostile arbiters operating under the guise of copyright'; A. Lewis, 'Playing Around with Barbie: Expanding Fair Use for Cultural Icons' (1999) 1 *Chicago-Kent Journal of Intellectual Property* 61; E. Gredley and S. Maniatis, 'Parody: A Fatal Attraction? Part 2 Trade Mark Parodies' [1997] EIPR 412, in particular at 420.

property.⁴⁶ The thrust of these critiques is that a work may have many meanings and these meanings are produced by society at large as much as by the author.⁴⁷ The problem with existing intellectual property law is not so much that it ignores these other contributions – the contributions made in fanzines, over the Internet and in everyday conversation – but more that it gives the owner the opportunity to restrict the development of certain alternative meanings. In particular, there is the danger that while owners may be happy to see positive, mainstream (but unanticipated) meanings develop, they may attempt to prevent the development of more critical readings, or readings that have a resonance for historically disadvantaged groups. Attempts have been made to illustrate the latter point by reference to the trade mark dispute that arose between a San Francisco athletics organisation and the US Olympic Committee, which refused to allow the athletics club to promote a sporting event it was organising as the 'Gay Olympic Games'.⁴⁸ Critics of the decision that upheld this refusal have argued that there is no other word that conjures up the same images of sporting excellence and success, leaving homosexual groups uniquely disadvantaged (the US Olympic Committee is quite happy for a wide variety of other organisations to use the word Olympic in the title of their events, hence the Police Olympics, the Canine Olympics, etc.⁴⁹).

Critics who subscribe to the above view have argued for the right to 'recode' works in circumstances that do not fit comfortably within established categories of exception such as criticism or review.⁵⁰ A number

---

⁴⁶ In treating these commentators as being concerned with free speech issues we are referring to the general nature of their critique. It should be acknowledged, however, that at least some of these commentators are not prepared to rely on 'freedom of expression' to justify their stance. See, e.g., Coombe, *Cultural Life*, ch. 6, arguing that 'Freedom of expression . . . is an area of legal doctrine ill-prepared to cope with postmodern conditions.' Coombe relies instead on a theory of speech based on Soviet theorist Mikhail Bakhtin's philosophy. For an illuminating discussion of this aspect of Coombe's work see P. Johnson, 'Can You Quote Donald Duck?: Intellectual Property in Cyberculture' (2001) 13 *Yale Journal of Law and the Humanities* 451.
⁴⁷ E.g. Coombe, *Cultural Life*, at pp. 133–4: 'The social deployment of texts always confounds the anticipations of their authors: the connotations of commodified form exceed those imagined in their inception'; K. Aoki, 'Adrift in the Intertext: Authorship and Audience "Recoding" Rights – Comment on Robert H. Rotstein, "Beyond Metaphor: Copyright Infringement and the Fiction of the Work"' (1993) 68 *Chicago-Kent Law Review* 805; P. Jaszi, 'On the Author Effect: Contemporary Copyright and Collective Creativity' (1992) 10 *Cardozo Arts and Entertainment Law Journal* 293.
⁴⁸ *San Francisco Arts and Athletics Club v. United States Olympics Committee* 483 US 522 (1987).
⁴⁹ See Coombe, *Cultural Life*, pp. 136–8, discussing the dissenting judgment of Judge Kozinski in the Court of Appeals for the Ninth Circuit.
⁵⁰ See Aoki, 'Adrift', arguing for a right to 'recode'; E. Fukumoto, 'The Author Effect After the "Death of the Author": Copyright in a Postmodern Age' (1997) 72 *Washington Law Review* 903, arguing for a broad right of 'pastiche'; W. Griesdorf, 'The Laugh of

of commentators have argued that the US case *Rogers* v. *Koons*[51] provides an example of where a broader right of reuse should have been recognised. That case concerned a dispute between Art Rogers, a photographer, and Jeff Koons, a sculptor and appropriation artist. Koons had purchased a postcard of one of Rogers' works in which a man and a woman are seated on a bench, each holding four puppies. Koons decided to make a sculpture based on this image. Having decided on materials, colours and dimensions he sent the postcard to artisans in Italy with instructions that the 'work must be just like photo – features of photo must be captured'.[52] The sculpture was subsequently exhibited by Koons in an exhibition entitled the 'Banality Show', which Koons argued was intended to act as a comment on the cliché-ridden imagery that dominates the mass media. Both at first instance and on appeal Koons was held to have infringed copyright in the photograph, Koons' argument that his actions fell within the fair use defence being rejected. For some commentators the *Koons* case provides a clear illustration of the sort of situation in which existing doctrines such as fair use are inadequate and in which a right to reuse or 'recode' a work should have been recognised.[53]

Some commentators have argued that the justification for a right to 'recode' works is particularly strong in the case of 'cultural icons', and that it ought not to matter whether such icons are protected by copyright, trade marks, personality rights or any other intellectual property regime.[54] This argument is predicated on the fact that cultural icons are by definition already extremely well known, so that the owner of the

    the Hypertext' (1994–5) 9 IPJ 1, arguing for a legal system oriented towards 'permitting uses'. See also D. Lange, 'At Play in the Fields of the Word: Copyright and the Construction of Authorship in the Post-Literate Millennium' (1992) 55(2) *Law and Contemporary Problems* 139, arguing that 'If intellectual property survives . . . there will be no . . . balances to be struck against the interests of creativity'; V. Tadros, 'A Few Thoughts on Copyright Law and the Subject of Writing', in L. Bently and S. Maniatis (eds.), 4 *Perspectives on Intellectual Property: Intellectual Property and Ethics* (London: Sweet & Maxwell, 1998), p. 127, refusing to prescribe reform in the absence of a 'new ethic of writing', but insisting that we should 'valorise certain forms of repetition'.

[51] 960 F 2d 301 (1992).

[52] *Ibid.*, 305. Rogers' photograph and a photograph of Koons' sculpture are reproduced in Samuels, *Illustrated Story of Copyright*, p. 194.

[53] Other commentators, however, see the case as one in which the fair use defence was simply misapplied. See, e.g., E. Ames, 'Beyond *Rogers* v. *Koons*: A Fair Use Standard for Appropriation' (1993) 93 *Columbia Law Review* 1473. It is also important to note that *Rogers* v. *Koons* was decided prior to the decision of the Supreme Court in *Campbell* v. *Acuff-Rose Music* 114 S Ct 1164 (1994), in which the Supreme Court expanded protection for parodies under the fair use defence: J. Okpaluba, 'Appropriation Art: Fair Use or Foul?', in D. McClean and K. Schubert (eds.), *Dear Images: Art, Copyright and Culture* (London: Ridinghouse, 2002).

[54] See A. Lewis, 'Playing Around with Barbie: Expanding Fair Use for Cultural Icons' (1999) 1 *Chicago-Kent Journal of Intellectual Property* 61; S. Cordero, 'Cocaine-Cola, The Velvet Elvis, and Anti-Barbie: Defending the Trademark and Publicity Rights to

image or sign in question will already have had ample opportunities to make money from its exploitation. It is also said that it is highly unlikely that a 'recoding' of such an image or sign will be sufficient to displace its core meaning or damage its iconic status, so that the owner will still be able to charge for its mainstream exploitation in the future.[55] The financial incentive that copyright provides for the creation of works will therefore be left intact.[56]

Thus far we have identified at least three ways in which copyright and freedom of expression can be said convincingly to intersect. A fourth theme developed by proponents of the view that copyright can impose restrictions on freedom of expression relates to the evidential importance of being allowed to reproduce extracts from a work. According to this view, it is essential that copyright does not become a means of suppressing facts or a tool of private censorship.[57] More specifically, it has been said that conservative accounts of the relationship between copyright and freedom of expression ignore the danger that without the freedom to quote, any expression will lack authority and may be ignored as a result. It is possible to reinterpret Nimmer's examples of when it will be 'necessary' to reproduce photographs and films as being examples of evidentially important works. Another example is provided by the US case *Meeropol* v. *Nizer*,[58] which Denicola has used to illustrate when, in his view, free speech interests should take precedence over copyright

---

Cultural Icons' (1998) 8 *Fordham Intellectual Property, Media and Entertainment Law Journal* 599. See also, e.g., N. Klein, *No Logo* (London: Flamingo, 2001), at p. 182, arguing: 'Copyright and trademark laws are perfectly justifiable if the brand in question is just a brand, but increasingly that's like saying that Wal-Mart is just a store. The brand in question may well represent a corporation with a budget larger than that of many countries . . . When we lack the ability to talk back to entities that are culturally and politically powerful, the very foundations of free speech and democratic society are called into question.'

[55] But cf. J. Hughes, '"Recoding" Intellectual Property Rights and Overlooked Audience Interests' (1999) 77 *Texas Law Review* 923, 962–3, doubting this point.

[56] In the case of trade marks it is said that there will be no likelihood of consumer confusion since the reuse will normally be textual or on different goods, or the context will make it clear that the product in question is not produced by the trade mark owner. Nor will there be a risk of dilution, since the iconic status of the brand will protect its core meaning for consumers. But cf. B. Isaac, *Brand Protection Matters* (London: Sweet & Maxwell, 2000), implicitly adopting the view that all brands are 'fragile'.

[57] See P. McCoy Smith, 'Copyright, Suppression and the Problem of the Unpublished Work: Lessons from the Patent Law' (1991) 19 *AIPLA Quarterly Journal* 309; R. Denicola, 'Copyright and Free Speech: Constitutional Limitations on the Protection of Expression' (1979) 67 *California Law Review* 283; E. Volokh and B. McDonnell, 'Freedom of Speech and Independent Judgment Review in Copyright Cases' (1998) 107 *Yale Law Journal* 2431; R. Burrell, 'Defending the Public Interest' [2000] EIPR 394.

[58] 560 F 2d 1061 (1977).

protection.[59] The background to *Meeropol* was that the plaintiffs' parents had been executed for espionage. While awaiting execution they wrote a number of letters that were published in a collection shortly after their death, but which had been out of print for nearly twenty years by the time the case came to trial. The defendants in the case had reprinted extracts from the letters in a book that examined the impact of the trial on the parents. The plaintiffs alleged, *inter alia*, infringement of copyright in the letters. Although the final outcome of the dispute is unclear because the reported decisions relate to a claim and counterclaim for summary judgment which were refused, Denicola lends strong support to the district court's conclusion that

> It is not sufficient, as the plaintiffs suggest, for the defendants . . . to resort to 'the obvious device of not quoting them directly'. To do so would have prevented them from fully and accurately conveying the [parents'] own expression, which in this situation may be essential to an accurate rendition of the relevant thoughts themselves.[60]

Illustrating the problem II

From the above it can be seen that there is a variety of ways in which copyright can be said to conflict with freedom of expression. Even if some of the illustrations of the intersection between copyright and freedom of expression are open to doubt, or even if the theoretical underpinnings of some of the claims examined above are questionable (for example, critiques of copyright based on attacks on romantic notions of authorship have been met with increasingly confident responses[61]), when viewed as a whole, it can be seen that the argument that copyright protection does affect freedom of expression is extremely convincing. Moreover, it is possible to supplement the above analysis by reference to a range of other cases. This is particularly important because supporters of the status quo in copyright tend not to confront head-on examples of where copyright seems to be overreaching, but rather choose to emphasise the problems that owners have in enforcing their rights.[62] The suggestion

---

[59] Denicola, 'Copyright', 307–9.
[60] 417 F Supp 1201 (1976), 1212 (per Gagliardi, District Judge).
[61] See D. Saunders, 'Dropping the Subject: An Argument for a Positive History of Authorship and the Law of Copyright', in B. Sherman and A. Strowel (eds.), *Of Authors and Origins* (Oxford: Clarendon, 1994); L. Bently, 'Copyright and the Death of the Author in Literature and Law' (1994) 57 *Modern Law Review* 973; Sherman and Bently, in particular pp. 36–42.
[62] Samuels, *Illustrated Story of Copyright*, p. 204, provides a good example, concluding his fair use chapter with the following statement: 'We've now seen so many doctrines

is that the problems identified by more critical commentators are unlikely to arise and are a distraction from the key issues of the need to deal with piracy and widespread unauthorised private copying.[63] Furthermore, it is sometimes suggested that the adverse publicity that any attempt to rely on copyright as a tool of censorship is likely to generate for the owner is usually a sufficient deterrent to prevent misuse.

However, it is simply not true to say that the problems with which we are concerned are unlikely to arise. On the contrary, it is possible to point to a considerable number of cases in which an attempt has been made to use copyright to censor adverse comment or to prevent information from being placed in the public domain. We will turn to many of the relevant cases in due course, but in the United Kingdom, for example, attempts have been made to rely on copyright to prevent adverse comment on the Church of Scientology,[64] to stop the release of information that a breathalyser was faulty,[65] to prevent the reproduction of evidence that cast doubt on claims about a murderous conspiracy on the part of the security services,[66] to limit criticism of a journalist's preferred choice of leader of a political party,[67] to prevent details of a meeting between the Prime Minister and a leader of an opposition party from being made public,[68] to prohibit the reproduction of a letter written by a firm of solicitors that threatened its recipient with legal action,[69] and to restrict further information about a drug that was known to cause birth defects from being placed in the public domain.[70] In Australia there was an attempt to rely on copyright to prevent a journalist from exposing a lack of integrity in the Australian government's policy towards Indonesia and East Timor.[71] In Canada, copyright was used to prevent striking

---

limiting copyright that it's hard to believe copyright owners ever win law suits at all. Between the difficulties of discovering violations . . . and the limitations on enforcing rights highlighted here, there are certainly a lot of hurdles along the way. Maybe that's the reason Congress grants such broad rights . . . to those copyright owners who are successful in navigating the hurdles – to compensate successful copyright owners for the difficulties in enforcing their rights.'

[63] The tendency to ignore the relationship between copyright and freedom of expression can also be seen in the work of some keen advocates of the right to freedom of expression who are prepared to accept without analysis that existing copyright law is adequate to protect free speech. See, e.g., E. Barendt, *Freedom of Speech* (Oxford: Clarendon, 1985), pp. 62–3.
[64] *Hubbard* v. *Vosper* [1972] 2 QB 84.   [65] *Lion Laboratories* v. *Evans* [1985] QB 526.
[66] *Hyde Park* v. *Yelland* [2001] Ch 143.   [67] *Beloff* v. *Pressdram* [1973] 1 All ER 241.
[68] *Ashdown* v. *Telegraph Group* [2002] Ch 235.
[69] *Musical Fidelity* v. *Vickers* [2003] FSR 898.
[70] *Distillers* v. *Times Newspapers* [1975] QB 613.
[71] *Commonwealth of Australia* v. *Fairfax* (1981) 147 CLR 39.

workers from lampooning their employer's motif.[72] In the United States, in addition to some of the examples considered in the previous section, there have been attempts to use copyright to stop anti-abortionists from quoting from material collected by pro-abortionists,[73] to prevent criticism of a candidate standing for re-election to public office,[74] to stop artists from using Barbie dolls in works critical of the imagery used to market such toys to young girls,[75] and by the Church of Scientology to limit criticism of L. Ron Hubbard.[76]

It may also be worth noting that attempts have been made to use other forms of intellectual property protection to suppress certain types of speech. These cases illustrate further that the mere fact that bringing an action may generate adverse publicity for the intellectual property owner is not a sufficient safeguard. To take but two examples, in the United States the Mattel Corporation attempted to use trade mark law and other forms of protection for business reputation to prevent the pop group Aqua from using the word 'Barbie' in a song that was highly critical of the values with which Barbie is associated.[77] In the United Kingdom one of the factors that motivated Mothercare, the children's clothes retailer, to sue the publisher of a book entitled *Mother Care/Other Care* for trade mark infringement was Mothercare's dislike of the central thesis of the book, namely, that mother-centred childcare is not necessarily superior to other types of childcare arrangement.[78]

Given the examples set out above and given that it is difficult to tell the extent to which claimants are able to use the existence of potential copyright liability as leverage in disputes that never come to trial, there is every reason to suppose that the ability of copyright to impinge on freedom of expression is a matter of very real concern. Moreover, if owners fare relatively well when using intellectual property rights to suppress adverse comment (as opposed, say, to relying on the law of defamation), this will increasingly lead owners to frame their complaint in intellectual property terms. At the political or legislative level it may also lead to attempts to recast issues in intellectual property terms. For example,

---

[72] *Cie Générale des Établissements Michelin – Michelin & Cie v. CAW Canada* (1996) 71 CPR (3d) 348.
[73] *Maxtone-Graham v. Burtchaell* 803 F 2d 1253 (1986).
[74] *Keep Thompson Governor Committee v. Citizens for Gallen Committee* 457 F Supp 957 (1978).
[75] *Mattel v. Pitt* 229 F Supp 2d 315 (2002); *Mattel v. Walking Mountain Productions* 353 F 3d 792 (2003).
[76] *New Era Publications v. Henry Holt* 695 F Supp 1493 (1988).
[77] *Mattel v. MCA Records* 28 F Supp 2d 1120 (1998).
[78] See *Mothercare v. Penguin Books* [1988] RPC 113, in particular at 116; Mothercare believed that its customers would be 'horrified' by the message of the book.

Volokh notes that in the light of the US Supreme Court striking down legislation prohibiting burning the American flag there have been attempts to justify such a ban on the basis that the government owns an intellectual property right in the flag.[79]

The case examples we chose to set out above give some indication of where we believe the most serious potential conflicts between copyright and freedom of expression lie. In order to justify our selection it is necessary to explain something of how we understand freedom of expression. We then turn to consider the implications of this understanding, and in so doing regroup and reinterpret some of the examples given by other commentators of the circumstances in which copyright can interfere with freedom of expression.

Our starting point is that there are a number of good reasons for avoiding placing restrictions on expressive freedom. These are reflected in the host of rationales that have been put forward for freedom of expression.[80] Most importantly for present purposes, freedom of expression contributes to the advancement of knowledge,[81] it is associated with self-fulfilment and the exercise of autonomy, and it is a precondition for democratic government.[82] If these values are taken seriously it becomes evident that the potential conflict between copyright and freedom of expression is extremely broad – insofar as copyright can limit our understanding by preventing a work from being reinterpreted, can limit subsequent authors'

---

[79] See E. Volokh, 'Freedom of Speech and Intellectual Property: Some Thoughts after *Eldred, 44 Liquormart, Saderup*, and *Bartnicki*' (2003) 40 *Houston Law Review* 697, 700 and see, generally, R. Goldstein, *Flag Burning and Free Speech* (Lawrence, Kans.: University Press of Kansas, 2000). See also T. Emerson, *Toward a General Theory of the First Amendment* (New York: Random House, 1966), p. 19, arguing that exceptions to freedom of expression 'must be clear-cut, precise and readily controlled. Otherwise the forces that press toward restriction will break through the openings, and freedom of expression will become the exception and suppression the rule.'

[80] Campbell, for example, identifies seven separate rationales and this is not an exhaustive list: T. Campbell, 'Rationales for Freedom of Communication', in T. Campbell and W. Sadurski (eds.), *Freedom of Communication* (Sydney: Dartmouth, 1994), noting that 'if free speech is special, then it may be so for a combination of reasons rather than the unique application of one overriding rationale' (at p. 19). For other overviews of the rationales for freedom of expression see, e.g., Barendt, *Freedom of Speech*, ch. 1; Emerson, *Toward a General Theory*, ch. 1; W. Sadurski, *Freedom of Speech and Its Limits* (Dordrecht: Kluwer, 1999), ch. 1; R. Wright, *The Future of Free Speech Law* (New York: Quorum Books, 1990), pp. 2–12.

[81] A claim that is not dependent on acceptance of the broader Millian argument that freedom of expression is a precondition for the emergence of truth, an argument which is now widely regarded as problematic: Campbell, 'Rationales', pp. 23–33; Sadurski, *Freedom of Speech*, pp. 8–16. Cf. J. S. Mill, *On Liberty* (London: Penguin Classics, 1985), ch. 2.

[82] This justification also leads inevitably to the conclusion that the public has a right to access information relevant to the political process. Freedom of expression and freedom of information can thus be seen as two sides of the same coin.

artistic choices or can prevent information relevant to the political process from being placed in the public domain, freedom of expression is involved.

Equally, however, we do not believe that an absolute right of freedom of expression is justified. Rather, we start from the premise that 'the determination of what rights of free communication ought to be secured is a complex and open-ended matter which cannot be reduced to easy arguments from simple and straightforward premises'.[83] Treating freedom of expression as less than absolute ties in with much of the recent academic work on freedom of expression and accords with the limited nature of the right to freedom of expression guaranteed under Article 10(2) of the European Convention on Human Rights.[84] Moreover, we believe that the apparently widely shared intuition that copyright protection in some form is both ethically justified and socially useful tells us something important about the limits of freedom of expression and how those limits ought to be set.[85] More specifically, we believe that the complex interaction of the interests at stake in the copyright field suggests that the limits of freedom of expression have to be set in part by legislatures. We do not believe that freedom of expression should be treated as if it occupied some separate (higher) sphere removed from political decision-making.[86] As we explain below, this has important implications for resolving the tension between copyright and freedom of expression. However, before turning to our model it is perhaps worth making one further observation about our understanding of the scope of expressive freedom.

Implicit in what has been said so far is that we do not believe that the potential conflict between copyright and freedom of expression can be dismissed on the basis that freedom of expression only applies as against exercises of public power and not (as will usually be the case with copyright) as against exercises of private power. The most obvious reply to this potential objection is that since copyright protection flows from an exercise of legislative power, freedom of expression is in any event engaged. More importantly, however, to limit the operation of freedom of speech

---

[83] See Campbell, 'Rationales', p. 43.
[84] For discussion see J. Wadham, H. Mountfield and A. Edmundson, *Blackstone's Guide to the Human Rights Act 1998* (London: Blackstone, 1999), pp. 101–103 and the cases discussed therein.
[85] Similarly, Campbell, 'Rationales', p. 17, lists the potential utility and fairness of intellectual property rights as one of nine counters to the recognition of an absolute right of freedom of communication; Tushnet, 'Copyright', aims 'to make possible a rethinking of standard First Amendment Theory in light of copyright's constitutionality'.
[86] See J. Waldron, *Law and Disagreement* (Oxford: Clarendon 1999), p. 12, criticising the tendency to treat rights 'as though they could be dealt with on a different plane in law – on the solemn plane of constitutional principle far from the hurly-burly of legislatures'.

to exercises of public power would fail to reflect both the importance of and the political controversy surrounding the power of corporate actors.[87] More generally, the need to ensure that our human rights jurisprudence is relevant to a world in which transnational corporate actors wield considerable influence, in which the contracting out of government services is common, and in which there is widespread private ownership of spaces that perform a public function is something that is occupying human rights lawyers.[88]

Resolving the conflict

Thus far we have argued that the intersection between copyright and freedom of expression is much more significant than is normally assumed to be the case, that freedom of expression is compromised when someone is prevented from reusing a work to communicate a different message and even when someone is prevented from expressing the same message using words, images or symbols owned by another. This does not, however, mean that copyright protection is unjustifiable. Freedom of expression should not always override copyright. Rather, we believe that a distinction needs to be drawn between circumstances in which copyright prevents information relevant to the political process from being placed in the public domain and circumstances in which copyright interferes with the creative and interpretive activities[89] of later users/authors. In outline, we believe that freedom of expression needs to be given much greater weight in the first type of case than in the second.

Copyright and the democratic process

There is a longstanding body of literature that treats freedom of expression as being of most importance when it relates to the democratic

---

[87] See Drahos, 'Decentering Communication'; F. Macmillan, 'Towards a Reconciliation of Free Speech and Copyright', in E. Barendt et al. (eds.), *The Yearbook of Media and Entertainment Law 1996* (Oxford: Clarendon, 1996), p. 199. This is also implicit in Patricia Louglan's work in this area. See P. Loughlan, 'Looking at the Matrix: Intellectual Property and Expressive Freedom' [2002] EIPR 30.

[88] See, e.g., D. Shelton, 'Protecting Human Rights in a Globalized World' (2002) 25 *Boston College International and Comparative Law Review* 273; J. Paust, 'Human Rights Responsibilities of Private Corporations' (2002) 35 *Vanderbilt Journal of Transnational Law* 801; A. Aman, 'Globalization, Democracy, and the Need for a New Administrative Law' (2002) 49 *UCLA Law Review* 1687; W. Freedman, *Freedom of Speech on Private Property* (New York: Quorum, 1988); K. Gray and S. Gray, 'Civil Rights, Civil Wrongs and Quasi-Public Spaces' [1999] *European Human Rights Law Review* 46.

[89] This distinction is intended to give a sense of the scope of our categories; it is not intended to suggest that there is a clear division to be drawn between 'creative' activities on the one hand and 'interpretive' activities on the other.

process[90] and a number of recent commentators have also adopted this position.[91] Something similar can also be observed in ECHR jurisprudence.[92] This informs our particular concern that copyright might be used to suppress facts or evidence relating to a matter of genuine public interest and our belief that freedom of expression needs to be prioritised over the interests of the copyright owner in cases where there is any danger that information relevant to the political process will be prevented from entering the public domain.

Our approach leads inevitably to the need to draw a distinction between those works that contain information relevant to the political process or relating to matters of public interest and those that do not. We recognise that drawing such a distinction is inherently problematic, that there is no clear division between political and non-political communication and that, for example, there is a sense (or more accurately several senses) in which 'all art is political'. Nevertheless, we believe that it is possible to draw a sensible distinction (although one which leaves difficult cases at the margins) between works whose content relates directly to matters of public interest and works whose content is of only indirect relevance to the political process. Information directly relevant to the political process includes that relating to the conduct and fitness for office of politicians and public officials; the policies, funding, structure and behaviour of political parties, trade unions, religious bodies, universities and large corporations; the conduct and effectiveness of the armed forces; the operation of the courts and other tribunals; the views and conduct of public persons (including of those holding themselves up as

---

[90] In particular, see A. Meiklejohn, *Free Speech and its Relation to Self-Government* (New York: Harper & Brothers, 1948), e.g. at pp. 93–94: 'the principle of the freedom of speech is derived, not from some supposed "Natural Right," but from the necessities of self-government by universal suffrage . . . It is assured only to speech which bears, directly or indirectly, upon the issues with which voters have to deal – only, therefore, to the consideration of matters of public interest.'

[91] See, e.g., Barendt, *Freedom of Speech*, p. 299, arguing that the most convincing justification for free speech is that 'much political and social discussion should be immune from government suppression because it enables people to participate fully and knowledgeably in public affairs and to deal with government on a level of equality'; F. Schauer, *Free Speech: A Philosophical Enquiry* (Cambridge: Cambridge University Press, 1982), p. 46: 'No facet of the argument from democracy is conclusive, but it provides several reasons for treating political speech as a wholly different creature. It thus gives added force to the argument from uncertainty [that is, that we should allow or even encourage the expression of opposing views in order to have the opportunity of reviewing our beliefs (at p. 31)], when that argument is applied to questions of governmental policy, power and control.'

[92] See Wadham, Mountfield and Edmundson, *Blackstone's Guide*, p. 102 and the cases discussed therein; Hugenholtz, 'Copyright', p. 262.

role models); public health and public safety; and political, social and economic trends.[93]

Returning to some of the examples that we have already considered, we would group within this category Nimmer's concerns about copyright being used to censor photographs of the My Lai massacre and Denicola's concern that copyright ought not to be used to prevent information about the impact on the accused of a widely publicised trial from being made known. Similarly, we would include within this category attempts to prevent criticism of a government's foreign policy, or of a religious movement or of the person who founded that movement, or of a journalist's choice of leader of a political party or of the fitness for office of a political candidate.[94] A right to copy the work itself and not merely to describe its contents is essential because freedom of expression extends to 'not only the substance of the ideas and information expressed, but also the form in which they are conveyed'.[95] This right is most obviously important as regards visual material, since describing an image is no substitute for having access to the image itself. There are, however, numerous other examples of where having access to the form of the communication is essential. In particular, this is important in any case in which the publication is intended to place evidence in the public domain – in such cases members of the public ought to have the right to assess the evidence themselves and this in turn means that direct copying from the work that contains the evidence ought to be permissible. The absence of such a right also creates a serious imbalance as between the copyright owner and would-be critics. Whereas the copyright owner can selectively release extracts of documents or particular photographs or stills from a film that appear to support its case, critics will be limited to describing any contrary evidence they have seen.

Over the course of the next two chapters we develop a number of examples of where the present UK copyright regime fails to provide adequate safeguards to ensure that information relevant to the political process can be placed in the public domain. But in order to illustrate the above points it may be worth providing two examples at this point. First, it was seen in this chapter that Nimmer (who took a narrow view of when copyright and freedom of expression collide) believed that it would be 'intolerable'

---

[93] This list is based in part on an early attempt by the High Court of Australia to define 'political communication' in the context of Australia's constitutionally protected sphere of communication. See *Theophanous* v. *Herald & Weekly Times* (1994) 182 CLR 104, 124 (per Mason CJ, Deane and Gaudron JJ).
[94] See the examples set out in the subsection headed 'Illustrating the problem II'.
[95] *Jersild* v. *Denmark* (1995) 19 EHRR 1, 26.

if the owner of copyright in the photographs of the My Lai massacre could prevent their publication. Yet it will be seen in the next chapter that this is precisely what the UK's statutory regime would allow, since neither of the relevant fair dealing provisions would apply – as will be seen, fair dealing for the purpose of criticism and review does not apply to unpublished works and fair dealing for the purpose of reporting current events does not apply to photographs.

Our second example is drawn from the 'children overboard' controversy in Australia. In October 2001, shortly before a general election in which immigration was a major issue, a number of senior politicians claimed that during a recent naval operation to intercept a ship carrying asylum seekers, passengers on the ship had thrown children overboard so as to deter the navy from redirecting the vessel. To support this claim the government released close-up photographs that showed children being rescued from the water. It has since become clear that the 'children overboard story' was untrue and that the photographs of the children being rescued were taken not on the day the vessel was intercepted but on the following day, when the navy was forced to rescue passengers from their vessel because it was sinking.[96] Significantly, it later became clear that photographs other than those released by the government showed that the vessel was sinking at the time the children were being rescued. If these photographs had been leaked to journalists, under UK law they could not have been published without running the risk of infringing copyright. Nor would it be possible under UK law to publish copies of transcripts of telephone conversations between naval officers and government officials that provided evidence of who knew what and when. At best a journalist could describe the other photographs and the contents of the transcripts. Since this would not be sufficient to counter the impact of photographs showing children being pulled from the water, this would leave the government in an extremely favourable position.

In the light of examples such as those set out above and those that we develop over the course of the next two chapters, we argue that the United Kingdom's present approach to the exceptions needs to be liberalised so as to ensure that copyright can no longer impede the dissemination of political information – 'political' information being understood in a broad sense. In order to achieve this aim a much greater degree of flexibility needs to be built into the exceptions. As we explain in the final chapter, we believe that this flexibility can be achieved by modelling a new set of exceptions around the provisions of the Information Society Directive and

---

[96] These facts have been taken from the Australian Senate Select Committee, *Report on a Certain Maritime Incident* (Canberra: 23 Oct. 2002).

by supplementing these provisions with a limited public interest defence. Judges would be expected to apply such a system in a sensible manner. For example, we argue in Chapter 3 that a factor that ought to be taken into account when applying a public interest defence is whether the public will in any event have access to the work in the near future. This would prevent a journalist from relying on the public interest defence in order to publish a rival's forthcoming scoop.

As a final point, and one to which we will also return, we believe that our call for copyright to give way in cases where it imposes an obstacle to the dissemination of political information is reinforced by the fact that many of the works that will be at issue in this category of case will be outside the core of copyright protection. In Europe at least, it is widely accepted that copyright protection performs the dual roles of protecting the author's personal interests and providing opportunities for commercially exploiting the protected work.[97] Copyright now extends, however, to a range of other subject matter that cannot be said convincingly to embody the personality of a creator and which is often never intended for public dissemination. For example, copyright will normally subsist in internal memorandums, security videos, transcripts of telephone conversations and e-mails. This has come about because the legislature has thought it unwise to spell out in too much detail what 'a work' will look like and because the judiciary has been understandably reluctant to engage in consideration of the aesthetic merits of a work. These provide good practical reasons for the extension of copyright, and in many cases this extension has beneficial effects in that it means that copyright can supplement, *inter alia*, actions for breach of confidence and defamation. This is particularly important given that UK law does not recognise a general right of privacy. But this should not blind us to the fact that these are largely accidental benefits, and that copyright protection for non-artistic, non-commercially exploitable works may also have less desirable consequences. In particular, this is likely to be the case when copyright is being used to circumvent a public-policy-based limitation that would prevent the owner from relying on another cause of action, for example, because a claim for breach of confidence would be blocked by a public interest defence,[98] or because a claim for an interim injunction for defamation would be barred because the defendant intended to plead justification.[99] None of this is to be taken to indicate that we believe that our category of works containing information relevant to the political process is confined to works which only enjoy 'accidental' copyright protection. This is clearly

---

[97] *Musik-Vertrieb Membran v. GEMA* [1981] 2 CMLR 44, 64.   [98] See Chapter 3.
[99] *Bonnard v. Perryman* [1891] 2 Ch 269, 284; *Holley v. Smyth* [1998] QB 726.

not the case – photographs, even 'mere' snapshots, are within the core of copyright protection. Nevertheless, the fact that the works involved in dissemination of information cases will often have little inherent value does reinforce our belief that it is appropriate to prioritise freedom of expression in such cases.

Copyright and creative copying

In contrast to the type of case considered in the previous subsection, the capacity of copyright to interfere with later interpretive and creative activities raises concerns of a different order, but they are nevertheless concerns that are properly understood in freedom of expression terms. For example, copyright limits the amount of material that a biographer, historian or scientist can reproduce without seeking a licence. As such, copyright can limit that person's expressive freedom by reducing their ability to explore a topic fully and to do all they can to prove that their analysis is correct.[100] This may in turn inhibit the advancement of knowledge. Similarly, it has been seen that copyright can limit artistic choices by preventing an author from basing a sculpture on an earlier photograph, or from parodying or satirising an earlier work, and so on. This may well prevent an author from achieving the self-fulfilment that can be gained from unfettered artistic expression.

We have also indicated, however, that the type of concern outlined in the preceding paragraph does not justify curtailing copyright to the same degree as when copyright is inhibiting the free flow of information relevant to the political process. We have already put forward the view that the argument from democracy provides the strongest justification for freedom of expression. In addition, we take the position that copyright protection underpins a range of commercial activity that provides outlets through which authors are able to disseminate their works and which provide authors with the financial returns that can also be a precondition for self-fulfilment. Copyright protection also secures a degree of autonomy for authors by providing the means to prevent commercially insensitive uses of their works, in particular through the provision of moral rights (albeit that such rights are relatively limited in the United Kingdom). In the light of such considerations the task of reconciling the interests of the copyright owner with those of subsequent authors is inherently complex. What will become clear, however, is that the current UK system does not do nearly enough to protect the interests of later authors. Nor can it even be said that the limits of the current exceptions represent Parliament's

---

[100] A related point is made by Guibault, p. 31.

considered view as to where to set the boundaries of copyright, since, as we explain in Chapters 8 and 9, any such argument misdescribes the role the judiciary has played in setting the current limits of copyright law.

As part of our suggested package of reform measures we therefore recommend the extension of existing rights of criticism and review, the introduction of a new 'caricature, parody and pastiche exception' and a new right of use for the purposes of non-commercial scientific research. We also call for judges to look on users much more favourably and to bear in mind that exceptions that allow for the reinterpretation and creative reuse of earlier works play an important part in safeguarding freedom of expression. In particular, we would expect judges to look favourably at defendants who are reusing a work creatively in order to make a political statement such that the democratic justification for freedom of expression is at least partly engaged. We would therefore hope to see judges striving to protect defendants in cases like *Air Pirates*. We would also expect judges to look favourably on reuses that have a particular resonance for historically disadvantaged groups (for example, a novel that retells *Gone with the Wind* from a slave's perspective[101]), since such reuses have a significant political dimension. Such an approach would also help to ease the problem of having to distinguish between cases in which copyright is preventing the dissemination of information and cases in which copyright is inhibiting the creative reuse of a work which is intended to convey a political message. Even if a borderline case were held to fall within the latter category, it would still receive generous treatment.

Conclusion

In this chapter it has been argued that there is a significant tension between copyright and freedom of expression and that it is not appropriate to attempt to downplay this issue. We also have enough examples of attempts being made to use intellectual property rights as a tool of censorship to dismiss the argument that difficulties are unlikely to arise in practice. In the final section of this chapter we have drawn a distinction between the capacity of copyright to prevent the dissemination of information and its capacity to interfere with later creative and interpretive reuses, arguing that the former poses the more significant problem, but indicating that current UK law is inadequate to deal with either set of issues. In the next two chapters we seek to justify this final claim.

[101] Cf. *Suntrust Bank v. Houghton Mifflin Co* 268 F 3d 1257 (2001).

2 Fair dealing for the purposes of criticism, review and news reporting and related exceptions

Having demonstrated in the last chapter that exceptions covering activities such as criticism, review and news reporting are necessary in order to prevent copyright from conflicting unduly with freedom of expression, we turn in this chapter to consider the provisions of UK law that relate to such activities. The principal focus of this chapter is on two fair dealing exceptions, namely, fair dealing for the purpose of criticism or review and fair dealing for the purpose of reporting current events.[1] Consideration is also given, however, to a number of supplementary provisions, including, for example, the provision that allows for the reproduction of spoken words and provisions relating to the reporting of official proceedings. To some extent our analysis can only be provisional, given the dearth of case law interpreting the relevant exceptions post the implementation of the Information Society Directive. But given that the government decided to adopt a 'bolt-on' transposition of the Directive,[2] sticking as closely to the original wording of the 1988 Act as was reasonably possible, it seems safe to assume that the courts will continue to apply much the same principles when interpreting the newly modified provisions. We demonstrate that the relevant provisions are, in various respects, limited in scope, subject to important restrictions and uncertain in their application. Moreover, in addition to identifying various problems with the exceptions themselves, we also discuss various other obstacles that may prevent users from relying on the exceptions. In particular, we discuss the possibility that the copyright owner may be able to rely on some other cause of action to prevent a user from copying the work. This brings us to consider the controversial question of contracting out of the exceptions. We also consider a problem unique to the online environment, namely, that a copyright owner may be able to persuade an online service provider to take steps even against a user who has a good defence to a claim of copyright infringement.

---

[1] The exception allowing for fair dealing with a work for the purposes of research or private study, contained in s. 29 of the 1988 Act, is dealt with in Chapter 4.
[2] See Chapter 8 for a discussion of the 'bolt-on' transposition of EU law and the problems this can cause for users.

Fair dealing for the purposes of criticism, review and the reporting of current events: introduction

As we have already indicated, the most generous provisions that apply to the sorts of activities with which we are concerned in this chapter are the fair dealing provisions contained in section 30 of the 1988 Act. That section, as amended, provides as follows:

30. – (1) Fair dealing with a work for the purpose of criticism or review, of that or another work or of a performance of a work, does not infringe any copyright in the work provided that it is accompanied by a sufficient acknowledgement and provided that the work has been made available to the public.
(1A) For the purposes of subsection (1) a work has been made available to the public if it has been made available by any means, including –
(a) the issue of copies to the public;
(b) making the work available by means of an electronic retrieval system;
(c) the rental or lending of copies of the work to the public;
(d) the performance, exhibition, playing or showing of the work in public;
(e) the communication to the public of the work;
but in determining generally for the purposes of that subsection whether a work has been made available to the public no account shall be taken of any unauthorised act.
(2) Fair dealing with a work (other than a photograph) for the purpose of reporting current events does not infringe any copyright in the work provided that (subject to subsection (3)) it is accompanied by a sufficient acknowledgement.
(3) No acknowledgement is required in connection with the reporting of current events by means of a sound recording, film or broadcast where this would be impossible for reasons of practicality or otherwise.

It can be seen that this section allows works to be used for the purpose of criticism or review and for the purpose of reporting current events. It must be emphasised that it is only these specific types of use that gain the benefit of an exception; other types of use will not be privileged, no matter how 'fair' they may be.[3] When considering whether the section 30 provisions apply it is necessary to ask the following four questions:
   (i) Does the exception apply to the work in question?
   (ii) Is the use for one of the approved purposes?
   (iii) Is the use fair?
   (iv) Is there a sufficient acknowledgement?

---

[3] See *Beloff* v. *Pressdram* [1973] 1 All ER 241, 262: 'It is fair dealing directed to and consequently limited to and to be judged in relation to the approved purposes. It is dealing which is fair for the approved purposes and not dealing which might be fair for some other purpose or fair in general' (per Ungoed-Thomas J); *Pro Sieben* v. *Carlton* [1998] FSR 43, 49: 'the provisions are not to be regarded as mere examples of a general wide discretion vested in the courts to refuse to enforce copyright where they believe such refusal to be fair and reasonable' (per Laddie J).

It will be demonstrated that each of these requirements can create serious problems for users.

Does the exception apply to the work in question?

Excluded subject matter

The Act styles the fair dealing provisions as 'general' exceptions and, as such, they apply to a wide range of subject matter. The criticism and review exception applies to all *types* of work (but does not apply to unpublished works, as is explained below). Fair dealing for the purpose of reporting current events applies to nearly all types of work, but does not apply to photographs.[4] At first blush the exclusion of photographs from the current events exception may seem to be a matter of little consequence, given its narrow scope. Moreover, photographs came to be excluded from the current events exception because publishers of newspapers and magazines were worried that the current events exception might be used by rival publishers to reproduce photographs without payment – an apparently legitimate concern.[5] Closer analysis reveals, however, that the exclusion of photographs raises very real freedom of expression concerns. Nor was the exclusion required to protect publishers of newspapers and magazines, since a court would be extremely unlikely to conclude that the use of a rival's photograph without payment was 'fair', save in the most exceptional circumstances.[6]

The problem with the exclusion of photographs from the scope of the current events exception lies in its absolute nature, that it applies irrespective of the content of the photograph, the circumstances in which it was taken or the willingness of the copyright owner to grant permission for its publication. It is also important to bear in mind the rules on ownership in the UK. The Act provides that works created by an employee in the course of her employment vest in the employer,[7] including in cases where the employer is the Crown.[8] These rules on ownership, together with the absolute exclusion of photographs, mean that photographs taken by an army photographer or a spy plane[9] which cast doubt on the government's

---

[4] CDPA 1988, s. 30(2). Photograph is defined in s. 4(2) as 'a recording of light or other radiation on any medium on which an image is produced or from which an image may by any means be produced, and which is not part of a film'. The Act therefore provides a broad definition of 'photograph', but stills from a film do not fall within the definition.
[5] For the background see *Copinger*, para. 9.19.
[6] *Ibid.*   [7] CDPA 1988, s. 11(2).   [8] *Ibid.*, s. 163(1).
[9] If the plane were fully automated copyright would probably vest in the Crown by virtue of ss. 9(3) (authorship of copyright in computer-generated works) and 163(1) of the CDPA 1988.

claims that civilians had not been injured in an aerial attack could not be published without the government's consent. Nor could photographs taken by members of the security services which demonstrated, say, that they were conducting an illegal surveillance operation or that they were aware of the activities of a terrorist suspect but had failed to prevent that person's involvement in a subsequent terrorist attack. It is also possible to imagine examples where it would be undesirable to allow a private organisation to prevent the publication of a photograph in which it owned the copyright. If, for instance, the clearest evidence of what occurred at Bhopal during the 1984 disaster had been contained in photographs taken by a Union Carbide employee in the immediate aftermath of the explosion and ensuing gas leak, there is a good case to be made that copyright ought not to be capable of preventing those photographs from being placed in the public domain.[10]

It must also be emphasised that the problems created by the absolute exclusion of photographs from the current events exception cannot be overcome by relying on the criticism or review exception as an alternative. While a superficial reading of the fair dealing provisions might suggest that a defendant could instead argue that her intention was to criticise the behaviour of the organisation or personnel in question, such an argument is unlikely to be successful for three reasons: first, because in such a case there would be no criticism or review *of a work* as required by the Act (see 'Criticism or review of a work', below), second, because the courts have signalled that they will be wary of defendants attempting to use the criticism and review exception to circumvent the exclusion of photographs from the current events exception,[11] and third, because in many of the cases that cause most concern the photographs in question will be unpublished (see below).

Unpublished works

If even the narrow exclusion of photographs from the scope of the current events exception raises free speech concerns, far more serious problems are created by the way in which the Act treats unpublished works. Following the implementation of the Information Society Directive, the Act provides that the criticism and review exception only applies to works

---

[10] Depending on the precise nature of the employment a court might conclude that the photographs were not taken 'in the course of employment' (see, in particular, *Noah v. Shuba* [1991] FSR 14), but this would not provide assistance in a case where the employee remains loyal to the company or fears reprisals if she allows the photographs to be published.

[11] *Banier v. News Group Newspapers* [1997] FSR 812.

that 'have been made available to the public'.¹² The Act provides an open-ended definition of 'made available to the public',¹³ but specifically provides that issuing copies of a work to the public, making the work available online, performing or exhibiting the work in public and broadcasting the work will be sufficient to place a work in the public forum for these purposes.¹⁴ Despite this broad definition, works which have not been placed in the public forum by any means are now completely outside the scope of the criticism and review exception.

The exclusion of unpublished works from the scope of the criticism and review exception might be thought to be necessary in order to protect authors from having extracts of their works placed into the public domain before the work has been completed, such premature disclosure representing a serious threat to the creative process.¹⁵ Again, however, a court would be extremely unlikely to conclude that taking an extract from an unfinished work was 'fair'. Moreover, the exclusion is not confined to 'unfinished' works, but rather applies to all unpublished works, irrespective of how important the content of the work is for public debate. It is easy to imagine examples where the absolute exclusion of unpublished works from the criticism and review exception would cause very real free-speech problems, but it may be worth providing an illustration drawn from the facts of a real case. *Hubbard v. Vosper*¹⁶ concerned a dispute between the founder of the Church of Scientology, L. Ron Hubbard, and a former member of the Church who had written a book that was highly critical of it. In the book the defendant quoted from various unpublished works on Scientology written by Hubbard. An interlocutory injunction was granted in the High Court, but this was discharged by the Court of Appeal, which concluded that the defendants had an arguable fair dealing defence. A key part of the defendants' case was that the passages reproduced demonstrated that, until 1970 at least, Church doctrine had deemed that suppressive persons – a category which included those who were critical of the Church in public¹⁷ – were to be regarded as 'Fair Game', by which was meant 'without right for self, possessions or position'.¹⁸ This element of Church doctrine clearly had a considerable

---

[12] CDPA 1988, s. 30(1).
[13] *Ibid.*, s. 30(1A): a work will have been made available to the public 'if it has been made available by any means'.
[14] *Ibid.*
[15] See W. Fisher, 'Reconstructing the Fair Use Doctrine' (1988) 101 *Harvard Law Review* 1659, 1773–4, arguing forcefully against the disclosure of creative works before their creators deem them finished.
[16] [1972] 2 QB 84.
[17] See the extracts from Church documents cited by Megaw LJ, *ibid.*, 99.
[18] *Ibid.*, 93.

influence on the Court, Lord Denning MR noting that 'even on what we have heard so far, there is good ground for thinking that these courses contain such dangerous material that it is in the public interest that it should be made known'.[19]

With the absolute exclusion of unpublished works from the scope of the criticism or review exception, it is difficult to see any basis for concluding that the defendants in *Hubbard* would still have an arguable defence. Although the documents in question had been widely circulated within the Church, they had never been made publicly available and hence it could not be said that copies of the work had been 'issued to the public'.[20] Thus if the same facts were to arise today it seems that *Hubbard* v. *Vosper* would have to be decided differently.

In contrast to the criticism and review exception, no distinction is drawn between published and unpublished works for the purposes of the reporting current events exception. A *de novo* interpretation of section 30 might, therefore, lead us to conclude that the reporting current events exception applies equally to published and unpublished works. It is clear, however, that the government's intention was to preserve the existing system of permitted acts wherever possible, and the wording of the current events provision was simply left unchanged. Consequently, the courts are unlikely to adopt a completely fresh interpretation of the fair dealing provisions. They are far more likely to continue to apply pre-harmonisation case law. This indicates that any use that results in the publication of a substantial part of a previously unpublished work will not be 'fair'.[21]

It therefore seems that the reporting current events exception will also not be available in relation to unpublished works. There is some authority to suggest that even if a work has not been published to the world at large it may have been circulated to a sufficiently wide audience to make it fair to publish sections of it. It has been indicated that this might apply where a tract has been made broadly available within a religious community or where a report has been sent to all the shareholders of a public company.[22] The Court of Appeal has recently reiterated, however, that this exception

---

[19] *Ibid.*, 96.
[20] S. 18(2) defines 'the issue to the public of copies' (wording which is very similar, but not quite identical, to the language used in s. 30(1A)) as meaning '(a) the act of putting into circulation in the EEA copies not previously put into circulation in the EEA by or with the consent of the copyright owner, or (b) the act of putting into circulation outside the EEA copies not previously put into circulation in the EEA or elsewhere'. S. 18 is itself notoriously difficult to interpret. See J. Phillips and L. Bently, 'Copyright Issues: The Mysteries of Section 18' [1999] EIPR 133.
[21] *British Oxygen* v. *Liquid Air* [1925] 1 Ch 383; *Hyde Park* v. *Yelland* [2001] Ch 143.
[22] *Hubbard* v. *Vosper* [1972] 2 QB 84. It has also been suggested that there might be an exclusion allowing for the publication of extracts from unpublished government works:

is limited and does not replace the general rule that it will not be fair for the purpose of reporting current events to publish extracts from a previously unpublished work.[23] Thus although the rule that applies to reporting current events is somewhat less restrictive than that which applies to fair dealing for the purpose of criticism or review, the position is that it is not fair dealing to place a substantial part of a previously unpublished work in the public domain.

Is the use for an approved purpose?

As has already been emphasised, the fair dealing provisions will only apply if the use is for one of the approved purposes. The first question that needs to be addressed is how the purpose of the taking is to be assessed – should the defendant's purpose be judged objectively or ought it to be enough that the defendant honestly believed that her taking was for an approved purpose? This question had been left open, but in a number of recent decisions it has been indicated that the courts will apply an objective test when deciding whether the taking was for an approved purpose.[24] While the question of what standard of interpretation ought to be used is probably of fairly limited importance, the recent entrenchment of an objective test is a cause for concern. The danger is that judges may focus on what *they* would have done or might have been trying to achieve in the circumstances. This may lead them to take an unduly negative view of the intention behind the taking, particularly when dealing with unfamiliar art forms. Nor is it true to say that an objective standard is necessary to ensure that an honest but misguided defendant does not take too much, since even if the defendant's purpose were to be assessed subjectively, it would still be necessary to show that the taking was 'fair'.

The second, more important, issue that needs to be considered when asking whether the defendant's taking was for an approved purpose is what is meant by 'criticism or review of a work or a performance of a work' and what is meant by 'reporting current events'. The rest of this section is concerned with these questions.

Commonwealth of Australia v. *Fairfax* (1981) 147 CLR 39, 55 (High Court of Australia, per Mason J, sitting as a single judge). However, the only authority to support the existence of such an exception is a first instance Australian decision, and it is notable that the Court of Appeal made no reference to this possible exception when reiterating the general rule in *Yelland*. The existence of an exception allowing for the publication of extracts from unpublished government works is thus doubtful at best.

[23] *Hyde Park* v. *Yelland* [2001] Ch 143, 158–9.
[24] *Pro Sieben* v. *Carlton* [1999] FSR 610, 620; *Hyde Park* v. *Yelland*, 157; *Newspaper Licensing* v. *Marks and Spencer* [2000] 4 All ER 239, 249; *Copyright Licensing* v. *University of Auckland* (2002) 53 IPR 618, 625 (High Court of New Zealand); *CCH Canadian* v. *Law Society of Upper Canada* [2004] SCC 13 (Supreme Court of Canada). But cf. *Pro Sieben* v. *Carlton* [1998] FSR 43, 49.

The meaning of 'criticism' and 'review'

Any attempt to assess what is meant by use for the purposes of 'criticism' and 'review' is complicated by the fact that, for the most part, judges have refused to define these terms. Rather, it has been emphasised that they are 'expressions of wide and indefinite scope'.[25] In some cases judges have made reference to dictionary definitions of the words 'criticism' and 'review', but these definitions are themselves very broad. For example, in the Australian case *De Garis* v. *Neville Jeffress Pidler* Beaumont J adopted elements of the *Macquarie Dictionary*'s definitions of these words. He therefore concluded that 'criticism' means '(i) the act or art of analysing and judging the quality of a literary or artistic work; (ii) the act of passing judgment as to the merits of something; (iii) a critical comment, article or essay; a critique'.[26] 'Review' was defined to mean 'a critical article or report, as in a periodical, on some literary work, commonly some work of recent appearance; a critique'. More recently, in the New Zealand case *Copyright Licensing* v. *University of Auckland*, Salmon J adopted the *Shorter Oxford English Dictionary*'s definition of these terms and concluded that 'criticism' means '(i) the investigation of the text, character, composition and origin of literary documents; (ii) the art or practice of estimating the qualities and character of literary or artistic works'. 'Review' was defined to mean 'an account or criticism of a book, play, film, product *etc.*'.[27]

Judicial reluctance to set definite parameters for the criticism and review exception, the breadth of the dictionary definitions set out above and many of the cases all suggest that traditional practices of commenting on and criticising works will receive fairly generous protection. More complicated is the question of the extent to which the criticism and review exception can be interpreted in such a way as to allow for the creation of certain types of derivative work. UK law has no equivalent to the German 'free use' defence[28] or the French 'caricature, parody and pastiche' exception.[29] Consequently, works of parody and satire and other works that incorporate samples or extracts amounting to a substantial part of an earlier work will infringe unless the defendant can bring herself within the criticism and review exception. The question of whether the criticism and review exception could allow for the creation of some types of derivative work has attracted most attention in discussions of the law's treatment of parodies. As will be seen, it was formerly thought that parodies were entitled to special treatment under UK law, such that they

---

[25] *Pro Sieben* v. *Carlton*, 620 (per Robert Walker LJ).
[26] (1990) 18 IPR 292, 299 (Federal Court of Australia). [27] (2002) 53 IPR 618, 625.
[28] German Copyright Act 1965, Art. 24(1). This provision of German law is discussed in more detail in Chapter 7.
[29] French Intellectual Property Code 1992, Art. 122(5).

would rarely infringe copyright.[30] The courts have since retreated from this position, however, and it now seems that any parody that reproduces a substantial part of an underlying work[31] will infringe unless the parodist can bring herself within the criticism and review exception. There is limited UK authority to indicate that parodies might fall within this exception[32] and some persuasive authority to the same effect,[33] but there is also persuasive authority going the other way.[34] The dictionary definitions set out above also fail to provide much assistance – a parody may or may not amount to 'a critical comment' on an earlier work, etc.

Even if it were to be accepted that parodies fall within the criticism and review exception, and it must be emphasised that this is by no means certain, it seems likely that this is as broad a reading of 'criticism' and 'review' as the courts would be prepared to accept. Other types of derivative work are likely to fall outside the exception altogether. In *Pro Sieben* v. *Carlton* it was said that 'the nearer that any particular derivative use of copyright material comes to the boundaries [of the criticism and review exception], unplotted though they are, the less likely it is to make good the fair dealing defence'.[35] There may therefore be the danger that '[i]n order to be deemed "proper" criticism, a work had best be a rather obvious parody of the underlying work'.[36] It is notable, for example, that although

---

[30] See Chapter 9.
[31] This will frequently be the case because parodies depend on recognition of the work being parodied. See E. Gredley and S. Maniatis, 'Parody: A Fatal Attraction? Part 1: The Nature of Parody and its Treatment in Copyright' [1997] EIPR 339; M. Spence, 'Intellectual Property and the Problem of Parody' (1998) 114 *Law Quarterly Review* 594. It is sometimes said that the substantial part test is less likely to be satisfied in the case of parodies of literary works than of musical or artistic works, since in the case of literary works there may be less direct ways of summoning up the original in the minds of the audience. It must be remembered, however, that literary copyright protects not only the author's precise words, but also the work's structure, sequence and pattern of events. A good example of a potentially infringing literary parody is provided by the US case *Suntrust Bank* v. *Houghton Mifflin Co* 268 F 3d 1257 (2001), which concerned a parody of Margaret Mitchell's 1936 novel, *Gone with the Wind*. In that case it was held that the defendant's work was substantially similar to *Gone with the Wind*, but fell under the aegis of the fair use defence. For commentary see J. Grossett, 'The Wind Done Gone: Transforming Tara into a Plantation Parody' (2002) 52 *Case Western Law Review* 1113.
[32] *Williamson Music* v. *The Pearson Partnership* [1987] FSR 97, 103.
[33] *Channel Nine* v. *Network Ten* (2002) 55 IPR 112 (Federal Court of Australia – Full Court), 132: 'Criticism may involve an element of humour, or "poking fun at" the object of the criticism' (per Hely J).
[34] *Cie générale des établissements Michelin – Michelin & Cie* v. *CAW Canada* (1996) 71 CPR (3d) 348 (Federal Court of Canada – Trial Division), para. 66: 'criticism is not synonymous with parody. Criticism requires analysis and judgment of a work that sheds light on the original' (per Teitelbaum J).
[35] *Pro Sieben* v. *Carlton* [1999] FSR 610, 621 (per Robert Walker LJ).
[36] L. Greenberg, 'The Art of Appropriation: Puppies, Piracy and Post-Modernism' (1992) 11 *Cardozo Arts and Entertainment Law Journal* 1, 29, commenting on the outcome of *Rogers* v. *Koons* 960 F 2d 301 (1992), discussed in the previous chapter.

in a recent Australian case it was accepted that parody can amount to a form of criticism or review, the court went on to find that the rebroadcast of excerpts from the plaintiff's programmes infringed except in circumstances where there was direct comment on the excerpt.[37]

To summarise, 'criticism' and 'review' have been interpreted broadly, so that where the defendant has engaged in traditional practices of commenting on or reviewing a work she will have little difficulty in persuading the court that her taking was for an approved purpose. The dearth of provisions allowing for the creation of derivative works in the United Kingdom means, however, that it is also important to consider how far the criticism and review exception can be stretched. Once we move beyond traditional forms of comment and analysis any application of the criticism and review exception becomes much less certain.

Criticism or review of a work

The Act not only specifies that the taking must be for the purposes of 'criticism' or 'review', it also specifies that the taking must be for the purpose of criticising or reviewing *'that or another work or . . . a performance of a work'*. It will be seen that these words have an important limiting effect, but it is first necessary to consider the effect of these words more generally.

By providing that the taking can be for the purpose of criticising or reviewing 'that work or another work', the Act makes it clear that the work copied need not be the work criticised. It is therefore permissible to quote from other works on the same topic in the course of reviewing a work. By providing that the exception is available when reviewing a performance of a work, the Act makes it permissible to quote extracts from a play when reviewing a performance of a dramatic work. It is also clear from the cases that the requirement that the criticism or review be *of a work* does not limit the availability of the exception to criticism or review aimed at the surface of the work, that is, to the way the work is

---

[37] *Channel Nine* v. *Network Ten*. The facts of this case are complex. In outline, it concerned twenty separate occasions on which the defendant rebroadcast extracts from the plaintiff's programmes during *The Panel*, a weekly television programme that pokes fun at other television shows. In relation to nineteen of the extracts the defendant pleaded a fair dealing defence. It was eventually concluded that ten of the uses did not amount to fair dealing. The Court's reasoning has been criticised on the basis that the judges failed to display sensitivity to the ethos of programmes like *The Panel*. See M. Handler and D. Rolph, '"A Real Pea Souper": *The Panel Case* and the Development of the Fair Dealing Defences to Copyright Infringement in Australia' (2003) 27 *Melbourne University Law Review* 381, 410–13. This case subsequently went to appeal, but the issue of fair dealing was not considered: *Network Ten* v. *Channel Nine* [2004] HCA 14 (High Court of Australia).

written, filmed and so on. Rather, the cases indicate that criticism aimed at underlying thoughts, ideas, principles, philosophy or theology may still fall within the scope of the exception.[38] Moreover, provided the defendant can show that there has been a criticism or review of the work, the fact that the criticism or review is only intended as a springboard to facilitate some other criticism will not prevent the exception from applying. Thus in *Time Warner v. Channel 4*[39] it was held that taking substantial extracts from the plaintiff's film was fair dealing for the purposes of criticism and review, even though the main thrust of the defendants' programme was criticism of the decision to withdraw the work from circulation. In the course of the programme there was a review of the film which focused, in particular, on the level of violence in the film.

The cases also establish that the requirement that the criticism or review be *of a work* does not mean that the defendant is placed under an obligation to review the whole of a work in such a way as to 'do the work justice'. A reviewer is therefore permitted to focus on those aspects of a work that she finds particularly laudable or objectionable. Criticism of a single aspect of a work is therefore capable of constituting fair dealing.[40] Indeed, Robert Walker LJ has gone as far as to state '[i]f the fair dealing is for the purpose of criticism that criticism may be strongly expressed and unbalanced without forfeiting the fair dealing defence; an author's remedy for malicious and unjustified criticism lies (if it lies anywhere) in the law of defamation, not copyright'.[41]

Perhaps more surprisingly, it has recently been indicated that use of an extract from a work to criticise or review a genre of works may also fall within the scope of the exception, since in such a case there will be an implicit criticism or review of all works within that genre. This point came to be decided in *Pro Sieben v. Carlton*. The defendant had included a 30-second extract from the plaintiff's film in a television programme about chequebook journalism. The purpose of the inclusion was to criticise chequebook journalism as a practice. It therefore seemed that there was no criticism or review *of a work* as required by the Act. Laddie J adopted this literal interpretation at first instance, holding that the criticism and review defence could not apply.[42] However, this conclusion was reversed on appeal, the Court of Appeal holding that there had been a criticism or review of a work since the programme criticised 'various works representing the fruits of chequebook journalism'.[43] In other words, criticism of

---

[38] This point was established by *Hubbard v. Vosper* [1972] 2 QB 84 and now seems to be universally accepted.
[39] [1994] EMLR 1. The case concerned Stanley Kubrick's *A Clockwork Orange*, which had been withdrawn from distribution in the United Kingdom at Kubrick's request.
[40] *Ibid.*   [41] *Pro Sieben v. Carlton*, 619.   [42] [1998] FSR 43.   [43] [1999] FSR 610, 621.

the practice of chequebook journalism amounted to criticism of all works of chequebook journalism.

The requirement that the criticism or review be *of a work* does not, therefore, have some of the consequences that might have been attributed to this wording. In particular, the decision of the Court of Appeal in *Pro Sieben* represents a welcome extension of the exception. Yet even this decision, which stretches the language of the statute to breaking point, still does not catch some important situations in which the criticism and review exception ought to be available. The requirement that the criticism or review be *of a work* would still seem to mean that it would not be possible to rely on this section when quoting from a treatise on political theory when criticising political arrangements or from a book on moral philosophy when criticising someone's behaviour. Similarly, the alternative that the criticism or review be *of a performance of a work* would seem to exclude cases where there is no work underlying the performance. It therefore seems that it would not be possible to rely on this exception to quote from a treatise on juggling when reviewing a juggler's performance.

The recent case *Ashdown v. Telegraph Group*[44] illustrates some of the potential problems. One of the questions that arose in that case was whether the defendants' copying of portions of a confidential minute fell within fair dealing for the purpose of criticism or review. The minute related to a meeting between new Prime Minister Tony Blair and Paddy Ashdown, then leader of the Liberal Democrats,[45] shortly after the 1997 general election. The accompanying article argued that the public and Labour MPs had been misled about the intentions of Blair and Ashdown to form a coalition government. In rejecting the argument that this brought the use within the criticism and review exception, Sir Andrew Morritt VC said at first instance:

> what is required is that the copying shall take place as part of and for the purpose of criticising and reviewing the work. The work is the minute. But the articles are not criticising or reviewing the minute: they are criticising or reviewing the actions of the Prime Minister and the claimant in October 1997. It was not necessary for that purpose to copy the minute at all. In my judgment the articles do not come within section 30(1) because the purpose of copying the work was not its criticism or review.[46]

It therefore seems that despite broad readings of the requirement that the criticism or review be *of a work* or *a performance of a work* it may nevertheless impose an unjustifiable restriction on the ability of users

---

[44] [2001] Ch 685; [2002] Ch 149.   [45] The third-largest party in Parliament.
[46] [2001] Ch 685, 697–8. This reasoning was endorsed on appeal: [2002] Ch 149, 171.

to cite works in support of an argument, analysis or review. In the next subsection we turn to consider the reporting current events exception. It will be seen that this exception is also limited in a number of important respects.

The meaning of reporting current events

When considering what is meant by 'reporting current events' it is necessary to appreciate what 'event' means in this context, when an event will be treated as 'current' and when a use will be for the purpose of 'reporting' an event.[47] These will be considered in turn.

It has been said on a number of occasions that the reporting current events exception should be construed liberally,[48] and the courts have therefore adopted a fairly broad definition of 'events'. Matters which are the subject of political controversy will unquestionably be covered by the exception. Thus it has been said that articles dealing with the minimum wage, child labour or racial bias within an institution will all be privileged, as will articles reporting announcements from politicians or a central bank about a single currency.[49] It has also been indicated that matters of purely local significance can fall within the definition of 'events'. Perhaps more surprisingly, the courts have been prepared to accept that sporting fixtures can amount to 'events'[50] and there is reason to believe that other public spectacles, such as firework displays, might be covered.[51]

In contrast to the above, it has been said that comparisons of products of different retailers, lifestyle articles, fashion advice and personal interest stories will not fall within the scope of the exception.[52] However, even if the matter is seemingly trivial, the courts have indicated that they will be prepared to take what is interesting to the public into account. In this way sustained media coverage of an apparently trivial matter may be sufficient to bring it within the exception.[53] Overall, therefore, the requirement that

---

[47] It has been indicated that it is better to regard 'reporting current events' as a composite phrase and to avoid further dissection: *Pro Sieben* v. *Carlton* [1999] FSR 610, 620; *Newspaper Licensing* v. *Marks and Spencer* [2001] Ch 257, 270, 289. Ultimately, however, and as can be seen in these cases, questions about what is meant by the words 'current', 'events' and 'reporting' inevitably resurface.

[48] For example, see *Pro Sieben* v. *Carlton* [1999] FSR 610, 620; *Newspaper Licensing* v. *Marks and Spencer* [2001] Ch 257, 271; *Ashdown* v. *Telegraph Group* [2002] Ch 149, 172.

[49] *Newspaper Licensing* v. *Marks and Spencer* [2001] Ch 257, 290 (per Mance LJ).

[50] *BBC* v. *BSB* [1992] Ch 141, and see the Broadcasting Act 1996, s. 137.

[51] *Nine Network Australia* v. *Australian Broadcasting Corp* (1999) 48 IPR 333; under Australian law New Year's Eve celebrations were at least arguably 'newsworthy'.

[52] *Newspaper Licensing* v. *Marks and Spencer* [1999] RPC 536, 547.

[53] This comes across most clearly from *Pro Sieben* v. *Carlton* [1999] FSR 610, 625. See also Bently and Sherman, p. 205.

Is the use for an approved purpose?

the reporting relate to current *events* should cause relatively few problems for users.

Much more serious problems are created by the requirement that use be for the purpose of reporting *current* events. It has been held that the requirement that the events be 'current' does not mean that the exception is confined to very recent happenings,[54] and case law indicates that information directly relevant to the political process may have a particularly long shelf-life for these purposes.[55] It is also important to emphasise that the work itself need not have been produced recently; it needs only to have been used to report current events. Thus it has been said that old correspondence relating to a nuclear reactor that has just suffered a severe failure might be relevant to the reporting of current events.[56] Ultimately, however, the problem is that there is no exception that allows for the reproduction of material relating to newsworthy matters of history, no matter how important the topic. As it has been put by Lord Phillips MR, 'it is possible to conceive of information of the greatest public interest relating not to a current event, but to a document produced in the past. We are not aware of any provision of the 1988 Act which would permit publication in such circumstances.'[57]

If the temporal requirement that the events be 'current' causes problems for users, the fact that the use needs to be for the *reporting* of current events may further limit the availability of the exception. One area of uncertainty relates to the range of media activities that fall within the 'reporting' of events. A literal reading of the statute might suggest that it is only the communication of information that falls within the exception – 'reporting' does not obviously include commentary on events that are well known or the expression of opinion. This restrictive interpretation would seem to be supported by a recent New Zealand decision in which it was said that the 'work must be used for "reporting current events" and not

---

[54] *Pro Sieben* v. *Carlton* [1998] FSR 43, 54; it had been argued that the exception should be confined to events less than twenty-four hours old, but this interpretation was rejected.
[55] *Ashdown* v. *Telegraph Group* [2002] Ch 149, 172.
[56] *Associated Newspapers Group* v. *News Group Newspapers* [1986] RPC 515, 519; *Hyde Park* v. *Yelland* [1999] RPC 655, 661. Some commentators have also concluded that an event may be 'current' where an investigation is ongoing or where victims are seeking compensation: Laddie et al., 3rd edn, para. 20.15; Bently and Sherman, p. 204. The cases, however, do not support this conclusion: *Hyde Park Residence* v. *Yelland* [2001] Ch 143, 156–7; *Distillers* v. *Times Newspapers* [1975] QB 613, 625–6, leaving the issue open but doubting whether ongoing controversy would be sufficient.
[57] *Ashdown* v. *Telegraph Group* [2002] Ch 149, 166–7. Lord Phillips went on to note that the argument that disclosure and any accompanying controversy would be sufficient to make events 'current' would normally be rejected. However, he left open the possibility that the courts might accept this argument in a limited class of case, such as where a document becomes available at the Public Record Office under the 30-year rule.

for editorial or other purposes'.[58] Some support for this interpretation can also be gained from *Hyde Park* v. *Yelland*, where Aldous LJ concluded that use of stills from a film to prove the falsity of certain claims that had been made in the public forum could not be said to be for the purpose of *reporting* events.[59] If this interpretation is correct, then it seems that a range of news-related media activities, including some types of newspaper opinion piece and humorous topical news programmes, will not fall within the scope of the current events exception. Against this restrictive interpretation, it might be noted that two recent Australian cases indicate that the news reporting exception under Australian law extends to programmes that treat news items in an entertaining or amusing fashion.[60] Neither of these cases, however, contains a detailed discussion of what *reporting* means. The range of media activities that might fall within fair dealing for the purpose of reporting current events is therefore uncertain at best.

There is also now reason to suggest that the requirement that the use be for the purpose of *reporting* events may limit the availability of the exception to public acts, that is, to uses that serve to place information in the public domain. In *Newspaper Licensing* v. *Marks and Spencer* one of the questions that arose was whether the photocopying and distribution of articles from newspapers and magazines to key Marks and Spencer's personnel fell within the current events exception. This question was not finally decided, but in the Court of Appeal all three judges indicated that Marks and Spencer's actions did not fall within the exception. For Peter Gibson LJ, although it could be said that Marks and Spencer were reporting the appearance of the article, they could not be said to be reporting current events, since 'the language of the subsection . . . naturally connotes the public reporting of a recent newsworthy event'.[61] For Mance LJ the exception represents a public interest exception to copyright which cannot be extended to copying within a private organisation (although he left open the possibility that the private reporting of information to a public body might be permissible).[62] That the reporting of current

---

[58] *Copyright Licensing* v. *University of Auckland* (2002) 53 IPR 618, 626, citing *Copinger*, para. 9.19.
[59] [2001] Ch 143, 157. However, on the facts Aldous LJ concluded that it was arguable that the stills had been used for the purpose of reporting on the ongoing media coverage.
[60] *Nine Network Australia* v. *Australian Broadcasting Corp* (1999) 48 IPR 333 (Federal Court of Australia); *Channel Nine* v. *Network Ten* (2002) 55 IPR 112 (Federal Court of Australia – Full Court).
[61] *Newspaper Licensing* v. *Marks and Spencer* [2001] Ch 257, 271.
[62] *Ibid.*, 290. In contrast, Chadwick LJ took the view that the defendant's actions did fall within the 'reporting of current events', but indicated that he would have declined to treat the takings as 'fair': *ibid.*, 279–80.

events requires some element of public dissemination of information is also suggested by a recent New Zealand case in which it was indicated that copying by universities could not fall within the scope of the current events exception. Salmon J went further in that case, however, and stated, '[i]t is difficult to think of any circumstances where the reporting of current events would occur other than [through] some section of the news media.'[63]

Overall it can be seen that the restriction of section 30(2) to the 'reporting of current events' may impose further significant restrictions on the rights of media organisations to communicate information to the public. The recent indications that the exception may only be available in relation to public activities is also a matter for significant concern. The decision of the Court of Appeal in *Marks and Spencer* is at least open to the interpretation that any private distribution of part of a work will fall outside the scope of the exception. This means that distribution of information within political parties and non-governmental organisations (NGOs) would not be covered, even though such distribution falls squarely within the category of communications that are relevant to the political process. The related suggestion that the exception will only be available to media organisations is also a matter of significant concern in the electronic environment. One of the advantages of the Internet is said to be that it increases the ability of individuals to communicate their views to the world at large. This advantage of the Internet may be overstated, but this provides all the more reason to ensure that copyright law does not inhibit whatever potential the Internet does have for empowering individuals.

Is the use fair?

If the defendant can establish that the taking was for an approved purpose she will then have to convince the court that the taking was 'fair'. It is now clear that similar criteria of 'fairness' will be employed whether the use in question involves criticism or review or the reporting of current events. The leading judgment on the meaning of 'fairness' remains that of Lord Denning in *Hubbard* v. *Vosper*. Although Lord Denning concluded that the decision must ultimately be a matter of impression (a point that has since been reiterated on a number of occasions), he identified three factors that will ordinarily be relevant in determining whether a particular use is fair. He said:

---

[63] *Copyright Licensing* v. *University of Auckland* (2002) 53 IPR 618, 626.

You must consider first the number and extent of the quotations and extracts. Are they altogether too many and too long to be fair? Then you must consider the use made of them. If they are used as a basis for comment, criticism or review, that may be fair dealing. If they are used to convey the same information as the author, for a rival purpose, that may be unfair. Next, you must consider the proportions. To take long extracts and attach short comments may be unfair. But, short extracts and long comments may be fair.[64]

These three factors – how much has been taken? how much has been added? is the use for a rival purpose? – are sensible guiding principles. Problems may arise, however, if these factors are applied inflexibly or without regard to the type of work in question. For example, there are occasions when it ought to be permissible to reproduce the whole of a work. This may be particularly important in cases where the work is short.[65] Moreover, it needs to be remembered that Lord Denning's guiding principles were developed in the context of literary works and that they may need to be modified when dealing with other types of work. For example, in cases involving artistic works, when asking how 'much' of the work has been taken, the manner of reproduction should also be taken into account. A black and white photograph of a painting published in a newspaper should not necessarily be treated as a taking of 'the whole' of the work. It is therefore encouraging that in a recent decision the Canadian Supreme Court emphasised that consideration should be given generally to the nature of the work that has been copied and, more specifically, stated that it might sometimes be permissible to reproduce the whole of a photograph.[66]

It has also been indicated that another useful test for deciding whether the taking was fair is whether the user's purpose could have been achieved by other means.[67] As one factor that addresses the question of fairness this would seem a sensible test. The concern, as Bently and Sherman have noted, is that this factor may be applied as a test of necessity.[68] The danger

---

[64] [1972] 2 QB 84, 94.
[65] In *Hubbard* v. *Vosper* [1972] 2 QB 84, 98, Megaw LJ indicated that it might be permissible to reproduce a short work in its entirety. There is some authority to suggest that the taking of the whole of a work can never be fair dealing: *Zamacois* v. *Douville* [1943] 2 DLR 257 (Exchequer Court of Canada), but this case has now been implicitly overruled by *CCH Canadian* v. *Law Society of Upper Canada* [2004] SCC 13.
[66] See *CCH Canadian* v. *Law Society of Upper Canada*, paras. 56, 58. However, this was said in the context of the research and private study exception (see Chapter 4). See also S. Weil, 'Fair Use and the Visual Arts, or Please Leave Some Room for Robin Hood' (2001) 62 *Ohio State Law Journal* 835, arguing in the context of the United States that fair use rules developed in relation to literary works need to be modified when dealing with works of visual art.
[67] *Associated Newspapers Group* v. *News Group Newspapers* [1986] RPC 515, 519; *CCH Canadian* v. *Law Society of Upper Canada*, para. 57.
[68] Bently and Sherman, p. 199.

is that courts will take a restrictive view of when a taking is necessary and will be blind to the sorts of commercial factors that a media organisation will have to take into account. In contrast, Strasbourg jurisprudence makes it clear that it is not appropriate for courts 'to substitute their own views for those of the press as to what technique of reporting should be adopted'.[69]

A rather different problem with the test of fairness is that it fails to provide potential defendants with any certainty as to the amount that can safely be copied. Individual industries have attempted to work round this problem by creating their own codes of practice. For example, the major broadcasters in the United Kingdom have established a code of practice relating to the use of extracts taken from exclusive sports broadcasts for the purpose of reporting current events.[70] Similarly, there is a widespread understanding within the publishing industry that taking a single extract of up to 400 words from a work of prose will be fair for the purposes of the criticism and review exception.[71] The attraction of codes of this type is that they provide nuanced, industry-specific and subject-matter-specific guidelines. However, because industry guidelines lack official sanction there is the danger that even someone operating within the guidelines will be held to infringe. On the other hand, there may be a danger that industry guidelines will be applied mechanistically, the courts being insufficiently vigilant as to the parties responsible for their development.[72] The problem is that without some form of official oversight large industry players, who see themselves principally as owners of copyright material, will draw up the guidelines. As such they are likely to tend towards a restrictive definition of fair dealing. It is worth noting that the guidelines drawn up by broadcasters relating to the use of extracts of sporting events are more restrictive than the guidelines laid down by the courts. For example, the broadcasters' code restricts the showing of clips to inclusion in general news programmes. In contrast, it has been held by the courts that the inclusion of extracts in a specialist sports news programme can also fall within the reporting of current events exception.[73]

---

[69] *Jersild* v. *Denmark* (1995) 19 EHRR 1, 26.
[70] For a detailed discussion see T. Simpson, 'Exclusive Sports Broadcast Rights and Fair Dealing' [2001] EntLR 207.
[71] The Society of Authors provides further information on its website, www.societyofauthors.net/publications/index.html, 'Permissions Quick Guide'. See also L. Owen, *Selling Rights*, 2nd edn (London: Blueprint, 1994), p. 168.
[72] In *Sillitoe* v. *McGraw-Hill Book Co* [1983] FSR 545, the judge made reference to the guidelines drawn up by the Society of Authors and the Publishers Association when deciding the question of fairness and was heavily influenced by the fact that the defendants' actions fell outside these guidelines.
[73] *BBC* v. *BSB* [1992] Ch 141. See Simpson, 'Exclusive Sports Broadcasting Rights'.

Attribution of the work

The final hurdle that the defendant needs to clear is to demonstrate that the underlying work has been attributed to the author. The criticism and review exception is always dependent on 'sufficient acknowledgement' of the work.[74] Sufficient acknowledgement is also required for the current events exception,[75] but no acknowledgement is required in relation to reporting by means of a sound recording, film or broadcast, 'where this would be impossible for reasons of practicality or otherwise'.[76] Sufficient acknowledgement is defined to mean an acknowledgement identifying the work in question by its title or other description and identifying the author unless it is published anonymously.[77] The acknowledgement must be sufficient to allow a reasonably astute member of the relevant audience to understand who the author is.[78] However, where the author customarily identifies herself/itself in a particular fashion she/it cannot then complain that this form of identification is meaningless to the average member of the audience if the defendant subsequently adopts this form of identification. Thus in the *Pro Sieben* case it was held that the defendant's reproduction of the plaintiff's logo did adequately identify the plaintiff as the author of the film.

A requirement that the user acknowledge the source of material will ordinarily be unobjectionable. It is a matter of some concern, however, that the absence of a sufficient acknowledgement will automatically prevent the exception applying, even if the defendant acted in good faith. Particular problems are likely to arise in relation to entrepreneurial works, where the Act designates certain people or entities as the 'author' of the work. The fact that a user needs to mention these entities in order to rely on an exception may well come as a surprise. Consider, for example, a review of a film which incorporates clips or stills. In order to have the benefit of the fair dealing exception the reviewer must provide a sufficient acknowledgement. A reviewer might be forgiven for believing that providing the title of the film and the name of the director would be sufficient. This would not, however, be correct, since the Act designates the 'producer' of the film (normally the film production company) as well as the principal director as the author of a film.[79] The sufficient

---

[74] CDPA 1988, s. 30(1).   [75] *Ibid.*, s. 30(2).
[76] *Ibid.*, s. 30(3). Prior to the implementation of the Information Society Directive there was no requirement of sufficient acknowledgement at all in cases of reporting by means of a sound recording, film, broadcast or cablecast. Consequently, there is not yet any case law on when it is 'impossible' to provide an acknowledgement.
[77] CDPA 1988, s. 178.   [78] *Pro Sieben Media* v. *Carlton* [1998] FSR 43, 55.
[79] CDPA 1988, s. 9(2)(ab).

acknowledgement requirement has the capacity, therefore, to act as a trap for the unwary.

The requirement of sufficient acknowledgement may also create problems in cases where the creator of a derivative work, such as a parody, is attempting to bring themselves within the criticism and review exception. Even if it were accepted that some types of derivative work amount to forms of criticism or review, the requirement of sufficient acknowledgement might impose an artificial obligation on the author of the derivative work. For example, it has been pointed out that while it would be possible to acknowledge the work underlying a parody, this does not accord with ordinary publishing practice and would impose an artificial obligation on the parodist, since one of the benchmarks against which a parody can be judged is its success in making a connection with the work being parodied without any form of express reference.[80]

Summary

In the last chapter we demonstrated that the overlap between copyright and freedom of expression or freedom of information is more significant than most judges and commentators have been prepared to acknowledge. In particular, we drew out two rather different sets of problems. First, it was seen that there are circumstances in which copyright can be exercised in such a way as to prevent information, evidence and opinions from being placed in the public domain. As such, copyright can interfere directly with the effective functioning of the democratic process. Second, it was seen that copyright can interfere with the expressive interests of later authors. It was further seen that reconciling copyright and freedom of expression is a complex matter, particularly when it comes to reconciling the interests of the copyright owner with that of subsequent authors, such that there is plenty of scope for good faith disagreement over where to draw the boundary between copyright protection and expressive freedom. In contrast, in this chapter it has been seen that while there is plenty of room for disagreement about where to draw copyright's boundaries, the section 30 fair dealing exceptions are manifestly inadequate to reconcile copyright with freedom of expression or freedom of information. More specifically, it has been seen that the exclusion of photographs from the current events exception, the fact that neither exception applies to unpublished works, the fact that the criticism and review exception only applies to criticism or review *of a work* or *a performance of a work*, the fact

---

[80] *Copinger*, para. 9.18. See also L. Hutcheon, *A Theory of Parody* (London: Methuen, 1985).

that the news reporting exception only applies to the *reporting* of *current* events and the peculiarities of the sufficient acknowledgement requirement all mean that the section 30 exceptions are incapable of preventing copyright from imposing unjustifiable restrictions on the public's ability to communicate information and to express opinions on important matters. Moreover, the section 30 exceptions do not provide expressly for the interests of the creators of parodies and other types of derivative work at all. It is therefore hardly surprising that these provisions are incapable of reconciling copyright with the expressive interests of the creators of such works.

In the next two sections we consider a number of miscellaneous provisions that supplement the fair dealing exceptions. We have grouped these provisions in accordance with our two chief concerns: we begin by considering other provisions that relate to the communication of information before considering various provisions that might allow for the creation of derivative works. It will be seen that while many of these miscellaneous provisions are important in particular contexts, they are all limited in scope. Thus, even taken together, they do little to remedy the problems with the section 30 fair dealing exceptions that we have identified.

Miscellaneous provisions relating to the communication of information

There are three miscellaneous permitted acts that relate to the communication of information. Two of these provisions relate to the reporting of official proceedings. In order to ensure that copyright does not interfere with the operation of government, the Act provides that copyright will not be infringed by anything done for the purpose of parliamentary proceedings, judicial proceedings or the proceedings of royal commissions and statutory inquiries.[81] In addition, the Act provides that the reporting of such proceedings will not infringe copyright. The Act therefore recognises the importance of the public being informed about the operation of official bodies. The freedom to report official proceedings is fairly generous – 'parliamentary proceedings', 'judicial proceedings' and 'statutory inquiry' are broadly defined;[82] there is no temporal element,

---

[81] See CDPA 1988, ss. 45–46.

[82] 'Parliamentary proceedings' include proceedings of the Northern Ireland Assembly, the Scottish Parliament and the European Parliament; 'judicial proceedings' include proceedings before any court, tribunal or 'person having authority to decide any matter affecting a person's legal rights or liabilities' (arbitration proceedings are therefore covered: *London & Leeds Estates* v. *Paribas (No. 2)* [1995] 1 EGLR 102); 'statutory inquiry' means any inquiry or investigation conducted in pursuance of a duty imposed or power conferred by or under an enactment: CDPA 1988, ss. 46(4), 178.

Miscellaneous provisions

so the report can relate to proceedings from any point in the past; there is no quantitative restriction placed on the amount of material that can be reproduced; and the reporting can be done by any means. The reporting of official proceedings provisions only apply, however, to direct reporting. The Act does not allow for the copying of works which are themselves a published report of the proceedings in question.[83] Thus although it is permissible to report a speech made in Parliament without infringing any copyright in the speech itself or in any underlying work to which the member of parliament may make reference, it is not possible to rely on the reporting of parliamentary proceedings exception to justify copying from Hansard. Nevertheless, it remains true to say that the reporting of official proceedings exceptions are fairly broad. Ultimately, however, it must be remembered that these exceptions only apply to the reporting of specific forms of official activity. Although they are of considerable importance for freedom of expression in that they allow for the communication of information about the workings of government, they do not begin to solve the problems with the fair dealing provisions that we have identified.

The third provision that needs to be considered in this context is the provision allowing for the use of notes or recordings of spoken words.[84] This provision was introduced because the Act expressly recognises that copyright may subsist in a speaker's words when they are recorded by another person, irrespective of whether the speaker has consented to this 'fixation'.[85] There was concern that this might create problems for journalists and broadcasters who would find themselves unable to print or broadcast interviews and speeches without permission. A provision was therefore introduced that allows spoken words to be reproduced without infringing copyright.[86] The exception applies where a record[87] of spoken words has been made 'for the purpose of reporting current events' or 'for the purpose of communicating to the public the whole or part of the work'. Provided that the making of the record and the use of the work were not prohibited by the speaker, it is not an infringement of copyright in the words themselves or in an underlying work (such as the text of a prepared speech) to reproduce the record for either of the approved purposes.

The use of spoken words for the purpose of reporting current events is somewhat more generous than the related fair dealing exception because there is no requirement that the taking be 'fair' and hence there is no

---

[83] CDPA 1988, ss. 45(2), 46(2).   [84] *Ibid.*, s. 58.
[85] *Ibid.*, s. 3(3).   [86] *Ibid.*, s. 58(1).
[87] Record is not defined by the Act and can apparently be in any form – tape recording, written notes, etc.

quantitative restriction on the amount of copying that will be justified. In addition, there is no requirement of sufficient acknowledgement. The alternative, that the record be used for the purpose of communicating the work to the public, is wider still – there does not have to be any element of reporting current events under this limb. Again, however, although the reporting of spoken words exception provides a useful additional tool, its utility is limited to a very specific type of case.

Miscellaneous provisions relating to the creation of derivative works

It has been seen that the section 30 fair dealing exceptions make no direct allowance for the expressive interests of subsequent authors, and this has created interest in the extent to which the criticism and review exception could be extended to protect parodies and so on. However, when thinking about the protection of the expressive interests of subsequent authors in the United Kingdom there are two miscellaneous provisions that should also be mentioned.

Incidental inclusion

One provision that deserves to be mentioned in this context is the incidental inclusion provision. The Act contains a general provision that allows for the 'incidental inclusion' of copyright material in an artistic work, sound recording, film or broadcast.[88] 'Incidental' is not further defined in the Act. It has been held that 'incidental' bears its ordinary meanings of something which is 'casual or of secondary importance' or something which is 'not essential, subordinate, merely background, etc'.[89] It has also been cautioned, however, that reliance must not be placed on a search for synonyms,[90] and that there is no necessary dichotomy between that which is 'incidental' and that which is 'integral'.[91] The exception applies to all types of copyright subject matter, but is more limited as regards musical and related works than as regards other types of copyright

---

[88] CDPA 1988, s. 31(1). The section does not permit incidental inclusion in other types of work. Thus, for example, there can be no incidental inclusion of an earlier work in a literary or musical work. There is some discussion of this point in *Football Association Premier League* v. *Panini* [2004] FSR 1, 13–14 (per Mummery LJ).
[89] See *IPC Magazines* v. *MGN* [1998] FSR 431, 441; *Football Association Premier League* v. *Panini* [2003] FSR 698, 701–2, drawing on the definitions set out in the *Shorter OED, Copinger*, para. 9.26, and Laddie et al., 3rd edn, para. 20.17.
[90] *Football Association Premier League* v. *Panini* [2003] FSR 698, 702 (per Peter Smith J); *Football Association Premier League* v. *Panini* [2004] FSR 1, 14–15 (per Mummery LJ).
[91] *Football Association Premier League* v. *Panini* [2004] FSR 1, 12 (per Chadwick LJ).

subject matter. Where the work in question is a musical work, a lyrical work or a portion of a sound recording or broadcast that includes music or lyrics, copying is not to be regarded as 'incidental' if it is deliberate.[92] In contrast, in relation to other types of work the inclusion can be deliberate but still incidental.[93]

The incidental inclusion provision is of considerable practical importance. It is by virtue of this provision that a broadcaster can film a parade or a sporting event during which music can be heard in the background without having to obtain permission from the owners of copyright in the works reproduced.[94] In addition (and most importantly for present purposes) the incidental inclusion provision may secure a degree of artistic freedom for artists and directors. For example, it has been said that this provision means that no special permission would be needed to film in an art gallery or against the background of a play being performed in a theatre.[95] It is also possible that the incidental inclusion exception might protect an artist who included miniatures of earlier well-known paintings in the background of her own work, and perhaps even an artist who paints a picture or takes a photograph of a disabled soldier standing in front of a militaristic work.[96] It must be emphasised, however, that such examples are few and that, at best, the incidental inclusion exception secures a degree of artistic freedom for authors and directors in a small number of quite specific types of case.

Moreover, in the recent case *Football Association Premier League* v. *Panini*, the Court of Appeal adopted a restrictive interpretation of the incidental inclusion provision. The background to that case was that the Premier League licensed the production of an official sticker album, the stickers showing photographs of football players wearing their club strip. The defendant produced an unauthorised album and sticker set, which also pictured players in their club strips. The Premier League and a number of premiership clubs sued for infringement of copyright in the club logos and the premier league's logo, one or more logos being visible in the overwhelming majority of the defendant's stickers. The case turned on whether the defendant's use could be categorised as an incidental inclusion, but at both first instance and on appeal the Court showed little hesitation in rejecting this defence. This conclusion is surprising given the

---

[92] CDPA 1988, s. 31(3).
[93] *IPC Magazines* v. *MGN* [1998] FSR 431, 441; *Football Association Premier League* v. *Panini* [2004] FSR 1, 11.
[94] Cf. *Hawkes and Sons* v. *Paramount* [1934] Ch 593; Berne Convention, Art. 10bis(2).
[95] *Copinger*, para. 9.26.
[96] In the latter example, however, it might be difficult to persuade a court that the taking was merely 'incidental', particularly given the outcome in the *Panini* case, discussed below.

size of the logos as reproduced in the defendant's photographs and given that the defendant's intention was merely to show players in their club strips – the fact that the strips happened to include the logos was purely 'incidental'. It is also worth contrasting the outcome in this case with the outcome in *Trebor Bassett* v. *The Football Association*.[97] In *Trebor* it was held that it was not even arguable that the defendant's actions amounted to trade mark use, that case concerning the reproduction of the plaintiff's trade marked logo in photographs of football players wearing their football strip included in packets of confectionery. The judge in that case, Rattee J, noted: 'The logo appears on the card only because it is worn by the player whose photograph appears on the card as part of that player's England team football strip'.[98]

The implications of *Panini* for the type of case with which we are principally concerned are difficult to predict. In reaching its conclusion the Court of Appeal emphasised the commercial nature of the defendant's activities and seemed to leave open the possibility that a more liberal approach might be adopted in a case where the defendant was motivated by artistic considerations.[99] Nevertheless, the fact that the Court was so quick to find for the claimants in this case is worrying. It is also a cause for concern that the Court concluded that the 'incidentality' of the taking is to be assessed objectively; it is not necessary to inquire into the subjective intent of the user.[100] Moreover, even though the Court of Appeal left space for a court in a different type of case to adopt a different approach, in the short term at least, the *Panini* decision may serve to dissuade anyone from seeking to rely on the incidental inclusion exception.

Making of subsequent works by the same artist

The second permitted act that should be mentioned in this context is the provision allowing the author of an artistic work to copy portions of her earlier works even after she has assigned copyright in those works. Recognising that artists often draw on their own earlier work, the Act provides that where the author of an artistic work is not the copyright owner, she does not infringe the copyright by copying the work in making another artistic work, provided she does not repeat or imitate the main design of the earlier work.[101] It has been said that this provision might allow an architect to copy a particular design feature, such as a staircase, in a later building or it might allow the painter of a group portrait to

---

[97] [1997] FSR 211.   [98] *Ibid.*, 216.
[99] *Football Association Premier League* v. *Panini* [2004] FSR 1, 12, 15.
[100] *Ibid.*, 12.   [101] CDPA 1988, s. 64.

reuse sketches to produce individual portraits[102] or it might allow an artist to reproduce a 'trade mark' object or motif.[103] In this way the Act provides some protection for the expressive interests of authors as against copyright owners. Allowing artists to reuse portions of their earlier works does nothing, however, to protect third party artists or other types of author.

Other obstacles faced by users

All of the problems with the permitted acts examined thus far can be summarised as internal difficulties, that is, they relate to the way in which the permitted acts have been formulated, and to obstacles that will prevent a user from relying on an exception as against the owner of copyright. Over and above these problems, however, there might be other reasons why, in practice, a defendant will not be able to rely on the exceptions to reuse part of a work. In particular, the copyright owner may be able to rely on some other form of legal interest to prevent the user from making use of its work. Furthermore, in the electronic environment there is the possibility that the copyright owner may be able to persuade an online service provider to take steps even against a user who has a good defence to a claim for copyright infringement. The remainder of this chapter is concerned with these other obstacles that users may face.

The 'digital lock-up' and contractual exclusion of the exceptions

One external constraint on the ability of users to rely on the exceptions that has been widely discussed is the possibility that copyright owners will seek to exclude the operation of the exceptions through contract. In particular, there is concern that in the online environment attempts to exclude the operation of the exceptions will prove to be particularly common, with terms to this effect being embodied in automated licence agreements. Discussions of contractual exclusion are often tied to concerns about owners using technological measures of protection and legal protection for such measures to limit further the operation of the exceptions. The possibility that the operation of the exceptions may come to be excluded in the online environment is often referred to as the 'digital lock-up', and this has attracted considerable attention from commentators over recent years.[104] Many of these commentators have concluded

---

[102] *Hansard*, HL vol. 491, col. 191; vol. 493, col. 1187.
[103] *Copinger*, para. 9.92, giving the example of Magritte's chessmen or 'bilboquets'.
[104] In addition to some of the sources cited below, see, e.g., T. Vinje, 'A Brave New World of Technological Protection Systems: Will There Still be Room for Copyright?' [1996]

that the digital lock-up poses a substantial risk to users. This has led to proposals to render void contractual terms that seek to exclude the operation of the exceptions, and to loosen prohibitions on the circumvention of technological measures. Perhaps most significantly, in 2002 the Australian Copyright Law Review Committee turned its attention to the relationship between copyright and contract and recommended that contracting out be prohibited.[105]

Given our belief that certain types of exception are necessary to protect fundamental rights and interests, the ability of copyright owners to exclude the operation of the permitted acts is clearly a matter of concern to us. Nevertheless, we are somewhat less concerned about this problem than are many other commentators. We also believe that a careful distinction needs to be drawn between contracting out and the use of technological measures of protection, since the two methods of excluding the exceptions raise quite distinct issues. We turn first to contracting out.

One reason why we believe that it would be a mistake to place too much emphasis on the dangers posed by contracting out is that it is still not clear how often owners will seek to use contracting out terms. The clearest evidence of what is happening at the moment comes from the Australian Copyright Law Review Committee's Report,[106] and, despite the committee's conclusions, the evidence presented by the committee as to the extent of the problem is not overwhelming. Moreover, some of the evidence collected by the committee relates to attempts to exclude rights to decompile computer programs, clauses that would in any event be void under UK law (see below). The committee also acknowledged that a range of factors, including consumer resistance, is likely to shape how often copyright owners attempt to exclude the operation of the exceptions through contract, a point we believe needs to be emphasised.

Second, even if attempts to contract out do become commonplace, it is by no means clear that owners will succeed in excluding the operation of the exceptions. For example, doubts remain as to whether contractual

---

EIPR 431; J. Cohen, 'Copyright and the Jurisprudence of Self-Help' (1998) 13 *Berkeley Technology Law Journal* 1089; J. Cohen, 'WIPO Copyright Treaty Implementation in the United States: Will Fair Use Survive?' [1999] EIPR 236; T. Vinje, 'Copyright Imperilled?' [1999] EIPR 192; L. Lessig, *Code and Other Laws of Cyberspace* (New York: Basic Books, 1999), ch. 10; T. Brogan, 'Fair Use No Longer: How the Digital Millennium Copyright Act Bars Fair Use of Digitally Stored Works' (2002) 16 *Saint John's Journal of Legal Commentary* 691; T. Foged, 'US v. EU Anti Circumvention Legislation: Preserving the Public's Privileges in the Digital Age' [2002] EIPR 525; C. Correa, 'Fair Use in the Digital Era' (2002) 33 IIC 570.

[105] Copyright Law Review Committee, *Copyright and Contract* (Canberra, 2002).
[106] *Ibid.*

Other obstacles faced by users   69

terms seeking to exclude the operation of copyright exceptions would be deemed to be validly incorporated,[107] as to the enforceability of such terms[108] and as to how such terms would be interpreted.[109] These doubts are particularly important given our argument in later chapters that better protection for users depends in part on a change in judicial mindset and a greater willingness on the part of judges to look to general common law principles to rein in copyright law.[110]

Finally and most importantly, however, our concern about the possible contractual exclusion of the exceptions is tempered by the fact that this is an area in which UK and EU law already seems to be on the right track. As is the case elsewhere, the general position is that the permitted acts relate only to the question of infringement of copyright and do not affect any other right or obligation.[111] It is therefore generally possible to contract out of the permitted acts. There is, however, a growing list of circumstances in which it is not possible to contract out of the permitted acts, Parliament and the European legislator having recognised that it ought not to be possible to exclude the exceptions in certain circumstances. Thus it is no longer possible to contract out of fair dealing for the purpose of reporting current events as regards the inclusion of an extract from a broadcast in another broadcast.[112] Nor is it possible to contract out of the right enjoyed by the lawful user of a database to do anything which is necessary for the purpose of accessing and using the contents of the database.[113] Nor is it possible to contract out of the right to make a back-up copy of a computer program[114] or the rights to decompile or test a program.[115] The last of these prohibitions is particularly

---

[107] A detailed discussion is provided in *ibid.*, ch. 5. The Committee notes that under Anglo-Australian law a term cannot be incorporated after the acceptance of an offer. The Committee notes that this might well exclude terms found in many 'browsewrap agreements' where it is deemed that the act of browsing amounts to acceptance of terms.

[108] The right owner will be contracting in the course of business and the terms in question will not be 'individually negotiated'. Thus where the user is contracting as a consumer, that is, 'outside his trade, business, or profession', the Unfair Terms in Consumer Contracts Regulations 1999 (SI 1999 No 2083) will come into play. By virtue of reg. 5(1) a term is unenforceable if 'contrary to the requirement of good faith, it causes a significant imbalance in the parties' rights and obligations arising under the contract, to the detriment of the consumer'. For a comparative analysis see Guibault, in particular chs. 3 and 4.

[109] A creative judge could probably conclude that many of the existing terms purporting to exclude the operation of the exceptions do not have the desired effect. For example, a term of an agreement on a US site purporting to exclude an application of the fair use defence could well be deemed not to affect an application of the fair dealing provisions.

[110] See Chapters 6, 8, 9 and 10.

[111] UK law is somewhat unusual in having an express provision dealing with this issue: CDPA 1988, s. 28(1).

[112] Broadcasting Act 1996, s. 137.   [113] CDPA 1988, s. 296B.

[114] Computer Program Directive, Art. 9(1); CDPA 1988, s. 296A.   [115] *Ibid.*

significant, given the Australian Copyright Law Review Committee's finding that attempts to exclude decompilation provisions are particularly common.[116] Moreover, over and above the express prohibitions, it should be noted that the Copyright Tribunal has extensive powers to review the terms of licences granted by collecting societies. These powers would enable the tribunal to strike down contracting out provisions contained in licences issued by collective rights organisations.[117]

We are also of the opinion that a piecemeal approach to the question of whether it ought to be possible to exclude the operation of the permitted acts is preferable to the alternative – a blanket prohibition. It seems to us that a blanket prohibition on the exclusion of the permitted acts would be much too inflexible. For example, if an architect commissioned to design a new headquarters for a large commercial organisation were able to insist on a term that excluded that organisation's right to rebuild,[118] it is by no means clear that this term ought to be treated as null and void. Similarly, if two record companies were to reach agreement on reciprocal use, for payment, of digital sound samples taken from works within the other's repertoire, there would be nothing objectionable about a term that excluded reliance on the argument that the use was for the purpose of criticism or review or on the argument that the extract taken was merely an insubstantial part of the original work. As Lemley has put it, 'there must be some affirmative governmental policy benefit in order to justify overriding the public and private interests in enforcing contracts'.[119] Consequently, when setting out our preferred model for reform in the final chapter, we focus on what needs to be done to make the current, piecemeal, approach work effectively. In particular, we are concerned that a system needs to be put in place to ensure that new prohibitions on contracting out can be added quickly if evidence of inappropriate contracting out practices surfaces.

Copyright exceptions and technological measures of protection

Turning to the possibility that technological measures of protection may prevent a user from relying on the exceptions, we have already indicated that, as with contracting out, we are rather less concerned about this threat to users than are many other commentators. It is perhaps worth emphasising at the outset that we are concerned here only with the

---

[116] Copyright Law Review Committee, *Copyright and Contract*, para. 4.95.
[117] The role of the Copyright Tribunal is discussed in more detail in Chapter 4.
[118] Cf. CDPA 1988, s. 65.
[119] M. Lemley, 'Intellectual Property and Shrinkwrap Licenses' (1995) 68 *Southern California Law Review* 1239, 1274.

narrow question of the relationship between technological measures and the exceptions. Thus we are principally concerned with the possibility that a person who has lawful access to a work will not be able to reuse part of that work in reliance on one of the exceptions, either because a technological measure makes reproduction impossible or because it is unlawful for that person to decipher the encryption. We are not concerned here with the possibility that a user may not be able to afford to access a work in the first place. In contrast, some discussions of the problems posed by technological measures are underpinned by broader concerns about the possibility that a widespread move towards the online delivery of works on any form of fee-for-access basis may create a social divide between the 'digital haves' and the 'digital have-nots'. We do not deal with these broader concerns here because they are outside the scope of our project, but would note as an aside that we are wary of attempts to recast problems of poverty and social exclusion in terms of a 'digital divide'.[120]

When thinking about the threat to the exceptions posed by technological measures of protection, it is again worth emphasising that it may as yet be too early to know how often copyright owners will apply such measures to their works. Even if, as seems likely, use of such measures becomes widespread, when viewed solely in terms of the exceptions it seems inevitable that such measures will not be able to affect dramatically the availability of the exceptions as regards certain types of work. In particular, it seems highly unlikely that technological measures will be able to exclude the operation of the exceptions as regards works in textual form. Consider, for example, an online delivery service that provides users with copies of literary works or dramatic works in textual form. It is conceivable that a technological protection system might prevent users from saving a copy of a work to their hard drive or from cutting and pasting extracts from a work into another document. Leaving aside consumer resistance to such restrictions (which is likely to be considerable), such a system could not, however, prevent a user from copying extracts by hand and then typing these into another document. Moreover, if the system allowed a user to print out a version of a work, nothing could prevent the user from scanning the work electronically. Such methods of copying may be relatively slow and inconvenient, but they place the user in no worse a position than in cases where the work is only available in print form. There are, of course, other situations in which use for the purposes

---

[120] See R. Burrell, 'The Information Society: Chances and Challenges', in C. Heath and A. Kamperman Sanders (eds.), *Intellectual Property in the Digital Age: Challenges for Asia* (London: Kluwer, 2001), pp. 18–19, 21.

of criticism, review, news reporting and the like will require mechanical copying from the original. For example, we have emphasised the importance of users being allowed to reproduce photographic evidence in certain circumstances. Nevertheless, we believe that it is important to bear in mind that technological measures of protection may affect users differently according to the type of work in question.

Our approach to the relationship between the exceptions and technological measures of protection has also been coloured by the fact that we believe that Europe has adopted the right *approach* to this issue, although (as we explain below) it may be necessary to expand the coverage of the current provisions. In order to justify this conclusion it is necessary to pause and consider the ways in which the legislature might seek to ensure that users can continue to rely on the exceptions.

The most extreme response to concerns about the impact of technological measures on users would be to make the encryption of works illegal. However, as Sellars has noted, this would be 'anathema to copyright holders and technology manufacturers alike'.[121] Such a step could seriously shake the confidence of the copyright industries and, as far as we are aware, has not been seriously proposed.

A superficially attractive alternative might be to leave the use of technological protection measures entirely unregulated. Under such a system owners would be free to protect their works, but users would be free to decipher works themselves and to buy programs and devices designed to get round technological measures of protection. This approach would do nothing, however, to protect the interests of users per se. Rather, as Landes and Posner have argued, it would leave us with an arms race between copyright owners and the manufactures of circumvention devices, the position of users fluctuating according to which side is ahead.[122]

A third option is to permit the sale of circumvention devices, but to punish heavily those who use such devices to infringe copyright. It is important to emphasise, however, that while this approach is likely to be more attractive to copyright owners than the second option, it would still create exactly the same 'arms race' problem.[123]

A fourth option is to prohibit the manufacture and sale of circumvention devices, but to allow individual users to decipher works in order

---

[121] C. Sellars, 'Digital Rights Management Systems: Recent European Issues' [2003] EntLR 5, 8.

[122] W. Landes and R. Posner, *The Economic Structure of Intellectual Property Law* (Cambridge, Mass.: Harvard University Press, 2003), p. 44.

[123] It is therefore somewhat surprising to find Landes and Posner advocating this as even a partial solution to the problems thrown up by technological measures: *ibid.*, p. 45.

to take advantage of an exception. The problem with this approach is that it restricts the availability of the exceptions to a small subset of highly technologically literate users, that is, to those users who are personally able to decipher a technological protection system.[124] Users would therefore be left even worse off than under the second and third options.

If all of the options canvassed above are problematic, probably the best way forward is to adopt a 'fair use by design' approach.[125] This approach rests on encouraging copyright owners to build space for users into their copyright protection strategy. For example, owners might be persuaded to devise technological protection systems that are sophisticated enough to detect when the use is for an exempted purpose (although such systems are probably some way off) or to make non-encoded versions of works available to institutional users.[126] Should copyright owners fail to take appropriate steps, a mechanism can be put in place to force owners to make non-encrypted versions of works available. A fair use by design approach has a number of advantages over the alternatives. First, it places the interests of users centre stage, providing a positive mechanism to ensure that users can take advantage of the exceptions. In contrast, it was seen that, with the exception of an outright prohibition on the use of technological measures, the alternatives considered above merely provide users with lawful opportunities *to attempt* to decipher a work. Second, unlike some of the alternatives considered above, a fair use by design approach does not conflict with international obligations relating to the protection of technological protection measures contained in the 1996

---

[124] Precisely this concern has been raised about the copy control provisions of the Digital Millennium Copyright Act. See, e.g., D. Nimmer, 'How Much Solicitude for Fair Use is there in the Anti-Circumvention Provision of the Digital Millennium Copyright Act?', in N. Elkin-Koren and N. Netanel (eds.), *The Commodification of Information* (The Hague: Kluwer Law International, 2002), p. 220: 'the only users whose interests are truly safeguarded are those few who personally possess sufficient expertise to counteract whatever technological measures are placed in their path'; J. Therien, 'Exorcising the Specter of a Pay-per-Use Society: Toward Preserving Fair Use and the Public Domain in the Digital Age' (2001) 16 *Berkeley Technology Law Journal* 979, 1023: 'the fail-safe mechanism protects only the constitutional rights of users capable of circumventing TPSs on their own. This group is already an extremely small one. As TPSs become more advanced, even fewer people will possess the programming skills required to crack TPSs in order to exercise their constitutional use rights'; R. Van Den Elzen, 'Decrypting the DMCA: Fair Use as a Defense to the Distribution of DeCSS' (2002) 77 *Notre Dame Law Review* 673, 689: 'None of the exceptions allow an ordinary citizen, without the knowledge to develop his or her own circumvention technology, to make fair use, such as excerpting, of an encrypted DVD'.
[125] Coined by Dusollier: S. Dusollier, 'Exceptions and Technological Measures in the European Copyright Directive of 2001 – an Empty Promise' (2003) 34 IIC 62, 70.
[126] *Ibid.*

WIPO Treaties.[127] The political obstacles to the implementation of a fair use by design approach are therefore less formidable. Third, by setting up a tripartite regulatory encounter between owners, users and government in cases where owners have failed to take voluntary steps, the fair use by design approach helps to ensure that the needs of users are communicated directly to owners. This should broaden the perspective of owners (who tend inevitably to see the use of technological measures solely in terms of the need to prevent piracy) and may help ensure that at least some owners look at the problems created for users in good faith.[128]

It is significant, therefore, that it is the fair use by design approach that underpins the provisions of the Information Society Directive relating to technological measures of protection, provisions that have now been transposed into UK law through section 296ZE of the 1988 Act. This section applies where a technological protection system is preventing a user from carrying out one or more of the permitted acts listed in Schedule 5A of the Act.[129] In such a case a user or a representative of a class of users can issue a notice of complaint to the Secretary of State.[130] On receipt of a notice of complaint, the Secretary of State has extensive powers to investigate the complaint (in particular, to establish whether the owner has taken any voluntary measures to ensure exceptions remain available) and to compel owners and exclusive licensees to make available to a complainant the means of carrying out a permitted act.[131]

In substance we believe that systems of the type created by section 296ZE are the best means of dealing with the relationship between technological measures of protection and the exceptions. There are, however, two respects in which the current system may prove to be seriously flawed. First, it is important to emphasise that the Secretary of State's powers do not extend to material made available to the public online subject to a contractual agreement. Thus in relation to the distribution of works over the Internet, an area in which the application of technological measures is causing most concern, the Secretary of State's powers are extremely limited. Second, it is important to appreciate that the Secretary of State's powers only apply to some of the permitted acts, namely, those listed in the new Schedule 5A of the Act. Excluded from this schedule are the provisions to which we have given most attention in this chapter, that

---

[127] See WIPO Copyright Treaty 1996, Art. 11; WIPO Performances and Phonograms Treaty, Art. 18.
[128] As we noted in the Introduction to this work, we believe that it is important not to demonise copyright owners and their representatives or to assume that all owners will necessarily be opposed to a liberalisation of the exceptions even after the problems with the current regime are explained to them.
[129] Set out in Appendix 2, and see below.
[130] CDPA 1988, s. 296ZE(2).   [131] *Ibid.*, s. 296ZE(3).

is, fair dealing for the purposes of criticism and review and fair dealing for the purpose of news reporting. Consequently, the new powers given to the Secretary of State will do nothing to protect users seeking to rely on the most important of the provisions we examined in this chapter. (In contrast, as regards research and private study and the copying of works by institutional users, that is, the provisions we examine in Chapters 4 and 5, the new powers are much more satisfactory). The exclusion of much online material from the scope of the new powers and the restriction of these powers to certain of the permitted acts both flow from the Directive. In the final chapter we argue that both of these restrictions may well need to be removed if users are to be provided with a more satisfactory system of protection. However, this should not blind us to the fact that the overall approach adopted by the Directive remains the most sensible.

In contrast to some of the more alarmist pronouncements that have been made about the impact of contracting out and technological measures of protection on users, we have attempted to provide a realistic assessment both of the threat posed to users and of how user interests might best be safeguarded. In particular, we have suggested that it may be premature to place too much importance on these issues, but have argued that, in any event, the current legislative framework is based around the correct principles. None of this should be taken to indicate, however, that we are entirely unconcerned about the dangers posed by a 'digital lock-up'. Rather, we would emphasise that contracting out and the application of technological measures may cause yet further difficulties for users against a legislative background that does not do nearly enough to protect their interests. Moreover, although we have argued that the legislative framework dealing with contracting out and technological measures of protection is broadly appropriate, it has been seen that in both cases some reform will probably be required if the system is to function effectively – in the case of contracting out to ensure that new prohibitions can be added quickly, and in the case of technological measures to remove the exemption of material delivered online and to extend the Secretary of State's powers to include all of the permitted acts.

Copyright and the Internet: the role of online service providers

A third problem that users may face that is entirely confined to the online environment is that fear of liability may cause online service providers (OSPs) to take down material about which they receive a complaint, even though the user has a good defence to an action for infringement of copyright.

Implementation of the Information Society Directive has led to the introduction of a new exception which, *inter alia*, privileges the making of temporary copies so as to enable the transmission of works over a network between third parties.[132] Although this provision is important for OSP liability generally, it does not address the problem with which we are concerned here. More important for present purposes, therefore, are the provisions of the E-Commerce Directive, implemented into UK law by the Electronic Commerce Regulations 2002.[133] The E-Commerce Directive deals with OSP liability on a 'horizontal' basis, that is, it regulates service provider liability generally.[134] The Directive establishes three areas in which OSP liability is limited, namely, where the OSP acts as a 'mere conduit' for an unlawful transmission,[135] where the OSP has 'cached' unlawful material[136] and where the OSP has 'hosted' unlawful material.[137] In the copyright context it is the 'hosting' privilege that is likely to prove most important,[138] since it is this exception that covers the placing of material on to a site operated or controlled by an OSP. Problems may arise because the hosting exception only applies in the absence of knowledge on the part of the OSP.

Following the lead set by the United States in its 1998 Digital Millennium Copyright Act,[139] under the E-Commerce Directive the OSP 'must err in favour of removal of the material complained of'.[140] This is because the hosting exception no longer applies once the OSP becomes aware of 'facts or circumstances from which it would have been

---

[132] See CDPA 1988, s. 28A.   [133] (SI 2002 No 2013).
[134] 'Online service provider' is defined extremely broadly: E-Commerce Directive, Art. 2, recital 17; E-Commerce Regulations, reg. 2.
[135] E-Commerce Directive, Art. 12; E-Commerce Regulations, reg. 17. An OSP will be a 'mere conduit' for information where it does not initiate the transmission, does not select the receiver of the transmission and does not select or modify the information contained in the transmission. This would protect an OSP from liability in relation to its role in transmitting e-mails.
[136] E-Commerce Directive, Art. 13; E-Commerce Regulations, reg. 18. 'Caching' refers to the process of copying and temporarily storing information so as to facilitate access to it.
[137] E-Commerce Directive, Art. 14; E-Commerce Regulations, reg. 19. The 'hosting' exception is discussed in more detail, below.
[138] See V. McEvedy, 'The DMCA and the E-Commerce Directive' [2002] EIPR 65, 68–9, where the OSP has acted as a mere conduit it is unlikely to be approached by the owner given the transitory nature of the communications covered by this provision; in relation to caching the owner is likely to be more concerned to act against the source of the material.
[139] For a critical discussion of this aspect of the Digital Millennium Copyright Act see A. Yen, 'Internet Service Provider Liability for Subscriber Copyright Infringement, Enterprise Liability, and the First Amendment' (2000) 88 *Georgetown Law Journal* 1833.
[140] McEvedy, 'The DMCA', 65.

apparent ... that the activity or information was unlawful'.[141] The OSP is also placed under an express obligation to act expeditiously to remove information or disable access to it on obtaining the requisite awareness,[142] and the Directive and the implementing Regulations give little additional guidance as to when an OSP should refuse to take down or should restore material.[143] Given this legislative regime and given that (unlike traditional publishers) OSPs will often have little stake or interest in the content of the material they host, an OSP that receives a complaint about copyright infringement is likely to act to remove or block access to the material in question. Thus even a user with a very strong case that her actions fall within one or more of the permitted acts may well find that the OSP has chosen to remove or block access to her material.[144]

Moral rights

A fourth external constraint that users may face, and one which is not confined to the digital environment, is that any reuse of a portion of a work might infringe the author's moral rights, in particular the right of integrity. None of the permitted acts examined in this chapter provide a defence to an action for derogatory treatment. Thus there is at least a theoretical possibility that the use of an extract from a work for the purpose of criticism or review or the incidental inclusion of a portion of a work, and so on, might amount to a derogatory treatment.

In order to maintain an action for derogatory treatment it will be necessary for the author to demonstrate that there has been a 'treatment' of the work, that the treatment is derogatory and that the treatment has been communicated to the public.[145] In the majority of cases with which we are concerned the claimant will probably be able to establish that there has been a treatment of the work. 'Treatment' is defined as 'any addition to, deletion from or alteration to or adaptation of the work'.[146] While the position is not entirely clear, it is probably correct to say that any use of an

---

[141] E-Commerce Regulations, reg. 19(a)(i); E-Commerce Directive, Art. 14(1)(a).
[142] E-Commerce Regulations, reg. 19(a)(ii); E-Commerce Directive, Art. 14(1)(b).
[143] See McEvedy, 'The DMCA', 70; E. Sullivan, 'Lost in Cyberspace: A Closer Look at ISP Liability' [2001] EntLR 192, 192.
[144] See also Yen, 'Internet Service Provider Liability'. It is sometimes said that an OSP that wishes to take down material would have to tread carefully because blocking access to material might amount to a breach of contract with the user. However, this would only apply where there is a contractual relationship between the OSP and the user. Even if there is a contractual relationship the OSP could seek to exclude liability under the terms of the contract, and OSPs can safely assume that most users will not have the resources to bring an action against them.
[145] CDPA 1988, s. 80.   [146] *Ibid.*, s. 80(2)(a).

extract from a work will amount to a deletion of the remainder.[147] There will also normally be little difficulty in establishing that the treatment has been communicated to the public.[148] Much will therefore depend on whether the treatment is to be regarded as derogatory. The Act provides that a treatment is to be regarded as derogatory if 'it amounts to a distortion or mutilation of the work or is otherwise prejudicial to the honour or reputation of the author'.[149]

In the majority of cases a claimant is probably going to struggle to demonstrate that the reuse of an extract of a work amounts to a distortion or mutilation or is otherwise prejudicial to her honour or reputation, particularly as the courts seem to be moving towards an objective, defamation-style, test for determining when a treatment is derogatory.[150] Real problems may arise, however, where the defendant's work holds the claimant's work up to ridicule. It is not inconceivable, for example, that a highly critical review could be deemed to be prejudicial to an author's honour or reputation. Problems are also likely to arise in the case of parodies and similar works. Even if the creators of such works can bring themselves within the criticism and review exception they may still find themselves liable for derogatory treatment. Admittedly, we cannot be certain of these conclusions. A court could well conclude, for example, that provided any quotations are accurate there can be no infringement of the right of integrity since it will not be 'the treatment' which is prejudicial to the author's honour or reputation. But the uncertainty that surrounds the current position may well be sufficient to deter a defendant who receives threats of legal action from proceeding. More generally, it is a cause for concern that it remains far from clear how moral rights and the exceptions intersect in the United Kingdom.

Conclusion

In this chapter it has been seen that the United Kingdom's system of statutory permitted acts is extremely restrictive and, as such, creates a range of situations in which copyright can come into conflict with freedom of expression. Over and above problems with the permitted acts themselves, it has been seen that there are a range of external constraints

---

[147] The alternative interpretation, that in order for there to be a deletion there has to be some erasure of material from within the portion extracted, would render 'deletion' indistinguishable from 'alteration'.
[148] See CDPA 1988, ss. 80(3)–(6).   [149] *Ibid.*, s. 80(2)(b).
[150] See *Tidy* v. *Natural History Museum* (1998) 39 IPR 501; *Pasterfield* v. *Denham* [1999] FSR 168. Cf. Bently and Sherman, p. 249, arguing that the notion of 'honour' (which is a concept alien to UK law) suggests that there should be a subjective element to the test.

that might prevent a user from relying on an exception. Although we have placed less emphasis on some of these external constraints than have other recent commentators, taken together with the other problems we have identified in this chapter, it can be seen that the UK provisions relating to activities such as criticism, review and news reporting are in urgent need of reform.

3 The public interest defence

In the last chapter it was seen that the statutory provisions relating to activities such as criticism, review and news reporting are inadequate to safeguard freedom of expression or freedom of information. It is therefore important to consider whether these provisions might be supplemented by a 'common law' public interest defence, that is, a defence sitting outwith the statutory regime that would justify the publication of copyright material in certain circumstances. This question is complicated by the fact that two recent Court of Appeal cases reached different conclusions as to whether a public interest defence to actions for infringement of copyright exists at all in the United Kingdom, and even the case that accepted that such a defence does exist indicated that its scope is more limited than earlier authorities had seemed to suggest.

This chapter begins by considering the scope of this defence as it had apparently been established prior to the recent decisions of the Court of Appeal. Our aim in this section is to demonstrate that whilst these earlier authorities indicated (quite rightly) that the public interest defence is relatively limited in scope, in its early form the public interest defence added a degree of flexibility to the statutory scheme. In particular, in its early form the public interest defence provided an important additional safeguard in cases where the user was seeking to place evidence contained in an unpublished work into the public domain. As such, the defence provided some degree of additional protection for freedom of expression.

We then turn to consider the recent Court of Appeal decisions. We demonstrate that even if a public interest defence to actions for infringement of copyright does still exist in the United Kingdom, it now appears that it is only available in exceptional circumstances, such that it is unlikely to provide users with much additional protection.

In the third part of the chapter we turn to consider an argument that has frequently been put forward by opponents of a public interest defence, namely that the recognition of such a defence is unnecessary because a court could achieve the same result by relying on equitable principles and by being creative when awarding a remedy. We argue that considerable uncertainty surrounds these other mechanisms and that many of the objections that have been raised to the recognition of a public interest defence would also apply to any reliance on these devices.

In the final part of the chapter we turn to consider the other objections put forward by opponents of the public interest defence and demonstrate that none of these objections stands up to close scrutiny. Consequently we call for a public interest defence to be reinstated as part of the package of reform measures that we outline in the final chapter. However, for practical reasons we would like to see the judiciary reinstate a broad form of the public interest defence in advance of any statutory reform.

The public interest defence in its early form

Preliminary observations

Prior to the recent Court of Appeal decisions considered below, it had been indicated in a number of cases that there is a public interest defence to an action for infringement of copyright that sits alongside the statutory permitted acts.[1] It was on the strength of some of these earlier authorities that Parliament chose to include in the 1988 Act a provision that was designed to ensure that the courts would remain free to develop a public interest defence. Unfortunately, however, Parliament did so without clearly and unambiguously providing for such a defence.[2] We turn to consider the scope of the defence in detail shortly, but in outline the early cases that recognised the existence of a public interest defence indicated that its scope is roughly coterminous with the public interest defence in the law of confidence. Such a defence would allow for the reproduction of a substantial part of a work in so far as the portion of the work

---

[1] See *Beloff* v. *Pressdram* [1973] 1 All ER 241; *Commonwealth of Australia* v. *Fairfax* (1981) 147 CLR 39; *Queen* v. *James Lorimer & Co* (1984) 77 CPR 2d 262; *Lion Laboratories* v. *Evans* [1985] QB 526; *PCR* v. *Dow Jones Telerate* [1998] FSR 170; *Service Corporation* v. *Channel 4* [1999] EMLR 83; *Hyde Park* v. *Yelland* [1999] RPC 655 (per Jacob J at first instance); *Mars* v. *Teknowledge* [2000] FSR 138. Reference might also be made to the ambiguous comments of Lord Denning in *Fraser* v. *Evans* [1969] 1 QB 349, 362-3, and to the decision of Warner J in *Beggars Banquet* v. *Carlton* [1993] EMLR 349, 372, the cases 'evince a developing jurisdiction'.

[2] See CDPA 1988, s. 171(3): 'Nothing in this Part affects any rule of law preventing or restricting the enforcement of copyright on the grounds of public interest or otherwise.' Although a casual reading of this section might suggest that this amounts to express statutory recognition of a public interest defence, a technical construction focuses on the fact that this section only states that any existing defence is preserved. For a detailed account of the background to this provision see Chapter 8 and R. Burrell, 'Defending the Public Interest' [2000] EIPR 394.

reproduced contains information that in 'the public interest' should be made known.

When considering why a public interest defence is required, it is important to bear in mind both the limitations of the statutory provisions considered in the last chapter and the problems that copyright law can pose for freedom of expression explored in Chapter 1. In particular, it is important to appreciate that a wide range of material that is now 'clothed in copyright' – nearly all written and visual material will be protected by copyright. As was seen in Chapter 1, the concern is that the subsistence of copyright in things like security videos and internal memorandums might be used to prevent the public having access to important sources of information. Thus the danger is that copyright might be used to suppress evidence that a nuclear reactor is faulty, or that a drug has unacknowledged side effects or that a public official is guilty of serious wrongdoing. It was seen in the last chapter that no defence of fair dealing is likely to succeed in such a case, *inter alia*, because the work in question will invariably be unpublished. Nor is it adequate to say that the public should be content with a description of the contents of the work in question, since this would not always be a guarantee against a claim for infringement of copyright, it would deprive the public of an opportunity to see the evidence for themselves, and it would create a disparity between the publisher of the information and the copyright owner (who could selectively release copies of documents and other material to rebut accusations levelled against it). Moreover, even if it can be anticipated that a judge is likely to prove sympathetic to a defendant in a particular case, it would be impossible to reassure a client that she would be on safe ground if she chooses to reproduce a substantial part of a work, and this uncertainty may be sufficient to deter a potential defendant from proceeding.

Guidance as to when a public interest defence ought to be available, and how such a defence can be kept within reasonable bounds, can be gained from breach of confidence cases (where such a defence is now firmly established) as well as from the copyright cases that have recognised such a defence. In the remainder of this section we explore in detail how a broad form of the public interest defence might be expected to operate, indicating where the cases are silent how we believe the defence ought to be developed. The cases indicate that a public interest defence would only be available in relation to certain types of information, that it would often only justify disclosure of information to persons in a position of authority and not to the world at large, and that various other safeguards could be expected to evolve that would prevent the defence from being abused in copyright cases.

Type of information

When considering the type of information to which the defence might apply (or to be more precise the type of information that would have to be disclosed in the portion of the work reproduced) it is important to note that the courts have differentiated between matters that affect the public interest and matters which are merely 'interesting to the public'. In this way a distinction is drawn between matters which affect the welfare of the public and matters which the public is likely to find entertaining or amusing. It has been indicated that matters which genuinely affect the public interest include public health and public safety,[3] public morals,[4] the corruption of public officials,[5] and the competence of regulatory agencies.[6] A good illustration of the type of information to which the defence might apply is provided by *Lion Laboratories* v. *Evans*,[7] the most authoritative decision to recognise a public interest defence in the law of copyright. In that case it was held that the defendant was justified in publishing extracts from internal documents that demonstrated that the plaintiff's breathalyser was faulty, since failure to do so might have resulted in the wrongful conviction of a class of persons, in this case motorists.

It is submitted that as well as justifying publication in cases where the risk or threat is ongoing, there is also good reason to suggest that the public interest defence should apply to past accidents, errors, injustices or 'near misses'. This is not so as to encourage muck-raking, but rather because there is an increasing recognition that it is only by throwing light on past errors that mistakes can be avoided in the future. It is also better if there is public acknowledgement of past errors, otherwise institutional pressures may lead to the problem being overlooked or ignored.[8] On a rather different note we would also argue that if a public interest defence is to be available to expose corruption or wrongdoing, it ought also to be available as regards evidence that helps rebut any such charge that has been made in the public forum. This would catch cases such as *Hyde Park* v. *Yelland* (which has been mentioned in previous chapters and

---

[3] *Beloff* v. *Pressdram*, 260.
[4] *Service Corporation* v. *Channel 4* (treatment of the deceased in funeral homes).
[5] *Cork* v. *McVicar* (*The Times*, 31 Oct. 1984) (police corruption).
[6] *Jockey Club* v. *Buffham* [2003] QB 426 (inability to prevent corruption in horseracing).
[7] [1985] QB 526.
[8] Note, for example, the recent debates that have taken place in medical circles. See P. Barach and S. Small, 'Reporting and Preventing Medical Mishaps: Lessons from Non-Medical Near Miss Reporting Systems' (2000) 320 *British Medical Journal* 759; S. Mayor, 'English NHS to Set Up New Reporting System for Errors' (2000) 320 *British Medical Journal* 1689. More generally, see N. Pidgeon, 'Safety Culture and Risk Management in Organizations' (1991) 22 *Journal of Cross-Cultural Psychology* 129, 137, comparing the construction industry unfavourably with the aviation industry.

which is discussed in detail below), where the disclosure was intended to help rebut serious allegations about the behaviour of the security services.

A second class of case where a public interest defence should be available is where the information concerned is directly relevant to the political process. A good example of such a case is provided by *London Regional Transport* v. *The Mayor of London*,[9] a recent breach of confidence case. That case concerned a dispute over a report prepared by Deloitte and Touche which cast doubt on whether the government's preferred public–private partnership model of funding for the London Underground provided the best value for money. The question in the case was whether the Mayor of London was entitled to publish a redacted form of this report (with commercially sensitive information removed). It was held by the court at first instance and by a unanimous Court of Appeal that publication in this case was clearly in the public interest since the document related to a hotly contested political issue. This could only be resolved through the democratic process and democratic processes can only be effective if they are properly informed. This case is particularly significant for present purposes because if the facts had been slightly different London Regional Transport might have been able to claim copyright in the report. Given that it was the unanimous belief of the judges in *London Regional Transport* that the report should be placed in the public domain, it would be highly regrettable if a public interest defence were not also extended to a copyright action in similar circumstances. The *London Regional Transport* case is also significant in that it shows that the public interest defence in the law of confidence retains some degree of flexibility – Aldous LJ stated that the decision marked 'a modest extension of the law'.[10]

The third type of case in which a public interest defence should be available is where a public figure has deliberately set out to mislead the public. As the Press Complaints Commission Code of Practice recognises, in such circumstances the 'public interest includes . . . preventing the public from being misled by some statement or action of an individual or organisation'.[11] The application of this principle can again be illustrated by a recent breach of confidence case, *Campbell* v. *MGN*.[12] The claimant in this case, fashion model Naomi Campbell, accepted that the *Mirror* newspaper was justified in revealing the fact that she was a drug addict in light of the fact that she had gone out of her way to insist that,

---

[9] [2003] EMLR 88. [10] *Ibid.*, 110.
[11] Available at www.pcc.org.uk/cop/cop.asp. It has been indicated that courts can gain assistance from the Code: *A* v. *B Plc* [2003] QB 195, 209 (per Lord Woolf CJ).
[12] [2004] EMLR 247.

unlike many other models, she did not take drugs, stimulants or tranquillisers, and both the Court of Appeal and the House of Lords gave a strong indication that this concession had been made correctly.[13]

In contrast to the three classes of case outlined above, it has been stated that information which gratifies prurient curiosity or which is solely intended to cast public figures in a poor light is likely to be categorised as being merely interesting to the public. Such information will not, therefore, fall within the scope of the defence. It is perhaps worth reiterating, therefore, that the third category of case outlined above only applies where a public figure has set out to mislead the public. This point was emphasised in *Campbell*, the Court of Appeal and the House of Lords both emphasising that there is no general right under UK law to place evidence in the public domain in order to prove that a public figure has feet of clay.[14] The claimant in that case would have been entitled to have had information that she was a drug addict remain confidential had she not gone on record as asserting that she did not take drugs. Moreover, even in a case where there is a right to set the record straight the press may still

---

[13] See also *Campbell v. Frisbee* [2003] EMLR 76; *Theakston v. MGN* [2002] EMLR 398; *Woodward v. Hutchins* [1977] 1 WLR 760. The last of these cases should probably not now be applied, but it does illustrate the general point, as does the New Zealand case *Tucker v. News Media Ownership* [1986] 2 NZLR 716. For hostile commentary see R. Wacks, 'Pop Goes Privacy' (1978) 41 *Modern Law Review* 67.

[14] See respectively [2003] QB 633, 658; [2004] EMLR 247, 258, 290. Cf. *A v. B*. In that case it was held that a football player was not entitled to prevent details of an extramarital affair being published. This was not, however, because the revelations were treated as being in the public interest, but rather because the other party to the affair was not obliged to keep the existence of the affair secret. More generally, it needs to be appreciated that *A v. B* takes place against a background of the courts seeking to expand the sphere of information that can be protected through a confidence action so as to give effect to Article 8 ECHR (see *A v. B*, 202). This has led to the creation of a 'grey area' of information, that is, information that is entitled to some degree of legal protection, but which will have to give way to freedom of expression in a much broader range of circumstances than would be covered by the public interest defence. This interpretation of *A v. B* receives strong support from the Court of Appeal's decision in *Campbell* (at 658). Cases in this grey area of limited legal protection have little relevance in the copyright field. It might also be noted that when outlining this grey area in *A v. B* Lord Woolf drew on the Australian High Court case *Australian Broadcasting Corporation v. Lenah Game Meats* (2001) 185 ALR 1 and, in particular, on the judgment of Gleeson CJ. However, *Lenah Meats* deals only tangentially with the question of what information can be subject to an obligation of confidence, in large part because the respondents conceded that the information was not confidential, and yet there is a good argument to be made that the information in *Lenah Meats* was confidential in the traditional sense: D. Stewart, 'Protecting Privacy, Property and Possums' (2002) 30 *Federal Law Review* 177, 193–5; G. Taylor and D. Wright, 'Privacy, Injunctions and Possums: An Analysis of the High Court's Decision in *Australian Broadcasting Corporation v. Lenah Game Meats*' (2002) 26 *Melbourne University Law Review* 707, 716–18. It is therefore encouraging that some members of the House of Lords in *Campbell* expressed caution about placing reliance on *Lenah Meats*.

only go so far, hence the eventual finding in *Campbell* that the newspaper was not entitled to publish details of the claimant's treatment for her addiction.[15] It has also been recognised that general economic considerations will not justify an application of the public interest defence. For example, in *PCR* v. *Dow Jones Telerate* it was held that the public interest in the transparency of a market could not justify overriding copyright.[16] In this way courts have recognised that weighing general economic factors involves a form of complex economic assessment they may not be competent to make.[17]

The person to whom the disclosure is made

In addition to limiting the types of information to which the defence can apply, the courts have also placed limits on the person to whom the disclosure can be made. In particular, where the material in question provides evidence of a crime or other wrongdoing it has been said that it will normally only be appropriate to disclose the information to the police or to some other investigatory authority.[18] There are, however, circumstances in which general disclosure will be justified. In particular, the cases indicate that this will be the case where the information relates to the actions or workings of a public authority or to the behaviour of a public official.[19] Moreover, even if disclosure of information to the public is justified, this does not mean that a defendant no longer has to pay any regard to the confidential nature of the information – there may still be specific facts which must not be disclosed. Thus it has been indicated that the public interest defence could not justify disclosing the

---

[15] [2004] EMLR 247.
[16] [1998] FSR 170, 188. See also *Ernest Turner* v. *PRS* [1943] Ch 167, where it was held that the court could not take into account worker productivity as an aspect of the public interest when assessing whether a performance had taken place in public.
[17] Even amongst those who believe that cases should be decided strictly according to a principle of allocative efficiency, there are many who believe that judges will not usually be in a position to identify the most efficient outcome. See, e.g., F. Easterbrook, 'The Limits of Antitrust' (1984) 63 *Texas Law Review* 1. See also M. Jacobs, 'An Essay on the Normative Foundations of Antitrust Economics' (1995) 74 *North Carolina Law Review* 219, in particular at 222–3, 257, for a discussion of differing views of judicial competence amongst economic theorists of law.
[18] *Initial Services* v. *Putterill* [1968] 1 QB 396, 405–6. See also *Francome* v. *Mirror Group Newspapers* [1984] 1 WLR 892, preventing disclosure of conversations which were alleged to reveal that the plaintiff had breached jockey club regulations and possibly committed criminal offences because, on the facts, disclosure to the jockey club and/or the police would have sufficed; *Re A Company's Application* [1989] Ch 477, 481, holding that an ex-employee was justified in disclosing confidential documents to a financial regulatory authority and to the Inland Revenue in circumstances where if 'there were any question or threat of general disclosure by the defendant . . . there could be no answer to the claim for an injunction'.
[19] *Cork* v. *McVicar*; *Lion Laboratories* v. *Evans*; *Jockey Club* v. *Buffham*.

identity of informants even in a case where public disclosure was otherwise justified,[20] and there is good reason to believe that the publication of commercially sensitive information would not be justified where this is not relevant to the debate surrounding a politically sensitive issue.[21] The public interest defence would not, therefore, operate in the all-or-nothing way that some opponents seem to imply.

In the rare case where disclosure to the public is justified, a public interest defence to an action for infringement of copyright may well be necessary in order to put previously unpublished evidence into the public domain – the public will only be able to hold a public body to account and the democratic process can only work effectively if the public can see the evidence for themselves.

In the more common case where it is only disclosure to an official body that will be warranted, the person providing the evidence may have the benefit of an express statutory exception in the event that providing the evidence involves reproducing copyright material. However, this may not always be the case, as is demonstrated by *Woolgar v. Chief Constable of the Sussex Police*.[22] Although this was a breach of confidence case, it shows that interests other than the public's right to information can also be at stake in public interest cases and it helps illustrate how far copyright can now extend.[23] In *Woolgar* it was held that the police were justified in sending a copy of a taped interview with a suspect, a registered nurse, to the UK Central Council for Nursing (UKCC). It is important to appreciate that the plaintiff in this case might also have brought an action for copyright infringement because, as noted in the last chapter, the 1988 Act expressly recognises that copyright may subsist in a speaker's words when they are recorded by another person, irrespective of whether the speaker has consented to this 'fixation'. It seems that if (as is likely) the plaintiff's statement attracted copyright, the police would not have been able to rely on any of the express statutory exceptions, since their making a copy of the statement to send to the Central Council for Nursing was not *specifically authorised* by statute,[24] nor would they have fallen within the exception which allows for the use of notes or recordings of spoken words since the recording was not made for one of the relevant purposes.[25] The police might have been able to argue that their actions fell within the exception that allows for copying for the purposes of judicial proceedings, but it is doubtful whether 'judicial proceedings' would

---

[20] *Jockey Club* v. *Buffham*, 477.
[21] Cf. *London Regional Transport* v. *The Mayor of London* [2003] EMLR 88.
[22] [2000] 1 WLR 25.
[23] See also *Francome* v. *Mirror Group Newspapers*: under the 1988 Act the conversation recorded on the tape might well have attracted copyright protection.
[24] Cf. CDPA 1988, s. 50(1). [25] Cf. CDPA 1988, s. 58, and see Chapter 2.

extend to include proceedings before the UKCC.[26] Thus if infringement of copyright had been pleaded the police might well have been forced to rely on a public interest defence. Moreover, even if *Woolgar* could have been brought within the judicial proceedings defence, this defence would clearly not cover the making of copies of works intended for a range of other public bodies, including the police and government departments.[27] In such cases description of the contents of the original documents would clearly not be sufficient: public bodies generally have to see the evidence for themselves. This demonstrates that a public interest defence can be justified in part by reference to the public interest in the administration of justice and efficient administration more generally, as well as by reference to the public's right to information.

Other factors

If the courts have taken care to ensure that the public interest defence in the law of confidence is limited both as regards the types of information to which it extends and the person to whom disclosure can be made, other cases show that the courts would not allow the indefinite reproduction of copyright material, so that once the public is sufficiently aware of the information contained in the work, no further copying from the work would be justified. Thus in *Beggars Banquet* v. *Carlton*, Walton J concluded that the public interest could not justify indefinite copying from the film in question, although he allowed the defendants to rebroadcast their programme in this case as the programme was 'a particularly vivid and telling means of conveying [an] important message' and on the evidence there were 'still many people . . . who have not seen the programme'.[28]

There is also good reason to suppose that the courts would be circumspect when dealing with the relationship between a proposed application of the public interest defence and the express statutory exceptions. On the one hand, if the public interest defence is to serve any useful function then it clearly has to apply in circumstances where no statutory exception would be available. At times this may mean that a public interest defence should succeed in circumstances which are closely analogous to circumstances in which a statutory exception is available, but where the

---

[26] Cf. *Re a Solicitor* (5 Nov. 1996) (Court of Appeal) (*Lexis* Transcript): plaintiff argued that copying of documents placed before Solicitor's Disciplinary Tribunal infringed his copyright because proceedings before the Tribunal did not amount to 'judicial proceedings'. The copyright argument failed because, on the facts, the plaintiff had consented to the documents being placed before the Tribunal.

[27] Cf. CDPA 1988, s. 48, material must have been communicated to the Crown 'by or with the licence of the copyright owner'. Cf. also *Re A Company's Application*.

[28] [1993] EMLR 349, 372.

statutory exception is not available due to some limiting factor as, for example, where an unpublished work is used to criticise something other than a work or a performance of a work.[29] On the other hand, a court is clearly not going to allow the public interest defence to be used routinely in such a way as to undermine a compromise hammered out by the legislature. Thus if it has been specifically decided that no defence should be available in a particular category of case, no court would allow a public interest defence to succeed so as to reverse this decision.[30]

It may also be worth saying something expressly about a recent objection raised by Thomas to the recognition of a public interest defence to copyright infringement, namely that it 'would lead to arguably unfair results, especially in circumstances where the copyright-holder is innocent of any wrongdoing. For example, an investigative journalist who prepares a report demonstrating serious negligence on the part of a major pharmaceutical company may be left without redress should a fellow journalist obtain the report and publish it in a competing newspaper.'[31] The concern, therefore, is that the recognition of a public interest defence would leave those who take the time and trouble to discover important information vulnerable to having their efforts misappropriated. Thomas supports this argument by reference to the *Thatcher Diaries* case,[32] which concerned an attempt by a newspaper that had paid for exclusive serialisation rights to prevent another newspaper from publishing unauthorised extracts. Thomas asserts that the plaintiff's application for an interlocutory injunction was refused 'on the ground that the publication of the extracts by the third party was, in part, in the public interest . . .'[33]

On closer analysis, however, the above point seems to us to be misconceived. In particular, it should be noted that Thomas is primarily concerned with the operation of a public interest defence to actions for infringement of copyright. To reiterate, in the copyright context a public interest defence is required in order to allow documentary and photographic material that reveals certain types of information to be placed in the public domain. It ought not to apply to the expression a journalist used to relate a story. Thus, to return to Thomas' example, there is nothing in the copyright cases to suggest that a journalist could copy another's story in reliance on the public interest defence. Moreover, in so far as the second journalist merely copies the evidence on which the first journalist had intended to rely, the public interest defence to an action for infringement

---

[29] See Chapter 2. [30] *Mars v. Teknowledge*, 145–6.
[31] D. Thomas, 'A Public Interest Defence to Copyright Infringement?' (2003) 14 AIPJ 225, 232.
[32] *Times Newspapers v. MGN* [1993] EMLR 442.
[33] Thomas, 'Public Interest Defence', 232.

of *copyright* would not normally prejudice the first journalist, since in most cases she would not own the copyright in the evidential material (admittedly there might be exceptions to this, in particular, where the relevant evidence is contained in photographs taken by the first journalist, but in general it is safe to say that she will not be the copyright owner). The central issue, therefore, is whether the courts would be prepared to protect a journalist's scoop from misappropriation *through the law of confidence* in cases where the public interest defence would protect the journalist from a breach of confidence action brought by a third party (the potential existence of copyright in evidential material created by the journalist being merely a side issue). In other words, the key question is whether the first journalist would be able to bring an action for breach of confidence against the second journalist in respect of her story even though that story contains information which it is in the public interest to be made known. The courts have not addressed this question directly. The main grounds for refusing an injunction in the *Thatcher Diaries* case were (i) that the plaintiffs were unable to persuade the court that a satisfactory injunction could be drafted,[34] and (ii) that the court was unsure whether an action for breach of confidence could arise in a case where the plaintiff itself intended to publish the information in the future – a point that has now been resolved in favour of allowing claimants who intend the information to be published to bring an action.[35] In so far as the question of the public interest in publication was discussed at all in *Thatcher Diaries*, far from supporting Thomas' argument, it would seem to undermine it, Bingham MR stating in that case: 'I would for my part have little hesitation in accepting [the] argument that there is no public interest, in the strict sense, in the publication of the material about the Falklands War, and no doubt other highlights of Lady Thatcher's Prime Ministership, which would justify the publication of this material this

---

[34] In *Douglas v. Hello! (No 5)* [2003] EMLR 641, 718, Lindsay J described this feature of the case as 'odd'.

[35] See, in particular, *Douglas v. Hello! (No 5)*, Lindsay J commenting on Bingham MR's uncertainty on this point in *Thatcher Diaries* as follows: 'I respectfully doubt whether, even as to a wholly personal or individual confidence, an intention to publish should of itself invariably deny a claimant relief but it cannot sensibly deny relief in the case of a commercial secret. An inventor . . . might, for example, confide to a prospective manufacturer secret details of his invention which he hoped soon to make public by way of an application for a patent . . . In such cases it would be absurd, as I have already mentioned, if an intention to make the subject-matter of the confidence public should destroy confidentiality.' See also *Shelley Films v. Rex Features* [1994] EMLR 134; *Douglas v. Hello! (No 1)* [2001] QB 967; *Bloomsbury Publishing v. News Group Newspapers* [2003] FSR 842. Moreover, as Lindsay J also noted in *Douglas v. Hello (No 5)*, this point would seem to have been established long before *Thatcher Diaries* by cases such as *Fraser v. Thames TV* [1984] QB 44.

week rather than in ten days' time'.[36] This only provides limited support for permitting a court to take into account whether the public will have access to the information in the near future when deciding whether to accept a public interest defence. Nevertheless, we would strongly support the establishment of such a rule in both the copyright and breach of confidence contexts.

Summary

In breach of confidence cases the courts have done a good job of providing clear guidance as to the circumstances in which a public interest defence might be accepted. They have also built in other safeguards to ensure that the defence does not come to be abused, and there is no reason why still other such safeguards could not emerge. For example, it has been suggested that there is good reason to suppose that the courts would not allow the public interest defence to be used to justify copying from a work indefinitely.

The recent authorities

Despite the potential utility of the type of defence outlined above, two recent decisions of the Court of Appeal have thrown the scope of the public interest defence in copyright cases and its very existence into doubt. The first of these more recent cases was *Hyde Park* v. *Yelland*.[37] That case concerned an application for summary judgment for infringement of copyright against the *Sun* newspaper made by a company associated with Mohammed Al Fayed. The background to the case was the *Sun*'s reprinting of stills from a security video which the newspaper argued cast doubt on Al Fayed's claim that a conspiracy had been hatched to kill Diana Princess of Wales and his son Dodi Al Fayed in order to prevent their marriage. At first instance Jacob J held that the *Sun* had an arguable defence, both because the stills had arguably been used for the reporting of current events and because the *Sun*'s disclosure helped to refute serious allegations made in the public forum and thus was arguably in the public interest. In contrast, the Court of Appeal concluded that no defence of fair dealing for the purpose of reporting current events could succeed.[38]

In relation to the public interest defence the Court did not merely conclude that no public interest defence could succeed on the facts. Rather, the Court drastically curtailed judicial discretion to refuse to enforce

---

[36] *Times Newspapers* v. *MGN*, 447. [37] [2001] Ch 143. [38] See Chapter 2.

copyright on public interest grounds. Aldous LJ, with whom Stuart Smith LJ agreed, concluded that there is no general public interest defence to an action for infringement of copyright in the United Kingdom. Instead, Aldous LJ chose to reiterate that the courts have the power under their 'inherent jurisdiction' to refuse to enforce copyright if *the work* is immoral or injurious to the public.[39] Aldous LJ also implied that the courts have some further discretion in cases where the claimant is attempting to base a cause of action on an illegal or an immoral act, although, significantly, he failed to spell out the limits and consequences of this second form of discretion. But for Aldous LJ the courts have no jurisdiction to refuse to enforce copyright where the claimant is not guilty of wrongdoing and where the work, although itself innocuous, reveals information which affects the public interest. Nor did he give any examples of the sorts of situation in which it would be appropriate to exercise either of the forms of discretion he identified. Mance LJ, in a partially dissenting judgment, declined to go as far as Aldous LJ. He apparently accepted that the courts do have some discretion to refuse to enforce copyright on public interest grounds. However, he made it clear that this discretion is much more limited than in breach of confidence cases and that it could not be used in the same general area as covered by one of the statutory permitted acts. He also failed to give any examples of the sorts of situation in which it would be appropriate to exercise this discretion, such that it is difficult to imagine the circumstances in which a defendant could successfully rely upon the defence.

The very restrictive approach to matters affecting the public interest adopted by Aldous LJ in *Yelland* was subsequently confirmed by two decisions of the Vice-Chancellor,[40] who rejected the argument that the question of whether there is a public interest defence should be reinterpreted in the light of the coming into force of the Human Rights Act.

More recently, in *Ashdown* v. *Telegraph Group*[41] the Court of Appeal stepped back from outright rejection of the public interest defence. As was seen in the last chapter, the *Ashdown* case concerned an action for infringement of copyright in a confidential memorandum of a meeting between Tony Blair and Paddy Ashdown that had taken place shortly after the 1997 general election. The *Sunday Telegraph* obtained a copy of this minute from an unknown source and published sections of it, claiming that the memorandum demonstrated that the general public

---

[39] As to this jurisdiction see *AG* v. *Guardian (No 2)* [1990] 1 AC 109; *Glyn* v. *Weston Feature Film Co* [1916] 1 Ch 261.
[40] *Ashdown* v. *Telegraph Group* [2001] Ch 685; *Imutran* v. *Uncaged Campaigns* [2001] 2 All ER 385 (decided by the Vice-Chancellor on the same day as *Ashdown*).
[41] [2002] Ch 149.

had been misled about Blair and Ashdown's plans to form a coalition government. Although the Court was of the view that the defendant did not have an arguable case on the facts, it concluded that there are rare circumstances in which copyright can come into conflict with freedom of expression and hence in which a public interest defence will be available. In order to justify this departure from *Yelland*, the Court came to the surprising conclusion that the view that there is not a public interest defence to actions for infringement of copyright was not in fact supported by a majority in *Yelland*, since although 'Stuart Smith LJ agreed that the appeal should be allowed for the reasons given by Aldous LJ . . . [i]t does not seem to us that these reasons depended on the precise scope of the public interest exception identified by Aldous LJ'.[42]

It is important to emphasise that the decision in *Ashdown* only represents a limited relaxation of the approach taken in *Yelland*. It seems clear that the defence as recognised in *Ashdown* is more limited than the approach taken in the pre-*Yelland* cases.[43] This is clear not only from *Ashdown* itself, where it was said that the defence would only apply in 'very rare' circumstances, but also from the fact that the Court referred approvingly to Mance LJ's partially dissenting judgment in *Yelland*, which indicates that the public interest defence is of limited scope. Moreover, a further practical problem with the *Ashdown* formulation is that the decision in *Yelland* and the subsequent decisions of the Vice-Chancellor indicate that there are at least some members of the judiciary who would prefer to banish free speech interests from copyright altogether. *Ashdown* allows plenty of scope for a judge of this view to refuse to treat any given case as being sufficiently exceptional to warrant an application of the defence. It is also notable that there was no criticism of the actual outcome in *Yelland*, even though there was considerable force in the *Sun*'s assertion that their use of the stills was the only adequate way to rebut serious charges made in the public forum. Whilst the defendant's case in *Ashdown* was perhaps not as strong, it is our view that the argument that publication was justified merited much more careful consideration.[44]

---

[42] *Ibid.*, 249.
[43] This interpretation is shared by others: J. Griffiths, 'Copyright Law After Ashdown – Time to Deal Fairly with the Public' [2002] IPQ 240.
[44] In particular, because the information disclosed was directly relevant to the political process. Also see S. Lockyear, 'When Paddy Met Tony', *Guardian*, 30 July 2001: 'the Ashdown case is surely a good example of precisely when it is justifiable to copy the exact words of a copyright work because information about the Ashdown/Blair meeting had previously been published by other newspapers and the *Sunday Telegraph*'s purpose was to prove the existence and content of that meeting by publication of extracts from the minute itself'.

Given the unsatisfactory way in which the Court in *Ashdown* dealt with Stuart Smith LJ's judgment, it seems likely that the matter is in any event not finally decided, and that it will take a decision of the House of Lords to resolve once and for all the question of the scope of the public interest defence in copyright cases. Whilst this will give opponents of the defence the opportunity to have the partial reversal in *Ashdown* overturned, it will also provide an opportunity to have the exception reinstated in the broad form towards which the pre-*Yelland* cases seemed to point.

Can the same result be achieved by other means?

The argument that a public interest defence would be a useful, if limited, addition to the statutory permitted acts is, of course, seriously flawed if alternative and better established mechanisms exist to allow a court to achieve the same result. Some judges and commentators have indicated that such mechanisms are to be found in traditional equitable bars such as fraud and clean hands.[45] Other commentators have argued that same result could be achieved by a court refusing an injunction and otherwise being creative when awarding a remedy.[46] However, as Hamilton has also noted, one thing which is immediately noticeable is that few of these accounts contain a detailed analysis of the circumstances in which a court could rely on these alternate mechanisms.[47] In fact, further analysis demonstrates that considerable uncertainty surrounds many of the mechanisms upon which opponents of the public interest defence rely.

Turning first to clean hands, it should be noted that this principle is usually only thought to bar equitable relief,[48] but, for reasons that will be examined shortly, it is also important in this context to ensure that defendants are not liable for damages. More generally, any attempt to analyse the circumstances in which this principle will act as a bar to relief soon encounters the difficulty that the clean hands doctrine is highly fluid. In his seminal articles in the *Michigan Law Review*[49] Chafee summarised

---

[45] In particular, this argument is associated with Gummow J's long-standing opposition to the recognition of public interest defences: *Corrs Pavey Whiting & Byrne* v. *Collector of Customs* (1987) 10 IPR 53; *SmithKline & French* v. *Department of Community Services and Health* [1990] FSR 617; *Collier Constructions* v. *Foskett* (1990) 19 IPR 44.
[46] Laddie et al., 2nd edn, p. 127.
[47] A. Hamilton, 'Copyright and the Public Interest – Public versus Private Rights', Honours thesis, Monash University, 1995. The exception is Thomas, 'Public Interest Defence'.
[48] But note the related common law principle *ex turpi causa non oritur actio* (an action does not arise from a base cause) and see the comment of Chafee, 'Coming into Equity' [I], below.
[49] Z. Chafee, 'Coming into Equity with Unclean Hands' [I] (1949) 47 *Michigan Law Review* 877; Z. Chafee, 'Coming into Equity with Unclean Hands' [II] (1949) 47 *Michigan Law Review* 1065.

his position as follows: 'I propose to show that the clean hands doctrine does not definitely govern anything, that it is a rather recent growth, that it ought not to be called a maxim of equity because it is by no means confined to equity, that its supposed unity is very tenuous and it is really a bundle of rules relating to quite diverse subjects, that insofar as it is a principle it is at times not very helpful but is at times capable of causing considerable harm.'[50] Whilst more recent commentators have declined to go as far as Chafee, many have chosen to emphasise the uncertainty that surrounds the doctrine. Significantly, a number of these commentators have also argued that it would be better if clean hands cases were justified on more precise grounds and that the clean hands principle is at its most useful when it is used to underpin more definite equitable defences.[51]

Given the latter argument, it is interesting to note that both strands of cases that can be said to underpin a public interest defence in copyright law (that is, the public interest defence in the law of confidence and cases in which a court has refused to enforce copyright on the grounds that the work is immoral) can be said to have their foundation in the clean hands principle.[52] On this view, the argument that the public interest defence should be replaced by an application of the clean hands doctrine is entirely regressive. Moreover, given the uncertainty that surrounds clean hands, an application of this principle is much more likely to create uncertainty and is much more likely to act as 'an invitation to judicial idiosyncrasy'[53] than an application of a public interest defence in the form advocated in the previous section.

Not only is the application of the clean hands principle unpredictable, in so far as we can draw any conclusions about the operation of the doctrine, it can be seen that there are a number of reasons why it may not provide much assistance in copyright cases. First, it is often stated that general depravity will not bar a claim, rather, there must be 'an immediate and necessary relation to the equity sued for'.[54] This restriction alone

---

[50] 'Coming into Equity' [I], 878.
[51] See P. Pettit, 'He Who Comes into Equity Must Come with Clean Hands' [1990] *Conveyencer and Property Lawyer* 416, 422: 'The clean hands doctrine is perhaps no more than a background principle from which have developed particular equitable defences'. Similarly, see I. Spry, *The Principles of Equitable Remedies: Specific Performance, Injunctions, Rectification and Equitable Damages*, 6th edn (London: Sweet & Maxwell, 2001), p. 245.
[52] See respectively *Corrs Pavey Whiting & Byrne* v. *Collector of Customs*, 70–7 (per Gummow J), arguing that *Gartside* v. *Outram* can be explained on this basis; Chafee, 'Coming into Equity' [II], 1065–70, explaining *Glyn* v. *Weston Feature Film Co* and similar US cases on this basis.
[53] Cf. *SmithKline & French* v. *Department of Community Services and Health*, 663 (per Gummow J).
[54] *Dering* v. *Earl of Winchelsea* (1787) 1 Cox 318, 319 (per Eyre LC); *Collier Constructions* v. *Foskett* (per Gummow J). The same point is made by Hamilton, 'Copyright'. There

would justify a conservative judge in refusing to use the doctrine to deny relief in the type of case under consideration here. Second, the courts have already shown a reluctance to apply this principle in copyright cases.[55] Third, the doctrine seems to have declined in importance in general over recent years, perhaps making it less likely that a court would be willing to extend its application to a public interest case.[56]

Closer examination reveals that the other equitable principle relied upon by opponents of the public interest defence – fraud – is also unlikely to provide a satisfactory alternative to the public interest defence. The notion of equitable fraud tends to be used in a number of different ways. It is probably most commonly encountered as a device that can be used to set aside a transaction that is tainted in some respect.[57] However, it is still encountered in other guises, and ultimately it remains 'one of the three pillars that support the entire structure of the equitable jurisdiction'.[58]

---

are cases that suggest that the clean hands principle can have a broader application, but the status of these statements is uncertain, particularly given the tendency towards restricting the principle's application (see below). Thomas, 'Public Interest Defence', places particular reliance on *Kettles and Gas Appliances* v. *Hordern* (1934) 35 SR (NSW) 108, interpreting this case as a decision in which the clean hands principle was applied because the plaintiff's behaviour was to the detriment of the public as a whole. This case does not, however, support the proposition that general depravity can justify an application of the clean hands principle. Rather, in that case the plaintiff was treated as only being able to establish goodwill in the get-up of its kettles because of its having warded off other traders by dishonestly claiming that the design had been patented. Consequently, therefore, the plaintiff's unconscionable behaviour did have a direct relation to the equity sued for. Thomas seems to equate conduct which misleads the public with general depravity unrelated to the equity sued for. There is nothing in the case to suggest, for example, that a copyright owner who is flouting safety standards will be denied equitable relief as regards a copyright work that provides evidence of this misconduct. It is also noticeable that the judge in that case (Long Innes J) gave no indication that he thought that he was departing from established principle. Moreover, it might be noted that any other result in that case would have produced the anomalous result that a trader who successfully warded off potential competitors with a dishonest claim that a product was patented would have been in a better position than a trader who actually secured a patent, the courts discounting goodwill acquired at a time when no one else was in a position to manufacture the article in question: *Cellular Clothing* v. *Maxton* [1899] AC 326, 343–4 (per Lord Davey). Thus *Kettles and Gas Appliances* is probably best thought of as developing principles left latent in the law of passing off.

[55] See *British Leyland* v. *Armstrong Patents* [1982] FSR 481, 501–2 (Foster J); *Penguin Books* v. *India Book Distributors* [1985] FSR 120, 126–7, emphasising the general principle: 'The maxim . . . must not be taken too widely . . . It is not a maxim of which a defendant can take advantage. It is a self-imposed ordinance that closes the door of a court of equity to one tainted with iniquity or bad faith relative to the matter in which he seeks relief' (High Court of Delhi, per Rohatgi J).

[56] See Pettit, 'He Who Comes'; R. Meagher, D. Heydon and M. Leeming, *Meagher, Gummow and Lehane's Equity Doctrines and Remedies*, 4th edn (Sydney: Butterworths, 2002), p. 100, noting that 'In England, the tendency has probably been to restrict rather than enlarge the scope of the doctrine.'

[57] See J. McGhee, *Snell's Equity*, 30th edn (London: Sweet & Maxwell, 2000), p. 607.

[58] Meagher, Heydon and Leeming, *Meagher, Gummow and Lehane*, p. 450.

At this general level it might be argued that there would be room for a court to develop a jurisdiction to refuse to enforce copyright, but, as with any use of a clean hands defence, this would involve an act of judicial legislation that would take us deep into uncertain territory (indeed, the doctrines of fraud and clean hands are by no means entirely separate[59]).

The third mechanism relied on by opponents of the public interest defence is a more general discretion to refuse to award an injunction (that is, on grounds over and above those justified by reference to the clean hands principle, etc.). This third mechanism might at first seem more promising, but again a closer examination reveals that there are two key difficulties. The first, and most fundamental, objection to relying on the discretion to refuse to enforce an injunction is that in so far as a defendant will still be liable for damages this may not resolve the potential conflict between copyright and freedom of expression or a right to information. As a practical matter, damages awards may have a significant chilling effect on the actions of potential defendants. As a matter of principle creating what will, in effect, be a compulsory licence over copyright material seems inadequate to protect either the free speech interests of potential defendants or the non-financial interests of copyright owners. Alternatively, a court could perhaps decide to award only nominal damages, an award that could be justified by citing the low value of the types of work that will normally be involved in public interest cases.[60] The possibility of only awarding nominal damages was canvassed by Jacob J in *Yelland*, but was rejected as an artificial solution.[61] Not only do we agree with this analysis, we would also argue that a solution which saw a claimant emerge as the nominal victor but without a remedy fails to achieve legal transparency. Moreover, if a court were to award only nominal damages on the basis that the work has a low inherent value, this could set a dangerous precedent in other cases,[62] since in the more normal case copyright provides a useful additional tool to protect privacy and reputation, as has been recognised in the trend towards granting damages for mental distress and injury to feelings in copyright cases.[63]

---

[59] See I. Spry, *Principles of Equitable Remedies*, p. 245.
[60] This will not always be the case, however.
[61] [1999] RPC 655, 670: 'It seems to me that the whole question of nominal damages is at the end of this century far too legalistic. A plaintiff who recovers only nominal damages has in reality lost and in reality the defendant has established a complete defence.'
[62] *W v. Egdell* [1990] 1 Ch 359, provides a good example of where an unmeritorious plaintiff led the court to make some sweeping and unfortunate statements about the types of damage recoverable through a confidence action.
[63] It is now widely accepted that damages for injury to feelings and reputation ought to be available in copyright and confidence cases (see, e.g., Cornish and Llewelyn, pp. 332, 450–1) and there is growing, albeit still limited, authority to support the award of

98   The public interest defence

Second, irrespective of the argument that a mere refusal to grant an injunction does not provide an adequate safeguard for user interests, there are also questions about the circumstances in which a court is entitled to refuse an injunction. Whilst the mantra that injunctions are always discretionary has frequently been recited in this context, there are statements to the effect that there are certain classes of case where a court has no discretion to refuse to award an injunction.[64] Whilst these statements may be wrong[65] and whilst there are good reasons to think that, in any event, they do not apply to copyright cases,[66] they offer justification for not treating the mantra at face value. Such statements also draw attention to the fact that the courts have developed detailed guidelines for determining when an injunction should be made available. When considering these guidelines it is important to draw a distinction between final and interim injunctions. These will be considered in turn.

Significantly, there has been some recent judicial discussion of the circumstances in which a court in a copyright case may refuse a final injunction. These cases indicate that the discretion to refuse a final injunction in a copyright case is extremely limited and is to be guided by general principles relating to the refusal of injunctive relief.[67] The most important general guidelines that we have as to when it is appropriate to refuse an injunction remain those laid down by the Court of Appeal in *Shelfer v. City of London Electric Lighting Company*.[68] These guidelines and guidance from subsequent cases indicate a number of circumstances in which it may be appropriate to refuse an injunction. These include situations where the damage to the claimant's interests is small[69] and where there is no danger that an infringement will be repeated.[70] These guidelines would not seem to justify the refusal of an injunction in the type of case with which we are concerned. There is other authority to suggest that the public interest may occasionally justify a refusal to grant an injunction,[71]

---

damages for this kind of injury. See *Williams v. Settle* [1960] 1 WLR 1072; *Beloff v. Pressdram*; *Cornelius v. De Taranto* [2001] EMLR 329; *Nottinghamshire Healthcare v. News Group Newspapers* [2002] RPC 962.

[64] *Doherty v. Allman* (1878) 3 App Cas 709, 719–20, no discretion to refuse an injunction to enforce a negative contractual obligation (per Lord Cairns).

[65] See Spry, *Principles of Equitable Remedies*, ch. 5.

[66] See the cases referred to below.

[67] See *Ludlow Music v. Robbie Williams (No 2)* [2002] EMLR 585, 612–16; *PPL v. Maitra* [1998] 1 WLR 870, 878–79. For discussion see G. Harbottle, 'Permanent Injunctions in Copyright Cases: When Will They Be Refused?' [2001] EIPR 154, 157: 'the jurisdiction remains an exceptional one and none of the recent authorities suggest that its scope is likely to be extended beyond its extremely restricted boundaries'.

[68] [1895] 1 Ch 287.   [69] *Ibid.*   [70] See *Raleigh Cycle v. Miller* (1949) 66 RPC 23.

[71] *Wrotham Park v. Parkside Homes* [1974] 1 WLR 798, 810–11; *Miller v. Jackson* [1977] 1 QB 966 (per Lord Denning). See also *Chiron Corporation v. Organon Teknika (No 10)* [1995] FSR 325 (discussed below).

but this authority is limited, is not directly on point,[72] and has been subject to judicial criticism.[73] It is also important to note that some opponents of the public interest defence have also expressed their opposition to the use of a general public interest test when determining whether to grant injunctive relief. In particular, in his extrajudicial capacity, Gummow J has described the decision in *Miller* v. *Jackson* as 'a judicial aberration' and has complained that the case disregarded the decision in *Shelfer* and 'flouted the numerous judicial warnings against inventing novel heads of public policy'.[74] Moreover, even in one of the cases in which it was accepted that the general public interest might be a relevant factor when deciding whether to grant an injunction, it was held that the mere fact that it would be in the public interest to allow someone to reproduce the subject matter of the monopoly is not a sufficient reason to refuse an injunction in an intellectual property case.[75]

It is therefore clear that the traditional guidelines as to when it is appropriate to refuse a final injunction do not provide adequate protection for

---

[72] It is worth noting, for example, that in *Dennis* v. *Ministry of Defence* [2003] EnvLR 741 Buckley J treated *Miller* v. *Jackson* as shedding light on a 'principle in the law of nuisance' (at 751). Moreover, in the course of refusing to award an injunction on public interest grounds in this case he emphasised that 'the facts of this case are extreme' (e.g., at 758).

[73] See *Kennaway* v. *Thompson* [1981] QB 88, 93: 'Lord Denning MR's statement that the public interest should prevail over the private interest runs counter to the principles enunciated in *Shelfer*'s case and does not accord with Cumming-Bruce LJ's reason for refusing an injunction. We are of the opinion that there is nothing in *Miller* v. *Jackson* binding on us, which qualifies what was decided in *Shelfer*'s case. Any decisions before *Shelfer*'s case ... which give support to the proposition that the public interest should prevail over the private interest must be read subject to the decision in *Shelfer*'s case' (per Lawton LJ). More recently, in *World Wildlife Fund* v. *World Wrestling Federation Entertainment* [2003] EWCA Civ 401 CA Carnwarth LJ referred to Lord Denning's test in *Miller* v. *Jackson*, but made no comment on whether that case was rightly decided, preferring to emphasise that it could have no application on the facts. In contrast, Peter Gibson LJ and Blackburne J (sitting in the Court of Appeal) indicated that if other issues had been decided differently, they would have granted a stay of the injunction not on public interest grounds, but rather because the damage to the claimant was small (see paras. 71 and 61 respectively).

[74] R. Meagher, W. Gummow and J. Lehane, *Equity Doctrines and Remedies*, 3rd edn (Sydney: Butterworths, 1992), p. 547.

[75] *Chiron Corporation* v. *Organon Teknika (No 10)*: 'as a general rule, a defendant, who interferes with a proprietary right of a plaintiff and threatens to continue to do so, will be injuncted' (per Aldous J) – granting an injunction despite the benefit that would have been gained from widespread dissemination of the defendant's infringing product (test kits for the detection of hepatitis C). In contrast, in *Acohs* v. *Bashford Consulting* (1997) 37 IPR 542 Merkel J (in the Federal Court of Australia) indicated, without deciding, that the general public interest can justify the refusal of an injunction in a copyright case. In reaching this conclusion, however, he framed his judgment by reference to the English cases that recognise a public interest defence to actions for infringement of copyright, and he failed to consider the broader tests of when it is appropriate to refuse injunctive relief. It is therefore surprising that Thomas, 'Public Interest Defence', 235 places reliance on this decision.

users. Whilst it could be countered that it is the principles dealing with interim injunctions that are more important in this context, in a case where the claimant is seeking summary judgment (as was the case in both *Ashdown* and *Yelland*) it is the guidelines on final injunctions that will come into play.

In any event, when we turn to the principles relating to when an interim injunction should be refused, we see that here too it is not clear that relevant factors can be taken into account. On the contrary, under the *American Cyanamid* principles, one factor which the court should take into account is the adequacy of damages.[76] Given that the harm in public interest cases is likely to be to non-financial interests, damages are unlikely to be adequate. Furthermore, in cases of doubt the *American Cyanamid* principles indicate that the court should preserve the status quo. Given that works in public interest cases will almost invariably be unpublished, this would also suggest that an injunction should be granted. Nor would Laddie J's controversial reformulation of *American Cyanamid* in the *Series 5 Software* case[77] assist a defendant, since this places increased emphasis on the merits of the case and hence on who is likely to be successful at trial. There is some separate limited authority to suggest that the public interest may at times justify the refusal of an interim injunction, but the cases concerned are only first instance decisions and they fail to give any real guidance as to when this discretion can be exercised.[78] Moreover, one of these cases apparently draws on the public interest defence cases and is therefore now of questionable authority.[79]

A court that was considering whether to decline a final or an interim injunction on public interest grounds would therefore find only very limited support in the general authorities to support the refusal of an injunction and almost no guidance as to the circumstances in which it might be appropriate to exercise such a discretion. Support could instead be gained from section 12 of the Human Rights Act, which imposes special obligations on a court that is considering whether to grant relief that might affect the exercise of the right to freedom of expression. Before turning to the potential impact of section 12, it is worth making three preliminary points. The first is that Laddie, Prescott and Vitoria, the most influential exponents of the argument that there is no need for a public interest

---

[76] See *American Cyanamid* v. *Ethicon* [1975] AC 396.
[77] *Series 5 Software* v. *Clarke* [1996] 1 All ER 853.
[78] See *Solar Thompson* v. *Barton* [1977] RPC 537, 549; *Femis-Bank* v. *Lazar* [1991] 2 All ER 865, 872; *Beggars Banquet* v. *Carlton*. The other cases cited by Laddie et al., 2nd edn, p. 127, do not support this proposition: cf. *M'Beath* v. *Ravenscroft* (1839) 8 LJ Ch 208; *Harbottle* v. *National Westminster Bank* [1977] 2 All ER 862.
[79] *Beggars Banquet* v. *Carlton*.

defence, formed their view prior to the passage of the Human Rights Act. The second is that if we conclude that reliance must be placed on the Human Rights Act in order to reconcile the tension between copyright and freedom of expression then it is clear that copyright law does not resolve this conflict internally and is not therefore already adequately 'balanced'. The third point is that in order for section 12 to come into play a court must be satisfied that freedom of expression would be compromised by the grant of an injunction but, as has been seen, some members of the judiciary have refused to accept that there is any relationship between copyright and freedom of expression.

Turning to section 12, the key provision in this context is subsection 4.[80] That subsection provides:

The court must have particular regard to the importance of the Convention right to freedom of expression and, where the proceedings relate to material which the respondent claims, or which appears to the court, to be journalistic, literary or artistic material (or to conduct connected with such material), to–
 (a) the extent to which–
  (i) the material has, or is about to, become available to the public; or
  (ii) it is, or would be, in the public interest for the material to be published;
 (b) any relevant privacy code.

This provision, which makes specific reference to the public interest, could be used to underpin the refusal of both interim and final injunctions. However, this section was initially given a fairly cool reception, with judges taking the view that this section has not altered the test for deciding when injunctive relief should be available.[81] Whilst this may be beginning to change,[82] at present the impact of 12(4) on the type of case with which we are concerned is doubtful at best. Moreover, it has been seen that even if this section were used to deny injunctive relief this would not, by itself, be sufficient to reconcile copyright with freedom of expression.

Overall, the fairest conclusion is not that the alternative mechanisms relied upon by opponents of the public interest defence are necessarily inadequate to reconcile copyright with freedom of expression. Rather, it is that considerable uncertainty surrounds these mechanisms and this makes their adequacy for the task difficult to assess. On a practical level

---

[80] To date much of the attention has been focused on s.12(3), which provides that where free speech interests are at stake no 'relief is to be granted so as to restrain publication before trial unless the court is satisfied that the applicant is likely to establish that publication should not be allowed'. This provision would do little to assist a potential defendant, since in the absence of a public interest defence the claimant is 'likely' to be able to establish that she will be successful at trial. As to the test to be applied under s. 12(3), see *Cream Holdings v. Banerjee* [2003] Ch 650.

[81] See *Douglas v. Hello! (No 1)*; *Ashdown v. Telegraph Group*, 701.

[82] See *Theakston v. MGN*; *A v. B*; *Jockey Club v. Buffham*.

a creative judge who was keen to prevent copyright from being used inappropriately could probably stretch one of these other mechanisms to achieve the desired result. However, a conservative judge would be justified in criticising such a decision on precisely the same grounds that have been used to attack the public interest defence, namely, that the decision was insufficiently grounded by precedent and provides an invitation to judicial idiosyncrasy. It could therefore be said that the real battle is over the appropriate bounds of copyright and it is this argument that is important, not the precise mechanism by which copyright is constrained. Whilst this is true on one level, any move away from the public interest defence would represent a backwards step. It would represent a victory for those who would be happier to see free speech interests banished from copyright altogether and it would lead to much greater uncertainty. Moreover, any such uncertainty might not be merely short-term, since many of the alternative equitable principles on which opponents of the public interest defence rely suffer from inherent indeterminacy. An echo of this criticism is to be found in the *London Transport* case. In that case Sedley LJ concluded that the principle of proportionality developed by the European Court of Human Rights provides better guidance as to when the public interest defence to an action for breach of confidence should be available than a test based on the conscience of the recipient of the information.[83] Reliance on mechanisms other than the public interest defence would also be less likely to achieve legal transparency, with problems increasing the more these other mechanisms are stretched to achieve public policy goals. Consider, for example, the 'successful' claimant who is denied injunctive relief on the basis of a much extended clean hands principle and who is awarded only nominal damages. Not only would such a result be difficult to explain to the parties, it is also precisely the sort of outcome that brings the law into disrepute.

The objections of principle to a public interest defence

Having demonstrated that there are good reasons to support the existence of a public interest defence and that there is no clearly established alternative mechanism that could achieve the same result, it is now necessary to consider the various objections of principle that have been raised to the recognition of such a defence. These objections have been most fully developed by Laddie, Prescott and Vitoria.[84] It seems clear that these

---

[83] [2003] EMLR 88, 109.
[84] See Laddie et al., 2nd edn, pp. 126–31. The third edition of Laddie et al. does not deal with these arguments since the section in question was apparently written between the

arguments influenced the Court in *Yelland*[85] and it is likely that they would be raised in any future case. It is therefore important for advocates of the public interest defence to attempt to refute these objections of principle. These objections can be grouped under four headings, namely: (1) arguments to the effect that such a defence would be *illegitimate*; (2) arguments to the effect that such a defence would be *inappropriate*; (3) arguments to the effect that such a defence is *unnecessary*; and (4) arguments to the effect that such a defence would be *unworkable*. These will be dealt with in turn.

Is a public interest defence legitimate?

There are two main arguments which go to the question of the legitimacy of the public interest defence. The first argument is that to refuse to enforce copyright on the grounds of the public interest would be to expropriate the plaintiff's property without compensation. In effect, the argument is that a public interest defence would be constitutionally illegitimate.[86] This argument is also said to explain why a distinction should be drawn between copyright and other areas of the law where a public interest defence is unquestionably available, in particular the law of confidence.

One response to this argument might be to point out that the public interest defence will only involve a very limited expropriation of property, since the owner will remain free to exploit the work commercially and the copyrights affected will usually have little inherent value. Indeed, as we argued in Chapter 1, an interesting feature of the sorts of work that will usually be involved in public interest cases is that the subsistence of copyright will be almost entirely accidental. That is, copyright will subsist in things like security videos and internal memorandums because copyright has been extended to cover certain types of product irrespective of their form, merit or purpose. This extension has largely resulted from an appreciation on the part of the legislature that it is unwise to spell out in too much detail what 'a work' will look like and from an understandable reluctance on the part of the judiciary to engage in consideration of the aesthetic merits of a work. However, whilst these may provide good

---

first instance and appeal decisions in *Yelland*. See also J. Phillips, 'The Berne Convention and the Public Interest' [1987] EIPR 106.
[85] Although the Court of Appeal did not refer to Laddie et al.'s position, Laddie et al.'s views were cited by the plaintiff in *Yelland* and were considered at length by Jacob J at first instance.
[86] Laddie et al., 2nd edn, p. 127 and see the judgment of Aldous LJ in *Yelland* and of Morritt VC at first instance in *Ashdown*.

practical reasons for extending copyright to these types of work, if we return to first principles we can see that none of the theories that are usually used to justify copyright really explain why protection should be extended to works of this kind.[87] More specifically, there is no need to provide incentives for the creation of these works, nor in most cases can they be truly said to embody the personality of their creator.[88] In most cases the claimant will not even have thought about copyright protection until her legal advisor suggests that copyright law might be used to address her underlying grievance, which will usually be invasion of privacy and/or harm to reputation. Of course, as has already been suggested, in most cases the additional protection afforded by copyright to these interests will be desirable, but there are times when we should not allow copyright to be used in such a way as to get round a carefully considered limitation which has been built into the law of confidence and/or defamation.[89] The attempt to draw a distinction between copyright and confidence on the basis that the former is a property right is also unconvincing, since this rests upon a highly formalistic distinction which would be of little comfort to someone deprived of a valuable monopoly over information. Indeed, it is possible to argue that the disclosure of information controlled by confidence is a more damaging form of 'expropriation' than disclosure of information controlled by copyright, because the former may destroy the basis of monopoly, that is that the information be 'relatively' secret.[90] Moreover, as Jacob J pointed out at first instance in *Yelland*, some doubt remains as to whether it might not also be possible to classify at least some types of confidential information as property.[91]

---

[87] See also J. Waldron, 'From Authors to Copiers: Individual Rights and Social Values in Intellectual Property' (1993) 68 *Chicago Kent Law Review* 841, 851–2: 'From the innocuous premise: (1) If someone is morally deserving, then it is appropriate to reward him; we fallaciously infer: (2) If it is appropriate to reward someone, then that person must be morally deserving'.

[88] We leave aside Lockean labour theory as a justification for copyright because Locke's provisos are so open-ended that it is possible to justify just about any arrangement by reference to his theory of property.

[89] Cf. *Parfums Christian Dior* v. *Evora* [1998] RPC 166, 197: 'the protection conferred by copyright as regards the reproduction of protected works in a reseller's advertising may not, in any event, be broader than that which is conferred on a trademark owner in the same circumstances'. For discussion see A. Kur, 'The "Presentation Right" – Time to Create a New Limitation in Copyright Law' (2000) 31 IIC 308, in particular at 310: 'the problem [in the *Christian Dior* case] resulted not least from the fact that copyright protection has been extended into areas that until recently were considered to belong in the public domain or . . . were only subject to a different category of rights . . . It is easy to predict that this constellation will give rise to more problems in the future.'

[90] See *AG* v. *Guardian (No 2)*.

[91] [1999] RPC 655, 668 and see *Re Keene* [1922] 2 Ch 475, information may be held on trust; *Jeffrey* v. *Rolls Royce* (1962) 40 Tax Cas 443, information treated as property for

Is a public interest defence legitimate? 105

A second, more fundamental, response to the argument that a public interest defence would be illegitimate because it would expropriate the claimant's property without compensation, would be to question whether such expropriation might in any event not be justifiable in circumstances where the property is being used to interfere with other important interests, such as free speech. Concluding that a deprivation without compensation would be justified in these cases would also seem consistent with the relatively limited right to property guaranteed by Article 1, Protocol 1 of the European Convention on Human Rights. When deciding on the lawfulness of any interference with the enjoyment of property rights, the European Court of Human Rights employs a test of proportionality that would seem to point towards the public interest defence being legitimate.[92] As has been seen, the properties in question will usually have little inherent value, whilst the general interest that is being protected is also recognised in the Convention as a fundamental freedom. In addition, because the owner will remain free to exploit the work commercially, the application of the public interest defence is closer to the imposition of a control on the use of property than a deprivation and, as such, ought not to create a presumption of the need for compensation.[93]

A third response would be to point out that the argument is, in part, circular, since property can only be expropriated in circumstances where the owner has an enforceable right. This point will be developed in detail in Chapter 6, but in essence our argument is that to view the owner's rights as 'prior' to the exceptions is to make a political choice and a choice which is in some respects ahistorical.

The second argument that goes to the legitimacy of a public interest defence is that such a defence would be incompatible with the United Kingdom's international obligations. This in turn requires consideration of two interrelated sets of questions: first, to what extent is a public interest defence compatible with the Berne Convention? Second, to

---

tax purposes. For the position in the United States see *Ruckelshaus* v. *Monsanto* 467 US 986 (1984), government regulations requiring that trade secrets be revealed to a public authority and permitting that authority to use the information required for compensation under the Fifth Amendment of the US Constitution. See also D. Libling, 'The Concept of Property: Property in Intangibles' (1978) 94 *Law Quarterly Review* 103.

[92] See, generally, D. Rook, *Property Law and Human Rights* (London: Blackstone, 2001), in particular ch. 4.

[93] Anderson notes that the distinction between control of use and deprivation in the jurisprudence of the ECHR is 'untidy and unsatisfactory': D. Anderson, 'Compensation for Interference with Property' [1999] *European Human Rights Law Review* 543, 553. However, given the way in which copyright is normally conceptualised as 'a bundle of rights', it may be important in this context to note the approach adopted in *Baner* v. *Sweden* (1989) 60 DR 128, where it was held that where only one right in 'a bundle' is lost or restricted it will normally be appropriate to conceptualise this as a control of use rather than a deprivation. For discussion, see Rook, *Property Law*, pp. 92–4.

what extent is a public interest defence compatible with the Information Society Directive? In *Yelland* Aldous LJ concluded that a public interest defence was incompatible with the Berne Convention.[94] In particular, he asserted that 'there is no general power for courts of the signatories [to the Berne Convention] to refuse to enforce copyright if it is thought to be in the public interest of that State that it should not be enforced. Thus a general defence of public interest would appear to be contrary to this country's international obligations'.[95] Unfortunately, this conclusion does not seem to have been based on a detailed reading of Berne.[96] The only article of Berne referred to by Aldous LJ was Article 10, which is principally designed to allow for quotations of works that have been lawfully made available to the public. A public interest defence could not be justified under this article. However, such a defence might be justifiable under Article 9(2) and/or Article 17 of the Convention. The former Article allows member states to provide exceptions to the reproduction right so long as they satisfy the so-called three-step test. The scope of Article 9(2) and the three-step test are examined in detail in later chapters,[97] but for now it is worth noting that it is at least arguable that a public interest defence could be justified by reference to this Article. Still more importantly, Article 17 of Berne allows member states to '*permit*, control or to prohibit the circulation or protection of a work' (emphasis added). This exception is designed to ensure that copyright cannot be exercised in a way that would be contrary to *ordre publique*, a notion which would extend to cover many of the types of use in question here.[98] At the very least, Aldous LJ should have explained why he did not regard either of these Articles as sufficient to cover a public interest defence. Aldous LJ also failed to explain how the much broader discretion, which he accepts that the courts have, to refuse to enforce copyright altogether in cases where a work is obscene, or blasphemous or grossly immoral can be justified within the terms of the Convention.[99] Assuming that this discretion can be justified, for example under Article 17, then presumably a

---

[94] See also Phillips, 'Berne Convention'.   [95] [2001] Ch 143, 164.
[96] It is also worth noting that the particular work in question in *Yelland* (a security video) is not a Berne Convention work and hence the United Kingdom has no obligation to protect works of this kind.
[97] See Chapters 7 and 9.
[98] See Ricketson, para. 9.72. Admittedly, Art. 17 refers to the right of the *government* to exercise this right, but the Convention goes on to make it clear that the 'government' in this case includes all 'competent authorities'. There is no reason to suppose that a country is not entitled to designate the courts as the competent authority for this purpose, something which Parliament attempted to achieve in the 1988 Act.
[99] See *Glyn* v. *Weston Feature Film Co*; *Slingsby* v. *Bradford Patent Truck* [1906] WN 51; *AG* v. *Guardian Newspapers (No 2)* [1990] 1 AC 109. For the limits of this doctrine see *ZYX Music* v. *King* [1995] FSR 566.

much narrower discretion can also be justified. Accepting that the courts have the power to refuse to enforce copyright altogether in certain cases, whilst rejecting a public interest defence, also raises a more fundamental problem of consistency. As Jacob J said at first instance in *Yelland*,

> Once it is conceded, as it must be, that the courts in certain limited classes of case can refuse to recognise copyright altogether, the concession amounts to saying that none of the acts which Parliament has said are infringements are such. If the courts can do that then surely they can do the lesser thing of refusing to recognise a particular act as infringement when that act is in the public interest.[100]

It is therefore at the very least arguable that a public interest defence is compatible with the United Kingdom's obligations under the Berne Convention (and hence its obligations under TRIPS[101]). Turning to the question of whether such a defence is compatible with the Information Society Directive, it should be noted that Article 5(3)(e) of the Directive allows member states to provide an exception for the purposes of public security and to ensure the proper performance of official duties. In so far as the public interest defence is designed to protect public health or public morals or assist in the investigation of wrongdoing then this article would seem to provide a solid foundation for the defence. The more difficult question is whether the Directive would also allow for an exception in cases (as we advocate) where the publication relates to a matter which is genuinely in the public interest and where publication is intended to put important evidence into the public forum. One possible (if strained) reading would be to interpret the inherently slippery notion of 'public security' as also extending to this type of case. In support of this interpretation it could be argued that the public interest defence is intended to protect freedom of expression and that European Community legislation should be read as being compatible with the European Convention on Human Rights.[102] Some reliance could also be placed on the provisions of the Directive relating to the reporting of current events, although this would not provide assistance if the material reproduced related to matters that were no longer current. Nevertheless, taken together, it can be argued that these provisions provide a relatively firm foundation for the defence.

Further support for the argument that the defence is compatible with the Directive could be obtained by reinterpreting the nature of the public

---

[100] [1999] RPC 655, 667–8.
[101] See Chapter 7 for a discussion of the relation between Berne and TRIPS standards as regards copyright exceptions.
[102] See A. Arnull, A. Dashwood, M. Ross and D. Wyatt, *Wyatt and Dashwood's European Union Law*, 4th edn (London: Sweet & Maxwell, 2000), pp. 144–8 and the cases cited therein.

interest 'defence'. Article 9 of the Information Society Directive specifically states that the Directive is to apply without prejudice to national provisions relating to confidentiality. If the defence were reinterpreted as a rule to the effect that where the substance of a complaint is breach of confidence then a claimant cannot be in a better position by relying on copyright, then it could be argued that this rule could be preserved by virtue of Article 9.[103] Alternatively, the public interest 'defence' could be conceptualised not as a defence or as an exception but rather as a merely temporary refusal to enforce copyright in cases where the owner is attempting to abuse its monopoly. As such, the defence could be said to be analogous to the *abus de droit* principle under French law, which is sometimes used in copyright cases to prevent a copyright owner from exercising its rights inappropriately and which is thought to be unaffected by the Information Society Directive.[104]

Is a public interest defence appropriate?

The second objection identified by Laddie et al. is that a public interest defence would be inappropriate, because courts are often unsuited to the task of assessing the public interest. The argument that courts are unsuited to the task of assessing the public interest is a familiar one and depends on the assumption that an elected and democratically accountable body is in a better position to strike a compromise between the demands of different interest groups. In the words of Justice Frankfurter, 'how best to reconcile competing interests is the business of legislatures'.[105]

Whilst there is much to be said for leaving questions of public policy to the political process, it must also be recognised that there are times when it will be impossible to predict in advance where the public interest will lie. In these cases we are not so much concerned with the broad and prospective exercise best left to Parliament, but rather we are confronted with having to decide which of the two conflicting interests demands the greater protection in the circumstances. At this level we are obliged to give judges the discretion to decide where the public interest lies on an ad hoc basis. This was at least arguably recognised by Parliament in

---

[103] See also n. 89, above, for recognition by the ECJ that it is sometimes appropriate to prevent a claimant from being in a better position by relying on a 'subsidiary' right.
[104] See C. Caron, 'Abus de droit et droit d'auteur: une illustration de la confrontation du droit spécial et du droit comun en droit civil français' (1998) 176 RIDA 3.
[105] *Dennis v. United States* 341 US 494 (1951), 539–40. See also L. Frantz, 'The First Amendment in the Balance' (1962) 71 *Yale Law Journal* 1424, in particular at 1428.

the 1988 Act when it made express provision to ensure that the courts would continue to feel free to apply and develop a public interest defence. Moreover, as has been seen, when making this ad hoc assessment in public interest cases, the courts have shown themselves to be reluctant to take into account factors (such as general economic factors) that they may not be competent to assess.

Another important issue that goes to the appropriateness of a public interest defence arises from what was said by Jacob J at first instance in *Yelland*. When considering the relationship between the public interest defence and the ECHR, he said that 'balancing the "freedom of expression" conferred by Article 10 ECHR and the "right to respect for private life" conferred by Article 8 will involve the judges in just the same or a similar sort of exercise as is involved in judging whether there is a public interest defence'.[106] If this statement is correct, and public interest cases involve the sorts of consideration that judges are increasingly having to deal with under the Human Rights Act, there seems little point in insisting that judges are unsuited to the task of taking such factors into account in one narrow category of case. Finally, it may be worth pointing out an apparent inconsistency in Mr Justice Laddie's position. On the one hand, as we have seen, Laddie J is opposed to giving judges a broad discretion in public interest cases. On the other hand, in his extrajudicial capacity, Laddie J has argued for the introduction of a general fair use defence, maintaining that such a defence would give the courts 'the flexibility to prevent copyright from being abused'.[107]

Is a public interest defence necessary?

We have already dealt in passing with at least part of the argument that a public interest defence is unnecessary, but for the sake of completeness it is also worth confronting this argument directly. The claim that the defence is unnecessary has two strands. First, it is argued that the permitted acts taken together with general legal and equitable principles are sufficient to protect the interests that would be safeguarded by a public interest defence. Alternatively, it is argued that, at the very least, Parliament must have regarded the permitted acts as sufficient (and it is not for the courts to interfere with this assessment).

---

[106] [1999] RPC 655, 671.
[107] H. Laddie, 'Copyright: Over-Strength, Over-Regulated, Over-Rated?' [1996] EIPR 253, 258. See Chapter 9 for a detailed discussion of whether the United Kingdom should introduce a fair use defence.

The first argument, that the statutory permitted acts are sufficient to protect the public interest, has been buttressed by using the facts of *Lion Laboratories* v. *Evans* as an example. Laddie et al. argue that the defendants in that case might 'readily' have published extracts from the reports that indicated that the breathalyser was faulty if they had thought to rely on the fair dealing provisions.[108] Similarly, in *Yelland* Mance LJ used the fact that the fair dealing provisions were not discussed to throw doubt on whether *Lion Laboratories* was rightly decided.[109] Dealing first with the illustration, it is far from clear that the defendants in *Lion Laboratories* could have relied on a fair dealing defence at the time the case was decided, and today it is even less likely. Whilst there was undoubtedly criticism of the plaintiff's behaviour in that case, it is unlikely that there was any criticism or review of a work, although this is not entirely clear from the decision.[110] It is rather more likely that the defendants could have persuaded the Court that the use was for the purpose of reporting current events, but it is by no means certain that this argument would have been accepted. Most importantly, however, the documents in the *Lion Laboratories* case were unpublished. As was seen in the previous chapter, the fair dealing provisions have long had a very limited application as regards unpublished works, and implementation of the Information Society Directive has further restricted the availability of the fair dealing defences as regards unpublished material.

As to the general claim of sufficiency, we have demonstrated in this chapter that there is no other mechanism which is adequate to safeguard the interests that would be protected by a public interest defence. More generally, our primary aim in this first section of the book is to demonstrate that the United Kingdom's existing approach to the permitted acts creates serious difficulties for users in cases where there is little risk of harm to the economic and personal interests that copyright is intended to protect. That is not to say that a public interest defence would be able to remedy all of the difficulties with the existing provisions that we identify, but it would at least introduce some limited additional flexibility.

The alternative suggestion, that at the very least Parliament must have considered the express exceptions to be sufficient to protect the public interest, goes directly to parliamentary intention. As has already been suggested, and as is explained further in Chapter 8, far from believing that the statutory permitted acts would always be sufficient to protect

---

[108] Laddie et al., 2nd edn, para. 2.151. [109] *Hyde Park* v. *Yelland* [2001] 1 Ch 143, 172.
[110] Copyright Act 1956, s. 6(2), and see Chapter 2 for a detailed discussion of this requirement and the problems it creates.

the public interest, Parliament made specific provision to ensure that a separate public interest defence would be available, whilst leaving it to the courts to delineate the precise contours of this defence.

Is a public interest defence workable?

In addition to the three sets of objections to a public interest defence considered above, there seems to be a fourth, less frequently articulated objection, namely, that such a defence would be unworkable. In part this objection is tied up with concerns about the appropriateness of allowing judges to decide where the public interest lies. However, there is also a wider point here, which is simply that such a defence would be too unpredictable. That is, even if we can trust judges to arrive at the right result in any given case, the overall effect of such a defence would be to make the law uncertain. From this perspective, abandoning the relative certainty of the statutory permitted acts is a high price to pay for the flexibility of a common law defence.

On one level this objection is difficult to answer, because if it is to be useful a public interest defence has to retain a considerable degree of flexibility. However, it is important not to overemphasise the level of certainty that has to be sacrificed in order to achieve this flexibility. One of our concerns is to demonstrate that the operation of the permitted acts is often unpredictable and, more generally, we would argue that there is considerable force in the Realist critique that the added certainty provided by legislation is often chimerical. Moreover, whilst the circumstances in which a public interest defence ought to be available are not capable of precise definition, it was seen at the start of this chapter that it is possible to identify principles which can act as a useful guide when deciding whether the defence should apply.

Conclusion

Building on the problems with the permitted acts that we identified in the last chapter, we have focused here on a defence which, if fully reinstated, could provide a limited but important degree of additional flexibility. The reintroduction of a broad form of public interest defence is, however, only a small part of the solution we advocate. Given that we also call for statutory reform, it could be objected that our call for the judiciary to reinstate the defence is unnecessary, since the same result could be achieved as part of the legislative process. Whilst a legislative solution is a possibility (and one we would advocate should the House of Lords fail to act appropriately when a suitable case comes before it), a judicial solution is preferable, because even achieving the relatively modest reforms we advocate is likely to prove extremely difficult and we are conscious of the need to focus on practical ways of achieving the outcomes for which we argue. In addition, as will become clear from later chapters, one of our aims is to challenge judicial attitudes towards the exceptions. One way in which attitudes can be changed is by challenging the courts directly to reintroduce a defence that Parliament attempted to preserve.

4 Exceptions applying to education, research and private study

In this chapter and the next we focus on the exceptions that apply to institutional users of copyright such as schools, universities, libraries, archives, museums and galleries. Our principal focus in this chapter is on the exceptions that apply to educational establishments, but we also consider as a preliminary matter the fair dealing exception that allows use of a work for the purposes of research or private study.

The impact of copyright law on educational establishments has become highly controversial over recent years. On the one side, copyright owners have become more militant, concerned to protect their rights in the face of what they see as blatant and widespread unauthorised copying, and motivated by technological advances which they believe may drive them out of business. Publishers have also long emphasised that the works that are most frequently copied in educational establishments are works made for the educational market and consequently that broad educational copying exceptions would result in a decrease in the supply of those works that educational establishments find most useful. On the other side, educational establishments want to be able take advantage of the ease with which copies of works can now be made and have to respond to the changing expectations of students and to government pressure to take advantage of new technologies. Moreover, in higher education in particular, class sizes have grown considerably since the 1980s, with classes containing hundreds of students now the norm. Without the ability to distribute copies of works to students, pressure on library resources becomes intolerable, particularly since library budgets have often been cut over recent years. Within higher education there is also frustration at the fact that much of the material that is being copied has been produced by academics. In some cases this means that universities are being forced to pay for the copying of material produced by their employees. More generally, there is a widespread sense that most academics would be happy to have their work distributed free of charge, but that they are often forced to assign their copyright to publishers. This has led to interest in other ways in which academic work might be circulated, but moves towards an 'open source' model are hindered by the perception that it is still material published through traditional channels that counts most for promotion and research assessment purposes.

Implicit in what was said in the previous paragraph, it is the issue of 'classroom copying', that is, the distribution of copies of articles and extracts from other works to groups of students, that lies at the heart of recent controversies. The costs attached to classroom copying are clearly of crucial importance, but it should also be recognised that there is a danger of this question overshadowing all the other issues that arise in relation to the educational exceptions. Consequently, when looking at the education exceptions, we begin by looking at the exceptions that apply to other types of use within educational establishments, demonstrating that these provisions are unnecessarily restrictive. We then turn to consider the provisions relating to classroom copying and the associated licensing schemes. Although we are encouraged by moves towards an 'open source' model for the distribution of research and would like to see both the removal of the obstacles that prevent such a model from being more attractive to academic authors and moves towards distributing other types of work in this way, in the short to medium term at least we are prepared to accept that classroom copying ought not to be covered by an outright exception. There are, however, problems with the existing system of licensing for educational use. For example, it is often difficult for users to find out (or at least to find out quickly) what can and cannot be done legitimately under the current arrangements. In order to illustrate some of the problems that arise and to give a better sense of how the current arrangements operate in practice we consider as a case study the recent dispute between the Copyright Licensing Agency and higher education institutions.

Underpinning our analysis is, on the one hand, a firm belief in the value of education both for economic growth and in broader social terms. We are confident that universities, for example, play a distinctive and valuable role in modern societies, whilst recognising the need to be cautious about some of the more exaggerated claims that are made for their special status.[1] On the other hand, we also believe that a healthy education system is itself dependent on the flourishing of educational writing and publishing, and that in the absence of the proven effectiveness of a new means

---

[1] See A. Monotti and S. Ricketson, *Universities and Intellectual Property: Ownership and Exploitation* (Oxford: Oxford University Press, 2003), ch. 2, demonstrating that the role of the university has evolved continuously and that some of the claims that are made for the unique role of universities do not stand up to serious scrutiny, whilst maintaining that universities are still in some respects 'special'.

of distributing educational works, proposals to extend dramatically the education exceptions need to be approached with caution.

Fair dealing for the purposes of research or private study

Overview

In this section we examine the provision that allows for fair dealing with a work for the purposes of research and private study, found in section 29 of the 1988 Act. This section is dealt with here because, in practice, its operation is closely intertwined with the activities of institutional users of copyright. For example, it will be seen in the next chapter that the Act contains various provisions allowing librarians and archivists to make copies on behalf of readers. However, these provisions do not apply in cases where readers make copies for themselves using a self-service photocopier or a handheld scanner. In these cases the question of whether or not copyright has been infringed will be determined primarily by reference to the research and private study exception. More generally, it is the research and private study exception that protects academics who copy works in order to further their research and students who collect material in the course of preparing to write an essay or sit an examination. Consequently, the research and private study exception is highly important for educational establishments, libraries, and so on. Unfortunately, however, the current provision also suffers from a number of serious defects and its scope has been limited still further as a result of the way in which the Information Society Directive has been implemented. The government insisted that the introduction of these further restrictions was required by the Directive, but in the final chapter we demonstrate that there are other ways to implement the Directive that would, for example, retain some types of copying for commercial research within the scope of the exception.

Scope of the exception

For present purposes the key parts of section 29 of the 1988 Act, as amended, provide as follows:

(1) Fair dealing with a literary, dramatic, musical or artistic work for the purposes of research for a non-commercial purpose does not infringe any copyright in the work provided that it is accompanied by a sufficient acknowledgement.
(1B) No acknowledgement is required in connection with fair dealing for the purposes mentioned in subsection (1) where this would be impossible for reasons of practicality or otherwise.

(1C) Fair dealing with a literary, dramatic, musical or artistic work for the purposes of private study does not infringe any copyright in the work.
(2) Fair dealing with the typographical arrangement of a published edition for the purposes of research or private study does not infringe any copyright in the arrangement.
(3) Copying by a person other than the researcher or student himself is not fair dealing if –

...

> (b) in any other case, the person doing the copying knows or has reason to believe that it will result in copies of substantially the same material being provided to more than one person at substantially the same time and for substantially the same purpose.

In order to determine whether this section applies it is therefore necessary to ask four questions similar to those examined in Chapter 2 that apply to the other fair dealing provisions,[2] namely: (1) Does the exception apply to the work in question? (2) Is the use for one of the approved purposes? (3) Has there been a sufficient acknowledgement? (4) Is the use fair?

One of the most serious problems with the research and private study exception is that section 29 only applies to a narrow range of copyright subject matter, that is, to literary, dramatic, musical and artistic works and to the typographical arrangements of published editions.[3] This is now entirely unsatisfactory and fails to reflect the importance of non-authorial works for both study and research. It can also lead to some counterintuitive results. For example, a researcher who copied a substantial part of a sound recording for the purpose of private study would infringe copyright in the recording itself, but not in any underlying musical work. It is difficult to see why the rights of the owner of copyright in the sound recording ought to be given greater protection in such a case.

There is little UK authority as to the meaning of 'research' and 'private study', but it has been held in other Commonwealth jurisdictions that both terms are to be given their ordinary dictionary definitions.[4] Thus it has been said that 'research' means the 'diligent and systematic inquiry or investigation into a subject in order to discover facts or principles', and 'study' has been held to include 'the application of the mind

---

[2] That is, fair dealing for the purposes of criticism, review and the reporting of current events.
[3] CDPA 1988, ss. 29(1), (1C), (2). It might also be noted that computer programs are now largely excluded from the scope of the research and private study exception (despite being treated by the Act as a form of literary work), but copying a computer program for the purposes of research or study may fall instead within s. 50B (decompilation of computer programs) or the new s. 50BA (observing, studying and testing computer programs).
[4] *De Garis v. Neville Jeffress Pidler* (1990) 18 IPR 292 (Federal Court of Australia).

to the acquisition of knowledge, as by reading, investigation or reflection'.[5] More recently, the Canadian Supreme Court has emphasised that '"Research" must be given a large and liberal interpretation in order to ensure that users' rights are not unduly constrained . . . Lawyers carrying on the business of law for profit are conducting research.'[6] Whilst these cases are likely to be treated as providing useful guidance, the statement of the Canadian Supreme Court must be read with caution because the research exception is now (following implementation of the Information Society Directive) expressly confined to 'non-commercial' research, a point to which we return below. Leaving this point aside for now, however, it seems to us that it is not so much the definitions of 'research' and 'private study' that are likely to cause problems, but more that the Act makes no allowance for the reuse of material in a subsequent research paper, essay or thesis.

Copying for the purposes of research or study can be divided into two stages. During the early stages of writing an article, conference paper, essay or thesis, any copying that is done usually consists of obtaining extracts of earlier published and unpublished works. Such copies are made for a variety of reasons – to allow reading to be done at the researcher's convenience, because material is held in a distant library or archive to which the researcher has to travel and does not have time to read all potentially relevant material on site, and sometimes because the researcher has not finally decided what questions she is asking and thus may need to review the material several times. A second type of copying occurs when the researcher's results are presented, for example, in an essay, thesis, published paper or book and the researcher wishes to make reference to source material. On a casual reading it might well be thought that fair dealing for 'the purposes of research' would extend to protect this second type of use. However, section 29(3)(b) of the Act provides that 'copying by a person other than the researcher or student himself is not fair dealing if . . . the person doing the copying knows or has reason to believe that it will result in copies of substantially the same material being provided to more than one person at substantially the same time and for substantially the same purpose'. It seems that this was intended to ensure that the research and private study exception could not be used to justify classroom copying, but its effect is to prevent entirely any reliance

---

[5] *Ibid.*, 298–9. *De Garis* was referred to approvingly in *Television New Zealand* v. *Newsmonitor Services* [1994] 2 NZLR 91, 105 (High Court of New Zealand). The judge in that case, Blanchard J, also added, however, that 'research involves the study of things, including written materials or those captured in electronic form' (at 105). Similarly, see *Copyright Licensing* v. *University of Auckland* (2002) 53 IPR 618, 629.

[6] *CCH Canadian* v. *Law Society of Upper Canada* [2004] SCC 13, para. 51.

on the research exception to justify the inclusion of a substantial part of an earlier work in a published research paper, etc.

The way in which section 29(3)(b) is worded also leads to a range of arbitrary distinctions. For example, an academic who personally makes a number of copies of a research paper she has written, which includes substantial quotes from earlier works, and who distributes these at a conference might still fall within the aegis of the research exception. In contrast, the research exception could not apply if she e-mails the paper to the conference organiser and that person makes the copies. In response to such problems it might be objected that the research and private study exception should be treated as entirely irrelevant in such cases because such use falls within fair dealing for the purpose of criticism or review. However, as we explain in the final chapter, there might be circumstances in which a right to reuse extracts for research purposes would provide protection above and beyond that afforded by the criticism and review provision. Moreover, if the research exception is to be read as applying only to the first stage of research, that is, to the collection of materials stage, then the requirement of sufficient acknowledgement is anomalous.[7] This is because the only person to see the copied extracts is likely to be the researcher herself. Nor is it entirely clear how such a requirement will operate – presumably the researcher would be given a reasonable period of time between making the copy and adding the relevant information to the copy by hand if the pages reproduced do not happen to contain the relevant information. Most fundamentally, however, if the research exception is to be read as applying only to the first stage of research, it is unclear how much it adds to the private study exception, and yet the Act draws a distinction between them – there is no requirement of sufficient acknowledgement if the copy is made for the purposes of private study.

The most important case to deal with the requirement of fairness as it applies to the research and private study exception is the recent Canadian Supreme Court case *CCH Canadian v. Law Society of Upper Canada*.[8] The Court indicated that many of the factors to be taken into account are similar to those used to determine whether a taking is fair for the purposes of the criticism, review and news reporting exceptions. Thus attention will be paid to how much material has been copied, the effect of the dealing on the market for the work, whether the defendant's purpose could have been achieved by other means, and the nature of the work copied.[9] The Supreme Court also indicated, however, that in relation

---

[7] That is, an acknowledgement identifying the work in question by its title or other description and identifying the author unless it is published anonymously: CDPA 1988, s. 178.
[8] [2004] SCC 13.   [9] *Ibid.*, paras. 53–60.

to the research and private study exceptions, a further relevant factor is what happens to a copy after it has been made. In particular, if the copy is subsequently destroyed this will aid a finding that the taking was fair.[10] By and large these factors seem sensible, but again, as with the criticism, review and news reporting exceptions, a problem with the test of fairness is that it fails to provide potential defendants with any certainty as to the amount that can safely be copied. This causes real problems for institutional users.

Implications for institutional users

A longstanding problem for institutional users, particularly libraries, is that it is very difficult for them to know how much a student or researcher is entitled to copy when relying on the fair dealing exception. This problem has been exacerbated by the newly added complication of having to identify those researchers whose work is of a commercial nature, commercial research now falling outside the research and private study exceptions.[11] The question of how much students and researchers are entitled to copy is important to institutional users because of concern that if students or researchers copy beyond that which is 'fair', institutions may be held liable for authorising copyright infringement. The Australian case *Moorhouse* v. *University of New South Wales*[12] has long been representative of these concerns – in that case an Australian university was held liable for authorising copyright infringement through its provision of self-service photocopiers, despite having posted copyright warning notices next to the machines. There has long been room for argument about whether a UK court would reach a similar decision,[13] and the recent decision of the Canadian Supreme Court in the *CCH* case[14] has probably made it much less likely that *Moorhouse* would be followed. Nevertheless, in the absence of clear authority to this effect, institutions are likely to continue to be

---

[10] *Ibid.*, para. 55.
[11] The latter point is not immediately obvious from s. 29, but is made clear by s. 178, which defines private study so as to exclude 'any study which is directly or indirectly for a commercial purpose'. Cf. *Television New Zealand* v. *Newsmonitor Services*, 106: 'I am inclined to think that a corporation can engage in private study, as when its personnel endeavour to place themselves in a position to be better able to perform their functions in or related to the corporation' (per Blanchard J).
[12] (1975) 13 CLR 1.
[13] In particular, in *CBS Songs* v. *Amstrad* [1988] RPC 567, the House of Lords appeared to take a very different approach to the question of authorisation. But cf. Laddie et al., 3rd edn, para. 33.18, taking the view that despite *Amstrad* 'it is thought that UK courts would reach a similar conclusion to that in *Moorhouse*'.
[14] See *CCH Canadian* v. *Law Society of Upper Canada*, in particular para. 41, describing *Moorhouse* as 'inconsistent with previous Canadian and British approaches'.

cautious in controlling what researchers and students copy, in some cases excessively so.[15] Uncertainty over how much students and researchers can copy also undermines institutional users in licensing negotiations, since they have no clear sense of the initial entitlement, such that they may be persuaded to take out a licence that gives little or nothing beyond what the statute allows.

The education exceptions: overview

Having looked at the research and private study exception and how it relates to the activities of institutional users of copyright, we now turn to look at the education exceptions contained in sections 32–36A of the 1988 Act. These are:
  (i) things done for the purposes of instruction or examination (s. 32);
  (ii) anthologies for educational use (s. 33);
  (iii) performing, playing or showing a work in the course of the activities of an educational establishment (s. 34);
  (iv) recording by educational establishments of broadcasts (s. 35);
  (v) reprographic copying by educational establishments of passages from published works (s. 36); and
  (vi) lending of copies by educational establishments (s. 36A).

With one exception (s. 32) the education provisions of the 1988 Act only apply to 'educational establishments'. In contrast to the narrowness of many of the exceptions, the term 'educational establishment' is itself widely drawn and thus the Act starts from a wide base of inclusion. 'Educational establishment' is defined as including any school, university, university college, institution providing further education, college of education or theological college.[16] In addition, home teachers employed by a local authority to cater for the needs of pupils who cannot attend school can also rely on these provisions.[17]

Things done for the purposes of instruction or examination

Section 32 of the 1988 Act deals with two quite different issues, namely, copying for the purpose of instruction and copying for the purpose of

---

[15] As experienced by the authors when, in conducting research for this book, one of them was prevented from copying on a self-service photocopier in the British Library a twelve-page chapter from a Canadian government report of just over 100 pages. The report in question advocated the introduction of a more liberal system of exceptions, an irony apparently lost on the member of staff concerned.

[16] CDPA 1988, s. 174; Copyright (Educational Establishments) (No 2) Order 1989 (SI 1989 No 1068).

[17] See the Copyright (Application of Provisions relating to Educational Establishments to Teachers) (No 2) Order 1989 (SI 1989 No 1067).

examination. These will be dealt with in turn, but as an introductory point it is important to note that implementation of the Information Society Directive has led to section 32 being amended in a number of important (and unsatisfactory) respects.

Copying for the purpose of instruction

It has already been noted that, unlike the other education exceptions, section 32 is not confined in its application to education establishments and thus the provisions allowing for copying in the course of instruction apply broadly and would extend, for example, to training courses run within any organisation. However, implementation of the Information Society Directive has led to a distinction being drawn between instruction for a commercial purpose and instruction for a non-commercial purpose. The effect of this distinction is that instruction for a non-commercial purpose gets the benefit of a more generous exception.

In cases where the instruction is for a *non-commercial* purpose section 32(1) of the Act applies. That section provides that copyright in a literary, dramatic, musical or artistic work is not infringed by its being copied in the course of instruction or of preparation for instruction provided certain conditions are satisfied, namely: (1) that the copying is done by a person giving or receiving instruction; (2) that it is not done by means of a reprographic process; and (3) that it is accompanied by a sufficient acknowledgement. One key characteristic of this section is that there is no quantitative restriction on the amount of material that can be copied under this section, and thus it would allow a teacher to copy the whole of a poem on to a whiteboard and pupils in the class to copy the entire poem into their notes.

In contrast, where the instruction is for a *commercial* purpose section 32(2A) applies. That section provides that copyright in a literary, dramatic, musical or artistic work is not infringed by its being copied in the course of instruction or of preparation for instruction provided that the work (1) has been made available to the public;[18] (2) amounts to a fair dealing; (3) is done by a person giving or receiving instruction; (4) is not done by means of a reprographic process; and (5) is accompanied by a sufficient acknowledgement. Thus the two key differences between this

---

[18] A work will have been made available to the public if it has been made available by any means, including by the issue of copies to the public, by making the work available by means of an electronic retrieval system, by the rental or lending of copies of the work to the public, by the performance, exhibition, playing or showing of the work in public, or by the communication to the public of the work. But in determining whether a work has been made available to the public no account shall be taken of any unauthorised act: CDPA 1988, ss. 32(2B), 30(1A).

exception and the exception described in the previous paragraph are that this provision only applies to published works and contains a restriction on the amount of material that can be copied (by virtue of the fact that the taking has to be 'fair').

Given the distinction drawn in section 32 between commercial and non-commercial instruction it is frustrating that clearer guidance has not been provided as to when instruction is to be treated as being for a commercial purpose. Without such guidance it would seem arguable that independent schools and universities can only rely on the narrower exception. However, it is our view that 'commercial use' should be given a restricted interpretation in this context, and it is notable that the British Library and the Copyright Licensing Agency seem agreed upon such an interpretation.[19]

In addition, it is important to appreciate that the proviso that the copying must not be done by means of a reprographic process curtails severely the usefulness of the above exceptions. By disallowing the use of reprographic copying techniques, the Act makes it clear that this section cannot be used to distribute photocopied extracts of works to students. However, the Act defines reprographic process broadly, as including copying 'involving the use of an appliance for making multiple copies' and, in the case of works in 'electronic form', copying by electronic means.[20] This definition means that it is not possible to rely on section 32 to photocopy material onto an acetate for use on an overhead projector (since this involves the use of an appliance for making multiple copies) nor to cut and paste material onto a PowerPoint slide (copying by electronic means). Thus in relation to literary, dramatic, musical and artistic works the Act only provides protection for old-fashioned teaching methods.[21]

The elements of section 32 considered thus far only apply in relation to literary, dramatic, musical and artistic works. However, if the instruction is for a *non-commercial* purpose and the work in question is a sound recording, film or broadcast, then copying may be permissible under 32(2), provided that (1) the copying results in the making of a film or film soundtrack; (2) the copying is done in the course of instruction or of the preparation for instruction in the making of films or film soundtracks; (3) the copying is done by the person giving or receiving instruction; (4) it is accompanied by a sufficient acknowledgement. This

---

[19] See the Joint Note from the British Library and the Copyright Licensing Agency, 'Changes to UK Copyright Law', available at www.cla.co.uk/directive/BL-CLA-FAQ.doc, setting out a range of hypothetical scenarios.
[20] CDPA 1988, s. 178.
[21] See also Chapter 8, where we return to the legislative history of this provision.

provision is important for burgeoning media studies courses, but this provision is, as usual, limited in its application and will cause problems for students who wish to send copies of their work to potential employers (as is common practice) (such copies not being made 'in the course of instruction').

Copying for the purpose of examination

Section 32 also provides that copyright is not infringed by anything done for the purposes of an examination by way of setting the questions, communicating the questions to the candidates or answering the questions.[22] It is therefore permissible by virtue of this section to set out substantial parts of a copyright work (including whole poems, maps and photographs) on an examination paper for the candidate to comment on, translate, and so on. This section also means that a translation produced by a candidate will not infringe and, more generally, allows candidates to reproduce substantial sections of a work by way of answer (despite the likely undesirability of this in the eyes of the examiner). This section would also allow long passages of a work to be read aloud by a teacher in examinations designed to test aural comprehension.[23] It is not, however, possible to photocopy sheet music for candidates taking music exams by virtue of this provision.[24] This reflects the fact that this sector of the publishing industry is in a precarious position.[25] A further restriction on the scope of this provision must also be noted. Following implementation of the Information Society Directive, this provision only applies if the questions are accompanied by a sufficient acknowledgement. The problem with such a requirement is that it prevents examiners from testing whether candidates are able to identify the source of a quote. There is a safeguard in section 32(3A), but this is unlikely to provide much assistance, since this section only states that no acknowledgement is required where this would be 'impossible for reasons of practicality or otherwise'. It is highly unlikely that inconsistency with pedagogical aims would be sufficient to bring a case within the category of when it would be 'impossible' to provide an acknowledgement.

---

[22] CDPA 1988, s. 33(3).
[23] Although such use might in any event not infringe on the basis that there would be no public performance of the work and might also be covered by s. 34 (considered below) or s. 59 (the reading or recitation in public by one person of a reasonable extract from a published literary or dramatic work does not infringe any copyright in the work if it is accompanied by a sufficient acknowledgement).
[24] CDPA 1988, s. 32(4).
[25] J. Gurnsey, *Copyright Theft* (Aldershot: Aslib Gower, 1995), pp. 19–20.

Anthologies for educational use

The anthologies for educational use exception contained in section 33 of the 1988 Act has antecedents going back to 1911,[26] but the current provision is hedged around with so many limitations that it is difficult to imagine anyone seeking to rely on it. Section 33 allows the inclusion of a 'short passage' from a published literary or dramatic work in a collection which is intended for use in educational establishments. The exception does not apply to other classes of copyright work and thus is inappropriate for many items, such as photographs, video clips and sound recordings, which might be used in a multimedia work. Moreover, in order to fall within section 33 four conditions must be satisfied. First, the collection must be described as being for use in educational establishments both in its title and in any advertisements issued by or on behalf of the publisher. Second, it must consist 'mainly of material in which no copyright subsists', thus ruling out collections of passages of modern works, for these will be protected by copyright. Third, the work from which the passage is taken must itself not be intended for use in an educational establishment, ruling out many publications by academics. Finally, the inclusion must be accompanied by sufficient acknowledgement.[27] Even if these conditions are satisfied, no more than two excerpts from copyright works by the same author (either alone or in collaboration with others) may be published in collections by the same publisher over any period of five years.[28] The utility of this section is limited still further by the uncertainty surrounding what is meant by the term 'short passage' (what is 'short' but more than 'substantial' having yet to be determined) and by the term 'mainly' as used in relation to the requirement that the anthology must consist 'mainly of material in which no copyright subsists'. In many respects section 33 is a historical aberration that fails to protect the interests of educational establishments or educational publishers. It seems likely that its abolition would cause little hardship.

Performing, playing and showing works in educational establishments

The general rule is that only the owner of a work protected by copyright, such as a poem, a play or a piece of music, has the right to perform it in public. However, section 34 of the Act provides that the performance of a literary, dramatic or musical work in an educational establishment before

---

[26] See Copyright Act 1911, s. 2(1)(iv).
[27] CDPA 1988, ss. 33(1).   [28] *Ibid.*, ss. 33(2), 32(3).

an audience consisting of teachers, pupils and other persons directly connected with the activities of the establishment (a category that is expressly declared not to include parents[29]) by a teacher or pupil, or by any other person for the purposes of instruction, is not a public performance for the purposes of infringement of copyright.[30] In addition, the Act provides that the playing or showing of a sound recording, film or broadcast in an educational establishment before an audience of teachers and pupils is not a playing or showing of the work in public for the purposes of infringement of copyright.[31] This latter provision is particularly important, given that most educational establishments now make extensive use of video material, for example on topics in the news. This is encouraged by modern teaching methods, since it can help keep student attention and is sometimes a more efficient way of imparting information. It must be emphasised, however, that this section does not allow a recording to be made of a broadcast before it is shown. Such copying is covered by section 35 of the 1988 Act (considered below). Another feature of this section that is worthy of note is that it takes effect by limiting the scope of the right to control public performance of a work, rather than by providing a defence to an action for infringement. It seems that this reverses the burden of proof[32] and may have other unforeseen consequences. For example, it could well be held that a term in an agreement for the purchase of a copy of a film or a sound recording that purported to exclude 'exceptions' or 'defences' would be insufficient to cover section 34. The exclusion of parents from the category of those who are to be treated as persons directly connected with the activities of the establishment is also worthy of comment. This substantially reduces the importance of section 34 for schools, at least as regards performances of literary, dramatic and musical works. More generally, the exclusion of parents is indicative of the grudging attitude that has been taken towards the provision of copyright exceptions in the United Kingdom. At the time of the passage of the 1988 Act the government insisted that this limitation was necessary in order to comply with the Berne Convention. It was said that this was because Berne does not allow for the provision of exceptions in relation to the public performance right.[33] However, this argument does not support the government's conclusion[34] and is difficult to square with the

---

[29] *Ibid.*, s. 34(3).   [30] *Ibid.*, s. 34(1).   [31] *Ibid.*, s. 34(2).
[32] *Copinger*, para. 9.34.   [33] *Hansard*, HL vol. 493, col. 1167.
[34] Having concluded that Berne leaves member states with discretion to limit the definition of 'public' performance, it seems reasonable to suppose that this discretion would extend to allowing a performance in front of pupils, teachers and parents. It must also be remembered that in the pre-TRIPS era member states had extensive freedom and there is an excellent case to be made that a provision that extended to parents would in any event be compatible with TRIPS.

half-hearted approach that was taken to complying with Berne standards in other areas.[35]

Lending of copies by educational establishments

Implementation of the Rental Right Directive resulted in an extension[36] of the right to control rental[37] and the introduction of a new public lending right.[38] However, Article 5(3) of the Rental Right Directive gives member states the power to exempt from the lending right entirely certain categories of establishment. In reliance on Article 5(3) the government introduced section 36A of the 1988 Act, which, in full, states, 'Copyright in a work is not infringed by the lending of copies of the work by an educational establishment.' This is clearly an important provision – without its introduction the lending right would have had serious implications for the library budgets of education establishments. In some respects it is also a surprisingly broad exception, in that the class of persons to whom a library of an educational establishment can lend is not limited in any way. Thus a university library that extends borrowing privileges to alumni or which allows members of the public full library privileges on payment of a fee (for example, a law library that has a scheme for allowing legal practitioners to use library facilities) would, it seems, still fall within section 36A. However, it will be seen in Chapter 5 that this is largely explained by the somewhat unusual nature of the public lending right.

The licensing provisions

Having looked at various miscellaneous provisions that apply to educational establishments, we now turn to consider two provisions that only take effect if copyright owners have failed to make licences available on reasonable terms. These exceptions are thus quite different from the other provisions we have examined. The intention is not that these exceptions will ever be relied on, but rather that owners will be forced to

---

[35] For example, as regards moral rights.
[36] Prior to implementation of the Directive, under UK law the rental right only applied to films, sound recordings and computer programs.
[37] That is, the right to control making a work available on terms that it will or may be returned, for direct or indirect economic or commercial advantage: CDPA 1988, s. 18A(2).
[38] That is, the right to control making a work available on terms that it will or may be returned, otherwise than for direct or indirect economic or commercial advantage through an establishment which is accessible to the public: CDPA 1988, s. 18A(2).

make licences available. The Secretary of State is then given certain powers as regards such licences and the Copyright Tribunal has the power to review their terms, should, for example, educational establishments remain dissatisfied. These exceptions should thus be seen as part of a broader framework for regulating copyright licensing in the educational sector and, more generally, alongside the extensive powers that have been given to the Copyright Tribunal to regulate certain copyright licences and licensing schemes.[39]

We begin our analysis by looking at section 35, which applies to the recording of broadcasts by educational establishments, and then turn to consider section 36, which applies to reprographic copying by educational establishments. In both cases we try to provide a sense of how these provisions relate to the licensing arrangements that have been put in place and the broader framework of controls, but in order to provide a fuller picture of these issues we conclude this chapter by examining as a case study the recent dispute between the Copyright Licensing Agency and higher education institutions.

Recording of broadcasts by educational establishments

Section 35 of the 1988 Act provides that a recording of a broadcast may be made by or on behalf of an educational establishment for non-commercial educational purposes without infringing copyright in the broadcast or in any underlying work, provided that there is a sufficient acknowledgement of the broadcast.[40] The Act further provides that copyright will not be infringed by the communication to the public of such a recording by a person situated within the premises of an educational establishment provided that the communication cannot be received by any person situated outside the premises of that establishment.[41] However, as has already been seen, section 35 would only apply in the absence of a certified licensing scheme. 'Certified' in this context means certified by the Secretary of State under section 143 of the Act. This section provides that a licensing

---

[39] See, generally, *Copinger*, ch. 29.   [40] CDPA 1988, s. 35(1).
[41] *Ibid.*, s. 35(1A). This latter provision should be seen alongside s. 34(2) of the Act (discussed above) which excludes from the right to control public performance the playing or showing of a sound recording, film or broadcast in an educational establishment. Section 35(1A) is intended to allow internal electronic communication within educational establishments: 'Implementation of the Copyright Directive (2001/29/EC) and Related Matters – Transposition Note', available at www.patent.gov.uk/copy/notices/2003/copy_direct3a.htm. There are, however, some curious and potentially significant differences between the new provision and s. 34(2), in particular, as regards the permissible composition of the audience.

scheme may be certified if the Secretary of State is satisfied that it enables the works to which it applies to be identified with sufficient certainty and if it sets out clearly the terms on which licences will be granted, including terms as to payment.[42] Moreover, and again as has already been noted, even if there is a certified licensing scheme in operation, it may still be referred to the Copyright Tribunal, in particular, if an educational establishment should feel that the proposed terms are unreasonable. The Educational Recording Agency Ltd runs the principal scheme in operation at present,[43] with a separate scheme applying to programmes made by the Open University.[44]

Reprographic copying by educational establishments

Section 36 of the 1988 Act covers reprographic copying by educational establishments. It has already been seen that this section does not apply if licences are available authorising the copying in question.[45] In practice, licences to cover reprographic copying are administered by the Copyright Licensing Agency Ltd (CLA), which enters into agreements with colleges, schools and universities (and representative bodies for such institutions). We shall return to licensing arrangements shortly. It should first be noted, however, that section 36 of the Act allows reprographic copying of up to 1 per cent of any published, literary, dramatic or musical work where the copy is made by or on behalf of an educational establishment for the purposes of non-commercial instruction and it is accompanied by a sufficient acknowledgement.[46] Copying in accordance with this section will not infringe copyright in the work itself or in the typographical arrangement.[47] An entitlement to copy 1 per cent of a work does not, even without further restriction, seem very generous, particularly given that this provision is only designed to strengthen the hand of educational establishments and to prevent bargaining breakdown. But in any event it should be noted that the entitlement to copy 1 per cent of a work applies not to any single act of copying, but rather to the activities of

---

[42] CDPA 1988, s. 143(2).
[43] See the Copyright (Certification of Licensing Scheme for Educational Recording of Broadcasts and Cable Programmes) (Educational Recording Agency Limited) Order 1990 (SI 1990 No 879) (as amended by orders in 1992, 1993, 1994, 1996, 1998 and 1999 and by the 2003 Copyright and Related Rights Regulations).
[44] Copyright (Certification of Licensing Scheme for Educational Recording of Broadcasts) (Open University) Order 2003 (SI 2003 No 187) (as amended by the 2003 Copyright and Related Rights Regulations).
[45] CDPA 1988, s. 36(3).
[46] But no acknowledgement is required where this would be 'impossible for reasons of practicality or otherwise': CDPA 1988, s. 36(1A).
[47] CDPA 1988, s. 36(1B).

an entire educational establishment in any one quarter, that is, in any period 1 January to 31 March, 1 April to 30 June, and so on. Thus, if forced to rely on this provision, a college of further education, for example, would find that it could not copy more than 1 per cent of a work in the course of a term, even though the English department and the drama department might require part of the same work. Monitoring compliance with section 36 would also impose significant administrative costs on an institution. It must therefore be doubted whether section 36 achieves its aim of ensuring that publishers have an incentive to enter into licensing arrangements.

As a practical matter it is worth noting that some US publishers, for example, do not fall within the CLA scheme. In such cases the statutory scheme applies, but this is so limited that educational establishments will almost certainly have to contact the publisher directly – a slow and time-consuming process, and there is anecdotal evidence to suggest that written requests for a licence from such publishers are not infrequently ignored. It should also be noted, that unlike licensing schemes under section 35, there is no requirement that the Secretary of State approve licences before the statutory scheme is displaced. Instead section 36(3) provides that licences cannot be less favourable than the statutory scheme. Since it is difficult to imagine such a licence ever being offered, this provides little additional security for educational establishments and in practice, of course, licences covering photocopying in educational establishment are more favourable than the statutory regime as regards the amount of material that can be copied. The Secretary of State does, however, have the power under section 137 of the Act to extend the coverage of educational reprographic licences and licensing schemes so as to include works of a description similar to those already covered.[48] In addition, and most importantly from the perspective of educational establishments, licences and licensing schemes operated by licensing bodies such as the CLA can be referred to the Copyright Tribunal. The licence covering photocopying for teaching purposes in higher education has recently been the subject of review by the Copyright Tribunal following a dispute over the reasonableness of the terms of the current licence, attempts to exclude certain subject matter from its ambit, and in the light of stalled negotiations for a successor licence. This is discussed further below.

---

[48] The Secretary of State may only exercise this power in cases where works have been unreasonably excluded from the scope of the licensing scheme and only if including them within the scheme would not conflict with the normal exploitation of the works or unreasonably prejudice the legitimate interests of the copyright owners. See also ss. 138–140 of the 1988 Act for the Secretary of State's powers to vary or discharge an order, and to order inquiries.

Case study: copyright licensing in higher education

Background

It has been seen that copyright licensing schemes are a key component of the regulation of the use of copyright works in education. This section considers the recent reference of the licence to photocopy in higher education to the Copyright Tribunal. The Tribunal's decision is important as it will inevitably have a considerable impact on copyright licensing in other areas of education, such as in schools and further education colleges, as well as on other activities, such as digitisation and digital distribution, which form the subject matter of separate licensing arrangements. It also demonstrates the interplay of public policies in this controversial area.

The reference to the Copyright Tribunal was made on behalf of higher education institutions by Universities UK (UUK), a body on which university vice-chancellors and principals sit.[49] The parties to the action were UUK, as applicant; the CLA as respondent; and the Design and Artists Copyright Society (DACS) as intervenor.[50] The background to the dispute was as follows. There had long been tension between universities and the CLA, in particular over the question of course packs (discussed below).[51] A new licence was finally agreed between the CLA and UUK[52] acting on behalf of higher education institutions in March 1998, to take effect from 1 April 1998. The terms were actually negotiated on behalf of UUK by a copyright subcommittee, and it appears that little attention was paid by the main committee to copyright or to the difficulties the subcommittee encountered. At that time, and against the background of other key issues facing the sector, copyright was seen as a matter of little importance to most vice-chancellors. The copyright subcommittee doubtless did its best, but negotiations were held in a difficult climate. The result was an agreement that caused near chaos when it came to be implemented, forcing changes to teaching and library practices and giving less freedom to copy despite the payment of higher fees.

---

[49] Formerly the Committee of Vice-Chancellors and Principals of the Universities of the United Kingdom.

[50] DACS acts as the agent of artists in the licensing of their rights, in much the same way as the CLA acts as agent for authors and publishers and their representatives. In 1998 DACS appointed the CLA to act as its agent in granting the right to make reprographic copies of its members' works.

[51] See further S. Picciotto, 'Copyright Licensing: The Case of Higher Education Photocopying in the United Kingdom' [2002] EIPR 438, 440. More generally, see U. Suthersanen, 'Copyright and Educational Policies: A Stakeholder Analysis' (2003) 23 *Oxford Journal of Legal Studies* 585.

[52] At the time the Committee of Vice-Chancellors and Principals of the Universities of the United Kingdom, but referred to here as UUK for convenience and to avoid confusion.

Most controversial were the provisions of the licence dealing with the compilation of course packs. The exclusion of course packs from the CLA licence had long been a matter of concern to higher education institutions. This was because in order to produce a course pack academics, or in some cases copyright officers, had to spend time obtaining copyright clearance through the CLA's Copyright Licensing Rapid Clearance Service or CLARCS. This system was slow and administratively cumbersome. Moreover, costs were usually passed on to students, which proved unpopular with staff and students alike. Not only was the course pack exclusion maintained under the 1998 licence, the definition of a course pack was extended. The new guidelines stated that where a lecturer or tutor wished to distribute copyright materials to students on a genuinely ad hoc basis, he or she could do so, provided that the copying was limited to the following:

(i) no more than one chapter from a book, or one article from a journal/periodical, or one single case report from a law report; or
(ii) no more than 5 per cent of a given work, whichever is greater.

The guidelines also stated that poems, short stories and short literary works could be copied in their entirety as long as a maximum of ten pages was not exceeded. There was no definition of ad hoc copying, but it was generally thought to mean 'one-off'. More extensive copying for classroom use fell under the course pack provisions. A course pack was defined as

a compilation of materials (whether bound or loose-leaf) of four or more photocopied extracts from one or more sources, totalling over 25 pages of copyright material, designed to support a module or course of study, irrespective of whether the materials are copied at the start of the course, or at intervals during the duration of the course, *or are placed in the short loan reserve or equivalent for systematic copying by students at intervals throughout the course.*[53]

The extended course pack provisions had a significant impact on libraries. Before the 1998 licence took effect, libraries often took deposits from teaching staff of a limited and agreed number of copies of extracts from books and journals. These were kept in the short loan collection of the library to be consulted by students. When the 1998 course pack provisions were implemented the ability of a library to keep copies on short loan in this way was severely curtailed. The new guidelines made it clear that short loan collections could not be used to circumvent the provisions of the licence regarding course packs (see the definition set out above). Librarians pointed out that the guidelines only covered items 'placed in

---

[53] Emphasis added.

the short loan reserve or equivalent '*for systematic copying by students*' and did not, therefore, cover items placed in the short loan collection so that they could be read. However, the CLA insisted that if students had any opportunity to make a photocopy of an item placed on short loan it fell within the course pack definition. Nor was it even possible to obtain clearance through CLARCS for library holdings.

Matters came to a head in 1999. First, the CLA produced a supplementary protocol to the main CLA licence concerning the photocopying of artistic works. In a letter to vice-chancellors,[54] the research and compliance manager of the CLA pointed out that the photocopying of separate illustrations and photographs in published editions was expressly excluded from the terms of the CLA licence. The licence was silent as regards the copying of artistic works which formed part of the text of a page, but the research and compliance manager argued that the CLA licence was a text-only licence and that illustrations, maps and diagrams integrated into text could not be copied under its terms. The CLA, as agent for DACS, offered a supplementary agreement, but for a fee. Some universities signed up to this supplementary agreement, but many refused to do so. All regarded the CLA proposal with great concern and, as the Copyright Tribunal pointed out subsequently, the CLA must have appreciated that its actions would not stand up to the scrutiny of the Tribunal, because they withdrew the supplementary agreement shortly before the commencement of the reference in July 2000.

The second development in 1999 was that DACS invited universities to join its slide collection licensing scheme. This covered the reproduction of artistic works (broadly defined) on slides, acetates or transparencies.[55] From the universities' perspective one problem was that they often had no idea what slides were being used or by whom. This made it difficult to assess whether the terms offered by DACS were reasonable, since they could not easily ascertain how many works administered by DACS were being reproduced. Surveying staff would also have been difficult since the copyright issues at stake were complex and a good deal of information would thus have had to be elicited. To take but one example, there would clearly be no need to pay for the reproduction of an artistic work that was out of copyright. However, to produce a slide from a photograph of such a work might require a licence, but not if the photograph was taken by the academic planning to make the slide or another person who gave permission for the slide to be made. Moreover, the photographer's

---

[54] Dated 3 June 1999.
[55] That is, the making of copies of artistic works and their subsequent use for the purposes of teaching.

permission would not be required if the making of the slide was covered by an exception, in particular, if the slide was originally made by an academic for the purposes of research or private study (once lawfully made no further permission to show the slide would be required since the right to control the showing of a work in public does not extend to artistic works[56]). Even if the photographer's permission were required, copyright in the work might not be administered by DACS. In addition to these practical difficulties there was also a cultural obstacle – universities had not had to pay for this use of copyright works in the past.

The disputes over the DACS slide collection scheme and the supplementary protocol to the CLA licence, coming as they did on the back of the course pack controversy, proved too much for the universities, which decided that they had to take action. They therefore brought a reference to the Copyright Tribunal challenging the CLA licence.[57]

The Copyright Tribunal decision

References were made to the Copyright Tribunal under sections 118 and 119 of the 1988 Act. These sections give the Tribunal wide-ranging powers to make such orders as the Tribunal determines to be reasonable in the circumstances. The Tribunal was therefore able to look at the situation in the round, taking account of a broad range of factors. Three principal questions had to be determined by the Tribunal in *Universities UK v. Copyright Licensing Agency*,[58] namely:

(i) How much money should universities be required to pay under a licensing scheme for the photocopying by their staff and students of the literary and artistic copyright materials contained in books and journals?
(ii) Should there be a unitary licensing system, or a two-tier system in which an additional fee and advance clearance is required for course packs?
(iii) What was meant by the exclusion from the licensing scheme of 'separate illustrations, diagrams and photographs'?

It is not proposed to dwell on the first question. Although the fee set by the Copyright Tribunal is of great importance to the parties involved, the method by which it was computed is largely beyond the remit of this book. However, the wide disparity between the highest fee requested by

---

[56] CDPA 1988, s. 18.
[57] No reference was brought over the DACS slide collection licensing scheme. DACS was an intervenor in the UUK reference because of its interest in the photocopying of artistic works (see below).
[58] [2002] EMLR 693.

the CLA (£13.09 per FTE[59]) and the lowest fee offered by UUK (60p per FTE) is worth noting. In the event, the Copyright Tribunal set the fee at £4.00 per FTE[60], an increase over the then cost of £3.25 per FTE, the increase being largely for an increase in the coverage of the licence, which was extended to cover the making of course packs and the inclusion of a greater range of artistic works. Ultimately, therefore, the Tribunal came down much closer to the university side.

As to the second question, the Tribunal decided that there should be a unitary licensing system and that the separate treatment of course packs and the requirement for CLARCS clearance should be removed. This will reduce substantially the administrative burden on university staff and, in effect, restores the position to that which pertained before 1993, to the great relief of all in the higher education sector, and with significant potential implications for the amendment of licences applying to further education colleges and to schools.

In relation to the third question, the Tribunal held that the current licence was not a text-only licence, as the CLA had asserted. The exclusion of 'separate illustrations, diagrams and photographs' was ambiguous, but it probably meant separate artistic works which were both (a) on a separate page, and (b) not necessary for the understanding of the text.[61] However, the scope of this exclusion did not seem to have been discussed or clarified by the CLA or UUK at the time of negotiations for the agreement, and there was much subsequent disagreement as to its meaning. By the time of the hearing both sides accepted that a different approach was required and the Tribunal therefore extended the scope of the licence and raised the royalty rate to take account of the broader reach of the amended terms.

Certain other matters have also been laid to rest by the decision of the Tribunal. One point of contention had been reading lists or syllabus sheets distributed by lecturing staff and directing students to certain texts. The CLA argued that these were invitations to copy. The Tribunal rejected this contention, stating, 'the mere distribution of a reading list, without any instructions to copy, is not in our view an infringement of copyright'.[62] The Tribunal also showed awareness of the problematic interaction between the uncertain scope of the research and private study exception and the need for institutional users to secure licences (see the section 'Fair dealing for the purposes of research or private study', above).

Throughout their deliberations the Copyright Tribunal showed sensitivity to the needs of the higher education system and described the

---

[59] 'Full time equivalent' – a measure of student numbers.
[60] But this will increase each year in line with the Retail Price Index.
[61] *UUK* v. *CLA*, 779.   [62] *Ibid.*, 762–3.

relationship between publishers, authors and the education system as a 'symbiotic one'.[63] *UUK* v. *CLA* does much to safeguard the interests of higher education establishments. Commenting on the decision, Diana Warwick, chief executive of UUK, said, 'We are delighted at this outcome and that the issue has finally been resolved with a licence that is workable for all concerned. Universities UK now looks forward to working with the CLA, universities, publishers and authors under the much improved framework ordered by the Tribunal.'[64]

Conclusion

Of the exceptions that we have looked at in this chapter, it has been seen that the research and private study exception suffers from a number of serious defects. In particular, it applies to a limited range of subject matter, fails to distinguish between different stages of research and gives no clear guidance as to the quantity of material that can be copied in reliance on this exception. Not only does the latter problem cause difficulty for students and researchers, it also causes problems for institutional users. Moreover, the problems faced by such institutions have been exacerbated by the recent exclusion of commercial research from the scope of the research and private study exception. As regards the miscellaneous education exceptions examined in this chapter, it has been seen that these too suffer from certain defects and that the instruction and examination provision and the performances in educational establishments provisions, in particular, ought to be extended. In contrast, we have been somewhat less critical of the provisions that only take effect in the absence of licensing arrangements. We have noted that in cases where licences are not available the statutory exception relating to reprographic copying is inadequate. But insofar as licences are available, we believe that the overall approach adopted at present (at least in the light of *UUK* v. *CLA*) is one that might productively be continued, although, as we noted at the outset, we believe that the development of other models for the distribution of educational material and scholarly research is something that should continue to be explored.

---

[63] *Ibid.*, 763, noting: 'A healthy publishing industry is important in general, but of particular importance to those in education. Wholesale exemption from the copyright laws for educational establishments would be damaging to the publishing industry, and in consequence damaging to education. On the other hand the publishing industry depends on academic authors for much of its raw material. If education is burdened too heavily with copyright restrictions, teaching and scholarship is discouraged, to the disadvantage of the public interest in general, and the publishing industry in particular.'
[64] Universities UK Media release, 26 April 2002, available at www.universitiesuk.ac.uk/mediareleases.

5 The library and archive provisions and related exceptions

The libraries and archive sections of the 1988 Act,[1] even in their amended form, are complex and old-fashioned, and they draw unnecessary and inappropriate distinctions between institutions in a sector that has changed rapidly over recent years. However, the outcome of the law reform process in 2003 has not been unwelcome to people working within the sector. Those who run libraries and archives were expecting far worse, and since the 2003 Regulations[2] came into force there has been a collective sigh of relief. This relief may, however, be short-lived, for the changes made to the law in the United Kingdom have been minimal, freezing in time a set of provisions which were long overdue for radical reform.

The libraries and archives sections allow officially sanctioned persons to make copies of a work and, in appropriate circumstances, to supply these copies to other institutions and to individuals – typically, a librarian supplying a library reader.[3] The person making the copy will therefore be a professional person working in a sector traditionally held in special regard by the state as a holder and provider of information. Public policies regarding dissemination and preservation of knowledge, culture and heritage for the public benefit therefore come into play. The question to be considered is the extent to which furtherance of these policies justifies the provision of copyright exceptions or, to load the question rather differently, the extent to which copyright protection is justified in circumstances in which it interferes with the work of libraries and archives.

It is important to acknowledge that the dissemination and preservation of knowledge, culture and heritage is not limited to libraries and archives. A range of other institutions, the media and private individuals also play an essential role. It might therefore be asked whether there is any justification for singling out libraries and archives for special treatment. However, to grant wide-ranging exceptions to cover all circumstances in

---

[1] CDPA 1988, ss. 37–44A.
[2] The Copyright and Related Rights Regulations 2003 (SI 2003 No 2498).
[3] The exception is s. 44, which has a somewhat different function and effect. This section is discussed in detail below.

which copying is intended to preserve or disseminate knowledge, culture and so on would be to go too far – indeed, it is difficult to see what scope would be left for copyright under such a system. We are therefore prepared to start from the premise that libraries and archives have a distinctive (albeit evolving) role within society that justifies their special treatment within copyright law. Nevertheless, it is worth focusing on the narrower question of why similar provisions have not been extended to institutions such as museums and galleries, particularly to non-profitmaking, public-sector institutions. Not only do such institutions (broadly speaking) play a similar role in society, there is a political imperative towards greater cross-sectoral working, and the distinction between different types of institution is becoming increasingly blurred. For example, a person who goes to a museum will now expect to see (and perhaps touch or read) objects such as sculptures, paintings, books and manuscripts. The public expects material to be determined more by themes than by categories of information and materials. One of the themes of this chapter is that the interests of institutions other than libraries and archives are not adequately accounted for within the current statutory regime, but we also argue that libraries and archives are themselves poorly served by the existing (newly modified) provisions.

Overview of the existing exceptions

In outline, the library and archive exceptions enable librarians, and in some cases archivists, to perform certain tasks without infringing copyright (the so-called library exceptions or library privileges), namely:

(i) copying by librarians of articles in periodicals, or of parts of published works, for users who require them for research or private study (ss. 38 and 39);

(ii) lending books within the public lending right scheme (s. 40A);

(iii) supplying copies of articles or published editions to another library so as to expand that library's collection (s. 41);

(iv) making replacement copies of a work for preservation purposes (s. 42);

(v) supplying copies of unpublished works (s. 43);

(vi) making a copy of an article of cultural or historical importance or interest before that article is exported from the United Kingdom (s. 44); and

(vii) making a copy of a non-print publication by a library of legal deposit (s. 44A).

It is important to emphasise that, for the most part, the above provisions are designed to allow librarians to make copies. Where readers make their own copies of copyright works held by a library, the above provisions do not apply. As was seen in the last chapter, where the reader uses a self-service photocopier or a privately owned handheld scanner, the fair dealing provisions relating to research and private study may apply. It was also seen, however, that librarians, archivists and related professions still have to take account of copyright in such cases, and that the uncertainty surrounding the scope of the research and private study exception causes significant problems for those faced with policing the activities of readers. These problems have been made much worse by the newly added complication of having to distinguish between those researchers whose work is of a commercial nature and those whose work is purely private. As we explain in the final chapter, we believe that in appropriate circumstances the division between librarian copying and copying by readers ought to be abolished, and that librarians ought to be able to rely directly on an expanded research and private study provision.

The library provisions should also be seen alongside a number of miscellaneous provisions that allow for the copying of public records (s. 49) and of material open to public inspection and on official registers (s. 47), and that allow for the recording of folksongs and of broadcasts for archival purposes (ss. 61 and 75). These provisions are also considered in this chapter, as too is the provision relating to advertisement of the sale of artistic works (s. 63), this last provision being important for galleries in particular. Before turning to examine the scope of the current provisions, however, we first consider in more detail the role of the institutions with which we are concerned in this chapter.

Defining libraries, archives, museums and galleries and the role of such institutions

It has never been easy to define a library, an archive, a museum or a gallery or to assign to such institutions clear and distinctive roles. Both tasks are becoming more difficult as time goes by. In part this is because external factors such as political pressure and technological and social change are forcing these institutions to adapt, but it is also because those working within the sector are questioning traditional assumptions about their role. Despite these difficulties it is nevertheless possible to describe their features and functions in general terms.

Libraries have traditionally been viewed as repositories of printed material, particularly books, but for several years they have been adding audiovisual material to their collections. More recently, libraries have sought to provide readers with access to electronic resources, including the Internet. This expansion of the range of library holdings and facilities (which has often come at the expense of book purchasing) has occurred in part because important sources of information, including scholarly works, are increasingly being produced in non-print-based forms. In addition, however, this expansion has been driven by the desire of libraries to transform themselves into more general centres for community information. Inevitably, these factors have impacted differently depending on the type of library in question – something that should remind us that libraries come in many different forms. Some provide broad public services to communities that themselves have divergent needs. Others are much more specialised, including, for example, picture, newspaper and film libraries. In so far as such a diverse range of organisations can be said to share a common role, the function of a library is to provide readers with opportunities for self-directed learning by giving them 'the ability to search for information and to develop knowledge actively and independently'.[4]

In contrast to libraries, whose holdings are normally made up principally of published material, archives comprise the documentation that accumulates naturally over time as the product of the business of organisations or individuals. Most of the material contained in an archive will therefore be unique or will exist in a handful of copies. It follows that the management of archival material has to be different, and dominated by preservation needs. Archives are held by a variety of establishments, including universities, businesses and a variety of charitable organisations. The most important archives, however, are, on the one hand, a small number of large centralised institutions, such as the Public Record Office (PRO) at Kew, which is responsible for the records of central government and, on the other hand,[5] the network of county or local record offices that exist throughout England, Scotland and Wales.[6] Archival material is retained for its enduring usefulness and historical value to its creator and/or the public. Archives thus provide a form of institutional or collective memory.

Museums are probably still most clearly established in the public perception as repositories of old artefacts displayed in a static manner,

---

[4] European Bureau of Library, Information and Documentation Associations (EBLIDA) policy statement, 'Lifelong Learning, the Role of Archives and Libraries' (2 April 2002), available at www.eblida.org/topics/lifelong/lifelonglearning.htm.

[5] This distinction is somewhat simplistic, however, because some records of central government that are of particular relevance to a particular locale are in the care of local record offices with PRO approval. This adds extra complexity to the copying practices of local record offices, which must apply the Public Records Rules when copying this material.

[6] There is no such network of record offices in Northern Ireland, where PRONI (the Public Record Office of Northern Ireland) carries the principal responsibility for archives and records.

although the public is also now used to museums seeking to enrich the experience they offer through the use of interactive displays, sound recordings, films and even artificially generated smells. Like the other institutions under consideration here, museums vary widely, ranging from national institutions to small, even one-room, establishments dealing with local matters or special themes. Museum collections vary accordingly, ranging from fragments of pottery to industrial machinery to clothing and costumes. Museums share with archives the concern for unique, irreplaceable items and consequently they tend to be similarly concerned with preservation issues. Thus it has been said, 'Museums and archives – both modern institutions for preserving relics of the past – were close to each other in principle at their moments of origin.'[7] Probably to a greater extent than the other institutions with which we are concerned, museums have gone through a prolonged period of introspection as their role in controlling our perceptions of history has been challenged by commentators who have set out to 'explore the consequences of particular forms of representation in terms of the distribution of power: who is empowered or disempowered by certain modes of representation'.[8] These issues have arisen, in particular, in debates about the representation of indigenous cultures[9] and the way in which museums have prioritised particular epistemologies,[10] and in debates about whether historical artefacts removed from developing countries ought to be returned.[11] Carol Duncan has therefore argued:

> Museums and museum practices can become objects of fierce struggle and impassioned debate. What we see and do not see in our most prestigious ... museums – and on what terms and whose authority we do or don't see it – involves much larger questions of who constitutes the community and who shall exercise power to define its identity.[12]

---

[7] D. Chakrabarty, 'Museums in Late Democracies' (2002) 9 *Humanities Research* 5, 8.
[8] S. Macdonald, 'Exhibitions of Power and Powers of Exhibition: An Introduction to the Politics of Display', in S. Macdonald (ed.), *The Politics of Display: Museums, Science, Culture* (London: Routledge, 1998), p. 4.
[9] See, e.g., M. Anderson and A. Reeves, 'Contested Identities: Museums and the Nation in Australia', in F. Kaplan (ed.), *Museums and the Making of 'Ourselves': The Role of Objects in National Identity* (London: Leicester University Press, 1994), in particular pp. 86–91, 118–19.
[10] See, e.g., Chakrabarty, 'Museums'.
[11] See, e.g., K. Warren, 'A Philosophical Perspective on the Ethics and Resolution of Cultural Properties Issues', in P. Messenger (ed.), *The Ethics of Collecting Cultural Property* (Albuquerque: University of New Mexico Press, 1989).
[12] C. Duncan, 'Art Museums and the Ritual of Citizenship', in I. Karp and S. Levine (eds.), *Exhibiting Cultures: The Poetics and Politics of Museum Display* (Washington: Smithsonian Institution Press, 1991), p. 102.

However, despite the controversy that has come to surround the operation of museums, it is still largely accepted that they are institutions with important roles to play in the preservation of historically significant artefacts and in allowing us to engage productively with other cultures and the lives of previous generations.

When considering the definition of 'gallery' it should be remembered that most museums display the bulk of their collections in rooms or spaces referred to as galleries. In this context, however, we are principally concerned with institutions devoted to the exhibition (and sometimes sale) of works of fine and applied art, but even in this context it should be noted that the word 'gallery' is often used to describe both the principal display areas within such institutions and the institutions themselves. Galleries also vary widely in size and scope. Like museums, galleries 'exist to give people an opportunity to engage with the creations of their own and other societies, and perhaps to find inspiration and enjoyment in that engagement. They can be imagined as guardians of cultural memory.'[13]

While the above descriptions are somewhat simplistic and are in danger of becoming outdated (for example, there is an increasing trend towards referring to collections of films and sound recordings and certain special interest collections as 'archives'[14]), it is to be hoped that they provide a sense of the activities of the institutions with which we are concerned in this chapter. Collectively, these institutions play a vital role in preserving and promoting access to cultural resources and providing opportunities for self-education.

In outlining the basic features of different types of institution we are not attempting to indicate that they have clearly distinct functions – on the contrary, and as we have already indicated, we believe that as well as there being significant variety within each sector there is a significant overlap between them. For example, many public libraries hold a local studies collection, which often includes some original archival material as well as maps, newspapers and photographs. Most local record offices maintain a reference collection of printed works that may constitute the best local 'library' provision of its kind. Museums are similarly complex and variable. They will certainly hold reference collections of books to support the work of the curators and may even have a designated 'library'.

---

[13] N. Korn and P. Wienand, 'Public Access to Art, Museums, Images and Copyright: The Case of Tate', in D. McClean and K. Schubert (eds.), *Dear Images: Art Copyright and Culture* (London: Ridinghouse, 2002), p. 227.
[14] Cf. CDPA 1988, ss. 61 and 75 (discussed below).

Similarly, galleries have libraries as essential components of curatorial expertise.

If there has long been a significant overlap between different types of institution, recent pressure towards increased collaboration is making the interrelationship still more fluid. In particular it is government policy to promote 'cross domain' working between libraries, archives, museums and galleries.[15] This is part of a wider educational, cultural and social agenda which is prioritising measures designed to aid 'lifelong learning' and that improve access to education and cultural resources, with the use of new technologies being heavily advocated. Museums and galleries, libraries and archives are seen as key contributors, and are being actively encouraged to work together in order to make progress towards these broad goals. The recent report by the Regional Museums Task Force on the future of regional museums in England, *Renaissance in the Regions: A New Vision for England's Museums*,[16] provides an overview of the ways in which museums and related bodies are responding to such directional influence. Furthermore, the devolved administrations in Scotland, Wales and Northern Ireland have all adopted this central policy whilst working out the details for their own communities. In short, government policy is changing the objectives and the working practices of publicly funded museums and galleries, libraries and archives in unprecedented ways, with emphasis on access, outreach, drawing in new audiences and educational provision, and on working with and exploiting the potential of new technology. Educational networks, electronic portals and digitisation projects have proliferated, both at the national and local levels.

It is instructive to contrast the pressures and developments described above with the approach adopted in the 1988 Act.

Divisions within the 1988 Act

The 1988 Act fails to reflect the changes to the structure and functions of libraries, archives, museums and galleries outlined above. Some sections of the Act (ss. 37, 40A, 42, 43, 44) apply to both libraries and to archives, others only to libraries (ss. 38, 39, 41, 44A), but none applies to archives alone. Museums and galleries are not mentioned at all. It should be acknowledged, however, that an archive, a museum or a gallery with a library section (for example, with holdings on art, architecture or family

---

[15] This work is being led by the Museums, Libraries and Archives Council, a strategic body set up in 2000.
[16] Available at www.resource.gov.uk/documents/rennais.pdf.

history) may, in relation to its library collection, be classified as a library for the purposes of the rules under discussion. Similarly, an archive section in a library, gallery or museum may be treated as an archive. Thus our concern is not so much that the existing provisions do not extend to museums and galleries, but more that the Act fails to accommodate the special needs of such institutions and, above all, places obstacles in the way of institutions digitising their catalogues.

Continuing the theme of division of the sector, it will be seen that not even all libraries are treated in the same way under the current regime. In particular, it will be seen that whereas some of the exceptions apply to libraries in general, other provisions only apply to not-for-profit libraries. Whilst this is the sort of distinction that commends itself to copyright lawyers, it may well be one that eludes the diligent researcher who has travelled from afar.

In addition to drawing distinctions between different types of institution, the Act also draws divisions according to the type of work in question. In particular, it is important to appreciate that the library exceptions are largely confined to the copying of literary, dramatic or musical works, to any illustrations accompanying such works, and to the typographical arrangement of a published edition. Consequently, artistic works, for example, are for the most part outside the scope of the exceptions. It was presumably thought either that there would be no demand for the copying of other types of work or that a broader exception would be open to abuse. However, limiting the library and archive exceptions to literary, dramatic and musical works, accompanying illustrations and typographic arrangements has the consequence of taking sound recordings, films, photographs and maps outside the scope of the exceptions. These restrictions cause significant problems in practice.

Wider coverage under the directive

We outline our vision of reform in detail in the final chapter, but it is worth pausing at this point to emphasise that the Information Society Directive is not responsible for the current unsatisfactory position. Rather, the library provisions considered below are in essence the same as when originally enacted in 1988. As we noted at the start of this chapter, the minimal changes to UK law in this area have been largely welcomed, but this is because the majority of stakeholders were concerned that implementation of the Directive would lead to the library exceptions being curtailed dramatically. In contrast, we argue in the final chapter that there would have been other, very different, ways of implementing the Directive and that were the Directive to be implemented 'in full' the position would be much improved. This argument will be developed in detail later, but for now it should be noted that the relevant provisions of the Directive apply to all of the institutions with which we are concerned in this chapter.[17]

Another important feature of the Directive is that the range of materials to which an exception may apply is not limited in any way. Thus any new exceptions could permit the reproduction of all categories of copyright works and not just literary, dramatic or musical works, accompanying illustrations and typographic arrangements, as is the case at present.

Finally, it should be noted that the Directive makes specific provision to allow (subject to certain limitations) for the making available on dedicated terminals digitised versions of works contained in the collections of libraries, museums and so on.[18] Such an exception is important because most public museums and galleries are legally bound under their governing instruments to promote the public enjoyment and understanding of art, craft, design, local history, science and so on.[19] Such obligations cannot now be fulfilled without the reproduction of images of works contained in their collections. Furthermore, a great deal of public money (for example, from the New Opportunities Fund) is being spent on digitisation projects. Admittedly, the relevant provision of the Directive does not go so far as to permit the placing of digitised images of works on the Internet (because of the requirement that access be by means of dedicated terminals located on the premises of relevant institutions[20]). Nevertheless, the provision remains significant, and it is worth noting that the Directive does not state expressly that the 'dedicated terminals' must only provide access to the works of the establishment in which the terminal is located. The Directive is thus open to the interpretation that intranet services across libraries, educational establishments, museums and archives would fall within the scope of the permitted exception.

The Directive has therefore paved the way for a much more satisfactory approach. It is to be hoped that the government will pay attention to its

---

[17] See, in particular, Information Society Directive, Art. 5(2)(c), which applies to 'publicly accessible libraries, educational establishments or museums, or . . . archives'. Although galleries are not mentioned specifically in the text of Art. 5(2)(c), it is clear that galleries can, in appropriate cases, be included as 'museums of art'.

[18] Information Society Directive, Art. 5(3)(n).

[19] See further P. Weinand, A. Booy and R. Fry, *A Guide to Copyright for Museums and Galleries* (London: Routledge, 2000), p. 42.

[20] As confirmed by Recital 40 of the Directive, which states that 'an exception or limitation should not cover uses made in the context of on-line delivery of protected works or other subject-matter'.

own agenda for changes in the heritage sector and implement appropriate changes to copyright law. Such changes are urgently required given the limitations of the current provisions.

The existing library exceptions

Introduction

Although the library exceptions have a similar general function, it is helpful to subdivide the relevant provisions into three groups, namely (1) those that allow librarians to make and supply copies of works or parts of works directly to readers (ss. 38, 39 and 43); (2) those that allow librarians to make and supply copies to other libraries and for internal purposes (ss. 41, 42 and 44A); and (3) miscellaneous provisions relating to the lending of works and the making of copies of works as a condition of export (ss. 40A and 44).

Supplying copies to readers: overview

The provisions with which we are concerned at present relate only to copying by or on behalf of librarians. As stated above, where a library user uses a self-service photocopier, the provisions relating to fair dealing apply. In practice, with so many self-service photocopiers in libraries and with readers doing so much of the copying themselves, the provisions in question apply mainly to requests for copies made as part of an interlibrary document service (interlibrary loans). Consequently, much of the debate has focused on the exchange of request forms between libraries and on the narrow questions of whether this can be done electronically and, if so, whether electronic signatures can be used.

In order for the exceptions to apply, librarians must satisfy themselves that the statutory requirements for the operation of the relevant sections are being met. In practice this requires librarians to ensure that users sign declaration forms, since librarians are able to rely on such forms if an action for copyright infringement is brought against them. Sample declaration forms are to be found in Schedule 2 of the Library Regulations.[21] The Library Regulations set out two forms – Form A and Form B. Form A is intended to be used by readers requesting a copy of an article in a periodical or part of a published work (that is, copying covered by ss. 38 and 39 of the 1988 Act); Form B relates to copies of

---

[21] The Copyright (Librarians and Archivists) (Copying of Copyright Material) Regulations 1989 (hereafter, the Library Regulations) (SI 1989 No 1212).

unpublished works (that is, copying covered by s. 43 of the 1988 Act). Using Form A as an example,[22] the reader has to declare that she
(a) has not previously been supplied with a copy of the same material by the librarian making that copy or by any other librarian;
(b) will not use the copy except for research for a non-commercial purpose or private study and will not supply a copy of it to any other person; and
(c) that to the best of the reader's knowledge, no other person with whom she works or studies has made or intends to make, at or about the same time as this request, a request for substantially the same material for substantially the same purpose.

Further, the library user must declare that she understands that if the declaration is false in a material particular, the copy made by the librarian will be an infringing copy and hence that she will be liable for infringement of copyright as if she had made the copy herself.

The only significant change made to Form A by the 2003 amendments was the inclusion in (b) above of the requirement that the research be for a non-commercial purpose. If the research is commercial, the user will have to purchase from the library a sticker under the Copyright Licensing Agency (CLA) Sticker Scheme.[23] The Sticker Scheme allows, for example, for the copying of one chapter from a book, one article from a periodical, one case from a published law report, or one poem in an anthology.[24] This scheme provides an important mechanism for facilitating commercial research; however, it also suffers from certain drawbacks, most notably that it does not cover copying from works produced by publishers not affiliated with the CLA.[25]

Provided the relevant form has been completed, a librarian is entitled to rely on the reader's declaration that she requires the copy for the purposes of private study or non-commercial research unless the librarian is aware that the declaration is false in a material particular.[26] The librarian must also be 'satisfied' that the reader's request is not similar to that of another person (that is, is not a request for substantially the same material at substantially the same time and for substantially the same purpose)[27] and is not related to that of another person (that is, is not relevant to

---

[22] The wording of Form B differs in detail but is similar in overall effect.
[23] For further details see the Copyright Licensing Agency guide, 'The CLA Sticker Scheme', available at www.cla.co.uk/directive/leaflet.pdf. The fee payable under this scheme (at the time of writing £9.00) is returned to the CLA by the library and thence from the CLA to the copyright holders in the usual way.
[24] Ibid.   [25] See also see Chapter 4.
[26] CDPA 1988, s. 37(2)(a); Library Regulations, reg. 4(3).
[27] CDPA 1988, s. 40(2)(a); Library Regulations, reg. 4(2)(b)(i).

the same course of study).[28] In practice completed copies of the relevant forms must be saved by the library or archive in order to exonerate the librarian in the event of any accusation that library facilities were used to infringe copyright. However, it is no exaggeration to say that this can pose an administrative nightmare. Most libraries keep these forms in boxes in roughly chronological order – they are not catalogued. It seems that forms are generally kept for six years, that is, for the period in which proceedings for infringement of copyright must be commenced,[29] but it has been pointed out that this does not provide an absolute safeguard[30] and that in order to be completely certain forms would have to be kept for six years and a day after the expiry of the copyright term.[31] Such a measure would clearly not be practical for the majority of libraries. The storage costs (which are in any event significant) would be enormous. So too would be the retrieval costs in the event of an action and the costs of administering a system under which forms were only destroyed a given period of time after the expiry of copyright. This in turn leads us to a more general criticism of the current provisions, namely, that they impose significant costs on institutions whilst arguably doing little, if anything, to prevent abuses.[32]

Copying of articles in periodicals and of parts of published works

Having outlined the basic features of the exceptions that allow for copies to be supplied directly to readers, we now turn to consider the scope of individual permitted acts, starting with sections 38 and 39 of the 1988 Act, which allow for the copying of articles in periodicals and parts of published works respectively.

The first point to note is that sections 38 and 39 apply only to 'prescribed' libraries. These are specified in the Library Regulations and defined to include the five UK 'copyright libraries', libraries administered by a local authority or by a library authority, school libraries and the libraries of most other educational establishments, and libraries administered by a government department or by an agency administered by a minister of the crown (the latter would include NHS hospital libraries). In addition to these specific categories, the Library Regulations also include

---

[28] CDPA 1988, s. 40(2)(b); Library Regulations, reg. 4(2)(b)(ii).
[29] Limitation Act 1980, s. 2.
[30] This is for a variety of reasons, but perhaps the most obvious is that there might be a dispute as to the date on which the copying occurred and as to whether a declaration form was ever completed at all.
[31] T. Padfield, *Copyright for Archivists and Users of Archives*, 2nd edn (London: Facet Publishing, 2004), pp. 124–5.
[32] Similarly, see *Copinger*, para. 9.40.

within the definition any 'other library conducted for the purpose of facilitating or encouraging the study of bibliography, education, fine arts, history, languages, law, literature, medicine, music, philosophy, religion, science (including natural and social science) or technology, or administered by any establishment or organisation which is conducted wholly or mainly for such a purpose'.[33] Libraries conducted for profit, or which are administered by a body conducted for profit, are, however, specifically excluded.[34] It was thought at one time that the definition of a prescribed library would change when the Directive was implemented, but this has not occurred.

Section 38 of the 1988 Act permits the librarian of a prescribed library to make and supply a copy of an article in a periodical without infringing any copyright in the text, in any illustrations accompanying the text or in the typographical arrangement.[35] An 'article' in a periodical is defined in the 1988 Act as 'including an item of any description',[36] but a 'periodical' is not defined. It has been seen that a copy may only be supplied (1) to a reader who has declared that she requires the copy for the purposes of private study or non-commercial research; and (2) if the librarian is satisfied that the request is not similar or related to that of another person (see preceding subsection 'Supplying copies to readers: overview'). In addition, the librarian must ensure (3) that the reader is not supplied with more than one copy of an article or more than one article contained in the same issue of a periodical;[37] and (4) that the reader pays for the copy a sum not less than the cost (including a contribution to the general expenses of the library) attributable to its production.[38]

Section 39 of the Act permits the librarian of a prescribed library to make and supply 'from a published edition' a copy of part of a literary, dramatic or musical work (other than an article in a periodical). A copy may only be supplied under this section if a number of conditions are satisfied. These conditions are identical to those that apply to section 38, as set out in the last paragraph, except that in place of (3), above, the librarian must ensure that the reader is not supplied with more than one copy of the same material or more than a reasonable proportion of a work.[39]

Unfortunately, sections 38 and 39 suffer from a number of defects. We have already alluded to a number of these. Most obviously, these provisions only apply to a limited range of copyright subject matter in a

---

[33] Library Regulations, Sched.1, Part A. As to the 'copyright libraries', see n. 76 below and accompanying text.
[34] Library Regulations, regs. 3(1), 3(5).   [35] CDPA 1988, s. 38(1).
[36] *Ibid.*, s. 178.   [37] *Ibid.*, s. 38(2)(b); Library Regulations, reg. 4(2)(c)(i).
[38] CDPA 1988, s. 38(2)(c); Library Regulations, reg. 4(2)(d).
[39] CDPA 1988, s. 39(2)(b); Library Regulations, reg. 4(2)(c)(ii).

way that fails to reflect the increasing importance of non-textual media for study and research.[40] We have also noted that these provisions are administratively cumbersome but probably do little to protect copyright owners, for example, because readers can lie on declaration forms safe in the knowledge that they are highly unlikely to be sued for copyright infringement. Yet the system is such that it leads inevitably to difficult confrontations between librarians and readers who find the system time-consuming and intrusive. Sections 38 and 39 also suffer from other, more specific, problems. For example, the Act makes no attempt to define what amounts to a 'reasonable proportion' for the purposes of section 39 – an area of significant uncertainty for librarians. Librarians must also be diligent in ensuring that they do not accidentally reproduce the whole of a work when relying on section 39 or copy more than a single article in a periodical in reliance on section 38. There is a danger that this might occur inadvertently if a librarian is asked to copy, say, a one-page poem contained in an anthology or the letters page from a journal (each letter being a separate 'article' for the purposes of the Act[41]).

Other problems flow from the restrictions placed on the provision of multiple copies. As regards limitations on the provision of copies to different readers who require them for the same purpose or as part of the same course of study, it can be difficult for library staff to know if multiple copies are being requested, especially if the copiers are operated by a number of people. As Sandy Norman argues, staff cannot be expected to check records retrospectively. The Library Association therefore considers that recognition of duplicate requests must be left to the memory of the staff concerned, but they should do their best to act responsibly.[42] This would seem a sensible position, but one that can still have arbitrary and frustrating results if readers discover that some members of library staff are willing to provide the copy but others are not. Such a system also places a significant premium on a reader being the first to request a copy, since, in practice, the fact that other readers require substantially the same material will not come to light until subsequent requests are made. As regards the limits that apply to individual readers, it is unsatisfactory that the Act does not contain a cut-off period after which a further copy of the same material, or a second article from an issue of a periodical or a second extract from a work can be supplied. Read literally,

---

[40] This problem should also be viewed alongside the restricted scope of the research and private study exception considered in the last chapter.

[41] As noted above, s. 178 of the 1988 Act defines an article in a periodical as 'including an item of any description'.

[42] S. Norman, *Copyright in Further and Higher Education Libraries*, 4th edn (London: Library Association Publishing, 1999), p. 16.

the Act prevents the supply of a second copy, second article or second extract, irrespective of how many years later the request is made. In practice, this causes readers few problems because the fact that the copy has been requested outside the terms of the Act will never be detected. There might, however, be fields of research where detection is likely because of the small number of librarians and readers involved. Any time limit would have to be long enough to prevent readers from using the library provisions to obtain entire copies of a work or entire issues of a periodical for a single programme of research or course of study without payment, but nevertheless the introduction of such a limit is highly desirable.

Yet further difficulties flow from the fact that sections 38 and 39 do not allow librarians to take advantage of 'new' technologies.[43] For example, it has been pointed out that it will not ordinarily be possible to supply a copy of an article in a periodical or a portion of another type of work by fax[44] or by e-mail[45] in reliance on sections 38 and 39.

Copying of unpublished works

The third exception that allows copies to be supplied directly to readers is contained in section 43 of the 1988 Act. Unlike sections 38 and 39, which apply to published material, section 43 allows for the making of copies of unpublished works. It is important to emphasise that this provision is supplemented by certain transitional provisions, which are of considerable practical importance. In effect these transitional provisions preserve an additional set of exceptions for works made before 1 August 1989 (that is, the date the Act came into force). We begin by looking at the current provisions that apply to all works irrespective of when they were made,[46] before turning to consider the transitional provisions.

---

[43] See, generally, S. Norman, 'The Electronic Environment: The Librarian's View' [1996] EIPR 71.

[44] Laddie et al., 3rd edn, para. 33.36, pointing out that sending a fax will almost certainly involve making a copy to be fed into the fax machine that will not be supplied to the reader.

[45] Laddie et al., 3rd edn, para. 33.37, pointing out that the process of scanning a work into a computer will involve making a number of further electronic copies that will not be supplied to the reader. Nor would the new exception contained in s. 28A provide any assistance, because, *inter alia*, a copy of a scanned work saved onto the hard drive of the computer being used to send the copy would not be a 'transient or incidental' temporary copy, even if the file were erased immediately after the copy was sent as an attachment.

[46] Cf. *Copinger*, para. 9.48; Laddie et al., 3rd edn, para. 33.15, both taking the view that s. 43 only applies to works made after 1 Aug. 1989. The key issue is the interrelationship between CDPA 1988, Sched. 1, para. 3 (new provisions to apply to existing works) and Sched. 1, para. 16 (preservation of provisions of the 1956 Act). Since para. 16 does not *expressly provide* that s. 43 does not apply to pre-existing works (cf. Sched. 1, para. 3) the better view is that s. 43 applies to all works, irrespective of when they were made.

The existing library exceptions

Section 43 allows librarians and archivists of any library or archive (although the Act refers to 'prescribed' libraries and archives, all libraries and archives in the United Kingdom are prescribed for the purposes of this section[47]) to make and supply a copy of the whole or part of an unpublished literary, dramatic or musical work (and accompanying illustrations[48]) held by the library or archive. This exception is further limited by a number of conditions, many of which are similar to those considered in relation to sections 38 and 39. Thus a copy may only be supplied (1) to a reader who has declared (using Form B) that she requires the copy for the purposes of private study or non-commercial research;[49] and the librarian must ensure (2) that the reader is not supplied with more than one copy of the same material;[50] and (3) that the reader pays for the copy a sum not less than the cost (including a contribution to the general expenses of the library) attributable to its production.[51] In addition, however, copying is only permitted under this section if (4) the copyright owner has not prohibited copying of the work.[52]

The fourth of the above conditions is worthy of special note. Many of those who deposit unpublished works in an archive wish to restrict copying or access, and it is important that the wishes of such people are respected so that others will have the confidence to deposit their own works. Limiting the exception to cases in which consent to copying has not been withheld is thus, broadly speaking, justifiable. The Act also seeks to safeguard librarians and archivists, since liability will only be imposed if, at the time the copy was made, the librarian or archivist knew or ought to have been aware of the fact that copying had been prohibited (although good practice ought to dictate that the terms of deposit are readily available for consultation by staff making copies[53]). However, linking the restriction on copying to the copyright owner's consent can produce unfortunate results not envisaged by Parliament. One consequence of consent being linked to copyright ownership in this way would seem to be that a person who derives title from the person depositing the material can impose more onerous restrictions on its use than the depositor intended. This creates the danger that future owners will attempt to

---

[47] Library Regulations, regs. 3(2), 3(4).
[48] There is, of course, no reference to copyright in the typographical arrangement of a published edition because this section applies only to unpublished works.
[49] CDPA 1988, s. 43(3)(a); Library Regulations, reg. 7(2)(a)(i).
[50] CDPA 1988, s. 43(3)(b); Library Regulations, reg. 7(2)(b).
[51] CDPA 1988, s. 43(3)(c); Library Regulations, reg. 7(2)(c).
[52] CDPA 1988, s. 43(2)(b).
[53] In practice, terms of deposit are normally noted on the computer system.

limit access to material that they believe casts the depositor in a poor light. Tying the requirement of consent to copyright ownership also means that, in theory at least, if person A deposits her personal papers in an archive and those papers contain letters written by A and letters written to A by B, A can only restrict copying of her letters under this section. A cannot use this section to restrict the copying of B's letters, for copyright in them vests in B. Only B or B's successor in title can prohibit copying of letters that she has written. This would not seem to provide adequate protection for A's interests. In short, therefore, there are circumstances in which the scheme created by the Act would seem to provide insufficient protection for the interests of either the depositor or the public.

It is also worth drawing attention to some of the more general problems with section 43. In particular, it should be noted that this section also applies only to a limited range of subject matter. It does not apply, for example, to the copying by librarians or archivists of unpublished sound recordings[54] or films, nor does it apply to artistic works, other than accompanying illustrations – maps and photographs are thus excluded from the operation of this provision. These restrictions must also be viewed alongside the limited scope of the research and private study provision. It will be remembered that fair dealing for the purposes of research or private study only applies to literary, dramatic, musical and artistic works and to the typographical arrangement of a published edition. It would not, therefore, be possible to rely on the fair dealing provision as an alternate means of making a copy of an unpublished film or sound recording held by a library or archive.

It would be possible to seek to rely on the research and private study exception so as to make a copy of unpublished artistic works such as maps and photographs. However, the delicate nature of such works means that curators will rarely permit anyone other than trained staff to copy them. There is nothing in the Act, if it is read literally, to prevent a librarian or an archivist acting as the reader's agent in such cases, such that copying of an unpublished map or photograph could well be held to fall within the aegis of the section 29 fair dealing defence. Confusion on this point may arise because of section 29(3), which provides that copying by a librarian is not fair dealing if 'he does anything which regulations under section 40 would not permit to be done under section 38 or 39'. This provision is sometimes treated as though it excludes librarians and archivists from seeking to rely on the research and private study exception in all circumstances. It is therefore important to emphasise that this limitation has a more restricted effect. It would not preclude a librarian or archivist from seeking to rely

---

[54] But note the limited exception contained in s. 61(3), discussed below.

on the research and private study exception when operating outside the terms of sections 38 and 39 altogether, as would be the case when making a copy of an unpublished artistic work. In practice, however, it seems that the uncertainty that surrounds the extent to which it is fair for the purposes of research or private study to copy an unpublished work or the whole of an artistic work means that librarians and archivists will not seek to rely on a section 29 defence. In this context it is notable that Padfield, in his guide to copyright for archivists, states that 'in the great majority of cases, archivists should be very wary of providing copies of copyright artistic works (including most maps, drawings and photographs) in their collections'.[55]

Having examined the scope of section 43, we move on to the additional transitional provisions which, it will be remembered, apply to works created before 1 August 1989. The transitional provisions in question have the effect of keeping in force the relevant provisions of the 1956 Copyright Act, subject to certain modifications.[56] The provisions in question are contained in section 7 of the 1956 Act. The effect of that section is such that where an unpublished literary, dramatic or musical work has been open to public inspection in any institution in the United Kingdom, it may be copied by any person without infringing copyright in the work or in any accompanying illustrations, so long as (1) the work was created before 1 August 1989;[57] (2) more than fifty years have elapsed from the end of the calendar year in which the author died; (3) the work is more than 100 years old; and (4) the copy is made for the purposes of research or private study, or with a view to publication. As has already been noted, these transitional provisions remain of considerable practical importance, and the fact that this section allows for reproduction for the purposes of publication is particularly noteworthy. It is important to appreciate, however, that this section was originally intended to run alongside the 1956 Act's very different approach to copyright duration. Under the 1956 Act copyright in an unpublished literary, dramatic or musical work was often perpetual. The 1988 Act abolished perpetual copyright and converted the term for unpublished works (that is, unpublished as of 1 August 1989) into a fixed period of fifty years.[58] The continued operation of the

---

[55] Padfield, *Copyright*, p. 104. In reaching this conclusion he argues: 'there are special provisions for copying on behalf of a researcher by an archivist or librarian . . . Because of this, it seems that the defence of fair dealing would not for the most part be available to a librarian or archivist who supplied copies outside the terms of those special provisions'.
[56] See CDPA 1988, Sched. 1, para. 16.
[57] A work is taken to have been made on the date it was completed: *ibid.*, Sched. 1, para. 1(3).
[58] This fixed term was subsequently increased in some cases so as to comply with the Term Directive.

provisions of the 1956 Act should thus be seen as part of a complex set of transitional arrangements dealing with copyright term, rather than as creating a peculiarly broad exception.

Supply of copies to other libraries

We now turn to consider those provisions that allow librarians to make and supply copies to other libraries (rather than to readers directly) and for internal purposes. The broadest of the three exceptions that permit copying for such purposes is contained in section 41 of the 1988 Act. This section, which is sometimes described as allowing for 'interlibrary copying for stock', contains, in effect, two quite different exceptions. The first exception applies only to single articles in periodicals. As regards such works, the Act states that the librarian of a prescribed library may make and supply to another prescribed library a copy of an article without infringing copyright in the text of the article, or in the typographical arrangement or in any accompanying illustrations.[59] Provided that only one copy is supplied[60] and provided that the receiving library pays for the copy 'a sum not less than the cost (including a contribution to the general expenses of the library) attributable to its production',[61] the exception applies. This provision therefore allows a library 'to make limited additions to its collection by acquiring for its readers articles from journals to which it does not subscribe'.[62]

The second exception is more generous in scope, but is also subject to much tighter controls. It allows the librarian of a prescribed library to make and supply to another prescribed library a copy of several articles in the same issue of a periodical or the whole or part of a published edition of a literary, dramatic or musical work, without infringing copyright in the text of the material copied, or in the typographical arrangement or in any accompanying illustrations.[63] In order for this provision to apply three conditions have to be satisfied, namely: (1) the requesting library must provide a written statement indicating that it does not know, and could not by reasonable inquiry ascertain, the name and address of a person entitled to authorise the making of the copy;[64] (2) only a single copy can

---

[59] All libraries in the United Kingdom are prescribed libraries for the purpose of making and supplying copies, but the receiving library must either be a library falling within Part A of Sched. 1 of the Library Regulations (see above n. 34 and accompanying text) or must be a not-for-profit library based outside the United Kingdom: Library Regulations, regs. 3(2), 3(3).

[60] Library Regulations, reg. 5(2)(a).   [61] *Ibid.*, reg. 5(2)(c).   [62] *Copinger*, para. 9.44.

[63] As to the meaning of 'prescribed library' in this context see above n. 59.

[64] Library Regulations, reg. 5(2)(b).

be provided;[65] and (3) the receiving library must pay for the copy a sum not less than the cost (including a contribution to the general expenses of the library) attributable to its production.[66] This second exception is useful because in practice it is often very difficult to trace the copyright owner, for example, because copyright in the work was assigned to a company that has ceased trading. Overall, therefore, it can be said that the section 41 exceptions provide a useful, albeit limited, mechanism that libraries can use to add to their stock. These exceptions should be considered alongside the provisions of section 42.

Preservation and the making of replacement copies

In outline, section 42 of the 1988 Act permits the librarian or archivist of a prescribed library or archive to make a copy of certain types of work contained in that institution's permanent collection in order to preserve or replace the original. The copy can then be placed in the permanent collection either in addition to or in place of the original. In addition, section 42 permits a copy to be made in order to replace in the permanent collection of another prescribed library or archive an item that has been lost, destroyed or damaged.[67] These provisions are, however, subject to a number of important restrictions that are contained primarily in the Library Regulations. The restrictions are that (1) the item to be copied must be held in the permanent collection for reference purposes only, that is, it must either not be available for loan at all or must only be available on loan to other libraries or archives for reference purposes;[68] (2) it must not be reasonably practicable to purchase a copy of the item concerned;[69] (3) if another library requests a copy, it must declare in a written statement that its copy has been lost, destroyed or damaged, that it is not reasonably practicable for it to purchase a replacement copy and that the copy will only be used for the approved purpose;[70] and (4) if another library requests a copy it must pay for it a sum not less than the cost (including a contribution to the general expenses of the library) attributable to its production.[71]

---

[65] *Ibid.*, reg. 5(2)(a).   [66] *Ibid.*, reg. 5(2)(c).
[67] For the purposes of s. 42 all libraries in the UK are prescribed libraries for the purpose of making and supplying copies, but the receiving library must either be a library falling within Part A of Sched. 1 of the Library Regulations (see above n. 34 and accompanying text) or must be a not-for-profit library based outside the United Kingdom: Library Regulations, regs. 3(2), 3(3). Similarly, all archives in the United Kingdom are prescribed archives for the purpose of making and supplying copies, but the receiving archive must be a not-for-profit archive within the United Kingdom: Library Regulations, reg. 3(4).
[68] *Ibid.*, reg. 6(2)(a).   [69] CDPA 1988, s. 42(2); Library Regulations, reg. 6(2)(b).
[70] Library Regulations, reg. 6(2)(c).   [71] *Ibid.*, reg. 6(2)(d).

In practice section 42 operates so as to allow libraries to replace out-of-print books that have become damaged or destroyed and to allow fragile material to be placed onto microfilm.[72] Such a provision is essential because deliberate damage to books is not uncommon and overused items fall to pieces. Unfortunately, however, this section suffers from a number of unnecessary limitations. The most serious limitation is that this section only applies to a limited range of copyright subject matter. This may not, however, be immediately apparent, because the section states that if the prescribed conditions are complied with a librarian or an archivist may make a copy 'from *any item* in the permanent collection of the library or archive' in order to preserve or replace it.[73] However, the section then goes on to state that it is only copyright in a literary, dramatic or musical work and in the typographical arrangement and in any accompanying illustrations that will not be infringed where reliance is placed on this section. In other words, section 42 only applies to the usual categories of works covered by the library and archive provisions and not, therefore, to most artistic works (including, for example, maps and photographs), nor to sound recordings or films. This is an area in which the law must be changed to facilitate the preservation of these other works. Many old films, sound recordings and photographs (including glass negatives and dangerous, cellulose nitrate film) are deteriorating and need copying for preservation purposes. It would be a sad state of affairs, and in some cases little short of a national disaster, if this work were not done because copyright permission could not be obtained.[74] We suspect that much of the preservation work of sound recordings, films and photographs is done in infringement of copyright.[75]

On a rather different note, it would also be useful if the Act specifically covered copying for other purposes related to the preservation of rare works. For example, it would be desirable if the Act also allowed copying for the purpose of obtaining insurance.

Legal deposit libraries: copying of non-print publications

The third provision that allows librarians to make copies of a work so as to expand and protect their holdings came into effect on 1 February 2004.

---

[72] See Padfield, *Copyright*, pp. 120–1.   [73] CDPA 1988, s. 42(1) (emphasis added).
[74] Often such permission cannot be obtained because the copyright owner cannot be identified.
[75] It should also be noted that s. 42 largely reproduces s. 7(5) of the Copyright Act 1956. It seems likely that at the time the 1956 Act was passed the preservation of sound recordings and films was not seen as a matter of great cultural or economic importance and/or such copying was regarded as difficult or impossible.

The existing library exceptions 157

This new provision was introduced by the Legal Deposit Libraries Act 2003 and is designed to protect the position of the 'legal deposit' or 'copyright' libraries, that is, the six libraries that have been entitled to receive a copy of everything published in the United Kingdom since the passage of the Copyright Act 1911.[76] The 2003 Act was designed to deal with the concern that non-print forms of publication, in particular, publication on the Internet, might undermine the special role the copyright libraries have in providing world-class library resources. To this end the 2003 Act amended the 1988 Act by introducing a new section (section 44A). This section allows a person acting on behalf of a deposit library to copy a work from the Internet without infringing copyright, provided that the work is of a description prescribed by regulations and is sufficiently connected to the United Kingdom (again as prescribed by regulations), and provided that all other prescribed conditions are complied with.[77] The Secretary of State is also empowered to make regulations to allow material that has been copied from the Internet to be reused in ways that would otherwise amount to an infringement and, more generally, to make provision such that other non-print publications acquired by the deposit libraries may be utilised without infringing copyright.[78] Furthermore, the Secretary of State can order that in addition to providing copies of works, publishers must provide a copy of any computer program and any information required to access the work.[79]

At the time of writing, no regulations under this section have been made, and the government has made it clear that it intends to implement the Act in stages following consultations with interested parties.[80] It is therefore difficult to predict what impact the introduction of section 44A will have or to know whether, in practice, its impact will extend much beyond the voluntary arrangements that are already in place between publishers and the copyright libraries.[81] This new exception is interesting, however, in that it represents an attempt to update the law relating to libraries in a way that stands in marked contrast to the approach that has been adopted to implementation of the Information Society

---

[76] Copyright Act 1911, s. 15. This provision has now been superseded by the 2003 Act. Prior to 1911 earlier copyright legislation also contained deposit requirements, and the origins of the deposit system in the United Kingdom can be traced back to the early seventeenth century: Laddie et al., 3rd edn, para. 33.19. The libraries in question are the British Library, the National Library of Scotland, the National Library of Wales, the Bodleian Library, Oxford, Cambridge University Library and the Library of Trinity College, Dublin.
[77] CDPA 1988, s. 44A(1). [78] Ibid., s. 44A(2); Legal Deposit Libraries Act 2003, s. 7.
[79] Legal Deposit Libraries Act 2003, s. 6.
[80] As to which, see www.culture.gov.uk/museums_and_galleries/legal_deposit.htm.
[81] See www.bl.uk/news/webcase.html.

Directive.[82] It is notable that the Legal Deposit Libraries Act 2003 began life as a private member's bill, a point to which we return in Chapter 8.

Lending of copies by libraries and archives

It was seen in the last chapter that implementation of the Rental Right Directive resulted in the introduction of a new public lending right.[83] It was also seen that although the Directive requires member states to introduce a lending right for most types of copyright subject matter, the Directive also allows member states to derogate from the lending right in certain circumstances. Thus the Directive allows member states to exempt certain establishments from the right.[84] More generally, the Directive allows member states to derogate from the lending right in cases where authors are provided with remuneration for such lending, and the Directive provides expressly that member states are entitled to take 'cultural promotion objectives' into account when determining the form and level of this remuneration.[85]

In reliance on the discretion outlined above, the UK government introduced section 40A of the 1988 Act. One effect of this section is that where a book[86] falls within 'the public lending right scheme',[87] a public library[88] may lend the work without infringing copyright.[89] The other effect of this section is to exempt entirely from the lending right prescribed not-for-profit libraries and archives other than 'public libraries'.[90] In other words, any prescribed library or archive which does not fall within the definition of a public library and which is not conducted for profit may lend to the public works of any description without infringing

---

[82] And see Information Society Directive, Art. 9: 'This Directive shall be without prejudice to provisions concerning . . . legal deposit requirements.'

[83] That is, the right to control making a work available on terms that it will or may be returned, otherwise than for direct or indirect economic or commercial advantage through an establishment which is accessible to the public: CDPA 1988, s. 18A(2).

[84] See Rental Rights Directive, Art. 5(3). Cf. CDPA 1988, s. 36A, and see Chapter 4.

[85] See Rental Rights Directive, Art. 5(1).

[86] Other types of work, including, most importantly, second recordings and films, are not covered by this exception. In contrast, s. 40A(2), considered below, applies to all types of work, but 'public libraries' are prevented from relying on this exception.

[87] That is, the system of remuneration for authors whose works are lent by public libraries created by the Public Lending Right Act 1979 (as amended).

[88] See CDPA 1988, s. 178: 'public library' means, in particular, a library administered by or on behalf of a library authority.

[89] *Ibid.*, s. 40A(1). This section was apparently introduced in reliance on Art. 5(1) of the Rental Rights Directive.

[90] CDPA 1988, s. 40A(2). This section was apparently introduced in reliance on Art. 5(3) of the Rental Rights Directive.

copyright.[91] These provisions are clearly of considerable practical importance for libraries and archives. They should, however, be seen alongside other provisions that cut down the scope of the public lending right under UK law.[92] Taken together these provisions reflect the limited nature of the public lending right under the Directive (a right which is not recognised at all under the international conventions relating to copyright). As such, these provisions define the limits of a right that sits at the margins of copyright law as much as they reflect the overriding interest that the public has in being able to borrow copyright works from libraries. This underscores the point that the permitted act provisions perform a range of different functions.[93]

Copy of a work required as a condition of export

The final provision to be found under the 'Libraries and Archives' heading in the 1988 Act applies where a copy of a work cannot be lawfully exported from the United Kingdom unless a copy is deposited in a library or archive. Section 44 therefore provides that 'if an article of cultural or historical importance or interest cannot lawfully be exported from the United Kingdom unless a copy of it is made and deposited in an appropriate library or archive, it is not an infringement of copyright to make that copy'. This section has to be understood in the context of domestic and European export controls that apply to important cultural goods.[94] In the case of documentary and photographic material, one option is to allow the work to be exported on condition that a copy of the work is deposited in a suitable library or archive. In recognition of the fact that the person seeking the export licence may well not be the copyright owner, the 1988 Act allows that person to make the required copy.[95] Thus although this provision is related to the achievement of important cultural objectives, its operation is quite different from that of the other library and archive provisions in that it provides a mechanism by which

---

[91] In effect, 'prescribed library' in this context has the same meaning in relation to s. 40A(2) as in relation to ss. 38 and 39 (see above n. 34 and accompanying text), except that public libraries are specifically excluded. See CDPA 1988, s. 40A(2); Copyright and Related Rights Regulations 1996 (SI 1996 No 2967), reg. 35. All not-for-profit archives are 'prescribed archives' for the purposes of this section.

[92] Namely, CDPA 1988, s. 36A (copyright not infringed by the lending of a work by an educational establishment – see Chapter 4) and s. 66 (power given to Secretary of State to grant compulsory licences for the lending of works).

[93] See the Introduction to this work.

[94] See, generally, the Department for Culture, Media and Sport Notice, *UK Export Licensing for Cultural Goods: Procedures and Guidance for Exporters of Works of Art and Other Cultural Goods*, Issue 5 (28 Feb. 2003); N. Palmer, *Art Loans* (London: Kluwer, 1997).

[95] For detailed discussion see *Copinger*, paras. 9.49–9.50.

works can be supplied to libraries and archives, rather than a mechanism to allow such bodies to make copies.[96]

Miscellaneous exceptions

In addition to the exceptions grouped under the 'Libraries and Archives' heading, there are a number of related provisions to be found in other portions of the permitted acts chapter of the 1988 Act. These provisions have much in common with the miscellaneous exceptions that we have examined elsewhere (in particular, in Chapter 2). Although these miscellaneous exceptions can be useful in particular circumstances, they do not begin to address the problems with the more general provisions that we have identified, and even some of these provisions are unduly limited. The miscellaneous provisions that are relevant to copying by libraries and archives and to the operation of institutional users of copyright more generally are those contained in section 47 (copying of material open to public inspection and on public registers), section 49 (copying of public records), section 61 (recording of folksongs for archival purposes), section 75 (recording of broadcasts for archival purposes) and section 63 (advertisement of the sale of artistic works). These provisions will be briefly examined in turn.

The first miscellaneous provision with which we are concerned is contained in section 47 of the 1988 Act. Section 47 allows for the reproduction of copyright material held on various types of public register.[97] For example, this section allows the copying of patent specifications, planning

---

[96] But see also Legal Deposit Libraries Act 2003, s. 9: where a person is required to deliver a copy of a work or subject matter needed to access another work to the copyright libraries, that delivery is to be taken 'not to breach any contract relating to any part of the work to which that person is a party' and 'not to infringe copyright, publication right or database right in relation to any part of the work or any patent'. For the context in which this provision operates see the subsection 'Legal deposit libraries: copying of non-print publications', above.

[97] In fact s. 47 contains three rather different exceptions, namely: (1) in relation to material that is open to public inspection pursuant to a statutory requirement, or is on a statutory register, copyright in the material as a literary work is not infringed by the copying of factual information contained in the work, but copies cannot be issued to the public by virtue of this exception (s. 47(1)); (2) in relation to material that is open to public inspection pursuant to a statutory requirement, copyright is not infringed by the copying or issuing to the public of copies of the material for the purpose of enabling the material to be inspected at a more convenient time or place or in order to facilitate some other statutory purpose (s. 47(2)); and (3) in relation to material that is open to public inspection pursuant to a statutory requirement or which is on a statutory register and which contains information about matters of general scientific, technical, commercial or economic interest, copyright is not infringed by the copying or issuing to the public of copies of the material for the purpose of disseminating information (s. 47(3)). In each case the copying must be done by or with the authority of an appropriate person.

applications and records held by the Registrar of Companies.[98] This section thus performs an important function in furthering the dissemination of information to the public, which is the principal reason for making information available through public registers.

The second exception with which we are concerned relates to the copying of public records. Section 49 of the Act provides that public records[99] which are open to public inspection may be copied and a copy may be supplied to any person without infringing copyright, provided that the copy is made by or with the authority of an appropriate person. This provision has much in common with the provision relating to the copying of material on public registers in that it also promotes access to material which it has been decided ought to be available to the public. It is also closely tied to the operation of public archives.

The third and fourth exceptions that are worth noting in this context are the provisions that allow for the recording of folksongs and broadcasts for 'archival' purposes (ss. 61 and 75 respectively). In relation to the recording of folksongs, the Act provides that a sound recording of unpublished lyrics of unknown authorship[100] can be made in order to deposit the recording with a designated body,[101] provided that the performer did not prohibit the making of the recording.[102] Once such a recording has been made, a single copy can then be supplied to persons who require them for research for a non-commercial purpose or for private study.[103] In relation to the recording of broadcasts, the Act provides that a designated body may record a broadcast for 'archival' purposes without infringing any copyright in the broadcast or in any underlying work.[104] Sections 61 and 75 are similar in effect, in that they both aim to provide a permanent record of potentially important works that might otherwise be lost – in the case of folksongs because of declining interest in preserving an oral tradition and in the case of broadcasts because of their evanescent nature. Both provisions are, however, extremely limited in scope. For example, the folksongs provision does not apply to musical

---

[98] See *Copinger*, para. 9.54.
[99] As defined by the Public Records Act (Northern Ireland) 1923, the Public Records (Scotland) Act 1937, the Public Records Act 1958, and the Government of Wales Act 1998.
[100] The heading 'folksongs' is thus merely a signpost: *Copinger*, para. 9.86.
[101] As to these bodies see the Copyright (Recording of Folksongs for Archives) (Designated Bodies) Order 1989 (SI 1989 No 1012).
[102] CDPA 1988, s. 61(2)(c).
[103] *Ibid.*, s. 61(4); Copyright (Recording of Folksongs for Archives) (Designated Bodies) Order 1989, reg. 3(2).
[104] CDPA 1988, s. 75(1). See, as to 'designated bodies' for the purpose of this section, Copyright (Recording for Archives of Designated Class of Broadcasts and Cable Programmes) (Designated Bodies) Order 1993 (SI 1993 No 74).

works unaccompanied by lyrics, and there is no right under the recording of broadcasts provision to allow copies to be supplied for research or private study purposes, even if the recording was made many years before and even if there is no other source from which a copy of the broadcast can be obtained.

The final miscellaneous provision with which we are concerned is different from the other provisions we have looked at in this chapter in that it is a provision that provides some protection for galleries. Section 63 of the 1988 Act provides that 'it is not an infringement of copyright in an artistic work to copy it, or to issue copies to the public, for the purpose of advertising the *sale* of the work'.[105] This provision recognises that attracting the public to the sale of artistic works may well require the ability to reproduce the work in auction catalogues and on other promotional material. It is sufficiently broad to cover a gallery that is exhibiting the works of one or more artists in cases where the works are available for purchase at the end of the exhibition, thus providing galleries with some limited protection. It is important to emphasise, however, that this section does not allow for works to be reproduced in order to advertise their exhibition more generally. Most museums and galleries and indeed libraries host exhibitions in order to entice the public through their doors. It seems only logical that they ought to be able to use copies of the items in their exhibitions in order to advertise the event. In most cases, of course, copyright owners will not object to such use, but including it within the remit of an exception would have the advantage that time would not then have to be spent by the hosting institution in obtaining the owner's consent. Moreover, as is so often the case in this area of copyright law, there is always the danger that it may be impossible to trace the owner. In contrast, it will be seen in the final chapter that the Information Society Directive allows member states to provide an exception to allow use for the purpose of advertising 'the public exhibition *or* sale of artistic works'.[106]

Conclusion

In this chapter we have argued that the current provisions relating to libraries and archives are unsatisfactory in a number of respects. In particular, we have argued that these provisions apply to an unduly limited range of subject matter, that they prevent librarians and archivists from

---

[105] CDPA 1988, s. 63(1) (emphasis added). The Act goes on to provide, however, that 'where a copy which would otherwise be an infringing copy is made in accordance with this section but is subsequently dealt with for any other purpose, it shall be treated as an infringing copy for the purposes of that dealing': CDPA 1988, s. 63(2).

[106] Information Society Directive, Art. 5(3)(j) (emphasis added).

passing on to their readers the benefits offered by new technologies, and that the needs of related institutions such as museums and galleries have not been adequately accounted for, for example, because of the restrictions that copyright imposes on the ability of these institutions to place digitised images of works held in their collections in electronic catalogues. We have also indicated that the Information Society Directive would allow many of these problems to be rectified if the UK government could be persuaded to undertake a radical overhaul of the exceptions.

Part II

How we got here

6 Markets and metaphors

> Perhaps the immobility of the things that surround us is forced upon them by our conviction that they are themselves and not anything else, by the immobility of our conception of them.
>
> Marcel Proust, *Swann's Way*[1]

The aim thus far has been to demonstrate that the United Kingdom's existing approach to the permitted acts brings copyright into conflict with a number of important rights and interests and causes a range of real difficulties for both individual and institutional users. We hope that this analysis will speak for itself to some extent. In particular, we hope that our exploration of the practical difficulties that users face in various circumstances will give owner representatives pause for thought and will help counteract their natural reflex to oppose measures that would liberalise the exceptions. In the next three chapters we build on this analysis by exploring some of the reasons why the United Kingdom has adopted an overly restrictive approach to the exceptions. We argue that a variety of factors – political, constitutional, institutional and accidental – together with judicial attitudes have to be accounted for. An exploration of these factors reveals that the current approach to the exceptions does not result from the adoption of a coherent or well thought through approach to copyright as a whole. In so far as copyright can be said to have been consciously shaped, our analysis suggests that for the most part it has been crafted to reflect the interests of powerful and well-organised groups that are able to operate effectively at both the national and international level. The vast majority of such organisations represent the interests of right holders.

We begin our analysis, however, by considering in this chapter various ideas and assumptions about copyright and the role of the exceptions which help to underpin the current (overly restrictive) regime. The argument is not that these understandings have been consistently 'written into' the present Act. As we have just noted, the Act does not embody a single

---

[1] Trans. C. K. Scott Moncrieff and T. Kilmartin (London: Vintage, 1996), p. 4.

conception of copyright, and the ideas that we explore in this chapter are not necessarily compatible with one another. Nevertheless, as we explain in Chapters 7 and 8, it is possible to identify cases where these understandings appear to have influenced legislators and policy makers directly. More generally, these understandings provide a language through which elements of the present system can be justified. This is important because, as Netanel notes, 'Naked self-interest can only go so far in shaping the contours of a legal regime. The most robust policy ideas are informed by a cogent rhetorical framework that eases their way to general acceptance.'[2] Our principal claim is that the ideas we explore in this chapter provide frameworks of this kind.

In the remainder of this chapter we focus on three claims that are made about copyright exceptions and the way in which they ought to be interpreted which help to justify the adoption of an overly restrictive approach. These are, first, that exceptions should only be available in cases where the owner is unlikely to licence the use in question; second, that the permitted acts have to be interpreted narrowly since they are exceptions to a property right; and, third, that copyright represents a 'balance' between competing interests. In examining these claims about the exceptions we inevitably touch on broader questions about the nature of copyright. As has already been suggested,[3] this is because debates about the proper scope of the copyright exceptions are to a large extent another opportunity to discuss the fundamental questions of the justifications for and the proper role of a copyright system, even if starting with the potential users of copyright works, rather than the potential owners, tends to cast these familiar questions in a new light.

Exceptions, licences and market failure

Perhaps the single most influential argument that has been used to support a maximalist vision of copyright is that copyright exceptions should only be available in the absence of appropriate licensing arrangements. In other words, if someone wishes to make use of a work they should first and foremost expect to have to pay for that use. Use should only be free if it would be impossible or at least impractical to obtain a licence in the particular circumstances in question. This 'licensing' argument is often encountered in the context of discussions about legislative reform and the way in which the law should be adapted to fit new technologies.

---

[2] N. Netanel, 'Copyright and a Democratic Civil Society' (1996) 106 *Yale Law Journal* 283, 306.
[3] See the Introduction to this work.

In particular, it is often said that new technologies will lower transaction costs by allowing actors to deal directly with one another (because of disintermediation caused by the Internet) and by allowing for the development of automated licence agreements which will reduce the need to negotiate permissions on a case-by-case basis. It has therefore been said that the exceptions will be rendered increasingly unnecessary.[4]

In addition, many commentators would also like to see courts taking the availability of licences into account when applying the existing exceptions. Thus it has been said that the availability of licences should be taken into account when considering whether the defendant's actions were 'fair' for the purposes of fair use or fair dealing exceptions. For example, Paul Goldstein has argued that a distinction should be drawn between cases where a work itself is parodied and cases of satire, where part of a work is used to provide a critique of individuals or institutions or society in general, arguing that it is only cases of parody that should fall within the fair use defence, because 'the copyright owner who is not willing to license a parody of his work may be more than willing, at a reasonable price, to license use of his work as a vehicle for social comment'.[5] The

---

[4] See Report of the Working Group on Intellectual Property Rights, *Intellectual Property Rights and the National Information Infrastructure* (Washington, DC, 1995), p. 82; Australian Copyright Council, *Copyright in the New Communications Environment: Balancing Protection and Access* (Redfern: Centre for Copyright Studies, 1999); Australian Copyright Council, *Fair Dealing in the Digital Age* (Redfern: Centre for Copyright Studies, 1996), in particular p. 34; P. Goldstein, *Copyright's Highway: From Gutenburg to the Celestial Jukebox* (New York: Hill & Wang, 1994), p. 224; T. Bell, 'Fair Use vs. Fared Use: The Impact of Automated Rights Management on Copyright's Fair Use Doctrine' (1998) 76 *North Carolina Law Review* 557; M. Fraser, 'Fair is Foul and Foul is Fair: From Analogue to Digital Fair Dealing' (1998) 9 *Journal of Law and Information Science* 93. See also R. Merges, 'The End of Friction? Property Rights and Contract in the "Newtonian" World of Online Commerce' (1997) 12 *Berkeley Technology Law Journal* 115, taking the view that the market failure argument will inevitably lead to the abandonment of the fair use doctrine in the online environment and proposing an alternative redistributive justification for fair use.

[5] P. Goldstein, *Copyright: Principles, Law, and Practice* (Boston: Little, Brown, 1989, Supplement 1993), para. 10.2.1. Other commentators have adopted a very similar position. See, for example, R. Posner, 'When Is Parody Fair Use?' (1992) 21 *Journal of Legal Studies* 67. But for a strong attack on this distinction from an economic perspective see R. Merges, 'Are You Making Fun of Me? Notes on Market Failure and the Parody Defense in Copyright Law' (1993) 21 *AIPLA Quarterly Journal* 305, 311: 'a parodist's choice of a particular "weapon" as embodying something else that is the ultimate "target" is not accidental. Indeed, a successful parody might often be expected to parody both a copyrighted work and the values it represents. Surely, for example, a parody of 'Gone With the Wind' might use the movie as a weapon to parody romanticized notions of the Civil War and southern "gallantry", while successfully mocking some of the overdone aspects of the film itself. The second problem with Posner's "weapon"/"target" distinction is his assumption that a copyright holder will normally license parodies of the first sort, but not the second. This seems wrong, at least in those cases where the "target" of the parody

influence of the licensing argument can clearly be observed in fair use cases in the United States.[6]

From a formalistic legal perspective the question of the relationship between the availability of licences and the provision of an exception is entirely circular, except in cases where the legislation specifically provides that an exception is not to be available if the owner has made licences available,[7] since, of course, users whose actions are covered by an exception do not need to seek a licence. It is therefore important to appreciate that the licensing argument invariably forms part of an economic analysis of copyright in which the exceptions are treated as legitimate only in so far as they are designed to overcome market failure, that is, circumstances in which the parties are unlikely to agree a licence. For example, it is often said that this may occur because the transaction costs of negotiating a licence may outweigh the value of that licence.

The more traditional and most influential economic rationale for copyright protection is that copyright operates as an incentive for the creation of certain types of cultural product. The underlying premise of the incentive theory is that a work will only be created if the expected revenues exceed the cost of expression and the cost of making and distributing copies. In addition, the price of a successful work must compensate for the risk of failure.[8] Copyright is needed as an incentive because creating a copyright work is often a time-consuming and expensive business, but once a work has been created it can usually be reproduced quickly and cheaply. This is said to create an almost classic public goods problem as, in the absence of copyright protection, others would be tempted to free ride – either potential purchasers would copy the work for themselves or rival publishers would emerge who would be able to undercut the author or first publisher, since they would not have to cover the cost of expression and, if they waited until a work was a proven success, neither would they have to bear the risk of failure. Thus without copyright protection no one would bother to create or publish copyright works or, at the very least, the market would become skewed towards cheap to produce, faddish works from which authors and publishers might be able to recoup their investment by relying on lead-time

---

is a set of values or cultural assumptions deeply cherished by the copyright holder or at least widely held by the segment of the public loyal to her.'

[6] See, e.g., *American Geophysical Union* v. *Texaco* 60 F 3d 913 (1994); *Princeton University Press* v. *Michigan Document Services* 99 F 3d 1381 (1996).

[7] The UK Act does contain a limited number of exceptions of this kind: CDPA 1988, ss. 31B–D, 35, 36, 60, 74. See Chapter 4 for more detail.

[8] The terminology employed here has been taken from an article by Landes and Posner that remains the single most important article on the economics of copyright law. See W. Landes and R. Posner, 'An Economic Analysis of Copyright Law' (1989) 18 *Journal of Legal Studies* 325.

Exceptions, licences and market failure

alone.[9] Incentive theorists who support the licensing argument do so on the basis that it is in cases of market failure that there is least danger that incentives will be eroded.[10]

The more recent approach to copyright economics, sometimes referred to as the 'neoclassical' approach, sees copyright not only as providing incentives for the creation of works, but also as a mechanism that facilitates the exchange of rights and hence ensures that works become transferred to actors who value them most highly, thereby perfecting the market for copyright works. As such, it is said that the owner's rights should extend to all economically valuable uses of a work.[11] Advocates of this maximalist vision of copyright insist not only that the exceptions be confined to cases of market failure, but also that even where it appears that transaction costs might lead to market failure, copyright owners must be given the opportunity to develop collective licensing or similar arrangements that will reduce transaction costs.[12] They therefore tend to favour a model in which exceptions are confined not merely to cases of likely market failure, but rather to cases where a defendant can prove actual market failure on the facts.[13]

---

[9] See *ibid.*, 332. It should be noted, however, that in Landes and Posner's later work they place less emphasis on the incentives to create provided by intellectual property rights. See W. Landes and R. Posner, *The Economic Structure of Intellectual Property Law* (Cambridge, Mass.: The Belknap Press of Harvard University Press, 2003), in particular pp. 9–10.

[10] See W. Gordon, 'Fair Use as Market Failure: A Structural and Economic Analysis of the Betamax Case and its Predecessors' (1982) 82 *Columbia Law Review* 1600, e.g. at 1604: 'The same economic considerations that guide the copyright system as a whole can also be used to suggest models of resolving the conflicts, providing a method of applying fair use both to achieve desirable dissemination and to avoid the erosion of incentives', and at 1618: 'Fair use should be denied whenever a substantial injury appears that will impair incentives' (but cf. Professor Gordon's later work, below n. 15); Landes and Posner, 'Economic Analysis', 357–8; R. Towse, *Creativity, Incentive and Reward: An Economic Analysis of Copyright and Culture in the Information Age* (Cheltenham: Edward Elgar, 2001), pp. 14, 142.

[11] See, e.g., Merges, 'Are You Making Fun of Me?', 306: 'And, it is important to point out, the literature has progressed beyond the point where a crude "incentive" story passes for analysis in every case'; Goldstein, *Copyright's Highway*, p. 236: 'the best prescription for connecting authors to their audiences is to extend rights into every corner where consumers derive value from literary and artistic works'. An excellent summary of the neoclassical position is provided by Netanel, 'Copyright'.

[12] See P. Goldstein, 'Preempted State Doctrines, Involuntary Transfers and Compulsory Licenses: Testing the Limits of Copyright' (1977) 24 *UCLA Law Review* 1107; M. Einhorn, 'Miss Scarlett's License Done Gone!: Parody, Satire, and Markets' (2002) 20 *Cardozo Arts and Entertainment Law Journal* 589; Bell, 'Fair Use'; D. Smith, 'Collective Administration of Copyright: An Economic Analysis' (1986) 8 *Research in Law and Economics* 137 (implicitly adopting this approach). See also Netanel's discussion, 'Copyright', 320–1.

[13] See Merges, 'Are You Making Fun of Me?' (but compare his later work, 'The End of Friction?'). For critical discussion see E. Kitch, 'Can the Internet Shrink Fair Use?' (1999) 78 *Nebraska Law Review* 880, pointing out that such an approach itself imposes

Aside from the specifics of the licensing argument, it is perhaps also worth drawing attention to the hostility to state intervention which underpins much economic analysis of law. From this perspective, overriding private property interests in order to further broad social goals such as increasing access to information or lowering the cost of education is always objectionable, as is clear from Posner's famous analogy: 'as we do not suppose that writers should be allowed to steal paper and pencils in order to reduce the cost of satire, neither is there a compelling reason to subsidize social criticism by allowing writers to use copyrighted materials without compensating the copyright holder'.[14]

As has already been indicated, the most important feature of the market failure argument is that it is often used to support demands for the curtailment of copyright exceptions in the digital environment, it being argued that the lowering of transaction costs between user and owner will eliminate the justification for the exceptions. Some economically minded commentators have challenged this conclusion by emphasising that the presence of high transaction costs is only one example of market failure,[15] or have argued that the non-exhaustible nature of intellectual goods undermines many of the traditional economic assumptions on which the market failure analysis rests,[16] or have proposed alternative, distributive, justifications for the exceptions.[17] More commonly, however, opposition to the licensing argument has come from commentators who are opposed to economic analysis of copyright more generally or who

---

transaction costs and noting, 'There is no case that suggests that George could not make use of Sam's copyrighted work because George knew Sam, knew his phone number, and knew he owned the copyright' (at 886); M. Africa, 'The Misuse of Licensing Evidence in Fair Use Analysis: New Technologies, New Markets and the Courts' (2000) 88 *California Law Review* 1145, discussing the problems that inevitably accompany the use of evidence as to the availability of licences.

[14] Posner, 'When Is Parody Fair Use?', 73. This point has recently been reiterated by Landes and Posner, *Economic Structure*, p. 158.

[15] L. Loren, 'Redefining the Market Failure Approach to Fair Use in an Era of Copyright Protection Systems' (1997) 5 *Journal of Intellectual Property Law* 1; B. Depoorter and F. Parisi, 'Fair Use and Copyright Protection: A Price Theory Explanation' (2002) 21 *International Review of Law and Economics* 453; W. Gordon, 'Market Failure and Intellectual Property: A Response to Professor Lunney' (2002) 82 *Boston University Law Review* 1031, arguing against a restrictive reading of her seminal article 'Fair Use as Market Failure' and insisting that 'to inquire into market failure is simply to ask, when can we as a society not safely rely on the bargain between owner and user to achieve social goals' and that her concern is with the broad notion of when 'markets let us down' (at 1037 and 1039, respectively). See also W. Gordon, 'Excuse and Justification in the Law of Fair Use: Commodification and Market Perspectives', in N. Elkin-Koren and N. Netanel (eds.), *The Commodification of Information* (The Hague: Kluwer Law International, 2002).

[16] G. Lunney, 'Fair Use and Market Failure: *Sony* Revisited' (2002) 82 *Boston University Law Review* 975. See also Guibault, pp. 86–7.

[17] Merges, 'The End of Friction?'.

are critical of the essentially conservative conclusions that most advocates of economic analysis draw. This is because, as has been seen, disputes over the scope of the copyright exceptions are often little more than a veneer disguising more fundamental disputes about the functions of and justifications for a copyright system. It is therefore impossible to separate objections to the licensing argument from objections to economic analyses of copyright as a whole. Opposition to economic analysis of copyright has taken a variety of forms. Rather than attempting to summarise the range of nuanced positions that individual commentators have taken, for present purposes it makes more sense to focus on the general thrust of the claims made by those opposed to economic analysis. More specifically, it is possible to identify three broad lines of attack that have been adopted by those opposed to the dominant economic models of copyright.

One line of attack has been to build alternative models of copyright with a view to demonstrating that copyright is not primarily about markets and wealth maximisation, but rather that it is a recognition of the natural right that authors have over their creations, that it provides the underpinnings of institutions necessary for a healthy democratic civil society, that it provides the best mechanism for striking a balance between our desire to reward authors whilst safeguarding other important interests, or that it is a result of lobbying pressure which is defended by an elite that 'has reason to support legal rules that reinforce the premise that rewards in a market system mirror intelligence, education, and effort'.[18] The precise role that the exceptions are said to play and the circumstances in which it is said that an exception ought to be available vary dramatically according to which of these alternative justifications or explanations is adopted, but, generally speaking, advocates of these alternative justifications or explanations would recognise that many of the exceptions are a reflection of some overriding non-monetisable interest. Such interests might include free speech, privacy, access to information, efficient public administration and the preservation and extension of cultural resources. From this perspective, the defences are best thought of not as 'exceptions' that represent a deviation from the marketplace norm of full property rights, but as 'users' rights' that are an integral and fundamental aspect of copyright law.[19]

---

[18] S. Sterk, 'Rhetoric and Reality in Copyright Law' (1996) 94 *Michigan Law Review* 1197, 1248.

[19] See, e.g., D. Vaver, *Copyright Law* (Toronto: Irwin Law, 2000), p. 190. Vaver's view has now been endorsed by the Supreme Court of Canada: *CCH Canadian* v. *Law Society of Upper Canada* [2004] SCC 13, para. 48. See Chapter 10 for a discussion of the rhetorical use of the language of 'users' rights'.

A second, related, approach adopted by some opponents of economic analysis of copyright has been to draw on objections to economic analysis of law in general. In particular, critics have focused on the wealth-maximisation principle on which economic theories of law rest. This is said to 'offer an essentially cold, hard and, in consequence, inordinately narrow vision of human nature'.[20] At its most fundamental this leads to the objection that, irrespective of its predictive power, a law and economics approach cannot account for all the values that copyright law ought to enshrine. Thus it has been doubted whether an analysis of copyright law that takes wealth-maximisation as its only value can properly respect artistic freedom and creativity.[21] Whilst an economic analysis of intellectual property rights may be less counterintuitive than an analysis of adoption laws that treats children as commodities,[22] it cannot satisfy completely anyone who accepts that, at least at its most serious, 'this is a branch of law which protects some of the finer manifestations of human achievement'.[23] Leaving this criticism aside, a law and economics approach built around *homo economicus*, rather than how people actually are, will inevitably wrongly predict the behaviour of actors in the copyright field.

Both of the above points can be illustrated by considering Landes and Posner's argument that moral rights do not, in fact, benefit authors. Such rights are normally said to be of most value as between the author and future assignees of copyright. For Landes and Posner, however, this means that authors do not gain anything from having such rights. Relying on traditional economic assumptions, Landes and Posner argue that potential assignees of copyright will take any (moral) rights retained by

---

[20] N. Duxbury, *Patterns of American Jurisprudence* (Oxford: Clarendon, 1997), p. 397. See also R. West, 'Authority, Autonomy and Choice: The Role of Consent in the Moral and Political Visions of Franz Kafka and Richard Posner' (1985) 99 *Harvard Law Review* 384, in particular at 388, arguing: 'Posner's actors, despite the ordinariness of the situations in which they find themselves, are not recognizable as ourselves or our neighbours. His wealth-maximizing, racially discriminating employer, his wealth-maximizing criminal who decides how best to use his opportunity time and his burglar's tools, and his wealth-maximizing tort victim who is compensated ex ante for an accident uncompensated ex post do not resemble the bigoted bosses, petty thieves, or the impoverished and paraplegic accident victims we may work with, know or be. The inner lives of Posner's characters, although engaged in such familiar situations are strikingly unrecognizable. They are not we, and their stark inner lives are not ours.'

[21] A. Yen, 'Restoring the Natural Law: Copyright as Labor and Possession' (1990) 51 *Ohio State Law Journal* 517, 542. More generally, see J. Coleman, *Markets, Morals and the Law* (Cambridge: Cambridge University Press, 1988), in particular pp. 111–15.

[22] Cf. E. Landes and R. Posner, 'The Economics of the Baby Shortage' (1978) 7 *Journal of Legal Studies* 323, e.g. at 327, where they argue: 'The thousands of children in foster care . . . are comparable to an unsold inventory stored in a warehouse.'

[23] Cornish and Llewelyn, p. 3.

the author into account when negotiating terms as to payment and will reduce the amount they are prepared to pay for an assignment of copyright accordingly.[24] On the other hand, they argue that even in the absence of statutory moral rights protection, authors can negotiate for control of the integrity of the work, a right to be named and so on.[25] Implicit in this analysis, however, is that artistic control is and ought to be monetisable, that there is nothing to choose between a world in which authors receive greater remuneration but lose all control over how their work is exploited or a world in which authors receive less payment but retain a degree of artistic control. But once we abandon the narrow set of values on which traditional law and economics rests, we can see that there might be good reasons for preferring the latter state of affairs.

If we turn to the predictive power of traditional law and economics analysis, it can be seen that the assumption that, in the absence of statutory moral rights protection, the right to control, say, the artistic integrity of a work will gravitate towards the actor who values it most highly (in effect, an application of the Coase Theorem) is now open to serious doubt. In particular, 'behavioural law and economics' (that is, a law and economics approach built around empirical evidence as to how people actually behave) teaches us that initial entitlements do matter. 'Endowment effects' (a manifestation of a more general phenomenon of 'loss aversion') mean that actors often weigh losses more heavily than gains.[26] This means that even if a right of integrity were fully transferable the grant of such a right to authors, rather than leaving them to negotiate for such a right, might well lead to more authors retaining artistic control since, because of endowment effects, authors may well value artistic control more highly when they start with a right of integrity than when they are forced to negotiate for artistic control. However, perhaps the still more important point to be drawn from behavioural law and economics is that we should be wary of even this conclusion in the absence of evidence as to how authors and potential assignees actually behave.

None of the above should be taken to indicate that we would not accept that *homo economicus* remains a useful analytical device with which to test standard assumptions about copyright. Landes and Posner have performed an important service in drawing our attention to the potentially

---

[24] Landes and Posner, 'Economic Analysis', 327; Landes and Posner, *Economic Structure*, p. 291.
[25] Landes and Posner, *Economic Structure*, p. 277.
[26] See C. Jolls, C. Sunstein and R. Thaler, 'A Behavioral Approach to Law and Economics', in C. Sunstein (ed.), *Behavioral Law and Economics* (New York: Cambridge University Press, 2000), pp. 17–19; D. Kahneman, J. Knetsch and R. Thaler, 'Experimental Tests of the Endowment Effect and the Coase Theorem', *ibid*.

negative impact of moral rights protection on authors' remuneration. Ultimately, however, law and economics only provides one potentially productive way of looking at copyright law. We should be equally prepared to look at copyright law through the eyes of the otherworldly artist in her garret and through the eyes of the movie executive who insists that she is concerned to ensure that good films are made, not merely films that will make the most money.[27]

The third, and in some respects most ambitious, approach adopted by opponents of economic analysis of copyright has been to attack such analysis on its own terms. At its most general this attack has come from commentators who have criticised the nature of the research that has been conducted in this area. In particular, and similarly to one of the points made above, it has been said that most of the economists working in this field have failed to conduct empirical research. But without such research economics is little more than 'applied moral philosophy'.[28] Nor is this simply an argument for economists to change their methodology, since it has been said that 'the empirical information necessary to calculate the effect of copyright law on the actions of authors, potential defendants and consumers . . . is probably uncollectable'.[29] Moreover, it has been argued that even if this data could be collected this would not solve the problems of economic analysis. The difficulty is that unlike economic analyses of other areas, such as criminal law, where there is an agreed goal (in the case of criminal law, that crime should be reduced), there is no agreement on the appropriate trade-off between production and dissemination of copyright works.[30]

Other critics within this third category have focused on the idea that copyright is necessary to provide incentives for the creation of copyright works. One argument is that there are other ways of generating incentives that may be at least as efficient as copyright protection; for example,

---

[27] Real-life examples of major players within the copyright industries who insist that they are not merely concerned with making money are not hard to find. Economists are often dismissive of such claims, but research across a variety of fields indicates that corporate executives are not just wealth maximisers. See I. Ayres and J. Braithwaite, *Responsive Regulation: Transcending the Deregulation Debate* (Oxford: Oxford University Press, 1992), pp. 22–3 and the sources referred to therein.

[28] See G. Priest, 'What Economists Can Tell Lawyers about Intellectual Property' (1986) 8 *Research in Law and Economics* 19, 22; and noting: 'I do not believe that it is unfair to say that the entire literature . . . of which I am aware has consisted of little more than assumptions. As a consequence, this literature [has] taught us almost nothing, nor has it guided research or thinking so that an approach with a firmer empirical base could be developed' (at 20). See also S. Light, 'Parody, Burlesque and the Economic Rationale for Copyright' (1979) 11 *Connecticut Law Review* 615, 621.

[29] Yen, 'Restoring the Natural Law', 542–3.   [30] See Priest, 'Economists'.

reliance could instead be placed on a system of state-funded rewards.[31] A more common argument is that there are many types of work that are currently protected by copyright that would be created in the same numbers even in the absence of copyright protection. Thus it has been said that works of fine art would still be created both because such works are often created for non-economic reasons and because the creators of such works have the possibility of selling the original, sometimes for large sums.[32] Similarly, it has been argued that there is no need to provide copyright protection for commissioned photographs or for architectural works[33] or for legal judgments[34] or for works created by salaried academics.[35] In reply it is sometimes said that even if authors often do not require an incentive to create works, publishers and other distributors will still need an incentive to distribute these works to the public. However, it has been pointed out that this has no application in the digital environment,[36] or to those types of artistic work that are not principally communicated to the public through the distribution of copies, or to photographs which are valued for their news content.[37] Moreover, one prominent commentator has suggested that even in other cases the history of copyright suggests that in the absence of legal protection publishers might still be able to make a profit by relying on their lead-time and by developing various other strategies to maximise their revenue.[38]

---

[31] See S. Shavell and T. Van Ypersele, 'Rewards versus Intellectual Property Rights' (2001) 44 *The Journal of Law and Economics* 525, 525: 'the intellectual property system does not enjoy any fundamental advantage over the reward system'. However, it should be noted that the authors confine their substantive analysis to the patent system, and they give little consideration to the political or constitutional objections to a reward system.

[32] See D. Gifford, 'Innovation and Creativity in the Fine Arts: The Relevance and Irrelevance of Copyright' (2000) 18 *Cardozo Arts and Entertainment Law Journal* 569.

[33] See Sterk, 'Rhetoric', in particular at 1213–14, 1225–6.

[34] D. Vaver, 'Intellectual Property: The State of the Art' (2000) 116 *Law Quarterly Review* 621, 631.

[35] *Ibid.* Cf. Landes and Posner, 'Economic Analysis', 331.

[36] See R. Ku, 'The Creative Destruction of Copyright: Napster and the New Economics of Digital Technology' (2002) 69 *University of Chicago Law Review* 263. Ku's analysis, however, is heavily reliant on the mythology of the information society and the transformative power of digital technologies. For criticism of this starting point see R. Burrell, 'The Information Society: Chances and Challenges', in C. Heath and A. Kamperman Sanders (eds.), *Intellectual Property in the Digital Age: Challenges for Asia* (London: Kluwer, 2001).

[37] See Gifford, 'Innovation'; Sterk, 'Rhetoric'.

[38] See S. Breyer, 'The Uneasy Case for Copyright: A Study of Copyright in Books, Photocopies and Computer Programs' (1970) 84 *Harvard Law Review* 281. See also A. Yen, 'A Preliminary Economic Analysis of Napster: Internet Technology, Copyright Liability, and the Possibility of Coasean Bargaining' (2001) 26 *University of Dayton Law Review* 247. But cf. Landes and Posner, 'Economic Analysis'; B. Tyerman, 'The Economic Rationale for Copyright Protection for Published Books: A Reply to Professor Breyer' (1971) 18 *UCLA Law Review* 1100; D. Long, 'First, "Let's Kill all the Intellectual

At the very least there is a strong argument that for all but the most expensive works (such as large-budget films) sufficient incentives could be provided to creators and distributors through a much more limited set of rights than copyright law currently provides.

A rather different critique of the incentive argument is that proponents of this justification for copyright have failed to explain the mechanism by which copyright provides an incentive to authors and publishers, given that there is widespread ignorance as to the nature and scope of copyright protection. As Jessica Litman puts it,

> much of the literature repackaging copyright in theoretical terms proceeds from the assumption that authors' creation of works is influenced by their awareness of the intricacies of the system. For those theorists who model the copyright law in economic or utilitarian terms, the assumption inheres in their approach: It is difficult to speak of the incentives supplied by a legal regime without relying on the convention that those whom the law seeks to prod are aware of the goodies that it offers as a bribe.[39]

There is certainly room for argument about this claim at the general level of whether copyright acts as an incentive to creation. In particular, it might be argued that there is general awareness of the financial rewards secured by successful creators and entrepreneurs in the copyright industries, and that it is this awareness that acts as an incentive. (By analogy, it could be noted that the mere fact that most members of the general public are not aware of the details of the sanctions attached to particular criminal offences does not mean that the criminal law fails to operate as a deterrent.) But when we turn to the argument that too much fair use or fair dealing will undermine incentives, it can be seen that this claim requires further elaboration. Given widespread ignorance as to the way in which the copyright system functions, it is clear that an expansion of the exceptions (which will pass unnoticed except by a handful of copyright lawyers) will not in itself lessen incentives. That is, actors will not take a change in the law into account directly when deciding whether to create or invest in a work. An expansion of the exceptions could thus only indirectly lessen incentives by reducing revenues. In order for the licensing argument to be convincing, therefore, it would have to be shown that authors and publishers are sensitive to small decreases in profit when, in fact, it has been seen that there is a good case to be made that for many types of work even a radical curtailment of copyright would not result in a decrease in supply.

Property Lawyers!": Musings on the Decline and Fall of the Intellectual Property Empire' (2001) 34 *John Marshall Law Review* 851.

[39] J. Litman, 'Copyright as Myth' (1991) 53 *University of Pittsburgh Law Review* 235, 241.

Yet a further line of attack has come from commentators who have emphasised the gulf between what economic analysis of copyright purports to offer and what it delivers in practice. The attraction of economic analysis is that it purports to offer certainty by providing us with definite criteria against which we can judge the effectiveness of our existing levels of copyright protection. Vague talk of balancing rights and interests can be replaced by a single criterion of effectiveness, namely, do our existing provisions maximise economic efficiency? In practice, however, economic theorists have often lent towards a maximalist vision of copyright, ignoring the barriers to creation thrown up by an overly broad copyright system. To the extent that they have tried to take account of other interests, economists have come 'dangerously close to the mushy balancing analysis from which economics was supposed to provide surcease'.[40] This inability of economics to provide greater certainty than other models of copyright perhaps explains why much economic analysis has tended to lend strong support to existing arrangements. As Boyle notes, 'it also makes one a little skeptical to note that [economic analyses] tend to track the existing case law with surprising fidelity'.[41]

An attempt has been made in this section to explain the relationship between the licensing argument and a particular set of justifications for copyright law. User groups will have to confront the licensing argument and its economic foundations head-on in the near future as copyright maximalists insist that the Internet and related technologies can lower transaction costs and hence will render the exceptions increasingly unnecessary. It is to be hoped that sufficient material has been presented here to demonstrate that the economic justification for copyright is far from uncontroversial, and that we have good cause to question the values on which economic analysis rests and to be sceptical about its predictive power. It has also been indicated that there are other, very different, justifications for copyright in which the exceptions are conceptualised as having a very different, sometimes even central, role. This should not, however, be taken to indicate that any one of these alternative justifications is by itself satisfactory. As was indicated in the Introduction to this work, a common problem shared by all of the dominant theories of copyright is that they are too limited in their outlook and their prescriptions are too inflexible. As a consequence they often cannot account adequately for the complexity of modern copyright statutes or all of the diverse range of subject matters now protected by copyright. The obvious

---

[40] J. Boyle, *Shamans, Software and Spleens* (Cambridge, Mass.: Harvard University Press, 1996), p. 39.
[41] *Ibid.*, p. 219.

reply is that theorists are concerned not with what copyright is or what copyright does, but rather with what copyright ought to be or ought to do. However, this defence sits uneasily alongside the tendency of many theorists to ground their theories in current copyright practice and to treat those elements that do not fit as anomalies.[42] Yet these 'anomalies' are often long-standing and will have formed the basis of agreements and entrenched understandings as much as any other aspect of copyright law. There comes a point when an element of a system becomes so engrained that if a theory can only account for it as an anomaly the presumption has to be that it is the theory that needs to be re-examined. Whilst this latter criticism has no application to less commonly encountered 'blue skies' theories of copyright, such theories are even more blind to the disruption to existing interests and expectations that the implementation of their models would entail, and the models themselves often feel crude compared with the complexity and diversity of the industries and activities underpinned by copyright law.

Copyright as a form of property

The second commonly held assumption that we should like to challenge, or at least subject to more rigorous analysis, is that because copyright is a form of property the exceptions must be read narrowly. This belief is inseparably linked to some notion of the sanctity of property. Its effects can be seen in recent UK cases that have adopted a restrictive interpretation of the exceptions.[43] Moreover, in the context of trade marks, the European Court of Justice (ECJ) has used this form of reasoning to support an expansive reading of the right of the owner of a mark to prevent importation.[44] If left unchallenged there is a danger that the ECJ could apply a similar logic to justify a restrictive reading of the relevant provisions of the Information Society Directive.[45]

One fundamental challenge to thinking about copyright as a form of property comes from commentators who have argued that the 'metaphor' of property provides an inappropriate description of the subject matter of intellectual property rights[46] and who have called for the language of

---

[42] See, e.g., Netanel, 'Copyright'; Landes and Posner, 'Economic Analysis'; Merges, 'Are You Making Fun of Me?'; Yen, 'Restoring the Natural Law'; L. Patterson and S. Lindberg, *The Nature of Copyright: A Law of Users' Rights* (Athens, Ga.: University of Georgia Press, 1991); L. Lacey, 'Of Bread and Roses and Copyrights' [1989] *Duke Law Journal* 1539, all of whom draw on current law and practice to support their theories.

[43] See *Hyde Park v. Yelland* [2001] Ch 143; *Ashdown v. Telegraph Group* [2001] Ch 685, and see the discussions of these cases in Chapters 2 and 3.

[44] *Silhouette v. Hartlauer* [1998] 2 CMLR 953.   [45] See also Chapter 10.

[46] See Vaver, 'Intellectual Property', 632–4; J. Litman, *Digital Copyright* (New York: Prometheus, 2001), p. 81; C. Craig, 'Locke, Labour and Limiting the Author's Right: A

property to be replaced with the language of monopoly privileges.[47] A rather different, but equally fundamental, challenge to thinking about copyright as a property right comes from Streeter's work on collecting societies. Streeter argues persuasively that the collective administration of copyright transforms its character so that it becomes the basis of a highly bureaucratic regime in which owners and users alike are confronted by a system that employs complex formulae to determine entitlements and liabilities.[48] Such a system, which results in 'welfare payments' being made to authors,[49] and which is heavily regulated by the state because of the monopolistic nature of collecting societies, is impossible to reconcile with calls to respect the sanctity of copyright.

Even if we leave the above challenges aside, there are a number of flaws in the argument that the proprietary nature of copyright means that the exceptions have to be interpreted in a restrictive fashion. One problem with this argument is that it is dependent on the rights of owners being treated as somehow 'prior' to the exceptions. It is as if the owner is seen as having some pre-existing natural estate over which the state has created rights of way. A similar sense of the respective priorities between owners and users can be seen in assertions that the exceptions represent a 'tax' on copyright owners, as, for example, can be found in the 1995 report of the US Working Group on Intellectual Property Rights, which stated, 'The Working Group rejects the notion that copyright owners should be taxed – apart from all others – to facilitate the legitimate goal of "universal access".'[50] Yet it is equally possible to see the exceptions as markers which help determine what rights the owner actually has. Indeed, some of the United Kingdom's permitted act provisions quite clearly take this form. In particular, reference has already been made to

---

Warning Against a Lockean Approach to Copyright' (2002) 28 *Queen's Law Journal* 1, 57: 'The powerful and mesmerizing badge of "property", whose force is compounded by the natural law tradition's labour-to-property equation, is not a helpful model for copyright. Instead of facilitating our analysis, it takes over our understanding and distorts our policy decisions.'

[47] See P. Drahos, *A Philosophy of Intellectual Property* (Aldershot: Dartmouth, 1996), p. 223, and, more generally, his attack on the 'proprietarian creed'.

[48] T. Streeter, 'Broadcast Copyright and the Bureaucratization of Property' (1992) 10 *Cardozo Arts and Entertainment Law Journal* 567. See also M. Kretschmer, 'The Failure of Property Rules in Collective Administration: Rethinking Copyright Societies as Regulatory Instruments' [2002] EIPR 126; R. Merges, 'Contracting into Liability Rules: Intellectual Property Rights and Collective Rights Organizations' (1996) 84 *California Law Review* 1293; Bently and Sherman, p. 270.

[49] Streeter, 'Broadcast Copyright', 576.

[50] Working Group on Intellectual Property Rights 1995, *Intellectual Property Rights*, p. 84. For criticism of the strong pro-owner bias of this report see P. Samuelson, 'The Copyright Grab' [1996] (Jan.) *Wired*, 57; M. Davison, 'Some Implications of the US Working Group's Report on Intellectual Property and the National Information Infrastructure' (1995) 6 *Journal of Law and Information Science* 228.

the provisions relating to typefaces that establish a distinctive and limited form of copyright.[51] Reference could also be made to the permitted acts provisions that take effect by defining certain activities in such a way that they fall outside the scope of the owner's exclusive rights,[52] or to the provisions that reinforce the limited duration of copyright.[53] In contrast, the type of provisions with which we are principally concerned can be thought of in a number of different ways. In certain respects it does make sense to think of them as exceptions, but they too can be treated as marking out the rights the owner actually has. This was recognised by the Australian Copyright Law Review Committee, which, when commenting on the fair dealing provisions in Australia, noted that 'fair dealing is not a defence to infringement; rather, it defines, the boundaries of copyright owners' rights'.[54]

Once it has been recognised that it is equally possible to see the permitted acts as partly defining the scope of the property, it can be seen that it does not automatically follow that these provisions should be interpreted narrowly. It can also be seen that referring to the permitted act provisions as 'exceptions' can itself be unhelpful in so far as it reinforces the idea that this aspect of copyright is somehow outside the core of the system. A concern about the potential significance of the language being employed to describe the permitted acts has led some commentators to refer to the permitted acts as 'users' rights'.[55] While we refer to the permitted acts and other defences as exceptions throughout most of this work,[56] as part of the package of reform measures we propose we also call for the permitted acts to be restyled as users' rights (although we accept that the language of users' rights is itself not unproblematic).

On a more abstract level it is interesting to note that in so far as the nature of copyright as a property right is given any thought, it seems to be assumed that copyright is a property right *over a work*. Somewhat bizarrely therefore (given the intangible nature of intellectual property rights) it is as if copyright is being treated as a right over a *thing*. In the classic formulation of property rights given by Blackstone, it is as if

---

[51] See CDPA 1988, ss. 54–55 and see the Introduction to this work.
[52] As was seen in Chapter 4, s. 34 of CDPA 1988 provides that the performance of a literary, dramatic or musical work in an educational establishment is 'not a public performance for the purpose of infringement of copyright', thereby taking such performances outside the owner's exclusive right of performance.
[53] See CDPA 1988, ss. 57, 66A, which allow a user to copy a work at a time when it is reasonable to assume that copyright has expired.
[54] Australian Copyright Law Review Committee, *Simplification of the Copyright Act 1968 Part 1: Exceptions to the Exclusive Rights of Copyright Owners* (Canberra: 1998), para. 4.01.
[55] See, e.g., Vaver, *Copyright Law*, p. 190. More generally, see Patterson and Lindberg, *Nature of Copyright*.
[56] See the Introduction to this work for further explanation.

copyright were a form of 'that sole and despotic dominion which one man claims and exercises over the external things of the world, in total exclusion of the right of any other individual in the universe'.[57] Most recent property theorists, however, have chosen to treat property rights as a set of relations.[58] Treating property as a category of relations allows us to account for the host of restrictions and limitations that are placed on property rights in modern societies. It allows us to recognise that property rights are 'always subject to limitations based on the rights of other individuals in the universe'.[59] Reinterpreting copyright in this way would further undermine the assumption that the permitted acts have to be read narrowly. This is because once we think about copyright as creating a set of relationships, rather than creating rights over a thing, we are forced to recognise that there is nothing 'exceptional' about giving an owner one set of rights as against a commercial publisher and a very different set of rights as against a student or researcher.

A rather different problem with thinking about copyright as a property right flows not so much from this categorisation per se, but more from the asymmetry that exists between our understanding of intellectual property and our understanding of other forms of personal property. Logically, the fact that copyright is a property right should only push us a very limited way towards strong rights, since copyright constantly intersects with other forms of personal property – copyright controls what people can do with their computers, their photocopiers and their CD collections. It might therefore be expected that much of the thinking about the permitted acts would have to be concerned with attempting to reconcile the conflict that occurs when these different spheres of ownership collide. That this is not the case is probably due in large part to the very different states of health of intellectual property law on the one hand and the rest of personal

---

[57] W. Blackstone, *Commentaries on the Laws of England*, 5th edn (Oxford: Clarendon, 1773), vol. 2, p. 2.
[58] See F. Cohen, 'Dialogue on Private Property' (1954) 9 *Rutgers Law Review* 357. See also W. Hohfeld, *Fundamental Legal Conceptions* (New Haven: Yale University Press, 1923), p. 28: 'Sometimes [the word 'property'] is employed to indicate the physical object to which various legal rights, privileges, etc., relate; then again – with far greater discrimination and accuracy – the word is used to denote the legal interest (or aggregate of legal relations) appertaining to such physical object.' In contrast, in his theory of property, Penner puts the 'thing' centre stage, but in doing so concludes that intellectual property rights are not a true form of property. See J. Penner, *The Idea of Property in Law* (Oxford: Clarendon, 1997), in particular at p. 118, where, in the course of reviewing late-nineteenth-century discussions of the nature of intangible property, he notes, 'These authors' views on intellectual property are similarly stimulating: not one of them embraces the idiotic fiction that intellectual property constitutes property in ideas (patents) or expressions (copyright). They see it for what it is, a certain class of rights to monopolies.'
[59] Cohen, 'Dialogue', 362.

property law on the other. Whereas intellectual property is an expanding domain that has attracted a great deal of scholarly attention over recent years, the rest of our law of personal property 'is in a bad state . . . interest has ebbed away and with it understanding'.[60]

The neglect of personal property is particularly acute as regards the subcategory which intersects with copyright most often, that is, choses in possession. As a result there is no agreement and very little debate about what rights flow from ownership of a chose in possession – does the owner have the right to use the goods for their 'ordinary' purpose? Does the owner have a right of repair? or the right to replace consumable components from whatever source they choose? When does a subsequent purchaser get the benefit of a licence (express or implied) between the copyright owner and the original owner of the goods? From time to time the courts have turned their attention to these issues. Most notably, in *British Leyland* v. *Armstrong*[61] the House of Lords considered whether an owner of tangible personal property might have a right of repair. The case arose out of a dispute between British Leyland and a manufacturer of spare parts. British Leyland alleged that Armstrong, which made its own spares for British Leyland cars, had indirectly infringed its copyright in drawings for exhaust pipes. The House of Lords held that there was no infringement because a purchaser of a car has a right to repair the vehicle and that right extends to the purchase of parts from competing manufacturers. Lord Templeman's speech, with which Lord Scarman agreed, is particularly significant. Lord Templeman based his decision on an extension of the land law principle of non-derogation from grant, concluding that the vendor of a car could not use property it retained (in this case copyright) so as to render the car unfit for the purpose for which it was sold.[62]

Subsequent cases, however, have made it clear that the right of repair will only apply in the most exceptional circumstances, to the point that it is at least arguable that the right of repair has been abolished.[63] In *Canon Kabushiki Kaisha* v. *Green Cartridge*[64] Lord Hoffmann, for the Privy

---

[60] P. Birks, 'Personal Property: Proprietary Rights and Remedies' (2000) 11 *King's College Law Journal* 1, 1. A similar point is made by Professor Bridge: M. Bridge, *Personal Property Law*, 2nd edn (London: Blackstone Press, 1996), p. vii. See also A. Bell, *A Modern Law of Personal Property in England and Ireland* (London: Butterworths, 1989), p. 23, who notes that the incoherence of the category of personal property has helped to transform intellectual property into 'a third category, alongside real and personal property'.
[61] [1986] AC 577.   [62] *Ibid.*, 641.
[63] G. Llewellyn, 'Does Copyright Law Recognise a Right to Repair?' [1999] EIPR 596; Bently and Sherman, p. 227.
[64] [1997] AC 728.

Council, pointed out that in land law non-derogation from grant is based on the presumed intention of the parties, whereas Lord Templeman's decision was clearly not based on any form of implied licence. Thus, according to Lord Hoffmann, the decision in *British Leyland* 'cannot be regarded as truly founded upon any principle of the law of contract or property'.[65] Lord Hoffmann therefore thought that the decision in *British Leyland* was better explained on public policy grounds and that the right to repair will only arise when the potential injustice to consumers is plain and obvious. A further important restriction was placed on the right of repair by Jacob J in *Mars* v. *Teknowledge*,[66] who concluded that such a right could not arise in a case where infringement of copyright in a computer program or a database is alleged, since these areas have now been harmonised at the European level and the relevant directives do not provide for a right of repair.

Although there is nothing wrong as such with the reasoning in *Canon* and *Mars*, these cases illustrate that at present any attempt to restrain copyright by relying on rights inherent in the ownership of personal property is always going to be vulnerable to the charge that there is no precedential or theoretical justification to underpin such rights. If a right of repair were to be understood as an aspect of the law of personal property, rather than as an exceptional application of public policy, Jacob J's point in *Mars* would also carry much less weight – the right to repair would then be seen as flowing from a separate and unharmonised system of property rights.

It is also instructive to contrast the lack of any sense that the ownership of tangible personal property ought to place limits on the exercise of copyright with what happens in the rarer situation where copyright intersects with the ownership of land. Here the law expressly provides that the reconstruction of a building (for whatever purpose) will not infringe any copyright in the building or in any preliminary drawings or plans.[67] Similarly, it has been held that employing an architect to prepare plans for the purpose of obtaining planning permission carries with it an implied right to build the building contained in the plans.[68] Mention could also

---

[65] *Ibid.*, 737.
[66] [2000] FSR 138. *United Wire* v. *Screen Repair Services* [2000] 4 All ER 353 is also instructive. In this case Lord Hoffmann rejected the argument that the owner of a patented product has a right of repair (cf. *Solar Thompson* v. *Barton* [1977] RPC 537), preferring the interpretation that the ability to repair an article flows merely from the residual freedom that is left to the owner of tangible property once the patent owner's right to control the 'making' of a product has been delineated.
[67] CDPA 1988, s. 65.
[68] *Blair* v. *Osborne & Tomkins* [1971] 2 QB 78, but cf. *Stovin-Bradford* v. *Volpoint* [1971] Ch 1007.

be made of the extremely restricted right of integrity enjoyed by architects in the United Kingdom.[69]

In calling for much more thought to be given to the question of what rights should flow from other forms of ownership we are not necessarily calling for the development of specific rights of repair, transfer and so on. Such rights might well prove to be too rigid and might not be able to account for the very different interests that can be at stake in different items of personal property – cars, laser printers and CDs should not necessarily be equated for these purposes. Instead, by focusing attention on the intersection between copyright and other forms of property, we hope to achieve two things. First, we hope to counteract further the presumption that the proprietary nature of copyright necessarily points to any particular interpretation of the permitted acts and other defences. Second, while we are not arguing for the adoption of hard-and-fast rules, we hope that judges in individual cases will be more amenable to the development of principles grounded in the proprietary rights of personal property owners that could be used to keep intellectual property rights in check.

The potential significance of the approach we advocate can be illustrated by reference to a recent Canadian patent decision, *Monsanto* v. *Schmeiser*.[70] The case in question arose out of an action brought by Monsanto against a Saskatchewan farmer, Percy Schmeiser, for infringement of a patent for genetically modified (GM) seed. It seems that the GM variety was present on the defendant's land as a result of earlier contamination from neighbouring farms. Nevertheless, it was held that the defendant had infringed the patent, patent infringement being a matter of strict liability. In the course of his defence the defendant raised a number of arguments, the most interesting of which was that the plaintiff should be taken to have waived or abandoned its patent rights as a result of the uncontrolled release of the invention, by analogy with the law of admixture. Regrettably, this argument was rejected out of hand. It appears that it was thought that the law of admixture could have no application, perhaps because, in principle, the tangible and intangible properties remained wholly distinct.

The law of admixture is not, however, confined to cases where the properties have become intermingled in such a way that the respective parts and portions have become indistinguishable. Admixture can also occur in cases of 'accession', that is, where one chattel has become attached

---

[69] See CDPA 1988, s. 80(5).
[70] *Monsanto* v. *Schmeiser* [2001] FCT 256; [2002] FCA 309; [2004] SCC 34. For a detailed analysis of this case and its implications see M. Lee and R. Burrell, 'Liability for the Escape of GM Seeds: Pursuing the "Victim"?' (2002) 65 *Modern Law Review* 517.

to a dominant chattel, with the consequence that the whole becomes the property of the owner of the principal goods.[71] Here, the analogy with the facts in *Schmeiser* would seem much stronger – although the defendant owned the seeds he was unable to sell them or use them to grow the next year's crop without implicating the patent owner's rights. Admittedly, in order for the accession doctrine to apply it also has to be shown that the inferior chattel could not be separated without causing serious damage to the newly formed whole. But if we return to first principles and ask what underlies this separability test in accession cases, we can see that the aim is to prevent an owner from being inconvenienced by the unlooked-for presence of 'other' property. The effect of the doctrine is to prevent the owner of that other property from exercising the paradigmatic right of ownership, that is, to take possession of the property in question. Viewed in this light, it seems perfectly sensible to argue that in a case like *Schmeiser* the owner of the intangible should be prevented from exercising their key right, that is, the right to exclude others from reproducing the subject of the monopoly.

By drawing attention to the fact that it is possible to draw an analogy with the law of admixture in some (perhaps rare) types of intellectual property cases, we are not suggesting that the courts should radically expand the interests of owners of tangible personal property at the expense of the owners of copyright and other forms of intellectual property. As with our call for the judges to reinvigorate the public interest defence, we are not claiming that judicial creativity in this area would solve the problems with the current permitted acts. Applications of the law of admixture or of a rediscovered principle of non-derogation from grant should not become common, and in any event such tools are unlikely to be of much assistance in the type of case with which we are principally concerned. More than anything our call is for a change of mindset and a refusal to accept that the proprietary nature of copyright is necessarily determinative of any substantive issue.

Copyright law and notions of balance

The third and perhaps most widely shared assumption about copyright that we should like to question is the assertion that the boundaries of copyright have been and ought to continue to be set by a process of 'balancing'. More specifically, it is frequently said that copyright does or should represent a balance between the interests of authors, publishers and users. At first glance this assertion may seem to be a harmless (and

---

[71] See G. McCormack, 'Mixture of Goods' (1990) 10 *Legal Studies* 293, 295.

meaningless) truism, since all legal rights represent a balance to some extent. However, in the copyright field the notion of balance seems to have acquired an elevated status, as if balance were something that we should consciously strive for and even at times as if it were capable of determining whether particular types of use should fall within the exclusive rights of the copyright owner. The language of balance has now even found its way into the international conventions relating to copyright. For example, the preamble to the 1996 WIPO Copyright Treaty states that the signatories recognise 'the need to maintain a balance between the rights of authors and the larger public interest, particularly education, research and access to information, as reflected in the Berne Convention'. The preamble to the 1996 WIPO Performances and Phonograms Treaty contains an almost identical statement, and one of the express aims of the TRIPS Agreement is to ensure that 'the protection and enforcement of intellectual property rights should contribute to . . . a balance of rights and obligations'.[72]

Despite the ubiquitous use of the language of balance in copyright debates and despite the imprimatur of the international conventions, there is a semantic ambiguity associated with the notion of 'balance' which makes its use in this context problematic. Amongst other things, the word 'balance' can mean 'an apparatus for weighing' and 'a harmony of proportion and design'.[73] Further reflection reveals that the notion of balance is being used in both these senses in copyright debates. At times it is asserted that when designing copyright legislation we need to balance competing interests against one another. Here the notion of balance is being used as if it were a mechanism or a process (in effect, using 'balance' in the first sense identified). On other occasions it is asserted that the balance of copyright must be preserved. In particular, in the context of debates about the application of copyright to digital technologies, it is often said that the balance that existed in the analogue environment must be replicated in the digital environment. Here balance is being used in the sense of a harmony of proportion and design. The danger comes when we fail to be alert to the slippage that can take place between these two different uses of the word 'balance'.

The importance of the linguistic shift that can take place between the two meanings of 'balance' is perhaps best illustrated by considering the claim that copyright laws have always been formulated by a process of balancing, a claim which is usually followed by a call for this balance to be maintained. A moment's reflection shows that there is a non sequitur here. The first claim, that copyright laws have in the past been formulated

[72] Art. 7.   [73] *Shorter OED.*

by a *process* of balancing, simply tells us that in the past other interests have been set off against copyright, a claim which can be justified by reference to a host of legislative materials and judicial decisions. The second claim, that this balance should be maintained, assumes that in the past this process has achieved the 'correct result', a claim which needs to be supported by detailed argument. That this error in logic is not immediately obvious has much to do with the different meanings of the word 'balance'. Linguistically it is a small step from saying that copyright laws have been formulated by a *process* of balancing to saying that copyright laws represent the *correct balance*, since the word 'balance' already carries with it some notion of 'correctness'.

In order to illustrate further the above point, it is worth revisiting the argument that copyright can at times impose an illegitimate restriction on freedom of speech. Those who employ the notion of balance as an explanation for how copyright laws have been formulated in the past frequently counter this argument with the assertion that free speech interests are already adequately represented within the structure of copyright law: they must already be adequately represented since copyright has always *involved a balance* between competing interests. Thus it has been said that free speech is adequately protected by the idea/expression dichotomy, and that the 'relevant' public interest in free speech is satisfied by the fair dealing exceptions.[74] The greatest danger in this type of reasoning is that it closes off alternative explanations for why the development of the copyright regime has taken a particular path. In particular, it closes off explanations that see judicial decisions or legislative intervention solely, or even primarily, in terms of the successful assertion of a particular pressure group's interests. It allows what may look like naked partisanship to be explained in terms of the readjustment of the balance which, it can be assumed, must have come to favour unduly some opposing interest.

The slippage that can take place once we accept that it is appropriate to talk about copyright law having been formulated by a process of balancing in the past may also suggest that user groups and pro-user commentators who try to appropriate the language of balance are misguided. In particular, they run the risk that they will, at best, preserve the existing settlement in the digital environment without challenging the strong pro-owner bias of many of the existing provisions. For example, Christopher May, when attacking the post-TRIPS international regime, suggests that the primary aim of reformers should be to 'rebalance' legislation, which

---

[74] *Ashdown v. Telegraph Group*, 696: 'The balance between the rights of the owner of the copyright and those of the public has been struck by the legislative organ of the democratic state itself in the legislation it has enacted.'

he seems to assume could be achieved by returning to something like the pre-TRIPS position: 'Political action could promote a programme to return intellectual property to the balance between production and distribution that obtained prior to the rise of the information society.'[75] The problem with this argument is that while a return to the pre-TRIPS position might benefit developing countries, if one takes the view that the laws of developed countries have unduly favoured owners for many years, then, within the developed world, returning to the position of a few years ago would bring little benefit (indeed, May ignores the fact that implementing the TRIPS Agreement required little legislative amendment in most developed countries).

Turning aside from the linguistic confusion associated with the idea of balance, the other thing that is striking about the use of the notion of balance in the copyright context is that it tells us very little about how to proceed in practice. On the whole we are left without any sense of how weight is to be attributed to differing interests or even as to which interests are to enjoy a place on the scales. It is therefore hardly surprising that notions of balance have been used to support a range of radically different proposals or that they have been employed by virtually every interest group involved in recent debates about where to draw copyright's boundaries. When used in this indeterminate way, it is difficult to escape the conclusion that notions of balance are being used to provide a fine-sounding justification for solutions that are favoured for ideological or financial reasons. Thus, as has been argued elsewhere, unless notions of balance are subjected to sustained analysis and refinement they can only be of limited utility.[76] At the very least, as Nimmer puts it, 'wherever one comes out on th[e] balancing question, it is important that the conclusion be based not on tacit assumptions, but upon articulated premises'.[77] In order to arrive at a refined notion of balance we would need to be clear about

---

[75] C. May, *A Global Political Economy of Intellectual Property Rights* (London: Routledge, 2000), p. 179. Similarly, see A. Quaedvlieg, 'Copyright's Orbit round Private, Commercial and Economic Law – the Copyright System and the Place of the User' (1998) 29 IIC 420.

[76] See L. Bently and R. Burrell, 'Copyright and the Information Society in Europe: A Matter of Timing as well as Content' [1997] *Common Market Law Review* 1197, 1215. More generally, see L. Frantz, 'The First Amendment in the Balance' (1962) 71 *Yale Law Journal* 1424, in particular at 1434–5, who provides a scholarly account of different notions of balance and the extent to which their use is inevitable. See also T. Emerson, 'Toward a General Theory of the First Amendment' (1963) 72 *Yale Law Journal* 877; A. Stone, 'The Limits of Constitutional Text and Structure: Standards of Review and the Freedom of Political Communication' (1999) 23 *Melbourne University Law Review* 668, 687–91.

[77] M. Nimmer and D. Nimmer, *Nimmer on Copyright* (New York: Matthew Bender, looseleaf), para. 1.69.

what exactly is being balanced – are we concerned with rights, interests or expectations? We would also need to know the extent to which these matters are commensurable and, to the extent they are commensurable, the relative importance they are to enjoy.[78]

A third difficulty with the language of balance is that it may help to suggest that the interests of copyright owners and users should always be seen in oppositional terms – the interests of one group constantly have to be set off or 'balanced' against those of another. Whilst this may inevitably be the way in which copyright owners and user groups see disputes, it does not follow that it is appropriate for legislatures and policy makers to view conflicts of interest in this way. The danger is that the complex nature of the interrelationship that exists between different interests in the copyright field and the complex nature of cultural creation will become lost. For example, the language of balance encourages us to try to set off the general public interest in education against the rights of copyright owners and our connected desire to provide incentives for the creation of new works. Yet in many respects this approach creates a false dichotomy, since the creation of and market for at least some types of work are also determined in part by levels of education.

It can now be seen that although it is frequently said that the boundaries of copyright should be formulated by a process of balancing, when this idea is examined in more detail it seems to obscure more than it reveals. This vagueness or indeterminacy explains how notions of balance have come to support radically different agendas. Nevertheless, in spite of this indeterminacy, it seems that the language of balance may exert an unlooked-for conservative influence.

Conclusion

In this chapter we have attempted to subject some of the dominant ideas and assumptions about copyright and the exceptions to critical analysis. We have argued that further reflection suggests that these ideas and assumptions are, in various respects, either contestable or unhelpful or that they do not support the conclusions that are usually drawn from them. More generally, we hope that our analysis reinforces the need to be

---

[78] See also T. Bell, 'Escape from Copyright: Market Success vs. Statutory Failure in the Protection of Expressive Works' (2001) 69 *University of Cincinnati Law Review* 741, 787: 'Even if they could measure all the relevant economic, legal, technological, and cultural factors, moreover, politicians could not balance such incommensurable values.' Refreshingly, Bell is entirely dismissive of the idea that copyright represents a balance, arguing that 'Thanks to their inevitable ignorance of the pertinent variables, legislators could not strike a balance if they wanted to; thanks to the influence of the copyright lobby they may not even care to try' (at 746).

circumspect when confronted with calls to make copyright fit a particular theoretical model and the fact that we need to be aware of the persuasive power of metaphors and be vigilant as to which parties are responsible for their development.[79] In the remainder of this second section we explore some of the other reasons why users receive a poor deal under the present copyright regime.

---

[79] See P. Samuelson, 'Law and Computers: The Quest for Enabling Metaphors for Law and Lawyering in the Information Age' (1996) 94 *Michigan Law Review* 2029; D. Johnson and K. Marks, 'Mapping Electronic Data Communications onto Existing Legal Metaphors: Should We Let Our Conscience (and Our Contracts) Be Our Guide?' (1993) 38 *Villanova Law Review* 487; Craig, 'Locke, Labour', 57–8.

7 Copyright in supranational fora

Having looked at some of the ways of thinking about copyright that underpin an overly restrictive regime, in this chapter and the next we consider the barriers that users face in getting their voices heard during legislative and policy-making processes. We argue that at every level – international, regional and national – user groups face obstacles that limit substantially their opportunities to shape decision making in the copyright field. In this chapter we focus on international and regional fora and the particular difficulties that users have in getting their voices heard at a supranational level. The majority of our analysis is concerned with the European legislative process because the most concrete steps affecting the exceptions have been taken at this level. We argue that, for a variety of reasons, the interests of users have been inadequately represented at the European level. In part this is because of political, financial and institutional constraints, but we also argue that the logic that is driving the harmonisation process and the Commission's starting point have also played an important role.

Before turning to the above, it is important to explain what may seem like a contradiction in, on the one hand, our criticising the European legislative process as paying insufficient attention to the needs of users and, on the other hand, our insisting that the Information Society Directive provides an opportunity for fundamental reform that could provide the foundation for a much fairer system of exceptions.[1] This apparent contradiction is explained by the fact that although the final form of the Directive leaves room for a fairly generous system of exceptions, this is not because the European legislative process responded to the needs of users. Rather, it is because member states were keen to limit disruption to their existing arrangements. Member states therefore insisted on provisions with sufficient flexibility to allow them to keep their lists of exceptions more or less intact. A similar conservatism or inertia can be seen at the international level. Here too it has been a desire to avoid disruption, rather

---

[1] This argument is developed in detail in Chapter 10.

than a desire to protect the interests of users per se, which has provided the greatest check on the tendency towards ever stronger rights. This suggests that we should not be sanguine about the likely direction of future developments, since over time the resistance of national governments may weaken as copyright becomes ever more harmonised.[2]

The logic of harmonisation

In order to understand why the European copyright agenda has developed in the way that it has, it is important to appreciate that the ongoing process of harmonisation of copyright has been driven by a desire to remove potential obstacles to the internal market. Thus, compared with how national governments and legislatures are likely to view the process of copyright reform, copyright reform in Europe has been driven by a narrow set of concerns. We believe that this narrow focus on achieving a single market is one factor that helps to explain why users face an uphill struggle in getting their voices heard in Europe.[3]

It has been clear since the 1970s that differences between national copyright systems might present barriers to trade, despite the best efforts of the ECJ to minimise such barriers through the doctrine of exhaustion of rights.[4] While wholesale harmonisation was deemed to be impossible at least in the short term (see 'The Commission's understanding of copyright II', below), the Commission set out to remedy potential problems for the internal market by dealing with specific rights or individual subject matters, in particular as regards new technologies, where it was deemed wise to harmonise before further divergences developed. Even within the piecemeal approach to reform adopted by the Commission, at a number of points the process and extent of harmonisation has been limited by the political impossibility of achieving reform in certain areas or beyond a certain point. As a result, the process of harmonisation has sometimes progressed in a way that would strike an outsider as bizarre. For example, the resistance of some member states to the harmonisation of the artists' resale right or *droit de suite* resulted in the passage of the *Droit*

---

[2] J. Ginsburg, 'Toward Supranational Copyright Law? The WTO Panel Decision and the "Three–Step Test" for Copyright Exceptions' (2001) 187 RIDA 3.

[3] See also H. Jehoram, 'The EC Copyright Directives, Economics and Authors' Rights' (1994) 25 IIC 821; L. Bently and R. Burrell, 'Copyright and the Information Society: A Matter of Timing as well as Content' [1997] *Common Market Law Review* 1197, 1202.

[4] See *Deutsche Grammophon* v. *Metro* [1971] ECR 487; *Music Vertrieb Membran* v. *GEMA* [1981] ECR 147, but cf. *Warner Bros* v. *Christiansen* [1988] ECR 2605; *EMI Electrola* v. *Patricia* [1989] ECR 79.

de Suite Directive being delayed for several years,[5] and has resulted in a piece of legislation that sets rights at a low level and which is unlikely to achieve complete harmonisation before 2012.[6] Given the disproportionate amount of time and energy that is taken up when a measure encounters sustained opposition from powerful lobby groups with the ear of one or more national governments, there may be a natural temptation for the Commission to harmonise rights at a level that satisfies the interests of powerful owner representative groups.[7] In other words, the Commission may be tempted to choose the path of least resistance to achieving its goal of removing barriers to the achievement of a single market.

The Commission's narrow focus may also make it difficult to revisit legislation that has harmonised rights at the wrong level. Indeed in many respects a poorly formulated harmonised regime can be more difficult to alter than divergent national regimes. This is because once a harmonised regime has been established the principal justification for Community action (that is, the need to remove barriers to the single market) will have been lost. The rights of copyright owners may have been set at the wrong level, but they will have been set at that level in every member state. Moreover, this difficulty has to be considered alongside the inevitable institutional constraints that may prevent the Commission from revisiting an issue – the European legislative agenda is busy and Community initiatives tend to create the impression of effective reform, with the result that it can then be difficult to reopen a debate once the legislative agenda has moved on.[8]

The difficulties created by the Commission's narrow focus on achieving harmonisation does not, however, mean that we believe that its role

---

[5] There was considerable concern in the United Kingdom, which was shared in Austria to some extent, that the effect of harmonisation would be to drive sales of modern artworks outside the European Union, in particular, to New York or Geneva. For discussion see D. Booton, 'A Critical Analysis of the European Commission's Proposal for a Directive Harmonising the *Droit de Suite*' [1998] IPQ 165.

[6] Art. 10 of the *Droit de Suite* Directive provides that it need not be implemented until 1 January 2006 (this can be contrasted with the implementation period for other copyright directives which has tended to be around eighteen months). In addition, Art. 8 sets out certain transitional provisions, the effect of which is that member states which do not at present have a *droit de suite* can restrict the right to living artists for another four years, until 1 January 2010. Moreover, if a member state requests it, that period can be extended for yet a further two years, subject to consultation with the Commission. Given the level of opposition to the Directive in certain quarters it seems likely that complete harmonisation will not be achieved until 2012.

[7] It is worth noting that the *Droit de Suite* Directive, which encountered the most sustained opposition of any of the directives in the copyright field, and which was heavily watered down from the Commission's original proposals, concerned the rights of authors rather than rights owned by the copyright industries.

[8] See S. Weatherill, *Law and Integration in the European Union* (Oxford: Clarendon, 1995), pp. 160–1.

should be restricted, since we also accept that developing an effective system of exceptions will require the harmonisation of at least certain types of provision. In particular, we believe that exceptions that allow part of a work to be reused in a later, commercially significant, work need to be harmonised if producers of such works are to have the confidence to market them throughout the Community.[9] Rather than retreating from harmonisation, we would therefore prefer to see the Commission adopting a broader understanding of its role in the copyright sphere. This is a far from radical suggestion since the Commission has already indicated that it sees itself as having such a role. For example, after the Term Directive was adopted the Commission issued a statement that the Directive

> constitutes a sign for all interested parties within and outside the Community: the Community is an entity and continues to assert its identity. This includes the protection of intellectual property rights in order to guarantee and further the development of the cultural richness of Europe.[10]

Similarly, recent copyright directives have made express reference to the broader social and cultural goals of the Community.[11] The problem is that such goals seem to have had little influence on the actual content of the legislation.

Some commentators have argued that the copyright directives lay the foundations for a distinctive European economic and cultural strategy on copyright, based on the goals of promoting creativity, supporting the cultural industries sector and ensuring that works are widely disseminated.[12] It is not, however, possible to achieve these goals, nor is it possible to ensure that the broader social and cultural objectives of the European Community are met,[13] unless intervention in the copyright field is planned to achieve more than the mere harmonisation of national rules. In this respect we would add our voice to those who have called for the Commission to move beyond its 'obsession' with the establishment of a

---

[9] See also Chapter 10, where we outline our vision of reform in detail.
[10] [1993] 12 WIPR 318.
[11] See, e.g., Information Society Directive, recital 12: 'Adequate protection of copyright works and subject-matter of related rights is also of great importance from a cultural standpoint. Article 151 of the Treaty requires the Community to take cultural aspects into account in its action'; *Droit de Suite* Directive, recital 5: 'Under Article 151(4) of the Treaty the Community is to take cultural aspects into account in its action under other provisions of the Treaty.'
[12] H. Comte, 'A Step Towards a Copyright Europe' (1993) 158 RIDA 2.
[13] As to such goals and objectives see EC Treaty, Art. 3(m) (goal of promoting research and technological development); and Art. 3(p) (goal of promoting education and training and 'the flowering of the cultures of the Member States').

single market.[14] As long as this remains the Commission's sole focus there will always be the temptation to harmonise along the path of least resistance by ensuring the support of powerful (right holder) lobby groups. Moreover, it has been seen that until the Commission changes its starting point it will be difficult to persuade it to revisit an issue once rights have been harmonised.

The Commission's understanding of copyright I: market failure, the copyright balance and property rights

The Commission's starting point and restricted focus can cause problems for users, but so too can its understanding of copyright and the role of the exceptions. In this respect the lead-up to the Information Society Directive is particularly instructive, since at various points the Commission seems to have been influenced by the ideas and assumptions about copyright that we subjected to critical analysis in the last chapter, namely, that the exceptions are best understood as applying in circumstances in which market failure is likely, that copyright is a balance, and that only narrow exceptions should be granted since copyright is a property right. It ought to be apparent that our argument is not that the adoption of these understandings is the only, or even the most important, explanation for why users have received a poor deal at the European level. Nevertheless, we do believe that the examples given here, taken together with those set out in the next chapter, provide firm evidence of the detrimental effects that these understandings of copyright have had for users.

The most striking example of the Commission's reliance on the market failure argument in the lead-up to the Information Society Directive is to be found in the Green Paper that preceded the Directive, entitled 'Copyright and Related Rights in the Information Society' (hereafter, the Green Paper).[15] Here the Commission considered whether copyright should be extended to uses that take place in private. At the time when the Green Paper was published, most countries in the Community recognised to some extent that copying and performance in private did not amount to an infringement of copyright. More specifically, a number of countries, including France, Germany, the Netherlands and Spain provided

---

[14] See, e.g., R. Whish, *Competition Law*, 4th edn (London: Butterworths, 2001), p. 19; Bently and Sherman, p. 16, noting the Commission's search for the 'holy grail of an internal market'.
[15] COM(95)383 final. The Green Paper was triggered by the Bangemann Report, *Europe and the Global Information Society – Recommendations of the High-Level Group on the Information Society to the Corfu European Council* (Brussels: European Commission, 1994).

a broad private use exception,[16] whilst other countries, including the United Kingdom, privileged private use through a number of more specific provisions.[17] In the Green Paper the Commission asserted that the justification for private use exceptions lay in the inability of right owners to police private spaces and hence to monitor infringements or dictate the terms of licences. It therefore concluded: 'where there is the technical means to limit or prevent private copying there is no further justification for what amounts to a system of statutory licensing'.[18] Admittedly, by the time the 'Follow-up to the Green Paper on Copyright and Related Rights in the Information Society' (hereafter, the Follow-up) was issued, the Commission had modified its position somewhat, recognising that privacy concerns are also relevant to the provision of private use exceptions.[19] Nevertheless, it is significant that the Commission was initially prepared to adopt a version of the market failure argument, and was prepared to use this to draw dramatic conclusions about the future of private use defences, without giving any consideration to other potential justifications for the existence of private use exceptions. In contrast, if the Commission had accepted that private use defences are not a consequence of likely market failure, but rather that they are grounded in other concerns, such as a right to privacy, then technological developments that allow private spaces to be monitored would have been regarded as a cause for considerable concern, and not as a reason for curtailing private use exceptions.[20]

The Green Paper and the Follow-up also relied heavily on the language of balance to justify their proposals. At various points in these documents

---

[16] It seems that most of these countries will preserve their private use defences in modified form following the implementation of the Information Society Directive. See also the section 'The Commission's understanding of copyright II', below.

[17] See CDPA 1988, ss.18 (limiting the performance right to public performances), 29 (fair dealing for the purpose of private study), 70 (time-shifting for private and domestic purposes), and 71 (photographs of broadcasts for private and domestic purposes). These provisions have been preserved in amended form following implementation of the Information Society Directive.

[18] Green Paper, p. 50.   [19] See Follow-up, Ch. 2, Part 3.

[20] It is also worth noting that there is other evidence that the market failure argument is beginning to win broad acceptance in Europe. For example, in a recent article on copyright exceptions and technological measures of protection under the Information Society Directive, Séverine Dusollier, a Belgian academic, has asserted (in a generally pro-user piece) that in countries such as France and Belgium the exceptions are based principally on market failure: S. Dusollier, 'Exceptions and Technological Measures in the European Copyright Directive of 2001 – An Empty Promise' (2003) 34 IIC 62, 63, 67. In the case of France at least, this interpretation is difficult to square with Gillian Davies' historical analysis of the evolution of the exceptions under French law. See G. Davies, *Copyright and the Public Interest*, 2nd edn (London: Sweet & Maxwell, 2002), pp. 159–69.

the Commission stated that its aim was to maintain the 'copyright balance' in the new environment. For example, in the Green Paper it was argued:

In order for the potential of the information society to be realised to the full, it will be necessary to maintain a balance between the interests of the parties concerned (rightholders, manufacturers, distributors and users of services as well as network operators).[21]

Similarly, in the Follow-up it was stated that: 'a fair balance of rights and interests between the different categories of rightholders, as well as between rightholders and rightusers, must be safeguarded'.[22] By insisting on the need to 'maintain' and 'safeguard' the copyright balance, the Commission was apparently using the language of balance to indicate that it believed that rights and exceptions had been set at the appropriate level in the analogue environment.

At no point did the Commission attempt to justify its conclusion that the level at which rights and exceptions had been set was appropriate. Moreover, in order for such an assertion to make sense in the European context, it would be necessary to show that every member state had set rights and exceptions at roughly the same level – if 'balance' in this context means a harmonious design and different countries had traditionally set rights and exceptions at different levels, then some countries must have got the 'balance' wrong. Alternatively, it could be argued that the reference to balance in this context was intended to refer to the fact that national governments have adjusted copyright to fit particular local circumstances. But if this were the case difficult questions would have to be asked about the Commission's entire harmonisation programme.

It is therefore difficult to escape the conclusion that, as so often happens, the Commission was using the language of balance to provide a fine-sounding justification for measures that it favoured for political and ideological reasons. At best the Commission could have been using the language of balance as a metaphor for the political process of responding to interest group representation. Yet in order for there to be 'balance' in this sense, the legislative process would have to be open to as many voices as possible. In contrast, for reasons that will be examined shortly, the European legislative process is often inaccessible to user groups. What is certain is that irrespective of how the Commission intended the language of balance to be understood, the Commission's initial proposals looked less like a balance than a flagrant giveaway to the copyright

---

[21] Green Paper, p. 7; see also pp. 15, 16, 32. [22] See Follow-up, Ch. 1, Part 3.

industries.[23] In the Green Paper and the Follow-up the question that was asked was always 'are the rights of content owners sufficiently strong in the digital environment?', and never 'has the digital environment rendered the rights too strong?' It is therefore no surprise that the early versions of the Directive would have drastically curtailed the exceptions.[24]

The influence of the third understanding that we examined in the last chapter, that the exceptions must be narrowly drawn because of the proprietary nature of copyright, is perhaps most obviously visible in the Commission's repeated insistence that rights must be harmonised at a high level. In part the Commission has justified this insistence on the basis that strong rights are necessary for the creation of a vibrant and competitive cultural industries sector.[25] In addition, however, the Commission has repeatedly stressed that harmonisation must not adversely affect the interests of existing copyright owners, an approach that is closely bound up with the belief that reducing the standard of protection would amount to an appropriation of property without compensation.[26] The practical consequence of this position is that the Commission will not even consider certain harmonisation models. For example, the Commission automatically veered towards the upwards harmonisation of the copyright term, rather than standardising protection at life plus fifty years, which is the international standard set out in the Berne Convention and was the ordinary term of protection in the vast majority of member states. Similarly, the Commission never even entertained the possibility of removing barriers to trade created by different levels of protection for artists' resale rights by abolishing the *droit de suite* throughout the European Union. This is not to suggest that either the downwards harmonisation of the term of protection or the abolition of the *droit de suite* would necessarily have been desirable, but these examples do illustrate a further aspect of the Commission's approach that tends towards the grant of strong rights and hence leads to a poor deal for users.

---

[23] Cf. P. Samuelson, 'The Copyright Grab' [1996] (Jan.) *Wired* 57, discussing the 1995 Report of the US Working Group on Intellectual Property Rights. See also Bently and Burrell, 'Copyright'.

[24] See Proposal for a European Parliament and Council Directive on the harmonisation of certain aspects of copyright and related rights in the Information Society COM(97)628 final. This would have restricted member states' freedom to provide optional exceptions to eight cases.

[25] E.g., Information Society Directive, recital 9.

[26] E.g., see the Term Directive, recital 9: 'Whereas due regard for established rights is one of the general principles of law protected by the Community legal order; whereas, therefore, a harmonization of the terms of protection of copyright and related rights cannot have the effect of reducing the protection currently enjoyed by rightholders in the Community . . .'

The Commission's understanding of copyright II: harmonisation and the copyright families

In addition to there being good evidence that the Commission has at points been influenced by certain general ideas about copyright and the exceptions that were shown to be unhelpful in the last chapter, the Commission has also been influenced by a particular understanding of the nature of the differences between national copyright regimes in Europe. Most significantly, the Commission has started with the presumption that the copyright laws of member states are based on different traditions of 'author's right' and 'copyright'. It is usually said that the fundamental distinction between copyright and author's right or *droit d'auteur* systems flows from the different historical origins of the two approaches and is reflected in marked differences between the rules of the two types of system. Most important for present purposes is the alleged difference in the way in which the systems treat the exceptions.

It is said that copyright systems conceptualise copyright as a grant from the state designed to produce a particular outcome, namely, to increase the supply of copyright works. If, however, copyright protection would be likely to fail to achieve this goal in particular circumstances or if there are circumstances in which copyright would impact negatively on other socially desirable goals, the legislature will have few reservations in making an exception available or removing or limiting copyright in some other way.[27] In contrast, it is said that *droit d'auteur* countries recognise copyright protection as a reflection of the natural right that authors have over their creations. Most commonly it is said that this right flows from the act of creation itself, the resulting work being an embodiment of the author's personality. It follows from this understanding of copyright as a natural right of authors that exceptions will only be available in very rare circumstances and not merely because to override copyright would further some desirable end. This is because, to adopt Ronald Dworkin's famous formulation, rights 'trump' goals.[28]

It has been suggested that the Commission's belief that variations between national laws are best understood in terms of the differences between the families of 'copyright' and 'author's right' was a factor in the Commission's rejection of the United Kingdom's proposal that the Information Society Directive should only limit member states' freedom to provide exceptions by reference to the Berne/TRIPS three-step

---

[27] C. Waelde and H. MacQueen, 'From Entertainment to Education: The Scope of Copyright?' [2004] IPQ 259, 265; and see, generally, Sterling, ch. 10.
[28] R. Dworkin, *Taking Rights Seriously* (London: Duckworth, 1981), p. xi.

test.[29] More generally, seeing the process of harmonisation in the context of a belief in the traditions outlined above might have a number of consequences for the way in which the exceptions are understood. One potential consequence is that since the vast majority of member states would ordinarily be said to adhere to the author's right tradition, the belief may develop that the majority of member states are unconcerned about the effect of copyright on the public interest. The greatest danger, however, is that the legislative process will be shaped by a perception that the biggest potential obstacle to harmonisation is the existence of different national traditions, thereby distracting attention from the core issue that all copyright systems have to face, that is, how to manage relationships between authors, owners and users.

A number of other commentators have expressed the concern that a belief in the traditions of 'copyright' and 'author's right' may have an unhelpful impact on the harmonisation process,[30] and there is now a body of literature that challenges traditional historical accounts of the origins of the two systems,[31] the belief that systems from within the same family share similar rules[32] and the belief that there are marked differences of substantive law as between the two families.[33] For example, in her work on copyright in the late eighteenth century in France and the United States, Ginsburg argues persuasively that 'the differences between the US and the French copyright system are in fact neither as extensive nor as venerable as typically described'.[34] Most important for present purposes, however, is Davies' work on copyright and the public interest.[35] Davies demonstrates that French and German copyright laws have always taken account of the broader public interest. More specifically, she points to

[29] S. Von Lewinski, 'Recent Developments in Europe Relating to the Digital Environment', paper delivered at the Copyright Society of Australia, Sydney, March 2002. As to the three-step test, see 'The international forum', below.

[30] G. Davies, 'The Convergence of Copyright and Authors' Rights – Reality or Chimera?' (1995) 26 IIC 964; Bently and Sherman, p. 28.

[31] See Davies, 'Convergence'; J. Ginsburg, 'A Tale of Two Copyrights: Literary Property in Revolutionary France and America', in B. Sherman and A. Strowel (eds.), *Of Authors and Origins* (Oxford: Clarendon, 1994); Sherman and Bently, in particular at pp. 216–17.

[32] W. Cornish, 'The Notions of Work, Originality and Neighbouring Rights from the Viewpoint of Common Law Traditions', paper delivered at the WIPO Symposium, Paris, June 1994 (summarised in Davies, 'Convergence'), emphasising the difference between US copyright law and the 'Commonwealth' tradition.

[33] See Davies, 'Convergence'; A. Strowel, '*Droit d'auteur* and Copyright: Between History and Nature', in Sherman and Strowel, *Of Authors and Origins*, arguing that the difference lies more in the 'interpretative framework within which the rights are posited'; L. Bently, 'European and International Copyright Harmonisation: Reflections on the Legal Traditions', paper delivered at the University of Wales, Aberystwyth, March 1997, arguing that differences result as much from different notions of contract as from different understandings of copyright.

[34] Ginsburg, 'Tale of Two Copyrights', p. 134.   [35] Davies, *Copyright*.

the fact that the discussions that have taken place at various stages in France and Germany about the justifications for a copyright system have invariably focused on issues beyond the natural rights of authors, the fact that copyright has always been of limited duration in both countries, and the fact that both France and Germany have long provided for a range of exceptions and defences.[36] Indeed, in relation to the exceptions, it might be noted that before the Copyright Act 1911 there were no statutory exceptions to copyright infringement in the United Kingdom, whereas the laws of a number of civil law countries contained such provisions much earlier.[37]

On a rather different note, even if the traditional account of the nature and basis of the *droit d'auteur* tradition is accepted, this does not lead to the conclusion that this tradition inevitably points towards very weak exceptions, since asserting that authors have a natural right over their works does not tell us what the right encompasses. As Drahos explains, within the dominant natural law tradition at least, the rules of positive law are not seen as 'being a mirror reflection of some metaphysical counterpart'. Rather, it is accepted that it is the state that will define the precise nature and scope of all rights, including property rights, within the overall framework set by natural law.[38] Returning to one of the themes explored in the last chapter, if we conceptualise the 'exceptions' not as rights of way over the copyright owner's property granted by the state to further the interests of some other class of persons, but rather as fence posts that help define what rights an owner actually has, it can be seen that there is not necessarily any connection between the assertion of a natural right of authors and the scope of provisions that safeguard the interests of users.

It is interesting to note that the above analysis is broadly in line with the conclusions of the German Federal Constitutional Court in the *School Books* case.[39] Shortly after the passage of the 1965 German Copyright Law there were a number of challenges to the constitutional validity of certain sections of that law. These challenges focused on the validity of various exceptions contained in the legislation. In effect, the argument was that the provision of the exceptions in question violated Article 14 of

---

[36] *Ibid.*, in particular chs. 6 and 7.
[37] English and French versions of some of these early provisions can be found in A. Birrell, *Seven Lectures on the Law and History of Copyright in Books* (London: Cassell & Co., 1899), pp. 182–5. The evolution of the exceptions in the United Kingdom is considered in more detail in Chapter 9.
[38] P. Drahos, 'Intellectual Property and Human Rights' [1999] IPQ 349, 351. See further St Thomas Aquinas, *Summa Theologica*, trans. T. Gilby (Cambridge: Blackfriars, 1966), vol. 28, in particular pp. 143–55, noting, for example, that human law may be altered to reflect 'the changed conditions of life' (at p. 145).
[39] This case is reported in English at (1972) 3 IIC 394.

the Basic Law, which guarantees that property will not be appropriated without equitable compensation. In rejecting these challenges[40] the Court held that although copyright is a property right protected within the meaning of Article 14, it does not follow that all uses of a work have to fall within the copyright owner's exclusive right, since it is for the legislature to determine the precise content of property rights. Most significantly, the Court stated:

> Since there is no pre-existing and absolute definition of property and since the content and function of property are capable and in need of adapting to social and economic situations, the [Basic Law] has put the legislature in charge of defining the scope and limits of property . . . This applies also for the economic rights of the author, which, just as [with] tangible property rights, need shaping by the legal order. The legislature, however, being bound by the [Basic Law], may not deal with this at random. In defining the privileges and duties that make up the content of this right, it must preserve the fundamental substance of the property guarantee while at the same time also keeping in line with the other constitutional provisions.[41]

It has been seen that it is possible to question both the accuracy of accounts that divide copyright systems into distinct families and the belief that a natural rights account of copyright inevitably leads to extremely narrow exceptions. In addition, a consideration of the scope of copyright exceptions in the member states of the European Union casts further doubt on the idea that there is any marked difference in the way in which member states treat users that is grounded in systemic traditions of copyright and author's right. It is hoped that the first section of this study will have cast considerable doubt on any suggestion that all 'copyright' countries provide generous protection for users. It has also been seen that the dominant models of economic analysis, which have gained considerable prominence in common law countries over recent years, are antithetical to user interests. A consideration of the political process in the United Kingdom, which we turn to in the next chapter, and the history of the evolution of the fair use and fair dealing defences in the United Kingdom, which we turn to in Chapter 9, discredit further the idea that user interests are placed centre stage in copyright countries. Moreover, whilst a detailed survey of the substantive provisions of the laws of continental European countries is beyond the scope of this study, an outline of some of the provisions relating to copyright exceptions in civil law countries may be enough to indicate that the other half of the claim that is

---

[40] The Court did, however, hold in relation to the educational anthologies exception that authors were entitled to be remunerated for use of their works.
[41] (1972) 3 IIC 394, 396. Also see Gillian Davies' discussion of this case: Davies, *Copyright*, pp. 203–5.

usually made for the impact of the traditions on copyright exceptions – that exceptions in author's right countries are always drawn very narrowly – should also be treated with caution.

Perhaps the most obvious example of where many author's right countries have historically provided relatively generous exceptions is in relation to private use. It has already been noted that, prior to the passage of the Information Society Directive, a number of European countries, including France, Germany, the Netherlands and Spain, provided a broad private use defence that went considerably further than the (largely unchanged) provisions of UK law relating to private reproduction and performance.[42] Most notably, perhaps, German law contained a provision making it lawful to 'make copies of a work for private use'.[43] This broad provision was supplemented by other provisions allowing single copies of a work to be made for a range of more specific purposes, including 'for personal scientific use',[44] for 'inclusion in personal files',[45] and, in the case of broadcast works, 'for personal information concerning current events'.[46] Admittedly, implementation of the Information Society Directive has resulted in these provisions being narrowed somewhat. For example, the general private use provision has been restricted in cases where the copying is done mechanically,[47] and the provision allowing for copies of a work to be made for personal scientific use now only applies to the production of paper versions and to analogue copying.[48] Nevertheless, even in modified form, the provisions relating to private copying in Germany remain relatively generous compared with their UK counterparts.

In response to the observation that many civil law countries have long treated private use more generously than has the United Kingdom, it might be pointed out that the relevant provisions need to be seen alongside the levies on blank tapes and recording equipment that most continental European countries operate in one form or other.[49] However, whilst such levies provide an important stream of revenue for certain types of copyright owner, it should be remembered that not all types of owner benefit

---

[42] As to these provisions of UK law see above n. 17 and accompanying text.
[43] Copyright Law 1965, Art. 53(1).
[44] *Ibid.*, Art. 53(2)(1).   [45] *Ibid.*, Art. 53(2)(2).   [46] *Ibid.*, Art. 53(2)(3).
[47] *Ibid.*, Art. 53(1). For commentary in English see A. Dietl, M. Donnseif and V. Grassmuck, 'Germany', available at www.fipr.org/copyright/guide/germany.htm (explaining that this amendment was aimed at copy shops).
[48] Copyright Law 1965, Art. 53(2). For commentary see Dietl, Donnseif and Grassmuck, 'Germany'.
[49] For an excellent, if dated, study of the operation of such levies see G. Davies and M. Hung, *Music and Video Private Copying* (London: Sweet & Maxwell, 1993), in particular ch. 6.

from such levies. Moreover, whilst such provisions may increase the price of recording equipment and blank tapes, they still ultimately leave users with much greater freedom than is the case in the United Kingdom. In addition, it should be noted that at various points the United Kingdom has given very serious consideration to the introduction of a system of levies even in the absence of broad private use rights.[50]

More generally, an analysis of German law makes an interesting case study of the way in which civil law countries deal with the exceptions. The German provisions relating to the exceptions are to be found in Chapter VI of the 1965 Copyright Law, as amended most recently by the legislation implementing the Information Society Directive in German law.[51] It has been seen that implementation of the Information Society Directive has resulted in the scope of some exceptions being restricted. Equally, however, a new exception for the benefit of persons with a disability has been introduced,[52] other exceptions have been extended to ensure that they cover use over the Internet and, generally speaking, German law continues to allow for the copying of works for a wide range of purposes. These include allowing

(i) copies to be made for the administration of justice and public safety;[53]
(ii) copying for the purpose of including part of the work in a collection intended for religious or educational use;[54]
(iii) recording of broadcasts for use in schools;[55]
(iv) the reproduction of public speeches;[56]
(v) reproduction for the purpose of reporting current events;[57] and
(vi) reproduction for the purposes of quotation.[58]

Although a number of the above provisions are hedged around with conditions that limit their operation, many of them remain broader than their UK counterparts. For example, whilst the German provisions

---

[50] See G. Dworkin and R. Taylor, *Blackstone's Guide to the Copyright, Designs and Patents Act 1988* (London: Blackstone, 1989), p. 162: 'until the very last moment [before the passage of the 1988 Act] the UK Government had decided that in some areas there was no alternative to the introduction of a compulsory levy on blank recording tape'.
[51] *Gesetz zur Regelung des Urheberrechts in der Informationsgesellschaft*, 10 Sept. 2003.
[52] Copyright Law 1965, Art. 45a.   [53] *Ibid.*, Art. 45.
[54] *Ibid.*, Art. 46. See also Art. 52a, which allows for small portions of a work to be published on access-controlled parts of a network service.
[55] *Ibid.*, Art. 47.   [56] *Ibid.*, Art. 48.
[57] See *ibid.*, Art. 49(1) (reproduction and distribution of material contained in newspaper, broadcasts, etc. concerning current events); Art. 49(2) (reproduction and distribution of works relating to 'news of the day'); Art. 50 (visual and sound reporting of news of the day; this provision has now been extended to cover reporting over the Internet).
[58] *Ibid.*, Art. 51.

allowing for news reporting are complex, they are less restrictive than fair dealing for the purpose of reporting current events.[59]

Moreover, in addition to the provisions of Chapter VI of the 1965 law, Article 24 continues to allow for 'free use' of a work. More specifically, Article 24(1) provides that 'an independent work created by the free use of the work of another may be published and exploited without the consent of the author of the used work'. Case law on the effect of this article is limited, and commentators agree that it has to be interpreted narrowly and must not be conflated with a US-style fair use exception.[60] Nevertheless, it can provide a German court with a flexible tool when dealing with questions of transformative use that goes well beyond anything available to a UK court in similar circumstances.[61] It has been used by German courts to fashion protection for parodies[62] and could well be used to provide protection for artists who reuse portions of an earlier work.[63]

It must also be remembered that a court in continental Europe might have a number of other avenues open to it to ensure that copyright remains within appropriate bounds. It was noted in Chapter 3 that French law has an *abus de droit* doctrine, which has been used on occasion to prevent copyright owners from enforcing their rights.[64] It was also seen in Chapters 2 and 3 that copyright protection for factual works can cause particular problems. When dealing with such works there might well be cases in which a court could use the flexible, creativity-based, standard of originality found in civil law systems to deny a work copyright protection altogether. In particular, it is important to note that German courts have expressly acknowledged that the originality standard can be varied in the light of policy considerations,[65] and a French commentator has expressed the view that a flexible application of the originality standard would be preferable to the court relying on the *abus de droit* doctrine in certain types of copyright case.[66]

To summarise, it has been seen that the Commission has started with the presumption that the copyright laws of member states are based on different traditions of 'author's right' and 'copyright'. It has also been seen

---

[59] CDPA 1988, s. 30(2), and see Chapter 2.
[60] See Sterling, *ibid.*, and the sources cited therein. The US fair use defence is considered in more detail in Chapter 9.
[61] Sterling, p. 361, in relation to transformative use: 'The "free use" concept is not so far distant, it is thought, from the approach adopted by US courts.'
[62] *Alcolix* (1994) 25 IIC 605.
[63] *Ibid.*, 609, may allow for reuse of cartoon character in painting.
[64] C. Caron, 'Abus de droit et droit d'auteur: une illustration de la confrontation du droit spécial et du droit commun en droit civil français' (1998) 176 RIDA 2.
[65] See *Silver Thistle* (1997) 28 IIC 140, in particular at 142. See also Sterling, p. 301.
[66] See Caron, 'Abus de droit', 68–70.

that the usual understanding of the nature of the differences between these traditions includes the belief that copyright countries provide more generous exceptions and are more concerned with the interests of users than are civil law countries. We have argued that this belief does not stand up to serious analysis – the idea that there are distinct traditions of copyright and author's right is problematic, it does not follow that a natural-rights-based justification for authors' rights leads inevitably to narrow exceptions, and a comparative analysis of the scope of the exceptions in the United Kingdom and Germany casts doubt on the idea that civil law countries provide less generous protection for users. Nevertheless, the belief that there are distinct traditions of copyright and author's right is one that has become deeply entrenched in the Commission's psyche and hence this belief 'undoubtedly will continue to have an impact on the way the law develops'.[67] In our immediate context it has been seen that this belief has further helped create a climate at the European level that is antithetical to the interests of users. This is because it leads the Commission to see the harmonisation process in terms of the need to reconcile competing traditions, rather than in terms of how best to reconcile the interests of authors, owners and users.

Opportunities for participation

If user groups face difficulties because of the ways in which copyright and the harmonisation process are presented and understood at a European level, they also face a number of other, more practical, obstacles in getting their voices heard. One problem that most user groups have to contend with is a relative lack of resources. Wilma Mossink, head of the Legal Department of the Dutch Open University and legal adviser to FOBID (the umbrella organisation for libraries and documentation and information centres in the Netherlands), who has considerable experience of lobbying on copyright issues at the European level, complains that user groups have to contend with a very uneven playing field. She argues that library groups and other user representatives find it very difficult to shape the legislative agenda. Unlike owner representatives, most user groups cannot afford to employ dedicated lobbyists and are held back at every turn by a lack of resources. Moreover, Mossink complains that these difficulties are compounded by a lack of interest in copyright reform amongst those who ought to be the natural allies of user groups. In particular, she argues that MEPs in the socialist bloc seem to regard copyright

---

[67] Bently and Sherman, p. 28.

Opportunities for participation 209

as an esoteric subject with which they need not concern themselves.[68] It is therefore interesting to note that a leading commentator on the evolution of the Directive has stated that 'The European Parliament in most cases has proposed strengthening the protection.'[69] Mossink argues that lack of interest in copyright matters is also shared by many consumer organisations, perhaps because they believe that it is too difficult to translate concerns about copyright into the issues that consumers actually care about, such as the price of CDs and photocopying.[70]

Many of Mossink's views are echoed by Teresa Hackett, the director of EBLIDA – the European Bureau of Library, Information and Documentation Associations – which is a non-governmental umbrella organisation that promotes the interests of libraries and archives at the European level. She has several years' experience of lobbying the EU on the Information Society Directive and other Community initiatives. She argues that user groups face an uphill struggle for a variety of reasons, but in addition to mentioning a lack of resources and expertise in lobbying and the general mismatch between user groups and organisations such as IFPI, Walt Disney and Vivendi, she also places considerable importance on the 'hostility of policy makers towards the user view'.[71]

Many of the above difficulties do not seem capable of being resolved easily. In addition, it should be noted that some interests that fall under the broad heading of 'user interests' are of only recent origin (particularly in relation to the Internet) and there is an inevitable time lag between the emergence of an interest group and its ability to operate effectively as it begins to familiarise itself with legislative and policy-making processes. The fact that users are inevitably going to face an uphill struggle to get their voices heard, however, means that there is an even greater need to ensure that the legislative process is arranged in such a way as to make it accessible and open to the views of as many groups as possible. Unfortunately this has often not been the case in the past. In this respect the background to the Information Society Directive is once again instructive. The Green Paper was intended to promote discussion and following its publication there was an opportunity for consultation. However, the timescale established by the Green Paper made it almost inevitable that only well-informed groups that were already geared up to respond would provide input. In this respect the subsequent document,

---

[68] Interview with Wilma Mossink, Canberra, 13 Feb. 2002.
[69] S. Von Lewinski, 'Proposed EC Directive on Copyright and Related Rights in the Information Society as It Progresses' (1999) 30 IIC 767, 778, commenting on the Opinion of the European Parliament on the Proposal for an Information Society Directive.
[70] Interview, Canberra, 13 February 2002.
[71] E-mail correspondence with the authors, April 2002.

'Replies from Interested Parties', which underpinned many of the reforms proposed in the Follow-up is revealing: almost all the submissions were from large, often transnational, organisations such as the Association of American Publishers, the Association of Commercial Television in Europe, the American Film Marketing Association and the Association Littéraire et Artistique Internationale. Although subsequent discussions took place in Brussels and Florence, these do not appear to have broadened significantly the range of groups that sought to influence the Commission.[72]

Commentators elsewhere have expressed similar concerns about the disproportionate influence that established industry groupings have had over the copyright legislative process. For example, Patry, writing in the context of the United States, has argued that lack of copyright expertise in Congress, reductions in congressional support staff and internal congressional rules all combine to help produce this result.[73] Similarly, Litman has raised the concern that copyright law reform in the United States has long been dominated by well-established parties, and that in the resulting negotiations between the copyright industries and institutional users such as libraries, it is the copyright industries that have invariably come out on top.[74] The problems identified by Patry and Litman should also be seen alongside our analysis in the next chapter, where we demonstrate that the UK legislative process has also failed to respond to the needs of users. The fact that problems with legislative processes are universal, however, means that European institutions need to be particularly vigilant when considering how best to ensure that the interests of users are represented – it should not become an excuse for inactivity.

It is sometimes said in reply to concerns about the difficulties user groups face in getting their voices heard that the position is not as bad as critics maintain, since the consumer electronics industry, which can afford to employ lobbyists and so on, will often battle on behalf of users. In support of this argument it might be noted that the European Association of Consumer Electronics Manufacturers (EACEM) did raise concerns about the likely impact of the Commission's proposals in the run-up to the adoption of the Information Society Directive,[75] arguing that consumer access to information would be impeded and that the European electronics industry would suffer. However, there is little to suggest that

---

[72] Hearings were held in Brussels in January 1996 and a conference was held in Florence in June 1996.
[73] See W. Patry, 'The Second Annual Tenzer Distinguished Lecture in Intellectual Property: Copyright and the Legislative Process: A Personal Perspective' (1996) 14 *Cardozo Arts and Entertainment Law Journal* 139.
[74] See J. Litman, *Digital Copyright* (New York: Prometheus, 2001).
[75] See, e.g., www.loehneysen.de/copy-docs/q&a.doc.

electronics manufacturers have had much influence during European copyright law-making processes, and it is significant that EACEM has felt that it has not always been given adequate opportunities to be involved in the consultation process for European legislation.[76] Moreover, irrespective of how effective the consumer electronics industry has been at presenting its case, Litman has argued persuasively that

> The folks who make tape recorders . . . also have their own agendas. Their interests may often accord with the public's, but where they diverge, the electronics industry . . . will look out for themselves. They are not, in other words, effective substitutes for a public advocate.

More generally, the problems faced by users in Europe need to be seen in the context of the democratic deficit which is now almost universally accepted to exist at the European level.[77] To be fair to the Commission, it has recognised that there is a need for greater openness and for more opportunities for participation, and that European legislative and policy-making processes are often seen as distant and Byzantine. In July 2001 the Commission published a White Paper on European Governance,[78] which identified public participation as one of five 'principles of good governance'.[79] As part of its subsequent reforms the Commission has adopted a communication on 'Interactive Policy Making' which includes a consultation mechanism designed to allow for public reaction to be given to new initiatives.[80] Commentators have also lent their support to a shift towards a more deliberative model of European government, in large part because it seems to provide an alternative to reforming the Community around a notion of representative democracy – reforms which may be difficult to achieve and which raise awkward theoretical questions.[81]

---

[76] See www.radio.gov.uk/topics/convergence/forum/brema/eacem.htm.
[77] The heart of the problem is that power has moved to a legislator that is not directly chosen and cannot be directly removed from office by popular vote. This problem is compounded by the added 'distance' between EU bodies and citizens, the complex EU committee structure and the weakening of judicial control over legislation. See P. Craig, 'The Nature of the Community: Integration, Democracy and Legitimacy', in P. Craig and G. de Burca (eds.), *The Evolution of EU Law* (Oxford: Oxford University Press, 1999), in particular pp. 23–7. Also see D. Curtin, *Postnational Democracy: The European Union in Search of a Political Philosophy* (The Hague: Kluwer, 1997), ch. 5; S. Douglas-Scott, *Constitutional Law of the European Union* (Harlow: Pearson Education, 2002), ch. 3; L. Siedentrop, *Democracy in Europe* (London: Penguin, 2000).
[78] *European Governance: A White Paper* COM(2001) 428 final. [79] *Ibid.*, p. 10.
[80] IPM – C(2001)1014. See further www.europa.eu.int/yourvoice.
[81] See Curtin, *Postnational Democracy*, in particular ch. 6; K. Armstrong, 'Rediscovering Civil Society: the White Paper on Governance' (2002) 8 *European Law Journal* 102; M. Lee, 'Public Participation, Procedure and Democratic Deficit in EC Environmental Law' (2003) 3 *Yearbook of European Environmental Law* 193.

Greater publicity for the Commission's copyright plans, providing much more time for public consultation and providing a clear trail of decision making are, however, only a first step. The concern has also been raised that the Commission seems to see deliberative democracy solely in instrumental terms – that it will increase public acceptance of the European project.[82] Consequently, the mechanisms for increased participation that the Commission is currently considering are modest and may result in participation being confined to well-organised, previously recognised, 'safe' groups.[83] In contrast, as Lee points out, genuine concern with democratic reform would entail an understanding of participation not merely as a way of increasing public acceptance of the Commission's plans, but also as a mechanism that might result in some plans being abandoned altogether and which might even lead to the adoption of a much more modest European project.[84]

On a more positive note, even within existing constraints there are steps user groups can take to increase their effectiveness. One is to agree a shared set of policy objectives in advance to ensure that legislators are confronted with a single alternative vision of the appropriate boundaries of copyright protection. During the debates about the Information Society Directive the user lobby formed an alliance called EFPICC (European Fair Practice in Copyright Campaign). As well as including libraries and educational groups, EFPICC brought in organisations representing the disabled, sections of the consumer electronics industry and listener and viewer organisations. The EFPICC campaign was widely regarded as more successful than earlier interventions and may provide a good template for political action in the future. Such large alliances may make it easier for less established user groups to get their concerns on to the political agenda. In addition, less established groups can take steps to familiarise themselves with existing copyright principles and language so that they can present their proposals in a form that will make them

---

[82] See e.g., the *Governance White Paper*, p. 10: 'Improved participation is likely to create more confidence in the end result'. For a general critique of the White Paper see A. Cygan, 'The White Paper on European Governance – Have Glasnost and Perestroika Finally Arrived to the European Union?' (2002) 65 *Modern Law Review* 229, arguing that the White Paper contains 'much self-indulgent debate by the Commission on its successes and blaming others for failures' (at 230).

[83] Lee, 'Public Participation'; P. Magnette, 'European Governance and Civic Participation: Can the European Union be Politicised?', in Jean Monnet Working Paper No.6/01, Symposium: 'Mountain or Molehill? A Critical Appraisal of the Commission White Paper on Governance' (available at www.jeanmonnetprogram.org/papers/01/010901.rtf), e.g. at p. 3: 'Far from breaking with the Community method, these participatory mechanisms constitute extensions of existing practices, and are underpinned by the same philosophy.'

[84] Lee, 'Public Participation'; Cygan, 'White Paper', 235–6.

more difficult to dismiss as irrelevant or naive. Again, there are already signs that newly established groups are taking steps of this kind. For example, the Electronic Frontier Foundation's interventions and proposals are becoming increasingly sophisticated.

Another aspect of the strategy of user groups that may need to be reconsidered is whether such groups have been too reactive in their stance. For the most part user groups have focused on the preservation of national regimes of exceptions. In future they may wish to consider whether it would not be better to argue for positive lists of harmonised users' rights, since there are cases where national variations may, in effect, render the exceptions useless. For example, a producer of a multimedia work aimed at a pan-European market would face considerable uncertainty if it wished to rely on the exceptions, rather than procuring a licence, to include an extract of an earlier work in its product – it would be both difficult and costly to ensure that the inclusion of the extract did not infringe in every member state. Works modified so as to make them suitable for a disabled audience would face similar problems. Calling for more pan-European exceptions would also allow user groups to appropriate the language of harmonisation for themselves. The EFPICC campaign may mark the first steps in this direction since it was concerned with the interests of European users as a whole and aimed to provide a template for national lobbies. Happily, there may also be signs that MEPs are beginning to take the user view seriously as copyright issues gain increasing media attention in the light of cases such as *Napster*.[85] But it must be emphasised that these are merely the first signs that a more level playing field may eventually be possible. For now, users continue to face considerable obstacles in getting their voices heard.

The Information Society Directive and the importance of official inertia

Thus far we have seen that the general climate within which copyright matters are being decided at the European level and a range of practical obstacles create serious problems for user groups trying to shape the legislative agenda. At the start of this chapter we referred to what may appear to be an inconsistency between this argument and our view that the Directive could be used to provide the foundation for a much fairer system of permitted acts in the United Kingdom. We further explained that this apparent contradiction disappears once it is appreciated that

---

[85] E-mail correspondence between Teresa Hackett and the authors, April 2002, referring to *A & M Records* v. *Napster* 239 F 3d 1004 (2001).

the single most important factor that shaped the final list of exceptions found in the Information Society Directive was the desire of member states to limit the disruption to their existing arrangements. Commenting on the history of the evolution of the Directive, Von Lewinski noted that the exceptions were 'provisions that the Member States are naturally unwilling to abandon' and added that this reluctance meant that the provisions relating to exceptions and limitations were 'amongst the most difficult aspects of harmonisation'.[86] As a result member states insisted on the inclusion of no fewer than twenty different heads of permissible exception in addition to a general saving provision allowing member states to retain existing minor exceptions which relate solely to analogue use. Importantly, some of the heads of permissible use are themselves fairly broad, for example, allowing use for 'purposes *such as* criticism or review'.[87] In contrast, the Commission's initial proposal for a draft directive contained only a very limited number of optional exceptions and hence would have drastically expanded copyright protection at the expense of users.[88] Evidence that it was political opposition from member states (and not recognition by the Commission of the importance of protecting user interests) that led to the final version of the Information Society Directive adopting a relatively liberal approach is also to be found in the text of the Directive itself. Even in the final version of the Directive the Commission felt that it was necessary to insist on the inclusion of only one mandatory exception, namely, a provision relating to certain acts of temporary reproduction that occur over an electronic network.[89] If the Commission had been genuinely concerned with the protection of users it would, in contrast, have done far more to ensure the substantive harmonisation of provisions relating, say, to criticism and review. Ironically, if the Commission had moved forward in this way, it is more likely that it would have achieved its goal of removing barriers to the achievement of a single market.[90]

As long as the Commission views the exceptions as lamentable political constraints on its ability to achieve its harmonisation goals we have good cause to be concerned about the likely shape of future developments. Moreover, it should be noted that the inertia of member states that constrained the Commission's ability to restrict the exceptions through the Information Society Directive is closely related to the 'bolt-on' method

---

[86] Von Lewinski, 'Proposed EC Directive', 778.
[87] Information Society Directive, Art. 5(3)(c). [88] See above, n. 24.
[89] Contained in Art. 5(1) of the Information Society Directive.
[90] See Chapter 10 for a detailed discussion of the impact of the Information Society Directive and the possibility of using it as a basis for achieving a greater degree of harmonisation than seems likely at present.

of implementing European legislation. In the next chapter it will be seen that this minimalist approach to the transposition of European directives into domestic law has itself caused unnecessary additional difficulties for users.

Summation

Thus far it has been seen that the Commission's limited objectives, its understanding of copyright and various practical obstacles have combined to push the concerns of users off the European legislative agenda. It can therefore be said that if users get a poor deal at present in the United Kingdom this is due in part to the fact that at the European level few steps have been taken to protect their interests. With the type of exceptions with which we are principally concerned, member states have, at most, been left with discretion to carve out a sphere of protection for users. Owner lobbyists then have a chance to persuade national governments either not to exercise this discretion at all or to exercise it only to a very limited extent. Moreover, even though users may have been sheltered to some extent by the conservatism or inertia of national governments, in so far as this is part of a more general desire to limit the impact of European directives, it will be seen that this too has had negative consequences for users.

The international forum

If the poor deal received by users at present in the United Kingdom is due in part to the fact that the European harmonisation process has been concerned with the harmonisation of the rights of owners rather than the rights of owners *and* users, much the same can be said about the international process of harmonisation. Given the conscious efforts of the European Community to set copyright policy at a global level, these failings are in some respects interconnected – when the Community acts on the international stage it does so in the light of its own harmonisation programme and its understanding of the appropriate level of copyright protection.[91] The most significant consequence of the exclusive focus on the harmonisation of rights, rather than rights and exceptions, is that at the international level, as at the European level, there is no minimum

---

[91] The influence of the Community on the development of international copyright law is perhaps most obvious in the 1996 WIPO Copyright Treaty and the 1996 WIPO Performances and Phonograms Treaty. See further Von Lewinski, 'Proposed EC Directive', 768.

standard of protection for users. Equally, however, it must be noted that the international conventions have left member states with considerable freedom in this area. The explanation for this apparent inconsistency is once again to be found in the reluctance of states to sacrifice their existing exceptions.

The importance of the desire of member states to be able to leave existing provisions in place is perhaps most clearly evident from the background to the harmonisation of the reproduction right and exceptions to it at the 1967 Stockholm Revision of the Berne Convention. Right from the earliest proposals for harmonisation of the reproduction right it was recognised that 'care would be required to ensure that this provision did not encroach upon exceptions that were already contained in national legislation'.[92] But again, this need to preserve national freedom of action was regarded as something to be lamented: 'it would be vain to suppose that countries would be ready at this stage to abolish these exceptions to any appreciable extent'.[93] The 1965 Committee of Governmental Experts decided that express mention should be made of the more common and important exceptions, such as private use, and that this short list of express exclusions should be supplemented by a general provision that would require other exceptions to meet certain conditions. These proposals proved controversial, however, as some member states attempted to amend the express list to bring the wording more in line with the formulation in their own law,[94] and other member states attempted to expand the range of the express exceptions. Ricketson suggests that it was the latter range of amendments that eventually led to the plans for an express list being dropped altogether,[95] a view that corresponds with the recollection of one of those present for the discussions at Stockholm.[96] The final form of the Stockholm revision only limited member states' freedom to provide an exception to the reproduction right in the following terms:

> It shall be a matter for legislation in the countries of the Union to permit the reproduction of such works in certain special cases, provided that such reproduction does not conflict with a normal exploitation of the work and does not unreasonably prejudice the legitimate interests of the author.[97]

---

[92] Ricketson, p. 479, citing the Report of the 1963 Study Group. See also M. Fiscor, 'How Much of What? The Three-Step Test and its Application in Two Recent WTO Dispute Settlement Cases' (2002) 192 RIDA 110.

[93] Fiscor, *ibid.*, citing the Diplomatic Record of the Stockholm Conference.

[94] See Ricketson, p. 480, discussing, for example, the French proposal to substitute 'private use' with 'individual or family use'.

[95] *Ibid.*, p. 481.

[96] Conversation with Professor Adrian Sterling, IFPI's representative at Stockholm, November 2000.

[97] Berne Convention, Art. 9(2).

The hurdle that this provision sets up, usually referred to as the 'three-step test', has traditionally been interpreted by member states as leaving them with considerable freedom. However, the concern is that more recent events may result in this freedom being eroded. Most significantly, the three-step test has now been incorporated into the TRIPS Agreement as a general restriction on the circumstances in which a member state may provide for an exception.[98] Thus unlike the Berne provision, which only applies to exceptions to the reproduction right, the TRIPS provision applies to all of the exclusive rights of the copyright owner. The fear expressed by a number of commentators is that the dispute settlement procedure will see a restrictive interpretation being placed on the three-step test, thereby reducing member states' room to operate.[99] In support of this fear it is possible to point to the negotiating history of the TRIPS Agreement where, once again, user interests were largely ignored.[100]

At present it is too early to say whether fears about the likely effect of the TRIPS Agreement will prove to be justified. Thus far there has only been one case on copyright exceptions. That case concerned whether certain newly introduced exceptions to the performance right in musical works under US law were compatible with the TRIPS Agreement. The decision, which went in part against the United States, does little to clarify the position, in large part because key passages in the decision are open to more than one interpretation,[101] but also because the extent to which the Dispute Settlement Body will adopt the principle of *stare decisis* is as yet unclear.[102] Consequently, it is not even possible to answer the most basic questions about the scope of the three-step test.[103] Moreover, there have been recent developments in other areas that may help steer the Dispute Settlement Body towards a liberal interpretation of the relevant provision of TRIPS. For example, the Doha Ministerial Statement on

---

[98] TRIPS Agreement, Art. 13.
[99] See, e.g., L. Helfer, 'World Music on a US Stage: A Berne/TRIPS and Economic Analysis of the Fairness in Music Licensing Act' (2000) 80 *Boston University Law Review* 93, 103, 184; R. Okediji, 'Toward an International Fair Use Doctrine' (2000) 39 *Columbia Journal of Transnational Law* 75.
[100] See C. May, *A Global Political Economy of Intellectual Property Rights* (London: Routledge, 2000); P. Drahos, 'Global Property Rights in Information: The Story of TRIPS at the GATT' (1995) 13 *Prometheus* 6.
[101] Cf. Ginsburg, 'Toward Supranational', 59: 'the Panel decision may have clarified the terms of reference, but it may not have made future outcomes any more predictable'.
[102] A similar point is made by Ginsburg, 'Toward Supranational', 7, and Okediji, 'Toward an International Fair Use Doctrine', 90. For general discussion of the use of precedent in the dispute settlement system see R. Bhala, 'The Precedent Setters: De Facto *Stare Decisis* in WTO Adjudication' (1999) 9 *Journal of Transnational Law and Policy* 1; J. Felgueroso, 'TRIPS and the Dispute Settlement Understanding: The First Six Years' (2002) 30 *AIPLA Quarterly Journal* 165, 223–5.
[103] See also Chapter 9, where the question of whether a general fair use defence is compatible with the TRIPS Agreement is discussed.

patent protection for pharmaceuticals points to the fact that Articles 7 and 8 of TRIPS, which emphasise the social welfare and public interest aspects of intellectual property protection, are relevant when construing the substantive provisions of the Agreement.[104] Cases on the permissible scope of patent exceptions also point towards a fairly liberal interpretation of the freedom of member states to set the boundaries of intellectual property protection.[105] Also to be welcomed is the controversial decision of the World Trade Organisation (WTO) to accept and consider *amicus curiae* briefs.[106] Although it might be objected that this decision will give owner groups yet another means of influence, as Robert Howse has pointed out, corporate interests already have ways of making their point of view known through their access to politicians, delegates and ambassadors.[107] In contrast, it may provide groups that lack resources with a relatively low-cost method of making their voice heard.

However, even if the TRIPS Agreement is interpreted in such a way as to preserve the freedom of action member states enjoyed under the Berne Convention, this does not mean that there may not still be reason for alarm about the direction in which TRIPS is taking us. Returning to the US performing rights case, it is noticeable that the provisions in question were designed not to protect a fundamental interest of users, but rather were merely designed to reduce the liability to pay copyright fees for certain types of business. As such, therefore, the decision might not be thought to provide much cause for concern. Yet it is important to note that the provisions in question were part of a political deal done in the United States which also saw the term of protection being extended to life plus seventy years.[108] In many respects, therefore, the decision provides a nice illustration of the potential dangers of a system that provides minimum standards of protection for right owners and maximum standards of protection for users. If a country chooses to go beyond the minimum standard of protection required (in this case by extending the

---

[104] See Declaration on the TRIPS Agreement and Public Health (WT/MIN(01)/DEC/2) adopted on 14 Nov. 2001 at the 4th WTO Ministerial Conference in Doha.
[105] See in particular WT/DS114/R (Dispute between the EU and Canada).
[106] See WT/DS58/AB/R (Shrimp/Turtle dispute between India, Malaysia, Pakistan and Thailand, and the United States).
[107] R. Howse, 'Membership and its Privileges: The WTO, Civil Society, and the *Amicus* Brief Controversy' (2003) 9 *European Law Journal* 496, in particular at 509. Similarly, see G. Dinwoodie, 'The Development and Incorporation of International Norms in the Formation of Copyright Law' (2001) 62 *Ohio State Law Journal* 733, 771, also taking the view that the involvement of non-governmental third parties in WTO proceedings through *amicus* briefs is a welcome development.
[108] See M. LaFrance, 'Congress Trips Over International Law: WTO Finds Unfairness in Music Licensing Act (2001)' 11 *De Paul-LCA Journal of Art and Entertainment Law* 397, 419.

term of protection beyond life plus fifty years) the decision is unassailable under international law,[109] but if a country goes too far in providing protection for users this may be declared to be incompatible with the TRIPS Agreement. If the country in question then complies with the ruling of the TRIPS panel without undoing the entire package of measures, the rights of owners will have been ratcheted up without any commensurate increase in the protection for users, leaving a level of protection in place to which the legislature might never have been willing to agree.[110]

Conclusion

When the main barrier preventing the rights of users from being eroded is a belief that reform would be too politically awkward or would cause too much disruption to existing arrangements, there is little reason to be confident about the likely direction of future developments. In relation to the main theme of this second section of the book, we can say that if users are getting a bad deal at present this is in part because at the international and European levels there is little interest in protecting the interests of users per se. Users are therefore confined to what they can get at the national level, but as rights are expanded and strengthened at the supranational level, governments and national legislatures are left with less and less room in which to manoeuvre. Moreover, even in the space remaining, user groups still have to compete with owner representatives who try to persuade national governments to go even further than international and regional instruments require. As will be seen in the next chapter, in the United Kingdom at least, user groups also face obstacles when operating at a national level which, even if they are not as great as the obstacles considered in this chapter, are nevertheless daunting.

---

[109] Attempts to challenge the constitutional validity of the extension of term in the United States also failed: *Eldred* v. *Ashcroft* 536 US 186 (2003).

[110] At the time of writing, however, the United States has yet to change its law, having chosen instead to pay compensation of $1.1 million a year for a three-year period to the end of 2004. European right holders regard this level of compensation as inadequate and are seeking to persuade the European Commission to revisit this issue at the WTO in 2005. See, e.g., British Music Rights' comments on the DTI's preparations for a Trade and Investment White Paper, available at www.bmr.org/html/submissions/submission95.htm.

8   Copyright in the domestic arena

Having identified some of the problems faced by users at the supranational level, in this chapter we turn our attention to the domestic political arena. As has already been indicated, the principal theme of this chapter is that at the domestic level too users face formidable obstacles in getting their voices heard and hence in shaping the legislative agenda. We begin by providing examples of where the unhelpful ideas and assumptions about copyright that we identified in Chapter 6 have contributed to an overly restrictive approach being taken to the exceptions. We suggest that problems caused by the adoption of these ideas and assumptions have been exacerbated by the way in which departmental responsibilities are divided in the United Kingdom. These factors, in turn, feed into another feature of the exceptions in the United Kingdom, which is that the permitted act provisions are very tightly drafted. This can create problems for users that are in some sense accidental (in that they do not result from a conscious decision to deny users protection in a given set of circumstances) and result from the failure of the draftsman to anticipate a particular issue or scenario or from generally poor draftsmanship. However, whilst such problems can be categorised as accidental, they are also inevitable, given an approach to drafting that attempts to define every possible situation in which an exception might apply. Yet a further problem for users flows from the way in which the government has implemented European directives, with additional restrictions being added on to existing exceptions so as to make them compatible with European law, when there would have been other, more radical (but potentially less restrictive) ways of implementing the directives.

It is also worth making two other preliminary points about the treatment of users in the domestic forum. The first is to reiterate that the United Kingdom has to operate within the overall limits set by the international conventions and the European directives. With the exception of a small number of mandatory minor exceptions introduced by the directives, the relevant international instruments provide for compulsory rights for owners, but merely optional exceptions for the benefit of users.

Such a system strongly favours right owners. This is because owners' representatives are given a further opportunity at the domestic level to argue for a maximalist version of copyright, by insisting that government and Parliament ought not to introduce an exception, even in circumstances where the relevant international instruments would allow for such a provision. In contrast, user groups will be hampered by the government's need to remain within the limits that have been set at the supranational level. The second point to note is that in the course of our analysis in this chapter it will be seen that it is Parliament, not government, which has tended to be most concerned about the protection of user interests. This provides further cause for concern about the effect of a shift in the law-making process in the copyright field from the domestic to the European level – not only do user groups find it difficult to operate effectively at the European level, the shift also results in decreased parliamentary oversight of the actions of government.

The final theme that we begin to explore in this chapter, and which we continue in the next, is the relationship between the courts and Parliament. Commentators who are critical of the United Kingdom's system of permitted acts have usually seen the problems solely in terms of problems with the existing legislation. Consequently, when considering options for reform they have tended to focus solely on legislative solutions. For example, it will be seen in the next chapter that one liberalising measure that is commonly advocated is that the United Kingdom replace its fair dealing provisions with a more general, US-style, fair use defence. Whilst we share the view that there needs to be a fundamental overhaul of the existing provisions, we believe that careful thought also needs to be given to how the judiciary is likely to react to legislative reform. We demonstrate that courts have been too ready to assume that Parliament must have intended to confine protection for users within narrow limits. Courts have also shown themselves to be reluctant to develop alternative safeguards for users. Whilst this reluctance may be understandable given traditional understandings of the relationship between the legislature and the judiciary, we argue that in highly technical areas of law this traditional understanding may misdescribe the way in which Parliament is likely to proceed when crafting legislation.

Understandings of copyright

In Chapter 6 we identified three beliefs about copyright and the role of the exceptions that have unhelpful implications for users. Those beliefs are that the exceptions are best understood as circumstances in which market failure is likely, that the exceptions must be narrowly drawn and narrowly interpreted because copyright is a property right, and that copyright represents a 'balance'. In the last chapter we identified examples of where these understandings of copyright appear to have influenced the Commission with detrimental results for users. In much the same way, we believe that it is possible to identify examples of where these understandings of copyright and closely allied beliefs have had an impact at the domestic level.

The clearest examples of the market failure argument being used to justify a restrictive approach to the exceptions in the United Kingdom are provided by the debates during the passage of the 1988 Act relating to those provisions that only take effect in the absence of an approved licensing scheme. It was seen in Chapter 4 that some of the provisions relating to educational copying operate in this way.[1] Whilst these are unquestionably the most important provisions that take this form, mention should also be made of the provision which allows for the reproduction of scientific or technical abstracts,[2] the provision which allows for the making of subtitled copies of broadcasts,[3] and the recently introduced provision which allows multiple copies of a work to be made for use by visually impaired persons,[4] none of which apply if a licensing scheme (meeting certain conditions) is in place.[5] During the passage of the 1988 Act it was made clear that the licensing approach is founded on the premise that it is for the market to determine how much users should pay for the right to reproduce copyright material. The provision of an exception is designed to reduce the risk of bargaining breakdown by creating an incentive for owners to enter into negotiations and to reach agreement.[6] As it was put for the government during debates on the educational copying provisions, it was believed that: 'The determination of the price educational establishments pay for copies . . . is a matter for negotiation between the licensing body and the educational establishments . . . It is not for the legislature to pick a royalty rate out of the air.'[7]

---

[1] CDPA 1988, ss. 35(2), 36(3).   [2] *Ibid.*, s. 60.   [3] *Ibid.*, s. 74.
[4] *Ibid.*, ss. 31B–C.   [5] *Ibid.*: see, respectively, ss. 31D, 60(2), 74(4).
[6] Nor can users refuse to negotiate, since in some cases users are likely to want to go beyond what the permitted act allows and in other cases it would be possible for the relevant minister to impose a licensing scheme upon them. It is perhaps worth contrasting this approach with that recommended by Robert Merges, a leading exponent of economic analysis of intellectual property rights. Merges argues that in cases of possible bargaining breakdown it is preferable to 'modify property rule entitlements so as to increase slightly the risk that the [user] can escape entirely from the . . . property right' than to attempt to fix the price through a compulsory or statutory licence: R. Merges, 'Contracting into Liability Rules: Intellectual Property Rights and Collective Rights Organizations' (1996) 84 *California Law Review* 1293, 1316. This point was made in the context of a discussion of the relationship between 'improvers' and 'pioneers' in patent law, but is representative of Merges' general approach.
[7] *Hansard*, HL vol. 493, col. 1171, per Lord Beaverbrook, rejecting alternative proposals for statutory educational licensing schemes.

Understandings of copyright

It would be idle to suggest that the government applied a market failure understanding of the role of the exceptions consistently, since at times other justifications were used to explain a particular approach. Indeed, opponents of the government's plans to extend the research exception to include commercial research pointed to the inconsistency in the government's approach in insisting that educational establishments enter into negotiations with copyright owners, whilst providing industry with an outright exception.[8] Nor would it be sensible to suggest that a version of the market failure argument was the only factor that led the government to adopt a restrictive approach to educational copying. But at the very least a (much simplified) version of the market failure argument provided the government with a language by means of which it could justify its restrictive approach.

Just as it cannot be proved that the market failure argument caused the government to adopt a particular approach to the educational exceptions in 1988, it is difficult to say conclusively what effect the belief that copyright represents a balance between competing interests had on the final form of legislation. One thing that is striking, however, is that the idea that copyright represents a 'balance' is to be found throughout the long process that eventually resulted in the passage of the 1988 Act. For example, the Whitford Committee made the following observation in the introduction to its report on copyright reform:

On the whole, we agree with the generally held view that the balance between the rights of the copyright owner on the one hand and the exceptions in favour of copyright users on the other is about right, and that no abrupt change in the balance is called for.[9]

Towards the end of the passage of the bill through the Lords it was said by the responsible minister that the government's approach 'in many ... parts of the Bill' was 'to try to find a balance between conflicting interests'.[10] Other references to the copyright balance are to be found throughout the parliamentary debates that accompanied the passage of the legislation.[11]

---

[8] *Hansard*, HC SCE, col. 183. It should be remembered that the limitation of fair dealing for the purposes of research to 'research for a non-commercial purpose' is a consequence of the implementation of the Information Society Directive. Under the original provisions of the 1988 Act commercial research was included within the scope of the exception.
[9] *Report of the Committee to Consider the Law on Copyright and Designs*, Cmnd 6732 (1977), para. 16.
[10] *Hansard*, HL vol. 495, col. 633 (per Lord Beaverbrook).
[11] See *Hansard*, HL vol. 491, col. 99: 'As has been said many times in debates on this Bill, copyright is a question of balance between the different participants' (per Viscount Brentford). And see, e.g., *Hansard*, HL vol. 491, cols. 77, 332; HL vol. 493, col. 1145; HC SCE, col. 176.

More recent use of the language of balance is to be found in the UK government's Regulatory Impact Assessment of the regulations to implement the Information Society Directive where, for example, it is stated:

> The government's aim in preparing these Regulations has been to seek to maintain as far as possible the existing balance between the interests of the various stakeholders – in particular, existing exceptions have been limited only to the extent considered necessary to comply with the Directive.[12]

It is also worth noting that the Copyright Directorate (the branch of government that has responsibility for copyright policy) states on its web pages that it sees its role as ensuring that copyright represents 'an appropriate balance' and 'the right balance'.[13]

Although it is impossible to say with certainty what effect beliefs in the copyright balance have had, as was suggested in the previous two chapters, the concern is that this way of thinking about copyright may lead to the adoption of a conservative approach to questions of reform. It leads us to assume that the normative work has already been done, and done well. The language of balance is therefore a technique by which to close off debate as to the purposes and proper boundaries of copyright law. As can be seen from the comment of the Whitford Committee, if the starting point is that copyright already represents a 'balance' between competing interests, this makes it almost inevitable that the conclusion that will be arrived at is that any reform should be limited to ensuring that the trade-off between access and control is not unduly altered by new technologies and new methods of reproducing and disseminating copyright works. It is likely to discourage a fundamental reappraisal of the system and probably helps underpin comments such as that made on behalf of the government during the passage of the bill through the Committee stage of the Commons, that in relation to library copying, '[T]he 1956 Act was satisfactory. It met the needs of users and producers, and to move from it will worsen and confuse the position.'[14]

A belief in the copyright balance may also lead to a search for retrospective, policy-oriented, explanations for why a particular type of use falls within or outside the exceptions. For example, in this chapter we explore why sound recordings came to be included and then excluded from the ambit of the research and private study exception. As we explain below, it seems that the question of whether sound recordings ought to fall within the ambit of the private study exception was not considered at all at the

---

[12] Para. 4.7. Available at www.patent.gov.uk/copy/notices/2003/copyria.pdf.
[13] www.patent.gov.uk/copy/policy/index.htm.   [14] *Hansard*, HC SCE, col. 226.

Understandings of copyright

time of the passage of the 1911 and 1956 Acts. This is quite probably because the technology available for reproducing sound recordings at the time meant that it would not ordinarily have been possible for a student or researcher to make a copy of a sound recording. When the Whitford Committee came to examine this question, however, it was asserted that a decision had been taken in 1956 to exclude sound recordings from the scope of the exception so as to prevent home tapers from arguing that they had a defence.[15] A belief in the copyright balance may encourage a search for this type of justification, which pays no attention to the history of the relevant provisions. This is because the alternative explanation, that what might appear to be a key change in the scope of sound recording copyright was merely a product of the way in which the relevant provisions were drafted, sits very uncomfortably alongside a belief that copyright represents a careful weighing of competing interests.

The impact of the categorisation of copyright as a property right is at least as difficult to assess as the impact of the other beliefs about copyright that we identified, but again it is possible to point to a number of examples of where the language of property was used to justify calls for a maximalist copyright regime. For example, opponents of the government's decision to refuse to extend copyright protection beyond life plus fifty years relied in part on an analogy with other forms of property, it being said that 'I do not think that Members of the Committee would be happy with the notion that 50 years after their death all their property would become public property.'[16] Similarly, in debates on the appropriateness of a right to seize infringing articles and the circumstances in which an order for delivery up of infringing articles should be made, much was made of the analogy with the return of stolen tangible property.[17] Most significant for present purposes, however, are the claims that were made for the sanctity of copyright as a property right during the debates on the permitted acts provisions. An extreme example of such a claim was provided by Lord Willis, who in the course of a debate on the research and private study exception stated that he believed 'in the sacred principle that the copyright belongs to the author'.[18] More measured use of the language of property during the debates on the exceptions included praise for

---

[15] *Report of the Committee to Consider the Law on Copyright and Designs*, Cmnd 6732 (1977), para. 674. It should be noted, however, that the Whitford Committee recommended the introduction of a general defence that would have applied to all copyright subject matter.
[16] *Hansard*, HL vol. 490, col. 1152 (per Lord Wyatt of Weeford). But compare the comment of Lord Hailsham who, in reply, argued that in the case of intellectual property rights, 'We are also talking about monopoly': *Hansard*, HL vol. 490, col. 1175.
[17] *Ibid.*, HL vol. 501, cols. 246–7, 248–9.   [18] *Ibid.*, HL vol. 491, col. 98.

the government for its stated commitment 'to preserve as far as possible the rights of copyright owners'.[19]

Isolated statements of the kind noted above, particularly when made from the back benches, do not tell us much about how or in what ways ideas about copyright as a property right shaped the legislation. Nevertheless, they provide some further evidence to support our argument that unsophisticated accounts of the nature of property rights help to underpin a maximalist copyright regime.

The DTI's mandate

Having identified a number of examples of where the ideas and assumptions about copyright that we examined in Chapter 6 seem to have had unhelpful consequences for users, we now turn to consider other factors that may lead to users receiving a poor deal in the United Kingdom. One such factor may be the way that departmental responsibilities are divided. In particular, there is the concern that the Department of Trade and Industry (DTI), which has responsibility for developing copyright policy and drafting primary and secondary copyright legislation, does not have responsibility for, and is not used to considering, the interests of copyright users. Attempting to assess the impact of this type of structural or institutional factor on the final form of copyright law and policy is clearly very difficult. However, many of those working within government treat the division of departmental responsibilities as the key to understanding why and how particular decisions are made in the copyright field.[20] User representatives with experience of lobbying in a number of countries have also commented that where the trade ministry is responsible for copyright, users face additional difficulties.[21] More generally, there is a long-standing body of academic literature that supports the view that the way in which the executive branch is structured can have significant implications for how government operates.[22] Moreover, we believe that

---

[19] *Ibid.*, HL vol. 491, col. 122 (per Lord Lloyd of Hampstead).
[20] This point was made forcibly by a senior civil servant with the Australian (Commonwealth) government in a conversation with one of the authors at a conference in Brisbane on 8 Feb. 2002.
[21] E-mail correspondence with Toby Bainton of SCONUL (Society of College, National and University Libraries), Oct. 2002. SCONUL's mission is to 'improve the quality and extend the influence of the libraries in higher education, and the national libraries, in the United Kingdom and Ireland' (see www.sconul.ac.uk).
[22] See, e.g., F. Bland, *Planning the Modern State: An Introduction to the Problem of Political and Administrative Re-organization* (Sydney: Angus & Robertson, 1945), in particular at p. 94, noting the problems of 'departmentalism'; D. Chester and F. Wilson, *The Organisation of British Central Government*, 2nd edn (London: Allen & Unwin, 1968), in particular ch. 11; M. Flinders, 'Governance in Whitehall' (2002) 80 *Public Administration* 51, in particular at 55–7.

a comparison of the United Kingdom and Australia provides at least some evidence to support our claim that the way in which departmental responsibilities are divided in the United Kingdom may have negative consequences for users.

In Australia, responsibility for the Copyright Act 1968, including responsibility for drafting legislative amendments, rests with the Attorney-General's Department.[23] As such, the final form of legislation is controlled by a department which is not directly responsible for promoting the growth of the copyright industries. Since 1993 the Department of Communications, Information Technology and the Arts (DCITA) has had joint responsibility with the Attorney-General's Department for most copyright policy matters. While DCITA is responsible for information and communications industries development and promoting e-commerce and business online, this department also has responsibility for the cultural sector, including support for libraries, museums and the arts. This mixed portfolio may explain why in both formal and informal meetings with the authors DCITA staff have always seemed much more pro-user than might have been expected.

Whilst we do not wish to suggest that the Australian system of permitted acts is perfect or that it ought to provide a template for reform, there are a number of respects in which Australian law is superior to UK law in its treatment of users. In relation to those areas that are of particular concern to us, that is, circumstances in which copyright can impact negatively on freedom of speech, freedom of information, access to cultural resources and the provision of education, there are a number of features of Australian law that are worthy of attention. As regards freedom of speech or freedom of information, it is notable that Australia's reporting exception is not confined to 'current events' but rather extends to 'news' in general.[24]

As regards the provision of education and library services, Australia's provisions are both broader in scope and less onerous to comply with than their UK counterparts. For example, the Australian research and private study exception is not confined to authorial works and hence applies to all copyright subject matter.[25] The legislation also provides

---

[23] See Administrative Arrangements Order 2001 (Australia) (Gazette S468, 27 Nov. 2001), amended by Order in Council 20 Dec. 2001 (Gazette GN2, 16 Jan. 2002). This Order sets out which ministers and departments are responsible for each of the Acts of the Australian Parliament.

[24] Copyright Act 1968 (Cth), ss. 42, 103B. For judicial confirmation see *Commonwealth of Australia v. Fairfax* (1980) 147 CLR 39, 56: 'I am inclined to allow that "news" ... is not restricted to ... "current events"' (per Mason J); *Channel Nine v. Network Ten* (2002) 55 IPR 112, 131; *Wigginton v. Brisbane TV* (1992) 25 IPR 58, 62.

[25] Copyright Act 1968 (Cth), ss. 40, 103C.

guidance both as to the quantity of material that can be copied by virtue of the research and private study exception[26] and the factors that will be taken into account when deciding whether any given taking is fair.[27] Still more importantly, the provisions relating to educational copying operate as a compulsory licence that extends to the creation of study packs. This avoids the problems encountered in the United Kingdom, where (as was seen in Chapter 4) the Copyright Licensing Agency may not have a mandate to authorise copying from a particular work. It is also interesting to note that the original compulsory licence provisions in Australia were replaced in 1989 by a new regime that was specifically designed to reduce the costs associated with complying with the statutory provisions, in particular by reducing the need for record keeping.[28] There also seems to be a general sense that the current educational copying provisions are working well.[29] Whilst the provisions relating to library copying have rather more in common with their UK counterparts, the Act again attempts to provide greater certainty by providing guidance as to the amount of a work that can be copied and, through a recent set of amendments, this attempt to provide clarity as to the amount that can be safely copied has been extended to works in digital form. Overall, therefore, it is safe to say that users are better protected in Australia than in the United Kingdom.

In contrast to the position in Australia, where the Attorney-General's Department is not directly responsible for the copyright industries, it has already been noted that in the United Kingdom it is the DTI that has principal responsibility for both copyright law and policy. Moreover, unlike DCITA, the DTI has no responsibility for libraries, museums or the cultural sector more generally. Admittedly, although the DTI has no responsibility for the cultural sector, it does have responsibility for consumer issues, and it is worth noting that Melanie Johnson MP, when Parliamentary Secretary for Consumer Affairs within the DTI, lent her support to attempts to introduce new permitted acts for the benefit of the visually impaired by means of a private member's bill.[30] In general, however, the DTI's consumer portfolio seems to have little bearing on how the department sees copyright issues. It was seen in the last chapter that consumer groups tend to give copyright issues a low priority and

---

[26] *Ibid.*, ss. 40(3), 10.   [27] *Ibid.*, ss. 40(2), 103C(2).
[28] See J. McKeough and A. Stewart, *Intellectual Property in Australia*, 2nd edn (Sydney: Butterworths, 1997), p. 184.
[29] *Ibid.*, both these authors coming from education.
[30] See M. Johnson MP, 'Launch of Copyright Guidelines for Visually Impaired People', 31 Oct. 2001, available at www.dti.gov.uk/ministers/archived/JohnsonM311001.html and see the Copyright (Visually Impaired Persons) Act 2002.

government agencies concerned with consumer matters may well follow their lead. More generally, the concern has been expressed that the coexistence of trade and consumer portfolios in the same department is an uneasy one at best, and one that may result in consumer issues being neglected.[31] In fairness to the DTI it should also be said that the Copyright Directorate (the branch of the DTI that has responsibility for copyright matters) does emphasise its commitment to consultation with users.[32] The list of organisations consulted in relation to the implementation of the Information Society Directive also demonstrates that this commitment is taken seriously.[33] Nevertheless, the user representatives we spoke to felt that they faced an uphill struggle in influencing the DTI, and it has to be emphasised once again that user groups have to contend with a relative lack of resources.[34]

It might, of course, be expected that other departments that do have responsibility for industries or sectors that make heavy use of copyright material might seek to influence copyright policy. That is, it might be expected that the interests of users would be represented within government by other departments, such as the Department for Culture, Media and Sport (which is responsible for libraries, museums and the cultural sector more generally) and the Department for Education and Skills. In practice, however, these departments seem to have little impact in the copyright field. In this context it is instructive to consider the background to the bill that eventually became the Copyright Act 1956. The creation of a draft Copyright Bill took place earlier than would normally have been the case because it was noted that 'several Departments are interested in copyright and the existence of a draft Bill would . . . greatly facilitate inter-departmental discussion'.[35] Yet despite this concern within government to enable communication between departments, there is little in the official record to indicate that departments other than the Board

---

[31] See, e.g., M. Childs, 'Listening to the Voice of the Consumer', *Guardian*, 24 Aug. 2000; M. Harrison, 'TUC Slates Hewitt over Shake-up at the DTI', *Independent*, 23 Nov. 2001.
[32] www.patent.gov.uk/copy/policy/index.htm.
[33] Such organisations included the Chartered Institute of Librarians and Information Professionals, the Educational Copyright Users Forum, the Museums Copyright Group, the Music Users Council and individual universities. See Consultation Paper on UK Implementation of the EC Directive on the Harmonisation of Certain Aspects of Copyright and Related Rights in the Information Society, Annex C – Draft Regulatory Impact Assessment: List of those Consulted Directly on the Draft Amendments in Annex A of the Consultation Paper of 7 Aug. 2002, available at www.patent.gov.uk/about/consultations/eccopyright/annexc.htm.
[34] E-mail correspondence with Toby Bainton of SCONUL, Oct. 2002, arguing that 'the money to employ full-time lobbyists is crucial'.
[35] Public Record Office Document: CAB21/3725 (note to the Lord Privy Seal dated 2 July 1953).

230 Copyright in the domestic arena

of Trade (the forerunner to the DTI) had much of an impact on the final form of the 1956 Act. Why this should have been the case can only be a matter of conjecture, but lack of copyright expertise, lack of interest in such a technical area of the law and the hectic reform programme of Attlee's postwar Labour governments (1945–51) may all have played a part. It is even perhaps possible that the early creation of a draft bill may have had the result opposite to that intended, since this may have created a sense within the Board of Trade that the bulk of the work had been done and a natural reluctance to reopen fundamental issues.

In summary, while the impact of the division of departmental responsibilities on the final form of legislation and policy making is impossible to assess with any degree of certainty, indications from those working within government, the experiences of user representatives, academic accounts of the way in which the civil service operates, a comparative analysis of the position in Australia and the United Kingdom, and some limited historical evidence all suggest that this may be a factor which helps to account for the difficulties user groups have faced in getting their voices heard in the United Kingdom.

Draftsmanship and the inevitable accident

When considering why users have received a poor deal in the United Kingdom, another factor that needs to be kept in mind is that some of the restrictions faced by users may result not from a set of conscious decisions, but rather from the fact that the legislation was poorly drafted or was drafted without proper account being taken of particular factual scenarios or likely technological developments. We begin by identifying three examples of where users seem to face problems of this kind, two drawn from within our core areas of concern and a third relating to the permitted act designed to allow for the copying of artistic works on public display. We then turn to consider why such problems occur and the extent to which such problems are inevitable, given the United Kingdom's current approach to the permitted acts.

One example of where an exception has been rendered of limited utility relates to the provision designed to allow for copying in the course of instruction.[36] As was seen in Chapter 4, this exception does not apply if the copying is done by means of a 'reprographic process'. A 'reprographic process' is defined by the Act as including copying 'involving the use of an appliance for making multiple copies' and, in the case of works

---

[36] CDPA 1988, s. 32.

in 'electronic form', copying by electronic means.[37] Consequently, it was seen that whilst a teacher may copy a substantial portion of a work onto a whiteboard, the teacher may not cut and paste material from an electronic database on to a PowerPoint slide or photocopy material onto an acetate for use on an overhead projector. Not only do these restrictions create real problems in practice, they sit uneasily alongside government pressure on teachers to utilise new technologies when delivering courses. Nevertheless, it might be argued that such restrictions are necessary in order to prevent educational copying provisions from being abused (although such an argument would be unconvincing, given that the Act also makes provision to ensure that copies made by virtue of this section cannot be subsequently dealt with[38]). For present purposes, however, the interesting feature of this provision is that the restrictions in question seem to have been designed to ensure that this exception could not be used to justify the production of multiple copies for distribution amongst a body of students.[39] That they now extend beyond this and exclude commonly used methods of projecting or presenting a single copy of a work is due to an understandable failure to anticipate the ways in which technology and teaching practices would develop.

A second, somewhat more complicated, example of where the permitted acts have come to be unintentionally limited relates to the exclusion of sound recordings from fair dealing for the purposes of research or private study. As was noted in Chapter 4, the exclusion of sound recordings and other non-authorial works fails to reflect the importance of non-textual media for both study and research. It also creates the counterintuitive situation that a researcher who copied a substantial part of a sound recording for the purpose of private study would infringe copyright in the recording, but not in any underlying musical work. The background to the exclusion of sound recordings from the scope of fair dealing for the purposes of research and private study is complex.

Under the 1911 Act it seems that the private study exception did apply to copyright in sound recordings. However, this was because the provisions relating to musical works were deemed to apply to sound recordings, subject to certain alterations (for example, relating to the term of protection).[40] At the time, the question of whether the fair dealing provision ought to apply to sound recording copyright or what that might

---

[37] *Ibid.*, s. 178.   [38] *Ibid.*, s. 32(5), and see Chapter 4.
[39] At least this is how the limitation was understood at the time: G. Dworkin and R. Taylor, *Blackstone's Guide to the Copyright, Designs and Patents Act 1988* (London: Blackstone, 1989), p. 173.
[40] Copyright Act 1911, s. 19.

mean given the state of technology at the time was never considered.[41] In contrast, under the 1956 Act sound recordings were excluded from the scope of the research and private study exception, but again there is no evidence that this was the result of a conscious decision to limit the rights of users in respect of sound recordings.[42] Thus sound recordings were first brought within the scope of the research and private study exception and then excluded from it, apparently without any thought being given to this issue one way or the other.[43] The most likely explanation seems to be that prior to the invention and widespread diffusion of tape recorders the question of whether sound recordings ought to be within the scope of the exception was a non-issue.[44] This would explain why the edition of *Copinger and Skone James on Copyright* which followed the passage of the 1956 Act did not even note the change.[45] In the lead-up to the 1988 Act there was some discussion of the question of whether the private study exception should apply to sound recordings, but this issue became tangled up with, and was overshadowed by, the questions of whether the United Kingdom should introduce a blank tape levy[46] and

---

[41] Cf. *Hansard*, HC vol. 28, cols. 1945–57; vol. 29, cols. 1254–2174; HL 1911, vol. X, cols. 45–6, 115–17, 205, 451–3; Public Record Office Documents BT103/711; BT209/477; BT209/620; BT209/621; BT209/1113; CAB37/103/31; CAB37/106/41; HO45/10616/195426; LO3/429; TS27/22.

[42] Cf. Gregory Committee, *Report of the Copyright Committee*, (Cmd. 8662) (1952), paras. 38–54; *Hansard*, HC vol. 558, cols. 685–719, 759–69; HL vol. 194, cols. 903–5, 1067–90, 1097–111; vol. 195, cols. 920–30; 1055–76; vol. 196, cols. 744–6; Public Record Office Documents: BT103/682; BT209/532; BT209/533; BT209/534; BT209/1118; BT209/1119; BT209/1128; BT281/12; BT281/13; BT281/14; BT281/15; CAB21/3725.

[43] During the passage of the 1956 Act Lord Chorley proposed an amendment to what became s. 6(1) that would have extended the scope of the research and private study exception to 'any work'. His motive for doing so, however, was the concern that artistic works were not included in the scope of the provision, and the amendment was withdrawn when it was brought to his attention that use of artistic works for the purposes of research or private study was covered by what became s. 9(1) of the 1956 Act. See *Hansard*, HL vol. 194, cols. 903–5.

[44] Interest in recording sounds magnetically dates back to the nineteenth century, and experimental tape recorders were produced in the 1930s, but it was not until Philips developed the audio cassette in the 1960s that tape recorders became portable and consumer ownership took off. See J. McWilliams, *The Preservation and Restoration of Sound Recordings* (Nashville: American Association for State and Local History, 1979), in particular pp. 15–19; M. Chanan, *Repeated Takes: A Short History of Recording and its Effects on Music* (London: Verso, 1995), in particular p. 153.

[45] See F. Skone James and E. Skone James, *Copinger and Skone James on Copyright*, 9th edn (London: Sweet & Maxwell, 1958), pp. 291–3.

[46] See, e.g., *Report of the Committee to Consider the Law on Copyright and Designs*, Cmnd 6732 (1977), in particular para. 674. As was noted earlier in this chapter, the Whitford Committee explained the exclusion of sound recordings from the research and private study exception on the basis that 'The reason no doubt, is to deprive those who make their record collections by taping others' records, rather than by purchase,

a 'time shifting' exception.[47] Consequently, the interests of researchers as such received very little attention, and by 1988 the question was seen in terms of whether the private study exception should be 'extended' to include sound recordings.

Our third example relates to the provision that enables certain works on public display to be represented without infringing copyright.[48] Section 62 of the 1988 Act provides that copyright in buildings, and in models for buildings, sculptures or works of artistic craftsmanship which are on public display will not be infringed by making a graphic work representing it, or by making a photograph or film of it, or by broadcasting a visual image of it.[49] Furthermore, copyright is not infringed 'by the issue to the public of copies, or the communication to the public, of anything whose making was, by virtue of this section, not an infringement of the copyright'.[50]

It seems that this provision was designed to safeguard the interests not only of members of the public who wish to take a photograph or sketch of a building, sculpture or similar work, but also the interests of artists, film makers, broadcasters and postcard designers who might well wish to include a representation of such a work in their painting, photograph or film. However, the major commentaries on copyright note that in practice this section offers very little protection.[51] This is because the permitted act would only seem to extend to copyright in the finished work, it would seem not to protect against a claim of indirect infringement in underlying drawings or plans.[52] Thus someone who takes a photograph of a building or sculpture might still infringe copyright in the architect's or sculptor's preliminary drawings, since the section would only seem to apply to copyright in the building or sculpture itself.

An analysis of the evolution of the above section, the origins of which go back to the 1911 Act, strongly suggests that the above limitation was

---

of any excuse that they were doing it for private study.' See further G. Davies and M. Hung, *Music and Video Private Copying* (London: Sweet & Maxwell, 1993), p. 157, for a description of the lobbying that surrounded the question of whether a blank tape levy should be included in the 1988 Act and the government's vacillation on this issue.

[47] Such an exception was introduced: CDPA 1988, s. 70.
[48] *Ibid.*, s. 62.   [49] *Ibid.*, s. 62(2).   [50] *Ibid.*, s. 62(3).
[51] *Copinger*, para. 9.90; Laddie et al., 3rd edn, para. 20.76.
[52] The difficulty is created by the fact that s. 62 applies to 'buildings' and 'sculptures, models for buildings and works of artistic craftsmanship, if permanently situated in a public place or in premises open to the public'. S. 62(2) states that 'copyright *in such a work*' is not infringed by doing any of the permitted acts provided for in the remainder of the section (emphasis added). This would seem to limit the protection afforded by s. 62 to copyright in the building, sculpture, etc., itself. This interpretation can be reinforced by drawing a contrast with s. 65, which allows for the reconstruction of buildings, which applies to copyright 'in the building' and 'in any drawings or plans in accordance with which the building was ... constructed'.

never intended.[53] The current provision only received very brief attention during the passage of the 1988 Act. It therefore appears that the wording of section 62 resulted from the draftsman having paraphrased the equivalent provisions of the 1956 Act, which also failed to cover copyright in preliminary drawings and plans.[54] Whilst the provision in the 1956 Act also received fairly scant attention, the available evidence suggests that Parliament intended the provisions in the 1956 Act to have the same effect as those of the 1911 Act,[55] and the provisions of the 1911 Act were not so limited.[56] This would therefore seem to provide another clear example of where an exception has come to be limited (in this case to such an extent as to render it virtually useless) without any conscious decision to this effect having been taken.

However, as we have already tried to indicate, whilst the above and similar problems can be represented as accidental, such difficulties are also inevitable, given an approach that sees protection for users as 'exceptional' and therefore only to be made available in the most carefully defined circumstances. As Mr Justice Laddie has put it in his extrajudicial capacity:

It is as if every tiny exception to the grasp of the copyright monopoly has had to be fought hard for, prised out of the unwilling hand of the legislature and, once conceded, defined precisely and confined within high and immutable walls. This approach also assumes that Parliament can foresee, and therefore legislate for, all possible circumstances in which allowing copyright to be enforced would be unjustified. Based on this approach, we now have an Act in which there are 49 sections of numbingly detailed exceptions to copyright infringement.[57]

Providing a fairer, more workable, system for users will require a change towards a looser, more open-ended style of drafting. In the final chapter we argue that the Information Society Directive provides a solid foundation for precisely such a system of users' rights.

---

[53] Cf. Copyright Act 1911, s. 2(1): 'the following acts shall not constitute an infringement of copyright . . . (iii) the making or publishing of paintings, drawings, engravings, or photographs of a work of sculpture or artistic craftsmanship, if permanently situate in a public place or building, or the making or publishing of paintings, drawings, engravings, or photographs (which are not in the nature of architectural drawings or plans) of any architectural work of art'. The 1911 Act did not, therefore, confine the exception to copyright in the particular types of work to which the section referred expressly. Provided the reproduction was for permitted purposes there would have been no infringement of copyright in the work itself or in any underlying work.

[54] Cf. Copyright Act 1956, ss. 9(3), 9(4), and see *Copinger*, para. 9.90.

[55] See *Hansard*, HL vol. 195, col. 1048. [56] See above n. 53.

[57] H. Laddie, 'Copyright: Over-Strength, Over-Regulated, Over-Rated?' [1996] EIPR 253, 258.

Implementing directives: the method of transposition

A further factor that has had negative consequences for users is the way in which the various copyright directives have been implemented in the United Kingdom. It was seen in the last chapter that the United Kingdom, like many other countries, has been keen to preserve its existing list of permitted acts. More generally, member states have a tendency to implement European legislation in a way that creates minimal disruption to their existing arrangements. In practice this often leads them towards what has been described as the 'bolt-on' transposition of EU law, whereby existing statutes or regulations are modified through the addition or amendment of isolated provisions. Such an approach means that member states will often implement European directives in a manner that pays little regard to the underlying spirit or purpose of the legislation. It also means that the interpretation of harmonised provisions will be approached by national courts operating within very different frameworks, thereby making differences of interpretation almost inevitable.[58]

The 'bolt-on' transposition of European law and its effects can be seen in the copyright field. In relation to the permitted acts this style of transposition has tended to work as follows. As has been seen, the copyright directives have provided for lists of exceptions. In some cases these provisions have been compulsory. For example, the Computer Program Directive contains provisions relating to the making of back-up copies, to decompilation and to error correction.[59] Provisions of this kind have been transposed by member states adding new provisions to their existing lists of exceptions. Thus the United Kingdom introduced three new permitted acts to comply with its obligations under the Computer Program Directive.[60] Although problems of drafting have arisen in these cases, in particular when the wording of the directives has not been followed exactly, overall it can be said that harmonisation through the introduction of mandatory exceptions has been effective, subject to the general problem that the interpretive frameworks within which the harmonised provisions operate remain very different between member states.

'Bolt-on' transposition has caused more serious problems in cases where a directive has contained merely optional provisions relating to copyright exceptions. In such cases the directives have provided that member states may provide for certain types of exception, subject to

---

[58] See, generally, D. Dimitrakopoulos, 'The Transposition of EU Law: Post-decisional Politics and Institutional Autonomy' (2001) 7 *European Law Journal* 442, in particular at 451.
[59] Computer Program Directive, Arts. 5 and 6.
[60] See CDPA 1988, ss. 50A–C.

certain conditions. When implementing provisions of this type, the United Kingdom has concentrated on maintaining its existing list of permitted acts. It has therefore matched its existing provisions against the optional provisions in the directives and has then 'bolted on' any additional limitations or conditions that the directives seem to require. The danger with the 'bolt-on' approach in this second category of case is that an existing permitted act will become narrowed still further by the introduction of some additional limitation or condition, whereas the directive in question would have allowed for a much broader exception. For example, it was seen in Chapter 2 that the criticism and review exception has become limited still further as a result of the implementation of the Information Society Directive. In contrast, it will be seen in Chapter 10 that if the government had been prepared to adopt a more fundamental overhaul of the permitted acts, users could have been provided with a much more extensive set of rights to reuse, comment on and criticise earlier works. Consequently, in outlining our vision of reform in the final chapter, we argue that the United Kingdom must abandon the 'bolt-on' transposition of EU law in favour of a much more fundamental overhaul of the permitted acts based on the provisions of the Information Society Directive.

European legislation and the erosion of parliamentary control

It has been seen that users find it difficult to operate at the European level and that the method of transposing European obligations creates further difficulties for users. In addition, from a domestic political perspective, there is a further reason for concern about the move to European lawmaking in the area of copyright exceptions, namely, that this transfer of responsibility will inevitably diminish parliamentary oversight.

The parliamentary history of the 1988 Act suggests that users may well be able to persuade individual legislators of the need to protect their interests. For example, during the passage of the bill there were back-bench attempts to introduce a general fair use defence, as had been recommended by the Whitford Committee but subsequently rejected by government.[61] There were also attempts to introduce specific amendments relating to a range of matters, including attempts to liberalise the educational anthologies exception,[62] to extend the amount of a work that could be copied by an educational establishment outside the terms of any

---

[61] See *Hansard*, HL vol. 491, cols. 89–91, and see Chapter 9 for a detailed discussion of various attempts to get general fair use style defences introduced in Commonwealth jurisdictions.
[62] See *Hansard*, HL vol. 491, cols. 135–6.

licence[63] and to extend the rights of the public as regards Acts of Parliament and court judgments.[64] Whilst these attempts were unsuccessful, they at least forced the government to explain and justify its approach. More successful was the sustained back-bench pressure that led to the incorporation of what became section 171(3) of the 1988 Act, a provision intended to preserve the public interest defence in the form established by the Court of Appeal in *Lion Laboratories*.[65] Other examples of where back-bench pressure helped persuade the government to support the introduction of a new provision are provided by the copyright in spoken words exception[66] and the exception relating to copyright in abstracts.[67] More recently, it was due to the efforts of Rachel Squire MP that the new exceptions for the benefit of visually impaired persons were introduced,[68] and it was thanks to Chris Mole MP that the new exception to allow the 'copyright' libraries to make copies of non-print publications was introduced.[69]

The above examples should not be taken to suggest that Parliament uniformly supported the extension of the exceptions. On the contrary, the exclusion of photographs from the reporting of current events exception had not been originally contemplated by government, but received sustained support in Parliament.[70] Similarly, the government's decision to include commercial research within the research and private study exception generated at least as much opposition as support in Parliament.[71] It would also be a mistake to attribute the government's change of heart in the examples considered above solely to back-bench pressure, since these changes of position may equally have resulted from more direct lobbying. Nevertheless, there is very real cause for concern that,

[63] See *ibid.*, HL vol. 493, col. 1169.   [64] See *ibid.*, HL vol. 493, cols. 1175–6.
[65] For a detailed account of the legislative history see R. Burrell, 'Defending the Public Interest' [2000] EIPR 394, and see Chapter 3 for a detailed discussion of the public interest defence, including the decision in *Lion Laboratories v. Evans* [1985] QB 526.
[66] See CDPA 1988, s. 58 (discussed in detail in Chapter 2). As to the legislative history see *Hansard*, HL vol. 491, cols. 116–20; HL vol. 493, cols. 1060–3; HL vol. 495, cols. 648–9; HC SCE, cols. 25–33.
[67] CDPA 1988, s. 60. As to the legislative history see *Hansard*, HL vol. 491, cols. 105–11; HL vol. 495, cols. 628–30, 648–9; HC vol. 138, cols. 143–5.
[68] See CDPA 1988, ss. 31A–C, and see the Copyright (Visually Impaired Persons) Act 2002 and the speech by Melanie Johnson, above n. 30. Squire introduced the 2002 Act as a private member's bill. This forced the government to take a position on the merits of providing exceptions for the benefit of the visually impaired and led ultimately to the government deciding to support Squire's bill.
[69] See CDPA 1988, s. 44A, and see Chapter 5.
[70] See *Hansard*, HL vol. 491, cols. 111–15; HL vol. 501, cols. 236–7; HC vol. 138, cols. 141–2; HC SCE, cols. 205–17.
[71] Following implementation of the Information Society Directive, commercial research no longer falls within the scope of this exception: CDPA 1988, s. 29(1), and see Chapter 4.

given the difficulties users face in making their voices heard in Brussels,[72] the practical effect of a move to European law-making will be that user interests will be marginalised still further as a result of the diminishment of parliamentary oversight.

The role of the judiciary

The final issue we wish to explore in this chapter concerns the relationship between the courts and Parliament. In exploring this relationship we are keen to develop two themes. The first theme, which we continue in the next chapter, is that the courts have not played a purely passive role in the restrictive approach to the exceptions that has been adopted in the United Kingdom. By and large commentators who believe that the current system of exceptions is unsatisfactory have focused almost exclusively on the need for legislative reform, with the introduction of a general, US-style, fair use defence being a commonly proposed solution. In the next chapter we explore the history of the evolution of the fair use exception and its subsequent replacement by the more restrictive fair dealing exceptions. We demonstrate that it was the judiciary which was largely responsible for the shift towards a much less flexible and much less generous approach to the exceptions between 1911 and 1956. We also consider more recent examples of where the courts have moved towards a more restrictive approach, despite the fact that there is no evidence that Parliament was unhappy with the more liberal approach that courts in earlier cases had developed. We therefore conclude that the judiciary has to bear considerable responsibility for the overly restrictive approach that has been taken towards copyright exceptions in the United Kingdom. As will be seen, this does not mean that we believe that judges have set out deliberately to undermine the position of users or imply that there are no decisions that adopt liberal interpretations of the existing exceptions. We do, however, believe that, viewed historically, it is possible to detect a pattern of judges failing to protect the interests of users. Consequently, any proposal that focuses solely on the need for legislative change must be treated with caution. Thought also needs to be given to how the judiciary is likely to respond to particular legislative developments.

The second theme we wish to explore here is why judges might be attracted to a restrictive reading of the exceptions in the first place. Part of the answer probably lies in judicial acceptance of the unhelpful ideas and assumptions about copyright that we explored in Chapter 6. In earlier chapters we noted briefly examples of where courts have relied on

---

[72] See Chapter 7.

ideas of the sanctity of property and a belief in the copyright balance to justify a restrictive application or reading of the exceptions. Thus it was noted that in *Hyde Park* v. *Yelland*[73] before the Court of Appeal and at first instance in *Ashdown* v. *Telegraph Group*,[74] the proprietary nature of copyright was used to justify the refusal to recognise a public interest defence. It was also seen that in *Ashdown* the language of balance was used to close off debate about whether the statutory permitted acts are sufficient to protect freedom of expression. These recent cases provide striking illustrations of the detrimental influence that inappropriate or contestable conceptions of copyright can have for users, and they are by no means isolated examples.

In the next chapter we discuss in detail *Hawkes and Sons* v. *Paramount Film Service*,[75] the most important fair dealing case to be decided under the Copyright Act 1911. It will be seen that Lord Hanworth's decision in that case is particularly antithetical to user interests, and it is therefore significant that he took a key principle of copyright law to be that 'copyright is a right of property, and [the owner] is entitled to come to the Court for the protection of that property, even though he does not show or prove actual damage'.[76] More generally, the language of property has been used to justify a pro-owner approach in cases in which the rights of the copyright owner have been given an expansive interpretation,[77] and in criminal cases in which it has been emphasised that piracy is a serious offence and hence for which tough penalties have been imposed.[78]

It is also possible to identify cases other than *Ashdown* in which the language of balance has been used to close off debate about the proper limits of copyright protection. For example, in *Universities UK* v. *Copyright Licensing Agency*[79] the Copyright Tribunal stated, 'In declining to create a wide generalised defence for educational establishments, the legislature has struck a balance between the interests of copyright owners on the one hand, and the interests of education and scholarship on the

---

[73] [2001] Ch 143.   [74] [2001] Ch 685.   [75] [1934] 1 Ch 593.   [76] *Ibid.*, 603.
[77] See e.g., *Ernest Turner* v. *PRS* [1943] Ch 167, which gave a broad definition to performances 'in public', Lord Greene noting: 'The owner of the copyright is entitled to be paid for the use of his property unless and until the legislature otherwise determines' (at 171).
[78] E.g., *R* v. *Carter* [1993] FSR 303, 304: 'it has to be borne in mind that counterfeiting of video films is a serious offence. In effect to make and distribute pirate copies of films is to steal from the true owner of the copyright, the property for which he has to expend money in order to possess it. It is an offence really of dishonesty'; *R* v. *Dukett* [1998] 2 CrAppR(S) 59, 60: 'Infringement of copyright is widespread. It does, in an ethical sense, involve stealing other men's property, and in its cumulative effect is able to cause serious damage to legitimate commercial and proprietary interests.'
[79] [2002] EMLR 693. This case is discussed in detail in Chapter 4.

other.'[80] Similarly, in the Court of Appeal in *Newspaper Licensing* v. *Marks and Spencer*[81] it was said, 'the defence of fair dealing is directed . . . to achieving a proper balance between protection of the rights of a creative author or the wider public interest, of which free speech is a very important ingredient'.[82] Again, the concern is that the assertion that copyright represents a balance stands in place of analysis of where the boundaries of copyright protection ought to lie. The language of balance is used to gloss over the tribunal's refusal to engage with the purposes of copyright protection. It closes off the need to search for imaginative ways of protecting users.[83]

It is rather more difficult to find examples of cases in which the market failure argument has influenced judges directly in the United Kingdom. Nevertheless, it is worth drawing attention to *Football Association Premier League* v. *Panini*,[84] a recent case (discussed in detail in Chapter 2) that adopts a restrictive reading of the incidental inclusion provision. In that case Chadwick LJ, who gave the leading judgment, chose to emphasise in his summary of the facts of the case that 'Panini's participation in the tender process indicates that it took the view that an exclusive licence was of value. Nevertheless, Panini now claims to be entitled to distribute stickers and an album without having obtained a licence from [the Football Association] or the premier league clubs'.[85] Thus although Chadwick LJ did not explicitly take the availability of licences into account when determining the scope of the incidental inclusion exception, he framed his judgment in a way that suggests he regarded the availability of licences to be a highly relevant factor.

We believe that these and similar cases provide further evidence of the influence of the unhelpful ideas about copyright that we have identified. However, over and above the effect that the adoption of these ideas has had, we believe that there may be other reasons why courts have been attracted to restrictive readings of the exceptions. In particular, we are concerned that traditional accounts of the legislative process cannot account for the way in which copyright legislation has taken shape and

---

[80] *Ibid.*, 763. As was seen in Chapter 4, we are generally supportive of the outcome in this case, but it is nevertheless notable that the Tribunal used the language of balance to close off the range of options it had to consider.

[81] [2001] Ch 257.   [82] *Ibid.*, 271.

[83] It might be objected that the language of balance is actually being used in these cases out of judicial deference to legislative outcomes. However, this argument would only be convincing if courts paid careful attention to parliamentary intention, which has not been true in the copyright field. Moreover, as is explained below, this argument rests on an account of the relationship between the courts and Parliament which misdescribes how copyright legislation is formed.

[84] [2004] FSR 1, discussed in detail in Chapter 2.   [85] *Ibid.*, para. 9.

may have led courts both to misread the aims of the legislation and to place too little importance on their own function. More specifically, we are concerned that much greater thought be given to the role that lobbying plays in shaping legislation and to the conservative way in which Parliament may choose to proceed when confronted with reform of highly technical areas of the law.

Perhaps the best way to illustrate our argument is by considering the claim that if legislators are unhappy with a judicial interpretation they can always reimpose their view by enacting another statute. This argument forms an obvious response to our criticism in the next chapter that the move away from a broad 'fair use' defence after 1911 did not accord with parliamentary intention – if this were genuinely the case Parliament would have taken steps to reinstate a fair use defence. Moreover, opponents of the public interest defence have used precisely this argument in the past. As was seen in Chapter 3, Parliament made specific provision in the 1988 Act to preserve the public interest defence in a broad form.[86] It was also seen, however, that the section in question does not actually provide for a defence, rather it only states that any existing defence is preserved. If, as opponents of the defence insist, we conclude that the pre-1988 Act authorities do not unambiguously provide for a public interest defence, then it can be said that the section in question does not bring such a defence into being. On this view the fact that Parliament may have been under a misapprehension as to the state of the authorities is not a matter for the courts. Parliament can always enact new legislation if it is concerned to make a public interest defence available.[87]

One obvious flaw with the argument that if Parliament is unhappy with a particular judicial interpretation it can always reimpose its view by enacting new legislation is that this ignores the reality of the legislative timetable and the particular difficulty in generating political interest in technical points of construction outside a wider review of the legislative framework. In addition, however, this argument sheds light on other ways in which traditional accounts of the legislative process fail to account for the nature and complexity of the forces that shape copyright legislation.

There is general recognition that the final form of legislation is often shaped by interest group pressure. Modern political theory also tends to take the importance of interest groups and lobbying for granted. Many lawyers, however, choose to ignore the effect of such pressure and hence continue to treat statutes as if they represented the wishes of one

---

[86] CDPA 1988, s. 171(3).
[87] Cf. Laddie et al., 2nd edn, para. 2.152, in particular n. 1.

individual with a coherent and rational plan.[88] The problem with this starting point is that it deflects attention from the range of interests that may become embedded in a modern statute. It glosses over the fact that statutes result from a complex and sometimes messy process of bargaining and compromise.[89] In the copyright field, in the United Kingdom at least, much of the process of bargaining and compromise has concerned the exceptions. One consequence of this process is that legislators may take the view that a new defence should be established or a defence with unsound foundations should be shored up as part of an overall settlement in which rights are also extended. The next time copyright is 'up for grabs' the whole process is repeated, such that restoring a defence that has been limited or removed altogether by the courts may involve a trade-off against rights that were strengthened previously. Thus, provided one accepts that the courts ought normally to respect the outcomes of the democratic or political process, it is important that the courts arrive at the correct interpretation first time round.[90]

A second respect in which traditional accounts of the relationship between the courts and Parliament may misdescribe the way in which copyright legislation is formed relates to the concern that Parliament has long shown for not upsetting (what it takes to be) established copyright principles. A common feature of debates on the reform of copyright law since at least 1911 is that Parliament has shown a desire to reform the law within the framework set by earlier judicial decisions. Thus a striking feature of the debates during the passage of the 1988 Act is that frequent reference was made to a number of key copyright cases, including *Walter v. Lane*,[91] *University of London Press v. University Tutorial Press*,[92] *Wham-O Manufacturing v. Lincoln*,[93] *Hensher v. Restawile*,[94] *Bauman v. Fussell*,[95] *British Leyland v. Armstrong*,[96] *Beloff v. Pressdram*[97] and *Hubbard v. Vosper*.[98] Significantly, these cases were treated not merely as a description of the law as it existed at the time, but also as if they provided illustrations of 'the' principles of copyright law. That is, they were largely

---

[88] See J. Waldron, *Law and Disagreement* (Oxford: Oxford University Press, 1999), in particular ch. 6.
[89] See also J. Litman, *Digital Copyright* (New York: Prometheus, 2001), who, writing in the context of the United States, has emphasised the importance of the legislative bargaining that takes place in the copyright field.
[90] A related point is made by Litman, *ibid.*, at p. 24, who emphasises that 'current law is the baseline against which proposals are negotiated'.
[91] *Hansard*, HL vol. 495, col. 610, leaving it for the courts to decide whether reporter's copyright exists in the UK.
[92] *Ibid.*, HL vol. 490, cols. 814, 815.   [93] *Ibid.*, HL vol. 491, col. 184.
[94] *Ibid.*, HL vol. 490, col. 847.   [95] *Ibid.*, vol. 490, col. 1186.
[96] *Ibid.*, vol. 490, col. 839; vol. 491, cols. 1090–1, 1092, 1095, 1113.
[97] *Ibid.*, HL vol. 491, col. 76; vol. 493, col. 1162.   [98] *Ibid.*, HL vol. 491, col. 86.

treated by all sides as if they provided a framework within which, broadly speaking, Parliament should seek to legislate. Indeed, at times the debates in Parliament centred on the question of how best to preserve the status quo, it being universally accepted that the principles developed in a particular line of cases continued to be appropriate. It is also interesting to note that Parliament took the unusual step of making specific provision so as to ensure that the courts would feel free to continue to apply existing authorities when interpreting the 1988 Act.[99]

The observation of parliamentary deference in the United Kingdom since 1911 is closely related to Katie Sykes' broader claim about the relative importance of judicial rule-making in the copyright field. In a memorable passage Sykes argues:

> Legislatures set up the basic parameters of copyright, but the way the doctrine takes shape is determined by the courts. It has been said that some statutes are like legislative hulls that have become encrusted with judicial barnacles. Copyright statutes are formed out of barnacles; the growth of the svelte Statute of Anne to our lengthy modern copyright statutes took place largely through the codification of judge-made developments.[100]

It seems that legislative deference in the copyright field is most likely caused by the impression that copyright is a technical and esoteric area of the law best left undisturbed by non-experts. This may in turn mean that lawyers are placed in charge of, or come to dominate, the reform process. It is worth noting, for example, that Lord Gorrell, a Law Lord, chaired the committee whose report led to the Copyright Act 1911,[101] and the Marquess of Reading KC originally chaired the 1952 committee that preceded the 1956 Act.[102] More recently, the Committee to Consider the Law on Copyright and Designs that reported in 1977 was chaired by Mr Justice Whitford, and its members included Edmund Skone James, copyright barrister and editor of *Copinger and Skone James on Copyright*, and William Wallace, barrister and Assistant Comptroller of the Patent

---

[99] See CDPA 1988, s. 172(3): 'Decisions under the previous law may be referred to for the purpose of establishing whether a provision of this Part departs from the previous law, or otherwise for establishing the true construction of this Part.'
[100] K. Sykes, 'Towards a Public Justification of Copyright' (2003) 61 *University of Toronto Faculty of Law Review* 1, 26.
[101] See *Report of the Committee on the Law of Copyright*, Cd. 4967 (1909).
[102] Reading acted as chairman throughout the committee's hearing of evidence, but resigned after he was appointed Under-Secretary of State for Foreign Affairs. He was replaced by Sir Henry Gregory, a senior civil servant at the Board of Trade. See *Hansard*, HC vol. 493, col. 19 (Written Answers). Harold Wilson, President of the Board of Trade at the time the committee was established, had wanted Mr Justice Lloyd Jacob to act as chairman. However, the Lord Chancellor refused to make Lloyd Jacob available because of concerns about judicial workload in the light of the introduction of legal aid: Public Record Office Document: LCO2/3888.

Office.[103] It is also worth noting that during the passage through Parliament of the 1988 Act Lord Denning, Lord Hailsham and other members of the judiciary sitting in the House of Lords intervened frequently. Another notable participant in the debates in the Lords was Lord Lloyd of Kilgerran, a member of the patent bar and editor of the 8th edition of *Kerly on Trade Marks*.[104] Similarly, in the Commons, the most active members of the standing committee that examined the bill tended to be those who were legally qualified.[105]

Work on post-revolutionary law-making has emphasised that lawyers will almost inevitably view legal reform through the lens of the prior law, with usually conservative consequences.[106] It is therefore interesting to note that it seems to have been the conservatism of the legally qualified members of the House of Lords that prompted Lord Williams of Elvel to comment during the passage of the bill: 'I very much hope that the Committee will not divide itself into lawyers versus the rest, because I see a danger in this.'[107] This deference to the judiciary and the influence of lawyers on the reform process must not be overemphasised; indeed, an account that placed too much importance on these factors would be incompatible with our emphasis on the importance of interest group pressure on the final form of legislation. We do, however, believe that a comprehensive account of how copyright legislation has evolved needs to move beyond orthodox accounts of the legislative process and that legislative deference in the copyright field is a factor that needs to be accounted for.

It should also be emphasised that we are not necessarily arguing that more frequent reference be made to the legislative history when interpreting statutes. In focusing on the history of various provisions, we are not arguing that the historical texts to which we refer should form the basis of a reinterpretation of the statute. Recourse to legislative history when interpreting statutes has been criticised on the basis that this conflates legislative efficacy with legislative authority.[108] Our aim is thus more to

---

[103] *Who's Who*, 1977 (London: A & C Black, 1977).
[104] *Who's Who*, 1988 (London: A & C Black, 1988).
[105] Tony Blair in particular was very active during the committee stage. Other legally qualified members of the committee included Nicholas Baker, partner at Frere Cholmeley, solicitors; Menzies Campbell, advocate at the Scottish Bar; Frank Doran, solicitor; Gerard Neale, solicitor; and John Taylor, solicitor: *Who's Who*, 1988 & 1989 (London: A & C Black, 1988, 1989).
[106] F. Feldbruge, *Russian Law: The End of the Soviet System and the Role of Law* (Dordrecht: Martinus Nijhoff, 1993), p. 74.
[107] *Hansard*, HL vol. 490, col. 821.
[108] Waldron, *Law and Disagreement*, p. 121. Similarly, see R. Dworkin, *Law's Empire* (London: Fontana, 1991), ch. 9. But cf. A. Marmor, *Interpretation and Legal Theory* (Oxford: Clarendon, 1992), ch. 8.

counter inaccurate or incomplete histories of why particular decisions were made. Having said that, however, it should be noted that even those opposed to the routine use of legislative history as an aid to statutory construction accept that there are cases in which it is appropriate to look to the parliamentary history. In particular, it has been said that this might be appropriate where there is an unopposed statement of the person responsible for steering the bill through the relevant chamber, since such a statement can legitimately be seen as an action of the legislature in its collective capacity and hence in one sense as part of the text of the statute.[109] Significantly, when conceptualised in this way, we are left with a stronger reason for respecting a limited class of statement than is provided by a more general, but looser, sense of when looking at the legislative history is appropriate. We would argue, for example, that statements made in Parliament that indicate that Parliament intended to preserve a broad form of the public interest defence fall squarely within this category.[110]

Conclusion

This chapter has focused on the difficulties that users face when operating at the domestic level. Not only are they forced to operate within limits that are set at the supranational level by systems and institutions that are indifferent to their interests, they also face formidable obstacles in getting their voices heard at the national level, sometimes because of factors similar to those operating at the supranational level and sometimes for other reasons.

The final issue that we began to explore towards the end of this chapter concerns the relationship between the courts and Parliament in the copyright field. We suggested that courts and lawyers have exerted considerable influence over copyright reform in recent years. Portrayals of the courts as an essentially neutral agency and suggestions that if the courts get it wrong we should be unconcerned because mistakes can always be rectified by Parliament are therefore seriously flawed. In the next chapter we go on to demonstrate that in a number of respects the courts have shown themselves to be unsympathetic to user interests. This helps to explain what might otherwise appear like a contradiction between, on the one hand, our looking at the negotiating history to understand how the exceptions evolved and, on the other hand, our insistence that the

---

[109] See Waldron, *Law and Disagreement*, pp. 145–6; Dworkin, *Law's Empire*, pp. 342–3. On this view the rules established by the House of Lords in *Pepper* v. *Hart* [1993] AC 593 as to when it is appropriate to look at *Hansard* would seem entirely appropriate.
[110] See Chapter 3, and Burrell, 'Defending'.

wording of the legislation cannot be looked at in isolation or through the lens of the negotiating history alone, since the meaning of legislative texts is not fixed and depends upon the judiciary's response to any given set of provisions. The main focus of the next chapter, however, is on the calls that have been made for the United Kingdom and other Commonwealth jurisdictions to introduce a general fair use defence. This forms part of our general focus in the final section of the book on options for reform of the present system.

Part III

Where we go from here

9 The fair use panacea

A principal theme of the first section of this book is that one of the major difficulties with the United Kingdom's present approach towards the exceptions is that it lacks flexibility. It was seen that in large part this is because the United Kingdom has a list of very specific exceptions, encompassing carefully defined activities. With the benefit of hindsight, it is possible to point to the Copyright Act 1911 as providing the template for this approach. This is particularly significant because the 1911 Act was an imperial measure. Although most former colonies and dominions have now had their own copyright legislation for a considerable number of years,[1] for the most part this legislation has tended to follow the imperial model developed in 1911. Thus Australia,[2] Canada,[3] India,[4] New Zealand,[5] Singapore[6] and South Africa[7] delineate the limits of copyright protection by way of an exhaustive list of specifically defined exceptions. This 'Commonwealth' approach is often contrasted with that adopted in the United States. Although US law does contain a number of specific exceptions,[8] it also has a general 'fair use' defence, contained in section 107 of the Copyright Act 1976.[9] Although this section provides a list of examples of the types of use that may constitute fair use (including, for example, criticism, comment and research), this list is merely illustrative. Thus the key difference between the fair use defence and Commonwealth fair dealing exceptions is that US courts can, and do, find that a defendant's use is fair and hence non-infringing in cases where the use in question does not fall within the statutory list. It is often said that the principal advantage of the fair use defence is that it remains a

---

[1] In Israel, however, the Copyright Act 1911 (as amended) remains the governing statute. See further J. Weisman, 'Israel', in M. Nimmer and P. Geller (eds.), *International Copyright Law and Practice* (New York: Matthew Bender, loose-leaf).
[2] Copyright Act 1968, ss. 40–73, 103A–112E.
[3] Copyright Act, RSC 1985, ss. 29–30.9, 31–32.2.
[4] Copyright Act 1957, ss. 52(1)(a)–(za).   [5] Copyright Act 1994, ss. 40–92.
[6] Copyright Act 1987, ss. 35–74.   [7] Copyright Act 1978, ss. 12–19B.
[8] See e.g., United States Copyright Act 1976, 17 USC, ss. 108(a)–(i).
[9] This provision is set out in full in Appendix 4, and see also the Introduction to this work.

highly flexible instrument. In contrast, defenders of the Commonwealth approach insist that the current approach offers certainty, whereas the fair use defence is dogged by pervasive unpredictability.

From time to time the wisdom of the Commonwealth approach has been called into question. For example, the 1977 Whitford Committee Report recommended that the UK adopt a general defence of fair use.[10] Similarly, in Canada a 1981 report for the Department of Consumer and Corporate Affairs[11] and a 1984 report for the Department of Consumer and Corporate Affairs and the Department of Communications recommended that Canada adopt a fair use defence modelled along US lines.[12] Whilst these recommendations were subsequently rejected[13] and whilst subsequent back-bench attempts to get a fair use defence incorporated into UK and Canadian law were unsuccessful,[14] interest in moving towards the US system remained. The recent focus on the exceptions has seen this interest become more sustained in several Commonwealth jurisdictions. In particular, the Australian Copyright Law Review Committee recommended the introduction of a general fair use defence in 1998[15] and the recent Australia–United States Free Trade Agreement

---

[10] *Report of the Committee to Consider the Law on Copyright and Designs*, Cmnd 6732 (1977), paras. 676–7: 'Any sort of work is likely to be of public interest, and the freedom to comment and criticise, to discuss and to debate, ought not, in principle, to be restricted to particular forms ("criticism" or "review" or "reporting current events") or particular media (newspapers, magazines, periodicals, broadcasting or cinematograph films) . . . We recommend a general exception in respect of "fair dealing" which does not conflict with a normal exploitation of the work or subject matter and does not unreasonably prejudice the legitimate interests of copyright owners.' See also para. 695 (summary of recommendations).

[11] B. Torno, *Fair Dealing: The Need for Conceptual Clarity on the Road to Copyright Revision* (Ottawa: Department of Consumer and Corporate Affairs, 1981).

[12] Government of Canada, *From Gutenberg to Telidon: A White Paper on Copyright: Proposals for the Revision of the Canadian Copyright Act* (Ottawa: Department of Consumer and Corporate Affairs/Department of Communications, 1984), pp. 35–49, e.g. at p. 39: 'The new Act will . . . provide both a definition of fair dealing (to be termed "fair use") and a prioritized list of factors to be considered in determining whether a particular use of a work is a fair use. "Fair use" will be defined as a use that does not conflict with the normal exploitation of the work or subject matter and does not unreasonably prejudice the legitimate interests of the copyright owner.'

[13] In the United Kingdom see *Reform of the Law relating to Copyright, Designs and Performers' Protection: A Consultative Document*, Cmnd 8302 (1981), para. 6: 'in view of the difficulties already experienced by copyright owners in protecting their rights, the Government does not feel it would be justified in making an amendment which might result in further encroachments into the basic copyright'.

[14] See, respectively, *Hansard*, HL vol. 491, cols. 89–91; Copyright Act (Fair Use) Bill 1991; and *Hansard* (Canada), Commons 1991, vol. IV, pp. 4794–804.

[15] Copyright Law Review Committee, *Simplification of the Copyright Act 1968, Part 1: Exceptions to the Exclusive Rights of Copyright Owners* (Canberra, 1998), paras 6.07–6.08: 'The Committee is strongly of the view that an approach that seeks to deal with each specific case is undesirable. First, it cannot be comprehensive in its coverage because it is

has revived interest in this proposal. Similarly, a number of commentators have indicated that they believe that a fair use defence would have a number of advantages over the current Commonwealth approach.[16] Unsurprisingly, this interest in moving towards the US system has come almost exclusively from commentators who believe that an overreaching copyright law imposes unnecessary costs on consumers of copyright works, may stifle creativity and may impact negatively on other socially important goals and on other rights and interests: it is only natural that such commentators should look towards more generous provisions that already exist elsewhere.

Calls for the introduction of a fair use defence have met opposition from two very different quarters. Predictably, it has come from industry representatives and from commentators who are untroubled by the dangers of an overreaching copyright law and who believe that copyright needs to

---

not possible to predict new uses to which the technological developments may give rise (or how they will affect copyright owners and users). Second, each new circumstance that needs to be dealt with simply adds to the complexity of the legislation . . . The Committee's recommended model simplifies the existing plethora of fair dealing provisions and addresses the real limitations of the current provisions, which are that they are inflexibly linked to specific purposes and are difficult to apply to new technologies.' For discussion of the Committee's proposals see P. Treyde, 'Simplification of the Exceptions to the Exclusive Rights Comprising Copyright' (1998) 9 *Journal of Law and Information Science* 77.

[16] See e.g., S. Handa, 'Reverse Engineering Computer Programs Under Canadian Copyright Law' (1995) 40 *McGill Law Journal* 621, but dealing only with the narrow issue of the reverse engineering of computer programs and putting forward various alternatives; H. Laddie, 'Copyright: Over-Strength, Over-Regulated, Over-Rated?' [1996] EIPR 253, 258; D. Fewer, 'Constitutionalizing Copyright: Freedom of Expression and the Limits of Copyright in Canada' (1997) 55 *University of Toronto Faculty Law Review* 175, 233–4, arguing that the courts could use constitutional principles to read such a defence into the Canadian Copyright Act; L. Bien, 'Canadian Visual Resources and Canadian Copyright' (1997) 12 *Visual Resources* 421, 422–3, also considering more limited amendments to Canada's fair dealing provisions; A. Mason, 'Public-Interest Objectives and the Law of Copyright' (1998) 9 *Journal of Law and Information Science* 7, 14; R. Coombe, *The Cultural Life of Intellectual Properties* (Durham, N.C.: Duke University Press, 1998), pp. 331–3; G. McLay, 'Being Fair to Users: The Welcome Arrival of a New, More Liberal Approach to Fair Dealing' (1999) 2 *New Zealand Intellectual Property Journal* 135, 136; J. Griffiths, 'Preserving Judicial Freedom of Movement – Interpreting Fair Dealing in Copyright Law' [2000] IPQ 164, 175; J. de Beer, 'Canadian Copyright Law in Cyberspace: An Examination of the Copyright Act in the Context of the Internet' (2000) 63 *Saskatchewan Law Review* 503, 512–13; L. Longdin, 'Shall We Shoot a Messenger Now and Then? Copyright Infringement and the On-line Service Provider', in C. Rickett and G. Austin (eds.), *International Intellectual Property and the Common Law World* (Oxford: Hart, 2000), pp. 70–1; J. Oliver, 'Copyright, Fair Dealing, and Freedom of Expression' (2000) 19 *New Zealand Universities Law Review* 89, 103; K. Janus, 'Defending the Public Domain in Copyright Law: A Tactical Approach – Part I' (1999–2000) 14 IPJ 379, 387; J. Okpaluba, 'Digitisation, Culture and Copyright Law: Digital Sampling, A Case Study', PhD thesis, University of London, 2000, pp. 340, 348–51.

be strengthened in the light of recent technological advances.[17] For such commentators, a fair use defence would undermine the position of right holders by introducing a highly unpredictable factor at a time when many copyright owners already face considerable uncertainty. Indeed, as has been seen, many would go further and argue that many of the existing exceptions should be further restricted or repealed altogether, arguments which tend to be reinforced by the claim that the existing exceptions and defences are justified only in so far as they relate to circumstances in which market failure is likely.[18]

Perhaps more surprisingly, opposition to the introduction of a more general defence has also come from commentators who are broadly supportive of the aims of those calling for the introduction of such a defence, but who are sceptical about what a fair use defence might achieve or emphasise that such a defence might also have a number of drawbacks.[19] The problem with this debate between pro-user commentators is that it has tended to focus on a narrow range of issues. In particular, much of the debate about the relative merits of a fair use defence has focused on the familiar themes of flexibility and certainty. As has already been indicated, a fair use defence is said to offer flexibility at the expense of certainty, whilst the current approach is said to offer certainty but is very rigid.[20] As with most flexibility/certainty debates, underpinning the respective positions are different attitudes towards judicial discretion and the respective roles of the legislature and the judiciary. Whilst this debate is undoubtedly important, it fails to address two crucial issues. First, it fails to examine critically the nature of the current regime of exceptions. In contrast, we hope that sufficient evidence has been presented in the first part of this book to make it clear that the current approach does not, in fact, provide certainty for users. Thus to a large extent the strongest argument for the current approach rests on an illusory foundation. The second issue that this debate fails to address, and which provides the focus for this chapter,

---

[17] See, e.g., M. Fraser, 'Fair Is Foul and Foul Is Fair: From Analogue to Digital Fair Dealing' (1998) 9 *Journal of Law and Information Science* 93.

[18] See Chapter 6.

[19] See S. Ricketson, 'Simplifying Copyright Law: Proposals from Down Under' [1999] EIPR 537, arguing that such a defence would create uncertainty and hence would lead to more litigation; L. Bently, 'Copyright's Futures: To Expand or Contract' (1999) 1(2) *Digital Technology Law Journal* (online), echoing Ricketson's concerns; D. Vaver, *Copyright Law* (Toronto: Irwin Law, 2000), p. 190, emphasising that fair use is no 'users' panacea'; M. Doherty and I. Griffiths, 'The Harmonisation of European Union Copyright Law for the Digital Age' [2000] EIPR 17, concerned about the impact of such a defence on European harmonisation.

[20] But cf. M. De Zwart, 'Seriously Entertaining: *The Panel* and the Future of Fair Dealing' (2003) 8 *Media and Arts Law Review* 1, 12, arguing that 'The key advantage of the fair dealing test is its flexibility.'

is how judges in the United Kingdom and elsewhere would react to the introduction of a fair use exception. Worryingly, both sides seem to work on the assumption that the judiciary, if armed with a fair use defence, could be trusted to protect users; it is just that for some commentators the uncertainty that such a defence would create is too high a price to pay. To put it another way, both sides seem to assume that judges lack the appropriate tools to protect users; the disagreement is about whether the legislature should equip the judiciary with an all-purpose device or a series of carefully crafted instruments.

In contrast, it has already been seen from our discussion of the public interest defence in Chapter 3 that if judges are unable to protect users at present, this is at least in part because they have divested themselves of a tool that could have been used to keep copyright protection within more appropriate bounds. In this chapter we identify other examples of courts closing off avenues that could have been used to constrain copyright. We also argue that all too often commentators have inadvertently aided this process. Thus unless the introduction of a fair use exception were accompanied by a transformation in judicial attitudes (and to a lesser extent in the attitudes of commentators) it would be unlikely to do much to improve the current position. Less controversially, we also argue that before adopting fair use as a model for change it is important to consider how fair use operates in practice in the United States and that thought needs to be given to the possibility that future developments may lead to the sclerosis of fair use provisions, therefore depriving them of their main advantage. This chapter begins, however, by considering the history of the fair use and fair dealing exceptions in the United Kingdom. The principal aim of this section is to demonstrate that, in stark contrast to the received history of these exceptions, it is possible to narrate a history of their evolution that casts serious doubt on the ability and willingness of the judiciary to act as the custodian of user interests.

The evolution of the fair use defence and its abolition by the judiciary

The dominant history of the evolution of the copyright exceptions in the United Kingdom begins with the Statute of Anne 1710, which is usually said to be the oldest copyright statute in the world.[21] Commentators generally begin by noting that the Statute of Anne did not provide for any exceptions or defences of the type that we would expect to find in

---

[21] But cf. Sherman and Bently, in particular, pp. 119–28, who argue that copyright did not take on its modern form until the middle of the nineteenth century.

a modern copyright statute. It therefore fell to the judiciary to protect the interests of other publishers and the public interest more generally. But it is said that the judiciary rose to this challenge 'remarkably early',[22] the principle that there are circumstances in which the reproduction of part of another work without the copyright owner's consent is justified being first recognised in 1740 by the decision of Lord Hardwicke, the Lord Chancellor, in *Gyles* v. *Wilcox*.[23] In that case the plaintiff sought an injunction to prevent the defendant from publishing a book entitled *New Crown Law*, which was an abridgement and partial translation of Sir Matthew Hale's *Historia Placitorum Coronae*, the 'copy of which' was owned by the plaintiff. Having decided that a 'real and fair abridgement' would not infringe copyright, but being unable to decide the extent of the copying on the evidence before him, the Lord Chancellor referred the matter to a master, who found that the abridgement contained 35 sheets and the original 275, and this was deemed to be a fair abridgement in the circumstances. It has been argued that this case shows that the 'right to make a fair abridgement was judicially created out of fear that the benefit from otherwise infringing works, which depended upon the use of the original work, would be lost'.[24]

Cases after *Gyles* v. *Wilcox* reaffirmed the principle that fair abridgements would not infringe copyright, and extended the principle by bringing quotation and criticism within the scope of the exception.[25] Simultaneously, however, the courts began to restrict the amount of the earlier work that could be taken,[26] such that by 1900 the initially generous fair abridgement exception had largely been abandoned,[27] whilst reviews and limited quotations were protected by a 'fair use' defence. For some

---

[22] W. Patry, *The Fair Use Privilege in Copyright Law*, 2nd edn (Washington, DC: Bureau of National Affairs, 1995), p. 3. See also K. Puri, 'Fair Dealing with Copyright Material in Australia and New Zealand' (1983) 13 *Victoria University of Wellington Law Review* 277, 278: 'The concept of "fair dealing" has been applied from times immemorial. It has existed before statute. It is perhaps as old copyright protection itself.' In contrast, Bradshaw traces the evolution of fair use back to the decision of Lord Ellenborough in *Cary* v. *Kearsley*, decided in 1802, and Judge Oakes traces its evolution to Lord Mansfield's direction to the jury in *Sayre* v. *Moore* in 1785, but they too see the fair use exception as a judicially created defence to an otherwise broad right created by Parliament. See, respectively, D. Bradshaw, 'Fair Dealing as a Defence to Copyright Infringement in UK Law: An Historical Excursion from 1802 to the Clockwork Orange Case 1993' [1995] *Denning Law Journal* 67, 68–9; J. Oakes, 'Copyrights and Copyremedies: Unfair Use and Injunctions' (1990) 18 *Hofstra Law Review* 983.

[23] (1741) 2 Atk 141.   [24] Patry, *Fair Use Privilege*, p. 7.

[25] See *Wilkins* v. *Aikin* (1810) 17 Ves 422; *Whittingham* v. *Wooler* (1817) 2 Swanst 428; *Mawman* v. *Tegg* (1826) 2 Russ 385; *Bell* v. *Whitehead* (1839) 8 LJ Ch 141.

[26] See, in particular, *Cary* v. *Longman and Rees* (1801) 1 East 357.

[27] See D. Vaver, 'Abridgments and Abstracts: Copyright Implications' [1995] EIPR 225 and the cases discussed therein.

commentators this narrowing of the fair abridgement/fair use exception reflects an increasing awareness of the effect of reviews and (above all) of abridgements on the market for the original work;[28] for others this process demonstrates the increasing influence of romantic conceptions of authorship after 1800.[29] But on either interpretation the essentials of the story remain the same – the judiciary created a fair use/fair abridgement defence and then set about confining its application. Moreover, whilst commentators may differ on the question of whether the judiciary was right to restrict the fair use exception, in any event judges are seen as championing non-owner interests more effectively than Parliament. This image of the judiciary as the best champion of user interests is further reinforced by the history that is told of the 1911 Act: when Parliament did finally step in to provide for a series of exceptions it did so in a very restrictive way, replacing a general fair use defence with the much less flexible fair dealing provisions. Thus, to summarise, the dominant history of the evolution of the copyright exceptions in the United Kingdom is a tale of judicial activism in which the judiciary is presented as creating a series of exceptions almost out of thin air in order to rein in an overly broad right created by Parliament. As such this is a history that would seem to favour the introduction of a general fair use defence – the courts have shown themselves willing to protect user interests in the past and could be trusted to do so again. In addition, this history might be taken to suggest that the introduction of a general fair use defence would not be entirely alien to Commonwealth copyright jurisprudence.[30]

However, it is possible to tell a history of the evolution of the fair use exception and its subsequent replacement by the fair dealing provisions that casts serious doubt on the image of the judiciary as the defender of user interests. Although, as has been seen, *Gyles* v. *Wilcox* established that a 'real and fair abridgement' would not infringe copyright, it should be noted that the starting point for this conclusion was almost the exact opposite of that which would be taken today. The Statute of Anne provided that 'the author of any book or books . . . shall have the sole liberty of printing and reprinting such book and books'. Read literally, the result of this wording would have been that unless it could be shown that the defendant had *reprinted* the plaintiff's book there would be no infringement. Yet almost from the outset the courts did not proceed in this way. By starting with the unobjectionable proposition that making a merely colourable alteration to an earlier work would not be sufficient to

---

[28] Patry, *Fair Use Privilege*, ch. 2, in particular p. 18.
[29] L. Bently, 'Copyright and the Death of the Author in Literature and Law' (1994) 57 *Modern Law Review* 973.
[30] Torno, *Fair Dealing*; Okpaluba, 'Digitisation', pp. 340–1.

avoid the statute, the courts were able to expand copyright protection well beyond cases that could meaningfully be described as a case of reprinting. In this light the fair abridgement cases begin to look rather different. Far from representing a judicial restriction on an unlimited right granted by Parliament, these cases begin to look much more like an attempt to set a limit on a judicial extension of copyright from being a right to control reprinting to being a right to control copying of more than a *de minimis* part of a work. Claims that fair abridgement was created out of the fear that the 'benefit from *otherwise infringing* works would be lost' should therefore be treated with a considerable degree of scepticism.[31] Moreover, in this light, subsequent cases which narrowed the fair abridgement/fair use principle look much less like an attempt to step back from an overly broad judicially created exception and much more like a further extension of owners' rights, such that by the time *Harper* v. *Biggs*[32] came to be decided in 1907 a court was prepared to hold that the publication of ten pages of the plaintiff's book over the course of several issues of a periodical amounted to an infringement, despite the fact that under the relevant statute the test for infringement remained, in essence, 'has the defendant reprinted the plaintiff's book?'[33]

Turning to the abolition of the fair use defence and its replacement by the fair dealing exceptions, we find that here too it is possible to tell a very different story of the intended effect of the 1911 Act. Unfortunately, the evidence of what the fair dealing provision was intended to achieve is limited. For example, the 1909 Royal Commission report that preceded the 1911 Act did not contain detailed proposals on copyright exceptions,[34] and there is little in the government papers for the

---

[31] Patry, *Fair Use Privilege*, p. 7 (emphasis added). But cf. L. Lape, 'Transforming Fair Use: The Productive Use Factor in Fair Use Doctrine' (1995) 58 *Albany Law Review* 677, 680–8, arguing that although the fair abridgement cases had some connection with the later development of the fair use defence, their influence has been overstated; L. Weinreb, 'Fair Use' (1999) 67 *Fordham Law Review* 1291, emphasising that in the early cases the question of whether the defendant's use was fair was inseparable from the test for infringement.

[32] (1907) [1905–1910] MacCC 168.

[33] The statute in question was the Copyright Act 1842. S. 15 of that Act provided that copyright was infringed by any person who 'shall . . . print or cause to be printed, either for sale or exportation, any book in which there shall be subsisting copyright'. Interestingly, Seville charts various attempts by Talfourd, the chief advocate of copyright reform in the 1840s, to clarify the position in relation to copying of parts of a work by trying to extend copyright protection to parts of volumes, by extending the definition of infringement and by introducing special provisions relating to abridgements. But these provisions were dropped from successive versions of the bills that eventually led to the passage of the 1842 Act. See C. Seville, *Literary Copyright Reform in Early Victorian England: The Framing of the 1842 Copyright Act* (Cambridge: Cambridge University Press, 1999), in particular, Appendix II.

[34] See the *Report of the Committee on the Law of Copyright*, Cd. 4967 (1909).

The evolution of the fair use defence   257

intervening years to indicate what was intended.[35] However, the evidence that is available suggests that Parliament did not intend the introduction of the fair dealing provision to mark the start of a more restrictive or less flexible approach to the copyright exceptions. For example, it was stated by the minister responsible for steering the bill through the Lords that 'All we propose to do is to declare that for the future the principle of fair dealing which the Courts have established is to be the law of the Code ... All that is done here is to make a plain declaration of what the law is and to put all copyright works under the same wording.'[36] The suggestion that the fair dealing provision was merely intended to codify the existing law also corresponds with the general aims of the 1911 Act.[37] Moreover, the absence of any prolonged discussion about the fair dealing provision can perhaps itself be taken to indicate that no one at the time thought of this provision as marking a new departure, since other new developments, such as the extension of the term of protection, led to heated debates.

Information about what the 1911 Act was intended to achieve can also be gleaned from the self-governing dominions which, unlike the colonies, had to pass implementing legislation in order for the 1911 Act to come into operation.[38] Particularly important for present purposes are the debates in Australia surrounding the passage of the Copyright Act 1912, which implemented the 1911 Act into Australian law.[39] Although these debates do not provide a positive indication that the intention was to preserve fair use, it is important to appreciate that the 1912 Act replaced the Copyright Act 1905 (a purely domestic piece of legislation) and that Act provided for a fair use defence in unambiguous terms.[40] The fact that replacement of Australia's statutory fair use defence with the fair dealing

---

[35] But see BT209/477: proposed right of private use in the 910 bill led to hostile lobbying. A government note on a music industry proposal to limit any exception to 'making fair extracts' or 'otherwise fairly dealing ... for purposes of criticism or review', concludes that this 'merely state[s] ... the existing law'.
[36] *Hansard*, HL 1911, vol. X, col. 117.
[37] See G. Robertson, *The Law of Copyright* (Oxford: Clarendon, 1912), p. vi; Sherman and Bently, pp. 135–6.
[38] Copyright Act 1911, s. 25(1).
[39] For judicial confirmation that the 1912 Act brought the 1911 Act into force in Australia and did not amount to an independent exercise of legislative power see *The Gramophone Company v. Leo Feist Incorporated* (1928) 41 CLR 1.
[40] See Copyright Act 1905, s. 28: 'Copyright in a book shall not be infringed by a person making an abridgment or translation of the book for his private use (unless he uses it publicly or allows it to be used publicly by some other person), or by a person making fair extracts from or otherwise fairly dealing with the contents of the book *for the purpose of a new work*, or for the purposes of criticism, review, or refutation, or in the ordinary course of reporting scientific information' (emphasis added). That this was intended to create a fair use defence finds strong support in the parliamentary debates: *Commonwealth of Australia, Parliamentary Debates* 1905, vol. 27, pp. 2912–13 (per Senator Keating, the minister responsible for the passage of the bill through the Senate).

provision did not attract any comment also suggests that no one at the time thought that the 1911 Act marked a break with the past as regards fair use.[41]

Further evidence that the 1911 Act was not intended to have the restrictive effect now attributed to it can perhaps also be gained from the Act itself. Section 2(1)(i) of that Act provided that copyright would not be infringed by 'Any fair dealing with any work for the purposes of private study, research, criticism, review, or newspaper summary'. It is instructive to contrast this single provision with the much more detailed provisions of the current UK Act.[42] Unlike the current provisions, it would be possible to argue that the approved purposes were intended to be read together as mere examples of potential fair dealings. Even read as an exhaustive list of approved purposes, the 1911 provision would seem to be more flexible than its modern equivalent and could have been taken to allow, for example, a defendant to quote from a treatise on political theory when criticising certain political arrangements, from a book on moral philosophy when criticising someone's behaviour or from a treatise on juggling when reviewing a juggler's performance, activities which would seem not to fall within the scope of the current exception.[43]

The reaction of leading commentators in the period immediately after the passage of the 1911 Act also supports the suggestion that the fair dealing provision was not intended to have the effect now attributed to it. Most importantly, J. M. Easton, the author of the fifth edition of *Copinger on Copyright*, published in 1915, was happy to cite pre-1911 fair use cases as if they continued to be good law. Commenting on the effect of section 2(1)(i) he stated, 'It is not very clear why the provision authorising fair dealing with any work . . . should have been expressly inserted in the Act, for fair dealing for other purposes has always been . . . permitted and, presumably, it was not intended to cut down the rights of fair user previously enjoyed under the old law.'[44] A not dissimilar view was taken by E. J. MacGillivray in his guides to the 1911 Act.[45] Moreover, there also seems to have been the perception that the newly introduced substantial

---

[41] During the second reading of the bill in the Senate important differences between the 1911 and 1905 Acts were identified and debated, but the fair dealing provision was not discussed (see *Commonwealth of Australia, Parliamentary Debates*, vol. 64, pp. 1333–9).

[42] See Chapter 2. [43] See Chapter 2.

[44] J. Easton, *The Law of Copyright in Works of Literature, Art, Architecture, Photography, Music and The Drama by the Late Walter Arthur Copinger*, 5th edn (London: Stevens & Haynes, 1915), p. 144. Bizarrely, the only other commentator to note this passage adopts a teleological interpretation of the 1911 Act and refers to this passage as 'artful', despite having also noted that this view seemed to accord with parliamentary intention: Bradshaw, 'Fair Dealing', at 73.

[45] E. MacGillivray, *The Copyright Act, 1911* (London: Stevens & Sons, 1912), p. 28; E. MacGillivray, *Guide to the Copyright Act, 1911* (London: Publishers' Association, 1912),

part test would be flexible enough to allow the courts to take a whole range of policy factors into account and, as such, would provide another avenue through which to preserve the fair use case law.[46]

In contrast to the contemporary view of what the 1911 Act was intended to achieve, by the early 1950s the dominant view had become that the fair dealing exceptions were confined to the list of approved purposes and that the purposes themselves were to be construed relatively narrowly. Thus the Gregory Committee, which reported in 1952, was of the view that the substantial part test should be considered separately from the fair dealing provision and that the list of approved purposes in section 2(1)(i) was to be treated as exhaustive. It also came to the conclusion that the fair dealing provision was unduly, and probably unintentionally, restrictive and therefore proposed a variety of amendments which it regarded as liberalising measures. Most significantly, the committee noted that it had been advised that the criticism and review exceptions might well not cover a case where the work from which the extract was taken was not itself the subject of the criticism or review.[47] The committee therefore recommended that the fair dealing provision be amended to make it clear that fair dealing would apply equally whether the criticism or review was of the work from which the extract was taken or another work, a recommendation which was acted upon in the 1956 Act. Yet this conclusion was drawn despite the fact that the 1911 Act provided that *any* fair dealing with *any* work for the purposes of criticism or review would not infringe copyright.

The gradual development of the restrictive view adopted by the Gregory Committee can be charted across successive editions of *Copinger*. As has been seen, the fifth edition, published in 1915, took the view that, taken together, the fair dealing provision and the substantial part test meant that the position under the 1911 Act had not been substantially altered. In contrast, the sixth edition, published in 1927, stated that 'the limitation of purposes in regard to which the defence of fair dealing can be set up has probably not altered the law, but it has prevented any attempt

---

pp. 16–17. MacGillivray's precise views are not easy to determine, but his stance seems to have been that the fair use case law was preserved by the 'research', 'criticism' and 'review' exceptions, whilst the 'private study' exception drew upon principles left latent in the case law. In contrast, his view of the 'newspaper summary' exception was that this was 'a new right'.

[46] See Easton, *Law of Copyright*, p. 137: 'The exclusive right of the owner is to produce or reproduce the work "or any substantial part thereof" in any material form. Whilst, therefore, it is recognised that it is not every abstraction from the work of another which constitutes a piracy, the amount taken must not exceed the limits of what is fair.'

[47] *Report of the Copyright Committee*, Cmd 8662 (1952), para. 40.

to extend the defence to new purposes'.[48] Equally significantly, it was said that the substantial part test 'is not to be considered as co-extensive with "fair user" under the old law'.[49] By the time the eighth edition was published in 1948 it could be declared that 'the question of whether a substantial part has been taken is quite distinct from whether there has been "fair user"',[50] although the old fair use cases were still treated as being of some assistance in illustrating when a taking would be treated as substantial. This outline should not be taken to suggest that the cases decided in this period were uniformly restrictive of the exceptions or that they develop the law in a linear fashion. On the contrary, we see judges in individual cases leaving open avenues for the protection of users. However, subsequent cases and the commentaries invariably emphasised the restrictive parts of earlier judgments or chose to read ambiguous judgments in a restrictive way, leaving ways of expanding protection for users unexplored.

The first case to mark a move towards a more restrictive approach was *University of London Press* v. *University Tutorial Press*.[51] While this case is now best remembered for providing a definition of 'literary work' and a partial definition of 'originality', another question that fell to be decided was whether the republication of the plaintiff's examination papers fell within the fair dealing exception. In rejecting an application of the fair dealing provision, Peterson J failed to explore the relationship between the pre-1911 fair use cases and the new section and was apparently prepared to treat the substantial part test and the fair dealing provision wholly separately. On the other hand, he also failed to distinguish properly fair dealing for the purpose of criticism and fair dealing for the purpose of private study, perhaps indicating that he believed that the section should be interpreted as a whole. Moreover, on the facts, no question of substantiality arose, since the defendants had taken the entirety of some of the examination papers. Peterson J also emphasised the competing nature of the defendants' publication, which was entirely in accordance with the old cases. Nevertheless, this case came to be seen as restrictive of the fair dealing provision and has been used to support the proposition that the private study exception 'only covers the case of a student copying out

---

[48] F. Skone James, *Copinger on the Law of Copyright*, 6th edn (London: Sweet & Maxwell, 1927), p. 122. It is also important to note that F. E. Skone James took over as editor from J. M. Easton (Walter Copinger's son-in-law) between the fifth and sixth editions and appears to have pushed a more consistently pro-owner line than either of his predecessors.
[49] *Ibid.*, p. 120.
[50] F. Skone James, *Copinger and Skone James on the Law of Copyright*, 8th edn (London: Sweet & Maxwell, 1948), p. 136.
[51] [1916] 2 Ch 601.

a book for his own use, but not the circulation of copies among other students'.[52]

British Oxygen v. *Liquid Air*[53] saw further important restrictions being placed on the fair dealing provision, Romer J holding that fair dealing for the purposes of criticism, review and newspaper summary could not justify copying from an unpublished work.[54] He also indicated (without actually deciding) that criticism must be confined to 'criticism of a work as such', which could be taken to indicate both that the criticism must be directed at the work from which the extract is taken[55] and that the criticism should be directed towards the work itself and not to underlying thoughts or ideas.[56] Significantly, Romer J left open the question of whether there could be a defence outside the statute that would permit a defendant to publish a previously unpublished document if the intention was to vindicate and clear her character since, on the facts, this was not the intention of the defendants,[57] but this latter aspect of the case does not seem ever to have been picked up in later cases, despite the fact that it would have provided a foundation from which to develop an important form of protection for users.

Perhaps the most important case in this period, however, is *Hawkes and Sons* v. *Paramount Film Service*,[58] a decision of the Court of Appeal. This case concerned a dispute between the owner of the musical copyright in 'Colonel Bogey' and the producer of newsreels shown in cinemas. The newsreel in question was filmed at the opening of a school. It was possible to make out some twenty seconds of the plaintiff's work which was being played by a band which happened to be present at the opening. The defendants argued both that no substantial part of the plaintiff's work had been taken and that their film amounted to fair dealing for the purpose of newspaper summary. Both of these arguments were accepted at first instance, but were rejected on appeal. The leading judgment, given by Lord Hanworth, was particularly restrictive. Dealing first with the substantial part test, he stated: 'when one deals with the word "substantial", it is quite right to consider whether or not the amount of the musical march that is taken is so slender that it would be impossible to

---

[52] See Skone James, *Copinger*, 8th edn, p. 137; *Sillitoe* v. *McGraw Hill Book Co* [1983] FSR 545, 558. But cf. R. Barker, *Photocopying Practices in the United Kingdom* (London: Faber & Faber, 1970), p. 20, for a rather more careful analysis.
[53] [1925] 1 Ch 383.
[54] *Ibid.*, 393. This limitation is discussed in detail in Chapter 2.
[55] See the advice given to the Gregory Committee, above n. 47 and accompanying text.
[56] If this was the intention then this aspect of the decision has now been overturned by the decision of the Court of Appeal in *Hubbard* v. *Vosper* [1972] 2 QB 84. See Chapter 2 for further discussion.
[57] [1925] 1 Ch 383, 393–4.   [58] [1934] 1 Ch 593.

recognise it'.⁵⁹ Romer LJ dealt with the substantial part test in similar terms, concluding that a substantial part had clearly been taken since 'every one who heard the march played through would recognise [the part taken] as being the essential air of the "Colonel Bogey" march'.⁶⁰ From this point the substantial part test is increasingly seen as operating as little more than a *de minimis* threshold, leaving protection of users to the (entirely separate) fair dealing exception.⁶¹ Thus we now find decisions to the effect that the reproduction of one grid and two sequences of five letters from a compilation of between 700 and 750 sets of grids and sequences of letters amounted to the reproduction of a substantial part of the work,⁶² that a 127-bit 'look up table', that is a string of 127 ones and zeroes, amounted to a substantial part of a computer program⁶³ and that under two lines of a song's lyrics formed a substantial part of a literary work.⁶⁴

In relation to the fair dealing exception itself, the decision in *Hawkes* v. *Paramount* is also restrictive, all three judges on appeal concluding that the newsreel did not fall within the fair dealing provision. Lord Hanworth took the view that 'the collocation of the words "criticism, review, or newspaper summary" clearly points to the review or to notices of books which appear in newspapers, and not to anything of the nature that was done in the present case'.⁶⁵ Slesser LJ adopted a similar, if somewhat less extreme, interpretation, concluding that the 'proviso must be dealt with strictly, and when it says "newspaper summary" it means newspaper

---

⁵⁹ *Ibid.*, 602.   ⁶⁰ *Ibid.*, 609.
⁶¹ In *Johnstone* v. *Bernard Jones Publications* [1938] 1 Ch 599, 603, Morton J relied on *Hawkes* v. *Paramount* when reaching the conclusion that the substantial part test is wholly separate from the question of whether the taking was fair, but (in line with the modern approach) he also concluded that the amount of the original work which has been taken is relevant to the question of fairness.
⁶² *Express Newspapers* v. *Liverpool Daily Post* [1985] FSR 306, 311: 'a substantial part of the work is being published, because that is the only part of the work that on that day will be any matter of consequence to anybody' (per Whitford J). However, it should be noted that the judge in this case in any event held that the individual grids and sequences were to be treated as separate works.
⁶³ *Autodesk* v. *Dyason* [1992] RPC 575 (High Court of Australia). See also *Network Ten* v. *Channel Nine* [2004] HCA 14, para. 100: 'The test of "substantial part" under the Act . . . has been applied restrictively as little more than a *de minimis* threshold' (High Court of Australia, per Kirby J).
⁶⁴ *Ludlow Music* v. *Robbie Williams* [2001] FSR 271. The position in the United States is even clearer. See, in particular, *Newton* v. *Diamond* 349 F 3d 591 (2003), 594: 'even where the fact of copying is conceded, no legal consequences will follow from that fact unless the copying is substantial . . . The principle that trivial copying does not constitute actionable infringement has long been a part of copyright law . . . This principle reflects the legal maxim, *de minimis non curat lex* (often rendered as, "the law does not concern itself with trifles").'
⁶⁵ [1934] 1 Ch 593, 604.

summary and nothing else'.⁶⁶ Thus both on the question of how the substantial part test is to be understood and on the scope of the fair dealing exception we find a majority in *Hawkes* v. *Paramount* adopting a restrictive reading of the Act.

Yet when we take the judgments of Slesser LJ and Romer LJ in isolation, we can see that they are much less restrictive than the result in the case might lead us to suppose. Thus although Slesser LJ concluded that the fair dealing provision should be read narrowly, uniquely in this period (and significantly for the argument presented here) he also concluded that the substantial part test preserved the fair use case law. For Slesser LJ, therefore, the fair dealing provision 'added to the protection given to a defendant'.⁶⁷ From the starting point that the (generous) fair use exception was in any event preserved, it seems entirely reasonable to conclude that the fair dealing provision should be read narrowly. In contrast, Romer LJ was prepared to adopt a fairly broad interpretation of the fair dealing provision, being prepared to include a newsreel within the scope of the newspaper summary exception, but (as has been seen) adopted a narrow interpretation of the substantial part requirement. It is therefore important to reiterate that the claim that is being made here is not that judges set out to restrict the exceptions in a systematic or methodical way, but rather that judges and commentators reacted to the restrictive elements of individual judgments, often without asking what, precisely, was at issue in individual cases and without placing these statements in a broader interpretive framework. The consequence was that by the time the Gregory Committee reported in 1952 the dominant view was that positive steps needed to be taken to liberalise the fair dealing exceptions.

Summation

Whilst there is much historical work that remains to be done on the background to the 1911 Act and early judicial reaction to it, it is hoped that sufficient evidence has been presented here to cast doubt on the view that it was Parliament's intention to restrict the scope of the copyright exceptions in 1911 and that the judiciary merely reacted to this. When considered alongside the fact that it is possible to see the early fair use cases not so much as an attempt to carve out a sphere of protection for users, but rather as an attempt to place a limit on rights which had been extended well beyond the wording of the statute, we have a first reason to doubt the assumption that all that has prevented judges from adequately

⁶⁶ *Ibid.*, 608. ⁶⁷ *Ibid.*, 607.

safeguarding user interests is an absence of appropriate legislative tools. Further doubt is cast on this assumption when we turn to look at two areas where the fair dealing provisions are particularly inadequate, namely, cases of parody and situations where copyright conflicts with a right of access to information. In relation to the latter conflict, it was seen in Chapter 3 that the courts have recently restricted the public interest defence, despite Parliament having taken positive steps to ensure that the courts would remain free to develop an earlier line of authority. Similarly, as we explain in the next section, in relation to parodies the judges have divested themselves of a tool that could have been used to protect parodists and they have done so despite the fact that there is no evidence that Parliament was unhappy with the more liberal approach that courts in earlier cases had developed.

Protecting parodies

While the major commentaries on UK copyright[68] and academic accounts of parody and its treatment under intellectual property law[69] differ to some extent on the question of whether a parody will be treated in exactly the same way as other potential infringements of copyright, the dominant view is that whether a parody infringes will be determined by reference to normal copyright principles. Thus if a parody reproduces a substantial part of a copyright work it will infringe unless the defendant can bring herself within the criticism or review exception. In contrast, the US Supreme Court has been able to use the fair use exception to fashion relatively generous rights for the parodist.[70] It is therefore no surprise to find parodies discussed as one of the areas in which a general fair use defence might prove useful.[71] For many years, however, it was thought that parodies already enjoyed a special status in the United Kingdom, such that a finding of copyright infringement would be unusual.

The case which seemed to establish the principle that parodies are entitled to special treatment was *Glyn* v. *Weston Feature Film Co.*[72] That case concerned an action brought by the author of a controversial novel (justifying adultery) against the producers of a film that was intended as a burlesque of this novel. Younger J held that there was no infringement,

---

[68] *Copinger*, para. 7.34; Laddie et al., 3rd edn, para. 3.142.
[69] See M. Spence, 'Intellectual Property and the Problem of Parody' (1998) 114 *Law Quarterly Review* 594; E. Gredley and S. Maniatis, 'Parody: A Fatal Attraction? Part 1: The Nature of Parody and its Treatment in Copyright' [1997] EIPR 339.
[70] See *Campbell* v. *Acuff-Rose Music* 114 S Ct 1164 (1994) and see Chapter 2.
[71] See Vaver, *Copyright Law*, p. 190; Okpaluba, 'Digitisation', p. 340.
[72] [1916] 1 Ch 261.

both because a substantial part of the work had not been reproduced and because the plaintiff's work was of such a 'cruelly destructive tendency' that the court should refuse to enforce copyright. In addition, however, he indicated that a parody or burlesque would not infringe in cases where the defendant 'has bestowed such mental labour upon what he has taken and has subjected it to such revision and alteration as to produce an original result'.[73] Although this latter statement was only *obiter*, it was subsequently followed by McNair J in *Joy Music* v. *Sunday Pictorial Newspaper*,[74] who stated that it provided him 'with a very clear indication as to the way in which I should decide this interesting question as to whether a parody can be held to be an infringement'. Applying Younger J's test to the facts, McNair J concluded that there was no infringement of the copyright in the lyrics of the plaintiff's song 'Rock-a-Billy', since the defendant's newspaper article 'was produced by sufficient independent new work . . . to be in itself, not a reproduction of the original "Rock-a-Billy", but a new original work derived from "Rock-a-Billy"'.[75] McNair J therefore concluded that the defendant had not reproduced a substantial part of the plaintiff's work.

While the limits of the jurisdiction to provide special dispensation for parodies were not adequately delineated in the two cases considered above, they at least seemed to provide a starting point from which it would have been possible to develop a more carefully considered doctrine, accommodating either the view that parodies are entitled to very extensive protection[76] or the view that some, but not all, types of parody need the benefit of an outright exception.[77] Alternatively, the case law could have developed in such a way as to distinguish between parody and satire, privileging the former, but not the latter.[78] Our concern in this chapter is not with which of these avenues or interpretations would have been most desirable, but merely with the fact that there was a point at which it would have been possible to move in any one of these directions.

However, as has already been suggested, more recent cases have insisted that parodies are to be treated no differently from other potentially infringing works. Thus in *Schweppes* v. *Wellingtons*,[79] Falconer J was

---

[73] *Ibid.*, 268.   [74] [1960] 2 WLR 645.   [75] *Ibid.*, 651.
[76] See Gredley and Maniatis, 'Parody', pp. 343–4; E. Gredley and S. Maniatis, 'Parody: A Fatal Attraction? Part 2: Trade Mark Parodies' [1997] EIPR 412, 420; Janus, 'Defending the Public Domain', 71.
[77] See Spence, 'Intellectual Property', 615–20.
[78] See, e.g., P. Goldstein, *Copyright: Principles, Law, and Practice* (Boston: Little, Brown & Co., 1989), para. 10.2.1, who argues that a distinction should be drawn between cases where a work itself is parodied and cases of satire, where part of a work is used to provide a critique of individuals or institutions or society in general. See also Chapter 6.
[79] [1984] FSR 210.

prepared to grant summary judgment in a case where the plaintiff alleged infringement of copyright in its labels for bottles of Indian tonic water, concluding that the fact that the defendant's work was claimed to be a parody was not even arguably relevant when determining whether there was an infringement:

> The fact that the defendant in reproducing his work may have himself employed labour and produced something original, or some part of his work which is original, is beside the point if none the less the resulting defendant's work reproduces without the licence of the plaintiff a substantial part of the plaintiff's work. The test every time in my judgment is, as the statute makes perfectly plain: Has there been a reproduction in the defendant's work of a substantial part of the plaintiff's work . . . If [*Joy Music*] is to be explained on any other basis then I think it was wrongly decided.[80]

The *Schweppes* case was followed in *Williamson Music* v. *The Pearson Partnership*,[81] where an interlocutory injunction was granted to the exclusive licensees of copyright in the song 'There is Nothin' Like a Dame' from the Rodgers and Hammerstein musical *South Pacific* against the defendant advertising agency for allegedly parodying its musical work in an advert for a bus company. Judge Paul Baker QC reiterated that the only question to be decided is whether a substantial part of the work has been taken and it is clear from the rest of his judgment that he believed that the question of substantiality should be decided in the normal way.[82]

Since there has been no indication that the courts would be willing to return to the earlier approach, it now seems reasonable to conclude that a nascent exception for parodies has been killed off by two judgments which do not consider the potential rationale for affording parodies special treatment, the history or function of the substantial part test, or whether it was appropriate to decide the extent to which parodies are entitled to special treatment in cases which were arguably not examples of true parody at all[83] and which pay little attention to what was actually said in *Glyn* and

---

[80] *Ibid.*, 212–13.   [81] [1987] FSR 97.
[82] Also see the Australian case *AGL Sydney* v. *Shortland County Council* (1989) 17 IPR 99, which seems to adopt a similar approach. Although Foster J noted that Younger J's statement in *Glyn* had won considerable approval, he went on to state: 'However, as it is of the essence of parody that the work parodied must be evoked in the mind of the hearer or viewer to fulfil the purpose of the parodist, the question must necessarily remain whether an infringement of copyright has occurred as a result of a substantial taking from the parodied work. This question must necessarily arise from the application of the provisions of ss. 14 and 31 of the Act. The statute grants no exemption, in terms, in the case of works of parody or burlesque' (at 105).
[83] Cf. *AGL Sydney* v. *Shortland County Council*, where Foster J concluded that in any event the defendant's 'reply advertisement' was probably not a parody, which he defined as 'a humorous or satirical imitation of a serious piece of literature or writing' (at 105).

Joy Music. It is difficult to imagine a judicial interpretation that extended the rights of owners being treated in such a cavalier fashion.

It is also instructive to contrast the reaction of commentators to the move away from special treatment for parodies with the reaction to the judicial creation of a public interest defence. Although, as noted above, there are some differences of detail on the question of whether a parody will be treated in exactly the same way as any other infringement – some commentators argue that courts still have room to be sympathetic when applying the substantial part test,[84] whilst others take the view that the fact that a defendant's work is a parody is wholly irrelevant when assessing whether the claimant's work has been infringed[85] – no one has argued that since we have four conflicting first instance decisions the position is entirely unclear or taken the point that since the more recent judgments were not delivered after a full trial they are arguably of more limited authority than the earlier decisions. In contrast, it has been seen that the creation of a public interest defence outside the statute by the Court of Appeal in *Lion Laboratories* was met with considerable scepticism from commentators who questioned the precedential basis of the defence,[86] whether it complied with the United Kingdom's international obligations,[87] and its rationale,[88] and who argued that since there were no cases where at full trial it had been held that the defendant did not infringe because of this defence the matter could not yet be regarded as settled.[89] This is not, of course, to suggest that these accounts of the public interest defence were in any sense inappropriate. Rather, the point is that when approaching a judicial extension of protection for users, judges and commentators alike tend to adopt a mindset very different from that when approaching an extension of the protection afforded to owners. Unless this mindset changes we could rapidly see a general fair use defence becoming as inflexible as the present arrangements.

The fair use defence: current practice and future developments

The aim thus far has been to demonstrate that the judiciary has been partly responsible for the development of an overly restrictive approach to the copyright exceptions. This final section has a rather different

---

[84] See Laddie et al., 3rd edn, para. 3.142; Spence, 'Intellectual Property', 617.
[85] *Copinger*, para. 7.34.
[86] J. Phillips, 'The Berne Convention and the Public Interest' [1987] EIPR 106; Laddie et al., 2nd edn, paras. 2.150–2.153.
[87] Phillips, 'Berne Convention'. [88] Laddie, et al., 2nd edn, paras. 2.150–2.153.
[89] *Ibid*.

focus – the argument here is that before a fair use defence is adopted as a model for change it is important to understand the context in which the fair use defence operates at present in the United States. This in turn requires an appreciation not only of practical arrangements and the specific environments in which the fair use defence operates, but also consideration of certain aspects of US legal culture. Moreover, it is important to look towards the future to try to gain both an appreciation of the context in which a fair use defence will have to operate and the forces that are likely to shape the way in which general defences will evolve. What follows is not intended to be a detailed exploration of these issues, rather the aim is merely to identify some of the things that would require careful and prolonged consideration before the fair use defence could be adopted as a model for change.

In order to understand how the fair use defence operates in practice in the United States it is important to appreciate that a complex web of understandings, agreements and policy statements support the legislative provisions. These other elements of the US copyright milieu are particularly important for institutional users of copyright material, such as universities and libraries, since they provide such users with an important degree of certainty around which they can structure their own copyright policies.[90] The most important and best known of these 'external' influences on fair use is the Agreement on Guidelines for Classroom Copying in Not-for-Profit Educational Institutions with Respect to Books and Periodicals, which attempts to lay down minimum standards for educational fair use and which was included in the final House of Representatives' report on the Copyright Act 1976. Other educational guidelines exist in relation to sheet music and off-air recording of broadcasts.[91] Of course it would also be possible to copy such guidelines, but this might not have the desired result, since the agreements in question were reached after protracted negotiations between interested parties over a number of years and have since enjoyed broad support of a kind that may be difficult to reproduce. A further important consideration is that the limits of fair use have been shaped by a series of high-profile cases and out-of-court settlements.[92] Not only has this litigation impacted directly on the way in

---

[90] See K. Crews, *Copyright, Fair Use, and the Challenge for Universities: Promoting the Progress of Higher Education* (Chicago: University of Chicago Press, 1993), in particular ch. 5. See also Chapters 4 and 5 for a discussion of the difficulties that the absence of clear guidelines creates for institutional users in the United Kingdom.

[91] As to which see Crews, *ibid.*

[92] See, e.g., *Sony Corp. v. Universal City Studios* 464 US 417 (1984); *Basic Books v. Kinko's Graphics* 758 F Supp 1522 (1991); *American Geophysical Union v. Texaco* 802 F Supp 1 (1992); *Campbell v. Acuff-Rose Music*; *Princeton University Press v. Michigan Document Services* 99 F 3d 1381 (1996); *A & M Records v. Napster* 239 F 3d 1004 (2001).

which the fair use defence is understood, it has also impacted on the way the above-mentioned guidelines have been received and implemented.[93] Again, this is an aspect of the fair use defence that might prove impossible to replicate.

Turning from the practical operation of the fair use defence to more abstract questions of legal culture, Fitzgerald has argued convincingly that the fair use defence in the United States is closely bound up with constitutional guarantees of free speech, deep respect for a private sphere of home and family life kept relatively free from regulation and vigorous notions of free competition underpinned by antipathy towards monopolies.[94] Although, as Fitzgerald himself emphasises, this does not mean that it would necessarily be unproductive to use the US provision as a model for change, it is beholden on us to think carefully about how a fair use defence would be likely to operate in a legal environment in which the principles that underpin and reinforce the fair use defence in the United States do not enjoy the same prominence.[95] This, in turn, brings us back to the principal theme of this chapter – that everything depends on the likely judicial response to the introduction of a fair use defence – and should give further pause for thought about what the reaction to a general fair use defence is likely to be.

In relation to the future operation of the fair use defence, one concern, which has already been considered, is that copyright exceptions of all descriptions may become redundant in the digital environment. As has been seen, the fear is that copyright owners will only make their works available online subject to contractual terms and conditions that will prevent users from seeking to rely on an exception and will further protect their works through technological measures that will limit reproduction. However, it has also been seen that it would almost certainly be undesirable to prohibit all contractual terms that set out to exclude the operation of an exception and that it would be both undesirable and impractical to prevent owners from relying on technological measures of

---

[93] See Crews, *Copyright*, in particular ch. 3.
[94] B. Fitzgerald, 'Underlying Rationales of Fair Use: Simplifying the Copyright Act' (1998) 2 *Southern Cross University Law Review* 153.
[95] See also N. Netanel, 'Asserting Copyright's Democratic Principles in the Global Arena' (1998) 51 *Vanderbilt Law Review* 217, 274: 'a legal rule or doctrine often operates quite differently, or carries very different symbolic content, when transplanted from the source to the host jurisdiction. Even if a rule is transplanted word-for-word, it may effectively be modified in substance or simply rendered irrelevant in the host country.' For a discussion of the problems of legal transplants more generally, see O. Kahn-Freund, 'On Uses and Misuses of Comparative Law' (1974) 37 *Modern Law Review* 1; I. Dozortsev, 'Trends in the Development of Russian Civil Litigation During the Transition to a Market Economy' (1993) 19 *Review of Central and East European Law* 513.

protection altogether.[96] Thus if a fair use defence were to be introduced it would probably be necessary to distinguish between uses capable of being excluded by contract or through technological measures and uses which should remain free in all circumstances. Since each subcategory of fair use would have to be dealt with separately and since this process would have to be repeated as new practices capable of constituting fair use evolved, at least part of the key advantage of a fair use defence (that it provides flexibility for the future) would be lost.[97] Such a process can already be observed to some extent in the United States, where the Digital Millennium Copyright Act authorises the Librarian of Congress in consultation with the Register of Copyrights to exempt particular fair use practices from the ban on the circumvention of technological safeguards.[98]

Aside from technological change, the most important influence on the US fair use defence will probably be the international conventions relating to copyright and, in particular, the TRIPS Agreement because of its strong enforcement mechanism. A number of commentators have expressed doubt as to whether a general fair use defence is compatible with TRIPS at all.[99] As has been seen, in relation to the exceptions the

---

[96] See Chapter 2.
[97] See M. Leaffer, 'The Uncertain Future of Fair Use in a Global Information Marketplace' (2001) 62 *Ohio State Law Journal* 849, arguing that the United States will have to move towards a system of 'bright-line exceptions and limitations to copyright that will resemble the fair use conception in civil law countries' (at 849).
[98] 17 USC, s. 1201(a)(1). For criticism of this provision of the DMCA see, *inter alia*, D. Burk and J. Cohen, 'Fair Use Infrastructure for Rights Management Systems' (2001) 15 *Harvard Journal of Law and Technology* 41; J. Therien, 'Exorcising the Specter of a Pay-Per-Use Society: Toward Preserving Fair Use and the Public Domain in the Digital Age' (2001) 16 *Berkeley Technology Law Journal* 979. See also Leaffer, 'Uncertain Future', 858: 'This rule-making process signifies a major divergence from the traditional nature of the fair use inquiry. The authority vested in the Librarian of Congress to identify and exempt specific categories of works differs sharply from the flexible open-ended fair use process. This will inevitably lead to a number of discrete, narrowly drafted, bright-line exceptions.' The most recent rules were issued by the Librarian of Congress on 28 Oct. 2003. These are available at www.copyright.gov/1201/.
[99] Compare J. Reichman, 'Universal Minimum Standards of Intellectual Property Protection under the TRIPS Component of the WTO Agreement' (1995) 29(2) *International Lawyer* 345, 369, concluding that TRIPS 'is potentially more restrictive than the broad fair-use doctrine fashionable in the United States'; R. Dreyfuss and A. Lowenfeld, 'Two Achievements of the Uruguay Round: Putting TRIPS and Dispute Settlement Together' (1997) 37 *Vanderbilt Journal of International Law* 275, 306: 'whether the [fair use and TRIPS] provisions are consistent with one another is not at all clear. Yet, it seems to us that panels ought to tread lightly in this area'; R. Okediji, 'Toward an International Fair Use Doctrine' (2000) 39 *Columbia Journal of Transnational Law* 75, in particular at 116–30, concluding that the fair use doctrine is probably inconsistent with TRIPS; G. Dworkin, 'Exceptions to Copyright Exclusivity: Is Fair Use Consistent with Article 9(2) Berne and the New International Order?', in H. Hansen (ed.), *International Intellectual Property Law and Policy*, Vol. 4 (New York: Juris Publishing, 2000), arguing that making the fair use defence expressly subject to the three-step test would be sufficient;

key provision of the Agreement is Article 13.¹⁰⁰ That Article provides: 'Members shall confine limitations or exceptions to exclusive rights to certain special cases which do not conflict with a normal exploitation of the work and do not unreasonably prejudice the legitimate interests of the right holder.' The question of whether the fair use defence is compatible with this provision is complicated and beyond the scope of this work.¹⁰¹ However, perhaps the key issue is whether the fair use defence is confined to 'certain special cases' as required by Article 13. The question is whether a 'special case' has to be set out in advance by the legislature or whether it is enough that there are broad principles in place which can then be applied in individual cases by the judiciary.¹⁰² Significantly, the Australian Copyright Law Review Committee glossed over this issue when recommending the adoption of a fair use defence,¹⁰³ apparently taking the realpolitik view that given US dominance in international copyright matters it is highly unlikely that the Dispute Settlement Body of the WTO would ever declare the US fair use provision to be incompatible with TRIPS.¹⁰⁴ Although the committee's view was formed prior to the decision of the WTO on section 110(5) of the US Copyright Act going

---

S. Ricketson, *WIPO Study on Limitations and Exceptions of Copyright and Related Rights in the Digital Environment* (Geneva: WIPO, 2003), in particular p. 69, doubting whether the US defence is compatible with the three-step test.

¹⁰⁰ See also Chapter 7.
¹⁰¹ Okediji, 'Towards an International Fair Use Doctrine' provides a thorough treatment. Some of the more important issues are the extent to which reference ought to be made to the *travaux préparatoires* when interpreting Berne and TRIPS, the extent to which Art. 13 should be read in conjunction with Arts. 7 and 8 of the TRIPS Agreement (which emphasise the social welfare and public interest aspects of intellectual property protection), whether similar (but arguably more generous) provisions in the subsequent WIPO Copyright Treaty might influence the way in which TRIPS is interpreted and, above all, the extent to which the WTO should defer to national legislatures in the area of exceptions. See also L. Helfer, 'A European Human Rights Analogy for Adjudicating Copyright Claims Under TRIPS' [1999] EIPR 8, 14–15, arguing that in the area of exceptions and limitations the WTO should 'permit courts, legislatures and administrative bodies a wide margin of appreciation to set the balance they consider appropriate' and that 'violation of Article 13 should be reserved for exceptional cases'; T. Newby, 'What's Fair Here Is Not Fair Everywhere: Does the American Fair Use Doctrine Violate International Copyright Law?' (1999) 51 *Stanford Law Review* 1633, taking a similar position.
¹⁰² The latter interpretation was implicitly adopted by the United States government in its reply to the questions on the fair use doctrine put to it by the European Union as part of the Review of Legislation on Copyright and Related Rights conducted by the Council for Trade-Related Aspects of Intellectual Property Rights. See WT/IP/Q/USA/1, part IV (Replies to Questions Posed by The European Communities and their Member States) and also note the replies given to the Australian and New Zealand governments.
¹⁰³ See above n. 15 and accompanying text.
¹⁰⁴ For criticism of this unprincipled view see F. Macmillan, 'Adapting the Copyright Exceptions to the Digital Environment' (1999) 1(2) *Digital Technology Law Journal* (online); L. Docker, 'The Demise of Fair Dealing' (2000) 17 *Copyright Reporter* 112.

(in part) against the United States,[105] declaring the fair use defence to be incompatible with TRIPS would strike at the heart of the United States' present arrangements and likely US reaction to such a ruling is difficult to predict.[106] Moreover, the decision itself does little to clarify the position of the fair use defence, primarily because (as was noted in Chapter 7) key passages in the decision are open to more than one interpretation[107] and because the extent to which the Dispute Settlement Body will apply a doctrine of precedent is as yet unclear.[108] At most it can be said that whilst there are certain parts of the decision that seem antithetical to such a defence, other aspects could be taken to support the view that a general fair use defence is in fact compatible with the TRIPS Agreement. Most significantly, the Dispute Settlement Body stated that in order to demonstrate that an exception is confined to 'certain special cases', as required by Article 13, 'there is no need to identify explicitly each and every possible situation to which the exception could apply, provided that the scope of the exception is known and particularised. This guarantees a sufficient degree of legal certainty.'[109]

Nevertheless, even if a general fair use defence is broadly compatible with TRIPS, this does not mean that the need to comply with TRIPS will not influence the way in which the fair use defence develops in the future. In particular, courts may respond to TRIPS by attempting to

---

[105] WT/DS160/R (15 June 2000) and note the subsequent arbitration proceedings: WT/DS/160/12 (15 Jan. 2001). For detailed analysis see J. Ginsburg, 'Toward Supranational Copyright Law? The WTO Panel Decision and the "Three-Step Test" for Copyright Exceptions' (2001) 187 RIDA 2; S. Henry, 'The First International Challenge to US Copyright Law: What Does the WTO Analysis of 17 USC 110(5) Mean to the Future of International Harmonization of Copyright Laws Under the TRIPS Agreement?' (2001) 20 Pennsylvania State International Law Review 301.

[106] Cf. Ginsburg, 'Toward Supranational', 7, noting that the impact of WTO decisions will be determined in part by the willingness of member states to comply with them, a point brought home by the US decision, for the moment at least, to pay compensation to European copyright owners rather than amending s. 110(5) (see Chapter 7). Also cf. Dworkin, 'Exceptions', arguing that there is little likelihood that the United States would be prepared to abandon fair use, with Okediji, 'Toward an International Fair Use Doctrine', arguing that in the present climate the United States might well be prepared to abandon the defence.

[107] Cf. Ginsburg, 'Toward Supranational', 59: 'The Panel decision may have clarified the terms of reference, but it may not have made future outcomes any more predictable.'

[108] A similar point is made by Ginsburg, ibid., 7, and Okediji, 'Toward an International Fair Use Doctrine', 90. For general discussion of the use of precedent in the dispute settlement system see R. Bhala, 'The Precedent Setters: De Facto *Stare Decisis* in WTO Adjudication' (1999) 9 *Journal of Transnational Law and Policy* 1; J. Felgueroso, 'TRIPS and the Dispute Settlement Understanding: The First Six Years' (2002) 30 *AIPLA Quarterly Journal* 165, 223–5.

[109] WT/DS160/R, para. 6.108.

set out categories of fair use that are rather more definite,[110] so that even if such a defence never becomes truly closed, it will nevertheless become much more difficult to bring new practices within that which is permitted. Whilst this possibility remains hypothetical at present,[111] it further underlines the need for us to think carefully about how the fair use defence is likely to develop in the future and to bear in mind the possibility that there might be pressures that will inevitably lead to its ossification.

From a more narrow UK perspective, advocates of a fair use defence must consider how such a defence would relate to the ongoing process of copyright harmonisation within the European Union. Most immediately, they need to consider how their advocacy of a fair use defence relates to the Information Society Directive, which is incompatible with a general fair use defence.[112] This does not, of course, mean that talk of introducing a fair use defence has to be abandoned, since it would be equally possible to argue that the Directive should be amended or that such a defence should be introduced at an international level.[113] Alternatively, advocates of a fair use defence could adopt the argument that the Information Society Directive lacks a proper legal basis and is invalid because it 'does not harmonise national rules, does not facilitate the free movement of goods or the freedom of services, and does not remove distortions to competition'.[114] If this argument were to be accepted by the ECJ then the United Kingdom would remain free to develop its own policy in this area.

However, the ECJ has already shown itself to be keen to avoid the disruption that would be caused if it were to declare a controversial and long-fought-over Directive to be invalid.[115] Moreover, even if the

---

[110] See also P. Geller, 'Can the GATT Incorporate Berne Whole?' [1990] EIPR 423, 425, arguing that there are two separate claims that might be made against the United States under the WTO system: (1) that the fair use defence is per se in violation of TRIPS standards; and (2) that while not objectionable per se US courts have overstepped the bounds of the three-step test when applying the defence.
[111] But see I. Ayers, 'The Future of Global Copyright Protection: Has Copyright Law Gone Too Far?' (2000) 62 *University of Pittsburgh Law Review* 49, 76–85, arguing that in a series of recent cases courts have begun to apply the fair use defence 'parsimoniously'; M. Bunker, 'Eroding Fair Use: The "Transformative" Use Doctrine After *Campbell*' (2002) 7 *Communication Law and Policy* 1.
[112] See Chapter 10 for a detailed discussion of the Directive's effects.
[113] Cf. Okediji, 'Toward an International Fair Use Doctrine', arguing for the introduction of an 'international fair use standard'.
[114] B. Hugenholtz, 'Why the Copyright Directive Is Unimportant, and Possibly Invalid' [2000] EIPR 499, 502, drawing an analogy with the Tobacco Advertising Directive.
[115] See A. Scott, 'The Dutch Challenge to the Bio-Patenting Directive' [1999] EIPR 212, discussing the challenge that the Dutch government, supported by Italy and Norway (as a member of the EEA), filed to Directive 98/44/EC of the European Parliament and of

Directive were held to be invalid it seems unlikely that the Commission would move very far from its current approach (still less abandon attempts at harmonisation altogether). Attempts to amend the Directive or to introduce an international fair use defence would face still more formidable obstacles. It therefore makes more sense to focus on alternative and more readily achievable ways of safeguarding the interests of users.

Conclusion

The focus in this chapter has been on the argument put forward by a number of pro-user commentators that the United Kingdom and other countries should consider adopting a fair use defence. Whilst we share many of the concerns of these commentators, particularly as regards the rigidity of the current approach, calls to adopt a fair use defence seem to us to be misplaced for a variety of reasons. First, in so far as such calls focus attention on the need for legislative reform, they distract attention from the role the judiciary has played in restricting the availability of the exceptions. As has already been made clear, this is not to suggest that judges have systematically tried to undermine the position of users or that there are not decisions that adopt a liberal interpretation of the existing exceptions.[116] Rather the claim is that over a longer period it is possible to detect a pattern of judges failing to take adequate account of the interests of users. As such, any proposal that focuses solely on the need for legislative reform should be treated with caution, since without a change in attitudes any new defence may soon become as inflexible as the current arrangements. Second, advocates of a fair use defence have for the most part failed to consider how a US-style fair use defence might operate in a very different legal environment – in so far as the question of legal culture has been addressed at all by proponents of a fair use defence, it has been to indicate that a shared history suggests that such a defence would not be entirely alien to the United Kingdom's copyright system. Third, advocates of a fair use defence have failed to take account of the forces that are likely to shape the way in which general defences will operate in the future.

the Council on the legal protection of biotechnological inventions. This challenge was dismissed by the ECJ on 9 Oct. 2001: *Kingdom of the Netherlands* v. *European Parliament and the Council of the European Union* [2001] ECR I-7079. Scott argues that the Dutch challenge had some merit, but correctly predicted that: 'Given the political ramifications of a decision to annul this measure, and the effort expended in its legislative passage, it is likely that the Court of Justice will be at pains to avoid such an outcome' (at 215).

[116] For example, *BBC* v. *BSB* [1991] 3 All ER 833; *Time Warner* v. *Channel 4* [1994] EMLR 1; *Pro Sieben Media* v. *Carlton* [1998] FSR 43; [1999] FSR 610. These cases are discussed further in Chapter 2.

Conclusion

Building on the above analysis and on the analysis in earlier chapters, we believe that proposed reforms need to be judged against a number of criteria. It needs to be recognised that the existing approach, whereby an attempt is made to define precisely every possible situation in which an exception might apply, is unsustainable: it prevents courts from responding flexibly to technological advances or to changes in artistic practices, it is an approach which will almost inevitably lead to poor drafting and it does not, contrary to what defenders of this approach would maintain, create certainty. A move towards a much more open system is therefore imperative. However, rather than advocating the introduction of a fair use defence, we argue in the next chapter that a better approach would be to look to the Information Society Directive as providing an opportunity for fundamental reform by providing a list of flexible, but not entirely open-ended, provisions. Provided such provisions were supplemented by minimum standards around which institutional users could safely structure their copyright policies, this approach could represent the beginnings of a much better deal for users. In addition, however, pro-user commentators must strive to ensure that their vision of a limited copyright comes to be accepted by the legislature, by the judiciary and by the majority of commentators. In the final chapter we build on these insights to outline our vision for reform of the exceptions.

10 A model for reform

Having rejected the most commonly prescribed solution to the problems created by the United Kingdom's current approach to protecting users, in this final chapter we outline our vision for reform. As we have indicated at a number of points, we believe that, despite its unpromising history, the Information Society Directive provides a good starting point from which to build a fairer system of exceptions. Although there are aspects of the Information Society Directive that are less than ideal, using the Directive as our starting point has the key advantage that the political obstacles to reform are much less formidable – any other model would almost certainly require amendment or repeal of the Directive in order to be implemented. Our vision of reform has been arranged around four principles. These are: (1) reform must lead to a more *flexible* system; (2) any new approach must create a *workable* system; (3) a new system should be restyled as a system of *users' rights*; (4) in the future there needs to be far more *public participation*. We begin by explaining and justifying the adoption of these principles before turning to consider what a system of rights for users based around the Information Society Directive might look like.

A flexible system

One principle that we believe should drive reform is that the resulting system must be more flexible than the existing one, which is characterised by an exhaustive list of closely defined exceptions. We have indicated that we believe that the rigidity of the current approach makes it unsustainable in the long term. In particular, we have attempted to demonstrate that it is an approach that makes it impossible for a court to respond flexibly to technological developments or new artistic practices. It also leads inevitably to poor drafting because the draftsman is forced to spell out the circumstances in which an exception is intended to apply in an inordinate amount of detail. More generally, it can be said that users are prejudiced under the current system because whereas rights are described in open-ended and technologically neutral terms, the 'exceptions' are defined by reference to specific acts and specific technologies of reproduction and representation. As the Australian Copyright Law Review Committee has noted, this approach creates injustice because it is often impossible to predict in advance the precise circumstances in which it would be desirable to make an exception available. It has also resulted in the legislation becoming ever more complex as new exceptions are added over time.[1]

A move towards a more flexible system is therefore imperative. The Information Society Directive provides an important opportunity for fundamental reform in this respect because it provides a list of flexible, but not entirely open-ended, provisions. Not only would a system modelled along these lines provide a much better deal for users, there is a good argument that it is only this approach that can ensure compliance with the Information Society Directive. Another practical reason for moving towards a more open-ended system of exceptions is that to some extent the Directive itself makes the United Kingdom's existing approach unsustainable. It can be argued that the present approach rests on Parliament responding to identifiable problems for users by making a new, specific exception available.[2] Irrespective of questions as to whether this accurately describes how the UK system has operated in the past, or whether such a system could ever function effectively, the Directive prohibits the application of such an approach in the future. This is because the Directive contains an exhaustive list of 'exceptions' – although it also contains a saving for 'minor exceptions', this only applies to provisions that already exist under national law and only to provisions that apply exclusively in the analogue environment.[3]

A workable system

A second principle that we believe should inform any reform proposals is that the system should be workable, by which we mean that working

---

[1] See Australian Copyright Law Review Committee, *Simplification of the Copyright Act 1968, Part 1: Exceptions to the Exclusive Rights of Copyright Owners* (1998), paras. 6.07–6.08: 'The Committee is strongly of the view that an approach that seeks to deal with each specific case is undesirable. First, it cannot be comprehensive in its coverage because it is not possible to predict new uses to which the technological developments may give rise (or how they will affect copyright owners and users). Second, each new circumstance that needs to be dealt with simply adds to the complexity of the existing legislation ... The Committee's recommended model simplifies the existing plethora of fair dealing provisions and addresses the real limitations of the current provisions, which are that they are inflexibly linked to specific purposes and are difficult to apply to new technologies.'

[2] See the analysis of the Australian Copyright Law Review Committee, *ibid.*

[3] Information Society Directive, Art. 5(3)(o).

within the rules should not be unduly onerous for those who have to deal with copyright as part of their ordinary working lives. One problem with the existing provisions, particularly as they affect institutional users, is that working within the system is time-consuming and requires too much advance planning. In practice, the consequence of this is that even those who are properly informed about the restrictions that copyright imposes routinely infringe copyright. Copyright owners are apparently well aware of this fact, but for the most part seem content with a system in which they tolerate a considerable amount of infringing activity, because the cost of policing what happens in individual classrooms and libraries would be prohibitive, whilst retaining the threat to sue in exceptional cases. It is probably also hoped (with good cause) that even a largely hypothetical risk of liability will generate internal pressures within schools, universities and libraries to keep unauthorised reproduction pegged at a tolerable level. Indeed, the fear of litigation can often lead institutions to adopt an overly restrictive interpretation of the permitted acts.

Whilst copyright owners seem content with the present system, with its unspoken acceptance of a considerable level of infringement, we believe that owners need to think carefully about the broader political and social significance of a system in which it is universally accepted that copyright will be routinely infringed. Stephen Fox, a senior lawyer with the Australian Attorney General's Department, has argued that the future of the copyright system is still not secure. According to Fox the future of the system will be determined in a battle for the 'hearts and minds' of the public. He argues that whilst what he dubs 'Barlow's new paradigm' (i.e. that copyright should be abolished) may have been rejected at the international or political level, there is still a real possibility that it will come to be accepted at the social level, and if this occurs it will create an unprecedented crisis for the copyright system.[4] If this analysis is correct, copyright owners may wish to consider carefully whether a system that is routinely ignored may help to foster the belief that copyright is

---

[4] S. Fox, 'The Future of Copyright Enforcement', paper delivered at the conference Shaping the New Agenda: Emerging Issues for Copyright, Brisbane, 8 Feb. 2002 (although it might be noted that this probably overstates Barlow's position – see Chapter 1). See also J. Garon, 'Normative Copyright: A Conceptual Framework for Copyright Philosophy and Ethics' (2003) 88 *Cornell Law Review* 1278, who sees copyright threatened by the public's loss of faith in the copyright system and who argues: 'The combination of copyright's intangible nature, an accepted norm rejecting corporate greed, the perception that copyright should not constrain legitimate unauthorized users, and the overstatement of copyright's economic reward create a normative culture where theft of intellectual property is no longer regarded as an illegal, unethical, or antisocial act . . . Only after copyright holders identify the root sources of the cultural attitudes toward piracy can they begin to fashion a meaningful response. To the extent that the norms reflect flaws within the legal regime of copyright itself, Congress must address those concerns to eliminate the erosion of copyright.'

unimportant and unjustifiable and hence in the long term may undermine the entire copyright edifice. A related point is that advocates of strong intellectual property protection are often dismissive of hypothetical situations in which intellectual property rights would conflict with other important rights and interests. For example, it is often said that an owner would never sue in these cases because of the political backlash that such an action would cause. However, advocates of strong rights might do well to consider whether even theoretical liability in such cases provides outright opponents of the copyright system with an important propaganda tool.

A law of users' rights

A third principle that we believe should underpin a new approach relates to the language used to describe the system. We believe that the new provisions should be styled as users' rights, rather than as 'exceptions', 'defences' or 'permitted acts'. There are, however, a number of potential objections to this change of language. One such objection is that the language of 'exceptions' is well understood and that to move away from it would cause unnecessary confusion. Moreover, both the TRIPS Agreement and the WIPO Copyright Treaty refer to 'limitations and exceptions' and hence the question might be asked whether a move towards the language of users' rights would place the United Kingdom in breach of its international obligations. In reply we would argue that although switching to the language of users' rights may appear to be a cosmetic reform, it is in fact both politically and psychologically important. As was explained in Chapter 6, the problem with the more traditional formulations is that they help to create the belief that provisions provided for the benefit of users are somehow not a central aspect of copyright law, that they are 'exceptional'. As such these formulations help reinforce the idea that provisions provided for the benefit of users must be framed and interpreted restrictively. By restyling the provisions as users' rights we hope to make it clear that users are to be treated very differently under any new regime. As regards the international conventions, it must be remembered that a divergence in the language used to describe a particular set of provisions will not place the United Kingdom in breach of its international obligations (at present the Act refers to 'permitted acts' rather than 'limitations and exceptions'). In so far as the concern is that *a new system* of users' rights would place the United Kingdom in breach, it needs to be remembered that the international conventions preserve a considerable degree of flexibility in this area.[5] Provided that the Dispute Settlement

---

[5] See Chapter 7.

Body of the WTO acts in a circumspect manner in this area (which is itself much more likely if attitudes towards users can be changed), there is no reason to believe that the system that we outline in this chapter would not be in conformity with the TRIPS Agreement and the United Kingdom's other international obligations.

A rather different objection is that, taken as a jurisprudential category, there is insufficient coherence in the idea of 'users' to talk in terms of 'users' rights'. More specifically, it can be objected that different users' rights are justified by very different societal interests; that 'users' are taken at various points to be individual critics, reviewers and parodists, the publishers and distributors of their works, and public institutions such as schools, universities, libraries and museums – groups that have little in common with one another; and that it would be equally possible to conceptualise the rights of users as including the right to access works that have fallen into the public domain because copyright has expired, the right to use unprotected general ideas, and so on. We accept that there is a good deal of force in the criticism that there is no coherent category of 'users'. Nonetheless, we still believe that the language of users' rights remains a useful rhetorical device with which to counter the overblown claims that are made for the sanctity of intellectual property rights. It is important to emphasise in this context that our analysis of the reasons for providing broad rights of criticism, review, educational use and so forth depend on the importance of the (albeit very different) interests that such rights protect. Nothing depends upon whether we group these rights into a single category. Similarly, in this chapter we include within 'users' rights' other types of provision that are currently treated as exceptions or permitted acts, provisions that are justified, *inter alia*, by the role they play in ensuring that copyright fits different types of subject matter.[6] For us the point is that such provisions perform an important function, and not that they relate to the interests of an identifiable class of 'users'.

The importance of public participation

The final principle that we believe should inform any proposal for reform is that far more effort needs to be made to ensure that a greater range of interested parties are given an opportunity to shape the legislation. It has been seen that the idea that copyright ought to represent 'a balance' is probably best understood as a call for legislatures and governments to take proper account of the views of authors, owners and users when formulating copyright legislation. Understood in this way the logical consequence

---

[6] See the Introduction to this work.

of the call for balance is that it is important that political and legislative processes be open to as many groups as possible. We have demonstrated that in the past the legislative process has often fallen far short of this openness and has been deaf to the voices of all but established industry groupings. Consequently, the principle of political equality has not been respected. Citizens who through institutional obstacles, the indifference of legislators or who through poverty, ignorance of the legislative process or lack of organisation cannot make their voices heard are not being treated as equals.[7] In order to achieve an acceptable level of openness, positive steps need to be taken to ensure that as many interests as possible are represented. For example, we have suggested that much more needs to be done to ensure that a wide range of opinion is represented on expert panels, that proposals must be much more widely publicised, and that consultation periods must be adequate to give groups that may have little familiarity with the legislative process time to respond.

We should also like to emphasise that there is a pragmatic reason for ensuring that the legislative process is opened up to as many groups as possible, namely, that it is far easier to regulate those who consent (in broad terms) to the regulation and those to whom the concepts employed make sense. This is particularly important if, as noted above, there is the real danger that the 'copyright paradigm' will be rejected at the social level. In order to obtain consent and understanding legislators will have to take positive steps to consult more widely. They will have to recognise that there are existing interest groups that are largely excluded from the debate but which can offer unique insights into the needs and views of different parts of society. Moreover, there is good reason to hope that if government strengthens the hand of existing user groups, this will send a signal that engagement is worthwhile and hence will provide an incentive for new organisations to form.[8]

Given our emphasis on the need for greater consultation it could be argued that it is incongruous for us to recommend building an alternative system of users' rights around the Information Society Directive. Again, however, we would argue that the political impossibility of renegotiating the Directive makes it desirable to attempt to work with the Directive when designing a new system of users' rights. In the remainder of this chapter we give an outline of what a system built around the Directive might look like. It is important to emphasise that the model we propose here is only offered tentatively and that it would be necessary to consult

---

[7] For the theoretical underpinnings of this claim see T. Christiano, *The Rule of the Many* (Boulder: Westview Press, 1996), in particular at p. 4.

[8] Cf. I. Ayres and J. Braithwaite, *Responsive Regulation: Transcending the Deregulation Debate* (Oxford: Oxford University Press, 1992), p. 14.

far more widely before developing detailed rules relating to institutional users, technological measures of protection and the contractual exclusion of the exceptions. Nevertheless, we hope that at the very least the model we propose will change attitudes towards the Directive and will create discussion about how the Directive could be best made to serve user interests. We begin our analysis by comparing the provisions of the Directive with those areas where the United Kingdom's existing provisions are particularly inadequate.

Working with the Directive: criticism, review and news reporting

In Chapter 2 we identified a number of serious shortcomings in the present UK provisions relating to criticism, review, news reporting and the like. In particular, it was noted that some types of work are excluded from the operation of the relevant fair dealing provisions, that the approved purposes are relatively narrow and that the requirement of sufficient acknowledgement can operate clumsily. It was also noted that while a range of other permitted acts supplement the fair dealing provisions these provisions are limited in scope.

The provisions of the Directive which cover broadly similar ground to the provisions considered in Chapter 2 are to be found in Article 5(3), subparagraphs (c), (d), (e), (f) and (k). It is worth setting out these subsections in full:

(3) Member States may provide for exceptions or limitations to the rights [of reproduction and communication to the public[9]] in the following cases:
. . .
> (c) reproduction by the press, communication to the public or making available of published articles on current economic, political or religious topics or of broadcast works or other subject-matter of the same character, in cases where such use is not expressly reserved, and as long as the source, including the author's name, is indicated, *or* use of works or other subject-matter in connection with the reporting of current events, to the extent justified by the informatory purpose and as long as the source, including the author's name, is indicated, unless this turns out to be impossible;[10]
>
> (d) quotations for purposes such as criticism or review, provided that they relate to a work or other subject-matter which has already been lawfully made available to the public, that, unless this turns out to be impossible, the source,

---

[9] But note Art. 5(4), which provides: 'Where the Member States may provide for an exception or limitation to the right of reproduction pursuant to paragraphs 2 and 3 [of Article 5], they may provide similarly for an exception or limitation to the right of distribution . . . to the extent justified by the purpose of the authorised act of reproduction.'

[10] Emphasis added; see the section 'News reporting', below.

including the author's name, is indicated, and that their use is in accordance with fair practice, and to the extent required by the specific purpose;
(e) use for the purposes of public security or to ensure the proper performance or reporting of administrative, parliamentary or judicial proceedings;
(f) use of political speeches as well as extracts of public lectures or similar works or subject-matter to the extent justified by the informatory purpose and provided that the source, including the author's name, is indicated, except where this turns out to be impossible;
. . .
(k) use for the purpose of caricature, parody or pastiche;
. . .

To reiterate, our suggestion is that the United Kingdom follow the wording of these provisions closely. This would result in more generous protection for users than is provided by the current provisions.

Criticism, review and parody

Dealing first with uses that are currently dealt with under the criticism and review provision, it is notable that the Directive's closest analogue, Article 5(3)(d), allows use for 'purposes *such as* criticism and review'. The mere fact that the Directive leaves open the precise grounds on which this users' right can apply provides a first indication that the Directive could be used as the basis for a more flexible, but not entirely open-ended, system. More specifically, the fact that the Directive allows use for purposes analogous to criticism and review may help to meet the concern of artists that the reproduction of elements of a work in order to 'comment' on a previous work or style may not fall within the criticism or review exception. Furthermore, the Directive does not require that the criticism or review be 'of a work', which would avoid a further significant problem with the current approach.[11] The requirement that the use be in accordance with 'fair practice' ought to be interpreted as requiring the court to take into account similar factors to those used at present to determine whether a taking is fair. Hence a court would have to continue to pay attention to how much the defendant has taken, how much the defendant has added and whether the works are in competition with one another. It has been seen that provided that these factors are not applied mechanistically they are largely sensible. The one minor amendment would be in the change of terminology – 'fair practice' being a more accurate description than 'fair dealing', which may create the misleading impression that there must be some form of contractual relationship between the parties.

[11] See Chapter 2.

Adopting the Directive as a model for reform would also result in the introduction of an express parody provision, Article 5(3)(k) allowing use for 'the purpose of caricature, parody or pastiche'. Consequently, it would no longer be necessary to force parodies within the criticism and review exception. It is also worth noting that the right of parody and caricature provided under the Directive is not subject to an acknowledgement requirement and, as such, the Directive avoids one of the situations in which the requirement to identify the author can operate very clumsily.[12] The precise circumstances in which this users' right should be available would require careful judicial elaboration, but at least some guidance could be gained from countries such as France, Spain and Germany, which already provide fairly generous protection for the creators of parodies and related types of derivative work.[13]

News reporting

Turning to the provisions relating to the reporting of news, it is to be noted that the most important provision of the Directive is Article 5(3)(c). This Article actually contains two discrete users' rights. The second part of the Article provides for 'use of works or other subject-matter in connection with the reporting of current events, to the extent justified by the informatory purpose and as long as the source, including the author's name, is indicated, unless this turns out to be impossible'. This right would be close to the United Kingdom's existing fair dealing provision. Whilst the Directive does not require the taking to be in accordance with 'fair practice', the fact that use is only allowed 'to the extent justified by the informatory purpose' could be taken to indicate that a similar range of factors ought to be considered. For example, the question of whether a taking is 'justified' could be decided by reference to how much has been taken relative to the informatory purpose. It is also notable that the Directive does not require that the work be previously published for this right to apply. Whilst the fact that a work is unpublished ought to be treated as going to the question of whether the taking is 'justified', it is to be hoped that the courts would adopt a more flexible approach to the reproduction of portions of unpublished works than has been the case under recent formulations of the test of 'fairness'.

---

[12] The Directive does not even require that the parodied work be published, but this is strange, since there is little justification for allowing unpublished works to be parodied.
[13] See, generally, Sterling, pp. 521–5; and see French Intellectual Property Code 1992, Art. 122(5); German Copyright Act 1965, Art. 24(1) ('free use') and *Alcolix* (1994) 25 IIC 605; Spanish Copyright Act: 1996, Art. 39; and L. Gimeno, 'Parody of Songs: A Spanish Case and an International Perspective' [1997] EntLR 18.

A right to report current events, similar to the existing fair dealing provision, would operate alongside the other right provided for by Article 5(3)(c), the right to reproduce 'published articles on current economic, political or religious topics or of broadcast works or other subject-matter of the same character, in cases where such use is not expressly reserved, and as long as the source, including the author's name, is indicated'. The wording of this provision is closely modelled on Article 10bis of the Berne Convention. By requiring the copyright owner to take positive steps to reserve the right of reproduction, this provision aims to ensure that articles on current events are as widely distributed as possible. Such a provision is useful because by placing the onus on the copyright owner to prohibit reproduction (which could normally be done easily and cheaply by simply adding a statement to the effect that the right of reproduction has been reserved at the end of the article, programme and so on) it ensures that users know that they can reuse the work without fear of infringement, without having to incur the delay and transaction costs involved in contacting the copyright owner. The justification for such a right is similar to one of the arguments that was traditionally used to support a copyright notice requirement, namely, that it places a substantial body of material into the public domain that no one is interested in protecting.[14] But unlike a general notice requirement, such a right would only allow copying for a limited time and would not have the draconian and potentially arbitrary effect of removing copyright protection altogether.[15]

In addition to the rights granted under Article 5(3)(c), Article 5(3)(e) would preserve and extend somewhat the already generous exception that applies to the reporting of official proceedings. Similarly, the right in Article 5(3)(f) to use political speeches and extracts from public lectures and similar works would cover much of the same ground as the reporting of spoken words exception currently found in section 58 of the 1988 Act.

Overall, therefore, there are good reasons to believe that a new system of users' rights modelled on the relevant provisions of the Directive would be a substantial improvement on the current position. Nevertheless, there are certain problems with the provisions of the Directive that relate to criticism, review, news reporting and the like. It is to these problems that we now turn.

---

[14] See M. Nimmer and D. Nimmer, *Nimmer on Copyright* (New York: Matthew Bender, looseleaf), para. 7.02, referring to the House of Representatives Report accompanying the 1909 US Copyright Act.
[15] Compare, most notoriously, *Dejonge & Co* v. *Breuker* 235 US 33 (1914), wrapping paper with twelve reproductions of an image and a single copyright notice on a strip at the edge of the paper held not to be protected since the notice had to be affixed to each image.

Problems with the Directive as regards criticism, review and news reporting

One problem with Article 5(3)(d), the criticism and review provision, is that it allows '*quotations* for purposes such as criticism or review'. The requirement that the use be for the purpose of 'quotation' should cause few difficulties in relation to literary and dramatic works – it ought to be possible to bring just about all situations in which a portion of a book, play and so on is reused within the ambit of 'quotation'. Moreover, even a dictionary definition would suggest that the reuse of part of a musical work in a later work would fall within the scope of the right, since one meaning of quotation is 'a short passage or tune taken from one piece of music to another'.[16] Quotation might seem less apt, however, to describe the reutilisation of parts of other types of work. For example, this wording could cause problems where an extract from a film is shown in the course of a television programme that criticises or reviews the work. It would therefore be necessary for 'quotation' to be interpreted broadly, in effect, quotation in this context would have to be treated as synonymous with 'taking'. Some support for this interpretation can be gained from Article 10(1) of the Berne Convention, which also refers to the right 'to make quotations from a work'. This is not thought to restrict the types of work to which the provision can apply. For example, the foremost commentator on Berne treats Article 10(1) as potentially allowing for the reproduction of the whole of an artistic work.[17]

A second problem with the right of criticism and review provided for in Article 5(3)(d) is that the right only applies where the 'use is in accordance with fair practice, *and to the extent required by the specific purpose*'. The effect of such a limitation is difficult to predict; much would depend on how what is 'required' were to be assessed. Hopefully the courts would not attempt to substitute their view of what was required for that of the defendant, but rather would interpret this requirement as imposing an obligation on them to subject the defendant's view of what was required to a test of reasonableness. Interpreted in this way, this limitation would cause few difficulties, although its presence does remain a matter of concern.

A final potential problem with the right of criticism and review provided for under the Directive is that it only applies to works that have been 'lawfully made available to the public'. Whilst, as has been seen, the fact that a work is unpublished is a relevant consideration when deciding whether to allow reuse of a substantial part of a work, a blanket rule

---

[16] *Oxford English Dictionary*, online edition.   [17] Ricketson, para. 9.23.

prohibiting any taking from an unpublished work is problematic[18] and is something that needs to be addressed.

The main difficulty with the news reporting right provided for in the second part of Article 5(3)(c) is that (as with the current provision) the right is confined to the reporting of current events; it does not apply to the reporting of news more generally. Taken together with the absolute exclusion of unpublished works from the scope of the criticism and review provision, some of the problems with the United Kingdom's existing scheme would remain if the Directive were adopted as the basis for reform. These difficulties would be alleviated, however, if a public interest defence were to continue to operate alongside the rights provided for by the Directive. We therefore turn to consider how such a defence would fit in with the Directive and our other proposals.

Supplementing the Directive: the public interest defence

In Chapter 3 we argued that, for practical reasons, we should like to see the judiciary reinstate a broad public interest defence prior to any legislative amendment, but it remains important to explain how such a defence would fit into the broader scheme of users' rights envisaged here. The first question is whether such a defence is compatible with the Information Society Directive at all. As we explained in Chapter 3, although such a defence is not expressly provided for, it could be argued that it falls within the penumbra of the Directive and is broadly justifiable (especially given its role in protecting freedom of expression) by reference to the provisions of the Directive relating to public security, the proper performance of official duties and the reporting of current events. More persuasively, perhaps, we have seen that it would be possible to reinterpret the public interest defence as a rule to the effect that where the substance of a complaint is breach of confidence, a claimant cannot be in a better position by relying on copyright. Given that the Directive applies without prejudice to national provisions relating to confidentiality this would provide an alternative way of justifying the defence.[19] Alternatively, we saw that the public interest defence could be conceptualised as a provision relating to the abuse of copyright, analogous to the *abus de droit* principle under French law, which is thought to be unaffected by the Directive. Finally, it could be said that the public interest defence will often be applied in cases where the work has a low level of originality and hence, in effect, will normally apply to unharmonised subject matter.[20]

---

[18] See Chapter 2.   [19] Information Society Directive, Art. 9.
[20] See Chapter 7 for a discussion of the ways in which civil law courts can manipulate the originality standard so as to achieve public policy goals.

There are therefore a number of ways in which the retention of a public interest defence could be justified. However, in order to make it clear that the public interest defence should only be applied in relatively rare circumstances – where the owner is attempting to use copyright to protect some other interest and where public health or safety or the administration of justice or rights to freedom of information and political communication are otherwise in danger of being jeopardised – then it may be better to retain the language of the public interest *defence* to make it clear that it sits outside the core body of users' rights.

Working with the Directive: private study and research, education, libraries and archives

It has been seen that even if the Directive is less than perfect, it could still form the basis of a substantially improved system of users' rights as regards criticism and comment, artistic freedom and freedom of information. In this section we turn to consider our second principal area of concern, that is, the rights of researchers, educational establishments, libraries, archives and related institutions, such as museums and galleries.[21] These are dealt with in Articles 5(2) and 5(3) of the Directive. Again it is worth setting out the relevant sections of the Directive in full:

(2) Member States may provide for exceptions or limitations to the reproduction right[22] . . . in the following cases:

   (a) in respect of reproductions on paper or any similar medium, effected by the use of any kind of photographic technique or by some other process having similar effects, with the exception of sheet music, provided that the rightholders receive fair compensation;
   (b) in respect of reproductions on any medium made by a natural person for private use and for ends that are neither directly nor indirectly commercial, on condition that the rightholders receive fair compensation which takes account of the application or non-application of technological measures referred to in Article 6 to the work or subject-matter concerned;
   (c) in respect of specific acts of reproduction made by publicly accessible libraries, educational establishments or museums, or by archives, which are not for direct or indirect economic or commercial advantage;
   . . .

---

[21] It should be noted that although the Directive does not refer expressly to galleries, it is clear that galleries can, in appropriate cases, be treated as 'museums of art'.

[22] But again note the effect of Art. 5(4), which provides: 'Where the Member States may provide for an exception or limitation to the right of reproduction pursuant to paragraphs 2 and 3, they may provide similarly for an exception or limitation to the right of distribution as referred to in Article 4 to the extent justified by the purpose of the authorised act of reproduction.'

(3) Member States may provide for exceptions or limitations to the rights [of reproduction and communication to the public[23]] in the following cases:
  (a) use for the sole purpose of illustration for teaching or scientific research, as long as the source, including the author's name, is indicated, unless this turns out to be impossible and to the extent justified by the non-commercial purpose to be achieved;
  . . .
  (n) use by communication or making available, for the purpose of research or private study, to individual members of the public by dedicated terminals on the premises of [publicly accessible libraries, educational establishments, museums and archives] of works and other subject-matter not subject to purchase or licensing terms which are contained in their collections;
  . . .

Unlike the provisions relating to criticism, review and news reporting, the above provisions of the Directive are not sufficiently detailed to form the basis of a workable system of users' rights by themselves. The provisions in question would therefore have to be supplemented by detailed national rules set out in either primary or secondary legislation. In considering how these provisions might apply, we turn first to copying by students and researchers and then to copying by institutional users of copyright.

Copying by students and researchers

It has been seen that copying for the purposes of study and research usually occurs in two quite distinct stages.[24] One type of copying occurs at the early stage of research, when a student or researcher gathers together copies of articles, extracts from books and other materials. The second type of copying occurs when the results of research are presented, for example, in an essay, thesis, published paper or book. One of the problems with the United Kingdom's approach is that no clear distinction has been drawn between these different stages of research. Together with restrictions intended to ensure that the research and private study exception does not apply to classroom copying, this has meant that the United Kingdom has adopted an unduly restrictive approach to the presentation of the fruits of research.

In contrast, the Directive could be used as the foundation for a much more sensible set of provisions. Our recommendation is that a much clearer distinction be drawn between the collection of materials, the presentation of results, and classroom and related forms of copying. It has been noted that the early stages of research will normally involve

---

[23] But again note the effect of Art. 5(4), considered above.   [24] See Chapter 4.

photocopying or some other mechanical method of reproduction of materials. Such copying falls within the scope of Articles 5(2)(a) and 5(2)(b) of the Directive. These provisions are too general to be transposed directly into UK law, but it would be possible to use them as the basis for maintaining a private study and research exception *designed to allow users to collect material*. (We deal with the presentation of results and classroom copying later.) We have in mind a provision along the following lines:

(1) Copyright in a literary, dramatic or artistic work or in the typographical arrangement of a published edition is not infringed by photographic reproduction for the purposes of research or private study, provided that the copying is in accordance with fair practice.
(2) (a) Copyright in a work is not infringed by reproduction on any medium for the purposes of non-commercial research or private study, provided that the copying is in accordance with fair practice.
   (b) This subsection shall not be taken to allow for the photographic reproduction of sheet music.
(3) (a) Copying by a person other than the researcher or student himself is not in accordance with fair practice if the person doing the copying knows or has reason to believe that it will result in copies of substantially the same material being provided to more than one person at substantially the same time and for substantially the same purpose.
   (b) This subsection shall not prevent a librarian or archivist from making more than one copy of the same material provided such copies are supplied to different students or researchers and provided such copies are individually requested.
(4) In determining whether the reproduction is in accordance with fair practice for the purposes of this section regard shall be had to all of the circumstances of the case, including:
   (a) the nature of the work;
   (b) the quality of the copy;
   (c) the defendant's motives;
   (d) the possibility of obtaining a copy of the work within a reasonable period of time and at an ordinary commercial price.
(5) Notwithstanding subsection (4) the reproduction shall be deemed fair practice –
   (a) if it is of a single article in a periodical, including any illustrations accompanying the text; or
   (b) if it amounts to no more than a single chapter or 10 per cent, whichever is greater, of a published edition; or

(c) in any other case if it amounts to no more than 10 per cent of the work.

(6) (a) A reproduction shall not be deemed fair practice by virtue of subsection (5) if it consists of copying a portion of a work or an article in an issue of a periodical within six months from the previous occasion that an extract from the work or an article in the same issue of a periodical was copied by virtue of that subsection, but

(b) where the copying is done by a person other than the student or researcher, liability shall not be imposed on that person by virtue of this subsection unless the person doing the copying knew or had reason to believe that the copying would result in the student or researcher being supplied with more than a single extract from a work or a single article from an issue of a periodical within the relevant period.

(7) For the purposes of this section 'photographic reproduction' means reproduction effected by the use of any kind of photographic technique or by some other process having similar effects.

Our preferred model is, admittedly, no less complex than the existing research and private study provision. Nevertheless, it would have a number of advantages over the present approach. In particular, it is worth emphasising that it would apply to all types of copyright work except sheet music. (The blanket exclusion of sheet music is a cause for some concern but is required by the Directive and can perhaps be justified by virtue of the precarious position of sheet music publishers.[25]) Our model would also have the advantage of providing users with a degree of certainty about the amount of material they could copy (with approved quantities being set out in subsection (5)), whilst retaining a more general right to copy outside the approved statutory quantities in appropriate cases (set out in subsection (4)). Moreover, by separating photographic reproduction from other forms of reproduction it is possible to keep some commercial research within the scope of the right. This is because Article 5(2)(a) of the Directive, which applies to photographic reproduction, unlike Article 5(2)(b) which applies to other forms of reproduction, does not require that the use be for a non-commercial purpose. In this way our model avoids the concern that librarians will be faced with the impossible task of attempting to police whether readers intend to use a photocopied extract for commercial purposes. This would also mean that small enterprises would not be prevented from acquiring low-cost photocopies of journal articles relevant to their business as is the case under the

---

[25] See J. Gurnsey, *Copyright Theft* (Aldershot: Aslib Gower, 1995), pp. 19–20.

newly amended UK regime, and it would prevent the copyright system from being brought into further disrepute as it would remove the incentive for businessmen and others involved in commercial research to lie to librarians and on forms used to obtain self-service photocopying cards.

On a rather different note, it should be emphasised that our proposed model would continue to exclude classroom copying from the scope of the research and private study exception (by virtue of subsection (3)). This is because we would prefer to see such copying dealt with through a separate set of provisions. We consider these provisions in the next section alongside our proposals to deal with other forms of copying by institutional users.

The other aspect of our approach that requires further elaboration relates to the requirement in Articles 5(2)(a) and 5(2)(b) that rightholders receive 'fair compensation' for use of their works. The Directive leaves member states a good deal of freedom when defining how fair compensation is to be calculated and the mechanism through which remittance is to be made.[26] Our preferred solution for dealing with this requirement is through a series of levies to be administered by appropriate collecting societies. For example, we would advocate the introduction of a small levy to be imposed on the cost of photocopies made by or on behalf of library users. Although such levies do impose costs on users, if tied to the type of regime envisaged here they would still leave users with much greater freedom than is the case in the United Kingdom at present.

In addition to the research and private study exception considered above, we would also like to see the introduction of a right privileging the inclusion of extracts from earlier works in research papers and related forms of publication. Such use is normally thought to fall within fair dealing for the purpose of criticism or review. However, a new right would remove uncertainty in cases where the extract is being used to provide supporting evidence without any obvious comment on or analysis of the work from which the extract was taken or some other work. It is at least arguable that such use does not fall within the scope of the current provision, and doubt might remain even if a new provision modelled on the Directive were to allow for use 'for purposes such as criticism or review'. Consequently, we propose the introduction of a new right that would allow a researcher to reuse a portion of an earlier work in the course of presenting her own argument or results that would not be dependent on

---

[26] Information Society Directive, recitals 35 and 37. Recital 35 even recognises that it may be appropriate to set the rate of compensation at zero 'where the prejudice to the rightholder would be minimal'. This provision is particularly important in so far as an extended research and private study exception would justify copying by hand, which would not attract levy payments.

proof that the inclusion was for the purposes of criticism or review or a closely related purpose – language that might not adequately capture all of the justifications for reusing material in a scientific paper, in a way that is probably much less true for the humanities.

The basis of an extended right of use for the purposes of research is to be found in the second part of Article 5(3)(a) of the Directive, which allows use for the purpose of non-commercial scientific research. This Article, if transposed into UK law, would create a new right allowing the republication of a portion of a work for the purposes of scientific research that would sit alongside rights of criticism, review and news reporting. The limitation in Article 5(3)(a) that reuse only be allowed 'to the extent justified by the non-commercial purpose to be achieved' would allow a court to take into account the sorts of factors that are currently used when assessing whether the taking was fair for the purposes of the criticism and review and news reporting exceptions. The Directive also makes the right of reuse for scientific purposes dependent on there being an indication of source, including of the author's name, except in cases where this is impossible. Again, such a limitation is entirely sensible and corresponds with normal scientific practice. (In contrast, it was seen in Chapter 4 that the requirement of sufficient acknowledgement that applies to the current research exception operates clumsily, since the current exception is largely confined to the first stage of research and at this stage the only person to see the copied extracts is likely to be the researcher herself.)

The main potential restriction on a right of use for scientific research based on Article 5(3)(a) of the Directive is that Article's requirement that the use be for a non-commercial purpose. It is to be hoped, however, that this limitation would be interpreted in such a way that the mere fact that a scientific paper was published in a commercial publication or has some commercial application would not be treated as taking the use outside the scope of the right. Attention should be focused instead on the intention of the person conducting the research. Provided that the researcher was primarily motivated by non-commercial ends the provision should still apply.[27] It is also to be hoped that 'scientific' research would be given a broad interpretation and would be treated as including research in technical fields such as engineering.

---

[27] Some support for a narrow interpretation of the requirement that the research be for a non-commercial purpose can perhaps be gained from recital 42 of the Directive, which provides: 'When applying the exception or limitation for non-commercial educational and scientific research purposes . . . the non-commercial nature of the activity in question should be determined by that activity as such. The organisational structure and the means of funding of the establishment concerned are not the decisive factors in this respect.'

Institutional users of copyright

When considering how the provisions of the Directive apply to institutional users of copyright, such as schools, universities and libraries, it is once again important to draw distinctions between different types of use. In this respect the existing legislation is a useful model for reform in so far as it draws attention to different types of potentially infringing activity. One type of use provided for under the existing legislation is copying in the course of instruction. Here the Directive provides for a direct solution. If, as advocated in the previous section, Article 5(3)(a) were transposed directly into UK law, a right to reproduce an extract for teaching purposes would be preserved. Unlike the existing provision, however, the right to make a copy for the purpose of illustration for teaching under the Directive would allow the use of mechanical methods of reproducing extracts intended to illustrate a particular proposition or technique. Consequently, it would allow extracts from a work to be copied onto a handout or onto a PowerPoint slide. However, there would continue to be a significant potential difficulty within any right of illustration for the purposes of teaching based on the Directive, namely, that it only applies where the use is for 'non-commercial' purposes. It was seen in Chapter 4 that this requirement has already led the United Kingdom to amend the section 32 teaching exception to exclude commercial use. The concern is that, unless interpreted narrowly, this could exclude universities and independent schools from relying on this provision, and the same concern would arise with any provision that is modelled more closely on the Directive. It is therefore worth restating our view that a narrow interpretation of 'commercial use' is appropriate in this context, and that the British Library and the Copyright Licensing Agency seem agreed on such an interpretation.[28]

A second type of use privileged by the existing provisions is copying for the purposes of examination.[29] It was seen that the purpose of this provision is to allow examiners to include extracts from works in examination papers. It was also seen that in its original form the relevant provision was relatively generous and caused few problems in practice. Implementation of the Information Society Directive has, however, led to this provision being made dependent on there being a sufficient acknowledgement of the work from which the extract was taken. Unfortunately, there are circumstances in which an acknowledgement requirement is inappropriate,

---

[28] See Chapter 4.
[29] See CDPA 1988, s. 32. This provision is discussed in detail in Chapter 4.

in particular, when one of the examiner's aims is to see whether candidates are able to identify the source of a quotation. It is therefore important to emphasise that it would be possible to remove the acknowledgement requirement and remain within the terms of the Directive. At present the United Kingdom justifies its retention of an examination provision by reference to Article 5(3)(a) of the Directive, which requires an indication of source.[30] Yet it is equally possible to justify an examination provision by reference to Article 5(2)(c) of the Directive, which allows for use as regards 'specific acts of reproduction made by publicly accessible ... educational establishments'. Unlike Article 5(3)(a), this Article does not require an indication of source. Once again, however, it is necessary to enter a caveat about the need for 'commercial use' to be interpreted narrowly, since Article 5(2)(c) is also restricted to non-commercial copying.

Other educational and library copying provisions relate to rights that are unaffected by the Information Society Directive. It is important to emphasise that the Directive harmonises only three of the exclusive rights of copyright owners, namely, the rights of reproduction, communication to the public and distribution. The provisions of the Directive relating to 'exceptions and limitations' are accordingly limited to these rights and hence 'exceptions' to other exclusive rights of the copyright owner are unaffected. The education and library copying provisions relating to performing rights[31] and rental and lending rights[32] are therefore unaffected by the Directive. Again, it would make sense to use the existing provisions as a template for reform, but account should be taken of the criticisms of these provisions discussed in Chapters 4 and 5. For example, it would be desirable if the scope of the educational performances provision were to be extended.

Thus far it has been seen that in relation to illustration for teaching, copying for inclusion in examinations, performances in educational establishments and exceptions to the lending right, the Directive either offers a preferable alternative to the current provisions or leaves member states with a free hand.

Much more controversial, however, are questions of what rights institutional users of copyright should have to make and supply copies of works to students, readers and so on and how such rights should apply in the digital environment. As we have already indicated, we believe that

---

[30] See 'Implementation of the Copyright Directive (2001/29/EC) and related matters Transposition Note', available at www.patent.gov.uk/copy/notices/2003/copy_direct3a.htm.
[31] CDPA 1988, s. 34.   [32] Ibid., ss. 36A, 40A.

many of the detailed rules of a new system should emerge from a dialogue between interested parties, but that all concerned must be prepared to move beyond merely tinkering with the existing system. It is also imperative that government be prepared to steer the debate and do its best to ensure that negotiations do not break down. Moreover, although we believe that it would be inappropriate for us to attempt to spell out what, precisely, a new system of rights for institutional users should look like, drawing on our analysis in Chapters 4 and 5 and on our analysis in the previous section of this chapter, there are a number of points that we should like to see being taken into account when a new scheme is being designed. These include the following.

1. A much more generous approach needs to be taken to the amount of material that can be copied by students and researchers who are involved in the early stages of research. At present there is a lack of clarity about the amount of material that can be copied outside the terms of any licence. In contrast, in the previous section we set out a research and private study exception that would give clear guidance as to the amounts that could safely be copied. It is also our view that librarians and archivists and those who work in museums and galleries ought to be able to rely directly on this provision. This would remove the complexity surrounding the current provisions relating to the supply of copies to users. Licences between institutional users and owners would then be negotiated from a much clearer understanding of what rights institutional users would enjoy in the absence of any agreement – something that would strengthen their bargaining power considerably. Such licences could be expected to cover those situations where permitting copying beyond the approved statutory quantities would seem justifiable, including, for example, where a special issue of a periodical is devoted to a single topic such that every article in that issue is relevant to the student or researcher's work.

2. Some of the more specific provisions authorising copying by institutional users, such as the provision allowing for the making of copies of works for preservation purposes, are much too narrow. Others are poorly designed; for example, it was seen that the provision allowing for the copying of unpublished papers by librarians fails to protect either the interests of the public or the interests of the depositor.

3. More needs to be done to ensure that institutional users can pass on to the public the benefits offered by new technologies. At the very least Article 5(3)(n) of the Directive ought to be transposed into UK law so as to allow institutional users to make available to the public digitised versions of works contained in their collections. Moreover, as we argued in Chapter 5, this article ought to be interpreted in such a way

as to allow intranet services to be developed across libraries, educational establishments, museums and archives.[33]

4. In relation to 'classroom copying', that is, the distribution of copies of articles and extracts from other works to groups of students, real difficulties arise in cases where the relevant collecting society does not have the authority to grant a licence for the copying of the work in question. Serious thought should therefore be given to the compulsory collective administration of educational copying rights.

5. In so far as our proposals may seem radical, it needs to be remembered that students, researchers and educators routinely ignore the restrictions imposed by copyright law. Our intuition is that if copyright were to be liberalised, the amount of infringing activity within libraries, schools and universities would decrease not merely because some currently infringing acts would be taken outside the scope of the copyright owner's monopoly, but also because voluntary compliance with copyright would increase. In other words, we believe that if the cost of compliance with copyright were to decrease this might lend copyright a greater legitimacy that would lead to respect for copyright being internalised. Such internalisation is unlikely so long as copyright is seen as overly restrictive and compliance is sought through coercion alone.[34]

Summation

It can now be seen that the Directive could be used as the foundation for a genuine system of users' rights. Admittedly, the Directive is also open to other, less pro-user, readings than that proposed here, but provided that the importance of protecting users is accepted, there is no reason why our reading should not be preferred. More specifically, we have argued that as regards rights of criticism, review, news reporting and the like, the Directive contains a number of provisions that could be transposed directly into UK law, with positive results for users. In the case of rights of research, private study and the rights of institutional users of copyright, the Directive contains some provisions that are suitable for direct transposition into UK law, but it would be

---

[33] To reiterate, the Directive does not state expressly that the 'dedicated terminals' must only provide access to the works of the establishment in which the terminal is located.

[34] There is now a good deal of evidence that coercive strategies alone are an ineffective mechanism for securing long-term compliance with legal standards. See C. Parker and J. Braithwaite, 'Regulation', in P. Cane and M. Tushnet (eds.), *The Oxford Handbook of Legal Studies* (Oxford: Oxford University Press, 2003), pp. 133–4, and the sources referred to therein.

necessary to supplement these provisions with other rules and guidelines based around the more open-ended provisions of the Directive. We have provided an indication as to the direction reform should take in cases where direct transposition is not possible, whilst recognising that some issues are best resolved through dialogue between owners and institutional users.

In the remainder of this chapter we explore how the system we have outlined would fit with other types of provision that are also grouped at present under the heading of permitted acts, how harmonisation in Europe can be made a reality, and what can be done to change judicial attitudes towards users. Towards the end of this chapter we also return to the controversial issues of contracting out and the relationship between users' rights and technological measures of protection. Before turning to these issues, however, we consider briefly the effect of Article 5(5) of the Directive.

The three-step test

One important issue that has yet to be considered is the place of the Berne/TRIPS three-step test in any system of users' rights constructed around the Information Society Directive. Article 5(5) of the Directive provides that all the exceptions provided for under the Directive are subject to their being 'applied in certain special cases which do not conflict with a normal exploitation of the work or other subject matter and do not unreasonably prejudice the legitimate interests of the rightholder'. The question that needs to be addressed is whether the three-step test should also be incorporated into domestic law or whether it should merely be treated as a general statement of principle intended to guide the actions of national governments. The UK government has chosen the latter interpretation, taking the view that the United Kingdom's existing provisions already satisfy the three-step test. We support this approach and would not wish to see the three-step test incorporated into national law as part of a reformed system of users' rights. As has been seen,[35] the three-step was never intended to fulfil the function now assigned to it in international instruments relating to copyright and it is too vague and open to too many different interpretations to make it a useful guide for national courts. Article 5(5) should therefore be treated as a general statement of principle capable of giving some limited guidance to the European Court of Justice when reviewing national law.

---

[35] See Chapter 7.

Other types of users' rights

In line with the general focus of this book, we have concentrated thus far on the provisions of the Information Society Directive that could be used to protect freedom of expression, freedom of information, artistic creativity and the provision of education and library services. However, as we identified at the outset of this project, there are a range of other types of provision which are grouped under the rubric of 'permitted acts', many of which perform functions very different from the provisions with which we are principally concerned. As part of the justification of our model it is important to explain how our vision of reform relates to these other types of provision. It probably makes most sense to divide these provisions into those which fall within the partially harmonised European copyright regime and those which fall outside this regime.

Other EU provisions

In addition to the provisions of the Information Society Directive considered already in this chapter, the Directive also allows member states to provide for users' rights in a range of other circumstances. Other permissible heads under the Directive include:
(1) ephemeral recordings made by broadcasters,[36]
(2) use for the benefit of people with a disability,[37]
(3) reproduction of artistic works permanently located in public,[38]
(4) incidental inclusion,[39]
(5) use for the purpose of advertising the public exhibition or sale of artistic works,[40] and
(6) use for the purpose of reconstructing a building.[41]

The 1988 Act contains provisions that correspond closely to each of the above. The provisions in question all predate the implementation of the Directive. Given the close correlation between the miscellaneous provisions of the Directive set out above and these permitted acts, the UK government was fully justified in preserving the provisions in question. We would also retain the substance of these provisions, whilst taking the opportunity to amend them where necessary. For example, it was seen in Chapter 5 that the current provision allowing for the use of artistic

---

[36] Information Society Directive, Art. 5(2)(d). Cf. CDPA 1988, s. 68.
[37] Information Society Directive, Art. 5(3)(b). Cf. CDPA 1988, ss. 31A–F, 74.
[38] Information Society Directive, Art. 5(3)(h). Cf. CDPA 1988, s. 62.
[39] Information Society Directive, Art. 5(3)(i). Cf. CDPA 1988, s. 31.
[40] Information Society Directive, Art. 5(3)(j). Cf. CDPA 1988, s. 63.
[41] Information Society Directive, Art. 5(3)(m). Cf. CDPA 1988, s. 65.

works in advertisements only applies where the sale of the work is being advertised. In contrast, Article 5(3)(j) of the Directive also applies where the public exhibition of a work is being advertised. Similarly, it was seen in Chapter 8 that the current provision relating to the copying of artistic works on public display is seriously flawed, and hence this provision would need to be reformed in the course of establishing a new system of users' rights in the United Kingdom.[42] Our preferred method of reform would, once again, be for the relevant provisions of the Directive to be transposed directly into UK law. This would remove much of the complexity surrounding the current provisions, and would provide judges with a much greater degree of flexibility to decide whether a particular use should be permitted.

Specific reference should be made to the incidental inclusion provision. As was seen in Chapter 2, this right is of considerable practical importance and is at least tangentially relevant to some of our core concerns. It is therefore worth drawing attention to the fact that Article 5(3)(i) allows, without qualification, for the incidental inclusion of a work in other material. If this provision were transposed into UK law it would be left to judges to prevent abuse. For example, it would be expected that in the vast majority of cases a court would refuse to treat the deliberate inclusion of a musical work in the background of a film or broadcast as an 'incidental' inclusion,[43] but would not be prevented from so doing in an exceptional case.

When considering other users' rights that might form part of any future regime, it must also be remembered that the Information Society Directive applies without prejudice to the other copyright directives.[44] This is important, since the Computer Program and Database Directives contain mandatory rights for users which have been implemented into UK law as sections 50A–D of the 1988 Act. These provisions would have to be retained. Similarly, the Information Society Directive applies without prejudice to the E-commerce Directive.[45] As was seen in Chapter 2, the latter provides 'horizontal' protection for online service providers (OSPs), that is, protection against financial and criminal liability in certain circumstances irrespective of the legal action they face.[46] These provisions would also have to form part of any future regime.

---

[42] See CDPA 1988, s. 62, and see Chapter 8.
[43] Cf. CDPA 1988, s. 32(3), and see Chapter 2.
[44] Information Society Directive, Art. 1(2), recital 20.   [45] *Ibid.*, recital 16.
[46] Cf. *ibid.*, recital 16: 'Liability for activities in the network environment concerns not only copyright and related rights but also other areas, such as defamation, misleading advertising, or infringement of trademarks, *and is addressed horizontally* in [the E-commerce Directive]' (emphasis added).

It was also seen in Chapter 2 that the provisions of the E-commerce Directive have to be read alongside the mandatory users' right contained in Article 5(1) of the Information Society Directive, which exempts from the reproduction right certain temporary acts of reproduction which are an integral and essential part of a technological process, including acts whose purpose is to enable 'a transmission in a network between third parties by an intermediary'. Article 5(1) of the Directive has now been implemented as section 28A of the 1988 Act, and again this provision would, in substance, have to be retained. To deal with the problem that OSPs may prove too ready to take down material about which they receive a complaint,[47] we should like to see a threats action introduced into UK copyright law, something that would only need action at the national level. Threats actions already exist in the United Kingdom in relation to trade marks, patents and designs.[48] Significantly, these provisions were introduced in recognition of the fact that the mere threat of litigation can deter people from conducting perfectly lawful activities,[49] which is precisely our concern. If modelled on the existing provisions, a threats action would provide a remedy to *any person aggrieved* by an unjustified threat to sue (a category that should be expressly declared to include persons who have material taken down by an OSP at the instigation of the copyright owner). In cases where the person making the threat is subsequently unable to establish infringement, the court would have the power to issue a declaration of non-infringement, grant an injunction and award damages. The introduction of a threats action might not, admittedly, prove to be a perfect solution because few users would have the resources to bring a threats action, but it might at least force owners to tread somewhat more carefully in their dealings with OSPs.

Unharmonised provisions

Thus far it has been seen that European law allows for or even requires the retention of a range of miscellaneous users' rights. In addition, however, the Information Society Directive leaves open a number of other avenues through which other types of users' rights can (and should) be preserved. First, and perhaps most importantly, Article 9 of the Information Society Directive states that it is to apply without prejudice to,

---

[47] See Chapter 2.
[48] See, respectively, Trade Marks Act 1994, s. 21; Patents Act 1977, s. 70; Registered Designs Act 1949, s. 26; CDPA 1988, s. 253 (unregistered design right). In other jurisdictions threats actions are already available in relation to threats to sue for infringement of copyright. See e.g., Australia, Copyright Act 1968, s. 202.
[49] See Bently and Sherman, p. 991.

inter alia, provisions relating to design rights, typefaces, access to cable or broadcasting services and the protection of national treasures.[50] This is significant because in the United Kingdom the relationship between copyright and these other subject matters, rights and interests is regulated in large part by the permitted acts. The effect of Article 9 seems to be that the United Kingdom is entitled to retain or even extend its provisions relating to copies required as a condition of export,[51] designs,[52] typefaces,[53] and cable retransmission.[54]

The second avenue left open by the Directive is the general saving for existing provisions of 'minor importance' found in Article 5(3)(o). That Article provides for

> use in certain other cases of minor importance where exceptions or limitations already exist in national law, provided they only concern analogue uses and do not affect the free circulation of goods and services within the Community.

Third, it must be remembered that the Information Society Directive only harmonises three of the exclusive rights of copyright owners, namely, the rights of reproduction, communication to the public and distribution. The provisions of the Directive relating to 'exceptions and limitations' are limited accordingly – 'exceptions' to the other exclusive rights of copyright owners are unaffected. Hence, as has already been noted in relation to educational and library copying, provisions relating to performing rights and rental and lending rights are unaffected by the Directive.[55]

It is often said that the Information Society Directive imposes a harmonised list of 'exceptions', but it can now be seen that to a certain extent this claim is incorrect. Rather, the Directive leaves member states with considerable freedom of action. Whilst this freedom is largely welcome as regards the types of users' rights under consideration in this section, it is also indicative of the failure of the Directive to achieve any real harmonisation at all. Aside from a few minor and consequential amendments most member states seem set to leave their existing provisions in place, just as the United Kingdom has done.

---

[50] Also see Information Society Directive, recital 60: 'The protection provided under this Directive should be without prejudice to national or Community legal provisions in other areas, such as industrial property, data protection, conditional access, access to public documents, and the rule of media exploitation chronology, which may affect the protection of copyright or related rights.'
[51] CDPA 1988, s. 44.   [52] *Ibid.*, ss. 51–53.   [53] *Ibid.*, ss. 54–55.
[54] *Ibid.*, ss. 73–73A.   [55] Cf. *Ibid.*, ss. 34, 36A, 40A, 59, 66.

Making harmonisation a reality

Some commentators have used the fact that the Directive is likely to fail to achieve any real harmonisation to argue that it is invalid.[56] It is important that we consider this argument in more detail, given both our support for the Directive and our argument that in some areas harmonisation is desirable since the practical consequence of differences in national rules may be to undermine users' rights altogether.

In considering the extent to which the Directive achieves its aims, it is again worth drawing a distinction between different types of users' rights. When it comes to provisions which, say, allow for use of a work in the course of a religious ceremony,[57] it is entirely appropriate that these matters be left to national law. Not only do such provisions have little impact on the operation of the internal market, they are often the sorts of provision that are most closely bound up with questions of national culture. Leaving such provisions unharmonised is also entirely consistent with the approach adopted in other copyright directives. For example, the Rental Right Directive allows member states to derogate from the public lending right,[58] and the *Droit de Suite* Directive leaves member states free to determine how the right is to operate in the case of works of art with a low resale value.[59]

Turning to the more fundamental users' rights, it is again possible to identify a number of areas where it seems perfectly reasonable to leave matters to member states. In particular, whilst provisions relating to private study and research, educational establishments, libraries and archives may be of fundamental importance, they too have little connection with the operation of the single market and can also involve questions of national culture.

It can therefore be seen that in relation to both miscellaneous users' rights and education and library provisions it is entirely appropriate that the Directive should only seek to set up very broad boundaries within which member states are free to operate. If the Directive is to be regarded as unsuccessful this must be because of its failure to harmonise those users' rights that allow part of a work to be reused in a later, commercially significant work. It is this type of provision that needs to be harmonised if producers are to have the confidence to market a work that incorporates

---

[56] B. Hugenholtz, 'Why the Copyright Directive is Unimportant, and Possibly Invalid' [2000] EIPR 499. See also Chapter 9.
[57] Cf. Information Society Directive, Art. 5(3)(g). At present there is no corresponding provision under UK law.
[58] Rental Right Directive, Art. 5. [59] *Droit de Suite* Directive, Arts. 3 and 4.

a substantial part of an earlier work throughout the Community without securing a licence. In other words, when thinking about harmonisation we need to be most concerned with provisions relating to activities such as criticism and review, parodies, news reporting and the publication of the results of research. Also within this category are provisions allowing works to be modified for the benefit of persons with a disability. At present it does appear that these types of provision are likely to remain unharmonised and hence it can legitimately be said that the Directive will have failed to achieve harmonisation in the areas where it is required most. However, it must be stressed that there is nothing inevitable about this failure – the failure results not from the Directive itself but rather from member states' desire to preserve not merely the general thrust of users' rights relating to reviews, news reports, parodies and so forth, but also the precise form and wording of their existing provisions. If, as we have proposed, member states were prepared to follow the wording of the Directive much more closely, harmonisation could become a reality, particularly if judges in individual member states showed a willingness to look to decisions decided under equivalent provisions elsewhere in Europe. Moreover, under such a system the European Court of Justice could play a more fundamental role and one with which it is familiar, rather than (as is likely to be the case) merely deciding whether a particular provision of national law is broadly compatible with the provisions of the Directive.

Overall it can be concluded that the Directive sets up general parameters within which member states have freedom of action and that this is entirely appropriate for most types of users' rights. In those areas where closer harmonisation is required the Directive may well fail to achieve its ends, but this is by no means an inevitable consequence of the wording of the Directive itself.

Changing attitudes

It is our firm belief that the regime of users' rights outlined in this chapter could provide the beginnings of a much better deal for users. However, as we have indicated in previous chapters, consideration also needs to be given to changing attitudes, particularly judicial attitudes, towards users' rights. Changing attitudes is an amorphous objective and progress will be difficult to measure. It is clear, however, that if it is to occur commentators (who have not always looked at decisions that narrow protection for users with a sufficiently critical eye) will have to challenge the ideas and assumptions about copyright which have been used to underpin a very restrictive regime. By challenging the belief that use should only be free in cases of market failure, that users' rights must be interpreted narrowly because copyright is a property right and that copyright legislation is 'balanced', we hope to have made a contribution to this process. Similarly, by pointing out some of the deficiencies in national and supranational legislative processes and by illustrating some of the limits imposed by the current provisions, we hope to raise awareness of the inconsistencies and general unfairness of the present system.

There is also good reason to hope that a fundamental overhaul of the existing permitted acts could, in itself, help to transform judicial attitudes. This is because a radical change of approach, even if inspired by the Information Society Directive, would hopefully be taken as a signal from Parliament that the judiciary should seek to further users' interests. It is significant that Mr Justice Laddie, one of the United Kingdom's leading intellectual property judges, has indicated that the United Kingdom should reform its existing approach to the exceptions.[60] Our call to restyle what are currently termed exceptions as users' rights should be understood in this context – the aim is to reinforce the idea that users are to be treated differently under the new regime. In this respect it may be possible to draw an analogy with the calls that were made for the incorporation of the European Convention on Human Rights into UK law prior to the passage of the Human Rights Act. For many commentators the point was not that existing common law principles were inherently unsuited to the protection of fundamental rights and freedoms, but rather that the judges were reluctant to use and develop existing principles in a sufficiently robust manner. If a complete overhaul of the permitted acts did lead to a transformation in judicial attitudes, judges might be more willing to use general legal principles creatively in order to keep copyright protection within more appropriate bounds. For example, we would lend strong support to a recent judicial suggestion that a court might imply a licence to reproduce a portion of a work in order to prevent copyright from interfering unduly with freedom of expression.[61]

---

[60] H. Laddie, 'Copyright: Over-Strength, Over-Regulated, Over-Rated?' [1996] EIPR 253.
[61] *Musical Fidelity* v. *Vickers* [2003] FSR 898, 907 (per Buxton LJ). The willingness of judges to use general legal principles to protect users is an issue of considerable importance in relation to contracting out. See Chapter 2 for a discussion of whether a court would enforce a term that seeks to override one or more users' rights.

Contractual exclusion and technological measures of protection

The final question that remains to be addressed is how our model for reform relates to the controversial issue of the relationship between users' rights, technological measures of protection and contractual provisions that seek to modify or exclude the operation of the 'exceptions'. It was seen in Chapter 2 that we are somewhat less concerned about the potential threat to users posed by technological measures of protection and contracting out than are many other commentators. Nevertheless, it is important to consider how a system of users' rights modelled on the Directive could deal with the dangers posed by a 'digital lock-up', both to see how specific problems that may arise could be resolved or in case our assessment of the overall danger posed to users is incorrect. Again, contracting out and circumvention of technological measures of protection need to be considered separately.

As regards contracting out, it should be noted that the Directive expressly states that it is to apply without prejudice to national contract rules.[62] This is significant, since one of the factors that shaped our attitude towards the contracting out issue is that UK law already seems to be on the right track – Parliament has recognised that it should not be possible to contract out of users' rights in certain circumstances or beyond certain limits, and the Copyright Tribunal has extensive powers to review the terms of licences granted by collecting societies.[63] In the short term, therefore, probably all that is required is some mechanism to ensure that if cases of contracting out being used inappropriately do arise then a new class of prohibition can be added swiftly. For example, in relation to agreements not already subject to its control, the Copyright Tribunal could be given the power to declare that provisions of contracts that exclude or modify one or more users' rights are of no effect on application of the Director General of Fair Trading. Alternatively, the power to declare certain provisions void could be given to the Secretary of State, similar to the newly introduced powers relating to technological measures of protection considered in Chapter 2.[64] If such ad hoc measures should prove inadequate then a more general prohibition on contracting out (as was recommended by the Australian Copyright Law Review Committee[65]) could still be introduced in the future.

In the longer term some action at the European level may also be desirable, again so as to ensure that differences between national rules

---

[62] Information Society Directive, Art. 9.   [63] See Chapter 2.
[64] See also CDPA 1988, s. 296ZE, Sched. 5A.
[65] Australian Copyright Law Review Committee, *Copyright and Contract* (Canberra, 2002).

do not prevent users from having the confidence to rely on their rights when marketing a product in more than one country. The most sensible approach would be to wait to see how national governments respond to the contracting out issue and then to adopt a minimal level of harmonisation by prohibiting certain terms throughout Europe, but leaving it to member states to add other prohibitions if they so wish. It is likely that the Commission would have a range of experience to draw upon. In addition to the United Kingdom's existing prohibitions on contracting out,[66] Belgium has introduced a general prohibition on contracting out in relation to databases.[67] But in any event in this respect the EU also seems to be on the right track already – both the Computer Program and Database Directives contain provisions prohibiting contracting out.[68] For example, under the Computer Program Directive it is not possible to contract out of the right to make back-up copies or the right to decompile.[69] It was seen in Chapter 2 that the Australian Copyright Law Review Committee's survey of online licence agreements noted that attempts to exclude decompilation provisions are particularly common.[70] Here EU law already provides a solution. Action at the European level would not only be consistent with the approach adopted in earlier directives, it would also correspond with the Commission's recent interest in the question of harmonisation of contract law generally in Europe[71] and its particular interest in the dramatic variations between national rules relating to copyright contracts.[72] Nor, despite what is sometimes claimed, is there anything in the Information Society Directive to indicate that the Commission is moving away from prohibiting at least certain forms of contracting out.[73]

---

[66] CDPA 1988, ss. 296A, 296B; Broadcasting Act 1996, s. 137.
[67] Australian Copyright Law Review Committee, *Copyright and Contract*, para. 6.10; Guibault, p. 219.
[68] Computer Program Directive, Art. 9(1); Database Directive, Arts. 6(1), 8(1).
[69] Computer Program Directive, Art. 9(1).
[70] Australian Copyright Law Review Committee, *Copyright and Contract*, para. 4.95.
[71] E.g., in July 2001, the Commission issued a *Communication to the Council and the European Parliament on European Contract Law* COM (2001) 398 final, and has now published reactions to this Communication; see, e.g.: www.europa.eu.int/comm/consumers/policy/developments/contract_law/comments/4.14.pdf.
[72] In particular, while most civil law countries place limits on freedom of contract and have principles of contractual interpretation that are designed to protect authors, the United Kingdom and Ireland place few restrictions on alienability and do not have special rules of contractual interpretation. The Commission has committed itself to establishing whether harmonisation is required.
[73] The confusion has been caused by Art. 6(4) (considered below), which provides that member states must exempt some uses from the prohibition on the circumvention of technological protection measures so as to ensure the continued availability of certain users' rights. However, the Directive goes on to provide that 'the provisions of the first and second subparagraphs [of Art. 6(4)] shall not apply to works or other subject matter

As regards technological measures of protection, the Information Society Directive already imposes a more harmonised regime. Article 6 of the Directive obliges member states to provide protection against the circumvention of technological measures of protection and against the manufacture and sale of devices that are primarily designed to facilitate such circumvention. However, in recognition of the concern that owners might attempt to use technological measures of protection to exclude the operation of users' rights, the Directive provides that owners must make available the means to circumvent to those entitled to the material under seven of the users' rights provided for in the Directive,[74] except where a work has been made available to the public online subject to a contractual agreement.[75] The seven rights in question probably represent those cases where technological measures are most likely to impact adversely upon users.[76] In other cases technological measures are unlikely to be as effective. For example, it was seen in Chapter 2 that any attempt to use technological protection measures to prevent reuse of part of a textual work for the purposes of criticism, review, parody, news reporting and the like is unlikely to be successful. Nevertheless, it is a cause for concern that the Directive does not provide a mechanism for ensuring that other users' rights remain available should technological measures cause problems in areas other than those catered for at present.

It was also seen in Chapter 2 that the Directive seeks to protect users by encouraging owners to build space for users into their copyright protection strategy, an approach Séverine Dusollier has dubbed 'fair use by

made available to the public on agreed contractual terms in such a way that members of the public may access them from a place and at a time individually chosen by them'. The Australian Copyright Law Review Committee interpreted this provision as meaning that contracts entered into over the Internet must prevail over users' rights. Moreover, because Art. 6(4) also applies to computer programs and databases the Committee concluded that this provision overrides the prohibitions on contracting out found in the Computer Program and Database Directives: Australian Copyright Law Review Committee, *Copyright and Contract*, paras. 6.28, 6.39. A literal interpretation of the Directive, however, suggests that this analysis is incorrect. The Directive only states that where a work has been made available pursuant to an online licence agreement there is no right to circumvent in order to ensure that users' rights remain available. The Directive does not say anything at all about the *validity of the terms of the agreement itself*. This also seems to be the interpretation adopted by the UK government, which has not amended the prohibition on contracting out for computer programs and databases so as to exclude online licences.

[74] The rights in question are those contained in Art. 5(2)(a) (reprographic copying), 5(2)(c) (copying by cultural institutions), 5(2)(d) (ephemeral recording of broadcasts), 5(2)(e) (reproduction of broadcasts by social institutions), 5(3)(a) (illustration for teaching or scientific research), 5(3)(b) (use for the benefit of people with a disability), 5(3)(e) (use for the purpose of public security).

[75] See below.

[76] And not that 'these provisions were considered somehow more vital'. Cf. Australian Copyright Law Review Committee, *Copyright and Contract*, para. 6.27.

design'.[77] Although Dusollier has concerns about the regime established by the Directive, she does note that one key advantage of the fair use by design approach is that it does not depend upon the user having the technical skills to circumvent the protection measure.[78] In contrast, a right to circumvent so as to take advantage of an exception is, in practice, restricted to a small subset of highly technologically literate users.[79] In cases where owners fail to take voluntary measures to protect users, member states *are obliged* to ensure that the seven rights mentioned above remain available.[80] In addition, member states are given the discretion to ensure that private copying rights falling within Article 5(2)(b) remain available.[81]

It is inevitable that uncertainty will remain at this stage about how easy users will find it to persuade the relevant government agencies to protect their interests, and some commentators are clearly sceptical about the willingness of member states to take action in this area. This scepticism may well prove to be justified and there may well be flaws with the procedures set up by individual member states.[82] Such problems are not, however, an inevitable consequence of the Directive. Overall, therefore, and bearing in mind that in Chapter 2 it was seen that there is no easy solution to the problems posed by technological measures, for the most part the scheme established by the Directive is sensible.

There are, however, two areas in which the Directive is potentially deficient and hence in which action at the European level may be required. The first reform that may be required is an extension of the range of provisions to which the power to ensure that a users' right remains available applies. Although the current provisions are likely to catch many of the cases in which technological measures impact adversely upon users, in the longer term other problems may well emerge. The second area in which reform may be required is in relation to technological measures that apply to material made available to the public online subject to a contractual agreement. Here member states are not obliged, and nor do they have the power, to ensure that users' rights remain available.[83] The extent to which this restriction will prove to be a problem in practice will

---

[77] S. Dusollier, 'Exceptions and Technological Measures in the European Copyright Directive of 2001 – an Empty Promise' (2003) 34 IIC 62, 70.
[78] *Ibid.*, 69–70.   [79] See Chapter 2.
[80] Information Society Directive, Art. 6(4) (para. 1).   [81] *Ibid.*, Art. 6(4) (para. 2).
[82] For the procedure in the United Kingdom see Chapter 2. For an outline of the procedures adopted in other member states see N. Braun, 'The Interface between the Protection of Technological Measures and the Exercise of Exceptions to Copyright and Related Rights: Comparing the Situation in the United States and the European Union' [2003] EIPR 496, 501–2.
[83] Information Society Directive, Art. 6(4) (para. 4).

depend on a number of factors, including the extent to which electronic access replaces more traditional forms of presenting and communicating works, the extent to which technological measures prove effective in combating piracy (and hence whether owners seek to rely on them) and levels of consumer resistance to technological measures. Nevertheless, this remains an aspect of the Directive that may well need to be revisited in the future.

Conclusion

As we indicated at the outset of this chapter, our aim here has not been to develop a fully fledged alternative system of users' rights, but rather to provide an outline of what a system of users' rights modelled on the Information Society Directive might look like. In many respects the model of reform outlined in this chapter is conservative – our proposals do not require action beyond the national level (at least not immediately) and can be justified by reference to the goal of achieving European harmonisation. By developing a model of this kind we hope to foster the belief that fundamental reform is achievable. In this respect our project is quite different from that of other commentators whose proposals would require the complete reshaping of the international conventions relating to copyright. This is not to suggest that such studies do not have their place, since they can play an important role in expanding our horizons, but our concern is both more immediate and more practical, and takes proper account of the disruption that any radical overhaul of the entire copyright system would create. As a final point, we should like to reiterate our call for owner representatives to rethink their approach to users' rights. In particular, we would urge them to think seriously about what effect an overreaching set of owners' rights has on the public perception of copyright at a time when the future of the entire system may not be as secure as recent legislative and political developments would seem to suggest.

Appendices

Appendix 1
Copyright, Designs and Patents Act 1988, Part I, Chapter III: 'Permitted Acts'

Introductory

Introductory provisions

28. – (1) The provisions of this Chapter specify acts which may be done in relation to copyright works notwithstanding the subsistence of copyright; they relate only to the question of infringement of copyright and do not affect any other right or obligation restricting the doing of any of the specified acts.

(2) Where it is provided by this Chapter that an act does not infringe copyright, or may be done without infringing copyright, and no particular description of copyright work is mentioned, the act in question does not infringe the copyright in a work of any description.

(3) No inference shall be drawn from the description of any act which may by virtue of this Chapter be done without infringing copyright as to the scope of the acts restricted by the copyright in any description of work.

(4) The provisions of this Chapter are to be construed independently of each other, so that the fact that an act does not fall within one provision does not mean that it is not covered by another provision.

General

Making of temporary copies

28A. Copyright in a literary work, other than a computer program or a database, or in a dramatic, musical or artistic work, the typographical arrangement of a published edition, a sound recording or a film, is not infringed by the making of a temporary copy which is transient or

---

Crown Copyright material is reproduced with the permission of the Controller of HMSO and the Queen's Printer for Scotland.

incidental, which is an integral and essential part of a technological process and the sole purpose of which is to enable –

(a) a transmission of the work in a network between third parties by an intermediary; or

(b) a lawful use of the work;

and which has no independent economic significance.

Research and private study

29. – (1) Fair dealing with a literary, dramatic, musical or artistic work for the purposes of research for a non-commercial purpose does not infringe any copyright in the work provided that it is accompanied by a sufficient acknowledgement.

(1B) No acknowledgement is required in connection with fair dealing for the purposes mentioned in subsection (1) where this would be impossible for reasons of practicality or otherwise.

(1C) Fair dealing with a literary, dramatic, musical or artistic work for the purposes of private study does not infringe any copyright in the work.

(2) Fair dealing with the typographical arrangement of a published edition for the purposes of research or private study does not infringe any copyright in the arrangement.

(3) Copying by a person other than the researcher or student himself is not fair dealing if –

(a) in the case of a librarian, or a person acting on behalf of a librarian, he does anything which regulations under section 40 would not permit to be done under section 38 or 39 (articles or parts of published works: restriction on multiple copies of same material), or

(b) in any other case, the person doing the copying knows or has reason to believe that it will result in copies of substantially the same material being provided to more than one person at substantially the same time and for substantially the same purpose.

(4) It is not fair dealing –

(a) to convert a computer program expressed in a low level language into a version expressed in a higher level language, or

(b) incidentally in the course of so converting the program, to copy it,

(these acts being permitted if done in accordance with section 50B (decompilation)).

(4A) It is not fair dealing to observe, study or test the functioning of a computer program in order to determine the ideas and principles which underlie any element of the program (these acts being permitted if done in accordance with section 50BA (observing, studying and testing)).

Criticism, review and news reporting

30. – (1) Fair dealing with a work for the purpose of criticism or review, of that or another work or of a performance of a work, does not infringe any copyright in the work provided that it is accompanied by a sufficient acknowledgement and provided that the work has been made available to the public.

(1A) For the purposes of subsection (1) a work has been made available to the public if it has been made available by any means, including –
    (a) the issue of copies to the public;
    (b) making the work available by means of an electronic retrieval system;
    (c) the rental or lending of copies of the work to the public;
    (d) the performance, exhibition, playing or showing of the work in public;
    (e) the communication to the public of the work,
but in determining generally for the purposes of that subsection whether a work has been made available to the public no account shall be taken of any unauthorised act.

(2) Fair dealing with a work (other than a photograph) for the purpose of reporting current events does not infringe any copyright in the work provided that (subject to subsection (3)) it is accompanied by a sufficient acknowledgement.

(3) No acknowledgement is required in connection with the reporting of current events by means of a sound recording, film or broadcast where this would be impossible for reasons of practicality or otherwise.

Incidental inclusion of copyright material

31. – (1) Copyright in a work is not infringed by its incidental inclusion in an artistic work, sound recording, film or broadcast.

(2) Nor is the copyright infringed by the issue to the public of copies, or the playing, showing or communication to the public, of anything whose making was, by virtue of subsection (1), not an infringement of the copyright.

(3) A musical work, words spoken or sung with music, or so much of a sound recording or broadcast as includes a musical work or such words, shall not be regarded as incidentally included in another work if it is deliberately included.

Visual impairment

Making a single accessible copy for personal use

31A. – (1) If a visually impaired person has lawful possession or lawful use of a copy ("the master copy") of the whole or part of –
>   (a) a literary, dramatic, musical or artistic work; or
>   (b) a published edition,

which is not accessible to him because of the impairment, it is not an infringement of copyright in the work, or in the typographical arrangement of the published edition, for an accessible copy of the master copy to be made for his personal use.

(2) Subsection (1) does not apply –
>   (a) if the master copy is of a musical work, or part of a musical work, and the making of an accessible copy would involve recording a performance of the work or part of it; or
>   (b) if the master copy is of a database, or part of a database, and the making of an accessible copy would infringe copyright in the database.

(3) Subsection (1) does not apply in relation to the making of an accessible copy for a particular visually impaired person if, or to the extent that, copies of the copyright work are commercially available, by or with the authority of the copyright owner, in a form that is accessible to that person.

(4) An accessible copy made under this section must be accompanied by –
>   (a) a statement that it is made under this section; and
>   (b) a sufficient acknowledgement.

(5) If a person makes an accessible copy on behalf of a visually impaired person under this section and charges for it, the sum charged must not exceed the cost of making and supplying the copy.

(6) If a person holds an accessible copy made under subsection (1) when he is not entitled to have it made under that subsection, the copy is to be treated as an infringing copy, unless he is a person falling within subsection (7)(b).

(7) A person who holds an accessible copy made under subsection (1) may transfer it to –
>   (a) a visually impaired person entitled to have the accessible copy made under subsection (1); or
>   (b) a person who has lawful possession of the master copy and intends to transfer the accessible copy to a person falling within paragraph (a).

(8) The transfer by a person ("V") of an accessible copy made under subsection (1) to another person ("T") is an infringement of copyright by V unless V has reasonable grounds for believing that T is a person falling within subsection (7)(a) or (b).

(9) If an accessible copy which would be an infringing copy but for this section is subsequently dealt with –
   (a) it is to be treated as an infringing copy for the purposes of that dealing; and
   (b) if that dealing infringes copyright, is to be treated as an infringing copy for all subsequent purposes.

(10) In subsection (9), "dealt with" means sold or let for hire or offered or exposed for sale or hire or communicated to the public.

Multiple copies for visually impaired persons

31B. – (1) If an approved body has lawful possession of a copy ("the master copy") of the whole or part of –
   (a) a commercially published literary, dramatic, musical or artistic work; or
   (b) a commercially published edition,
it is not an infringement of copyright in the work, or in the typographical arrangement of the published edition, for the body to make, or supply, accessible copies for the personal use of visually impaired persons to whom the master copy is not accessible because of their impairment.

(2) Subsection (1) does not apply –
   (a) if the master copy is of a musical work, or part of a musical work, and the making of an accessible copy would involve recording a performance of the work or part of it; or
   (b) if the master copy is of a database, or part of a database, and the making of an accessible copy would infringe copyright in the database.

(3) Subsection (1) does not apply in relation to the making of an accessible copy if, or to the extent that, copies of the copyright work are commercially available, by or with the authority of the copyright owner, in a form that is accessible to the same or substantially the same degree.

(4) Subsection (1) does not apply in relation to the supply of an accessible copy to a particular visually impaired person if, or to the extent that, copies of the copyright work are commercially available, by or with the authority of the copyright owner, in a form that is accessible to that person.

(5) An accessible copy made under this section must be accompanied by –
> (a) a statement that it is made under this section; and
> (b) a sufficient acknowledgement.

(6) If an approved body charges for supplying a copy made under this section, the sum charged must not exceed the cost of making and supplying the copy.

(7) An approved body making copies under this section must, if it is an educational establishment, ensure that the copies will be used only for its educational purposes.

(8) If the master copy is in copy-protected electronic form, any accessible copy made of it under this section must, so far as it is reasonably practicable to do so, incorporate the same, or equally effective, copy protection (unless the copyright owner agrees otherwise).

(9) If an approved body continues to hold an accessible copy made under subsection (1) when it would no longer be entitled to make or supply such a copy under that subsection, the copy is to be treated as an infringing copy.

(10) If an accessible copy which would be an infringing copy but for this section is subsequently dealt with –
> (a) it is to be treated as an infringing copy for the purposes of that dealing; and
> (b) if that dealing infringes copyright, is to be treated as an infringing copy for all subsequent purposes.

(11) In subsection (10), "dealt with" means sold or let for hire or offered or exposed for sale or hire or communicated to the public.

(12) "Approved body" means an educational establishment or a body that is not conducted for profit.

(13) "Supplying" includes lending.

Intermediate copies and records

31C. – (1) An approved body entitled to make accessible copies under section 31B may hold an intermediate copy of the master copy which is necessarily created during the production of the accessible copies, but only –
> (a) if and so long as the approved body continues to be entitled to make accessible copies of that master copy; and
> (b) for the purposes of the production of further accessible copies.

(2) An intermediate copy which is held in breach of subsection (1) is to be treated as an infringing copy.

(3) An approved body may lend or transfer the intermediate copy to another approved body which is entitled to make accessible copies of the work or published edition under section 31B.

(4) The loan or transfer by an approved body ("A") of an intermediate copy to another person ("B") is an infringement of copyright by A unless A has reasonable grounds for believing that B –
> (a) is another approved body which is entitled to make accessible copies of the work or published edition under section 31B; and
> (b) will use the intermediate copy only for the purposes of the production of further accessible copies.

(5) If an approved body charges for lending or transferring the intermediate copy, the sum charged must not exceed the cost of the loan or transfer.

(6) An approved body must –
> (a) keep records of accessible copies made under section 31B and of the persons to whom they are supplied;
> (b) keep records of any intermediate copy lent or transferred under this section and of the persons to whom it is lent or transferred; and
> (c) allow the copyright owner or a person acting for him, on giving reasonable notice, to inspect the records at any reasonable time.

(7) Within a reasonable time of making an accessible copy under section 31B, or lending or transferring an intermediate copy under this section, the approved body must –
> (a) notify each relevant representative body; or
> (b) if there is no such body, notify the copyright owner.

(8) A relevant representative body is a body which –
> (a) represents particular copyright owners, or owners of copyright in the type of copyright work concerned; and
> (b) has given notice to the Secretary of State of the copyright owners, or the classes of copyright owner, represented by it.

(9) The requirement to notify the copyright owner under subsection (7)(b) does not apply if it is not reasonably possible for the approved body to ascertain the name and address of the copyright owner.

Licensing schemes

31D. – (1) Section 31B does not apply to the making of an accessible copy in a particular form if –
> (a) a licensing scheme operated by a licensing body is in force under which licences may be granted by the licensing body

permitting the making and supply of copies of the copyright work in that form;

(b) the scheme is not unreasonably restrictive; and

(c) the scheme and any modification made to it have been notified to the Secretary of State by the licensing body.

(2) A scheme is unreasonably restrictive if it includes a term or condition which –

(a) purports to prevent or limit the steps that may be taken under section 31B or 31C; or

(b) has that effect.

(3) But subsection (2) does not apply if –

(a) the copyright work is no longer published by or with the authority of the copyright owner; and

(b) there are reasonable grounds for preventing or restricting the making of accessible copies of the work.

(4) If section 31B or 31C is displaced by a licensing scheme, sections 119 to 122 apply in relation to the scheme as if it were one to which those sections applied as a result of section 117.

Limitations, etc. following infringement of copyright

31E. – (1) The Secretary of State may make an order under this section if it appears to him that the making of copies –

(a) under section 31B; or

(b) under a licence granted under a licensing scheme that has been notified under section 31D,

has led to infringement of copyright on a scale which, in the Secretary of State's opinion, would not have occurred if section 31B had not been in force, or the licence had not been granted.

(2) The order may prohibit one or more named approved bodies, or one or more specified categories of approved body, from –

(a) acting under section 31B; or

(b) acting under a licence of a description specified in the order.

(3) The order may disapply –

(a) the provisions of section 31B; or

(b) the provisions of a licence, or a licensing scheme, of a description specified in the order,

in respect of the making of copies of a description so specified.

(4) If the Secretary of State proposes to make an order he must, before making it, consult –

(a) such bodies representing copyright owners as he thinks fit; and

(b) such bodies representing visually impaired persons as he thinks fit.

(5) If the Secretary of State proposes to make an order which includes a prohibition he must, before making it, consult –
    (a) if the proposed order is to apply to one or more named approved bodies, that body or those bodies;
    (b) if it is to apply to one or more specified categories of approved body, to such bodies representing approved bodies of that category or those categories as he thinks fit.

(6) An approved body which is prohibited by an order from acting under a licence may not apply to the Copyright Tribunal under section 121(1) in respect of a refusal or failure by a licensing body to grant such a licence.

Definitions and other supplementary provision for sections 31A to 31E

31F. – (1) This section supplements sections 31A to 31E and includes definitions.

(2) A copy of a copyright work (other than an accessible copy made under section 31A or 31B) is to be taken to be accessible to a visually impaired person only if it is as accessible to him as it would be if he were not visually impaired.

(3) "Accessible copy", in relation to a copyright work, means a version which provides for a visually impaired person improved access to the work.

(4) An accessible copy may include facilities for navigating around the version of the copyright work but may not include –
    (a) changes that are not necessary to overcome problems caused by visual impairment; or
    (b) changes which infringe the right (provided by section 80) not to have the work subjected to derogatory treatment.

(5) "Approved body" has the meaning given in section 31B(12).

(6) "Lending", in relation to a copy, means making it available for use, otherwise than for direct or indirect economic or commercial advantage, on terms that it will or may be returned.

(7) For the purposes of subsection (6), a loan is not to be treated as being for direct or indirect economic or commercial advantage if a charge is made for the loan which does not exceed the cost of making and supplying the copy.

(8) The definition of "lending" in section 18A does not apply for the purposes of sections 31B and 31C.

(9) "Visually impaired person" means a person –
    (a) who is blind;

(b) who has an impairment of visual function which cannot be improved, by the use of corrective lenses, to a level that would normally be acceptable for reading without a special level or kind of light;

(c) who is unable, through physical disability, to hold or manipulate a book; or

(d) who is unable, through physical disability, to focus or move his eyes to the extent that would normally be acceptable for reading.

(10) The Secretary of State may by regulations prescribe –

(a) the form in which; or

(b) the procedure in accordance with which,

any notice required under section 31C(7) or (8), or 31D(1), must be given.

(11) Any power to make regulations or orders is exercisable by statutory instrument subject to annulment in pursuance of a resolution of either House of Parliament.

Education

Things done for purposes of instruction or examination

32. – (1) Copyright in a literary, dramatic, musical or artistic work is not infringed by its being copied in the course of instruction or of preparation for instruction, provided the copying –

(a) is done by a person giving or receiving instruction,

(b) is not done by means of a reprographic process, and

(c) is accompanied by a sufficient acknowledgement,

and provided that the instruction is for a non-commercial purpose.

(2) Copyright in a sound recording, film or broadcast is not infringed by its being copied by making a film or film sound-track in the course of instruction, or of preparation for instruction, in the making of films or film sound-tracks, provided the copying –

(a) is done by a person giving or receiving instruction, and

(b) is accompanied by a sufficient acknowledgement,

and provided that the instruction is for a non-commercial purpose.

(2A) Copyright in a literary, dramatic, musical or artistic work which has been made available to the public is not infringed by its being copied in the course of instruction or of preparation for instruction, provided the copying –

(a) is fair dealing with the work,

(b) is done by a person giving or receiving instruction,

(c) is not done by means of a reprographic process, and

(d) is accompanied by a sufficient acknowledgement.

(2B) The provisions of section 30(1A) (works made available to the public) apply for the purposes of subsection (2A) as they apply for the purposes of section 30(1).

(3) Copyright is not infringed by anything done for the purposes of an examination by way of setting the questions, communicating the questions to the candidates or answering the questions, provided that the questions are accompanied by a sufficient acknowledgement.

(3A) No acknowledgement is required in connection with copying as mentioned in subsection (1), (2) or (2A), or in connection with anything done for the purposes mentioned in subsection (3), where this would be impossible for reasons of practicality or otherwise.

(4) Subsection (3) does not extend to the making of a reprographic copy of a musical work for use by an examination candidate in performing the work.

(5) Where a copy which would otherwise be an infringing copy is made in accordance with this section but is subsequently dealt with, it shall be treated as an infringing copy for the purpose of that dealing, and if that dealing infringes copyright for all subsequent purposes.

For this purpose "dealt with" means –

(a) sold or let for hire, offered or exposed for sale or hire; or

(b) communicated to the public, unless that communication, by virtue of subsection (3), is not an infringement of copyright.

Anthologies for educational use

33. – (1) The inclusion of a short passage from a published literary or dramatic work in a collection which –

(a) is intended for use in educational establishments and is so described in its title, and in any advertisements issued by or on behalf of the publisher, and

(b) consists mainly of material in which no copyright subsists,

does not infringe the copyright in the work if the work itself is not intended for use in such establishments and the inclusion is accompanied by a sufficient acknowledgement.

(2) Subsection (1) does not authorise the inclusion of more than two excerpts from copyright works by the same author in collections published by the same publisher over any period of five years.

(3) In relation to any given passage the reference in subsection (2) to excerpts from works by the same author –

(a) shall be taken to include excerpts from works by him in collaboration with another, and

(b) if the passage in question is from such a work, shall be taken to include excerpts from works by any of the authors, whether alone or in collaboration with another.

(4) References in this section to the use of a work in an educational establishment are to any use for the educational purposes of such an establishment.

Performing, playing or showing work in course of activities of educational establishment

34. – (1) The performance of a literary, dramatic or musical work before an audience consisting of teachers and pupils at an educational establishment and other persons directly connected with the activities of the establishment –

    (a) by a teacher or pupil in the course of the activities of the establishment, or

    (b) at the establishment by any person for the purposes of instruction,

is not a public performance for the purposes of infringement of copyright.

(2) The playing or showing of a sound recording, film or broadcast before such an audience at an educational establishment for the purposes of instruction is not a playing or showing of the work in public for the purposes of infringement of copyright.

(3) A person is not for this purpose directly connected with the activities of the educational establishment simply because he is the parent of a pupil at the establishment.

Recording by educational establishments of broadcasts

35. – (1) A recording of a broadcast, or a copy of such a recording, may be made by or on behalf of an educational establishment for the educational purposes of that establishment without thereby infringing the copyright in the broadcast, or in any work included in it, provided that it is accompanied by a sufficient acknowledgement of the broadcast and that the educational purposes are non-commercial.

(1A) Copyright is not infringed where a recording of a broadcast or a copy of such a recording, whose making was by virtue of subsection (1) not an infringement of copyright, is communicated to the public by a person situated within the premises of an educational establishment provided that the communication cannot be received by any person situated outside the premises of that establishment.

(2) This section does not apply if or to the extent that there is a licensing scheme certified for the purposes of this section under section 143 providing for the grant of licences.

(3) Where a copy which would otherwise be an infringing copy is made in accordance with this section but is subsequently dealt with, it shall be treated as an infringing copy for the purposes of that dealing, and if that dealing infringes copyright for all subsequent purposes. For this purpose "dealt with" means sold or let for hire or offered or exposed for sale or hire, or communicated from within the premises of an educational establishment to any person situated outside those premises.

Reprographic copying by educational establishments of passages from published works

36. – (1) Reprographic copies of passages from published literary, dramatic or musical works may, to the extent permitted by this section, be made by or on behalf of an educational establishment for the purposes of instruction without infringing any copyright in the work, provided that they are accompanied by a sufficient acknowledgement and the instruction is for a non-commercial purpose.

(1A) No acknowledgement is required in connection with the making of copies as mentioned in subsection (1) where this would be impossible for reasons of practicality or otherwise.

(1B) Reprographic copies of passages from published editions may, to the extent permitted by this section, be made by or on behalf of an educational establishment for the purposes of instruction without infringing any copyright in the typographical arrangement of the edition.

(2) Not more than one per cent. of any work may be copied by or on behalf of an establishment by virtue of this section in any quarter, that is, in any period 1st January to 31st March, 1st April to 30th June, 1st July to 30th September or 1st October to 31st December.

(3) Copying is not authorised by this section if, or to the extent that, licences are available authorising the copying in question and the person making the copies knew or ought to have been aware of that fact.

(4) The terms of a licence granted to an educational establishment authorising the reprographic copying for the purposes of instruction of passages from published works are of no effect so far as they purport to restrict the proportion of a work which may be copied (whether on payment or free of charge) to less than that which would be permitted under this section.

(5) Where a copy which would otherwise be an infringing copy is made in accordance with this section but is subsequently dealt with, it shall be

treated as an infringing copy for the purposes of that dealing, and if that dealing infringes copyright for all subsequent purposes. For this purpose "dealt with" means sold or let for hire, offered or exposed for sale or hire or communicated to the public.

Lending of copies by educational establishments

36A. Copyright in a work is not infringed by the lending of copies of the work by an educational establishment.

Libraries and archives

Libraries and archives: introductory

37. – (1) In sections 38 to 43 (copying by librarians and archivists) –
  (a) references in any provision to a prescribed library or archive are to a library or archive of a description prescribed for the purposes of that provision by regulations made by the Secretary of State; and
  (b) references in any provision to the prescribed conditions are to the conditions so prescribed.

(2) The regulations may provide that, where a librarian or archivist is required to be satisfied as to any matter before making or supplying a copy of a work –
  (a) he may rely on a signed declaration as to that matter by the person requesting the copy, unless he is aware that it is false in a material particular, and
  (b) in such cases as may be prescribed, he shall not make or supply a copy in the absence of a signed declaration in such form as may be prescribed.

(3) Where a person requesting a copy makes a declaration which is false in a material particular and is supplied with a copy which would have been an infringing copy if made by him –
  (a) he is liable for infringement of copyright as if he had made the copy himself, and
  (b) the copy shall be treated as an infringing copy.

(4) The regulations may make different provision for different descriptions of libraries or archives and for different purposes.

(5) Regulations shall be made by statutory instrument which shall be subject to annulment in pursuance of a resolution of either House of Parliament.

(6) References in this section, and in sections 38 to 43, to the librarian or archivist include a person acting on his behalf.

Copying by librarians: articles in periodicals

38. – (1) The librarian of a prescribed library may, if the prescribed conditions are complied with, make and supply a copy of an article in a periodical without infringing any copyright in the text, in any illustrations accompanying the text or in the typographical arrangement.
(2) The prescribed conditions shall include the following –
    (a) that copies are supplied only to persons satisfying the librarian that they require them for the purposes of –
(i) research for a non-commercial purpose, or
(ii) private study,
    and will not use them for any other purpose;
    (b) that no person is furnished with more than one copy of the same article or with copies of more than one article contained in the same issue of a periodical; and
    (c) that persons to whom copies are supplied are required to pay for them a sum not less than the cost (including a contribution to the general expenses of the library) attributable to their production.

Copying by librarians: parts of published works

39. – (1) The librarian of a prescribed library may, if the prescribed conditions are complied with, make and supply from a published edition a copy of part of a literary, dramatic or musical work (other than an article in a periodical) without infringing any copyright in the work, in any illustrations accompanying the work or in the typographical arrangement.
(2) The prescribed conditions shall include the following –
    (a) that copies are supplied only to persons satisfying the librarian that they require them for the purposes of –
(i) research for a non-commercial purpose, or
(ii) private study,
    and will not use them for any other purpose;
    (b) that no person is furnished with more than one copy of the same material or with a copy of more than a reasonable proportion of any work; and
    (c) that persons to whom copies are supplied are required to pay for them a sum not less than the cost (including a contribution to the general expenses of the library) attributable to their production.

Restriction on production of multiple copies of the same material

40. – (1) Regulations for the purposes of sections 38 and 39 (copying by librarian of article or part of published work) shall contain provision to the effect that a copy shall be supplied only to a person satisfying the librarian that his requirement is not related to any similar requirement of another person.

(2) The regulations may provide –
    (a) that requirements shall be regarded as similar if the requirements are for copies of substantially the same material at substantially the same time and for substantially the same purpose; and
    (b) that requirements of persons shall be regarded as related if those persons receive instruction to which the material is relevant at the same time and place.

Lending of copies by libraries or archives

40A. – (1) Copyright in a work of any description is not infringed by the lending of a book by a public library if the book is within the public lending right scheme. For this purpose –
    (a) "the public lending right scheme" means the scheme in force under section 1 of the Public Lending Right Act 1979, and
    (b) a book is within the public lending right scheme if it is a book within the meaning of the provisions of the scheme relating to eligibility, whether or not it is in fact eligible.

(2) Copyright in a work is not infringed by the lending of copies of the work by a prescribed library or archive (other than a public library) which is not conducted for profit.

Copying by librarians: supply of copies to other libraries

41. – (1) The librarian of a prescribed library may, if the prescribed conditions are complied with, make and supply to another prescribed library a copy of –
    (a) an article in a periodical, or
    (b) the whole or part of a published edition of a literary, dramatic or musical work,
without infringing any copyright in the text of the article or, as the case may be, in the work, in any illustrations accompanying it or in the typographical arrangement.

(2) Subsection (1)(b) does not apply if at the time the copy is made the librarian making it knows, or could by reasonable inquiry ascertain,

the name and address of a person entitled to authorise the making of the copy.

Copying by librarians or archivists: replacement copies of works

42. – (1) The librarian or archivist of a prescribed library or archive may, if the prescribed conditions are complied with, make a copy from any item in the permanent collection of the library or archive –
- (a) in order to preserve or replace that item by placing the copy in its permanent collection in addition to or in place of it, or
- (b) in order to replace in the permanent collection of another prescribed library or archive an item which has been lost, destroyed or damaged,

without infringing the copyright in any literary, dramatic or musical work, in any illustrations accompanying such a work or, in the case of a published edition, in the typographical arrangement.

(2) The prescribed conditions shall include provision for restricting the making of copies to cases where it is not reasonably practicable to purchase a copy of the item in question to fulfil that purpose.

Copying by librarians or archivists: certain unpublished works

43. – (1) The librarian or archivist of a prescribed library or archive may, if the prescribed conditions are complied with, make and supply a copy of the whole or part of a literary, dramatic or musical work from a document in the library or archive without infringing any copyright in the work or any illustrations accompanying it.

(2) This section does not apply if –
- (a) the work had been published before the document was deposited in the library or archive, or
- (b) the copyright owner has prohibited copying of the work,

and at the time the copy is made the librarian or archivist making it is, or ought to be, aware of that fact.

(3) The prescribed conditions shall include the following –
- (a) that copies are supplied only to persons satisfying the librarian or archivist that they require them for the purposes of –
  - (i) research for a non-commercial purpose, or
  - (ii) private study,

  and will not use them for any other purpose;
- (b) that no person is furnished with more than one copy of the same material; and

(c) that persons to whom copies are supplied are required to pay for them a sum not less than the cost (including a contribution to the general expenses of the library or archive) attributable to their production.

Copy of work required to be made as condition of export

44. If an article of cultural or historical importance or interest cannot lawfully be exported from the United Kingdom unless a copy of it is made and deposited in an appropriate library or archive, it is not an infringement of copyright to make that copy.

Legal deposit libraries

44A. – (1) Copyright is not infringed by the copying of a work from the internet by a deposit library or person acting on its behalf if –

(a) the work is of a description prescribed by regulations under section 10(5) of the 2003 Act,

(b) its publication on the internet, or a person publishing it there, is connected with the United Kingdom in a manner so prescribed, and

(c) the copying is done in accordance with any conditions so prescribed.

(2) Copyright is not infringed by the doing of anything in relation to relevant material permitted to be done under regulations under section 7 of the 2003 Act.

(3) The Secretary of State may by regulations make provision excluding, in relation to prescribed activities done in relation to relevant material, the application of such of the provisions of this Chapter as are prescribed.

(4) Regulations under subsection (3) may in particular make provision prescribing activities –

(a) done for a prescribed purpose,

(b) done by prescribed descriptions of reader,

(c) done in relation to prescribed descriptions of relevant material,

(d) done other than in accordance with prescribed conditions.

(5) Regulations under this section may make different provision for different purposes.

(6) Regulations under this section shall be made by statutory instrument which shall be subject to annulment in pursuance of a resolution of either House of Parliament.

(7) In this section –

(a) "the 2003 Act" means the Legal Deposit Libraries Act 2003;

(b) "deposit library", "reader" and "relevant material" have the same meaning as in section 7 of the 2003 Act;

(c) "prescribed" means prescribed by regulations made by the Secretary of State.

Public administration

Parliamentary and judicial proceedings

45. – (1) Copyright is not infringed by anything done for the purposes of parliamentary or judicial proceedings.

(2) Copyright is not infringed by anything done for the purposes of reporting such proceedings; but this shall not be construed as authorising the copying of a work which is itself a published report of the proceedings.

Royal Commissions and statutory inquiries

46. – (1) Copyright is not infringed by anything done for the purposes of the proceedings of a Royal Commission or statutory inquiry.

(2) Copyright is not infringed by anything done for the purpose of reporting any such proceedings held in public; but this shall not be construed as authorising the copying of a work which is itself a published report of the proceedings.

(3) Copyright in a work is not infringed by the issue to the public of copies of the report of a Royal Commission or statutory inquiry containing the work or material from it.

(4) In this section –

"Royal Commission" includes a Commission appointed for Northern Ireland by the Secretary of State in pursuance of the prerogative powers of Her Majesty delegated to him under section 7(2) of the Northern Ireland Constitution Act 1973; and

"statutory inquiry" means an inquiry held or investigation conducted in pursuance of a duty imposed or power conferred by or under an enactment.

Material open to public inspection or on official register

47. – (1) Where material is open to public inspection pursuant to a statutory requirement, or is on a statutory register, any copyright in the material as a literary work is not infringed by the copying of so much of the material as contains factual information of any description, by or with the authority of the appropriate person, for a purpose which does not involve the issuing of copies to the public.

(2) Where material is open to public inspection pursuant to a statutory requirement, copyright is not infringed by the copying or issuing to the public of copies of the material, by or with the authority of the appropriate person, for the purpose of enabling the material to be inspected at a more convenient time or place or otherwise facilitating the exercise of any right for the purpose of which the requirement is imposed.

(3) Where material which is open to public inspection pursuant to a statutory requirement, or which is on a statutory register, contains information about matters of general scientific, technical, commercial or economic interest, copyright is not infringed by the copying or issuing to the public of copies of the material, by or with the authority of the appropriate person, for the purpose of disseminating that information.

(4) The Secretary of State may by order provide that subsection (1), (2) or (3) shall, in such cases as may be specified in the order, apply only to copies marked in such manner as may be so specified.

(5) The Secretary of State may by order provide that subsections (1) to (3) apply, to such extent and with such modifications as may be specified in the order –

    (a) to material made open to public inspection by –
    (i) an international organisation specified in the order, or
    (ii) a person so specified who has functions in the United Kingdom under an international agreement to which the United Kingdom is party, or
    (b) to a register maintained by an international organisation specified in the order,

as they apply in relation to material open to public inspection pursuant to a statutory requirement or to a statutory register.

(6) In this section –

"appropriate person" means the person required to make the material open to public inspection or, as the case may be, the person maintaining the register;

"statutory register" means a register maintained in pursuance of a statutory requirement; and

"statutory requirement" means a requirement imposed by provision made by or under an enactment.

(7) An order under this section shall be made by statutory instrument which shall be subject to annulment in pursuance of a resolution of either House of Parliament.

Material communicated to the Crown in the course of public business

48. – (1) This section applies where a literary, dramatic, musical or artistic work has in the course of public business been communicated to the Crown for any purpose, by or with the licence of the copyright owner and a document or other material thing recording or embodying the work is owned by or in the custody or control of the Crown.

(2) The Crown may, for the purpose for which the work was communicated to it, or any related purpose which could reasonably have been anticipated by the copyright owner, copy the work and issue copies of the work to the public without infringing any copyright in the work.

(3) The Crown may not copy a work, or issue copies of a work to the public, by virtue of this section if the work has previously been published otherwise than by virtue of this section.

(4) In subsection (1) "public business" includes any activity carried on by the Crown.

(5) This section has effect subject to any agreement to the contrary between the Crown and the copyright owner.

(6) In this section "the Crown" includes a health service body, as defined in section 60(7) of the National Health Service and Community Care Act 1990, the Commission for Health Improvement, a Primary Care Trust established under section 16A of the National Health Service Act 1977, and a National Health Service trust established under Part I of that Act or the National Health Service (Scotland) Act 1978 and an NHS foundation trust and also includes a health and social services body, as defined in Article 7(6) of the Health and Personal Social Services (Northern Ireland) Order 1991, and a Health and Social Services trust established under that Order; and the reference in subsection (1) above to public business shall be construed accordingly.

Public records

49. Material which is comprised in public records within the meaning of the Public Records Act 1958, the Public Records (Scotland) Act 1937 or the Public Records Act (Northern Ireland) 1923, or in Welsh public records (as defined in the Government of Wales Act 1998), which are open to public inspection in pursuance of that Act, may be copied, and a copy may be supplied to any person, by or with the authority of any officer appointed under that Act, without infringement of copyright.

Acts done under statutory authority

50. – (1) Where the doing of a particular act is specifically authorised by an Act of Parliament, whenever passed, then, unless the Act provides otherwise, the doing of that act does not infringe copyright.

(2) Subsection (1) applies in relation to an enactment contained in Northern Ireland legislation as it applies in relation to an Act of Parliament.

(3) Nothing in this section shall be construed as excluding any defence of statutory authority otherwise available under or by virtue of any enactment.

Computer programs: lawful users

Back up copies

50A. – (1) It is not an infringement of copyright for a lawful user of a copy of a computer program to make any back up copy of it which it is necessary for him to have for the purposes of his lawful use.

(2) For the purposes of this section and sections 50B, 50BA and 50C a person is a lawful user of a computer program if (whether under a licence to do any acts restricted by the copyright in the program or otherwise), he has a right to use the program.

(3) Where an act is permitted under this section, it is irrelevant whether or not there exists any term or condition in an agreement which purports to prohibit or restrict the act (such terms being, by virtue of section 296A, void).

Decompilation

50B. – (1) It is not an infringement of copyright for a lawful user of a copy of a computer program expressed in a low level language –
  (a) to convert it into a version expressed in a higher level language, or
  (b) incidentally in the course of so converting the program, to copy it,
(that is, to "decompile" it), provided that the conditions in subsection (2) are met.

(2) The conditions are that –
  (a) it is necessary to decompile the program to obtain the information necessary to create an independent program which can be operated with the program decompiled or with another program ("the permitted objective"); and
  (b) the information so obtained is not used for any purpose other than the permitted objective.

(3) In particular, the conditions in subsection (2) are not met if the lawful user –

(a) has readily available to him the information necessary to achieve the permitted objective;
(b) does not confine the decompiling to such acts as are necessary to achieve the permitted objective;
(c) supplies the information obtained by the decompiling to any person to whom it is not necessary to supply it in order to achieve the permitted objective; or
(d) uses the information to create a program which is substantially similar in its expression to the program decompiled or to do any act restricted by copyright.

(4) Where an act is permitted under this section, it is irrelevant whether or not there exists any term or condition in an agreement which purports to prohibit or restrict the act (such terms being, by virtue of section 296A, void).

Observing, studying and testing of computer programs

50BA. – (1) It is not an infringement of copyright for a lawful user of a copy of a computer program to observe, study or test the functioning of the program in order to determine the ideas and principles which underlie any element of the program if he does so while performing any of the acts of loading, displaying, running, transmitting or storing the program which he is entitled to do.

(2) Where an act is permitted under this section, it is irrelevant whether or not there exists any term or condition in an agreement which purports to prohibit or restrict the act (such terms being, by virtue of section 296A, void).

Other acts permitted to lawful users

50C. – (1) It is not an infringement of copyright for a lawful user of a copy of a computer program to copy or adapt it, provided that the copying or adapting –
(a) is necessary for his lawful use; and
(b) is not prohibited under any term or condition of an agreement regulating the circumstances in which his use is lawful.

(2) It may, in particular, be necessary for the lawful use of a computer program to copy it or adapt it for the purpose of correcting errors in it.

(3) This section does not apply to any copying or adapting permitted under section 50A, 50B or 50BA.

Databases: permitted acts

Acts permitted in relation to databases

50D. – (1) It is not an infringement of copyright in a database for a person who has a right to use the database or any part of the database, (whether under a licence to do any of the acts restricted by the copyright in the database or otherwise) to do, in the exercise of that right, anything which is necessary for the purposes of access to and use of the contents of the database or of that part of the database.

(2) Where an act which would otherwise infringe copyright in a database is permitted under this section, it is irrelevant whether or not there exists any term or condition in any agreement which purports to prohibit or restrict the act (such terms being, by virtue of section 296B, void).

Designs

Design documents and models

51. – (1) It is not an infringement of any copyright in a design document or model recording or embodying a design for anything other than an artistic work or a typeface to make an article to the design or to copy an article made to the design.

(2) Nor is it an infringement of the copyright to issue to the public, or include in a film or communicate to the public, anything the making of which was, by virtue of subsection (1), not an infringement of that copyright.

(3) In this section –

"design" means the design of any aspect of the shape or configuration (whether internal or external) of the whole or part of an article, other than surface decoration; and

"design document" means any record of a design, whether in the form of a drawing, a written description, a photograph, data stored in a computer or otherwise.

Effect of exploitation of design derived from artistic work

52. – (1) This section applies where an artistic work has been exploited, by or with the licence of the copyright owner, by –

(a) making by an industrial process articles falling to be treated for the purposes of this Part as copies of the work, and

(b) marketing such articles, in the United Kingdom or elsewhere.

(2) After the end of the period of 25 years from the end of the calendar year in which such articles are first marketed, the work may be copied by making articles of any description, or doing anything for the purpose of making articles of any description, and anything may be done in relation to articles so made, without infringing copyright in the work.

(3) Where only part of an artistic work is exploited as mentioned in subsection (1), subsection (2) applies only in relation to that part.

(4) The Secretary of State may by order make provision –

(a) as to the circumstances in which an article, or any description of article, is to be regarded for the purposes of this section as made by an industrial process;

(b) excluding from the operation of this section such articles of a primarily literary or artistic character as he thinks fit.

(5) An order shall be made by statutory instrument which shall be subject to annulment in pursuance of a resolution of either House of Parliament.

(6) In this section –

(a) references to articles do not include films; and

(b) references to the marketing of an article are to its being sold or let for hire or offered or exposed for sale or hire.

Things done in reliance on registration of design

53. – (1) The copyright in an artistic work is not infringed by anything done –

(a) in pursuance of an assignment or licence made or granted by a person registered under the Registered Designs Act 1949 as the proprietor of a corresponding design, and

(b) in good faith in reliance on the registration and without notice of any proceedings for the cancellation or invalidation of the registration or for rectifying the relevant entry in the register of designs;

and this is so notwithstanding that the person registered as the proprietor was not the proprietor of the design for the purposes of the 1949 Act.

(2) In subsection (1) a "corresponding design", in relation to an artistic work, means a design within the meaning of the 1949 Act which if applied

to an article would produce something which would be treated for the purposes of this Part as a copy of the artistic work.

Typefaces

Use of typeface in ordinary course of printing

54. – (1) It is not an infringement of copyright in an artistic work consisting of the design of a typeface –
>   (a) to use the typeface in the ordinary course of typing, composing text, typesetting or printing,
>   (b) to possess an article for the purpose of such use, or
>   (c) to do anything in relation to material produced by such use;

and this is so notwithstanding that an article is used which is an infringing copy of the work.

(2) However, the following provisions of this Part apply in relation to persons making, importing or dealing with articles specifically designed or adapted for producing material in a particular typeface, or possessing such articles for the purpose of dealing with them, as if the production of material as mentioned in subsection (1) did infringe copyright in the artistic work consisting of the design of the typeface –

>   section 24 (secondary infringement: making, importing, possessing or dealing with article for making infringing copy),
>   sections 99 and 100 (order for delivery up and right of seizure),
>   section 107(2) (offence of making or possessing such an article), and
>   section 108 (order for delivery up in criminal proceedings).

(3) The references in subsection (2) to "dealing with" an article are to selling, letting for hire, or offering or exposing for sale or hire, exhibiting in public, or distributing.

Articles for producing material in particular typeface

55. – (1) This section applies to the copyright in an artistic work consisting of the design of a typeface where articles specifically designed or adapted for producing material in that typeface have been marketed by or with the licence of the copyright owner.

(2) After the period of 25 years from the end of the calendar year in which the first such articles are marketed, the work may be copied by making further such articles, or doing anything for the purpose of making such articles, and anything may be done in relation to articles so made, without infringing copyright in the work.

(3) In subsection (1) "marketed" means sold, let for hire or offered or exposed for sale or hire, in the United Kingdom or elsewhere.

Works in electronic form

Transfers of copies of works in electronic form

56. – (1) This section applies where a copy of a work in electronic form has been purchased on terms which, expressly or impliedly or by virtue of any rule of law, allow the purchaser to copy the work, or to adapt it or make copies of an adaptation, in connection with his use of it.

(2) If there are no express terms –
- (a) prohibiting the transfer of the copy by the purchaser, imposing obligations which continue after a transfer, prohibiting the assignment of any licence or terminating any licence on a transfer, or
- (b) providing for the terms on which a transferee may do the things which the purchaser was permitted to do,

anything which the purchaser was allowed to do may also be done without infringement of copyright by a transferee; but any copy, adaptation or copy of an adaptation made by the purchaser which is not also transferred shall be treated as an infringing copy for all purposes after the transfer.

(3) The same applies where the original purchased copy is no longer usable and what is transferred is a further copy used in its place.

(4) The above provisions also apply on a subsequent transfer, with the substitution for references in subsection (2) to the purchaser of references to the subsequent transferor.

Miscellaneous: literary, dramatic, musical and artistic works

Anonymous or pseudonymous works: acts permitted on assumptions as to expiry of copyright or death of author

57. – (1) Copyright in a literary, dramatic, musical or artistic work is not infringed by an act done at a time when, or in pursuance of arrangements made at a time when –
- (a) it is not possible by reasonable inquiry to ascertain the identity of the author, and
- (b) it is reasonable to assume –
(i) that copyright has expired, or
(ii) that the author died 70 years or more before the beginning of the calendar year in which the act is done or the arrangements are made.

(2) Subsection (1)(b)(ii) does not apply in relation to –
   (a) a work in which Crown copyright subsists, or
   (b) a work in which copyright originally vested in an international organisation by virtue of section 168 and in respect of which an Order under that section specifies a copyright period longer than 70 years.
(3) In relation to a work of joint authorship –
   (a) the reference in subsection (1) to its being possible to ascertain the identity of the author shall be construed as a reference to its being possible to ascertain the identity of any of the authors, and
   (b) the reference in subsection (1)(b)(ii) to the author having died shall be construed as a reference to all the authors having died.

Use of notes or recordings of spoken words in certain cases

58. – (1) Where a record of spoken words is made, in writing or otherwise, for the purpose –
   (a) of reporting current events, or
   (b) of communicating to the public the whole or part of the work,
it is not an infringement of any copyright in the words as a literary work to use the record or material taken from it (or to copy the record, or any such material, and use the copy) for that purpose, provided the following conditions are met.
(2) The conditions are that –
   (a) the record is a direct record of the spoken words and is not taken from a previous record or from a broadcast;
   (b) the making of the record was not prohibited by the speaker and, where copyright already subsisted in the work, did not infringe copyright;
   (c) the use made of the record or material taken from it is not of a kind prohibited by or on behalf of the speaker or copyright owner before the record was made; and
   (d) the use is by or with the authority of a person who is lawfully in possession of the record.

Public reading or recitation

59. – (1) The reading or recitation in public by one person of a reasonable extract from a published literary or dramatic work does not infringe any copyright in the work if it is accompanied by a sufficient acknowledgement.
(2) Copyright in a work is not infringed by the making of a sound recording or communication to the public, of a reading or recitation

which by virtue of subsection (1) does not infringe copyright in the work, provided that the recording or communication to the public consists mainly of material in relation to which it is not necessary to rely on that subsection.

Abstracts of scientific or technical articles

60. – (1) Where an article on a scientific or technical subject is published in a periodical accompanied by an abstract indicating the contents of the article, it is not an infringement of copyright in the abstract, or in the article, to copy the abstract or issue copies of it to the public.

(2) This section does not apply if or to the extent that there is a licensing scheme certified for the purposes of this section under section 143 providing for the grant of licences.

Recordings of folksongs

61. – (1) A sound recording of a performance of a song may be made for the purpose of including it in an archive maintained by a designated body without infringing any copyright in the words as a literary work or in the accompanying musical work, provided the conditions in subsection (2) below are met.

(2) The conditions are that –
    (a) the words are unpublished and of unknown authorship at the time the recording is made,
    (b) the making of the recording does not infringe any other copyright, and
    (c) its making is not prohibited by any performer.

(3) Copies of a sound recording made in reliance on subsection (1) and included in an archive maintained by a designated body may, if the prescribed conditions are met, be made and supplied by the archivist without infringing copyright in the recording or the works included in it.

(4) The prescribed conditions shall include the following –
    (a) that copies are only supplied to persons satisfying the archivist that they require them for the purposes of –
        (i) research for a non-commercial purpose, or
        (ii) private study,
        and will not use them for any other purpose, and
    (b) that no person is furnished with more than one copy of the same recording.

(5) In this section –
    (a) "designated" means designated for the purposes of this section by order of the Secretary of State, who shall not designate a body unless satisfied that it is not established or conducted for profit,

(b) "prescribed" means prescribed for the purposes of this section by order of the Secretary of State, and

(c) references to the archivist include a person acting on his behalf.

(6) An order under this section shall be made by statutory instrument which shall be subject to annulment in pursuance of a resolution of either House of Parliament.

Representation of certain artistic works on public display

62. – (1) This section applies to –
  (a) buildings, and
  (b) sculptures, models for buildings and works of artistic craftsmanship, if permanently situated in a public place or in premises open to the public.

(2) The copyright in such a work is not infringed by –
  (a) making a graphic work representing it,
  (b) making a photograph or film of it, or
  (c) making a broadcast of a visual image of it.

(3) Nor is the copyright infringed by the issue to the public of copies, or communication to the public, of anything whose making was, by virtue of this section, not an infringement of the copyright.

Advertisement of sale of artistic work

63. – (1) It is not an infringement of copyright in an artistic work to copy it, or to issue copies to the public, for the purpose of advertising the sale of the work.

(2) Where a copy which would otherwise be an infringing copy is made in accordance with this section but is subsequently dealt with for any other purpose, it shall be treated as an infringing copy for the purposes of that dealing, and if that dealing infringes copyright for all subsequent purposes.

For this purpose "dealt with" means sold or let for hire, offered or exposed for sale or hire, exhibited in public, distributed or communicated to the public.

Making of subsequent works by same artist

64. Where the author of an artistic work is not the copyright owner, he does not infringe the copyright by copying the work in making another artistic work, provided he does not repeat or imitate the main design of the earlier work.

Reconstruction of buildings

65. Anything done for the purposes of reconstructing a building does not infringe any copyright –
   (a) in the building, or
   (b) in any drawings or plans in accordance with which the building was, by or with the licence of the copyright owner, constructed.

Miscellaneous: lending of works and playing of sound recordings

Lending to public of copies of certain works

66. – (1) The Secretary of State may by order provide that in such cases as may be specified in the order the lending to the public of copies of literary, dramatic, musical or artistic works, sound recordings or films shall be treated as licensed by the copyright owner subject only to the payment of such reasonable royalty or other payment as may be agreed or determined in default of agreement by the Copyright Tribunal.

(2) No such order shall apply if, or to the extent that, there is a licensing scheme certified for the purposes of this section under section 143 providing for the grant of licences.

(3) An order may make different provision for different cases and may specify cases by reference to any factor relating to the work, the copies lent, the lender or the circumstances of the lending.

(4) An order shall be made by statutory instrument; and no order shall be made unless a draft of it has been laid before and approved by a resolution of each House of Parliament.

(5) Nothing in this section affects any liability under section 23 (secondary infringement: possessing or dealing with infringing copy) in respect of the lending of infringing copies.

Miscellaneous: films and sound recordings

Films: acts permitted on assumptions as to expiry of copyright, & c

66A. – (1) Copyright in a film is not infringed by an act done at a time when, or in pursuance of arrangements made at a time when –
   (a) it is not possible by reasonable inquiry to ascertain the identity of any of the persons referred to in section 13B(2)(a) to (d)

(persons by reference to whose life the copyright period is ascertained), and
(b) it is reasonable to assume –
(i) that copyright has expired, or
(ii) that the last to die of those persons died 70 years or more before the beginning of the calendar year in which the act is done or the arrangements are made.
(2) Subsection (1)(b)(ii) does not apply in relation to –
(a) a film in which Crown copyright subsists, or
(b) a film in which copyright originally vested in an international organisation by virtue of section 168 and in respect of which an Order under that section specifies a copyright period longer than 70 years.

Playing of sound recordings for purposes of club, society, & c

67. – (1) It is not an infringement of the copyright in a sound recording to play it as part of the activities of, or for the benefit of, a club, society or other organisation if the following conditions are met.
(2) The conditions are –
(a) that the organisation is not established or conducted for profit and its main objects are charitable or are otherwise concerned with the advancement of religion, education or social welfare, and
(b) that the sound recording is played by a person who is acting primarily and directly for the benefit of the organisation and who is not acting with a view to gain,
(c) that the proceeds of any charge for admission to the place where the recording is to be heard are applied solely for the purposes of the organisation, and
(d) that the proceeds from any goods or services sold by, or on behalf of, the organisation –
(i) in the place where the sound recording is heard, and
(ii) on the occasion when the sound recording is played, are applied solely for the purposes of the organisation.

Miscellaneous: broadcasts

Incidental recording for purposes of broadcast

68. – (1) This section applies where by virtue of a licence or assignment of copyright a person is authorised to broadcast –

(a) a literary, dramatic or musical work, or an adaptation of such a work,
(b) an artistic work, or
(c) a sound recording or film.

(2) He shall by virtue of this section be treated as licensed by the owner of the copyright in the work to do or authorise any of the following for the purposes of the broadcast –

(a) in the case of a literary, dramatic or musical work, or an adaptation of such a work, to make a sound recording or film of the work or adaptation;

(b) in the case of an artistic work, to take a photograph or make a film of the work;

(c) in the case of a sound recording or film, to make a copy of it.

(3) That licence is subject to the condition that the recording, film, photograph or copy in question –

(a) shall not be used for any other purpose, and
(b) shall be destroyed within 28 days of being first used for broadcasting the work.

(4) A recording, film, photograph or copy made in accordance with this section shall be treated as an infringing copy –

(a) for the purposes of any use in breach of the condition mentioned in subsection (3)(a), and

(b) for all purposes after that condition or the condition mentioned in subsection (3)(b) is broken.

Recording for purposes of supervision and control of broadcasts and other services

69. – (1) Copyright is not infringed by the making or use by the British Broadcasting Corporation, for the purpose of maintaining supervision and control over programmes broadcast by them, of recordings of those programmes.

(2) Copyright is not infringed by anything done in pursuance of –

(a) section 167(1) of the Broadcasting Act 1990, section 115(4) or (6) or 117 of the Broadcasting Act 1996 or paragraph 20 of Schedule 12 to the Communications Act 2003;

(b) a condition which, by virtue of section 334(1) of the Communications Act 2003, is included in a licence granted under Part I or III of that Act or Part I or II of the Broadcasting Act 1996; or

(c) a direction given under section 109(2) of the Broadcasting Act 1990 (power of OFCOM to require production of recordings etc).

(d) section 334(3) of the Communications Act 2003.

(3) Copyright is not infringed by the use by OFCOM in connection with the performance of any of their functions under the Broadcasting Act 1990, the Broadcasting Act 1996 or the Communications Act 2003 of –

(a) any recording, script or transcript which is provided to them under or by virtue of any provision of those Acts; or

(b) any existing material which is transferred to them by a scheme made under section 30 of the Communications Act 2003.

(4) In subsection (3), 'existing material' means –

(a) any recording, script or transcript which was provided to the Independent Television Commission or the Radio Authority under or by virtue of any provision of the Broadcasting Act 1990 or the Broadcasting Act 1996; and

(b) any recording or transcript which was provided to the Broadcasting Standards Commission under section 115(4) or (6) or 116(5) of the Broadcasting Act 1996.

Recording for purposes of time-shifting

70. – (1) The making in domestic premises for private and domestic use of a recording of a broadcast solely for the purpose of enabling it to be viewed or listened to at a more convenient time does not infringe any copyright in the broadcast or in any work included in it.

(2) Where a copy which would otherwise be an infringing copy is made in accordance with this section but is subsequently dealt with –

(a) it shall be treated as an infringing copy for the purposes of that dealing; and

(b) if that dealing infringes copyright, it shall be treated as an infringing copy for all subsequent purposes.

(3) In subsection (2), "dealt with" means sold or let for hire, offered or exposed for sale or hire or communicated to the public.

Photographs of broadcasts

71. – (1) The making in domestic premises for private and domestic use of a photograph of the whole or any part of an image forming part of a broadcast, or a copy of such a photograph, does not infringe any copyright in the broadcast or in any film included in it.

(2) Where a copy which would otherwise be an infringing copy is made in accordance with this section but is subsequently dealt with –

(a) it shall be treated as an infringing copy for the purposes of that dealing; and

(b) if that dealing infringes copyright, it shall be treated as an infringing copy for all subsequent purposes.

(3) In subsection (2), "dealt with" means sold or let for hire, offered or exposed for sale or hire or communicated to the public.

Free public showing or playing of broadcast

72. – (1) The showing or playing in public of a broadcast to an audience who have not paid for admission to the place where the broadcast is to be seen or heard does not infringe any copyright in –
  (a) the broadcast;
  (b) any sound recording (except so far as it is an excepted sound recording) included in it; or
  (c) any film included in it.

(1A) For the purposes of this Part an "excepted sound recording" is a sound recording –
  (a) whose author is not the author of the broadcast in which it is included; and
  (b) which is a recording of music with or without words spoken or sung.

(1B) Where by virtue of subsection (1) the copyright in a broadcast shown or played in public is not infringed, copyright in any excepted sound recording included in it is not infringed if the playing or showing of that broadcast in public –
  (a) forms part of the activities of an organisation that is not established or conducted for profit; or
  (b) is necessary for the purposes of –
    (i) repairing equipment for the reception of broadcasts;
    (ii) demonstrating that a repair to such equipment has been carried out; or
    (iii) demonstrating such equipment which is being sold or let for hire or offered or exposed for sale or hire.

(2) The audience shall be treated as having paid for admission to a place –
  (a) if they have paid for admission to a place of which that place forms part; or
  (b) if goods or services are supplied at that place (or a place of which it forms part) –
    (i) at prices which are substantially attributable to the facilities afforded for seeing or hearing the broadcast, or
    (ii) at prices exceeding those usually charged there and which are partly attributable to those facilities.

(3) The following shall not be regarded as having paid for admission to a place –
    (a) persons admitted as residents or inmates of the place;
    (b) persons admitted as members of a club or society where the payment is only for membership of the club or society and the provision of facilities for seeing or hearing broadcasts is only incidental to the main purposes of the club or society.

(4) Where the making of the broadcast was an infringement of the copyright in a sound recording or film, the fact that it was heard or seen in public by the reception of the broadcast shall be taken into account in assessing the damages for that infringement.

Reception and re-transmission of wireless broadcast by cable

73. – (1) This section applies where a wireless broadcast made from a place in the United Kingdom is received and immediately re-transmitted by cable.

(2) The copyright in the broadcast is not infringed –
    (a) if the re-transmission by cable is in pursuance of a relevant requirement, or
    (b) if and to the extent that the broadcast is made for reception in the area in which it is re-transmitted by cable and forms part of a qualifying service.

(3) The copyright in any work included in the broadcast is not infringed if and to the extent that the broadcast is made for reception in the area in which it is re-transmitted by cable; but where the making of the broadcast was an infringement of the copyright in the work, the fact that the broadcast was re-transmitted by cable shall be taken into account in assessing the damages for that infringement.

(4) Where –
    (a) the re-transmission by cable is in pursuance of a relevant requirement, but
    (b) to any extent, the area in which the re-transmission by cable takes place ("the cable area") falls outside the area for reception in which the broadcast is made ("the broadcast area"),
the re-transmission by cable (to the extent that it is provided for so much of the cable area as falls outside the broadcast area) of any work included in the broadcast shall, subject to subsection (5), be treated as licensed by the owner of the copyright in the work, subject only to the payment to him by the person making the broadcast of such reasonable royalty or other payment in respect of the re-transmission by cable of the broadcast

as may be agreed or determined in default of agreement by the Copyright Tribunal.

(5) Subsection (4) does not apply if, or to the extent that, the re-transmission of the work by cable is (apart from that subsection) licensed by the owner of the copyright in the work.

(6) In this section "qualifying service" means, subject to subsection (8), any of the following services –

(a) a regional or national Channel 3 service,

(b) Channel 4, Channel 5 and S4C,

(c) the public teletext service,

(d) S4C Digital, and

(e) the television broadcasting services and teletext service of the British Broadcasting Corporation;

and expressions used in this subsection have the same meanings as in Part 3 of the Communications Act 2003.

(7) In this section 'relevant requirement' means a requirement imposed by a general condition (within the meaning of Chapter 1 of Part 2 of the Communications Act 2003) the setting of which is authorised under section 64 of that Act (must-carry obligations).

(8) The Secretary of State may by order amend subsection (6) so as to add any service to, or remove any service from, the definition of "qualifying service".

(9) The Secretary of State may also by order –

(a) provide that in specified cases subsection (3) is to apply in relation to broadcasts of a specified description which are not made as mentioned in that subsection, or

(b) exclude the application of that subsection in relation to broadcasts of a specified description made as mentioned in that subsection.

(10) Where the Secretary of State exercises the power conferred by subsection (9)(b) in relation to broadcasts of any description, the order may also provide for subsection (4) to apply, subject to such modifications as may be specified in the order, in relation to broadcasts of that description.

(11) An order under this section may contain such transitional provision as appears to the Secretary of State to be appropriate.

(12) An order under this section shall be made by statutory instrument which shall be subject to annulment in pursuance of a resolution of either House of Parliament.

(13) In this section references to re-transmission by cable include the transmission of microwave energy between terrestrial fixed points.

Royalty or other sum payable in pursuance of section 73(4)

73A. – (1) An application to settle the royalty or other sum payable in pursuance of subsection (4) of section 73 (reception and re-transmission of wireless broadcast by cable) may be made to the Copyright Tribunal by the copyright owner or the person making the broadcast.

(2) The Tribunal shall consider the matter and make such order as it may determine to be reasonable in the circumstances.

(3) Either party may subsequently apply to the Tribunal to vary the order, and the Tribunal shall consider the matter and make such order confirming or varying the original order as it may determine to be reasonable in the circumstances.

(4) An application under subsection (3) shall not, except with the special leave of the Tribunal, be made within twelve months from the date of the original order or of the order on a previous application under that subsection.

(5) An order under subsection (3) has effect from the date on which it is made or such later date as may be specified by the Tribunal.

Provision of sub-titled copies of broadcast

74. – (1) A designated body may, for the purpose of providing people who are deaf or hard of hearing, or physically or mentally handicapped in other ways, with copies which are sub-titled or otherwise modified for their special needs, make copies of broadcasts and issue or lend copies to the public, without infringing any copyright in the broadcasts or works included in them.

(2) A "designated body" means a body designated for the purposes of this section by order of the Secretary of State, who shall not designate a body unless he is satisfied that it is not established or conducted for profit.

(3) An order under this section shall be made by statutory instrument which shall be subject to annulment in pursuance of a resolution of either House of Parliament.

(4) This section does not apply if, or to the extent that, there is a licensing scheme certified for the purposes of this section under section 143 providing for the grant of licences.

Recording for archival purposes

75. – (1) A recording of a broadcast of a designated class, or a copy of such a recording, may be made for the purpose of being placed in an archive maintained by a designated body without thereby infringing any copyright in the broadcast or in any work included in it.

(2) In subsection (1) "designated" means designated for the purposes of this section by order of the Secretary of State, who shall not designate a body unless he is satisfied that it is not established or conducted for profit.

(3) An order under this section shall be made by statutory instrument which shall be subject to annulment in pursuance of a resolution of either House of Parliament.

Adaptations

Adaptations

76. An act which by virtue of this Chapter may be done without infringing copyright in a literary, dramatic or musical work does not, where that work is an adaptation, infringe any copyright in the work from which the adaptation was made.

Appendix 2
Copyright, Designs and Patents Act 1988, s. 296ZE and Schedule 5A

296ZE Remedy where effective technological measures prevent permitted acts

(1) In this section –
"permitted act" means an act which may be done in relation to copyright works, notwithstanding the subsistence of copyright, by virtue of a provision of this Act listed in Part 1 of Schedule 5A;
"voluntary measure or agreement" means -
   (a) any measure taken voluntarily by a copyright owner, his exclusive licensee or a person issuing copies of, or communicating to the public, a work other than a computer program, or
   (b) any agreement between a copyright owner, his exclusive licensee or a person issuing copies of, or communicating to the public, a work other than a computer program and another party,
the effect of which is to enable a person to carry out a permitted act.
(2) Where the application of any effective technological measure to a copyright work other than a computer program prevents a person from carrying out a permitted act in relation to that work then that person or a person being a representative of a class of persons prevented from carrying out a permitted act may issue a notice of complaint to the Secretary of State.
(3) Following receipt of a notice of complaint, the Secretary of State may give to the owner of that copyright work or an exclusive licensee such directions as appear to the Secretary of State to be requisite or expedient for the purpose of -
   (a) establishing whether any voluntary measure or agreement relevant to the copyright work the subject of the complaint subsists; or
   (b) (where it is established there is no subsisting voluntary measure or agreement) ensuring that the owner or exclusive licensee of that copyright work makes available to the complainant the means of carrying out the permitted act the subject of the

complaint to the extent necessary to so benefit from that permitted act.

(4) The Secretary of State may also give directions -
   (a) as to the form and manner in which a notice of complaint in subsection (2) may be delivered to him;
   (b) as to the form and manner in which evidence of any voluntary measure or agreement may be delivered to him; and
   (c) generally as to the procedure to be followed in relation to a complaint made under this section;
   and shall publish directions given under this subsection in such manner as in his opinion will secure adequate publicity for them.

(5) It shall be the duty of any person to whom a direction is given under subsection (3)(a) or (b) to give effect to that direction.

(6) The obligation to comply with a direction given under subsection (3)(b) is a duty owed to the complainant or, where the complaint is made by a representative of a class of persons, to that representative and to each person in the class represented; and a breach of the duty is actionable accordingly (subject to the defences and other incidents applying to actions for breach of statutory duty).

(7) Any direction under this section may be varied or revoked by a subsequent direction under this section.

(8) Any direction given under this section shall be in writing.

(9) This section does not apply to copyright works made available to the public on agreed contractual terms in such a way that members of the public may access them from a place and at a time individually chosen by them.

(10) This section applies only where a complainant has lawful access to the protected copyright work, or where the complainant is a representative of a class of persons, where the class of persons have lawful access to the work.

. . .

Schedule 5A: Permitted Acts to which Section 296ZE Applies

section 29 (research and private study)
section 31A (making a single accessible copy for personal use)
section 31B (multiple copies for visually impaired persons)
section 31C (intermediate copies and records)
section 32(1), (2) and (3) (things done for purposes of instruction or examination)

section 35 (recording by educational establishments of broadcasts)

section 36 (reprographic copying by educational establishments of passages from published works)

section 38 (copying by librarians: articles in periodicals)

section 39 (copying by librarians: parts of published works)

section 41 (copying by librarians: supply of copies to other libraries)

section 42 (copying by librarians or archivists: replacement copies of works)

section 43 (copying by librarians or archivists: certain unpublished works)

section 44 (copy of work required to be made as condition of export)

section 45 (Parliamentary and judicial proceedings)

section 46 (Royal Commissions and statutory inquiries)

section 47 (material open to public inspection or on official register)

section 48 (material communicated to the Crown in the course of public business)

section 49 (public records)

section 50 (acts done under statutory authority)

section 61 (recordings of folksongs)

section 68 (incidental recording for purposes of broadcast)

section 69 (recording for purposes of supervision and control of broadcasts)

section 70 (recording for purposes of time-shifting)

section 71 (photographs of broadcasts)

section 74 (provision of sub-titled copies of broadcast)

section 75 (recording for archival purposes)

Appendix 3
Directive 2001/29/EC of the European Parliament and of the Council of 22 May 2001 on the harmonisation of certain aspects of copyright and related rights in the information society

THE EUROPEAN PARLIAMENT AND THE COUNCIL OF THE EUROPEAN UNION,
Having regard to the Treaty establishing the European Community, and in particular Articles 47(2), 55 and 95 thereof,
Having regard to the proposal from the Commission,
Having regard to the opinion of the Economic and Social Committee,
Acting in accordance with the procedure laid down in Article 251 of the Treaty,
Whereas:
(1) The Treaty provides for the establishment of an internal market and the institution of a system ensuring that competition in the internal market is not distorted. Harmonisation of the laws of the Member States on copyright and related rights contributes to the achievement of these objectives.
(2) The European Council, meeting at Corfu on 24 and 25 June 1994, stressed the need to create a general and flexible legal framework at Community level in order to foster the development of the information society in Europe. This requires, inter alia, the existence of an internal market for new products and services. Important Community legislation to ensure such a regulatory framework is already in place or its adoption is well under way. Copyright and related rights play an important role in this context as they protect and stimulate the development and marketing of new products and services and the creation and exploitation of their creative content.
(3) The proposed harmonisation will help to implement the four freedoms of the internal market and relates to compliance with the

European Communities' copyright in the European legislative material reproduced here is acknowledged.

fundamental principles of law and especially of property, including intellectual property, and freedom of expression and the public interest.

(4) A harmonised legal framework on copyright and related rights, through increased legal certainty and while providing for a high level of protection of intellectual property, will foster substantial investment in creativity and innovation, including network infrastructure, and lead in turn to growth and increased competitiveness of European industry, both in the area of content provision and information technology and more generally across a wide range of industrial and cultural sectors. This will safeguard employment and encourage new job creation.

(5) Technological development has multiplied and diversified the vectors for creation, production and exploitation. While no new concepts for the protection of intellectual property are needed, the current law on copyright and related rights should be adapted and supplemented to respond adequately to economic realities such as new forms of exploitation.

(6) Without harmonisation at Community level, legislative activities at national level which have already been initiated in a number of Member States in order to respond to the technological challenges might result in significant differences in protection and thereby in restrictions on the free movement of services and products incorporating, or based on, intellectual property, leading to a refragmentation of the internal market and legislative inconsistency. The impact of such legislative differences and uncertainties will become more significant with the further development of the information society, which has already greatly increased transborder exploitation of intellectual property. This development will and should further increase. Significant legal differences and uncertainties in protection may hinder economies of scale for new products and services containing copyright and related rights.

(7) The Community legal framework for the protection of copyright and related rights must, therefore, also be adapted and supplemented as far as is necessary for the smooth functioning of the internal market. To that end, those national provisions on copyright and related rights which vary considerably from one Member State to another or which cause legal uncertainties hindering the smooth functioning of the internal market and the proper development of the information society in Europe should be adjusted, and inconsistent national responses to the technological developments should be avoided, whilst differences not adversely affecting the functioning of the internal market need not be removed or prevented.

(8) The various social, societal and cultural implications of the information society require that account be taken of the specific features of the content of products and services.

(9) Any harmonisation of copyright and related rights must take as a basis a high level of protection, since such rights are crucial to intellectual creation. Their protection helps to ensure the maintenance and development of creativity in the interests of authors, performers, producers, consumers, culture, industry and the public at large. Intellectual property has therefore been recognised as an integral part of property.

(10) If authors or performers are to continue their creative and artistic work, they have to receive an appropriate reward for the use of their work, as must producers in order to be able to finance this work. The investment required to produce products such as phonograms, films or multimedia products, and services such as "on-demand" services, is considerable. Adequate legal protection of intellectual property rights is necessary in order to guarantee the availability of such a reward and provide the opportunity for satisfactory returns on this investment.

(11) A rigorous, effective system for the protection of copyright and related rights is one of the main ways of ensuring that European cultural creativity and production receive the necessary resources and of safeguarding the independence and dignity of artistic creators and performers.

(12) Adequate protection of copyright works and subject-matter of related rights is also of great importance from a cultural standpoint. Article 151 of the Treaty requires the Community to take cultural aspects into account in its action.

(13) A common search for, and consistent application at European level of, technical measures to protect works and other subject-matter and to provide the necessary information on rights are essential insofar as the ultimate aim of these measures is to give effect to the principles and guarantees laid down in law.

(14) This Directive should seek to promote learning and culture by protecting works and other subject-matter while permitting exceptions or limitations in the public interest for the purpose of education and teaching.

(15) The Diplomatic Conference held under the auspices of the World Intellectual Property Organisation (WIPO) in December 1996 led to the adoption of two new Treaties, the "WIPO Copyright Treaty" and the "WIPO Performances and Phonograms Treaty", dealing respectively with the protection of authors and the protection of performers and phonogram producers. Those Treaties update the international

protection for copyright and related rights significantly, not least with regard to the so-called "digital agenda", and improve the means to fight piracy world-wide. The Community and a majority of Member States have already signed the Treaties and the process of making arrangements for the ratification of the Treaties by the Community and the Member States is under way. This Directive also serves to implement a number of the new international obligations.

(16) Liability for activities in the network environment concerns not only copyright and related rights but also other areas, such as defamation, misleading advertising, or infringement of trademarks, and is addressed horizontally in Directive 2000/31/EC of the European Parliament and of the Council of 8 June 2000 on certain legal aspects of information society services, in particular electronic commerce, in the internal market ("Directive on electronic commerce"), which clarifies and harmonises various legal issues relating to information society services including electronic commerce. This Directive should be implemented within a timescale similar to that for the implementation of the Directive on electronic commerce, since that Directive provides a harmonised framework of principles and provisions relevant inter alia to important parts of this Directive. This Directive is without prejudice to provisions relating to liability in that Directive.

(17) It is necessary, especially in the light of the requirements arising out of the digital environment, to ensure that collecting societies achieve a higher level of rationalisation and transparency with regard to compliance with competition rules.

(18) This Directive is without prejudice to the arrangements in the Member States concerning the management of rights such as extended collective licences.

(19) The moral rights of rightholders should be exercised according to the legislation of the Member States and the provisions of the Berne Convention for the Protection of Literary and Artistic Works, of the WIPO Copyright Treaty and of the WIPO Performances and Phonograms Treaty. Such moral rights remain outside the scope of this Directive.

(20) This Directive is based on principles and rules already laid down in the Directives currently in force in this area, in particular Directives 91/250/EEC, 92/100/EEC, 93/83/EEC, 93/98/EEC and 96/9/EC, and it develops those principles and rules and places them in the context of the information society. The provisions of this Directive should be without prejudice to the provisions of those Directives, unless otherwise provided in this Directive.

(21) This Directive should define the scope of the acts covered by the reproduction right with regard to the different beneficiaries. This should be done in conformity with the acquis communautaire. A broad definition of these acts is needed to ensure legal certainty within the internal market.

(22) The objective of proper support for the dissemination of culture must not be achieved by sacrificing strict protection of rights or by tolerating illegal forms of distribution of counterfeited or pirated works.

(23) This Directive should harmonise further the author's right of communication to the public. This right should be understood in a broad sense covering all communication to the public not present at the place where the communication originates. This right should cover any such transmission or retransmission of a work to the public by wire or wireless means, including broadcasting. This right should not cover any other acts.

(24) The right to make available to the public subject-matter referred to in Article 3(2) should be understood as covering all acts of making available such subject-matter to members of the public not present at the place where the act of making available originates, and as not covering any other acts.

(25) The legal uncertainty regarding the nature and the level of protection of acts of on-demand transmission of copyright works and subject-matter protected by related rights over networks should be overcome by providing for harmonised protection at Community level. It should be made clear that all rightholders recognised by this Directive should have an exclusive right to make available to the public copyright works or any other subject-matter by way of interactive on-demand transmissions. Such interactive on-demand transmissions are characterised by the fact that members of the public may access them from a place and at a time individually chosen by them.

(26) With regard to the making available in on-demand services by broadcasters of their radio or television productions incorporating music from commercial phonograms as an integral part thereof, collective licensing arrangements are to be encouraged in order to facilitate the clearance of the rights concerned.

(27) The mere provision of physical facilities for enabling or making a communication does not in itself amount to communication within the meaning of this Directive.

(28) Copyright protection under this Directive includes the exclusive right to control distribution of the work incorporated in a tangible

article. The first sale in the Community of the original of a work or copies thereof by the rightholder or with his consent exhausts the right to control resale of that object in the Community. This right should not be exhausted in respect of the original or of copies thereof sold by the rightholder or with his consent outside the Community. Rental and lending rights for authors have been established in Directive 92/100/EEC. The distribution right provided for in this Directive is without prejudice to the provisions relating to the rental and lending rights contained in Chapter I of that Directive.

(29) The question of exhaustion does not arise in the case of services and on-line services in particular. This also applies with regard to a material copy of a work or other subject-matter made by a user of such a service with the consent of the rightholder. Therefore, the same applies to rental and lending of the original and copies of works or other subject-matter which are services by nature. Unlike CD-ROM or CD-I, where the intellectual property is incorporated in a material medium, namely an item of goods, every on-line service is in fact an act which should be subject to authorisation where the copyright or related right so provides.

(30) The rights referred to in this Directive may be transferred, assigned or subject to the granting of contractual licences, without prejudice to the relevant national legislation on copyright and related rights.

(31) A fair balance of rights and interests between the different categories of rightholders, as well as between the different categories of rightholders and users of protected subject-matter must be safeguarded. The existing exceptions and limitations to the rights as set out by the Member States have to be reassessed in the light of the new electronic environment. Existing differences in the exceptions and limitations to certain restricted acts have direct negative effects on the functioning of the internal market of copyright and related rights. Such differences could well become more pronounced in view of the further development of transborder exploitation of works and cross-border activities. In order to ensure the proper functioning of the internal market, such exceptions and limitations should be defined more harmoniously. The degree of their harmonisation should be based on their impact on the smooth functioning of the internal market.

(32) This Directive provides for an exhaustive enumeration of exceptions and limitations to the reproduction right and the right of communication to the public. Some exceptions or limitations only apply to the reproduction right, where appropriate. This list takes

due account of the different legal traditions in Member States, while, at the same time, aiming to ensure a functioning internal market. Member States should arrive at a coherent application of these exceptions and limitations, which will be assessed when reviewing implementing legislation in the future.

(33) The exclusive right of reproduction should be subject to an exception to allow certain acts of temporary reproduction, which are transient or incidental reproductions, forming an integral and essential part of a technological process and carried out for the sole purpose of enabling either efficient transmission in a network between third parties by an intermediary, or a lawful use of a work or other subject-matter to be made. The acts of reproduction concerned should have no separate economic value on their own. To the extent that they meet these conditions, this exception should include acts which enable browsing as well as acts of caching to take place, including those which enable transmission systems to function efficiently, provided that the intermediary does not modify the information and does not interfere with the lawful use of technology, widely recognised and used by industry, to obtain data on the use of the information. A use should be considered lawful where it is authorised by the rightholder or not restricted by law.

(34) Member States should be given the option of providing for certain exceptions or limitations for cases such as educational and scientific purposes, for the benefit of public institutions such as libraries and archives, for purposes of news reporting, for quotations, for use by people with disabilities, for public security uses and for uses in administrative and judicial proceedings.

(35) In certain cases of exceptions or limitations, rightholders should receive fair compensation to compensate them adequately for the use made of their protected works or other subject-matter. When determining the form, detailed arrangements and possible level of such fair compensation, account should be taken of the particular circumstances of each case. When evaluating these circumstances, a valuable criterion would be the possible harm to the rightholders resulting from the act in question. In cases where rightholders have already received payment in some other form, for instance as part of a licence fee, no specific or separate payment may be due. The level of fair compensation should take full account of the degree of use of technological protection measures referred to in this Directive. In certain situations where the prejudice to the rightholder would be minimal, no obligation for payment may arise.

(36) The Member States may provide for fair compensation for rightholders also when applying the optional provisions on exceptions or limitations which do not require such compensation.

(37) Existing national schemes on reprography, where they exist, do not create major barriers to the internal market. Member States should be allowed to provide for an exception or limitation in respect of reprography.

(38) Member States should be allowed to provide for an exception or limitation to the reproduction right for certain types of reproduction of audio, visual and audio-visual material for private use, accompanied by fair compensation. This may include the introduction or continuation of remuneration schemes to compensate for the prejudice to rightholders. Although differences between those remuneration schemes affect the functioning of the internal market, those differences, with respect to analogue private reproduction, should not have a significant impact on the development of the information society. Digital private copying is likely to be more widespread and have a greater economic impact. Due account should therefore be taken of the differences between digital and analogue private copying and a distinction should be made in certain respects between them.

(39) When applying the exception or limitation on private copying, Member States should take due account of technological and economic developments, in particular with respect to digital private copying and remuneration schemes, when effective technological protection measures are available. Such exceptions or limitations should not inhibit the use of technological measures or their enforcement against circumvention.

(40) Member States may provide for an exception or limitation for the benefit of certain non-profit making establishments, such as publicly accessible libraries and equivalent institutions, as well as archives. However, this should be limited to certain special cases covered by the reproduction right. Such an exception or limitation should not cover uses made in the context of on-line delivery of protected works or other subject-matter. This Directive should be without prejudice to the Member States' option to derogate from the exclusive public lending right in accordance with Article 5 of Directive 92/100/EEC. Therefore, specific contracts or licences should be promoted which, without creating imbalances, favour such establishments and the disseminative purposes they serve.

(41) When applying the exception or limitation in respect of ephemeral recordings made by broadcasting organisations it is understood that

a broadcaster's own facilities include those of a person acting on behalf of and under the responsibility of the broadcasting organisation.

(42) When applying the exception or limitation for non-commercial educational and scientific research purposes, including distance learning, the non-commercial nature of the activity in question should be determined by that activity as such. The organisational structure and the means of funding of the establishment concerned are not the decisive factors in this respect.

(43) It is in any case important for the Member States to adopt all necessary measures to facilitate access to works by persons suffering from a disability which constitutes an obstacle to the use of the works themselves, and to pay particular attention to accessible formats.

(44) When applying the exceptions and limitations provided for in this Directive, they should be exercised in accordance with international obligations. Such exceptions and limitations may not be applied in a way which prejudices the legitimate interests of the rightholder or which conflicts with the normal exploitation of his work or other subject-matter. The provision of such exceptions or limitations by Member States should, in particular, duly reflect the increased economic impact that such exceptions or limitations may have in the context of the new electronic environment. Therefore, the scope of certain exceptions or limitations may have to be even more limited when it comes to certain new uses of copyright works and other subject-matter.

(45) The exceptions and limitations referred to in Article 5(2), (3) and (4) should not, however, prevent the definition of contractual relations designed to ensure fair compensation for the rightholders insofar as permitted by national law.

(46) Recourse to mediation could help users and rightholders to settle disputes. The Commission, in cooperation with the Member States within the Contact Committee, should undertake a study to consider new legal ways of settling disputes concerning copyright and related rights.

(47) Technological development will allow rightholders to make use of technological measures designed to prevent or restrict acts not authorised by the rightholders of any copyright, rights related to copyright or the sui generis right in databases. The danger, however, exists that illegal activities might be carried out in order to enable or facilitate the circumvention of the technical protection provided by these measures. In order to avoid fragmented legal approaches that could potentially hinder the functioning of the internal market, there

is a need to provide for harmonised legal protection against circumvention of effective technological measures and against provision of devices and products or services to this effect.

(48) Such legal protection should be provided in respect of technological measures that effectively restrict acts not authorised by the rightholders of any copyright, rights related to copyright or the sui generis right in databases without, however, preventing the normal operation of electronic equipment and its technological development. Such legal protection implies no obligation to design devices, products, components or services to correspond to technological measures, so long as such device, product, component or service does not otherwise fall under the prohibition of Article 6. Such legal protection should respect proportionality and should not prohibit those devices or activities which have a commercially significant purpose or use other than to circumvent the technical protection. In particular, this protection should not hinder research into cryptography.

(49) The legal protection of technological measures is without prejudice to the application of any national provisions which may prohibit the private possession of devices, products or components for the circumvention of technological measures.

(50) Such a harmonised legal protection does not affect the specific provisions on protection provided for by Directive 91/250/EEC. In particular, it should not apply to the protection of technological measures used in connection with computer programs, which is exclusively addressed in that Directive. It should neither inhibit nor prevent the development or use of any means of circumventing a technological measure that is necessary to enable acts to be undertaken in accordance with the terms of Article 5(3) or Article 6 of Directive 91/250/EEC. Articles 5 and 6 of that Directive exclusively determine exceptions to the exclusive rights applicable to computer programs.

(51) The legal protection of technological measures applies without prejudice to public policy, as reflected in Article 5, or public security. Member States should promote voluntary measures taken by rightholders, including the conclusion and implementation of agreements between rightholders and other parties concerned, to accommodate achieving the objectives of certain exceptions or limitations provided for in national law in accordance with this Directive. In the absence of such voluntary measures or agreements within a reasonable period of time, Member States should take appropriate measures to ensure that rightholders provide beneficiaries of such exceptions or limitations with appropriate means of benefiting

from them, by modifying an implemented technological measure or by other means. However, in order to prevent abuse of such measures taken by rightholders, including within the framework of agreements, or taken by a Member State, any technological measures applied in implementation of such measures should enjoy legal protection.

(52) When implementing an exception or limitation for private copying in accordance with Article 5(2)(b), Member States should likewise promote the use of voluntary measures to accommodate achieving the objectives of such exception or limitation. If, within a reasonable period of time, no such voluntary measures to make reproduction for private use possible have been taken, Member States may take measures to enable beneficiaries of the exception or limitation concerned to benefit from it. Voluntary measures taken by rightholders, including agreements between rightholders and other parties concerned, as well as measures taken by Member States, do not prevent rightholders from using technological measures which are consistent with the exceptions or limitations on private copying in national law in accordance with Article 5(2)(b), taking account of the condition of fair compensation under that provision and the possible differentiation between various conditions of use in accordance with Article 5(5), such as controlling the number of reproductions. In order to prevent abuse of such measures, any technological measures applied in their implementation should enjoy legal protection.

(53) The protection of technological measures should ensure a secure environment for the provision of interactive on-demand services, in such a way that members of the public may access works or other subject-matter from a place and at a time individually chosen by them. Where such services are governed by contractual arrangements, the first and second subparagraphs of Article 6(4) should not apply. Non-interactive forms of online use should remain subject to those provisions.

(54) Important progress has been made in the international standardisation of technical systems of identification of works and protected subject-matter in digital format. In an increasingly networked environment, differences between technological measures could lead to an incompatibility of systems within the Community. Compatibility and interoperability of the different systems should be encouraged. It would be highly desirable to encourage the development of global systems.

(55) Technological development will facilitate the distribution of works, notably on networks, and this will entail the need for rightholders to

identify better the work or other subject-matter, the author or any other rightholder, and to provide information about the terms and conditions of use of the work or other subject-matter in order to render easier the management of rights attached to them. Rightholders should be encouraged to use markings indicating, in addition to the information referred to above, inter alia their authorisation when putting works or other subject-matter on networks.

(56) There is, however, the danger that illegal activities might be carried out in order to remove or alter the electronic copyright-management information attached to it, or otherwise to distribute, import for distribution, broadcast, communicate to the public or make available to the public works or other protected subject-matter from which such information has been removed without authority. In order to avoid fragmented legal approaches that could potentially hinder the functioning of the internal market, there is a need to provide for harmonised legal protection against any of these activities.

(57) Any such rights-management information systems referred to above may, depending on their design, at the same time process personal data about the consumption patterns of protected subject-matter by individuals and allow for tracing of on-line behaviour. These technical means, in their technical functions, should incorporate privacy safeguards in accordance with Directive 95/46/EC of the European Parliament and of the Council of 24 October 1995 on the protection of individuals with regard to the processing of personal data and the free movement of such data.

(58) Member States should provide for effective sanctions and remedies for infringements of rights and obligations as set out in this Directive. They should take all the measures necessary to ensure that those sanctions and remedies are applied. The sanctions thus provided for should be effective, proportionate and dissuasive and should include the possibility of seeking damages and/or injunctive relief and, where appropriate, of applying for seizure of infringing material.

(59) In the digital environment, in particular, the services of intermediaries may increasingly be used by third parties for infringing activities. In many cases such intermediaries are best placed to bring such infringing activities to an end. Therefore, without prejudice to any other sanctions and remedies available, rightholders should have the possibility of applying for an injunction against an intermediary who carries a third party's infringement of a protected work or other subject-matter in a network. This possibility should be available even where the acts carried out by the intermediary are exempted under Article 5. The conditions and modalities relating to such injunctions should be left to the national law of the Member States.

(60) The protection provided under this Directive should be without prejudice to national or Community legal provisions in other areas, such as industrial property, data protection, conditional access, access to public documents, and the rule of media exploitation chronology, which may affect the protection of copyright or related rights.
(61) In order to comply with the WIPO Performances and Phonograms Treaty, Directives 92/100/EEC and 93/98/EEC should be amended, HAVE ADOPTED THIS DIRECTIVE:

Chapter I
Objective and Scope

Article 1 Scope

1. This Directive concerns the legal protection of copyright and related rights in the framework of the internal market, with particular emphasis on the information society.
2. Except in the cases referred to in Article 11, this Directive shall leave intact and shall in no way affect existing Community provisions relating to:
   (a) the legal protection of computer programs;
   (b) rental right, lending right and certain rights related to copyright in the field of intellectual property;
   (c) copyright and related rights applicable to broadcasting of programmes by satellite and cable retransmission;
   (d) the term of protection of copyright and certain related rights;
   (e) the legal protection of databases.

Chapter II
Rights and Exceptions

Article 2 Reproduction right

Member States shall provide for the exclusive right to authorise or prohibit direct or indirect, temporary or permanent reproduction by any means and in any form, in whole or in part:
(a) for authors, of their works;
(b) for performers, of fixations of their performances;
(c) for phonogram producers, of their phonograms;
(d) for the producers of the first fixations of films, in respect of the original and copies of their films;

(e) for broadcasting organisations, of fixations of their broadcasts, whether those broadcasts are transmitted by wire or over the air, including by cable or satellite.

Article 3 Right of communication to the public of works and right of making available to the public other subject-matter

1. Member States shall provide authors with the exclusive right to authorise or prohibit any communication to the public of their works, by wire or wireless means, including the making available to the public of their works in such a way that members of the public may access them from a place and at a time individually chosen by them.
2. Member States shall provide for the exclusive right to authorise or prohibit the making available to the public, by wire or wireless means, in such a way that members of the public may access them from a place and at a time individually chosen by them:
   (a) for performers, of fixations of their performances;
   (b) for phonogram producers, of their phonograms;
   (c) for the producers of the first fixations of films, of the original and copies of their films;
   (d) for broadcasting organisations, of fixations of their broadcasts, whether these broadcasts are transmitted by wire or over the air, including by cable or satellite.
3. The rights referred to in paragraphs 1 and 2 shall not be exhausted by any act of communication to the public or making available to the public as set out in this Article.

Article 4 Distribution right

1. Member States shall provide for authors, in respect of the original of their works or of copies thereof, the exclusive right to authorise or prohibit any form of distribution to the public by sale or otherwise.
2. The distribution right shall not be exhausted within the Community in respect of the original or copies of the work, except where the first sale or other transfer of ownership in the Community of that object is made by the rightholder or with his consent.

Article 5 Exceptions and limitations

1. Temporary acts of reproduction referred to in Article 2, which are transient or incidental [and] an integral and essential part of a technological process and whose sole purpose is to enable:
   (a) a transmission in a network between third parties by an intermediary, or
   (b) a lawful use

of a work or other subject-matter to be made, and which have no independent economic significance, shall be exempted from the reproduction right provided for in Article 2.
2. Member States may provide for exceptions or limitations to the reproduction right provided for in Article 2 in the following cases:
   (a) in respect of reproductions on paper or any similar medium, effected by the use of any kind of photographic technique or by some other process having similar effects, with the exception of sheet music, provided that the rightholders receive fair compensation;
   (b) in respect of reproductions on any medium made by a natural person for private use and for ends that are neither directly nor indirectly commercial, on condition that the rightholders receive fair compensation which takes account of the application or non-application of technological measures referred to in Article 6 to the work or subject-matter concerned;
   (c) in respect of specific acts of reproduction made by publicly accessible libraries, educational establishments or museums, or by archives, which are not for direct or indirect economic or commercial advantage;
   (d) in respect of ephemeral recordings of works made by broadcasting organisations by means of their own facilities and for their own broadcasts; the preservation of these recordings in official archives may, on the grounds of their exceptional documentary character, be permitted;
   (e) in respect of reproductions of broadcasts made by social institutions pursuing non-commercial purposes, such as hospitals or prisons, on condition that the rightholders receive fair compensation.
3. Member States may provide for exceptions or limitations to the rights provided for in Articles 2 and 3 in the following cases:
   (a) use for the sole purpose of illustration for teaching or scientific research, as long as the source, including the author's name, is indicated, unless this turns out to be impossible and to the extent justified by the non-commercial purpose to be achieved;
   (b) uses, for the benefit of people with a disability, which are directly related to the disability and of a non-commercial nature, to the extent required by the specific disability;
   (c) reproduction by the press, communication to the public or making available of published articles on current economic, political or religious topics or of broadcast works or other subject-matter of the same character, in cases where such use is not expressly

reserved, and as long as the source, including the author's name, is indicated, or use of works or other subject-matter in connection with the reporting of current events, to the extent justified by the informatory purpose and as long as the source, including the author's name, is indicated, unless this turns out to be impossible;

(d) quotations for purposes such as criticism or review, provided that they relate to a work or other subject-matter which has already been lawfully made available to the public, that, unless this turns out to be impossible, the source, including the author's name, is indicated, and that their use is in accordance with fair practice, and to the extent required by the specific purpose;

(e) use for the purposes of public security or to ensure the proper performance or reporting of administrative, parliamentary or judicial proceedings;

(f) use of political speeches as well as extracts of public lectures or similar works or subject-matter to the extent justified by the informatory purpose and provided that the source, including the author's name, is indicated, except where this turns out to be impossible;

(g) use during religious celebrations or official celebrations organised by a public authority;

(h) use of works, such as works of architecture or sculpture, made to be located permanently in public places;

(i) incidental inclusion of a work or other subject-matter in other material;

(j) use for the purpose of advertising the public exhibition or sale of artistic works, to the extent necessary to promote the event, excluding any other commercial use;

(k) use for the purpose of caricature, parody or pastiche;

(l) use in connection with the demonstration or repair of equipment;

(m) use of an artistic work in the form of a building or a drawing or plan of a building for the purposes of reconstructing the building;

(n) use by communication or making available, for the purpose of research or private study, to individual members of the public by dedicated terminals on the premises of establishments referred to in paragraph 2(c) of works and other subject-matter not subject to purchase or licensing terms which are contained in their collections;

(o) use in certain other cases of minor importance where exceptions or limitations already exist under national law, provided that they only concern analogue uses and do not affect the free circulation of goods and services within the Community, without prejudice to the other exceptions and limitations contained in this Article.

4. Where the Member States may provide for an exception or limitation to the right of reproduction pursuant to paragraphs 2 and 3, they may provide similarly for an exception or limitation to the right of distribution as referred to in Article 4 to the extent justified by the purpose of the authorised act of reproduction.
5. The exceptions and limitations provided for in paragraphs 1, 2, 3 and 4 shall only be applied in certain special cases which do not conflict with a normal exploitation of the work or other subject-matter and do not unreasonably prejudice the legitimate interests of the rightholder.

Chapter III
Protection of Technological Measures and Rights-Management Information

Article 6 Obligations as to technological measures

1. Member States shall provide adequate legal protection against the circumvention of any effective technological measures, which the person concerned carries out in the knowledge, or with reasonable grounds to know, that he or she is pursuing that objective.
2. Member States shall provide adequate legal protection against the manufacture, import, distribution, sale, rental, advertisement for sale or rental, or possession for commercial purposes of devices, products or components or the provision of services which:
   (a) are promoted, advertised or marketed for the purpose of circumvention of, or
   (b) have only a limited commercially significant purpose or use other than to circumvent, or
   (c) are primarily designed, produced, adapted or performed for the purpose of enabling or facilitating the circumvention of,
   any effective technological measures.
3. For the purposes of this Directive, the expression "technological measures" means any technology, device or component that, in the normal course of its operation, is designed to prevent or restrict acts, in respect of works or other subject-matter, which are not authorised by the rightholder of any copyright or any right related to copyright as provided for by law or the sui generis right provided for in Chapter III of Directive 96/9/EC. Technological measures shall be deemed "effective" where the use of a protected work or other subject-matter is controlled by the rightholders through application of an access control or protection process, such as encryption, scrambling

or other transformation of the work or other subject-matter or a copy control mechanism, which achieves the protection objective.
4. Notwithstanding the legal protection provided for in paragraph 1, in the absence of voluntary measures taken by rightholders, including agreements between rightholders and other parties concerned, Member States shall take appropriate measures to ensure that rightholders make available to the beneficiary of an exception or limitation provided for in national law in accordance with Article 5(2)(a), (2)(c), (2)(d), (2)(e), (3)(a), (3)(b) or (3)(e) the means of benefiting from that exception or limitation, to the extent necessary to benefit from that exception or limitation and where that beneficiary has legal access to the protected work or subject-matter concerned.

A Member State may also take such measures in respect of a beneficiary of an exception or limitation provided for in accordance with Article 5(2)(b), unless reproduction for private use has already been made possible by rightholders to the extent necessary to benefit from the exception or limitation concerned and in accordance with the provisions of Article 5(2)(b) and (5), without preventing rightholders from adopting adequate measures regarding the number of reproductions in accordance with these provisions.

The technological measures applied voluntarily by rightholders, including those applied in implementation of voluntary agreements, and technological measures applied in implementation of the measures taken by Member States, shall enjoy the legal protection provided for in paragraph 1.

The provisions of the first and second subparagraphs shall not apply to works or other subject-matter made available to the public on agreed contractual terms in such a way that members of the public may access them from a place and at a time individually chosen by them.

When this Article is applied in the context of Directives 92/100/EEC and 96/9/EC, this paragraph shall apply mutatis mutandis.

Article 7 Obligations concerning rights-management information

1. Member States shall provide for adequate legal protection against any person knowingly performing without authority any of the following acts:
   (a) the removal or alteration of any electronic rights-management information;
   (b) the distribution, importation for distribution, broadcasting, communication or making available to the public of works or other subject-matter protected under this Directive or under Chapter III

of Directive 96/9/EC from which electronic rights-management information has been removed or altered without authority,

if such person knows, or has reasonable grounds to know, that by so doing he is inducing, enabling, facilitating or concealing an infringement of any copyright or any rights related to copyright as provided by law, or of the sui generis right provided for in Chapter III of Directive 96/9/EC.

2. For the purposes of this Directive, the expression "rights-management information" means any information provided by rightholders which identifies the work or other subject-matter referred to in this Directive or covered by the sui generis right provided for in Chapter III of Directive 96/9/EC, the author or any other rightholder, or information about the terms and conditions of use of the work or other subject-matter, and any numbers or codes that represent such information.

The first subparagraph shall apply when any of these items of information is associated with a copy of, or appears in connection with the communication to the public of, a work or other subject-matter referred to in this Directive or covered by the sui generis right provided for in Chapter III of Directive 96/9/EC.

Chapter IV
Common Provisions

Article 8 Sanctions and remedies

1. Member States shall provide appropriate sanctions and remedies in respect of infringements of the rights and obligations set out in this Directive and shall take all the measures necessary to ensure that those sanctions and remedies are applied. The sanctions thus provided for shall be effective, proportionate and dissuasive.
2. Each Member State shall take the measures necessary to ensure that rightholders whose interests are affected by an infringing activity carried out on its territory can bring an action for damages and/or apply for an injunction and, where appropriate, for the seizure of infringing material as well as of devices, products or components referred to in Article 6(2).
3. Member States shall ensure that rightholders are in a position to apply for an injunction against intermediaries whose services are used by a third party to infringe a copyright or related right.

Article 9 Continued application of other legal provisions

This Directive shall be without prejudice to provisions concerning in particular patent rights, trade marks, design rights, utility models, topographies of semi-conductor products, type faces, conditional access, access to cable of broadcasting services, protection of national treasures, legal deposit requirements, laws on restrictive practices and unfair competition, trade secrets, security, confidentiality, data protection and privacy, access to public documents, the law of contract.

Article 10 Application over time . . .

Article 11 Technical adaptations . . .

Article 12 Final provisions

1. Not later than 22 December 2004 and every three years thereafter, the Commission shall submit to the European Parliament, the Council and the Economic and Social Committee a report on the application of this Directive, in which, inter alia, on the basis of specific information supplied by the Member States, it shall examine in particular the application of Articles 5, 6 and 8 in the light of the development of the digital market. In the case of Article 6, it shall examine in particular whether that Article confers a sufficient level of protection and whether acts which are permitted by law are being adversely affected by the use of effective technological measures. Where necessary, in particular to ensure the functioning of the internal market pursuant to Article 14 of the Treaty, it shall submit proposals for amendments to this Directive.
. . .

Article 13 Implementation

1. Member States shall bring into force the laws, regulations and administrative provisions necessary to comply with this Directive before 22 December 2002. They shall forthwith inform the Commission thereof.
. . .

Article 14 Entry into force . . .

Article 15 Addressees

This Directive is addressed to the Member States.

Done at Brussels, 22 May 2001.

Appendix 4
United States Copyright Act 1976, 17 USC, s. 107

§ 107. Limitations on exclusive rights: Fair use

Notwithstanding the provisions of sections 106 and 106A, the fair use of a copyrighted work, including such use by reproduction in copies or phonorecords or by any other means specified by that section, for purposes such as criticism, comment, news reporting, teaching (including multiple copies for classroom use), scholarship, or research, is not an infringement of copyright. In determining whether the use made of a work in any particular case is a fair use the factors to be considered shall include –
(1) the purpose and character of the use, including whether such use is of a commercial nature or is for nonprofit educational purposes;
(2) the nature of the copyrighted work;
(3) the amount and substantiality of the portion used in relation to the copyrighted work as a whole; and
(4) the effect of the use upon the potential market for or value of the copyrighted work.
    The fact that a work is unpublished shall not itself bar a finding of fair use if such finding is made upon consideration of all the above factors.

Bibliography

SECONDARY SOURCES AND OFFICIAL REPORTS AND SIMILAR DOCUMENTS

Adams, J., 'Small Earthquake in Venezuela: The Database Regulations 1997' [1998] EIPR 129
  'The Reporting Exception: Does It Still Exist?' [1999] EIPR 383
Adelstein, R. and S. Peretz, 'The Competition of Technologies in Markets for Ideas: Copyright and Fair Use in Evolutionary Perspective' (1985) 5 *International Review of Law and Economics* 209
Adeney, E., 'The Moral Right of Integrity of Authorship: A Comparative View of Australia's Proposals to Date' (1998) 9 AIPJ 179
  'Authors' Rights in Works of Public Sculpture: A German/Australian Perspective' (2002) 33 IIC 164
Africa, M., 'The Misuse of Licensing Evidence in Fair Use Analysis: New Technologies, New Markets and the Courts' (2000) 88 *California Law Review* 1145
Allan, T., 'Parliamentary Sovereignty: Law, Politics, and Revolution' (1997) 113 *Law Quarterly Review* 443
Allen, D. and R. Jensen (eds.), *Freeing the First Amendment* (New York: New York University Press, 1995)
Alter, K., 'Resolving or Exacerbating Disputes? The WTO's New Dispute Resolution System' (2003) 79 *International Affairs* 783
Aman, A., 'Globalization, Democracy, and the Need for a New Administrative Law' (2002) 49 *UCLA Law Review* 1687
Ames, E., 'Beyond *Rogers* v. *Koons*: A Fair Use Standard for Appropriation' (1993) 93 *Columbia Law Review* 1473
Anassutzi, M., 'E-Commerce Directive 00/31' (2002) 13 *International Company and Commercial Law Review* 337
Anderson, D., 'Compensation for Interference with Property' [1999] *European Human Rights Law Review* 543
Anderson, G., 'Corporations, Democracy and the Implied Freedom of Political Communication: Towards a Pluralistic Analysis of Constitutional Law' (1998) 22 *Melbourne University Law Review* 1
Anderson, Margaret and A. Reeves, 'Contested Identities: Museums and the Nation in Australia', in F. Kaplan (ed.), *Museums and the Making of 'Ourselves': The Role of Objects in National Identity* (London: Leicester University Press, 1994)

Anderson, Mark, 'Applying Traditional Property Laws to Intellectual Property Transactions' [1995] EIPR 236

Anderson, Michael and P. Brown, 'The Economics Behind Copyright Fair Use: A Principled and Predictable Body of Law' (1993) 24 *Loyola University of Chicago Law Journal* 143

Anderson, Michael, P. Brown and A. Cores, 'Market Substitution and Copyrights: Predicting Fair Use Case Law' (1993) 10 *University of Miami Entertainment and Sports Law Review* 33

Antill, J. and P. Coles, 'Copyright Duration: The European Community Adopts Three Score Years and Ten' [1996] EIPR 379

Aoki, K., 'Adrift in the Intertext: Authorship and Audience "Recoding" Rights – Comments on Robert H. Rotstein, "Beyond Metaphor: Copyright Infringement and the Fiction of the Work"' (1993) 68 *Chicago-Kent Law Review* 805

Aquinas, St Thomas, *Summa Theologica*, trans. T. Gilby, Vol. 28 (Cambridge: Blackfriars, 1966)

Archives at the Millennium: The 28th Report of the Royal Commission on Historical Manuscripts 1991–1999 (HMSO, 1999)

Armstrong, K., 'Rediscovering Civil Society: The White Paper on Governance' (2002) 8 *European Law Journal* 102

Arnull, A., A. Dashwood, M. Ross and D. Wyatt, *Wyatt and Dashwood's European Union Law*, 4th edn (London: Sweet & Maxwell, 2000)

Arup, C., *The New World Trade Organisation Agreements: Globalizing Law Through Services and Intellectual Property Agreements* (Cambridge: Cambridge University Press, 2000)

Arup, C., and G. Tucker, 'Information Technology Law and Human Rights' in D. Kinley (ed.), *Human Rights in Australian Law* (Sydney: Federation Press, 1998)

Austin, G., 'Does The Copyright Clause Mandate Isolationism?' (2002) 16 *Columbia Journal of Law and the Arts* 17

'Valuing "Domestic Self-Determination" in International Intellectual Property Jurisprudence' (2002) *Chicago-Kent Law Review* 1155

'Copyright's Modest Ontology – Theory and Pragmatism in Eldred v. Ashcroft' (2003) 16 *Canadian Journal of Law and Jurisprudence* 163

Australian Copyright Council, *Fair Dealing in the Digital Age* (Redfern: Centre for Copyright Studies, 1996)

Copyright in the New Communications Environment: Balancing Protection and Access (Redfern: Centre for Copyright Studies, 1999)

Australian Copyright Law Review Committee, *Simplification of the Copyright Act 1968 Part 1: Exceptions to the Exclusive Rights of Copyright Owners* (Canberra: 1998)

Copyright and Contract (Canberra: 2002)

Australian Senate Select Committee, *Report on a Certain Maritime Incident* (Canberra: 23 October 2002)

Ayers, I., 'The Future of Global Copyright Protection: Has Copyright Law Gone Too Far?' (2000) 62 *University of Pittsburgh Law Review* 49

Ayres, I. and J. Braithwaite, *Responsive Regulation: Transcending the Deregulation Debate* (Oxford: Oxford University Press, 1992)

Bainbridge, D., 'The Copyright (Computer Software) Amendment Act (1985)' (1986) 49 *Modern Law Review* 214
  'Computer Programs and Copyright: More Exceptions to Infringement' (1993) 56 *Modern Law Review* 591
Baker, E., 'First Amendment Limits on Copyright' (2002) 55 *Vanderbilt Law Review* 891
Baker, T., 'The Property Concepts of Copyright Law' (1957) 22 *Missouri Law Review* 200
Band, J., 'The Digital Millennium Copyright Act: A Balanced Result' [1999] EIPR 92
Bangemann Report, *Europe and the Global Information Society – Recommendations of the High-Level Group on the Information Society to the Corfu European Council* (Brussels: European Commission, 1994)
Barach, P. and S. Small, 'Reporting and Preventing Medical Mishaps: Lessons from Non-medical Near Miss Reporting Systems' (2000) 320 *British Medical Journal* 759
Barendt, E., *Freedom of Speech* (Oxford: Clarendon, 1985)
Barendt, E., S. Bate, J. Dickens and T. Gibbons (eds.), *The Yearbook of Media and Entertainment Law 1996* (Oxford: Clarendon, 1996)
Barker, R., *Photocopying Practices in the United Kingdom* (London: Faber & Faber, 1970)
Barlow, J., 'Selling Wine without Bottles: The Economy of Mind on the Global Net', in P. Ludlow (ed.), *High Noon on the Electronic Frontier* (Cambridge, Mass.: MIT Press, 1996)
Barnes, J., *Authors, Publishers and Politicians: The Quest for an Anglo-American Copyright Agreement 1815–1854* (London: Routledge & Kegan Paul, 1974)
Barron, A., 'Copyright Law and the Claims of Art' [2002] IPQ 368
Baxi, U., 'Copyright Law and Justice in India' (1986) 28 *Journal of the Indian Law Institute* 497
Beddard, R., 'Photographs and the Rights of the Individual' (1995) 58 *Modern Law Review* 771
Beier, F. and G. Schricker (eds.), *GATT or WIPO? New Ways in the International Protection of Intellectual Property* (Weinheim: VCH, 1989)
Bell, A., *A Modern Law of Personal Property in England and Ireland* (London: Butterworths, 1989)
Bell, T., 'Fair Use vs. Fared Use: The Impact of Automated Rights Management on Copyright's Fair Use Doctrine' (1998) 76 *North Carolina Law Review* 557
  'Escape from Copyright: Market Success vs. Statutory Failure in the Protection of Expressive Works' (2001) 69 *University of Cincinnati Law Review* 741
Benson, C., 'Fair Dealing in the United Kingdom: *A Clockwork Orange*' [1995] EIPR 304
Bently, L., 'Sampling and Copyright Law: Is the Law on the Right Track? Part 1' [1989] *Journal of Business Law* 113
  'Sampling and Copyright Law: Is the Law on the Right Track? Part 2' [1989] *Journal of Business Law* 405
  'Ultraviolence: Conflicts between Markets and Authors' (1993–4) 4 *King's College Law Journal* 130

'Copyright and the Death of the Author in Literature and Law' (1994) 57 *Modern Law Review* 973

'European and International Copyright Harmonisation: Reflections on the Legal Traditions', paper delivered at the University of Wales, Aberystwyth, March 1997

'Copyright's Futures: To Expand or Contract?' (1999) 1(2) *Digital Technology Law Journal* (online)

Bently, L. and R. Burrell, 'Copyright and the Information Society in Europe: A Matter of Timing as Well as Content' (1997) 34 *Common Market Law Review* 1197

Bently, L. and S. Maniatis (eds.), *Intellectual Property and Ethics*, Perspectives on Intellectual Property 4 (London: Sweet & Maxwell, 1998)

Bently, L. and B. Sherman, 'Cultures of Copying: Digital Sampling and Copyright Law' [1992] EntLR 158

'Great Britain and the Signing of the Berne Convention in 1886' (2001) 48 *Journal of the Copyright Society of the USA* 311

Intellectual Property Law (Oxford: Oxford University Press, 2001)

Berg, M., 'Moral Rights and the Compulsory License for Phonorecords' (1979) 46 *Brooklyn Law Review* 67

Bergne, J., 'Curiosities of Copyright Law' (1888) 4 *Law Quarterly Review* 172

Bettig, R., *Copyrighting Culture: The Political Economy of Intellectual Property Rights* (Boulder: Westview, 1996)

Bettinger, T., 'Trademark Law in Cyberspace – The Battle for Domain Names' (1997) 28 IIC 508

Bhala, R., 'The Precedent Setters: De Facto *Stare Decisis* in WTO Adjudication (1999) 9 *Journal of Transnational Law and Policy* 1

Biagi, R., 'The Intersection of First Amendment Commercial Speech Analysis and the Federal Trademark Dilution Act: A Jurisprudential Roadmap' (2001) 91 *Trademark Reporter* 867

Bien, L., 'Canadian Visual Resources and Canadian Copyright' (1997) 12 *Visual Resources* 421

Birnhack, M., 'The Idea of Progress in Copyright Law' (2001) 1 *Buffalo Intellectual Property Law Journal* 3

Birks, P., 'Personal Property: Proprietary Rights and Remedies' (2000) 11 *King's College Law Journal* 1

Birrell, A., *Seven Lectures on the Law and History of Copyright in Books* (London: Cassell & Co., 1899)

Blackstone, W., *Commentaries on the Laws of England*, Vol. 2, 5th edn (Oxford: Clarendon, 1773)

Blakeney, M., *Trade-Related Aspects of Intellectual Property Rights: A Concise Guide to the TRIPS Agreement* (London: Sweet & Maxwell, 1996)

Blakeney, M. and F. Macmillan, 'Regulating Speech on the Internet' (1999) 1(1) *Digital Technology Law Journal* (online)

Bland, F., *Planning the Modern State: An Introduction to the Problem of Political and Administrative Re-organization* (Sydney: Angus & Robertson, 1945)

Booton, D., 'A Critical Analysis of the European Commission's Proposal for a Directive Harmonising the *Droit de Suite*' [1998] IPQ 165

Bouchard, M., 'Digital Distance Education: A Canadian Perspective', in H. Hansen (ed.), *International Intellectual Property Law and Policy*, Vol. 4 (New York: Juris Publishing, 2000)
Bowrey, K., 'Who's Writing Copyright's History?' [1996] EIPR 323
  'Ethical Boundaries and Internet Cultures', in L. Bently and S. Maniatis (eds.) *Intellectual Property and Ethics*, Perspectives on Intellectual Property 4 (London: Sweet & Maxwell, 1998)
  'The Outer Limits of Copyright Law – Where Law Meets Philosophy and Culture' (2001) 12 *Law and Critique* 75
Boyle, J., *Shamans, Software and Spleens* (Cambridge, Mass.: Harvard University Press, 1996)
  'A Politics of Intellectual Property: Environmentalism for the Net?' (1997) 47 *Duke Law Journal* 87
Bradshaw, D., 'Fair Dealing and the *Clockwork Orange* Case: "A Thieves Charter"?' [1994] EntLR 6
  'Fair Dealing as a Defence to Copyright Infringement in UK Law: An Historical Excursion from 1802 to the *Clockwork Orange* Case 1993' [1995] *Denning Law Journal* 67
  'Copyright, Fair Dealing and the *Mandy Allwood* Case: The Court of Appeal gets the Max out of a Multiple Pregnancy Opportunity' [1999] EntLR 125
Braun, N., 'The Interface between the Protection of Technological Measures and the Exercise of Exceptions to Copyright and Related Rights: Comparing the Situation in the United States and the European Union' [2003] EIPR 496
Brennan, D., 'The Three-Step Test Frenzy – Why the TRIPS Panel Decision Might Be Considered *Per Incuriam*' [2002] IPQ 212
  'Copyright and Parody in Australia: Some Thoughts on *Suntrust Bank* v. *Houghton Mifflin Company*' (2002) 13 AIPJ 161
Breyer, S., 'The Uneasy Case for Copyright: A Study of Copyright in Books, Photocopies, and Computer Programs' (1970) 84 *Harvard Law Review* 281
Bridge, M., *Personal Property Law*, 2nd edn (London: Blackstone, 1996)
British Copyright Council Submission to the European Commission, 'Digital Copyright in the Field of Copyright and Related Rights' [1996] EIPR 52
Brogan, T., 'Fair Use No Longer: How the Digital Millennium Copyright Act Bars Fair Use of Digitally Stored Copyrighted Works' (2002) 16 *Saint John's Journal of Legal Commentary* 691
Browes, R., 'Copyright: Court of Appeal Considers Fair Dealing Defence and Rejects Common Law Defence of Public Interest' [2000] EIPR 289
Brown, A., 'Post-Harmonisation Europe – United, Divided or Unimportant?' [2001] IPQ 275
Brown, I., 'Admixture of Goods in English Law' [1988] *Lloyd's Maritime and Commercial Law Quarterly* 286
Brownsword, R., 'Copyright Assignment, Fair Dealing and Unconscionable Contracts' [1998] IPQ 311
Brytha, G., 'The Justifications for the Protection of Author's Rights as Reflected in their Historical Development' (1992) 151 RIDA 53

Bunker, M., 'Eroding Fair Use: The "Transformative" Use Doctrine After *Campbell*' (2002) 7 *Communication Law and Policy* 1
Burk, D., 'Anticircumvention Misuse' (2003) 50 *UCLA Law Review* 1095
Burk, D. and J. Cohen, 'Fair Use Infrastructure for Rights Management Systems' (2001) 15 *Harvard Journal of Law and Technology* 41
Burkitt, D., 'Copyrighting Culture – The History and Cultural Specificity of the Western Model of Copyright' [2001] IPQ 146
Burrell, R., 'Defending the Public Interest' [2000] EIPR 394
  'The Information Society: Chances and Challenges', in C. Heath and A. Kamperman Sanders (eds.), *Intellectual Property in the Digital Age: Challenges for Asia* (London: Kluwer, 2001)
  'Reining in Copyright Law: Is Fair Use the Answer?' [2001] IPQ 361
  'The Future of Copyright Exceptions' in D. McClean and K. Schubert (eds.), *Dear Images: Art, Copyright and Culture* (London: Ridinghouse, 2002)
Burrell, R. and J. Stellios, 'Fair Dealing and Freedom of Expression in the United Kingdom' (2003) 14 AIPJ 45
Campbell, T., *The Left and Rights: A Conceptual Analysis of the Idea of Socialist Rights* (London: Routledge & Kegan Paul, 1983)
  'Rationales for Freedom of Communication', in T. Campbell and W. Sadurski (eds.), *Freedom of Communication* (Sydney: Dartmouth, 1994)
Campbell, T. and W. Sadurski (eds.), *Freedom of Communication* (Sydney: Dartmouth, 1994)
Cane, P. and M. Tushnet (eds.), *The Oxford Handbook of Legal Studies* (Oxford: Oxford University Press, 2003)
Caron, C., 'Abus de droit et droit d'auteur: une illustration de la confrontation du droit spécial et du droit commun en droit civil français' (1998) 176 RIDA 2
Carter, T., M. Franklin and J. Wright, *The First Amendment and the Fifth Estate: Regulation of Electronic Mass Media*, 5th edn (New York: Foundation Press, 1999)
Caviedes, A., 'International Copyright Law: Should The European Union Dictate Its Development?' (1998) 16 *Boston University International Law Journal* 165
Chadran, R., 'Copyright in Cyberspace: A Singapore Perspective' [2000] *Journal of Business Law* 192
Chafee, Z., 'Reflections on the Law of Copyright I' (1945) 45 *Columbia Law Review* 503
  'Reflections on the Law of Copyright II' (1945) 45 *Columbia Law Review* 719
  'Coming into Equity with Unclean Hands' [I] (1949) 47 *Michigan Law Review* 877
  'Coming into Equity with Unclean Hands' [II] (1949) 47 *Michigan Law Review* 1065
Chakrabarty, D., 'Museums in Late Democracies' (2002) 9 *Humanities Research* 5
Chalton, S., 'The Copyright and Rights in Databases Regulations 1997: Some Outstanding Issues on Implementation of the Database Directive' [1998] EIPR 178

Chanan, M., *Repeated Takes: A Short History of Recording and its Effects on Music* (London: Verso, 1995)
Chester, D. and F. Wilson, *The Organisation of British Central Government*, 2nd edn (London: Allen & Unwin, 1968)
Chisum, D. and M. Jacobs, *Understanding Intellectual Property* (New York: Matthew Bender, 1992)
Christiano, T., *The Rule of the Many* (Boulder: Westview Press, 1996)
Christie, A., 'The UK Design Copyright Exemption' [1989] EIPR 253
   'Reconceptualising Copyright in the Digital Era' [1995] EIPR 522
   'Simplifying Australian Copyright Law – the Why and the How' (2000) 11 AIPJ 40
   'A Proposal for Simplifying United Kingdom Copyright Law' [2001] EIPR 26
Cimino, C., 'Fair Use In the Digital Age: Are We Playing Fair?' (2002) 4 *Tulane Journal of Technology and Intellectual Property* 203
Ciolino, D., 'Rethinking the Compatibility of Moral Rights and Fair Use' (1997) 54 *Washington and Lee Law Review* 33
Coale, A., 'Fair Use: Considerations in the Emerging World of E-Books' (2002) 16 *Saint John's Journal of Legal Commentary* 727
Coble, H., 'Copyright's Past and Its Application to Copyright's Future' (2000) 47 *Journal of the Copyright Society of the USA* 1
Cohen, F., 'Dialogue on Private Property' (1954) 9 *Rutgers Law Review* 357
Cohen, J., 'Copyright and the Jurisprudence of Self-Help' (1998) 13 *Berkeley Technology Law Journal* 1089
   'WIPO Copyright Treaty Implementation in the United States: Will Fair Use Survive?' [1999] EIPR 236
   'Copyright and the Perfect Curve' (2000) 53 *Vanderbilt Law Review* 1799
Coleman, A., *The Legal Protection of Trade Secrets* (London: Sweet & Maxwell, 1992)
   Intellectual Property Law (London: Longman Law, Tax and Finance, 1994)
Coleman, J., *Markets, Morals and the Law* (Cambridge: Cambridge University Press, 1988)
Colston, C., 'Fair Dealing: What is Fair?' [1995] *Denning Law Journal* 91
Comte, H., 'A Step Towards a Copyright Europe' (1993) 158 RIDA 2
Conforti, J., 'Copyright and Freedom of Expression: A Privilege for News Reports' (1989–90) 5 IPJ 103
Conley, J. and J. Szoboscan, 'IP Rights and Competitive Advantage: Snow White Shows the Way' (2001) 110 *Managing Intellectual Property* 33
Coombe, R., *The Cultural Life of Intellectual Properties* (Durham, N.C.: Duke University Press, 1998)
   'Fear, Hope, and Longing for the Future of Authorship and a Revitalized Public Domain in Global Regimes of Intellectual Property' (2003) 52 *DePaul Law Review* 1171
Copinger, W., *The Law of Copyright in Works of Literature and Art*, 2nd edn (London: Stevens and Haynes, 1881)
   Copyright and Visually Impaired People – Consultation Paper (UK Patent Office, 2001)

Cordero, S., 'Cocaine-Cola, the Velvet Elvis, and Anti-Barbie: Defending the Trademark and Publicity Rights to Cultural Icons' (1998) 8 *Fordham Intellectual Property, Media and Entertainment Law Journal* 599

Cornish, G., 'Libraries and the Harmonisation of Copyright' [1998] EIPR 241

   Copyright – Interpreting the Law for Libraries, Archives and Information Services, 3rd edn (London: Library Association Publishing, 1999)

Cornish, W., 'Moral Rights Under the 1988 Act' [1989] EIPR 449

   'Authors in Law' (1995) 58 *Modern Law Review* 1

   'Copyright Across the Quarter Century' (1995) 26 IIC 801

Cornish, W. and D. Llewelyn, *Intellectual Property: Patents Copyright, Trade Marks and Allied Rights*, 5th edn (London: Sweet & Maxwell, 2003)

Correa, C., *Intellectual Property Rights, the WTO and Developing Countries: the TRIPS Agreement and Policy Options* (London: Zed Books, 2000)

   'Fair Use in the Digital Era' (2002) 33 IIC 570

Craig, C., 'Locke, Labour and Limiting the Author's Right: A Warning Against a Lockean Approach to Copyright' (2002) 28 *Queen's Law Journal* 1

Craig, P.,'The Nature of the Community: Integration, Democracy and Legitimacy', in P. Craig and G. de Burca (eds.), *The Evolution of EU Law* (Oxford: Oxford University Press, 1999)

   'Constitutions, Constitutionalism and the European Union' (2001) 7 *European Law Journal* 123

Craig, P. and G. de Burca (eds.), *The Evolution of EU Law* (Oxford: Oxford University Press, 1999)

Crews, K., *Copyright, Fair Use, and the Challenge for Universities: Promoting the Progress of Higher Education* (Chicago: University of Chicago Press, 1993)

Crick, B., *In Defence of Politics*, 4th edn (Harmondsworth: Penguin, 1992)

Curtin, D., *Postnational Democracy: The European Union in Search of a Political Philosophy* (The Hague: Kluwer, 1997)

Cygan, A., 'The White Paper on European Governance – Have Glasnost and Perestroika Finally Arrived to the European Union?' (2002) 65 *Modern Law Review* 229

Davies, G., 'The Public Interest in Collective Administration of Rights' [1989] *Copyright* 81

   Copyright and the Public Interest (Weinheim: VCH, 1994)

   'The Convergence of Copyright and Authors' Rights – Reality or Chimera?' (1995) 26 IIC 964

   'Technical Devices as a Solution to Private Copying', in I. Stamatoudi and P. Torremans (eds.), *Copyright in the New Digital Environment*, Perspectives on Intellectual Property 8 (London: Sweet & Maxwell, 2000)

   Copyright and the Public Interest, 2nd edn (London: Sweet & Maxwell, 2002)

Davies, G. and M. Hung, *Music and Video Private Copying* (London: Sweet & Maxwell, 1993)

Davison, M., 'Some Implications of the US Working Group's Report on Intellectual Property and the National Information Infrastructure' (1995) 6 *Journal of Law and Information Science* 228

'Australian Proposals for Copyright Reform: Some Unresolved Issues and Some Lessons from America' (1999) 1(1) *Digital Technology Law Journal* (online)

The Legal Protection of Databases (Cambridge: Cambridge University Press, 2003)

Deazley, R., 'Re-reading Donaldson (1774) in the Twenty-First Century and Why It Matters' [2003] EIPR 270

De Beer, J., 'Canadian Copyright Law in Cyberspace: An Examination of the Copyright Act in the Context of the Internet' (2000) 63 *Saskatchewan Law Review* 503

De Freitas, D., 'The Main Features of Copyright Protection in the Various Legal Systems' (1986) 28 *Journal of the Indian Law Institute* 441

De Mello, R., *Human Rights Act 1998: A Practical Guide* (Bristol: Jordan, 2000)

Denicola, R., 'Copyright and Free Speech: Constitutional Limitations on the Protection of Expression' (1979) 67 *California Law Review* 283

'Mostly Dead? Copyright Law in the New Millennium' (2000) 47 *Journal of the Copyright Society of the* USA 193

Department for Culture, Media and Sport, *UK Export Licensing for Cultural Goods: Procedures and Guidance for Exporters of Works of Art and Other Cultural Goods*, Issue 5 (28 February 2003)

Depoorter, B. and F. Parisi, 'Fair Use and Copyright Protection: A Price Theory Explanation' (2002) 21 *International Review of Law and Economics* 453

De Zwart, M., 'Seriously Entertaining: *The Panel* and the Future of Fair Dealing' (2003) 8 *Media and Arts Law Review* 1

Dickens, P., 'When Is an Authorisation an Authorisation?' [2000] EIPR 339

Dietl, A., M. Donnseif and V. Grassmuck, 'Germany' (online)

Dietz, A., 'The Protection of Intellectual Property in the Information Age – the Draft EU Copyright Directive of November 1997' [1998] IPQ 335

Dimitrakopoulos, D., 'The Transposition of EU Law: Post-decisional Politics and Institutional Autonomy' (2001) 7 *European Law Journal* 442

Dinwoodie, G., 'The Development and Incorporation of International Norms in the Formation of Copyright Law' (2001) 62 *Ohio State Law Journal* 733

Dixon, A. and M. Hansen, 'The Berne Convention Enters the Digital Age' [1996] EIPR 605

Docker, L., 'The Demise of Fair Dealing' (2000) 17 *Copyright Reporter* 112

Doern, G., *Global Change and Intellectual Property Agencies* (London: Pinter, 1999)

Doherty, M. and I. Griffiths, 'The Harmonisation of European Union Copyright Law for the Digital Age' [2000] EIPR 17

Douglas-Scott, S., *Constitutional Law of the European Union* (Harlow: Pearson Education, 2002)

Dozortsev, I., 'Trends in the Development of Russian Civil Litigation during the Transition to a Market Economy (1993) 19 *Review of Central and East European Law* 513

Drahos, P., 'Decentering Communication: The Dark Side of Intellectual Property', in T. Campbell and W. Sadurski (eds.), *Freedom of Communication* (Sydney: Dartmouth, 1994)

'Global Property Rights in Information: The Story of TRIPS at the GATT' (1995) 13 *Prometheus* 6

A Philosophy of Intellectual Property (Aldershot: Dartmouth, 1996)

'Intellectual Property and Human Rights' [1999] IPQ 349

'BITS and BIPS: Bilateralism in Intellectual Property' (2001) 4 *The Journal of World Intellectual Property* 791

Draper, W., 'Copyright Legislation' (1901) 17 *Law Quarterly Review* 39

Dreier, T., 'The Council Directive of 14 May 1991 on the Legal Protection of Computer Programs' [1991] EIPR 319

'Adjustment of Copyright Law to the Requirements of the Information Society' (1998) 29 IIC 623

Dreyfuss, R. and A. Lowenfeld, 'Two Achievements of the Uruguay Round: Putting TRIPS and Dispute Settlement Together' (1997) 37 *Vanderbilt Journal of International Law* 275

Drone, E., *A Treatise on the Law of Property in Intellectual Productions* (Boston: Little, Brown & Co., 1879)

Duncan, C., 'Art Museums and the Ritual of Citizenship', in I. Karp and S. Levine (eds.), *Exhibiting Cultures: The Poetics and Politics of Museum Display* (Washington: Smithsonian Institution Press, 1991)

Durie, R., 'Information as Property – Copyright and Confidential Information' (1985) 3(2) *Copyright Reporter* 22

Dusollier, S., 'Exceptions and Technological Measures in the European Copyright Directive of 2001 – An Empty Promise' (2003) 34 IIC 62

Duxbury, N., *Patterns of American Jurisprudence* (Oxford: Clarendon, 1997)

Dworkin, G., 'Exceptions to Copyright Exclusivity: Is Fair Use Consistent with Article 9(2) Berne and the New International Order?' in H. Hansen (ed.), *International Intellectual Property Law and Policy*, Vol. 4 (New York: Juris Publishing, 2000)

Dworkin, G. and R. Taylor, *Blackstone's Guide to the Copyright, Designs and Patents Act 1988* (London: Blackstone, 1989)

'By Accident or Design? The Meaning of "Design" under Section 51 CDPA 1988' [1990] EIPR 33

Dworkin, R., *Taking Rights Seriously* (London: Duckworth, 1981)

Law's Empire (London: Fontana, 1991)

Easterbrook, F., 'The Limits of Antitrust' (1984) 63 *Texas Law Review* 1

Easton, J., *The Law of Copyright in Works of Literature, Art, Architecture, Photography, Music and The Drama by the Late Walter Arthur Copinger*, 5th edn (London: Stevens & Haynes, 1915)

Edwards, R., 'Reading Down Legislation Under the Human Rights Acts' (2000) 20 *Legal Studies* 353

Ehrlich, C., *Harmonious Alliance: A History of the Performing Right Society* (Oxford: Oxford University Press, 1989)

Einhorn, M., 'Miss Scarlett's License Done Gone!: Parody, Satire, and Markets' (2002) 20 *Cardozo Arts and Entertainment Law Journal* 589

Eisenstein, M., 'An Economic Analysis of the Fair Use Defense in *Leibovitz v. Paramount Pictures Corporation*' (2000) 148 *University of Pennsylvania Law Review* 889

Elkin-Koren, N., 'Cyberlaw and Social Change: A Democratic Approach to Copyright Law in Cyberspace' (1996) 14 *Cardozo Arts and Entertainment Law Journal* 215

Elkin-Koren, N. and N. Netanel (eds.), *The Commodification of Information* (The Hague: Kluwer Law International, 2002)

Emerson, T., 'Toward a General Theory of the First Amendment' (1963) 72 *Yale Law Journal* 877

  Toward a General Theory of the First Amendment (New York: Random House, 1966)

Emmert, F., 'Intellectual Property in the Uruguay Round – Negotiating Strategies of the Western Industrialised Countries' (1990) 11 *Michigan Journal of International Law* 1317

Endeshaw, A., 'Treating Intellectual Capital as Property: The Vexed Issue' [2001] EIPR 140

Ercolani, S., 'Limitations and Exceptions in the Italian Copyright Legislation' [1999] EntLR 5

Estren, M., *A History of Underground Comics*, 3rd edn (Berkeley: Ronin Press, 1993)

European Bureau of Library, Information and Documentation Associations (EBLIDA) policy statement, *Lifelong Learning, the Role of Archives and Libraries* (2 April 2002)

European Fine Art Foundation (TEFAF), *The European Art Market in 2002: A Survey Follow-Up to the Green Paper on Copyright and Related Rights in the Information Society*, COM(96)final (Brussels: 20 November 1996)

Evans, J., 'Controlling the Use of Parliamentary History' (1998) 18 *New Zealand Universities Law Review* 1

Ezell, M. and K. O'Keeffe (eds.), *Cultural Artifacts and the Production of Meaning: The Page, the Image, and the Body* (Ann Arbor: University of Michigan Press, 1994)

Feather, J., *Publishing, Piracy, and Politics: A Historical Study of Copyright in Britain* (New York: Mansell, 1994)

Feldbruge, F., *Russian Law: The End of the Soviet System and the Role of Law* (Dordrecht: Martinus Nijhoff, 1993)

Felgueroso, J., 'TRIPS and the Dispute Settlement Understanding: The First Six Years' (2002) 30 *AIPLA Quarterly Journal* 165

Fellas, J., 'Laches as a Defence to Trademark and Trade Dress Infringement in the United States' [1999] EIPR 411

Fessenden, G., 'Peer to Peer Technology: Analysis of Contributory Infringement and Fair Use' (2002) 42 *Idea* 391

Fessler, A., 'The Next Frontier: Film Distribution over the Internet' [2000] EntLR 183

Fewer, D., 'Constitutionalizing Copyright: Freedom of Expression and the Limits of Copyright in Canada' (1997) 55 *University of Toronto Faculty Law Review* 175

Finer, S., H. Berrington and D. Bartholomew, *Backbench Opinion in the House of Commons 1955–59* (Oxford: Pergamon Press, 1961)

Firth, A., 'The Criminalisation of Offences Against Intellectual Property', in I. Loveland (ed.), *The Frontiers of Criminality* (London: Sweet & Maxwell, 1995)
Fiscor, M., 'How Much of What? The Three-Step Test and Its Application in Two Recent WTO Dispute Settlement Cases' (2002) 192 RIDA 110
Fisher, W., 'Reconstructing the Fair Use Doctrine' (1988) 101 *Harvard Law Review* 1659
Fitzgerald, B., 'Underlying Rationales of Fair Use: Simplifying the Copyright Act' (1998) 2 *Southern Cross University Law Review* 153
  'Software as Discourse? The Challenge for Information Law' [2000] EIPR 47
  'Commodifying and Transacting Informational Products Through Contractual Licences: The Challenge for Informational Constitutionalism', in C. Rickett and G. Austin (eds.), *International Intellectual Property and the Common Law World* (Oxford: Hart, 2000)
  'Intellectual Property Rights in Digital Architecture (Including Software): The Question of Digital Diversity' [2001] EIPR 121
  '(Australian) Constitutional Limits on Intellectual Property Rights' [2001] EIPR 103
  'Theoretical Underpinning of Intellectual Property: "I Am a Pragmatist but Theory Is My Rhetoric"' (2003) 16 *Canadian Journal of Law and Jurisprudence* 179
Fitzgerald, D., 'Magill Revisited' [1998] EIPR 154
Fitzpatrick, S., 'Copyright Imbalance: US and Australian Responses to the WIPO Digital Copyright Treaty' [2000] EIPR 214
Flinders, M., 'Governance in Whitehall' (2002) 80 *Public Administration* 51
Foged, T., 'US v. EU Anti Circumvention Legislation: Preserving the Public's Privileges in the Digital Age' [2002] EIPR 525
Fox, S., 'The Future of Copyright Enforcement', paper delivered at the conference, 'Shaping the New Agenda: Emerging Issues for Copyright', in Brisbane, 8 February 2002
Franzosi, M. and G. de Sanctis, 'Moral Rights and New Technology: Are Copyrights and Patents Converging?' [1995] EIPR 63
Frantz, L., 'The First Amendment in the Balance' (1962) 71 *Yale Law Journal* 1424
Fraser, M., 'Fair Is Foul and Foul Is Fair: From Analogue to Digital Fair Dealing' (1998) 9 *Journal of Law and Information Science* 93
Fraser, S., 'The Conflict between the First Amendment and Copyright Law and Its Impact on the Internet' (1998) 16 *Cardozo Arts and Entertainment Law Journal* 1
Freedman, W., *Freedom of Speech on Private Property* (New York: Quorum, 1988)
Freegard, M., 'Collective Administration: The Relationship between Authors' Organisations and Users of Works' [1985] *Copyright* 443
  '*Quis Custodiet?* The Role of Copyright Tribunals' [1994] EIPR 286
Friedman, D., 'In Defense of Private Orderings: Comments on Julie Cohen's "Copyright and the Jurisprudence of Self Help"' (1998) 13 *Berkeley Technology Law Journal* 1151

Froomkin, M., 'Anonymity and its Enmities' [1995] *Journal of Online Law* (online)

Fryer, W., *Readings on Personal Property*, 3rd edn (St. Paul: West Publishing, 1938)

Fukumoto, E., 'The Author Effect and the "Death of the Author": Copyright in a Postmodern Age' (1997) 72 *Washington Law Review* 903

Gaffney, F., 'The Fair Use of Unpublished Works: Where Privacy and Copyright Collide' (2001) 24 *Connecticut Law Review* 233

Gana, R., 'Has Creativity Died in the Third World? Some Implications of the Internationalization of Intellectual Property' (1995) 24 *Denver Journal of International Law and Policy* 109

Garben, S. and R. Hoy, 'Fair Dealing: Section 30(1) of the Copyright, Designs and Patents Act 1988 and the Case of *Matisse* v. *Phaidon*', in D. McClean and K. Schubert (eds.), *Dear Images: Art, Copyright and Culture* (London: Ridinghouse, 2002)

Garlick, M., 'Pricing Recorded Music in an Online World' [2000] EntLR 175

Garnett, K. and A. Abbott, 'Who is the "Author" of a Photograph?' [1998] EIPR 204

Garnett, K., J. Rayner James and G. Davies (eds.), *Copinger and Skone James on Copyright*, 14th edn (London: Sweet & Maxwell, 1999)

Garon, J., 'Normative Copyright: A Conceptual Framework for Copyright Philosophy and Ethics' (2003) 88 *Cornell Law Review* 1278

Geddes, A., *Protection of Individual Rights under EC Law* (London: Butterworths, 1995)

Geller, P., 'Can the GATT Incorporate Berne Whole?' [1990] EIPR 423

'Must Copyright Be For Ever Caught between Marketplace and Authorship Norms?', in B. Sherman and A. Strowel (eds.), *Of Authors and Origins* (Oxford: Clarendon, 1994)

'Copyright History and the Future: What's Culture Got To Do with It?' (2000) 47 *Journal of the Copyright Society of the USA* 209

Gendreau, Y., *The Retransmission Right: Copyright and the Rediffusion of Works by Cable* (London: ESC, 1990)

'A Technologically Neutral Solution for the Internet: Is It Wishful Thinking?', in I. Stamatoudi and P. Torremans (eds.), *Copyright in the New Digital Environment*, Perspectives on Intellectual Property 8 (London: Sweet & Maxwell, 2000)

'The Copyright Civilization in Canada' [2000] IPQ 84

Gerdsen, T., *Copyright: A User's Guide* (Collingwood: RMIT Press, 1996)

Gervais, D., 'Digital Distance Education: Exemption or Licensing', in H. Hansen (ed.), *International Intellectual Property Law & Policy*, Vol. 4 (New York: Juris Publishing, 2000)

Ghosh, S., 'Turning Gray into Green: Some Comments on Napster' (2001) 23 *Hastings Communication and Entertainment Law Journal* 563

Gibbons, T., *Regulating the Media* (London: Sweet & Maxwell, 1998)

Gifford, C., 'The Sonny Bono Copyright Term Extension Act' (2000) 30 *University of Memphis Law Review* 363

Gifford, D., 'Innovation and Creativity in the Fine Arts: The Relevance and Irrelevance of Copyright' (2000) 18 *Cardozo Arts and Entertainment Law Journal* 569

Gimeno, L., 'Parody of Songs: A Spanish Case and an International Perspective' [1997] EntLR 18

Ginsburg, J., 'Moral Rights in the Common Law System' [1990] EntLRev 121

'A Tale of Two Copyrights: Literary Property in Revolutionary France and America', in B. Sherman and A. Strowel (eds.), *Of Authors and Origins* (Oxford: Clarendon, 1994)

'Putting Cars on the "Information Superhighway": Authors, Exploiters, and Copyright in Cyberspace' (1995) *Columbia Law Review* 1466

'International Copyright: From a "Bundle" of National Copyright Laws to a Supranational Code?' (2000) 47 *Journal of the Copyright Society of the USA* 265

'Toward Supranational Copyright Law? The WTO Panel Decision and the "Three-Step Test" for Copyright Exceptions' (2001) 187 RIDA 3

'Berne without Borders: Geographic Indiscretion and Digital Communications' [2002] IPQ 111

Glover, J., *Humanity: A Moral History of the Twentieth Century* (London: Pimlico, 2001)

Glover, T., 'The Scope of the Public Interest Defence in Actions for Breach of Confidence' (1999) 6 *James Cook University Law Review* 109

Goebel, L., 'The Role of History in Copyright Dilemmas' (1998) 9 *Journal of Law and Information Science* 22

Goldberg, J., 'Now that the Future Has Arrived Maybe the Law Should Take a Look: Multimedia Technology and Its Interaction with the Fair Use Doctrine' (1995) 44 *American University Law Review* 919

Goldstein, P., 'Preempted State Doctrines, Involuntary Transfers and Compulsory Licenses: Testing the Limits of Copyright' (1977) 24 *UCLA Law Review* 1107

Copyright: Principles, Law and Practice (Boston: Little, Brown, 1989; supplement, 1993)

Copyright's Highway: From Gutenburg to the Celestial Jukebox (New York: Hill & Wang, 1994)

Goldstein, R., *Flag Burning and Free Speech* (Lawrence, Kans.: University Press of Kansas, 2000)

Golvan, C., 'Copyright and Writers: A Study in the Balancing of the Public Interests which Affect the Limits of the Protection Afforded to Literary Works by the Law of Copyright in Australia' [1987] EIPR 66

Goodhart, C., 'Economics and the Law: Too Much One-Way Traffic?' (1997) 60 *Modern Law Review* 1

Gordon, W., 'Fair Use as Market Failure: A Structural and Economic Analysis of the Betamax Case and its Predecessors' (1982) 82 *Columbia Law Review* 1600

'An Inquiry into the Merits of Copyright: The Challenge of Consistency, Consent, and Encouragement Theory' (1989) 41 *Stanford Law Review* 1343

'Reality as Artifact: From Feist to Fair Use' (1992) 55(2) *Law and Contemporary Problems* 93

'A Property Right in Self-Expression: Equality and Individualism in the Natural Law of Intellectual Property' (1993) 102 *Yale Law Journal* 1533

'Market Failure and Intellectual Property: A Response to Professor Lunney' (2002) 82 *Boston University Law Review* 1031

'Excuse and Justification in the Law of Fair Use: Commodification and Market Perspectives', in N. Elkin-Koren and N. Netanel (eds.), *The Commodification of Information* (The Hague: Kluwer Law International, 2002)

Gorman, R., 'Copyright Conflicts on the University Campus' (2000) 47 *Journal of the Copyright Society of the USA* 209

Gray, K. and S. Gray, 'Civil Rights, Civil Wrongs and Quasi-Public Spaces' [1999] *European Human Rights Law Review* 46

Greaves, R., 'Copyright: Public Interest and Statutory Powers under the Competition Act 1980' [1987] EIPR 3

Gredley, E. and S. Maniatis, 'Parody: A Fatal Attraction? Part 1: The Nature of Parody and Its Treatment in Copyright' [1997] EIPR 339

'Parody: A Fatal Attraction? Part 2: Trade Mark Parodies' [1997] EIPR 412

Greenberg, L., 'The Art of Appropriation: Puppies, Piracy and Post-modernism' (1992) 11 *Cardozo Arts and Entertainment Law Journal* 1

Griesdorf, W., 'The Laugh of the Hypertext' (1994–5) 9 IPJ 1

Griffith, J., *Parliamentary Scrutiny of Government Bills* (London: Allen & Unwin, 1974)

Griffith, J. and M. Ryle, *Parliament: Functions, Practice and Procedures* (London: Sweet & Maxwell, 1989)

Griffiths, J., 'Copyright Law and Censorship – The Impact of the Human Rights Act 1998', in E. Barendt and A. Firth (eds.), *Yearbook of Copyright and Media Law, 1999* (Oxford: Oxford University Press, 1999)

'Copyright in English Literature: Denying the Public Domain' [2000] EIPR 150

'Lives and Works – Biography and the Law of Copyright' (2000) 20 *Legal Studies* 485

'Preserving Judicial Freedom of Movement – Interpreting Fair Dealing in Copyright Law' [2000] IPQ 164

'Copyright Law After Ashdown – Time to Deal Fairly with the Public' [2002] IPQ 240

Gros, E., 'Copyright and the Photocopying of Specialist Journals' [1980] EIPR 275

Grossett, J., 'The Wind Done Gone: Transforming Tara into a Plantation Parody' (2002) 52 *Case Western Law Review* 1113

Groves, A., '*Princeton University Press* v. *Michigan Document Services, Inc.*: The Sixth Circuit Frustrates the Constitutional Purpose of Copyright and the Fair Use Doctrine' (1996) 31 *Georgia Law Review* 325

Guest, A., 'Accession and Confusion in the Law of Hire Purchase' (1964) 27 *Modern Law Review* 505

Guibault, L., *Copyright Limitations and Contracts: An Analysis of the Contractual Overridability of Limitations on Copyright* (The Hague: Kluwer Law International, 2002)

Gummow, W., 'International Intellectual Property and the Common Law World – Introduction', in C. Rickett and G. Austin (eds.), *International Intellectual Property and the Common Law World* (Oxford: Hart, 2000)

Gurnsey, J., *Copyright Theft* (Aldershot: Aslib Gower, 1995)
Gurry, F., *Breach of Confidence* (Oxford: Clarendon, 1984)
Haftke, M., 'Net Liability: Is an Exemption from Liability for On-line Service Providers Required?' [1996] EntLR 47
Hamilton, A., 'Copyright and the Public Interest – Public versus Private Rights', Honours thesis, Monash University, 1995
Hamilton, M., 'Copyright at the Supreme Court: A Jurisprudence of Deference' (2000) 47 *Journal of the Copyright Society of the USA* 317
Handa, S., 'Reverse Engineering Computer Programs Under Canadian Copyright Law' (1995) 40 *McGill Law Journal* 621
Handler, M., '*The Panel Case* and Television Broadcast Copyright' (2003) 25 *Sydney Law Review* 391
Handler, M. and D. Rolph, '"A Real Pea Souper": *The Panel Case* and the Development of the Fair Dealing Defences to Copyright Infringement in Australia' (2003) 27 *Melbourne University Law Review* 381
Hansen, H. (ed.), *International Intellectual Property Law and Policy*, Vol. 4 (New York: Juris Publishing, 2000)
Harbottle, G., 'Private Prosecutions in Copyright Cases: Should They Be Stopped?' [1998] EIPR 317
'Permanent Injunctions in Copyright Cases: When Will They Be Refused?' [2001] EIPR 154
Hardy, T., 'Property (and Copyright) in Cyberspace' [1996] *University of Chicago Legal Forum* 217
Harmon, L., 'Law, Art and the Killing Jar' (1994) 79 *Iowa Law Review* 367
Harrington, J., 'Access to Intellectual Property in the Light of Convergence: Should New Rules Apply?' [2001] EIPR 133
Harris, J., 'Private and Non-Private Property: What is the Difference?' (1995) 111 *Law Quarterly Review* 421
Harris, L., *Canadian Copyright Law*, 2nd edn (Ontario: McGraw-Hill Ryerson, 1992)
Hart, M., 'The Proposed Directive for Copyright in the Information Society: Nice Rights, Shame about the Exceptions' [1998] EIPR 169
Hawkins, C., 'Technological Measures: Saviour or Saboteur of the Public Domain?' (1998) 9 *Journal of Law and Information Science* 77
Hayhurst, W., *Intellectual Property Laws in Canada: The British Tradition, the American Influence and the French Factor* (Leeds: University Print Services, 1995)
Heath, C. and A. Kamperman Sanders (eds.), *Intellectual Property in the Digital Age: Challenges for Asia* (London: Kluwer, 2001)
Heide, T., 'The Berne Three-Step Test and the Proposed Copyright Directive' [1999] EIPR 105
'The Approach to Innovation under the Proposed Copyright Directive: Time for Mandatory Exceptions?' [2000] IPQ 215
'Copyright in the EU and US: What Access Right?' (2001) 48 *Journal of the Copyright Society of the USA* 363
Heker, H., 'The Publisher in the Electronic Age: Caught in the Area of Conflict of Copyright and Competition Law' [1995] EIPR 75

Helfer, L., 'A European Human Rights Analogy for Adjudicating Copyright Claims under TRIPS' [1999] EIPR 8
  'World Music on a US Stage: A Berne/TRIPS and Economic Analysis of the Fairness in Music Licensing Act' (2000) 80 *Boston University Law Review* 93
Hennessy, P., *Whitehall* (London: Secker & Warburg, 1989)
Henry, M., *Publishing and Multimedia Law* (London: Butterworths, 1994)
Henry, S., 'The First International Challenge to US Copyright Law: What Does the WTO Analysis of 17 USC 110(5) Mean to the Future of International Harmonization of Copyright Laws under the TRIPS Agreement?' (2001) 20 *Pennsylvania State International Law Review* 301
Heyne, P., 'The Foundations of Law and of Economics: Can the Blind Lead the Blind?' (1988) 11 *Research in Law and Economics* 53
Hickey, R., 'Dazed and Confused: Accidental Mixtures of Goods and the Theory of Acquisition of Title' (2003) 66 *Modern Law Review* 368
Hirsch, W., *Law and Economics*, 3rd edn (San Diego: Academic Press, 1999)
Hodgson, S., 'Intellectual Property Theft Emerging as Hot Issue in US Oil and Gas Industry' [1998] *Oil and Gas Journal* 26
Hoeren, T., *Copyright in Electronic Delivery Services and Multimedia Products* (Luxembourg: European Commission, 1995)
Hoeren, T. and U. Decker, 'Electronic Archives and the Press: Copyright Problems of Mass Media in the Digital Age' [1998] EIPR 257
Hoffman, B., 'Fair Use of Digital Art Images and Academia: A View from the Trenches of the Conference on Fair Use (CONFU)' (1997) 12 *Visual Resources* 373
Hohfeld, W., *Fundamental Legal Conceptions* (New Haven: Yale University Press, 1923)
Howse, R., 'Membership and its Privileges: The WTO, Civil Society, and the *Amicus* Brief Controversy' (2003) 9 *European Law Journal* 496
Hugenholtz, B., 'Fierce Creatures. Copyright Exceptions: Towards Extinction?', paper delivered at Imprimatur Conference, 1997
  'Why the Copyright Directive is Unimportant and Possibly Invalid' [2000] EIPR 499
  'Copyright and Freedom of Expression in Europe' in N. Elkin-Koren and N. Netanel (eds.), *The Commodification of Information* (The Hague: Kluwer Law International, 2002)
Hughes, J., '"Recoding" Intellectual Property Rights and Overlooked Audience Interests' (1999) 77 *Texas Law Review* 923
  'Fair Use Across Time' (2003) 50 *UCLA Law Review* 775
Hutcheon, L., *A Theory of Parody* (London: Methuen, 1985)
  Implementation of the Copyright Directive (2001/29/EC) and Related Matters – Transposition Note (UK Patent Office)(online)
Isaac, B., *Brand Protection Matters* (London: Sweet & Maxwell, 2000)
Jackson, M., 'Harmony or Discord? The Pressure toward Conformity in International Copyright Law' (2003) 43 *Idea* 607
Jacobs, M., 'An Essay on the Normative Foundations of Antitrust Economics' (1995) 74 *North Carolina Law Review* 219

Jacobson, N., 'Faith, Hope and Parody: *Campbell* v. *Acuff-Rose*, "Oh, Pretty Woman", and Parodists Rights' (1994) 31 *Houston Law Review* 955
Janus, K., 'Defending the Public Domain in Copyright Law: A Tactical Approach – Part I' (1999–2000) 14 IPJ 379
  'Defending the Public Domain in Copyright Law: A Tactical Approach – Part II' (2000–1) 15 IPJ 67
Jeroham, H., 'Freedom of Expression in Copyright Law' [1984] EIPR 3
  'The EC Copyright Directives, Economics and Authors' Rights' (1994) 25 IIC 821
  'Two Fashionable Mistakes' [2000] EIPR 103
  'The Future of Copyright Collecting Societies' [2001] EIPR 134
Johnson, D. and K. Marks, 'Mapping Electronic Data Communications onto Existing Legal Metaphors: Should We Let Our Conscience (and Our Contracts) Be Our Guide?', (1993) 38 *Villanova Law Review* 487
Johnson, M., 'Launch of Copyright Guidelines for Visually Impaired People' October 31, 2001 (online)
Johnson, P., 'Can You Quote Donald Duck?: Intellectual Property in Cyberculture' (2001) 13 *Yale Journal of Law and the Humanities* 451
Johnston, G., 'Copyright and Freedom of the Media: A Modest Proposal' [1996] EIPR 6
Joint Note, British Library and Copyright Licensing Agency, *Changes to UK Copyright Law* (online)
Jolls, C., C. Sunstein and R. Thaler, 'A Behavioral Approach to Law and Economics', in C. Sunstein (ed.), *Behavioral Law and Economics* (New York: Cambridge University Press, 2000)
Jones, N., 'Eurodefences: Magill Distinguished' [1998] EIPR 353
Jones, R., 'The Myth of the Idea/Expression Dichotomy in Copyright Law' (1990) 10 *Pace Law Review* 551
Jones, T., 'Property Rights, Planning Law and the European Convention' [1996] *European Human Rights Law Review* 233
Joseph, L., 'Human Rights versus Copyright: The Paddy Ashdown Case' [2002] EntLR 72
Julia-Barcelo, R., 'Liability for On-line Intermediaries: A European Perspective' [1998] EIPR 453
Jung, G., 'Copyright, Fair Use and Satire: *Dr Seuss Enterprises* v. *Penguin Books*' (1998) 13 *Berkeley Technology Law Journal* 119
Kahneman, D., J. Knetsch and R. Thaler, 'Experimental Tests of the Endowment Effect and the Coase Theorem', in C. Sunstein (ed.), *Behavioral Law and Economics* (New York: Cambridge University Press, 2000)
Kahn-Freund, O., 'On Uses and Misuses of Comparative Law' (1974) 37 *Modern Law Review* 1
Kamina, P., *Film Copyright in the European Union* (Cambridge: Cambridge University Press, 2002)
Kamperman Sanders, A., 'Unfair Competition and Ethics', in L. Bently and S. Maniatis (eds.), *Intellectual Property and Ethics*, Perspectives on Intellectual Property 4 (London: Sweet & Maxwell, 1998)

'The Legal Protection of Data and Databases', in C. Heath and A. Kamperman Sanders (eds.), *Intellectual Property in the Digital Age: Challenges for Asia* (London: Kluwer, 2001)

Kaplan, B., *An Unhurried View of Copyright* (New York: Columbia University Press, 1967)

Kaplan, F. (ed.), *Museums and the Making of 'Ourselves': The Role of Objects in National Identity* (London: Leicester University Press, 1994)

Karnell, G., 'The Berne Convention Between Authors' Rights and Copyright Economics – An International Dilemma' (1995) 26 IIC 193

Karp, I. and S. Levine (eds.), *Exhibiting Cultures: The Poetics and Politics of Museum Display* (Washington: Smithsonian Institution Press, 1991)

Katsh, M., *Law in a Digital World* (Oxford: Oxford University Press, 1995)

Katz, J., 'When Imitation is not Necessarily the Sincerest Form of Flattery – Intellectual Property Rights and Freedom of Expression' (2001) 2 *New Zealand Intellectual Property Journal* 342

Kay, J., 'The Economics of Intellectual Property Rights' (1993) 13 *International Review of Law and Economics* 337

Kearns, P., *The Legal Concept of Art* (Oxford: Hart, 1998)

Khan, A. and P. Hancock, 'Copyright in Australia – Fair Dealing for Research or Study Purposes' (2001) 20 *Journal of Legal Education* 505

Khlestov, N., 'WTO–WIPO Co-operation: Does It Have a Future?' [1997] EIPR 560

Kim, S., 'The Reinforcement of International Copyright for the Digital Age' (2002–3) 16 IPJ 93

Kinley, D. (ed.), *Human Rights in Australian Law* (Sydney: Federation Press, 1998)

Kitch, E., 'Can the Internet Shrink Fair Use?' (1999) 78 *Nebraska Law Review* 880

Kitching, C., *Archives: The Very Essence of our Heritage* (Chichester: National Council on Archives, 1996)

Klein, N., *No Logo* (London: Flamingo, 2001)

Koomen, K., 'Breach of Confidence and the Public Interest Defence: Is It in the Public Interest?' (1994) 10 *Queensland University of Technology Law Journal* 56

Korn, N. and P. Wienand, 'Public Access to Art, Museums, Images and Copyright: The Case of Tate', in D. McClean and K. Schubert (eds.), *Dear Images: Art Copyright and Culture* (London: Ridinghouse, 2002)

Kotler, J., 'Trade Mark Parody, Judicial Confusion and the Unlikelihood of Fair Use' (1999–2000) 14 IPJ 219

Kraft, N., 'The EC Directive on the *Droit de Suite*: A Contemporary Instrument for the Art World of the European Community?', LLM dissertation, University of London, 2002

Kravis, R., 'Does a Song by Any Other Name Still Sound as Sweet?: Digital Sampling and Its Copyright Implications' (1993) 43 *American University Law Review* 231

Kravitz, R., 'Trademarks, Speech and the Gay Olympics Case' (1989) 69 *Boston University Law Review* 131

Kretschmer, M., 'The Failure of Property Rules in Collective Administration: Rethinking Copyright Societies as Regulatory Instruments' [2002] EIPR 126

Krieg, P., 'Copyright, Free Speech, and the Visual Arts' (1984) 93 *Yale Law Journal* 1565

Ku, R., 'The Creative Destruction of Copyright: Napster and the New Economics of Digital Technology' (2002) 69 *University of Chicago Law Review* 263

'Consumers and Creative Destruction: Fair Use Beyond Market Failure' (2003) 18 *Berkeley Technology Law Journal* 539

Kudon, J., 'Form Over Function: Expanding the Transformative Use Test for Fair Use' (2000) 80 *Boston University Law Review* 579

Kur, A., 'The "Presentation Right" – Time to Create a New Limitation in Copyright Law' (2000) 31 IIC 308

Kurtz, L., 'Copyright and the National Information Infrastructure in the United States' [1996] EIPR 120

Lacey, L., 'Of Bread and Roses and Copyrights' [1989] *Duke Law Journal* 1539

Laddie, H., 'Copyright: Over-Strength, Over-Regulated, Over-Rated?' [1996] EIPR 253

Laddie, H., P. Prescott and M. Vitoria, *The Modern Law of Copyright and Designs*, 2nd edn (London: Butterworths, 1995)

Laddie, H., P. Prescott, M. Vitoria, A. Speck and L. Lane, *The Modern Law of Copyright and Designs*, 3rd edn (London: Butterworths, 2000)

LaFrance, M., 'Congress Trips Over International Law: WTO Finds Unfairness in Music Licensing Act' (2001) 11 *De Paul–LCA Journal of Art and Entertainment Law* 397

Lahore, J., G. Dworkin and Y. Smythe, *Information Technology: The Challenge to Copyright* (London: Sweet & Maxwell, 1984)

Lai, S., 'Database Protection in the United Kingdom: The New Deal and its Effects on Software Protection' [1998] EIPR 33

'Digital Copyright and Watermarking' [1999] EIPR 171

Landes, E. and R. Posner, 'The Economics of the Baby Shortage' (1978) 7 *Journal of Legal Studies* 323

Landes, W., 'Copyright, Borrowed Images and Appropriation Art: An Economic Approach' (2000) 9 *George Mason Law Review* 1

Landes, W. and R. Posner, 'An Economic Analysis of Copyright Law' (1989) 18 *Journal of Legal Studies* 325

The Economic Structure of Intellectual Property Law (Cambridge, Mass.: The Belknap Press of Harvard University Press, 2003)

Landy, B., 'Two Strands of the Fair Use Web: A Theory for Resolving the Dilemma of Music Parody' (1993) 54 *Ohio State Law Journal* 227

Lange, D., 'At Play in the Fields of the Word: Copyright and the Construction of Authorship in the Post-literate Millennium' (1992) 55(2) *Law and Contemporary Problems* 139

Lape, L., 'Transforming Fair Use: The Productive Use Factor in Fair Use Doctrine' (1995) 58 *Albany Law Review* 677

Latman, A., R. Gorman and J. Ginsburg, *Copyright for the Nineties*, 3rd edn (New York: Matthew Bender, 1989)

Lawrence, J., 'Donald Duck v. Chilean Socialism: A Fair Use Exchange', in J. Lawrence and B. Timberg (eds.), *Fair Use and Free Inquiry: Copyright Law and the New Media*, 2nd edn (Norwood: Ablex Publishing, 1989)

Lawrence, J. and B. Timberg (eds.), *Fair Use and Free Inquiry: Copyright Law and the New Media*, 2nd edn (Norwood: Ablex Publishing, 1989)

Lawson, R., 'Human Rights and Copyright' (2001) 145(6) *Solicitors Journal* 136

Leaffer, M., 'The Uncertain Future of Fair Use in a Global Information Marketplace' (2001) 62 *Ohio State Law Journal* 849

Lee, M., 'Public Participation, Procedure and Democratic Deficit in EC Environmental Law', in H. Somsen, H. Sevenster, J. Scott, L. Kramer and T. Etty (eds.), *Yearbook of European Environmental Law*, vol. 3 (Oxford: Oxford University Press, 2003)

Lee, M. and R. Burrell, 'Liability for the Escape of GM Seeds: Pursuing the "Victim"?' (2002) 65 *Modern Law Review* 517

Lefevre, K., 'The Tell-Tale "Heart": Determining "Fair" Use of Unpublished Texts' (1992) 55(2) *Law and Contemporary Problems* 153

Lehmann, M., 'Digitisation and Copyright Agreements', in I. Stamatoudi and P. Torremans (eds.), *Copyright in the New Digital Environment*, Perspectives on Intellectual Property 8 (London: Sweet & Maxwell, 2000)

Lehr, P., 'The Fair-Use Doctrine Before and After "Pretty Woman's" Unworkable Framework: The Adjustable Tool for Censoring Distasteful Parody' (1994) 46 *Florida Law Review* 443

Lemley, M., 'Intellectual Property and Shrinkwrap Licenses' (1995) 68 *Southern California Law Review* 1239

Lessig, L., *Code and Other Laws of Cyberspace* (New York: Basic Books, 1999)

Lester, D. and P. Mitchell, *Joynson-Hicks on UK Copyright Law* (London: Sweet & Maxwell, 1989)

Leval, P., 'Toward a Fair Use Standard' (1990) 103 *Harvard Law Review* 1105

Levin, B., *The Pirates and the Mouse* (Seattle: Fantagraphic Books, 2003)

Levy, K., 'Trademark Parody: A Conflict between Constitutional and Intellectual Property Interests' (2001) 69 *George Washington Law Review* 425

Lewis, A., 'Playing Around with Barbie: Expanding Fair Use for Cultural Icons' (1999) 1 *Chicago-Kent Journal of Intellectual Property* 61

Libling, D., 'The Concept of Property: Property in Intangibles' (1978) 94 *Law Quarterly Review* 103

Light, S., 'Parody, Burlesque and the Economic Rationale for Copyright' (1979) 11 *Connecticut Law Review* 615

Litman, J. 'Copyright, Compromise, and Legislative History' (1987) 72 *Cornell Law Review* 857
  'The Public Domain' (1990) 39 *Emory Law Journal* 965
  'Copyright as Myth' (1991) 53 *University of Pittsburgh Law Review* 235
  'Copyright Noncompliance (or Why We Can't "Just Say Yes" to Licensing)' (1997) 29 *New York Journal of International Law and Politics* 257
  Digital Copyright (New York: Prometheus, 2001)

Llewellyn, G., 'Does Copyright Law Recognise a Right to Repair?' [1999] EIPR 596

Long, D., 'First, "Let's Kill All the Intellectual Property Lawyers!": Musings on the Decline and Fall of the Intellectual Property Empire' (2001) 34 *John Marshall Law Review* 851

Longdin, L., 'Shall We Shoot a Messenger Now and Then? Copyright Infringement and the On-line Service Provider', in C. Rickett and G. Austin (eds.), *International Intellectual Property and the Common Law World* (Oxford: Hart, 2000)

Loren, L., 'Redefining the Market Failure Approach to Fair Use in an Era of Copyright Protection Systems' (1997) 5 *Journal of Intellectual Property Law* 1

Loughlan, P., 'Moral Rights (A View from the Town Square)' (2000) 5 *Media and Arts Law Review* 1

   'Protecting Culturally Significant Uses of Trade Marks (Without a First Amendment)' [2000] EIPR 328

   'Looking at the Matrix: Intellectual Property and Expressive Freedom' [2002] EIPR 30

   'The Marketplace of Ideas and the Idea/Expression Distinction of Copyright Law' (2002) 23 *Adelaide Law Review* 29

Lucas, A., 'Exploitation and Liability in the Light of Media Convergence' [2001] EIPR 275

Ludlow, P. (ed.), *High Noon on the Electronic Frontier* (Cambridge, Mass.: MIT Press, 1996)

Lukac, G. (ed.), *Copyright: The Librarian and the Law* (New Brunswick: Bureau of Library and Information Science, 1972)

Lunney, G., 'Fair Use and Market Failure: *Sony* Revisited' (2002) 82 *Boston University Law Review* 975

Lury, C., *Cultural Rights: Technology, Legality and Personality* (London: Routledge, 1993)

McAnanama, J., 'Copyright Law: Libraries and their Users have Special Needs' (1990–1) 6 IPJ 225

McClean, D. and K. Schubert (eds.), *Dear Images: Art, Copyright and Culture* (London: Ridinghouse, 2002)

McCormack, G., 'Mixture of Goods' [1990] 10 *Legal Studies* 293

McCoy Smith, P., 'Copyright, Suppression and the Problem of the Unpublished Work: Lessons from the Patent Law' (1991) 19 *AIPLA Quarterly Journal* 309

Macdonald, S. (ed.), *The Politics of Display: Museums, Science, Culture* (London: Routledge, 1998)

Macdonald-Brown, C. and L. Ferera, 'First WTO Decision on TRIPS' [1998] EIPR 69

McEvedy, V., 'The DMCA and the E-Commerce Directive' [2002] EIPR 65

McGhee, J., S*nell's Equity*, 30th edn (London: Sweet & Maxwell, 2000)

MacGillivray, E., *The Copyright Act, 1911* (London: Stevens & Sons, 1912)

   Guide to the Copyright Act, 1911 (London: Publishers' Association, 1912)

McJohn, S., 'Fair Use and Privatization in Copyright' (1998) 35 *San Diego Law Review* 61

   'Eldred's Aftermath: Tradition, the Copyright Clause, and the Constitutionalization of Fair Use' (2003) 10 *Michigan Telecommunications and Technology Law Review* 95

McKeough, J. and A. Stewart, *Intellectual Property in Australia*, 2nd edn (Sydney: Butterworths, 1997)

McLaren, K., 'Copyright: Fair Use or Foul Play' (1997) 12 *Visual Resources* 343

McLay, G., 'Being Fair to Users: The Welcome Arrival of a New, More Liberal Approach to Fair Dealing' (1999) 2 *New Zealand Intellectual Property Journal* 135

Macmillan, F., 'Towards a Reconciliation of Free Speech and Copyright', in E. Barendt, S. Bate, J. Dickens and T. Gibbons (eds.), *The Yearbook of Media and Entertainment Law 1996* (Oxford: Clarendon, 1996)

  'Adapting the Copyright Exceptions to the Digital Environment' (1999) 1(2) *Digital Technology Law Journal* (online)

Macmillan, F. and M. Blakeney, 'The Internet and Communication Carriers' Copyright Liability' [1998] EIPR 52

Macpherson, C., *The Political Theory of Possessive Individualism* (Oxford: Oxford University Press, 1962)

MacQueen, H., *Copyright, Competition and Industrial Design* (Edinburgh: Edinburgh University Press, 1995)

  'Copyright and the Internet', in L. Edwards and C. Waelde (eds.), *Law and the Internet: Regulating Cyberspace* (Oxford: Hart, 1997)

McWilliams, J., *The Preservation and Restoration of Sound Recordings* (Nashville: American Association for State and Local History, 1979)

Magnette, P., 'European Governance and Civic Participation: Can the European Union Be Politicised?' in Jean Monnet Working Paper No.6/01 Symposium: 'Mountain or Molehill? A Critical Appraisal of the Commission White Paper on Governance' (online)

Magnusson, D. and V. Nabhan, *Exemptions Under the Canadian Copyright Act* (Ottawa: Department of Consumer and Corporate Affairs, 1982)

Makeen, M., *Copyright in a Global Information Society: The Scope of Protection under International, US, UK and French Law* (London: Kluwer International, 2000)

Markesinis, B., 'Comparative Law – A Subject in Search of an Audience' (1990) 53 *Modern Law Review* 1

Marmor, A., *Interpretation and Legal Theory* (Oxford: Clarendon, 1992)

Martino, T. and D. Moseley, 'PPL and Performance Right Organisations: Half-Sisters in Copyright – Partners in Anti-trust?' [1985] EIPR 151

Marx, F., *The Administrative State: An Introduction to Bureaucracy* (Chicago: Chicago University Press, 1957)

Mason, A., 'Public-Interest Objectives and the Law of Copyright' (1998) 9 *Journal of Law and Information Science* 7

May, C., *A Global Political Economy of Intellectual Property Rights* (London: Routledge, 2000)

Mayor, S., 'English NHS to Set Up New Reporting System for Errors' (2000) 320 *British Medical Journal* 1689

Meagher, R., W. Gummow and J. Lehane, *Equity: Doctrines and Remedies*, 3rd edn (Sydney: Butterworths, 1992)

Meagher, R., D. Heydon and M. Leeming, *Meagher, Gummow and Lehane's Equity: Doctrines and Remedies*, 4th edn (Sydney: Butterworths, 2002)

Meiklejohn, A., *Free Speech and its Relation to Self-Government* (New York: Harper & Brothers, 1948)

Merges, R., 'Are You Making Fun of Me? Notes on Market Failure and the Parody Defense in Copyright' (1993) 21 *AIPLA Quarterly Journal* 305

  'Contracting into Liability Rules: Intellectual Property Rights and Collective Rights Organizations' (1996) 84 *California Law Review* 1293

  'The End of Friction? Property Rights and Contract in the "Newtonian" World of On-line Commerce' (1997) 12 *Berkeley Technology Law Journal* 115

Messenger, P. (ed.), *The Ethics of Collecting Cultural Property* (Albuquerque: University of New Mexico Press, 1989)

Mill, J. S., *On Liberty* (London: Penguin Classics, 1985)

Miller, C., 'Magill: Time to Abandon the "Specific Subject Matter" Concept' [1994] EIPR 415

MMC Report, *The British Broadcasting Corporation and Independent Television Publications Limited: A Report on the Policies and Practices of the BBC and ITP of Limiting the Publication by Others of Advance Programme Information*, Cmnd 9614 (HMSO, 1985)

  Collective Licensing: A Report on Certain Practices in the Collective Licensing of Public Performances and Broadcasting Rights in Sound Recordings, Cm 530 (HMSO, 1988)

  Performing Rights: A Report on the Supply in the UK of the Services of Administering Performing Rights and Film Synchronisation Rights, Cm 3417 (HMSO, 1996)

  The Supply of Recorded Music: A Report on the Supply in the UK of Pre-recorded Compact Discs, Vinyl Discs and Tapes Containing Music, Cm 2599 (HMSO, 1994)

Monotti, A., 'Allocating the Rights to Intellectual Property in Australian Universities: An Overview of Current Practices' (1999) 27 *Federal Law Review* 421

  'University Copyright in the Digital Age: Balancing and Exploiting Rights in Computer Programs, Web-based Materials, Databases and Multimedia in Australian Universities' [2002] EIPR 251

Monotti, A. and S. Ricketson, *Universities and Intellectual Property: Ownership and Exploitation* (Oxford: Oxford University Press, 2003)

Morgan, O., 'Advertising Works of Art for Sale – Copyright or Contract?' (2003) 14 AIPJ 21

Morrison, A., 'Distribution of MP3 Files over the Internet: Celestial Jukebox or Pirates' Bazaar?' [2000] *Computer and Telecommunications Law Review* 175

  'Computers – Infringement of Copyright on the Internet – Service Provider Liability' [2002] EIPR N130

  Multimedia Industry Advisory Report (Department of Trade and Industry, December 1995)

Myrick, R., 'Will Intellectual Property on Technology still Be Viable in a Unitary Market?' [1992] EIPR 298

Netanel, N., 'Copyright and a Democratic Civil Society' (1996) 106 *Yale Law Journal* 283

'Asserting Copyright's Democratic Principles in the Global Arena' (1998) 51 *Vanderbilt Law Review* 217

Newby, T., 'What's Fair Here Is Not Fair Everywhere: Does the American Fair Use Doctrine Violate International Copyright Law?' (1999) 51 *Stanford Law Review* 1633

Ng, C., 'When Imitation Is Not the Sincerest Form of Flattery: Fair Dealing and Fair Use for the Purpose of Criticism in Canada and the United States' (1996–7) 11 IPJ 183

Nikolinakos, N., 'Nature and Scope of Content Regulation for Online Services' [2000] *Computer and Telecommunications Law Review* 126

Nimmer, D., 'The End of Copyright' (1995) 48 *Vanderbilt Law Review* 1385

'How Much Solicitude for Fair Use Is There in the Anti-Circumvention Provision of the Digital Millennium Copyright Act?', in N. Elkin-Koren and N. Netanel (eds.), *The Commodification of Information* (The Hague: Kluwer Law International, 2002)

Nimmer, M., 'Does Copyright Abridge the First Amendment Guarantees of Free Speech and Press?' (1970) 17 *UCLA Law Review* 1180

Nimmer, M. and D. Nimmer, *Nimmer on Copyright* (New York: Matthew Bender, loose-leaf)

Nimmer, M. and P. Geller (eds.), *International Copyright Law and Practice* (New York: Matthew Bender, loose-leaf)

Norman, S., 'The Library's Use of the Network: The Role of Libraries in a Changing Environment', in *The Future is Already Here: Publishers and New Technologies*, Proceedings of the 3rd International Copyright Symposium (Milan: CEDAM, 1995)

'The Electronic Environment: The Librarian's View' [1996] EIPR 71

Copyright in Further and Higher Education Libraries, 3rd edn (London: Library Association Publishing, 1996)

Copyright in Further and Higher Education Libraries, 4th edn (London: Library Association Publishing, 1999)

Oakes, J., 'Copyrights and Copyremedies: Unfair Use and Injunctions' (1990) 18 *Hofstra Law Review* 983

Okediji, R., 'Copyright and Public Welfare in Global Perspective' (1999) 7 *Indiana Journal of Global Legal Studies* 117

'Toward an International Fair Use Doctrine' (2000) 39 *Columbia Journal of Transnational Law* 75

'Givers, Takers, and Other Kinds of Users: A Fair Use Doctrine for Cyberspace' (2001) 53 *Florida Law Review* 107

Okpaluba, J., 'Digitisation, Culture and Copyright Law: Digital Sampling, A Case Study', PhD thesis, University of London, 2000

'Appropriation Art: Fair Use or Foul?' in D. McClean and K. Schubert (eds.), *Dear Images: Art, Copyright and Culture* (London: Ridinghouse, 2002)

Oliver, J., 'Copyright, Fair Dealing, and Freedom of Expression' (2000) 19 *New Zealand Universities Law Review* 89

Owen, L., *Selling Rights*, 2nd edn (London: Blueprint, 1994)

Padfield, T., *Copyright for Archivists and Users of Archives*, 2nd edn (London: Facet Publishing, 2004)

Palmer, N., *Art Loans* (London: Kluwer, 1997)

Parker, C. and J. Braithwaite, 'Regulation', in P. Cane and M. Tushnet (eds.), *The Oxford Handbook of Legal Studies* (Oxford: Oxford University Press, 2003)
Parrinder, P., 'The Dead Hand of European Copyright' [1993] EIPR 391
Patry, W., *The Fair Use Privilege in Copyright Law* (Washington, DC: Bureau of National Affairs, 1985)
  The Fair Use Privilege in Copyright Law, 2nd edn (Washington DC: Bureau of National Affairs, 1995)
  'The Second Annual Tenzer Distinguished Lecture in Intellectual Property: Copyright and the Legislative Process: A Personal Perspective' (1996) 14 *Cardozo Arts and Entertainment Law Journal* 139
Patterson, L., 'Free Speech, Copyright and Fair Use' (1987) 40 *Vanderbilt Law Review* 1
Patterson, L. and S. Lindberg, *The Nature of Copyright: A Law of Users' Rights* (Athens, Ga.: University of Georgia Press, 1991)
Paust, J., 'Human Rights Responsibilities of Private Corporations' (2002) 35 *Vanderbilt Journal of Transnational Law* 801
Pearse, R., 'Library Open Distribution Systems and Copyright Infringement in Canada and the United States' (1994) 86 *Law Library Journal* 399
Pendleton, M., 'Chinese IP – Some Global Implications for Legal Culture and National Sovereignty' [1993] EIPR 119
Perle, E., 'Copyright Law and the Copyright Society of the USA 1950–2000' (2000) 47 *Journal of the Copyright Society of the USA* 209
Permulter, S., 'Convergence and the Future of Copyright' [2001] EIPR 111
Perritt, J., 'Protecting Technology Over Copyright: A Step Too Far' [2003] EntLR 1
Pettit, P., 'He who Comes into Equity Must Come with Clean Hands' [1990] *Conveyencer and Property Lawyer* 416
Phan, D., 'Will Fair Use Function on the Internet?' (1998) 98 *Columbia Law Review* 169
Phelan, D., *Revolt or Revolution: The Constitutional Boundaries of the European Community* (Dublin: Round Rall, Sweet & Maxwell, 1997)
Phillips, Jeremy, 'The Berne Convention and the Public Interest' [1987] EIPR 106
  'Copyright in Spoken Works – Some Potential Problems' [1989] EIPR 231
  'Life After Death' [1998] EIPR 201
  'When Is a Fact?' [2000] EntLR 116
  'The Risk that Rewards: Copyright Infringement Today' [2001] EntLR 103
Phillips, John, *Protecting Designs: Law and Litigation* (Sydney: Law Book Co., 1994)
Phillips, John and L. Bently, 'Copyright Issues: The Mysteries of Section 18' [1999] EIPR 133
Picciotto, S., 'Copyright Licensing: The Case of Higher Education Photocopying in the United Kingdom' [2002] EIPR 438
Pidgeon, N., 'Safety Culture and Risk Management in Organizations' (1991) 22 *Journal of Cross-Cultural Psychology* 129
Piele, K., 'Three Years After *Campbell* v. *Acuff-Rose Music, Inc.*: What is Fair Game for Parodists?' (1997) 18 *Loyola of Los Angeles Entertainment Law Journal* 75

Pinto, T., 'The Influence of the European Convention on Human Right on Intellectual Property Rights' [2002] EIPR 209

Pizer, J., 'The Public Interest Exception to the Breach of Confidence Action: Are the Lights About to Change?' (1994) 20 *Monash Law Review* 67

Plant, M., *The English Book Trade: An Economic History of the Making and Sale of Books*, 2nd edn (London: George Allen & Unwin, 1965)

Pollaud-Dulian, F. (ed.), *The Internet and Authors' Rights*, Perspectives on Intellectual Property 5 (London: Sweet & Maxwell, 1999)

Porter, H., 'European Union Competition Policy: Should the Role of Collecting Societies be Legitimised?' [1996] EIPR 673

Posner, R., 'When is Parody Fair Use?' (1992) 21 *Journal of Legal Studies* 67

PriceWaterhouseCoopers, *Final Report Study on Consumer Law and the Information Society* (17 August 2000)

Priest, G., 'What Economists Can Tell Lawyers about Intellectual Property' (1986) 8 *Research in Law and Economics* 19

Puri, K., 'Fair Dealing with Copyright Material in Australia and New Zealand' (1983) 13 *Victoria University of Wellington Law Review* 277

 'Librarians and Copyright Law' (1987) 17 *Victoria University of Wellington Law Review* 277

Quaedvlieg, A., 'Copyright's Orbit Round Private, Commercial and Economic Law – The Copyright System and the Place of the User' (1998) 29 IIC 420

Quentel, D., 'Bad Artists Copy. Good Artists Steal.: The Ugly Conflict Between Copyright Law and Appropriationism' (1996) 4 UCLA *Entertainment Law Review* 39

Radin, M., *Contested Commodities* (Cambridge, Mass.: Harvard University Press, 1996)

Rawls, J., *A Theory of Justice* (Oxford: Oxford University Press, 1973)

Reichman, J., 'Universal Minimum Standards of Intellectual Property Protection under the TRIPS Component of the WTO Agreement' (1995) 29(2) *International Lawyer* 345

Reinbothe, J. and S. Von Lewinski, *The EC Directive on Rental and Lending Rights and on Piracy* (London: Sweet & Maxwell, 1993)

Report of the Committee on the Law of Copyright, Cd. 4967 (HMSO, 1909)

Report of the Committee to Consider the Law on Copyright and Designs, Cmnd 6732 (HMSO, 1977)

Report of the Committee on the Future of Broadcasting, Cmnd 6753 (HMSO, 1977)

Report of the Copyright Committee, Cmd. 8662 (HMSO, 1952)

Report of the Royal Commission on Copyright of 1878, C 2036 (HMSO, 1878)

Report of the Working Group on Intellectual Property Rights, *Intellectual Property Rights and the National Information Infrastructure* (Washington DC, 1995)

Richardson, M., 'Freedom of Political Discussion and Intellectual Property Law in Australia' [1998] EntLR 3

Ricketson, S., 'Public Interest and Breach of Confidence' (1979) 12 *Melbourne University Law Review* 176

 The Berne Convention for the Protection of Literary and Artistic Works 1886–1986 (London: Kluwer and QMW, 1987)

'The Future of Australian Intellectual Property Law Reform and Administration' (1992) 3 AIPJ 1
'US Accession to Berne: An Outsider's Appreciation – Pt 1' (1992–3) 7 IPJ 233
'US Accession to Berne: An Outsider's Appreciation – Pt 2' (1993–4) 8 IPJ 87
'The Future of the Traditional Intellectual Property Conventions in the Brave New World of Trade-Related Intellectual Property Rights' (1995) 26 IIC 872
'The Challenge to Copyright Protection in the Digital Age – An Australian Perspective' paper presented at the Australian/OECD Conference in Canberra, February 1996
'Simplifying Copyright Law: Proposals from Down Under' [1999] EIPR 537
'The Boundaries of Copyright: Its Proper Limitations and Exceptions: International Conventions and Treaties' [1999] IPQ 56
WIPO Study on Limitations and Exceptions of Copyright and Related Rights in the Digital Environment (Geneva: WIPO, 2003)
The Law of Intellectual Property: Copyright, Designs and Confidential Information, 2nd edn (Sydney: LBC Information Services, loose-leaf)
Rickett, C. and G. Austin (eds.), *International Intellectual Property and the Common Law World* (Oxford: Hart, 2000)
Ries, K., 'Confidential Information and the Media' (1999) 15 *Queensland University of Technology Law Journal* 126
Rimmer, M., 'A Creature of Statute: Copyright and Legal Formalism' [2002] EntLR 31
'The Dead Poets Society: The Copyright Term and the Public Domain' (2003) 8(6) *First Monday* (online)
Robertson, G., *The Law of Copyright* (Oxford: Clarendon, 1912)
Robinson, L., 'Anticircumvention Under the Digital Millennium Copyright Act' (2003) 85 *Journal of the Patent and Trademark Office Society* 957
Roebuck, W., 'A Response to the DTI Consultation on the Electronic Commerce (EC Directive) Regulations 2002' (2002) 8 *Computer and Telecommunications Law Review* 163
Rook, D., *Property Law and Human Rights* (London: Blackstone, 2001)
Rose, Margaret, *Parody: Ancient, Modern and Post-Modern* (Cambridge: Cambridge University Press, 1993)
Rose, Mark, *Authors and Owners* (Cambridge, Mass.: Harvard University Press, 1993)
'The Author as Proprietor: *Donaldson* v. *Beckett* and the Genealogy of Modern Authorship', in B. Sherman and A. Strowel (eds.), *Of Authors and Origins* (Oxford: Clarendon, 1994)
Rose, R., 'The Political Status of Higher Civil Servants in Britain' in E. Suleiman (ed.), *Bureaucrats and Policy Making* (New York: Holmes & Meier, 1984)
Rosenlund, R., 'Compulsory Licensing of Musical Compositions for Phonorecords Under the Copyright Act of 1976' (1979) 30 *Hastings Law Journal* 683
Ross, J., '*The Panel Case* and the Desirability of Harm as a Requirement of Copyright Liability' (2002) 7 *Deakin Law Review* 201

Rubenfeld, J., 'The Freedom of Imagination: Copyright's Constitutionality' (2002) 112 *Yale Law Journal* 1

Ryan, C., 'Human Rights and Intellectual Property' [2001] EIPR 521

Sadurski, W., *Freedom of Speech and Its Limits* (Dordrecht: Kluwer, 1999)

Samuels, E., *The Illustrated Story of Copyright* (New York: Thomas Dunne, 2000)

Samuelson, P., 'The Copyright Grab' [1996] (Jan.) *Wired* 57

'Law and Computers: The Quest for Enabling Metaphors for Law and Lawyering in the Information Age' (1996) 94 *Michigan Law Review* 2029

'The US Digital Agenda at WIPO' (1997) 37 *Virginia Journal of International Law* 369

'Challenges for the World Intellectual Property Organisation and the Trade-related Aspects of Intellectual Property Rights Council in Regulating Intellectual Property Rights in the Information Age' [1999] EIPR 528

Saunders, D., 'Purposes or Principle? Early Copyright and the Court of Chancery' [1993] EIPR 452

'Dropping the Subject: An Argument for a Positive History of Authorship and the Law of Copyright', in B. Sherman and A. Strowel (eds.), *Of Authors and Origins* (Oxford: Clarendon, 1994)

Saw Cheng Lim, 'Is There a Defence of Public Interest in the Law of Copyright in Singapore' [2003] *Singapore Journal of Legal Studies* 519

Sayal, M., 'Copyright and Freedom of the Media: A Balancing Exercise?' [1995] EntLR 263

Schaefer, M., C. Rasch and T. Braun, 'Liability of On-line Service Providers for Copyright Infringing Third-Party Contents' [1999] EIPR 208

Schauer, F., *Free Speech: A Philosophical Enquiry* (Cambridge: Cambridge University Press, 1982)

'Free Speech in a World of Private Power', in T. Campbell and W. Sadurski (eds.), *Freedom of Communication* (Sydney: Dartmouth, 1994)

Schlosser, S., 'The High Price of (Criticizing) Coffee: The Chilling Effect of the Federal Trademark Dilution Act on Corporate Parody' (2001) 43 *Arizona Law Review* 931

Scott, A., 'The Dutch Challenge to the Bio-Patenting Directive' [1999] EIPR 212

Sellars, C., 'Digital Rights Management Systems: Recent European Issues' [2003] EntLR 5

Seville, C., 'Talfourd and His Contemporaries: The Making of the 1842 Copyright Act', in A. Firth (ed.), *The Prehistory and Development of Intellectual Property Systems*, Perspectives on Intellectual Property 1 (London: Sweet & Maxwell, 1997)

Literary Copyright Reform in Early Victorian England: The Framing of the 1842 Copyright Act (Cambridge: Cambridge University Press, 1999)

Shapiro, M., *Freedom of Speech* (Englewood Cliffs, N.J.: Prentice-Hall, 1966)

Shavell, S. and T. Van Ypersele, 'Rewards versus Intellectual Property Rights' (2001) 44 *The Journal of Law and Economics* 525

Shelton, D., 'Protecting Human Rights in a Globalized World' (2002) 25 *Boston College International and Comparative Law Review* 273

Shen Rengan, 'On the Assumption of the Nature of Commodities by Literary and Artistic Works vis-à-vis Copyright Protection' [1990] 3 *China Patents and Trade Marks* 61

Sherman, B., 'Remembering and Forgetting: The Birth of Modern Copyright Law' (1995–6) 10 IPJ 1

'Digital Property and the Digital Commons' in C. Heath and A. Kamperman Sanders (eds.), *Intellectual Property in the Digital Age: Challenges for Asia* (London: Kluwer, 2001)

Sherman, B. and L. Bently, *The Making of Modern Intellectual Property Law: The British Experience 1760–1911* (Cambridge: Cambridge University Press, 1999)

Sherman, B. and A. Strowel (eds.), *Of Authors and Origins* (Oxford: Clarendon, 1994)

Shiva, V., 'Intellectual Property Protection in the North/South Divide', in C. Heath and A. Kamperman Sanders (eds.), *Intellectual Property in the Digital Age: Challenges for Asia* (London: Kluwer, 2001)

Siedentrop, L., *Democracy in Europe* (London: Penguin, 2000)

Siebrasse, N., 'A Property Rights Theory of the Limits of Copyright' (2001) 51 *University of Toronto Law Journal* 1

Silberbauer, C., 'Abridgement and Breach of Copyright' (1951) 68 *South African Law Journal* 213

Simon, I., 'Picture Perfect' [2002] EIPR 368

Sinclair, M., 'Fair Is Not Always Fair: Media Monitors and Copyright' [1997] EIPR 188

Sindelar, L., 'Not So Fair After All – International Aspects of the Fairness in Music Licensing Act of 1998' (2001) 14 *Transnational Lawyer* 435

Singer, P., 'Mounting a Fair Use Defence to the Anti-Circumvention Provisions of the Digital Millennium Copyright Act' (2002) 28 *University of Dayton Law Review* 111

Sked, A. and C. Cook, *Post-War Britain: A Political History*, 4th edn (London: Penguin, 1993)

Skone James, F., *Copinger on the Law of Copyright*, 6th edn (London: Sweet & Maxwell, 1927)

Copinger on the Law of Copyright, 7th edn (London: Sweet & Maxwell, 1936)

Copinger and Skone James on the Law of Copyright, 8th edn (London: Sweet & Maxwell, 1948)

Skone James, F. and E. Skone James, *Copinger and Skone James on Copyright*, 9th edn (London: Sweet & Maxwell, 1958)

Smith, D., 'Collective Administration of Copyright: An Economic Analysis' (1986) 8 *Research in Law and Economics* 137

Smith, J., *Voice of the People: The European Parliament in the 1990s* (London: Royal Institute of International Affairs, 1995)

Sobel, L., 'Copyright! A Source of Friction between the United States and Ireland' [2001] EntLR 65

Soto, V., 'The Scale Tips in Favour of Parodists and Freedom of Speech Advocates, as "Other" Version of Gone With The Wind Held Fair Use under

Copyright Law: *Suntrust Bank* v. *Houghton Mifflin Co.*' (2002) 18 *Santa Clara Computer and High Technology Law Journal* 405

Spector, H., 'An Outline of a Theory Justifying Intellectual and Industrial Property Rights' [1989] EIPR 270

Spence, D., 'Shocking News' [2002] EntLR 27

Spence, M., 'Intellectual Property and the Problem of Parody' (1998) 114 *Law Quarterly Review* 594

Spry, I., *The Principles of Equitable Remedies: Specific Performance, Injunctions, Rectification and Equitable Damages*, 6th edn (London: Sweet & Maxwell, 2001)

Srikantiah, J., 'The Response of Copyright to the Enforcement Strain of Inexpensive Copying Technology' (1996) 71 *New York University Law Review* 1634

Stamatoudi, I., 'Are Sophisticated Multimedia Works Comparable to Video Games?' (2001) 48 *Journal of the Copyright Society of the USA* 467

Copyright and Multimedia Works: A Comparative Analysis (Cambridge: Cambridge University Press, 2002)

Stamatoudi, I. and P. Torremans (eds.), *Copyright in the New Digital Environment*, Perspectives on Intellectual Property 8 (London: Sweet & Maxwell, 2000)

Stammer, K., 'A Little Morality in a Digital World' (12 April 2001) *Managing Intellectual Property* (online)

Sterk, S., 'Rhetoric and Reality in Copyright Law' (1996) 94 *Michigan Law Review* 1197

Sterling, A. (ed.), *Intellectual Property and Market Freedom*, Perspectives on Intellectual Property 2 (London: Sweet & Maxwell, 1997)

'Creators' Rights and the Bridge Between Author's Right and Copyright' (1998) 29 IIC 302

'Philosophical and Legal Challenges in the Context of Copyright and Digital Technology' (2000) 31 IIC 508

'International Codification of Copyright Law: Possibilities and Imperatives' (2002) 23 IIC 270

World Copyright Law, 2nd edn (London: Sweet & Maxwell, 2003)

Stewart, D., 'Protecting Privacy, Property and Possums' (2002) 30 *Federal Law Review* 177

Stewart, S., *International Copyright and Neighbouring Rights*, 2nd edn (London: Butterworths, 1989; Vol. 2, 1993)

Still, K., '*American Geophysical Union* v. *Texaco, Inc.*: Expanding the Copyright Monopoly' (1995) 29 *Georgia Law Review* 1233

Stone, A., 'The Limits of Constitutional Text and Structure: Standards of Review and the Freedom of Political Communication' (1999) 23 *Melbourne University Law Review* 668

Stokes, S., 'Categorising Art in Copyright Law' [2001] EntLR 179

'Copyright and the Reproduction of Artistic Works' [2003] EIPR 486

Stott, W., 'Other People's Images: A Case History', in J. Lawrence and B. Timberg (eds.), *Fair Use and Free Inquiry: Copyright Law and the New Media*, 2nd edn (Norwood: Ablex Publishing, 1989)

Streeter, T., 'Broadcast Copyright and the Bureaucratization of Property' (1992) 10 *Cardozo Arts and Entertainment Law Journal* 567
  'Some Thoughts on Free Speech, Language and the Rule of Law', in D. Allen and R. Jensen (eds.), *Freeing the First Amendment* (New York: New York University Press, 1995)
Streibich, H., 'The Moral Right of Ownership to Intellectual Property: Part 1 – From the Beginning to the Age of Printing' (1975) 6 *Memphis State University Law Review* 1
Stromholm, S., 'Droit Moral – The International and Comparative Scene from a Scandanavian Viewpoint' (1983) 14 IIC 1
Suleiman, E. (ed.), *Bureaucrats and Policy Making* (New York: Holmes & Meier, 1984)
Sullivan, E., 'Lost in Cyberspace: A Closer Look at ISP Liability' [2001] EntLR 192
Sunstein, C. (ed.), *Behavioral Law and Economics* (New York: Cambridge University Press, 2000)
Suthersanen, U., 'Exclusions to Design Protection: A New Paradigm' in A. Sterling (ed.), *Intellectual Property and Market Freedom*, Perspectives on Intellectual Property 2 (London: Sweet & Maxwell, 1997)
  'Breaking Down the Intellectual Property Barriers' [1998] IPQ 267
  'Copyright and Educational Policies: A Stakeholder Analysis' (2003) 23 *Oxford Journal of Legal Studies* 585
Sykes, K., 'Towards a Public Justification of Copyright' (2003) 61 *University of Toronto Faculty of Law Review* 1
Szymanski, R., 'Audio Pastiche: Digital Sampling, Intermediate Copying, Fair Use' (1996) 3 *UCLA Entertainment Law Review* 271
Tackaberry, P., 'The Digital Sound Sampler: Weapon of the Technological Pirate or Palette of the Modern Artist?' [1990] 1 EntLR 87
Tadros, V., 'A Few Thoughts on Copyright Law and the Subject of Writing', in L. Bently and S. Maniatis (eds.), *Intellectual Property and Ethics*, Perspectives on Intellectual Property 4 (London: Sweet & Maxwell, 1998)
Taylor, G. and D. Wright, 'Privacy, Injunctions and Possums: An Analysis of The High Court's Decision in *Australian Broadcasting Corporation* v. *Lenah Game Meats*' (2002) 26 *Melbourne University Law Review* 707
Taylor, L., *Copyright for Librarians* (Hastings: Tamarisk, 1980)
Theakston, K. (ed.), *Bureaucrats and Leadership* (London: Macmillan, 2000)
Therien, J., 'Exorcising the Specter of a "Pay-per-Use Society": Toward Preserving Fair Use and the Public Domain in the Digital Age' (2001) 16 *Berkeley Technology Law Journal* 979
Thomas, A., 'MP3 Wars: The Battle for Copyright in Cyberspace' [2000] EntLR 165
Thomas, D., 'A Public Interest Defence to Copyright Infringement?' (2003) 14 AIPJ 225
Tierney, S., 'Press Freedom and the Public Interest: The Developing Jurisprudence of the European Convention of Human Rights' [1998] *European Human Rights Law Review* 419

Timkovich, E., 'The New Significance of the Four Fair Use Factors as Applied to Parody: Interpreting the Court's Analysis in *Campbell* v. *Acuff-Rose Music, Inc.*' (2003) 5 *Tulane Journal of Technology and Intellectual Property* 61

Tomkins, A., 'The Draft Constitution of the European Union' [2003] *Public Law* 571

Torno, B., *Fair Dealing: The Need for Conceptual Clarity on the Road to Copyright Revision* (Ottawa: Department of Consumer and Corporate Affairs, 1981)

Towse, R., *Creativity, Incentive and Reward: An Economic Analysis of Copyright and Culture in the Information Age* (Cheltenham: Edward Elgar, 2001)

Treece, J., 'Library Photocopying' (1977) 24 *UCLA Law Review* 1025

Treyde, P., 'Simplification of the Exceptions to the Exclusive Rights Comprising Copyright' (1998) 9 *Journal of Law and Information Science* 77

Tritton, G., *Intellectual Property in Europe* (London: Sweet & Maxwell, 1996)

Trosow, S., 'The Illusory Search for Justificatory Theories' (2003) 16 *Canadian Journal of Law and Jurisprudence* 217

Tucker, D., *Law, Liberalism and Free Speech* (Totowa, N.J.: Rowman & Allanheld, 1985)

Tunney, J., 'EU, IP, Indigenous People and the Digital Age: Intersecting Circles?' [1998] EIPR 335

Tushnet, R., 'Copyright as a Model for Free Speech Law: What Copyright Has in Common with Anti-pornography Laws, Campaign Finance Reform and Telecommunications Regulation' (2000) 42 *Boston College Law Review* 1

Twining, W., *Globalisation and Legal Theory* (London: Butterworths, 2000)

Tyerman, B., 'The Economic Rationale for Copyright Protection for Published Books: A Reply to Professor Breyer' (1971) 18 *UCLA Law Review* 1100

Underdown, E., 'The Copyright Question' (1886) 2 *Law Quarterly Review* 213

Universities UK Media release, 26 April 2002 (online)

Uphoff, E., *Intellectual Property and US Relations with Indonesia, Malaysia, Singapore and Thailand* (New York: South East Asia Program, 1991)

Van Caenegem, W., 'Communications Issues in Copyright Law', paper delivered at the Australian Law Teachers' Association 50th Anniversary Conference, 1995

  'Copyright, Communications and New Technology' (1995) 23 *Federal Law Review* 322

  'The Public Domain: *Scienta Nullis*' [2002] EIPR 324

Van Den Elzen, R., 'Decrypting the DMCA: Fair Use as a Defense to the Distribution of DeCSS' (2002) 77 *Notre Dame Law Review* 673

Vaver, D., 'Some Agnostic Observations on Intellectual Property' (1990–1) 6 IPJ 125

  'Abridgments and Abstracts: Copyright Implications' [1995] EIPR 225

  'Taking Stock' [1999] EIPR 339

  Copyright Law (Toronto: Irwin Law, 2000)

  'Intellectual Property: The State of the Art' (2000) 116 *Law Quarterly Review* 621

'Recreating a Fair Copyright System for the 21st Century (2000–1) 15 IPJ 123

Vick, D., 'The Internet and the First Amendment' (1998) 61 *Modern Law Review* 414

Vinje, T., 'Magill: Its Impact on the Information Technology Industry' [1992] EIPR 371

'A Brave New World of Technological Protection Systems: Will There Still be Room for Copyright?' [1996] EIPR 431

'Copyright Imperilled?' [1999] EIPR 192

Vivant, M., 'Le Droit d'Auteur, un Droit de l'Homme' (1997) 174 RIDA 61

Volokh, E., 'Freedom of Speech and Intellectual Property: Some Thoughts after *Eldred, 44 Liquormart, Saderup* and *Bartnicki*' (2003) 40 *Houston Law Review* 697

Volokh, E. and B. McDonnell, 'Freedom of Expression and Independent Judgment Review in Copyright Cases' (1998) 107 *Yale Law Journal* 2431

Von Lewinski, S., 'Copyright within the External Relations of the European Union and the EFTA Countries' [1994] EIPR 429

'The Role of Copyright in Modern International Trade Law' (1994) 161 RIDA 5

'A Successful Step Towards Copyright and Related Rights in the New Information Age: The New EC Proposal for a Harmonisation Directive' [1998] EIPR 135

'Proposed EC Directive on Copyright and Related Rights in the Information Society as It Progresses' (1999) 30 IIC 767

'Recent Developments in Europe Relating to the Digital Environment', paper delivered at the Copyright Society of Australia in Sydney, March 2002

Voon, T., 'Breach of Confidence by Government; Smith Kline and the TRIPS Agreement – Public Interest to the Rescue' (1998) 9 AIPJ 66

Wacks, R., 'Pop Goes Privacy' (1978) 41 *Modern Law Review* 67

Wadham, J. and H. Mountfield, *Blackstone's Guide to the Human Rights Act 1998* (London: Blackstone, 1999)

Waelde, C., and H. MacQueen, 'From Entertainment to Education: The Scope of Copyright?' [2004] IPQ 259

Waldron, J., 'From Authors to Copiers: Individual Rights and Social Values in Intellectual Property' (1993) 68 *Chicago Kent Law Review* 842

Law and Disagreement (Oxford: Clarendon, 1999)

Warnecke, A., 'The Art of Applying the Fair Use Doctrine: The Postmodern-Art Challenge to the Copyright Law' (1994) 13 *The Review of Litigation* 684

Warren, K., 'A Philosophical Perspective on the Ethics and Resolution of Cultural Properties Issues', in P. Messenger (ed.), *The Ethics of Collecting Cultural Property* (Albuquerque: University of New Mexico Press, 1989)

Warshofsky, F., *The Patent Wars: The Battle to Own the World's Technology* (New York: John Wiley, 1994)

Watson, A., *Legal Transplants: An Approach to Comparative Law* (Edinburgh: Scottish Academic Press, 1974)

Watson, M., 'Unauthorised Digital Sampling in Musical Parody: A Haven in the Fair Use Doctrine?' (1999) 21 *Western New England Law Review* 469

Watts, J. and F. Blakemore, 'Protection of Software Fonts in UK Law' [1995] EIPR 133

Weatherall, K., 'An End to Private Communications in Copyright? The Expansion of Rights to Communicate Works to the Public: Part 1' [1999] EIPR 342

'An End to Private Communications in Copyright? The Expansion of Rights to Communicate Works to the Public: Part 2' [1999] EIPR 398

Weatherill, S., *Law and Integration in the European Union* (Oxford: Clarendon, 1995)

Wei, G., 'Spare Parts and Copyright' (1998) 114 *Law Quarterly Review* 39

Weil, S., 'Fair Use and the Visual Arts, or Please Leave Some Room for Robin Hood' (2001) 62 *Ohio State Law Journal* 835

Weinand, P., A. Booy and R. Fry, *A Guide to Copyright for Museums and Galleries* (London: Routledge, 2000)

Weinreb, L., 'Fair's Fair: A Comment on the Fair Use Doctrine' (1990) 103 *Harvard Law Review* 1137

'Fair Use' (1999) 67 *Fordham Law Review* 1291

West, R., 'Authority, Autonomy and Choice: The Role of Consent in the Moral and Political Visions of Franz Kafka and Richard Posner' (1985) 99 *Harvard Law Review* 384

Whale, R., *Comment on Copyright* (London: British Copyright Council, 1969)

Wherry, T., *The Librarian's Guide to Intellectual Property in the Digital Age* (Chicago: American Library Association, 2002)

Whish, R., *Competition Law*, 4th edn (London: Butterworths, 2001)

Wilson, W., 'Privacy, Confidence and Press Freedom: A Study in Judicial Activism' (1990) 53 *Modern Law Review* 43

Wiseman, L., 'Educational Ownership and Use: An Opportunity to Rethink Copyright' (1998) 9 *Journal of Law and Information Science* 77

Copyright in Universities (Canberra: Australian Department of Education, Training and Youth Affairs, 1999)

Wolff, J., *The Social Production of Art* (London: Macmillan, 1981)

Xu Chao, 'On the Importance and Necessity of Establishing a System of Collective Administration of Copyright' [1996] 2 *China Patents and Trade Marks* 84

Yen, A., 'Restoring the Natural Law: Copyright as Labor and Possession' (1990) 51 *Ohio State Law Journal* 517

'When Authors Won't Sell: Parody, Fair Use and Efficiency in Copyright Law' (1991) 62 *University of Colorado Law Review* 79

'Internet Service Provider Liability for Subscriber Copyright Infringement, Enterprise Liability and the First Amendment' (2000) 88 *Georgetown Law Journal* 1833

'A Preliminary Economic Analysis of Napster: Internet Technology, Copyright Liability, and the Possibility of Coasean Bargaining' (2001) 26 *University of Dayton Law Review* 247

Yonover, G., 'The Precarious Balance: Moral Rights, Parody and Fair Use' (1996) 14 *Cardozo Arts and Entertainment Law Journal* 79

Yu, P., 'The Harmonization Game: What Basketball Can Teach about Intellectual Property and International Trade' (2003) 26 *Fordham International Law Journal* 218

'The Copyright Divide' (2003) 25 *Cardozo Law Review* 331

Yurkowski, R., 'Is *Hyde Park* Hiding the Truth? An Analysis of the Public Interest Defence to Copyright Infringement' (2002) 31 *Victoria University of Wellington Law Review* 1053

Zissu, R., 'US Fair Use in 1990: Where are We?' [1991] EntLR 20

NEWSPAPER ARTICLES

Childs, M., 'Listening to the Voice of the Consumer', *Guardian*, 24 August 2000

Harrison, M., 'TUC Slates Hewitt over Shake-up at the DTI', *Independent*, 23 November 2001

Lockyear, S., 'When Paddy Met Tony', *Guardian*, 30 July 2001

PUBLIC RECORD OFFICE DOCUMENTS

BT103/682, BT103/686, BT103/711, BT209/33, BT209/451, BT209/532, BT209/533, BT209/534, BT209/596, BT209/620, BT209/621, BT209/1113, BT209/1118, BT209/1119, BT209/1128, BT209/1361, BT281/12, BT281/13, BT281/14, BT281/15

CAB21/3725, CAB37/103/31, CAB37/106/41

HO45/10616/195426

LCO2/3888

LO3/429

TS27/22

Index

abstracts, 222, 237
abus de droit, 108, 207, 287
abuse of copyright, 287, 300
abuse of monopoly, 108
academics, works by, 177
access to information, *see* freedom of expression/information
accession, 186–7
acknowledgements
  anthologies for educational purposes, 124
  derivative works, 61
  educational copying, 128
  entrepreneurial works, 60–1
  examination exception, 123, 294–5
  fair dealing, 60–1, 62, 118
  forms, 60
  non-commercial scientific research, 293
  practicability, 60
  research and private study exception, 118
administration of justice, 206, 288
admixture, 186–7
advertisements, art sales, 138, 160, 162, 299–300
amicus curiae briefs, 218
anthologies
  educational purposes, 120, 124, 204, 236
  Germany, 204
  modern works, 124
  poems, 149
appropriation, 26
Aquinas, St Thomas, 203
architectural works, 177, 185–6, 233–4
archives, *see* libraries and archives
artistic works
  1956 Act, 232
  advertisement of sales, 138, 160, 162, 299–300
  droit de suite, 194–5, 200
  economic incentives, 177

exceptions, 3, 5
exhibitions, 162, 299
fair dealing, 58, 283
and idea/expression dichotomy, 22
incidental inclusion, 64–6
Information Society Directive, 299–300
instruction exception, 121
library copying, 143, 152
miniatures, 65, 89
photographs, 58
public display, 233–4, 299
recoding, 27–9
replacement copies, 156
research and study, 116, 152, 290
subsequent works by same artists, 66–7
term of copyright, 5
unpublished works, 152
value of copyright, 177
assignment, copyright, 174
Attlee, Clement, 230
Australia
  1905 Copyright Act, 257–8
  1912 Copyright Act, 257–8
  censorship by copyright law, 31
  'children overboard' controversy, 38
  computer programs, 70, 307
  Copyright Law Review Committee, 182, 250, 271, 277, 306, 307, 308
  departmental responsibilities, 227–8
  digital lock-up, 68
  educational copying, 228
  exceptions, 249, 277
  fair dealing, 182
  fair use, 250, 271
  freedom of expression, 21
  parodies, 266
  political communications, 37
  research/private study exception, 227–8
  users' rights, 227–8
Austria, 23, 195
authors' rights, 201–5, 207–8
Ayers, I., 273

Index

Baker, Nicholas, 244
balance of interests
  argument, 168
  closing debate, 239–40
  and copyright law, 187–91
  EU approach, 197, 198–200
  international instruments, 188
  and public participation, 280–1
  rhetoric, 8
  semantics, 188–9
  UK approach, 223–5
Bangemann Report, 197
behavioural law and economics, 175
Belgium, 307
Bell, T., 191
Bently, L., 58, 253, 289
Berne Convention
  educational exceptions, 125–6
  public interest defence, 105, 188
  Stockholm Revision, 216
  term of copyright, 200
  three-step test, 201, 217, 298
  and TRIPS, 2
Bhopal incident, 45
bibliographical studies, 148
biographies, 40
Blackstone, W., 182
Blair, Tony, 92, 244
blank tapes, levies, 205–6, 232
blind persons, 222, 228, 237
Bodleian Library, 157
Boyle, J., 179
breach of confidence, 39, 81, 82, 90–1, 104, 287
British Library, 122, 157, 294
broadcasts
  access to, 302
  archival copying, 138, 160, 161–2
  educational exception, 125
  ephemeral recordings, 299
  fair dealing, 60
  German educational exception, 206
  incidental inclusions, 64–6
  Information Society Directive, 299
  instruction exception, 122–3
  notes/recordings of spoken words, 63
  purpose of exceptions, 5–6
  recordings by educational establishments, 120, 127–8
  showing in educational establishments, 127
  subtitled copies, 222
buildings
  construction use, 299
  public display of models, 233–4
bureaucracy, 181

cable broadcasting, 5–6, 302
Cambridge University Library, 157
Campbell, Menzies, 244
Canada, 31, 249, 250
caricature, parody and pastiche exception
  see also parodies
  France, 49, 284
  Information Society Directive, 284
  law reform, 41
censorship, 29–30, 31–5
Chafee, Z., 94
changing attitudes, 304–5
Chorley, Lord, 232
choses in possession, 184–5
chrestomathies, 2
circumvention devices
  banning, 72–3
  non-regulation, 72
  regulation, 72
clean hands doctrine, 94–6, 102
Coase Theorem, 175
commentaries, 26–7
Commonwealth, 249–51
companies
  private study, 119
  registers, 161
compensation, fair compensation, 292
compulsory licensing, 19, 97, 228
computer programs
  back-up copies, 69, 235, 307
  copies to copyright libraries, 157
  decompilation, 68, 69–70, 307
  digital lock-up, 67–70, 308
  Directive, 235, 300, 307
  fair dealing, 262
  purpose of statutory provisions, 5
  research and study exception, 116
confidentiality
  breach of confidence, 39, 81, 82, 90–1, 104, 287
  and copyright law, 108
  national provisions, 287
  and public interest defence, 86–7
conservatism, 238–45
construction use, 299
consumer issues, 228–9
consumer organisations, 209, 228
contract
  digital lock-up, 67–70, 306, 308
  exclusions of exceptions, 67–70, 269–70, 306–7
  harmonisation of laws, 307
  unfair contract terms, 69
  and unlawful online material, 77

copyright
  alternative models, 173
  assignment, 174
  and authors' rights, 201–5, 207–8
  balance of interests, *see* balance of interests
  and creative copying, 40–1
  debates, 1
  and democratic process, 35–40, 84, 93, 288
  and designs law, 5
  economics, *see* economics
  exceptions, *see* exceptions
  fence posts, 203
  founding principle, 20
  and freedom of speech, *see* freedom of expression/information
  functions, 39, 299
  idea/expression dichotomy, 20–4
  ignorance of the law, 178
  infringement levels, 278–9, 297
  justification, 16, 18–19
  maximalists, 179
  and other rights, 279
  property right, 8, 168, 180–7, 200, 225–6, 239
  scope, 82
  UK attitudes, 221–6
  UK neglect, 229
  UK principles, 242–4
Copyright Directorate, 224, 229
copyright libraries, 147, 156–8
Copyright Licensing Agency
  and commercial use, 122, 294
  higher education dispute, 114, 130–5
  role, 128
  Sticker Scheme, 146
Copyright Licensing Rapid Clearance Service (CLARCS), 131, 134
Copyright Tribunal
  higher education dispute, 114, 130–5
  powers, 70, 127, 306–7
  referrals, 128, 129
corruption, 83–8
course packs, 130, 131–2, 134, 228
court judgments, 237
courts, *see* judiciary
Craig, C., 180–1
creative copying, 40–1
crime, public interest defence, 86
criticism and review exception
  acknowledgements, 60–1
  artistic works, 283
  and encryption, 75, 308
  fair dealing, 43–4
  fairness of use, 57–9
  Information Society Directive, 283–4, 286–7
  judicial interpretation, 261
  justification, 15
  law reform, 283–4
  meaning of criticism and review, 49–4
  parodies, *see* parodies
  published works, 286–7
  quotations, 286
  scope, 44–5, 236, 286
  unbalanced criticism, 52
  unpublished works, 45–7, 61, 62, 261
Crown employees, 44
culture
  cultural icons, recoding, 28–9
  Department for Culture, Media and Sport, 229
  EU control of cultural goods, 159–60
  EU objective, 196–7, 200
  national heritage, 156
  promotion, 158
  UK departmental responsibility, 228
current events, *see* reporting of current events

damages
  breach of copyright, 97
  and injunctions, 100
  nominal damages, 97, 102
databases, 231, 300, 307, 308
Davies, Gillian, 198, 202–3
defamation, 39, 104
democratic process
  and copyright, 35–40
  deliberative democracy, 212
  EU democratic deficit, 211
  and public interest defence, 84, 93, 288
Denicola, R., 29–30, 37, 269
Denning, Lord, 244
Department of Trade and Industry (DTI), 226–30
depravity, 95, 265
derivative works
  acknowledgement of original works, 61
  and fair dealing exception, 49–51, 62, 63
  freedom to copy, 25–6, 28
  generally, 64–7
  incidental inclusions, 64–6
  parodies, *see* parodies
  subsequent works by same artists, 66–7
  and synonyms, 64
design rights, 302

Index

Designs and Artists Copyright Society (DACS), 130, 132–3
designs law, 5
developing countries, 140
development, right to, 16
digital environment
  digital divide, 71
  digital lock-up, 67–70, 306, 308
  digital sound sampling, 26, 70
  economics, 172
  and fair use, 269–70
  new technologies, 168–9, 194, 231, 296
  pro-owner bias, 189
  value of copyright, 177, 263
directives
  bolt-on transposition, 235–6
  Information Society, see Information Society Directive
  UK implementation, 235–6
directors, incidental inclusions, 65
disability, see persons with disability
Doha Ministerial Statement, 217
Doran, Frank, 244
drafting of laws, 220, 230
Drahos, P., 203
dramatic works
  anthologies, 124
  educational performance exception, 124, 147
  instruction exception, 121
  interlibrary copying for stock, 154
  library copies of unpublished works, 151, 153
  library copying, 143, 148
  quotations, 286
  replacement library copies, 156
  research and study, 116, 152, 290
  term of copyright of unpublished works, 153
Dreyfuss, R., 270
droit d'auteur, 201–5
droit de suite, 194–5, 200
DTI, 226–30
Duncan, Carol, 140
Dusollier, Séverine, 198, 308–9
Dworkin, Ronald, 201, 270, 272

Easton, J. M., 258, 260
EBLIDA, 209
E-commerce Directive, 76–7, 300–1
economics
  alternative values, 173
  and behavioural law, 175
  and certainty of protection, 179
  digital environment, 172

economic approach to copyright, 170–3
  incentive mechanism, 178
  incentives theory of copyright, 170–3, 176–7
  market failure, 8, 168–80, 197–8, 222–3
  and moral rights, 174–5
  narrowness of vision, 174
  neo-classical approach, 171
  opposition to economic theory of copyright, 173–80
  quality of empirical research on copyright, 176–8
  and state intervention, 172
education exceptions
  anthologies, 120, 124, 204, 236
  Australia, 228
  copying, 120
  EU promotion of education, 196
  examination purposes, 120, 123, 294–5
  generally, 120–35
  Germany, 206
  higher education dispute, 114, 130–5
  Information Society Directive, 288–9
  instruction purposes, 120, 121–3
  lending copies, 120, 126
  market failure, 222
  modern works, 124
  overview, 120
  parents, 125–6, 152
  performances, 120, 124–6
  scope, 3
  study packs, 130, 131–2, 134, 228
  US copying practice, 268
educational establishments
  classroom copying, 114, 117, 292, 297
  copying, 120, 128–9
  impact of copyright law, 113–14
  importance of exceptions, 6
  law reform, 294–7
  lending copies, 120, 126
  libraries, 147
  licensing provisions, 126–9
  meaning, 120
  performances, 120, 124–6
  recordings of broadcasts, 120, 127–8
  supply of copies, 295–7
Educational Recording Agency, 128
EFPICC, 212, 213
Electronic Frontier Foundation, 213
e-mails, 39, 150, 154
employment, ownership of employees' works, 44–5
encryption, see technological measures of protection
endowment effects, 175

equity
  clean hands doctrine, 94–6, 102
  fraud, 94, 96–7
  and public interest defence, 80, 94–7
EU
  balance of interests rhetoric, 197
  Commission's understanding of copyright, 197–208
  compatibility with ECHR, 107
  and continental traditions, 201–8
  contracting out of exceptions, 306
  copyright directives, 196–7
  deliberative democracy, 212
  democratic deficit, 211
  digital lock-up, 69
  EU law and UK law, 220–1
  and fair use, 273–4
  Governance White Paper, 211
  harmonisation, see harmonisation
  implementation of directives, 235–6
  Information Society Directive, see Information Society Directive
  internal market, 194–5, 197, 303
  legislative process, 193–4
  market failure approach, 197–8
  parliamentary control over EU law, 236–8
  participation, 208–13
  piecemeal approach, 194
  technological measures of protection, 72
EU jurisprudence
  exhaustion of rights doctrine, 194
  freedom of expression, 23
  proportionality, 102, 105
  trade marks, 180
European Association of Consumer Electronics Manufacturers (EACEM), 210–11
European Convention on Human Rights, 36, 107, 109, 305
ex turpi causa non oritur actio, 94
examination exception, 120, 123, 294–5
exceptions
  see also specific exceptions
  approaches, 4–5
  Commonwealth countries, 249–51
  contractual exclusions, 67–70, 269–70, 306–7
  debate, 1–4, 368
  fair dealing, see fair dealing
  functions, 4–6
  Information Society Directive, 214, 299–301
  international instruments, 215–19
  or licensing, 168–80
  market failure claim, 168–80
  origins, 10
  and technological measures of protection, 70–5
  terminology, 10–11, 182, 279–80
  or users' rights, 10–11, 182, 279–80
  visually impaired persons, 228
exhaustion of rights doctrine, 194
exhibitions, artistic works, 233–4, 299
export, pre-export library copies, 137, 159–60, 207

fair compensation, 292
fair dealing
  1911 Act, 258, 259
  acknowledgements, 60–1, 62, 118
  approved purposes, 48–57
  Australia, 182
  codes of practice, 59
  criticism and review, see criticism and review exception
  derivative works, 49–51, 62, 63
  and economic incentives, 178
  excluded subject matters, 44–5, 61
  exclusion of photographs, 38, 44–5, 237
  and fair use, 249–50
  fairness principles, 57–9, 169–70
  Gregory Committee, 259
  inadequacy, 28, 61–2
  Information Society Directive problems, 286–7
  Information Society Directive provisions, 282–7
  instruction purposes, 121
  law reform, 221
  libraries, 145, 152–3
  meaning, 57–9
  news reporting, see reporting current events
  and non-substitutability, 25
  parodies, 49–51, 62, 63
  private study, see private study exception
  or public interest defence, 110, 127
  research, see research exception
  and technological measures of protection, 75
  UK copyright regime, 38
  uncertainty, 59
  unpublished works, 38
  unpublished works exclusion, 38, 45–8, 61, 62
  value, 9

Index

fair use
  abolition by judiciary, 253–64
  and digital environment, 269–70
  drawbacks, 252
  and EU law, 273–4
  fair abridgement, 254–6
  and fair dealing, 249–50
  flexibility, 252
  future, 269–74
  history of judicial interpretation, 253–64
  judicial interpretation, 253, 269
  opposition to, 251–3
  support, 250–3
  and TRIPS, 270–3
  uncertainty, 252–3
  United States, 4, 170, 207, 249–50
  US current practice, 267–9
fanzines, 27
fax copies, 150, 154
films
  acknowledgements, 60–1
  archives, 141
  educational exception, 125
  fair dealing, 60
  incidental inclusions, 64–6
  instruction exception, 122–3
  library copying, 143, 152
  public lending right, 158
  quotations, 286
  replacement library copies, 156
  showing in educational establishments, 127
  unpublished works, 152
fine arts, 148
Fitzgerald, B., 269
flexibility
  copyright exceptions, 38–39
  fair use, 252
  inflexibility of current position, 7, 249, 276–7
  inflexibility of judiciary, 238
  Information Society Directive, 277
  public interest defence, 111
  reform model, 276, 277
floodgates argument, 24
FOBID, 208
folksongs, copies, 138, 160, 161–2
Fox, Stephen, 278
France
  abus de droit, 108, 120, 207, 287
  caricature, parody and pastiche exception, 49, 284
  copyright system, 202–3
  market failure argument, 198
  private use, 197, 205

fraud, 94, 96–7
free riders, 170
free use defence, 49, 207
freedom of expression/information
  and appropriation, 26
  boundaries, 19–20
  case law, 31–5
  and commentaries, 26–7
  compulsory licence, 19, 228
  and copyright, 6, 15–20, 189
  and democratic process, 35–40
  evidential importance of quotations, 29–30
  Human Rights Act, 100–2
  and idea/expression dichotomy, 20–4
  illustrations of conflict, 24–5
  judicial attitudes, 21–3, 93, 101
  limits, 34
  non-substitutability argument, 24–5
  and parody, 25–6, 28
  photographs excluded from fair dealing, 44
  public interest defence, 288
  reasons for, 33–4
  recoding, 27–9
  resolution of conflict, 35–41
  substance and form, 37
  terminology, 15
  theory, 17–18
  US Constitutional guarantee, 269
  use of copyright as censorship, 29–30, 31–5

Garon, J., 278
Gay Olympics, 27
Geller, P., 273
Germany
  copyright and property right, 203–4
  copyright system, 202–3
  exceptions, 206–7
  free use defence, 49, 207
  parodies, 207, 284
  persons with disability, 206
  private use, 197, 205
  public policy, 207
Ginsburg, J., 202, 217, 272
GMOs, 186
Goldstein, Paul, 169, 171
Gone with the Wind, 41, 50, 169, 171, 286
goodwill, 96
Gordon, W., 25–6, 171, 172
Gorrell, Lord, 243
Gregory Committee, 232, 243, 259, 261

Hackett, Teresa, 209
Hailsham, Lord, 225, 244
Hale, Matthew, 254
Hamilton, A., 94
Hansard, 63, 245
harmonisation
  amendment process, 195
  Commission approach, 200, 201–8
  and continental traditions, 201–8
  contract laws
  Information Society Directive, 1–2, 201–8, 295, 302, 303–4
  and internal market, 194–5, 197, 303
  logic, 193, 194–7
  and national implementation, 235
  participation, 208–13
  realising, 303–4
health
  public health, 83, 99, 107, 288
  right to health, 16
Helfer, L., 271
historical studies, 148
Hohfeld, W., 183
honour, 78
Howse, Robert, 218
Hugenholz, B., 273
human rights
  ECHR jurisprudence, 36, 59
  free speech, *see* freedom of expression/ information
  impact of 1998 Act, 2, 17, 92, 100–2
  and IP rights, 16–20

idea/expression dichotomy, 20–4
illustrations
  educational copying, 132, 134
  evidential importance, 29, 37, 269
  and idea/expression dichotomy, 21
  interlibrary copying for stock, 154
  library copies of unpublished works, 151
  library copying, 143
immorality, 95, 265
imperial model, 249–51
incentive theories, 170–3, 176–7, 178
incidental inclusion, 64–6, 240, 299, 300
independent schools, 122, 294
India, exceptions, 249
indigenous cultures, 140
inertia
  Information Society Directive, 213–15
  international law, 193–4
inflexibility, current position, 7, 249, 276–7

information, *see* freedom of expression/ information
Information Society Directive
  balance of interests, 198–200
  copyrights as property rights, 200
  criticism and review, 283–4, 286–7
  digital copying, 144
  exceptions, 214, 299–301
  exhibitions of artistic works, 162
  fair dealing problems, 286–7
  fair dealing provisions, 282–3
  and fair use, 273–4
  flexibility, 277
  Green Paper, 197–200, 209–10
  harmonisation, 201–8, 295, 302, 303–4
  impact, xi, 1
  and inertia, 213–15
  institutional users, 288–9, 294–7
  libraries and museums, 143–5
  market failure approach, 197–8
  minor exceptions, 302
  news reporting, 284–5, 287
  non-commercial scientific research, 293
  parodies, 284
  private use, 205
  process, 197–200, 209–10, 212–13
  public interest defence, 107–8, 287
  reform model, 9–10, 38, 193–4, 276, 282–7, 297–8
  research and private study, 288–3
  supplemented with public interest defence, 287
  technological measures of protection, 74, 308–10
  UK implementation, 42, 76, 115, 121, 123, 157, 224, 229
  unharmonised provisions, 301–2
  and users' rights, 279, 281–7
  validity, 273–4, 303
infringement levels, 278–9, 297
injunctions
  and damages, 100
  discretion, 98–100
  interim injunctions, 100–1
  refusal, 97–101
injury to feelings, 97
institutional users
  administrative costs, 147
  education, *see* educational establishments
  exceptions, 113–15
  Information Society Directive, 288–9
  intranet services, 144, 297
  law reform, 294–7

Index

libraries and archives, *see* libraries and archives
museums, *see* museums and galleries
and new technologies, 296
research/private study exception, 119–20
supply of copies, 295–7
and technological measures of protection, 73, 75
warning notices, 119
instruction exception
  commercial purposes, 121–2
  drafting of legislation, 230–1
  generally, 120, 121–3
  non-commercial purposes, 121, 122
  reprographic processes, 122, 230–1
integrity
  architectural works, 186
  moral right, 77, 175
intellectual property rights
  economic rationale, 170–3
  and human rights, 16–20
  opposition to economic theory of copyright, 173–80
  and other rights, 279
  use for censorship, 32
interlibrary loans, 145
internal documents, 39, 82, 83, 103, 276
international law
  balance of interests rhetoric, 188
  exceptions, 2, 215–19
  inertia, 193–4, 213–15
  public interest defence, 105–8
  terminology, 279–80, 281–7
  and UK law, 220–1
Internet
  commentaries, 27
  contracts and encryption, 74
  and contractual exclusion of exceptions, 67–70
  copying by legal deposit libraries, 157
  digital lock-up, 67–70
  economics, 172
  e-mails, 39, 150, 154
  impact on exceptions, 169
  OSPs, *see* online service providers
  reporting of current events, 57
  temporary copies, 76, 301
  transaction costs, 179
intranet services, 144, 297
Ireland, 307
Israel, 249
Italy, 273

Jacob, Lloyd, 243
Johnson, Melanie, 228, 237

journalists
  news reporting, *see* reporting current events
  notes/recordings of spoken words, 63
  public interest defence, 89
  scoops, 39, 90
journals, 149
judicial proceedings, 62, 87–8, 177, 237
judiciary
  abolition of fair use defence, 253–4
  balance arguments, 239–40
  changing attitudes, 305
  copyright as property, 239
  and fair dealing reform, 221
  and freedom of expression, 93, 101
  history of fair use defence, 253–64
  ineffective protection of users, 9
  inflexibility, 238
  legislative correction of decisions, 241–4
  likely approach to fair use, 253, 269
  market failure argument, 240
  move to restrictive approaches, 238
  narrow interpretations, 238
  and parodies, 264–7
  and public interest defence, 93, 253
  references to legislative history, 244–5
  role, 221, 238–5

Kennedy, J. F., 25
Krieg, P., 26
Ku, R., 177
Kubrick, Stanley, 52, 287

Laddie, H., 102, 108, 109, 110, 234, 305
land law
  intersection with copyright, 185–6
  non-derogation from grant, 184, 185, 187
Landes, W., 72, 170, 171, 174–5
languages, 148
law reform
  case for reform, 6–10
  changing attitudes, 304–5
  counterclaims, 168
  criteria, 275, 276
  criticism and review, 283–4
  fair dealing, 221
  flexibility, 276, 277
  Information Society Directive model, 9, 276, 282–7, 297–8
  institutional users, 294–7
  news reporting, 284–5

law reform (cont.)
  public interest defence, 10, 39, 111–12, 287
  public participation, 276, 280–2
  research and private study, 289–3
  technological measures of protection, 306–10
  US model, 269
  users' rights, 276, 279–80
  workability, 276, 277–9
Leaffer, M., 270
Lee, M., 212
legal deposit libraries, 147, 156–8
legal studies, 148
legislative process
  1909 Royal Commission, 256
  1911 Act, 256–9
  1956 Act, 229–30
  1988 Act, 223–4, 236–7, 242–3
  erosion of parliamentary control over EU law, 236–8
  failures, 241
  implementation of directives, 235–6
  instruction exception, 230–1
  judicial reference to, 244–5
  and judiciary, 238–5
  parliamentary intentions, 234, 242–3, 263
  private members' bills, 228
  public display of building models, 233–4
  sound recordings exclusion, 231–3
  UK drafting, 220, 230–4
Lemley, M., 70
letters, 152
levies, 205–6, 232, 292
libraries and archives
  1988 divisions, 142–3
  2003 reforms, 136
  administrative burden, 147, 149
  commercial libraries, 148
  concerns, 3
  copies of articles, 147–50
  copies of non-print publications, 137, 156–8
  copies of part published works, 147–50
  copies of unpublished works, 137, 150, 296
  copies to other libraries, 137, 154–5
  copies to readers, 115, 145–7, 295–7
  copyright libraries, 147, 156–8
  declaration forms, 145–6, 149, 151
  defining, 138–42
  digitised copies of works, 144
  exceptions, 137–8, 145–62
  higher education, 113
  importance of exceptions, 6
  Information Society Directive, 143–5, 288–9
  interlibrary copying for stock, 154
  interlibrary loans, 145
  intranet services, 144
  law reforms, 294–7
  legal deposit libraries, 147, 156–8
  lending of copies, 158–9
  media restrictions, 152, 156
  microfilms, 156
  multiple copies, 149–50
  new directions, 142
  new technologies, 150
  non-textual media, 137, 149, 156–8, 237
  not-for-profit libraries, 143
  out-of-print books, 156
  permitted copying, 136
  pre-export copies, 137, 159–60, 207
  prescribed libraries, 147–8, 151, 154, 155, 158, 160
  public lending right scheme, 137, 158–9
  reasonable proportions, 149
  rentals, 126
  replacement copies, 137, 155–6, 296
  research/private study exception, 119–20, 137
  role, 138–9
  self-service photocopying, 138, 145
  short loan collections, 131–2
  special treatment, 136–7
  subject matters, 148
  time limits, 149–50
  transitional provisions, 153–4
  UK departmental responsibility, 228
  uncertainty, 149
  unpublished works, 137, 150, 296
  warning notices, 119
Library Association, 149
licensing
  compulsory licensing, 19, 97, 228
  and copyright exceptions, 168–80, 222
  course packs, 130, 131–2
  educational establishments, 126–9
  higher education dispute, 114, 130–5
  law reform, 296
  Secretary of State powers, 127, 129
lifelong learning, 142
limitation periods, 147
literary works
  anthologies, 124
  definition, 260
  educational performance exception, 124, 147
  fair dealing, 58

incidental inclusions, 64
instruction exception, 121
interlibrary copying for stock, 154
library copies of unpublished works, 151, 153
library copying, 143, 148
quotations, 286
replacement library copies, 156
research and study, 116, 152, 290
short works, 131
similar stories, 22
term of copyright of unpublished works, 153
literature studies, 148
Litman, Jessica, 178, 210, 211, 242
Lloyd of Hampstead, Lord, 226
Lloyd of Kilgerran, Lord, 244
lobbying power, 167, 195, 209, 210–11, 215, 233, 237, 241–2
Locke, John, 104, 180
logos, 60, 65–6
Lowenfeld, A., 270

MacGillivray, E. J., 258
Magritte, René, 67
making available to public, 46, 121
malice, 52
maps
  library copying, 143, 152
  replacement library copies, 156
market failure
  and EU commission, 197–8
  and exceptions, 8, 168–80
  and judiciary, 240
  UK attitudes, 222–3
May, Christopher, 189–90
media studies courses, 123
medical studies, 148
memorandums, 39, 82, 92, 103, 276
mental distress, 97
MEPs, 208, 213
Merges, Robert, 169, 222
microfilms, 156
Mill, John Stuart
miniatures, 65, 89
modern works, 124
Mole, Chris, 237
monopolies
  abuse of copyright monopoly, 108, 287, 300
  collecting agencies, 181, 225
  copyrights, 183
moral rights
  benefits, 40, 174–5, 176
  and Berne Convention, 126
  derogatory treatment, 77–8
  generally, 77–8
  integrity, 77, 175
  ridicule, 78
Mossink, Wilma, 208–9
multiple copies
  and instruction exception, 231
  law reform, 290
  libraries and archives, 149–50
  visually impaired persons, 222
museums and galleries
  1988 divisions, 142–3
  advertisement of sale of works, 138, 160, 162
  controversies, 140
  defining, 139–2
  digitised copies of works, 144
  discrimination against, 137, 143
  importance of exceptions, 6
  incidental inclusions, 65
  Information Society Directive, 143–5, 288–9
  law reform, 294–7
  new directions, 142
  Regional Museums Task Force, 142
  supply of copies, 295–7
  UK departmental responsibility, 228
musical studies, 148
musical works
  educational performance exception, 124, 147
  fair dealing, 261–2
  folksongs, copies, 138, 160, 161
  incidental inclusions, 64
  instruction exception, 121
  interlibrary copying for stock, 154
  library copies of unpublished works, 151, 153
  library copying, 143, 148
  quotations, 286
  replacement library copies, 156
  research and study, 116, 152, 231
  sheet music, 123
  term of copyright of unpublished works, 153
  and TRIPS, 217
My Lai massacre, 24, 37, 38, 49

Napster, 213
national heritage, 156
National Library of Scotland, 157
National Library of Wales, 157
Neale, Gerard, 244
near misses, reporting, 83
Netanel, N., 168, 171, 269

Netherlands, 197, 205, 208, 273
New Opportunities Fund, 144
new technologies, 150, 168–9, 194, 231, 296
New Zealand, 249
news reporting, *see* reporting current events
newspaper summaries, 262–3
NHS hospital libraries, 147
Nimmer, Melville, 24–5, 29, 37, 190
non-derogation from grant, 184, 185, 187
non-substitutability argument, 24–5
non-textual media
  libraries and archives, 137, 149, 152, 156–8, 237
  research/ private study, 231
Norman, Sandy, 149
Northern Ireland, 139, 142
Norway, 273
nuclear safety, 82

official proceedings
  judicial proceedings, 62, 87–8, 177, 237
  parliamentary proceedings, 61, 62, 63, 237
  published reports, 62, 63
  reporting, 61, 62–3
  statutory inquiries, 62
Okediji, R., 270, 271, 272, 273
online service providers
  caching unlawful material, 76
  conduits for unlawful material, 76
  E-Commerce Directive, 76–7, 300–1
  fear of liability, 75
  hosting unlawful material, 76
  role, 75–7
online services, *see* Internet
Open University, 128
originality, 260, 287
out-of-print books, 156

Padfield, T., 153
parents, and educational exceptions, 125–6, 152
parliamentary proceedings, 61, 62, 63, 237
parodies
  acknowledgement of original works, 61
  caricature, parody and pastiche exception, 41, 45, 49, 284
  and encryption, 308
  and fair dealing, 49–51, 62, 63
  fair use, 207
  and freedom of expression, 25–6, 28
  generally, 64–7
  Information Society Directive, 284

judicial interpretations, 264–7
protection, 264–7
and satire, 169, 265
special treatment, 264–7
participation
  EU legislative process, 208–13
  reform model, 276, 280–2
  or social rejection, 281
pastiches, *see* parodies
patents, 16, 160, 186, 218
Patry, W., 210
Penner, J., 183
performing rights, 295
periodicals
  interlibrary copying for stock, 154–5
  law reform, 291
  library copies of articles, 147–50
persons with disability
  Germany, 206
  Information Society Directive, 299
  visually impaired persons, 222, 228, 237
pharmaceuticals, 16, 31, 82, 218
philosophy, 148
photographs
  and anthologies, 124
  artistic works, of, 58
  definition, 44, 291
  educational copying, 132, 134
  evidential importance, 24–5, 37, 38
  exclusion from fair dealing, 38, 44–5, 237
  and freedom of expression, 24–5
  Information Society Directive, 291
  law reform, 290
  library copying, 143, 152
  replacement library copies, 156
  research and private study, 290, 291
  unpublished works, 152
  value of copyright, 177
piracy, 74, 239
planning applications, 160, 185
poems, 121, 131, 149
policing, 278, 291
political information
  see also democratic process
  copyright restrictions, 35–40
  fair dealing exception, 54
  meaning of political communication, 37
pornography, 18, 21
Posner, R., 72, 169–70, 171, 172, 174, 175
power groups, 167, 195, 209, 210–11, 215
Prescott, P., 102, 108, 110

Index

preservation copies, 137, 155–6, 296
Press Complaints Commission, 84
Priest, G., 176
privacy rights, 23, 39, 97
private study exception
  acknowledgements, 118
  Australia, 227–8
  companies, 119
  copying by other parties, 116, 117–18, 291
  copying in libraries, 137
  fair dealing exception, 115–20
  Information Society Directive, 288–9
  judicial interpretation, 118–19, 260–1
  law reform, 289–93
  non-commercial purposes, 117, 119, 138, 146, 159
  overview of exception, 115
  scenarios, 117–18
  scope of exception, 115–19, 152
  sound recordings, 116, 224–5, 231–3
  and technological measures of protection, 75
private use
  Berne Convention, 216
  and EU Commission, 197–8
  European approaches, 205–7
property rights
  choses in possession, 184–5
  copyrights as property right, 8, 168, 180–7, 200, 225–6, 239
  definition, 182
  Germany, 203–4
  land law, 185–6, 187
  limited ECHR right, 105
  neglect of personal property law, 183–4
  and public interest defence, 103–5
  repair rights, 184–5
  sanctity of property, 180, 225, 239
  and state intervention, 172
proportionality, 102, 105
public display, 233–4, 299
public goods, 170
public health, 83, 99, 107, 218, 288
public interest
  assessment, 108
  defence, *see* public interest defence
  reports of current events, 54, 56
  and TRIPS, 218, 271
public interest defence
  and abuse of monopoly, 108
  alternative means, 94–102
  appropriateness, 108–9, 111
  Berne Convention, 105

  common law defence, 80
  or compulsory licence, 97
  and confidentiality, 39, 81, 82, 86–7, 90–1
  early authorities, 81–91, 241
  economic considerations, 86
  and equity, 80, 94–7
  and express statutory exceptions, 88–9
  or fair dealing defence, 110, 127
  flexibility, 111
  France and Germany, 202
  indefinite reproduction, 88
  Information Society Directive, 107–8, 287
  and interesting matters, 83, 85
  international law, 105–8
  judicial attitudes, 93, 253, 267
  law reform, 10, 39, 111–12, 287
  legitimacy, 103–8
  literature, 21
  misleading information from public figures, 84
  necessity, 109–11
  objections of principle, 102–11
  past incidents, 83
  and political process, 84, 93
  and property rights, 103–5
  and prurience, 83, 85
  recent authorities, 91–4
  or refusal of injunctions, 97–101
  scope, 80
  statutory provision, 81
  subject areas, 83–6
  timing, 90
  to whom disclosed, 86–8
  uncertainty, 82, 111
  unfairness, 89–91
  workability, 111
public lending right, 126, 137, 158–9, 303
public morals, 83, 95, 107, 265
public order, 106
public policy
  and exceptions, 5
  Germany, 207
  judicial discretion, 108–9, 124
  and library sector, 136
  repair rights, 185
Public Record Office, 139
public records, 138, 160, 161
public registers, 138, 160–1
public safety, 83, 96, 107, 206, 288
public speeches, 206
Publishers Association, 59

quotations, 29–30, 206, 286

race discrimination, 18
reading lists, 134
Reading, Marquess of, 243
recoding, 27–9
recordings, *see* sound recordings
Regional Museums Task Force, 142
regulatory agencies, 83
Reichman, J., 270
religious studies, 148
religious use, 206, 303
rentals, 126, 155, 295
repair rights, 184–5
replacement copies, 137, 155–6, 296
reporting current events
  acknowledgements, 60–1
  currency of events, 55, 62
  defence, 91
  and encryption, 75, 308
  exclusion of photographs, 44–5, 237
  fair dealing, 43–4
  fairness of use, 57–9
  Germany, 207
  Information Society Directive, 284–5, 287
  law reform, 284–5
  meaning, 54–7, 288
  meaning of events, 54–5
  meaning of reporting, 55–7
  public domain, 285
  and public interest, 54, 56
  or public interest defence, 110
  scope of exception, 24–5, 44–5
  and unpublished works, 47–8, 61, 62
  use of spoken words, 63–4
reprographic processes, 122, 230–1
reputation, 78, 97, 104
research exception
  acknowledgements, 118
  Australia, 227–8
  commercial research, 146, 237, 291–2
  copying by other parties, 116, 117–18, 291
  copying in libraries, 137
  EU promotion of research, 196
  extracts from earlier works, 292–3
  fair dealing exception, 115–20
  importance of exceptions, 6
  Information Society Directive, 288–93
  judicial interpretation, 118–19
  law reform, 289–93
  meaning, 116–17
  non-commercial purposes, 117, 119, 138, 146, 148, 159, 223
  non-commercial scientific research, 41, 293

overview of exception, 115
scope of exception, 115–19, 152
and sound recordings, 116, 224–5, 231–3
and technological measures of protection, 75
types of copying, 117–18, 289
review exception, *see* criticism and review exception
reviews, meaning, 49
Ricketson, S., 216
ridicule, 78
right to life, 16
romantic notions of authorship, 26, 30

satire, 169, 172, 265
science studies, 148
scientific and technical abstracts, 222
SCONUL, 226
scoops, 39, 90
Scotland, 142
Scott, A., 273–4
sculptures, 233
security services, 45, 83, 84
security videos, 39, 82, 106
Sellars, C., 72
Seville, C., 256
sheet music, 123, 290, 291
Sherman, B., 58, 253, 289
short stories, 131
Singapore, 249
single market, 194–5, 197, 303
Skone James, Edmund, 243, 260
Skone James, F. E.
slides, 132–3
social sciences, 148
social welfare, 218, 271
Society of Authors, 59
sound recordings
  anthologies, 124
  archives, 141
  educational exception, 125
  exclusion from research/private study exception, 116, 224–5, 231–3
  fair dealing, 60
  incidental inclusion, 64–6
  judicial proceedings, 87–8
  library copying, 143, 152
  playing in educational establishments, 127
  public lending right, 158
  replacement library copies, 156
  spoken words, 63–4, 87–8
  technological development, 232
  unpublished works, 152

Index

South Africa, 249
Spain, 197, 205, 284
Spence, M., 25
spoken words, 63–4, 87–8, 237
sporting events, 54, 59, 65
Squire, Rachel, 237
state intervention, 172
statutory inquiries, 62
story lines, 22
Streeter, T., 181
study packs, 130, 131–2, 134, 228
surveillance photographs, 45
Sykes, Katie, 243
synonyms, 64

Taylor, John, 244
technological measures of protection
  banning circumvention devices, 72–3
  banning encryption, 72
  EU approach, 72
  and fair dealing exceptions, 75
  fair use by design, 73–5, 308
  generally, 70–5
  Information Society Directive, 74, 308–10
  institutional users, 73, 75
  and Internet contracts, 74
  law reform, 306–10
  non-regulation approach, 72
  non-regulation of circumvention devices, 72
  regulation of circumvention devices, 72
  research and private study exception, 75
  statutory complaints, 74–5
  trend, 3
  UK approach, 74–5
technology
  EU promotion, 196
  new technologies, 150, 168–9, 194, 231, 296
  scope of library copies, 148
  technical abstracts, 222
telephone transcripts, 38, 39
temporary copies, Internet, 76, 301
term of copyright
  artistic works, 5
  EU approach, 200
  extension, 225
  reform, 153
  Term Directive, 196
  twenty-year term, 16
  unpublished works, 153
terminology
  balance of interests, 188–9

exceptions or users' rights, 10–11, 182, 279–80
theatres, incidental inclusion, 65
Thomas, D., 89–6, 99
threats actions, 301
three-step test, 201, 217, 298
time-shifting, 233
trade marks
  EU jurisprudence, 180
  recoding, 28, 29
  scope of protection, 104
  use for censorship, 32
training courses, 121
transaction costs, 179
translations, 123
transnational organisations, 210
transparency
  alternatives to public interest defence, 102
  and nominal damages, 97
trials, restrictions, 37
Trinity College, Dublin, Library, 157
TRIPS
  copyright exceptions, 2, 279, 280
  dispute settlement procedure, 217–18
  effects, 217–19
  and fair use, 270–3
  public interest defence, 107
  regime, 189–90
  three-step test, 201, 217, 298
Tushnet, R., 22
typefaces, 5, 302
typographical arrangements, 143, 151, 154, 156, 290

uncertainty
  alternatives to public interest defence, 94, 101–2
  clean hands doctrine, 95
  current position, 7
  fair dealing, 59, 120
  fair use defence, 252–3
  library copying, 149
  public interest defence, 82, 111
  research/private study exception, 120, 138
unfair contract terms, 69
United Kingdom
  approach to exceptions, 4–5, 167
  balance of interests approach, 223–5
  copyright approaches, 221–6
  copyright as property right, 225–6
  departmental responsibilities, 226–7
  DTI's mandate, 226–30
  implementation of directives, 220

United Kingdom (*cont.*)
  legislation, *see* legislative process
  market failure approach, 222–3
  neglect of copyright issues, 229
  parliamentary oversight of government, 221
  poor deal for users, 8
  pre-1911 regime, 203
United States
  approach to exceptions, 4
  censorship, 32, 45
  classroom copying, 268
  Constitutional guarantees, 269
  copyright system, 202
  fair use, 4, 170, 207, 249–50, 268–73
  flag burning, 33
  freedom of expression, 16, 20, 23, 24
  legislative process, 210
  model for change, 269
  musical works, 217
  parodies, 264
  performing rights, 218–19
  unlawful material on Internet, 76
  use of IP law for censorship, 32
  Working Group on IP Rights, 181
universities
  see also educational establishments
  commercial purposes, 294
  copyright concerns, 113–14
  value, 114
unpublished works
  criticism and review exception, 286–7
  definition of making available to public, 46
  fair dealing exclusion, 38, 45–8, 61, 62, 110, 261
  library copying, 137, 150, 296
  news reports, 284
  parodies, 284
  photographs, 152
  and public interest defence, 82, 100
  publication for vindication purposes, 261
  term of copyright, 153
  terms of library deposits, 151–2
  transitional provisions, 153–4
user groups
  EU legislative process, 208–13
  UK legislative process, 229

users' rights
  Australia, 227–8
  diversity of interests, 280
  and DTI, 226–7
  and EU legislative process, 193–4
  or exceptions, 10–11, 182, 279–80
  and judiciary, 238–45
  and Parliament, 237
  positive lists, 213
  and reform model, 276, 279–80
  role, 173
  terminology, 10–11, 182, 279–80
  United Kingdom, 220–1

videos
  anthologies, 124
  educational exception, 125
  security videos, 82, 103, 106
visual works, *see* artistic works; illustrations; photographs
visually impaired persons, 222, 228, 237
Vitoria, M., 102, 108, 110
Volokh, F., 33
Von Lewinski, S., 214

Wales, 142
Wallace, William, 243
Warwick, Diana, 135
Whitford Committee, 223, 224, 225, 232, 236, 243, 250
Williams of Elvel, Lord, 244
Willis, Lord, 225
Wilson, Harold, 243
WIPO treaties
  balance of interests, 188
  copyright exceptions, 279, 281–7
  fair use, 271
  and technological measures of protections, 74
workability
  policing, 278
  public interest defence, 111
  reform model, 276, 277–9
WTO, 218, 271, 280
  see also TRIPS
Wyatt of Weeford, Lord, 225

Zapruder film, 25

Cambridge Studies in Intellectual Property

Titles in the series

Brad Sherman and Lionel Bently,
The Making of Modern Intellectual Property Law
0 521 56363 1

Irini A. Stamatoudi
Copyright and Multimedia Works
0 521 80819 7

Pascal Kamina
Film Copyright and the European Union
0 521 77053 X

Huw Beverley-Smith
The Commercial Appropriation of Personality
0 521 80014 5

Mark J. Davison
The Legal Protection of Databases
0 521 80257 1

Robert Burrell and Allison Coleman
Copyright Exceptions: The Digital Impact
0 521 84726 5

Lightning Source UK Ltd.
Milton Keynes UK
07 December 2010

163989UK00001B/274/P

9 780521 123440